DERIVATIVES LAW AND REGULATION

EDITORIAL ADVISORS

ASPEN SELECT SERIES

DERIVATIVES LAW AND REGULATION

Gary E. Kalbaugh
Special Professor of Law
Maurice A. Deane School of Law at Hofstra University

Wolters Kluwer
Law & Business

Published by Wolters Kluwer Law & Business in New York.

Wolters Kluwer Law & Business serves customers worldwide with CCH, Aspen Publishers, and Kluwer Law International products. (www.wolterskluwerlb.com)

To contact Customer Service, e-mail customer.service@wolterskluwer.com, call 1-800-234-1660, fax 1-800-901-9075, or mail correspondence to:

Wolters Kluwer Law & Business
Attn: Order Department
PO Box 990
Frederick, MD 21705

Printed in the United States of America.

1 2 3 4 5 6 7 8 9 0

ISBN 978-1-4548-5130-1

About Wolters Kluwer Law & Business

Wolters Kluwer Law & Business is a leading global provider of intelligent information and digital solutions for legal and business professionals in key specialty areas, and respected educational resources for professors and law students. Wolters Kluwer Law & Business connects legal and business professionals as well as those in the education market with timely, specialized authoritative content and information-enabled solutions to support success through productivity, accuracy and mobility.

Serving customers worldwide, Wolters Kluwer Law & Business products include those under the Aspen Publishers, CCH, Kluwer Law International, Loislaw, Best Case, ftwilliam.com and MediRegs family of products.

CCH products have been a trusted resource since 1913, and are highly regarded resources for legal, securities, antitrust and trade regulation, government contracting, banking, pension, payroll, employment and labor, and healthcare reimbursement and compliance professionals.

Aspen Publishers products provide essential information to attorneys, business professionals and law students. Written by preeminent authorities, the product line offers analytical and practical information in a range of specialty practice areas from securities law and intellectual property to mergers and acquisitions and pension/benefits. Aspen's trusted legal education resources provide professors and students with high-quality, up-to-date and effective resources for successful instruction and study in all areas of the law.

Kluwer Law International products provide the global business community with reliable international legal information in English. Legal practitioners, corporate counsel and business executives around the world rely on Kluwer Law journals, looseleafs, books, and electronic products for comprehensive information in many areas of international legal practice.

Loislaw is a comprehensive online legal research product providing legal content to law firm practitioners of various specializations. Loislaw provides attorneys with the ability to quickly and efficiently find the necessary legal information they need, when and where they need it, by facilitating access to primary law as well as state-specific law, records, forms and treatises.

Best Case Solutions is the leading bankruptcy software product to the bankruptcy industry. It provides software and workflow tools to flawlessly streamline petition preparation and the electronic filing process, while timely incorporating ever-changing court requirements.

ftwilliam.com offers employee benefits professionals the highest quality plan documents (retirement, welfare and non-qualified) and government forms (5500/PBGC, 1099 and IRS) software at highly competitive prices.

MediRegs products provide integrated health care compliance content and software solutions for professionals in healthcare, higher education and life sciences, including professionals in accounting, law and consulting.

Wolters Kluwer Law & Business, a division of Wolters Kluwer, is headquartered in New York. Wolters Kluwer is a market-leading global information services company focused on professionals.

To Fay Aurora Cirrincione

Summary of Contents

Contents

Preface

In keeping with common practice in the field of derivatives law, all references herein to the Commodity Exchange Act are to the named statute, not to the United States Code. The sole exception is for cases and materials that cite to the United States Code. These citations have been retained. For the reader's convenience, a Commodity Exchange Act-United States Code conversion table is included herein.

Throughout, some footnotes and citations have been omitted from cases and materials.

Part of the regulatory framework for derivatives is the regulation of security-based swaps by the Securities and Exchange Commission. Though the jurisdiction of the Securities and Exchange Commission over these products is discussed in Chapter 3, at the time of writing the implementation of this regulatory framework by the SEC had still not occurred and, therefore, it is not otherwise covered herein.

Though there are many rewards for writing this book (thanking those who contributed to its production is just one), my friendship with Richard A. Miller counts foremost among them. Richard, both through his establishment of the Futures and Derivatives Law Report and his continuing encouragement and contributions to the derivatives bar, has selflessly inspired and driven the academic study of derivatives law.

Richard offered his insight into every chapter, dedicating innumerable weekends to reviewing manuscript chapters (as he termed it "Coffee with Kalbaugh"). His influence on this work through both his detailed comments on drafts and the intellectual companionship he provided cannot be overstated. The author offers his warmest gratitude to Richard, without whom this work would not be possible.

The research and comments of Ariel Hazzard were superb. The foreign exchange chapter simply would not have come into being without the research and insight of Alexander F. L. Sand. Kristen Palermo has been an asset with every facet of the production of this work.

The author would also like to thank Professor Amy R. Stein for her efforts to teach him how to teach the law, Frederic M. Mauhs for his early encouragement and Marcy S. Cohen for her ongoing enthusiastic support. The chapter on manipulation owes a great debt to David Yeres. William T. Bagley and Robert G. Pickel, in addition to being preeminent contributors to the field of derivatives law in their own right, each showed great generosity with their time in relation to this book.

Thanks are also due to the author's parents, G. Edward Kalbaugh and Maria Christine Kalbaugh for their understanding and encouragement.

For well more than a year the author's wife, Kristin Kalbaugh, has patiently supported this project, even through the birth of their son. It has tested the boundaries of tolerance and the author thanks Kristin for being such a supremely dedicated spouse and mother.

ACKNOWLEDGMENTS

The author wishes to thank the following who kindly granted permission to reprint excerpts from the following materials:

Sean M. Flanagan, The Rise of a Trade Association: Group Interactions Within the International Swaps and Derivatives Association, 6 Harvard Negotiation Law Review 211 (Spring 2001). Reprinted by permission of the Harvard Negotiation Law Review via Copyright Clearance Center.

Gary E. Kalbaugh, The Erratic Journey of US Commodity Options Regulation 33 No. 10 Futures & Derivatives L. Rep. 1 (Nov. 2013). Reprinted with permission of Thomson Reuters.

Gary E. Kalbaugh and Richard A. Miller, Master Agreements for OTC Derivatives In Commercial Contracts: Strategies for Drafting and Negotiation (Vladimir R. Rossman & Morton Moskin, eds., 3d ed., Aspen Publishers 2014). Reprinted with permission of Aspen Publishers.

Lynn A. Stout, Uncertainty, Dangerous Optimism, and Speculation: An Inquiry into some Limits of Democratic Governance, 97 Cornell L. Rev. 1177 (2012). Reprinted with the permission of Cornell University.

CHAPTER 1
AN INTRODUCTION TO DERIVATIVES

A. INTRODUCTION AND SCOPE

1. *Why Study Derivatives Law?*

The topic of this book is the law and regulation applicable to participants in the derivatives market. All of the world's financial stock – i.e., outstanding equity, bonds, and loans – has been estimated to equal $211 trillion.[1] The estimated market value of the global derivatives market is over $19 trillion.[2] This is nearly 10% of the world's financial stock!

Due to its significant share of the global economy alone, derivatives law and regulation would be worthy of law school study. Add to that a new regulatory regime on a scale surpassing any Federal financial regulatory initiative since the 1930s and it is clear that the time to study derivatives law and regulation has never been better.

2. *Scope of this Book*

Throughout this book the terms "exchange-traded derivatives" and "off-exchange derivatives," also known as "over-the-counter derivatives" or "OTC derivatives," are used. They refer to the method of trading the same fundamental instrument, a derivative.

Exchange-traded derivatives have historically been more or less regulated. The market for off-exchange derivatives – i.e., derivatives traded by private bilateral contractual arrangement without use of an exchange or other centralized facility – is an estimated 10 times larger than the exchange-traded derivatives market.[3] This off-exchange derivatives market is only recently subject to significant regulation. This book examines the law and regulation of both "exchange-traded" and "off-exchange" derivatives. Each are big markets in themselves and much of the new regulation of the off-exchange derivatives market is influenced by the prevailing regulation of exchange-traded derivatives.

In this vein, it's important throughout this book to keep in mind the concept of "regulatory convergence." One way to define "regulatory convergence" is "the process by which the rules, regulations, or political institutions governing economic activity . . . become more similar."[4] The regulation of off-exchange derivatives represents regulatory convergence in that the manner of regulation is influenced by the existing regulatory regime applying to exchange-traded derivatives. Because on-exchange and off-exchange derivatives markets engage in similar economic activities, was regulatory convergence inevitable? And to what extent will regulatory convergence continue?

Before answering those questions, you might be asking yourself what exactly is a derivative?

B. WHAT ARE DERIVATIVES?

Later on, in Chapter 3, we will see how, through the definitions of "swap" and "security-based swap," derivatives have been defined for regulatory purposes.[5] For now, we will confine ourselves to introducing an economic definition of a derivative.

Economically, a derivative is fundamentally defined as an instrument whose value is derived from the value of an underlying asset. Therefore, a stock option, futures contract on a commodity, or a foreign exchange swap each fall within the economic definition of derivative. In this chapter, we will take a closer look at the economic elements of commonly traded derivatives. However, it is important to be mindful that the regulatory treatment of derivatives differs vastly depending on the type of derivative in question and how it is traded. This topic is one we will revisit in Chapter 3.

Derivatives can be sub-categorized into options, futures, and swaps. For each of these subcategories, an illustrative hypothetical will be provided, using the facts of the Law School Brewing Company. The examples used all involve the acquisition of wheat, a commodity fundamental to brewing the Law School Brewing Company's signature specialty brew, Study Break Wheat Beer. Keep in mind that, in addition to commodity derivatives, there are rate, credit, and equity derivatives, each of which we will briefly examine later in this chapter.

1. Option

An option is a contract whereby one party grants to the other a right, but not an obligation, to take a course of action.

Example: The Law School Brewing Company is unsure of how much wheat will be needed in a year's time. It could wait a year and then see what its needs are, but its management is concerned that the price of wheat could be a lot higher. A possible alternative strategy using a derivative would be for the Law School Brewing Company to buy an option to purchase a specified amount of wheat in a year's time.

In this example, we'll assume that the option is "cash-settled" meaning that, instead of physically delivering the commodity upon exercise of the option, the option seller will provide the buyer the difference between the market price and the price locked in by the option.

Pro: In a year's time, if the Law School Brewing Company finds out it does need wheat and the price of wheat is high, it will have locked in a lower price than the market price.

Con: If, in a year's time, the Law School Brewing Company finds out that it does not need wheat or the price of wheat is lower than the price locked-in by the option, it paid for an option it did not need.

To add numbers to the above facts, suppose that the Law School Brewing Company has purchased an option to "buy" (the implications of it being cash-settled are described below) 1,000 bushels of wheat[6] for $10,000 in one year's time[7] and has paid $1,000 for the option, an amount known as the "premium." Assuming that, at the time the Law School Brewing Company purchases the option, the market or "spot price" of wheat is $10 a bushel and the option provides the Law School Brewing Company the right to "purchase" the wheat for $10 a bushel (known as the "strike price") in a year's time, the option can be said to have been purchased "at-the-money," i.e., with the spot price equal to the strike price. If the strike price were less than the spot price, it would be said to be "out-of-the-money" and, if it were more than the spot price, it would be said to be "in-the-money."

To summarize:

Commodity	Today's Price/1,000 Bushels	Price for Option on 1,000 Bushels	Maturity of Option	Option Strike Price/1,000 Bushels
Wheat	$10,000	$1,000	1 Year	$10,000

The value of the wheat option to the Law School Brewing Company can be graphically illustrated as follows:

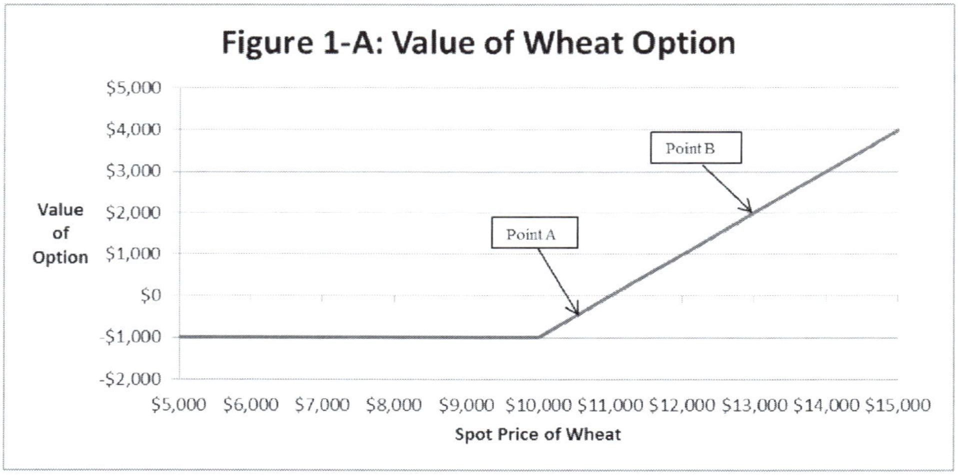

If the spot price of 1,000 bushels of wheat remains below $10,000, the option will expire worthless and the Law School Brewing Company will have wasted the $1,000 for the option premium. A spot price between $10,000 and $11,000 will result in the option having value, but not value in excess of the $1,000 paid by the Law School Brewing Company for the premium. For example, if the spot price were $10,500 ("Point A" in Figure 1-A), the Law School Brewing Company would exercise its option. Since it is "cash-settled," its counterparty would not deliver the wheat. Instead its counterparty would pay the Law School Brewing Company the current market price for the wheat ($10,500) minus the strike price fixed in the option ($10,000). The $500 paid to the Law School Brewing Company is still less than the premium of $1,000 which the Law School Brewing Company paid for the option.

Should the spot price for 1,000 bushels of wheat exceed $11,000, the option will have value in excess of the $1,000 paid. In other words, the Law School Brewing Company will be glad it purchased the option. For example, if the spot price for 1,000 bushels of wheat is $13,000 ("Point B" in Figure 1-A), the Law School Brewing Company's counterparty, upon exercise of the option by the Law School Brewing Company, will be required to pay the current market price for 1,000 bushels of wheat: $13,000 minus the $10,000 strike price locked in by the option. The $3,000 paid to the Law School Brewing Company is well in excess of the $1,000 premium it paid for the option.

2. *Futures or Forward Contract*

A futures contract is a contract to buy or sell an asset at a pre-agreed price and future date. Typically, when traded off-exchange a future is termed a "forward." For the regulatory distinction between futures and forwards, *see* Chapter 3. For the purposes of this section, both futures and forwards will be referred to as futures since their fundamental economic profiles are identical.

> Example: Last year, the Law School Brewing Company's management was unsure of how much wheat would be needed in a year's time and purchased an option. This year, it is certain that it will need a specified amount of wheat by year's end. It could wait a year to make its purchase but, of course, the price of wheat could be a lot higher. (It could be a lot lower, too.) A possible strategy using a derivative would be for the Law School Brewing Company to agree now to buy in a year's time a specified amount of wheat from a counterparty at a fixed price.
>
> Pro: In a year's time, if it finds out it does need wheat and the price of wheat is high, it will have locked in a lower price than the market price without paying for an option.
>
> Con: If, in a year's time, it finds out it does not need wheat or the price of wheat is lower than the price locked-in by the option, it still is required to perform on the contract and buy the specified amount of wheat for the agreed price.

As we did with the example using an option, let us add numbers to the above facts. Suppose that the Law School Brewing Company has agreed to purchase 1,000 bushels of wheat for $10,000 (the market value of 1,000 bushels of wheat at the time the contract is entered into) in one year's time. At the time the contract is entered into it is "at-the-money." Should wheat increase in price, the Law School Brewing Company will be "in-the-money." It will have made a good bargain because it will be able to purchase the wheat for $10,000 instead of the prevailing higher market price. Should the price of wheat decrease, the Law School Brewing Company will be "out-of-the-money." It will be locked in to purchase wheat at $10,000 even though it could buy the same amount of wheat for less at the prevailing market price.

To summarize:

Commodity	Today's Price/1,000 Bushels	Contract Settlement Date
Wheat	$10,000	1 Year

The value of the wheat futures contract to the Law School Brewing Company can be graphically illustrated as follows:

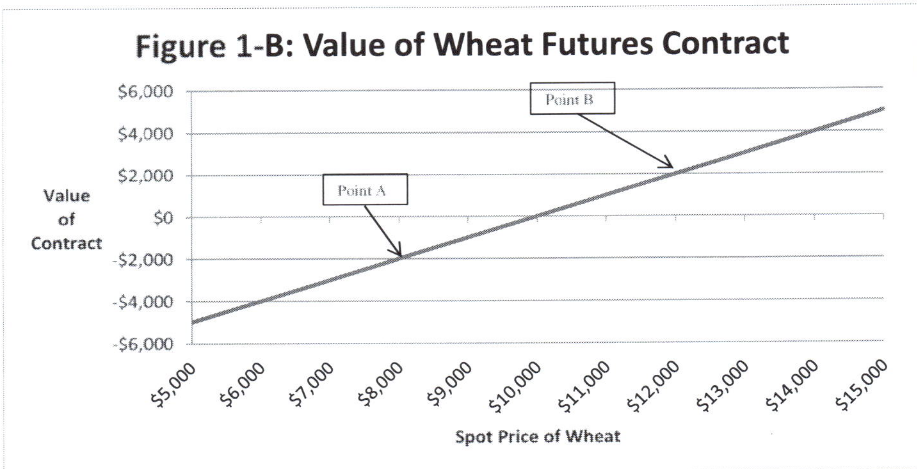

If the spot price were $8,000 for 1,000 bushels of wheat, the Law School Brewing Company will still be locked in by the futures contract to purchase 1,000 bushels of wheat for $10,000 ("Point A" in Figure 1-B).

If the spot price for 1,000 bushels of wheat is $12,000 for 1,000 bushels of wheat, the Law School Brewing Company will benefit because the futures contract will require that it pay only $10,000 for 1,000 bushels of wheat ("Point B" in Figure 1-B).

3. *Swap*

A swap is a contract to exchange assets periodically using predetermined pricing mechanisms.

> Example: Over the last two years, the Law School Brewing Company was unsure of how much wheat it would need in a year's time and entered into an option one year and a future the next. This year, it anticipates needing a specific amount of wheat each month. It could make its purchase each month as needed but, of course, the price of wheat is likely to vary monthly. In order to have certainty, therefore, the Law School Brewing Company might agree with a counterparty to a purchase of wheat monthly at a fixed price.

Historically, commodity swaps have traded off-exchange, though similar results could be achieved by entering into a series of commodities futures. Off-exchange commodity swaps are typically cash-settled, which means that the party fixing the price of the commodity pays that fixed amount and, in return, the other party pays the market price of the commodity.[8]

> Pro: It will be possible to anticipate and plan for wheat costs over the year and, if wheat increases in cost over the year, the Law School Brewing Company will have locked-in a lower price.
>
> Con: It is bound *ex ante* to the economic equivalent of the monthly purchases at a fixed price. If it finds out it does not need wheat or the price of wheat is lower than the price locked-in by the swap, it still is required to perform on the contract and pay its counterparty the fixed price agreed for the specified amount of wheat.

To add numbers to the above facts, the Law School Brewing Company has entered into a swap whereby on the first business day of each month (the "payment date") for one year (the day on which the one year period ends is the "maturity date") it will purchase 100 bushels of wheat (the so-called notional since the wheat itself will never be exchanged) for $1,000. If the first payment date is June 1 and the market price on that date is $980 for 100 bushels of wheat, the Law School Brewing Company must pay the difference between $1,000 and $980, or $20.[9] If, on the next payment date on July 1 the market price is now $1,050, the Law School Brewing Company will be paid the difference, $50.[10] The same calculation will be made – the difference between the "fixed price" agreed in the contract (paid by the Law School Brewing Company) and the "floating price," i.e., the market price, of 100 bushels wheat (paid to the Law School Brewing Company) – on each succeeding payment date. The floating price is determined by a commonly agreed external reference.

To summarize:

Commodity	Payment Dates	Maturity Date	Notional	Fixed Price	Floating Price
Wheat	First Business Day of Each Month	One Year	100 Bushels of Wheat	$1,000/100 Bushels of Wheat	Market Price on Payment Date for 100 Bushels of Wheat

Each monthly payment date is in effect a futures contract. Therefore, economically and graphically, each monthly payment can be illustrated using Figure 1-B above.

Due to the series of payment dates and the relevance of the market price of wheat at each of these payment dates, graphing the valuation of a wheat swap (or any swap) based on the value of wheat at the end of the contract is not feasible. Instead, the below table shows the cash flows that would occur on each payment date in a hypothetical scenario.

Figure 1-C: Hypothetical Swap Payments

Payment Date (for each month listed below, payment is due on the first business day)	Floating Rate (i.e., market value of 100 bushels of wheat on each payment date)	Fixed Rate (i.e., price per 100 bushels of wheat agreed by the parties at the inception of the swap)	Net Amount Payable (a positive number represents an amount payable to the Law School Brewing Company and a negative amount represents an amount payable from the Law School Brewing Company)
June	$980	$1,000	-$20
July	$1,050	$1,000	$50
August	$1,070	$1,000	$70
September	$1,120	$1,000	$120
October	$1,040	$1,000	$40
November	$1,050	$1,000	$50
December	$1,020	$1,000	$20
January	$950	$1,000	-$50
February	$940	$1,000	-$60
March	$920	$1,000	-$80

Payment Date	*Floating Rate*	*Fixed Rate*	*Net Amount Payable*
April	$960	$1,000	-$40
May	$970	$1,000	-$30
Total:[11]			$70

C. HOW ARE DERIVATIVES TRADED?

As previously noted, derivatives can be divided into products that have traditionally been traded on organized exchanges and those that historically have traded and settled off-exchange. Due primarily to the Dodd-Frank Wall Street Reform and Consumer Protection Act (which throughout we will refer to by its short title the Dodd-Frank Act or Dodd-Frank) categories of swaps that historically have been traded and settled off-exchange, may not necessarily trade and settle off-exchange.[12] We discuss this below and in more detail in Chapters 9 and 10.

1. *Exchange Traded Derivatives*

Exchange traded derivative are pre-established contracts outlining terms of trade "listed" as available for trading on a centralized exchange for settlement with a clearing house associated with that exchange.

2. *Off-Exchange Derivatives*

Off-exchange derivatives are bilaterally negotiated, traded, and settled. Where referencing physical commodities, they are typically settled in cash equivalents as opposed to physical delivery of the commodity in question. Some categories of derivatives formerly traded off-exchange are required by law and regulation to be traded on a centralized platform (known as a "swap execution facility" or "designated contract market") and/or to be centrally cleared. These requirements are discussed in Chapter 9.

They are typically documented by standardized documentation, namely the ISDA Master Agreement. The form of ISDA Master Agreement is produced by the industry association for the derivatives industry, the International Swaps and Derivatives Association, commonly known as "ISDA."

The ISDA Master Agreement is comprised of:

- A form ISDA Master Agreement, which is never directly modified by the parties;
- A supplementary Schedule containing the parties' customized terms;
- Confirmations evidencing each trade between the parties; and
- Optional sets of standardized definitions that the parties may incorporate by reference into the Schedule and/or the confirmations.

In Chapter 10 we discuss the documentation of off-exchange derivatives.

D. DERIVATIVES PRODUCT CATEGORIES

Note that, in a regulatory context, the term "swap" is used to describe an off-exchange derivative, even if the derivative itself is not necessarily a swap. In other words, most off-exchange futures and options are included[13] with the exception of options on a security (which are treated as a security) or options on foreign currency which are traded on a securities exchange.[14] The Commodity Futures Trading Commission (the "CFTC") is the primary regulator of most derivatives. For regulatory purposes, the CFTC has categorized the off-exchange derivatives which are subject to the CFTC's regulation as being divisible into four categories.

Commodity Futures Trading Commission Rule 1.3(iii)

17 C.F.R. § 1.3(iii)

. . . the terms major swap category, category of swaps and any similar terms mean any of the categories of swaps listed below. . . .

(1) Rate swaps. Any swap which is primarily based on one or more reference rates, including but not limited to any swap of payments determined by fixed and floating interest rates, currency exchange rates, inflation rates or other monetary rates, any foreign exchange swap . . . and any foreign exchange option other than an option to deliver currency.

(2) Credit swaps. Any swap that is primarily based on instruments of indebtedness, including but not limited to any swap primarily based on one or more broad-based indices related to debt instruments or loans, and any swap that is an index credit default swap or total return swap on one or more indices of debt instruments.

(3) Equity swaps. Any swap that is primarily based on equity securities, including but not limited to any swap based on one or more broad-based indices of equity securities and any total return swap on one or more equity indices.

(4) Other commodity swaps. Any swap that is not included in the rate swap, credit swap or equity swap categories.

Excluded from the above categories are credit or equity derivatives which reference a single security or loan or a "narrow-based security index." The primary regulator of these products is the Securities and Exchange Commission ("SEC").

The definition of "narrow-based security index" is complicated. However, a reference by a swap to nine or fewer securities is a reference to a "narrow-based security index." A reference to more than ten swaps requires application of a fairly complicated test to determine whether or not the reference is to a "narrow-based security index."[15]

Also, although nominally foreign exchange swaps are included in the "rate swap" category, the CFTC has limited jurisdiction over physically settled foreign exchange swaps, discussed in more detail in Chapter 3.[16]

Using the CFTC's categories, we will examine each more closely.

1. *Rate Swaps*

The CFTC category of "rate swaps" includes interest rate derivatives and foreign exchange derivatives.

a. Interest Rate Derivatives

In 2013, just over 75% of all off-exchange derivatives by market value were interest rate derivatives.[17] Interest rate derivatives are primarily used to fix exposure to interest rates. Because of its ubiquity and relative simplicity, the interest rate swap that serves to exchange a fixed rate of interest on a pre-agreed "notional amount" for a floating rate of interest on a pre-agreed "notional amount" is called a "plain vanilla" interest rate swap. Note how similar this is to the commodity swap example we used in Section B3 above, where on each payment date the Law School Brewing Company received the amount by which the market price (floating rate) on a specified amount of wheat (the notional) exceeded the fixed price (fixed rate) on the specified amount of wheat or, if the market price was lower than the fixed price, paid to its counterparty the amount by which the market price exceeded the fixed price on the specified amount of wheat.

An understanding of how a "plain vanilla" interest rate swap operates is essential to an understanding of derivatives.

…nerica National Trust and Savings

…2)

…dge. . . .

…tand the facts of this case and the legal issues …e a brief overview of derivative swap …act between two parties ("counterparties") to … specified intervals, calculated by reference to …ents based on a number of indices including …d security or commodity prices.

The "plain-vanilla" interest rate swap, the simplest and most common type of swap contract, obligates one counterparty to make payments equal to the interest which would accrue on an agreed hypothetical principal amount ("notional amount"), during a given period, at a specified fixed interest rate. The other counterparty must pay an amount equal to the interest which would accrue on the same notional amount, during the same period, but at a floating interest rate. If the fixed rate paid by the first counterparty exceeds the floating rate paid by the second counterparty, then the first counterparty must pay an amount equal to the difference between the two rates multiplied by the notional amount, for the specified interval. Conversely, if the floating rate paid by the second counterparty exceeds the fixed rate paid by the first counterparty, the fixed-rate payor receives payment. The agreed hypothetical or "notional" amount provides the basis for calculating payment obligations, but does not change hands.

For example, suppose Counterparties A and B enter into a five-year interest rate swap with the following characteristics: (1) Counterparty A agrees to pay a floating interest rate equal to LIBOR, the London Interbank Offered Rate; [i] (2) Counterparty B agrees to pay a 10% fixed interest rate; (3) both counterparties base their payments on a $1 million notional amount and agree to make payments semiannually. If LIBOR is 9% upon commencement of the first payment period, Counterparty B must pay A: (10%-9%) * $1 million * (.5) = $5,000. These net payments vary as LIBOR fluctuates and continue every six months for the term of the swap. If interest rates rise, the position of Counterparty B, the fixed-rate payor, improves because the payments it receives increase. For example, if LIBOR rises to 11% at the beginning of the next payment period, Counterparty B receives a net payment of $5,000 from A. Conversely, the position of Counterparty A, the floating-rate payor, improves when interest rates fall. The party whose position retains positive value under

---

[i] [N. 2] "LIBOR" stands for London Interbank Offered Rate, the rate at which top-rated banks in the European money market provide funding to each other. LIBOR is the most widely used floating index for interest rate swaps.

the swap is considered "in the money" while a party with negative value is considered "out of the money." As discussed previously, the $1 million notional amount never changes hands.

Almost all interest rate swaps are documented with (1) a confirmation and (2) master agreement. Typically, master agreements are standard form agreements prepared by the International Swaps and Derivatives Association ("ISDA"). The master agreement governs all interest swap transactions between the counterparties. It includes provisions generally applicable to all swap transactions including: payment netting, events of default, cross-default provisions, early termination events and closeout netting.

Most master agreements provide that, in the event of an early termination or default, the party in the money is entitled to collect "termination damages." Termination damages represent the replacement cost of the terminated swap contract and are generally determined by obtaining market quotations for the cost of replacing the swap at the time of termination. . . .

Interest rate swap agreements provide a powerful tool for altering the character of assets and liabilities, fine tuning risk expo
financing or speculating on interest rate fluctuations.
interest rate swaps to reduce exposure to adverse ch
to obtain financing characteristics unavailable throug
Interest rate swaps can modify a borrower's all-in fun
floating, floating-to-fixed or a combination of both.

Interest rate swaps have become an important p
domestic commerce, and the market for these instru
explosive growth. . . .

Thrifty refers to a fixed amount and a floating am
with respect to the Law School Brewing Company's co
terminology is also applicable to other categories of s
fixed amount is also referred to as the "fixed leg" of a
amount is referred to as the "floating leg" of the swa

b. Foreign Exchange Derivatives

Foreign exchange forwards are off-exchange transactions in which two parties agree to exchange a specified amount of one currency for a specified amount of another currency at an agreed-upon future date. If traded on-exchange they operate the same economically and are referred to as foreign exchange futures instead of forwards. An FX swap is a series of foreign exchange forwards, i.e., the parties agree to exchanges of currency at pre-agreed dates, often on a period basis, such as monthly. In a non-deliverable forward, commonly known as an "NDF," the parties net payments due on the payment date into a common currency instead of exchanging one currency for the other.

A typical cross-currency swap or cross-currency interest rate swap operates like an interest rate swap between two currencies. At the onset of the swap, one party ("Party A") provides a principal amount of a currency ("X") in exchange for a principal amount of another currency ("Y") from the other party ("Party B"). These amounts could be the actual amounts or notional equivalents depending on what the parties have agreed. On a periodic basis, Party A pays Party B interest on Y in exchange for the receipt of interest on X from Party B. The interest could be fixed, based on a floating reference, or one leg could be fixed and the other floating. At maturity, the parties return to each other (physically or notionally, as agreed) the principal exchanged at the onset of the swap.

2. *Credit Swaps*

The most common credit swap is a credit default swap.

Deutsche Bank AG v. AMBAC Credit Products, LLC

2006 WL 1867497 (S.D.N.Y. July 6, 2006)

Denis Cote, District Judge.

This is a dispute over a complex transaction between two sophisticated financial institutions. Although the instruments involved are somewhat abstruse, the central issue can be boiled down to a relatively straightforward question of contract interpretation: When was plaintiff Deutsche Bank AG ("DB") required to deliver a group of bonds to defendant Ambac Credit Products, LLC ("ACP")? DB claims that although the documents governing the disputed transaction set out a detailed timeline for delivery of the bonds, industry practice and other contractual provisions allowed for delivery well past the nominal deadline. Therefore, according to DB, ACP breached the contract when it refused to pay for the bonds DB tendered one month after the putative delivery date. . . .

The disputed transaction here is a species of credit derivative called a credit default swap ("CDS"). Credit derivatives are akin to insurance policies for holders of corporate bonds or other securities against downgrades in the credit of the issuing companies. They do this by transferring credit risk from a "protection buyer" to a "protection seller."[ii] A CDS is a common type of credit derivative in which the protection buyer makes a fixed payment to the protection seller in return for a payment that is contingent upon a "credit event" – such as a bankruptcy – occurring to the company that issued the security (the "reference entity") or the security itself (the "reference

---

[ii] [N. 2] A credit derivative is a synthetic instrument, however, and not all purchasers of such "protection" actually own the security covered by the transaction.

obligation"). The contingent payment is often made against delivery of a "deliverable obligation" – usually the reference obligation or other security issued by the reference entity – by the protection buyer to the protection seller. This delivery is known as the "physical settlement."[iii] Some CDS transactions, such as the one at issue here, are known as "portfolio" transactions, meaning they cover multiple reference entities and reference obligations.

CDS transactions are of relatively recent origin, having been developed in the mid-1990s. They are highly negotiated and are customarily based on standard terms published by the International Swaps and Derivatives Association, Inc. ("ISDA"). These terms may be modified for a particular transaction. At the time the transaction at issue here was executed, the 1999 ISDA Credit Derivatives Definitions ("1999 Definitions") provided the foundation for most CDS agreements[18]. . . .

Thus, once a credit event occurs, the parties have a strictly controlled time-frame in which to act. A buyer of protection must first deliver a [notice] and then the securities within the time frames allowed, or lose the right to obtain payment from the protection seller. Similarly, assuming the buyer has performed its obligations, the seller of protection must be prepared to make the required payment associated with the credit event within a defined and relatively short period of time following a credit event. . . .

Here, DB has utterly failed to show the existence of a market practice for credit default instruments that would have justified an expectation that it had an unlimited delivery window absent an express provision to that effect in the Confirmation. Its sole retained expert candidly admitted that she has no expertise whatsoever in the field of credit default obligations and did not disagree with any of the statements or analysis by ACP's expert, whose expertise within the field of credit default transactions was well established and unchallenged. At most, its own employees pointed to a handful of isolated CDS transactions in which late delivery of a physical settlement obligation was accepted. In none of these transactions was a non-dealer a party, and their relevance is therefore marginal at best. ACP, on the other hand, has shown through compelling evidence that the firm practice in the CDS marketplace was to require that delivery occur according to the timetable to which the parties had agreed. Under these circumstances, DB could not reasonably have expected that ACP would accept delivery after February 11 – and should have expected just the opposite.

Indeed, the evidence shows that DB itself understood in February 2004 that it had a firm obligation to deliver the [bonds] by the date it identified in the [notice] it sent to ACP, or within the five-business-day window that followed. In March, April, and May, as executives in the companies discussed ACP's refusal to accept DB's late-tendered bonds, DB never took the position that ACP was

---

[iii] [N. 3] The parties can sometimes settle transactions without a transfer of securities. This is known as a "cash settlement" and is not at issue here.

contractually bound to accept them. In fact, in a candid internal communication, it conceded it had "no leverage . . . at all" in the negotiations. . . .

For the foregoing reasons, each of DB's claims is denied in its entirety. The Clerk of Court shall enter judgment for the defendants and close the case. . . .

Credit default swaps that reference eight or fewer securities (excluding government securities) or loans are security-based swaps, subject to SEC jurisdiction. Those referencing government securities are swaps, subject to CFTC jurisdiction. A credit default swap referencing nine or more securities or loans is usually subject to CFTC jurisdiction. However, it is subject to a complicated test involving evaluation of relative concentration of each security and the depth of the markets in which the securities traded.

3. *Equity Derivatives*

Caiola v. Citibank, N.A., New York

295 F.3d 312 (2d Cir. 2002)

B.D. Parker Jr., Circuit Judge. . . .

Caiola, an entrepreneur and sophisticated investor, was a major client of Citibank Private Bank, a division of Citibank, from the mid-1980s to September 1999. During this relationship, Citibank assisted Caiola with a wide range of business and personal financial services. As a result of these transactions, which involved hundreds of millions of dollars, Caiola became one of Citibank's largest customers.

Beginning in the mid-1980s, Caiola undertook high volume equity trading, entrusting funds to Citibank who in turn engaged various outside brokerage firms. Caiola specialized in the stock of Philip Morris Companies, Inc. ("Philip Morris") and regularly traded hundreds of thousands of shares valued at many millions of dollars. To hedge the risks associated with these trades, Caiola established option positions corresponding to his stock positions.

As Caiola's trades increased in size, he and Citibank grew increasingly concerned about the efficacy of his trading and hedging strategies. Caiola's positions required margin postings of tens of millions of dollars and were sufficiently large that the risks to him were unacceptable unless hedged. But the volume of options necessary to hedge effectively could impact prices and disclose his positions – effects known as "footprints" on the market. In early 1994, Citibank proposed synthetic trading. A synthetic transaction is typically a contractual agreement between two counterparties, usually an investor and a bank, that seeks to economically replicate the ownership and physical trading of shares and options. The counterparties establish synthetic positions in shares or options, the values of which are pegged to the market prices of the related physical shares or options. The aggregate market values of the shares or options that underlie the synthetic trades are referred to as "notional" values and are treated as interest-bearing loans to the investor. As Citibank explained to Caiola, synthetic trading offers significant advantages to investors who heavily concentrate on large positions of a single stock by reducing the risks associated with large-volume trading. Synthetic trading alleviates the necessity of posting large amounts of margin capital and ensures that positions can be established and unwound quickly. Synthetic trading also offers a solution to the "footprint" problem by permitting the purchase of large volumes of options in stocks without affecting their price.

Taking Citibank's advice, Caiola began to engage in two types of synthetic transactions focusing on Philip Morris stock and options: equity swaps and cash-settled over-the-counter options. In a typical equity swap, one party (Caiola) makes periodic interest payments on the notional value of a stock position and also payments equal to any decrease in value of the shares upon which the notional value is based. The other party (Citibank) pays any increase in the value of the shares and any dividends, also based on the same notional value.

For example, if Caiola synthetically purchased 1,000 shares of Philip Morris at $50 per share, the notional value of that transaction would be $50,000. Because this notional value would resemble a loan from Citibank, Caiola would pay interest at a predetermined rate on the $50,000. If Philip Morris's stock price fell $10, Caiola would pay Citibank $10,000. If the stock price rose $10, Citibank would pay Caiola $10,000. Citibank also would pay Caiola the value of any dividends that Caiola would have received had he actually owned 1,000 physical shares.

Caiola also acquired synthetic options, which were cash-settled over-the-counter options. Because these options were not listed and traded on physical exchanges, their existence and size did not impact market prices. Caiola and Citibank agreed to terms regarding the various attributes of the option in a particular transaction (such as the strike price, expiration date, option type, and premium). They agreed to settle these option transactions in cash when the option was exercised or expired, based on the then-current market price of the underlying security.

Caiola and Citibank documented their equity swaps and synthetic options through an International Swap Dealers Association Master Agreement ("ISDA Agreement") dated March 25, 1994. The ISDA Agreement established specific terms for the synthetic trading. After entering into the ISDA Agreement, Caiola, on Citibank's advice, began to enter into "coupled" synthetic transactions with Citibank. Specifically, Caiola's over-the-counter option positions were established in connection with a paired equity swap, ensuring that his synthetic options would always hedge his equity swaps. This strategy limited the amount he could lose and ensured that his risks would be both controllable and quantifiable. . . .

Each synthetic transaction was governed by an individualized confirmation containing a number of disclaimers. A confirmation for Caiola's purchase of 360,000 cash-settled over-the-counter options dated December 9, 1998 ("Confirmation"), for instance, provides that each party represents to the other that "it is not relying on any advice, statements or recommendations (whether written or oral) of the other party," that each is entering the transaction "as principal and not as an agent for [the] other party," and that "[Caiola] acknowledges and agrees that [Citibank] is not acting as a fiduciary or advisor to [him] in connection with this Transaction." Further, the ISDA Agreement and accompanying Schedule, which governed the overall synthetic relationship, provides:

> This Agreement constitutes the entire agreement and understanding of the parties with respect to its subject matter and supersedes all oral communication and prior writings with respect thereto.
>
> [Caiola] has such knowledge and experience in financial, business and tax matters that render him capable of evaluating the merits and risks of this Agreement and the Transactions contemplated hereunder; [Caiola] is able to bear the economic risks of this Agreement and the Transaction contemplated hereunder; and, after appropriate independent investigations, [Caiola] has determined that this Agreement and the Transactions contemplated hereunder are suitable for him. . . .

Without Caiola's knowledge, Citibank, after its merger with Solomon Smith Barney, stopped entering into synthetic positions on Cailoa's behalf and, instead, entered into physical positions. These ended up exposing Caiola to losses he would not have suffered if the synthetic positions were retained. The court concluded that the swap positions were covered under SEC Rule 10b-5 (17 C.F.R. § 240.10b-5), an SEC rule prohibiting fraud in relation to securities transactions.

As with credit default swaps, equity derivatives that reference eight or fewer securities are security-based swaps, subject to SEC jurisdiction. An equity derivative referencing nine or more securities or loans may be a swap or security-based swap depending on the application of the test referenced in Section D2 above.

Because equity derivatives reference securities and can be a synthetic substitute for direct ownership of a security, they can trigger reporting requirements under securities and antitrust laws.

4. *Other Commodity Swaps*

The CFTC defines "other commodity swaps" as "Any swap that is not included in the rate swap, credit swap or equity swap categories." As a practical matter, the primary remaining category is commodity swaps.

We took a close look at commodity futures and options above in Section B2. Taking a closer look at commodity swaps we can discern that commodity swaps, like interest rate swaps, are comprised of a fixed and floating leg. The fixed leg is the price that is locked-in for the commodity. The floating leg is the market price of the commodity on each payment date.

Also included in this category would be swaps that are exotic in nature and, therefore, not easily categorized as a rate, credit, equity, or commodity swap. One example of such a derivative would be a weather derivative in which payment exchanges between the parties are correlated to specified weather events.

E. PRACTICAL APPLICATION OF DERIVATIVES

During the financial crisis that began in 2007 and referred to herein as the "Financial Crisis," derivatives were the subject of significant criticism discussed in Chapter 7. However, it is important to be mindful that derivatives also offer societal benefits. Some practical applications of derivatives were illustrated by our above examples with the Law School Brewing Company. Indeed, many companies use derivatives to manage risk, ranging from price volatility of commodities such as oil or cattle to interest rate volatility. For a company engaged in cross-border transactions requiring multiple currencies, foreign exchange derivatives may be an essential element for reducing the risk of currency fluctuations.

Many of the perceived benefits and shortcomings of derivatives were outlined before the Financial Crisis by the General Accounting Office.

United States General Accounting Office, Financial Derivatives – Actions Needed to Protect the Financial System

GAO/GGD 94-133 (May 18, 1994)

. . . The risks posed by derivatives use include (1) credit risk . . . ; (2) market risk (adverse movements in the price of a financial asset or commodity); (3) legal risk (an action by a court or by a regulatory or legislative body that could invalidate a financial contract); and (4) operations risk (inadequate controls, deficient procedures, human error, system failure, or fraud). These general types of risk exist for many financial activities, but the specific risks in derivatives activities are relatively difficult to manage, in part, because of the complexity of some of these products and the difficulties in measuring these risks. For example, because derivatives might be used in conjunction with other assets and liabilities, measuring the extent of market risks of derivative products alone is not sufficient to understand firms' total market risk. . . .

Derivatives are globally used financial products that have evolved to meet the demand for cost-effective protection against risks associated with rate and price movements. Derivatives essentially unbundle and transfer those risks from entities less willing or able to manage them to those more willing or able to do so. The values of derivatives are based on, or derived from, the value of an underlying asset, reference rate, or index – called the underlying. Common types of underlying assets are stocks, bonds, and physical commodities, such as wheat, oil, and lumber. An example of an underlying reference rate is the interest rate on the 3-month U.S. Treasury bill. An example of an underlying index is the Standard & Poor's 500 Index, which measures the performance of 500 common stocks.

Derivatives include customized and standardized contracts. Some derivatives are customized contracts between parties (also called counterparties) that include one or more negotiated terms in addition to price. These terms can include the quality and quantity of the underlying, time and place of delivery, and method of payment. Other derivatives are standardized contracts whose terms are fixed – except for price, which the market determines. Derivatives can be privately negotiated by the parties; these are called over-the-counter (OTC) derivatives. Derivatives also can be traded through central locations, called organized exchanges, where buyers and sellers or their representatives meet to determine derivatives prices; these are called exchange-traded derivatives. . . .

Market participants use derivatives (1) to hedge, or to protect against adverse changes in the values of assets or liabilities; (2) to speculate, or to assume risk in attempting to profit from anticipating changes in market rates or prices; and (3) to obtain more desirable financing terms.

Hedgers protect themselves from market risk, which is the exposure to the possibility of financial loss caused by adverse changes in the values of assets or liabilities. They protect themselves by entering into derivatives transactions whose values are expected to change in the opposite direction as the values of their assets or liabilities. For example, a hedger can protect asset values through derivatives transactions that increase in value as the asset values decline. The increases in values of the derivatives contracts (profits) will offset, or hedge, the decrease in values of the assets (losses).

In contrast, speculators take on risk in an attempt to profit from changes in the values of derivatives or their underlyings. Rather than owning the underlying, speculators can use derivatives as a more affordable way to attempt to profit from anticipating movements in market rates and prices. As speculators enter into transactions with hedgers and other speculators, they provide liquidity to the derivatives markets, thereby helping to ensure that high volumes of trading can occur without significantly affecting prices.

Some derivatives enable market participants to obtain more desirable financing in two ways. First, as we discuss later in this chapter, market participants can work together to take advantage of differences in the rates at which they borrow money. Second, an important by-product of hedging is the enhanced creditworthiness of the hedger. Banks will extend more favorable financing terms to firms that have reduced their market risk through hedging activities.

In achieving these purposes, derivatives can be more cost-effective than transactions in the underlying cash markets because of the reduced transaction costs and the leverage that derivatives provide. For example, instead of buying or selling $100,000 worth of U.S. Treasury bonds, a market participant can realize the benefits of buying or selling the same amount of bonds by using a derivatives contract and posting a deposit, called a margin, of only about 1,500, or 1.5 percent of the face amount of the bonds. Likewise, a market participant can achieve a result similar to buying or selling all of the stocks in the Standard & Poor's 500 Index by buying or selling a derivatives contract on this index for as little as 5 to 10 percent of the cost of the underlying stocks . . .

Although derivatives can provide economic benefits, dealers and end-users can experience extensive unanticipated losses if they do not carefully manage the risks associated with the use of derivatives. Several large U.S. and international firms have reported extensive losses from derivatives transactions as a result of unanticipated market movements and weaknesses in their risk-management systems. The Group of Thirty and bank regulators have also reported weaknesses in risk management systems of derivatives dealers and end-users. Although strong corporate governance is critical to the success of any risk management system, it is particularly crucial for managing the risks of complex and potentially volatile derivatives. Boards of directors, senior management, audit committees, and internal and external auditors all have key roles within the corporate governance system to manage the risks associated with derivatives.

The general types of risk associated with derivatives – credit, market, legal, and operations – exist for many financial activities. Therefore, risk-management policies and controls over such activities are also generally applicable to derivatives. However, the specific risks associated with derivatives activities are relatively difficult to manage, in part, because of the complexity of some of these products and the difficulties in measuring their risks.

Until the publication in 1993 of a report sponsored by the Group of Thirty, firms lacked comprehensive guidelines for evaluating their risk-management practices. That report recommended specific derivatives risk-management practices as benchmarks for firms' use. Subsequently, two federal bank regulators issued similar guidance on risk-management practices for the banks they supervise. Neither the Group of Thirty recommendations nor the federal bank regulators' guidance has the weight of federal regulations. However, the 15 major U.S. dealers that we visited described derivatives risk-management systems that generally conformed with them. The Group of Thirty report indicated that not all dealers fully complied with its recommendations. Also, bank regulators found some serious weaknesses in major dealers' risk-management systems. However, regulators and market participants said that improvements have been made in response to the recommendations and guidelines. . . .

Derivatives serve an important function in the global financial marketplace, providing end-users opportunities to better manage financial risks associated with their business transactions. The rapid growth and increasing complexity of derivatives reflects the increased demand from end-users for better ways to manage their financial risks and from speculators for lower cost ways to potentially profit from market volatility. They also reflect the innovative capacity of the financial services industry to respond to market demands. However, the combination of global involvement, concentration, and linkages among large derivatives dealers means that the sudden failure or complete withdrawal from trading of any of these dealers could heighten the risk of liquidity problems in the markets and pose risk to the others, including federally insured banks and the financial system. In cases of severe financial stress, the federal government is likely to intervene to keep the financial system functioning. . . .

Improving U.S. derivatives regulation without coordinating and harmonizing such actions with foreign regulators has at least two risks. First, U.S. financial institutions will remain vulnerable to a crisis that begins abroad and spreads to the United States as a result of the global linkages among financial institutions and markets. Second, regulation that market participants view as too severe could cause firms to move their derivatives activities outside of the United States. However, coordinating and harmonizing regulation worldwide has been difficult to achieve because countries have different legal requirements and different approaches to regulation.

Innovation and creativity are strengths of the U.S. financial services industry, and these strengths should not be eroded by excessive regulation. However, U.S. regulatory gaps and weaknesses must be addressed, especially considering the rapid growth in derivatives activity. Policymakers and regulators must strike a proper balance between (1) allowing the financial services industry to grow and innovate and (2) protecting the safety and soundness of the nation's financial system. Achieving this balance will require unprecedented cooperation among U.S. and foreign regulators, market participants, and members of the accounting profession. . . .

Given the weaknesses and gaps that impede regulatory preparedness for dealing with a crisis associated with derivatives, GAO recommends that Congress require federal regulation of the safety and soundness of all major U.S. OTC derivatives dealers. Regulators should attempt to prevent financial disruptions from turning into crises and resolve crises to minimize risks to the financial system. Thus, firms that become insolvent should be allowed to fail but to do so in an orderly fashion. . . .

As will be seen in the following chapter, only a few years after the 1994 Government Accounting Office report, off-exchange derivatives were exempted from most regulation. The questions the Government Accounting Office report raises, about the balance between having an innovative marketplace and risk-reducing regulation, remains as important today as in 1994, despite the belated adoption in 2010 of many of the GAO's recommendations.

QUESTIONS AND COMMENTS

1. Consider what risk the Law School Brewing Company might be exposed to if there were no derivative products available to hedge its wheat exposure. Would there be other ways to mitigate its risk?
2. What if, in addition to having wheat needs, the Law School Brewing Company, had a major barley supplier in Canada that required payment in Canadian dollars? What are some derivatives strategies that might be available to the Law School Brewing Company?
3. The SEC defines the categories of swaps that it primarily regulates more simply in [SEC Rule 240.3a67] by dividing them into "debt security-based swaps" and anything that is not a debt security-based swap. A debt security-based swap is defined as "[a]ny security-based swap that is based, in whole or in part, on one or more instruments of indebtedness (including loans), or on a credit event relating to one or more issuers or securities, including but not limited to any security-based swap that is a credit default swap, total return swap on one or more debt instruments, debt swap, debt index swap, or credit spread." Why is the SEC's categorization simpler than the CFTC's?
4. As discussed in greater detail in Chapter 3, the term "swap" is defined in § 1a(47) of the Commodity Exchange Act broadly to include some products that are not, strictly speaking, swaps. Why might that be the case? Does it matter whether the defined term corresponds to its external meaning?
5. Considering the important functions derivatives perform, why might an eminent financier such as Warren Buffet refer to them as "financial weapons of mass destruction"?[19]

CHAPTER 2
A REGULATORY HISTORY OF DERIVATIVES

A. ORIGINS

Derivatives have existed since ancient times as can be seen in this anecdote from Aristotle.

Aristotle, Politics
Book 1, Chapter 11

. . . Enough has been said about the theory of wealth-getting; we will now proceed to the practical part. . . .

It would be well also to collect the scattered stories of the ways in which individuals have succeeded in amassing a fortune; for all this is useful to persons who value the art of getting wealth. There is the anecdote of Thales the Milesian and his financial device, which involves a principle of universal application, but is attributed to him on account of his reputation for wisdom. He was reproached for his poverty, which was supposed to show that philosophy was of no use. According to the story, he knew by his skill in the stars while it was yet winter that there would be a great harvest of olives in the coming year; so, having a little money, he gave deposits for the use of all the olive-presses in Chios and Miletus, which he hired at a low price because no one bid against him. When the harvest-time came, and many were wanted all at once and of a sudden, he let them out at any rate which he pleased, and made a quantity of money. Thus he showed the world that philosophers can easily be rich if they like, but that their ambition is of another sort. . . .

Thales, by buying the future right to use the olive presses, entered into an economic derivative, a futures contract.

Derivatives in the United States also have a long history.

Lynn A. Stout, Uncertainty, Dangerous Optimism, and Speculation: An Inquiry into Some Limits of Democratic Governance

97 Cornell L. Rev. 1177 (2012)

. . . An early American example [of a derivative] was a type of derivative known as a "difference contract." Difference contracts were agreements between two parties that one would make a payment of money to the other determined by future changes in some market phenomenon, usually the market price for an agricultural commodity like wheat or corn. They were often formally structured like modern futures contracts, with one party promising to buy wheat at today's price and the other promising to purchase it, but with the contract to be performed at some future time. However, the parties further agreed that the contract would not be performed by actually delivering the wheat. Rather, the wheat "buyer" would pay the "seller" the difference between the contract price and the market price of wheat at the time of performance.

Not surprisingly, difference contract trading proved highly appealing to speculators. . . . Moreover, because difference contracts were essentially wagers, they could be used to bet on price declines and to take speculative positions virtually without cost – at least, until the bet came due. . . .

[The author notes that these "contracts for difference" were ultimately deemed unenforceable.]

[T]he common law did not try to stop those who wanted to use difference contracts to wager on the markets from doing so. It simply declined to subsidize speculators by allowing them to employ public courts to enforce their bets.[i] As a result, would-be speculators had to worry that their counterparties might not perform. A private solution to this enforcement problem soon emerged: privately organized futures exchanges. . . .

U.S. agricultural exchanges came to be dominated not by producers and consumers dealing in physical corn or cotton, but by traders exchanging "elevator receipts" representing a quantity of a commodity stored elsewhere (e.g., in a grain elevator). Soon elevator receipts morphed into "futures contracts" that called for delivery of the commodity in the future, at today's market price. However, most exchange-traded futures were not performed by actually delivering the corn or cotton. Rather, traders employed a "set off" process, purchasing a second, offsetting futures contract for delivery of the same quantity of the same goods on the same date. Futures contracts performed by set-off were just difference contracts by another name.

---

[i] [N. 88] *See Irwin v. Williar*, 110 U.S. 499, 508-09 (1884).

Nevertheless, traders who wanted to use exchange-traded futures for speculation rather than hedging generally did not worry their counterparties might use the common-law rule against difference contracts as an excuse not to perform. This is not because public courts enforced speculative futures contracts, but because anyone who wanted to trade on a futures exchange had to use the brokerage services of an exchange member who would guarantee the traders' performance. . . .

Outside of the confines of organized exchanges, the origins of which are said to go back to twelfth-century European trade fairs,[1] "bucket shops" flourished. Justice Holmes described bucket shops as "places wherein is permitted the pretended buying and selling of grain, etc., without any intention of receiving and paying for the property so bought, or of delivering the property so sold."[2] A year later, in *Gatewood v. North Carolina*, 203 U.S. 531 (1906), a bucket shop was described as "an establishment, nominally for the transaction of a stock exchange business, or business of similar character, but really for the registration of bets, or wagers, usually for small accounts, on the rise or fall of the prices of stock, grain, oil, etc. There being no transfer or delivery of the stock or commodities nominally dealt in."[3] Many of these bucket shops were deemed to be illegal gaming venues and there were various efforts to police them.

The Oxford English Dictionary cites the origin of the term "bucket shop" as a reference to low-end liquor shops.[4] An alternative explanation for the term implies that the term "bucket shop" derives from the practice of "bucketing" orders:

> The bucketing of grain-futures orders by their nonexecution in the pit was by no means confined to bucket shops prior to the enactment of laws against such practices. . . . Even after the Chicago Board of Trade sought to extirpate the bucket shops, members of the Board were in the habit of matching the orders of customers against each other instead of executing them in the pit.[5]

The Chicago Board of Trade engaged in a crackdown on bucket shops by hiring private investigators to see which of its members had telegraphic connections with bucket shops.[6] This resulted in the expulsion of members and, ultimately, the Chicago Board of Trade's efforts resulted in 281 indictments and 188 bucket shops being closed.[7]

These acts, and a Supreme Court decision in 1905 allowing for the organized exchanges to enjoin transmission of price quotations to bucket shops, led to the demise of bucket shops by 1916.[8]

B. THE FIRST ERA OF NATIONAL REGULATION, 1922-1991

1. *Grain Futures Act of 1922*

The first Federal effort to regulate futures was the Future Trading Act of 1921.[9] The Future Trading Act taxed grain futures traded on anything but a board of trade meeting statutory criteria and designated as such by the secretary of agriculture. In *Hill v. Wallace*, 259 U.S. 44 (1922), Chief Justice Taft ruled for the Supreme Court that this was an unconstitutional assertion of the tax power since its real objective was regulatory and denied that it was a regulation of interstate commerce because, *inter alia*, "interstate commerce" was never referenced in the statute.[10]

Heeding the chief justice's ruling, Congress passed the Grain Futures Act of 1922, the long title of which declared its grounding in Congress's constitutional authority to regulate interstate commerce: "An Act for the prevention and removal of obstructions and burdens upon interstate commerce in grain, by regulating transactions on grain future exchanges, and for other purposes." It was upheld by the Supreme Court in *Board of Trade of City of Chicago v. Olsen*, 262 U.S. 1 (1923).[11]

The motivation for the Grain Futures Act is stated in § 3:

> Transactions in grain involving the sale thereof for future delivery as commonly conducted on boards of trade and known as "futures" are affected with a national public interest . . . the transactions and prices of grain on such boards of trade are susceptible to speculation, manipulation, and control, and sudden or unreasonable fluctuations in the price thereof frequently occur, as a result of such speculation, manipulation, or control, which are detrimental to the producer or the consumer and the persons handling grain and products and by-products thereof in interstate commerce, and . . . such fluctuations in prices are an obstruction to and a burden upon interstate commerce in grain and the products and by-products thereof and render regulation imperative for the protection of such commerce and the national public interest therein.

Section 4 of the Act stated the broad prohibition that formed its core:

> It shall be unlawful for any person to . . . make or execute . . . any contract of sale of grain for future delivery on or subject to the rules of any board of trade in the United States . . . except (a) Where the seller is at the time of the making of such contract the owner of the actual physical property covered thereby, or is the grower thereof . . . or (b) Where such contract is

> made by or through a member of a board of trade which has been designated by the Secretary of Agriculture as a "contract market" . . .

In other words, grain futures that were available for trading on a board of trade could only be traded on a contract market designated by the secretary of agriculture by anyone other than an owner or grower of the grain in question. Section 5 of the statute outlined specific criteria for the secretary of agriculture to apply in determining whether to designate a board of trade as a contract market. A designated contract market failing to meet § 5's criteria could find its status as a designated contract market suspended or revoked by a commission comprised of the secretary of agriculture, secretary of commerce and U.S. attorney general.[12]

2. *Commodity Exchange Act of 1936*

The Commodity Exchange Act, nominally an amendment to the Grain Futures Act, established the Commodity Exchange Commission as a replacement for the commission establishec by the Grain Futures Act. As with the commission established by the Grain Futures Act, the Commodity Exchange Commission was comprised of the secretary of agriculture, secretary of commerce and the attorney general.[13] The scope of commodity futures that were required to be traded on a board of trade designated as a contract market were expanded beyond grain, i.e., "wheat, corn, oats, barley, rye, flax and sorghum,"[14] to include futures on cotton, rice, mill feeds,[15] butter, eggs, and Irish potatoes.[16] A registration regime was established for entities "engaged in soliciting or in accepting orders for the purchase or sale of any commodity for future delivery on or subject to the rules of any contract market and that, in or in connection [accepts money, securities or property to margin guarantee or secure such trades or contracts]," (known as "futures commission merchants") persons receiving commissions or other compensation for trading on the floor of a contract market (known as "floor traders").[17]

Over subsequent years, 12 amendments were made to the Commodity Exchange Act, further expanding its regulatory scope and including wool tops, fats and oils, cottonseed meal, cotton seed, peanuts, soybeans, soybean meal, wool, onions, livestock, livestock products, and frozen concentrated orange juice as commodities that, if traded for future delivery, were required to be traded on a board of trade designated as a contract market.

The table in Figure 2-A summarizes the amendments made to the Commodity Exchange Act between its enactment and 1970. As can be seen from Figure 2-A, save for a significant broadening of the Commodity Exchange Act's enforcement provisions in February 1968, the primary thrust of most of the amendments was an expansion of the definition of commodity and, therefore, the contracts of sale for future delivery required to be traded on a designated contract market.

Figure 2-A: Amendments to Commodity Exchange Act, 1936-1970		
Date of Amendment	Effect of Amendment	Citation
April 7, 1938	Added wool tops to definition of commodities.	75 P.L. 471
October 9, 1940	Added fats and oils, cottonseed meal, cottonseed, peanuts, soybeans, and soybean meal to definition of commodities.	76 P.L. 818
December 19, 1947	Provides for publication of names, addresses, and commodities purchased and sold of traders on Boards of Trade.	80 P.L. 392
August 28, 1954	Added wool to definition of commodities.	83 P.L. 690
June 16, 1955	Augmented investigatory powers of the secretary of agriculture and the Commodity Exchange Commission.	84 P.L. 82
July 26, 1955	Added onions to definition of commodities.	84 P.L. 174
July 24, 1956	Expanded hedging exemption from trading limits established by the Commodity Exchange Commission.	84 P.L. 778
August 28, 1958	Amendment of multiple statutes, including Commodity Exchange Act, regarding appeals procedures.	85 P.L. 791
August 28, 1958	Prohibited futures trading in onions.	85 P.L. 839
June 11, 1960	Amendment of multiple statutes, including Commodity Exchange Act, to account for use of certified mail in the same way as mail.	86 P.L. 507
February 19, 1968	Among other changes: - Added livestock and livestock products to definition of commodities; - Expanded definition of floor broker to include uncompensated individuals; - Expanded trading limits to broader "position	90 P.L. 258

	limits" with entities acting in concert deemed to be one entity; - Inserted antimanipulation provisions; and - Added penalties for violations.	
July 23, 1968	Added frozen concentrated orange juice to definition of commodities.	90 P.L. 418
January 19, 1970	Amendment of multiple statutes by Organized Crime Control Act of 1970 (including Commodity Exchange Act) to provide for procedural changes regarding testimony and witnesses.	90 P.L. 452

3. *Commodity Futures Trading Commission Act of 1974*

Outside of a fairly significant expansion in 1968, no major amendment to the Commodity Exchange Act had occurred since its passage in 1936. The Commodity Futures Trading Commission Act of 1974 overhauled the Commodity Exchange Act. Some of the reasons cited by legislators for this revision included:

- A cash market shortage of the commodities for which futures trading was subject to regulation;
- Concerns about recent frauds in the trading on markets outside the scope of regulation;
- A doubling of trading since 1969 in regulated markets and a quadrupling in the same period in unregulated markets;
- Protection of customers in unregulated markets since, among other things, there was no requirement in such markets to segregate customer funds;
- Perceived shortcomings in the designated contract markets' self-regulation particularly after 1968 amendments to the Commodity Exchange Act holding contract markets responsible for enforcement of their rules resulted in less rules; and
- Perennial concerns about offsetting sales with no *bona fide* economic purpose, i.e., wash sales, and bucketing of orders.[18]

The Commodity Futures Trading Commission Act resulted in the replacement of the Commodity Exchange Authority and Commodity Exchange Commission with an independent agency known as the Commodity Futures Trading Commission (referred to herein interchangeably as the "CFTC"), governed by five commissioners appointed by the president with the advice and consent of the Senate.

Shortly before enactment, a House of Representatives report summarized the scope of the changes to be implemented by the Commodity Futures Trading Commission Act.

House of Representatives Committee on Agriculture, Commodity Futures Trading Commission Act of 1974 Report

H.R. Rpt. 93-975 (April 4, 1974)

. . . [Title I provides that all] existing authority under the Commodity Exchange Act presently delegated to the Secretary of Agriculture and the Commodity Exchange Commission will be transferred to the new CFTC. All existing personnel of the CEA will be transferred to and become employees of the CFTC. Provision is made for a Secretary to the Commission, who will be responsible directly to the Commission members. . . . Certain responsibilities of the Commission may be delegated to CFTC staff, including an Executive Director who will perform the day to day functions of the operation of the Commission under the direction of the members of the Commission. In addition, the Commission will have its own General Counsel and legal staff as well as independent budgeting capability and its own Administrative Law Judges. Commission budgets are to be independent products of the Commission . . .

A customer reparation proceeding before the Commission will be authorized one year after date of enactment of the Act for handling customer complaints which arise from violations of the Act, particularly those which result in monetary damages to the customer. The Commission will have original jurisdiction to consider all such complaints which have not been resolved through the informal settlement procedure required of the contract markets and registered futures associations under the bill. . . . Initially, complaints would be considered by an Administrative Law Judge and then reviewed by the Commission before a final order is entered. A special judicial review of Commission decisions will be established for these proceedings which will allow either party adversely affected to appeal to the U.S. District Court.

The Commission will be directed to take into consideration the public interest designed to be protected by the antitrust laws of the United States before issuing any order, rule or regulation under the Act and before requiring or approving any bylaw, rule, regulation or resolution of a contract market or registered futures association.

Title II provides broad new authority to the new Commission over futures trading in a number of areas. All commodities trading in futures will be brought within federal regulation under the aegis of the new Commission, however, provision is made for preservation of Securities Exchange Commission jurisdiction in those areas traditionally regulated by it. [As noted below, this provision was subsequently broadened before enactment pursuant to the "Treasury Amendment."] "Commodity Trading Advisors" and "Commodity Pool Operators" will be brought within the purview of the Act and will be required to register with the Commission annually. Whether trading by floor brokers and futures commission merchants for their own accounts and at the same time trading for their customers will be allowed will be determined by the Commission after a hearing within six months after enactment and if allowed, the circumstances under which it shall be conducted will be determined by the Commission. [Such trading subsequently was allowed by the CFTC.[19]] The existing registration and examination for fitness requirement will be expanded to include all individuals handling customer accounts. . . . Contract markets will be required to establish their own customer claims settlement procedures complementing the Commission's procedures for the handling of customer complaints . . . and which will result in a voluntary informal settlement between the parties. Contract markets will be required to submit their bylaws, rules, regulations or resolutions which relate to the terms and conditions of futures contracts or other trading requirements to the Commission for its approval or disapproval.

The Commission will be given authority through the Attorney General to seek injunctions to stop any person from violating the Act or regulations thereunder and to stop any trader from controlling a commodity futures contract to the extent that he is effectively restraining trading in such contract but no injunction or mandamus will be issued *ex parte.* The Commission will have authority to impose monetary penalties . . . in both administrative and criminal proceedings for violations of the Act. The Commission will be authorized to require a contract market, after notice and hearings, to effectuate changes in its rules and practices which the Commission determines to be necessary for the protection of the public interest. The Commission will have authority to promulgate special rules and regulations for persons registered under the Act but who are not members of a contract market which may reasonably be required to protect the public interest. The Commission will have special emergency authority to direct contract markets to take such actions as it may deem necessary in "market emergency" situations, such as war, price controls, export embargoes, or significant intervention of a foreign government in the futures market, in order to facilitate the orderly training in or liquidation of any futures contract.

Title III provides enabling authority at the discretion of the Commission for persons registered under the Act and in the commodity trading business to establish a voluntary futures association or associations which would have authority to regulate the practices of its members in the public interest. [Ultimately, after additional amendments via the Futures Trading Act of 1982, this resulted in the formation of the National Futures Association, discussed further in Chapter 5.] Such an association would register with the Commission and establish a uniform code of professional conduct for those in the commodities business and have disciplinary authority over its members. It would also be required to establish a procedure for the settlement of claims and complaints against its members similar to that required of contract markets. Association rules and actions would be subject to review by the new Commission. Association activity would serve solely as a complement rather than a displacement to the authority of the new Commission.

Title IV makes it a felony for Commissioners, employees, or agents of the Commission to participate, directly or indirectly, in any transaction in either futures, options, or an actual commodity and it also makes it a felony for these same people to impart confidential information to others for the purpose of assisting them in participating in such transactions. . . .

One substantial difference between H.R. 13113, the predecessor bill to the Commodity Futures Trading Commission Act and the version enacted into law was a modification to the scope of the CFTC's jurisdiction. H.R. 13113 conferred jurisdictional authority on the CFTC for, in addition to the commodities historically within the Commodity Exchange Commission's purview, "all other goods and articles, except onions . . . and all services, rights, and interests in which contracts for future delivery are presently or in the future dealt in."

This broad scope was objected to by the Department of the Treasury. In a resulting compromise shortly before enactment, a new carve-out from the CFTC's jurisdiction was included with the above-quoted language, known as the "Treasury Amendment." (Note that it was an amendment to the bill before enactment, not to the enacted statute.)

The Treasury Amendment read:

> Nothing in this Act shall be deemed to govern or in any way be applicable to transactions in foreign currency, security warrants, security rights, resales of installment loan contracts, repurchase options, government securities, or mortgages and mortgage purchase commitments, unless such transactions involve the sale thereof for future delivery conducted on a Board of Trade.[20]

Alan Greenspan, Testimony of Federal Reserve Board Chairman Alan Greenspan on the Regulation of OTC Derivatives

Testimony before the House Committee on Banking and Financial Services (July 24, 1998) (available at http://www.federalreserve.gov/boarddocs/testimony/1998/19980724.htm) (accessed June 1, 2014)

The Commodity Futures Trading Commission Act of 1974 did not make any fundamental changes in the objectives of derivatives regulation. However, it expanded the scope of the [Commodity Exchange Act ("CEA")] . . . quite significantly. In addition to creating the CFTC as an independent agency and giving the CFTC exclusive jurisdiction over commodity futures and options, the 1974 Act expanded the CEA's definition of a "commodity" beyond a specific list of agricultural commodities to include "all other goods and articles, except onions, . . . and all services, rights, and interests in which contracts for future delivery are presently or in the future dealt in."

Given this broadened definition of a commodity and an equally broad interpretation of what constitutes a futures contract, a wide range of off-exchange transactions would have been brought potentially within the scope of the CEA. The Treasury Department was particularly concerned about the prospect that the foreign exchange markets might be found to fall within the Act's scope. Aside from the difficulty of manipulating these markets, Treasury argued that participants in OTC markets, primarily banks and other financial institutions, and large corporations, did not need the consumer protections of the Commodity Exchange Act. Consequently, Treasury proposed and Congress included a provision in the 1974 Act, the "Treasury Amendment," which excluded off-exchange derivative transactions in foreign currency (as well as government securities, and certain other financial instruments) from the newly expanded CEA. What the Treasury did not envision, and the Treasury Amendment did not protect, was the subsequent development and spectacular growth of a much wider range of OTC derivative contracts – swaps on interest rates, exchange rates, and prices of commodities and securities.

Even with the Treasury Amendment's carve-out, the seeds of jurisdictional disputes between the CFTC and SEC were sown.

4. Shad-Johnson Accord

The broad jurisdiction granted to the Commodity Futures Trading Commission under the Commodity Futures Trading Commission Act soon brought the Securities and Exchange Commission and the Commodity Futures Trading Commission into conflict.

The dispute originated over whether the CFTC or the SEC had jurisdiction over options and futures on securities. The CFTC argued that it was granted exclusive jurisdiction over options and futures on all commodities including securities. This was grounded in the grant of jurisdiction at that time to the CFTC over:

> accounts, agreements (including any transaction which is of the character of, or is commonly known to the trade as, an "option," "privilege," "indemnity," "bid," "offer," "put," "call," "advance guaranty," or "decline guaranty"), and transactions involving contracts of sale of a commodity for future delivery, traded or executed on a contract market designated

> pursuant to section 5 of this Act or any other board of trade, exchange, or market.
>
> With a carve-out specifying that:
>
> nothing contained in this section shall (i) supersede or limit the jurisdiction at any time conferred on the Securities and Exchange Commission or other regulatory authorities under the laws of the United States or of any State, or (ii) restrict the Securities and Exchange Commission and such other authorities from carrying out their duties and responsibilities in accordance with such laws.

Moreover, the CFTC's jurisdiction over futures contracts was with respect to commodities, i.e., "[All] goods and articles, except onions . . . and all services, rights, and interests." With respect to options, Commodity Exchange Act § 4c(a)(B) and § 4c(b) operated, at the time of the CFTC's establishment, to prohibit commodity options on the commodities historically subject to CFTC jurisdiction, i.e., wheat, cotton, rice, corn, oats, barley, rye, flaxseed, grain sorghums, mill feeds, butter, eggs, Solanum tuberosum (Irish potatoes), wool, wool tops, fats and oils (including lard, tallow, cottonseed oil, peanut oil, soybean oil, and all other fats and oils), cottonseed meal, cottonseed, peanuts, soybeans, soybean meal, livestock, livestock products, and frozen concentrated orange juice. Trading in all other commodity options was statutorily permitted, if CFTC regulations allowed for such trading.

Even this had a caveat, though, which stated:

> Nothing in this Act shall be deemed to govern or in any way be applicable to transactions in foreign currency, security warrants, security rights, resale of installment loan contracts, repurchase options, government securities, or mortgages and mortgage purchase commitments, unless such transactions involve the sale thereof for future delivery conducted on a Board of Trade.

In 1975, the SEC formally objected to the listing of futures as Government National Mortgage Association ("GNMA") securities by the Chicago Board of Trade, a CFTC-regulated entity. GNMA securities are securities backed by a pool of mortgages guaranteed by the GNMA, a U.S. government agency.

When the Chicago Board of Options Exchange, an SEC-regulated institution, listed options on GNMA securities in 1981, the Chicago Board of Trade sued the SEC, challenging its jurisdictional authority to authorize the listing of such options by one of its registrants. While the case was pending in the 7th Circuit (the 7th Circuit ultimately ruled in favor of the CFTC[21]), the agencies agreed to the Shad-Johnson Accord that, as enacted into statute:

- Granted the SEC jurisdiction over all securities-based options, including on indexes.
- Granted the CFTC jurisdiction over futures and options on futures referencing municipal securities and stock indexes.
- Prohibited single stock futures and options on single stock futures.[22]

However, as can be seen from the following case, the Shad-Johnson Accord did not provide a lasting resolution of questions on the extent of the SEC's and CFTC's relative jurisdictions.

Chicago Mercantile Exchange v. Securities and Exchange Commission

883 F.2d 537 (7th Cir. 1989)

Easterbrook, Circuit Judge. . . .

The CFTC regulates futures and options on futures; the SEC regulates securities and options on securities; jurisdiction never overlaps. Problem: The statute does not define either "contracts . . . for future delivery" or "option" – although it says that "'future delivery' . . . shall not include any sale of any cash commodity for deferred shipment or delivery". . . . [N]ewfangled instruments may have aspects of each of the prototypes. . .

A futures contract, roughly speaking, is a fungible promise to buy or sell a particular commodity at a fixed date in the future. Futures contracts are fungible because they have standard terms and each side's obligations are guaranteed by a clearing house. . . . Trading occurs in "the contract," not in the commodity. Most futures contracts may be performed by delivery of the commodity (wheat, silver, oil, etc.). Some (those based on financial instruments such as T-bills or on the value of an index of stocks) do not allow delivery. . . .

A security, roughly speaking, is an undivided interest in a common venture the value of which is subject to uncertainty. Usually this means a claim to the assets and profits of an "issuer". . . .

Securities usually arise out of capital formation and aggregation (entrusting funds to an entrepreneur), while futures are means of hedging, speculation, and price revelation without transfer of capital. So one could think of the distinction between the jurisdiction of the SEC and that of the CFTC as the difference between regulating capital formation and regulating hedging. Congress conceived the role of the CFTC in that way when it created the agency in 1974 to assume functions that had been performed by the Department of Agriculture but which were no longer thought appropriate for that Department as futures markets expanded beyond commodities into financial instruments. . . . Unfortunately, the distinction between capital formation and hedging falls apart when it comes time to allocate the regulation of options.

A call option is a promise by the writer to deliver the underlying instrument at a price fixed in advance (the "strike price") if the option is exercised within a set time. The buyer pays a price (the "premium") in advance for the opportunity; the writer may or may not own the instrument he promises to deliver. Call options are written "out of the money" – that is, the exercise price exceeds the market price at the outset. The writer will make money if by the time the option expires the market price is less than the strike price plus the premium (plus the interest earned on the premium in the interim); the buyer of the option hopes that the market price will rise above the strike price by enough to cover the premium, the time value of money, and the transactions costs of executing the option. . . .

The SEC consistently has taken the position that options on securities should be regulated as securities. For some years the CFTC maintained that options on securities should be regulated as futures because options are extrinsic to capital formation and because it is almost always possible to devise an option with the same economic attributes as a futures contract (and the reverse). Matters came to a head in 1980, when both agencies asserted jurisdiction over options on securities based on pools of notes. . . .

While the case was pending, the agencies reached a pact, which the SEC calls the Shad-Johnson Agreement and the CFTC calls the Johnson-Shad Agreement. (John Shad was the SEC's Chairman at the time, and Phillip Johnson the CFTC's.) This Accord (as we shall call it to avoid offending either agency) provided that jurisdiction over options follows jurisdiction over the things on which the options are written. So the SEC received jurisdiction of options on securities, while the CFTC got jurisdiction of options on futures contracts. . . .

Congress then enacted the Accord almost verbatim, producing the explicit reference to options in § 3(a)(10) of the '34 Act, the SEC savings clause in § 2a(i) of the CEA, and a small change in 7 U.S.C. § 6n to implement an understanding about pools. The legislature thought that this Accord would resolve things and restore a regime in which the SEC supervises capital formation and the CFTC hedging.

The legislation implementing the Accord left in place the premise [that] . . . if an instrument is both a security and a futures contract, then the CFTC's jurisdiction is exclusive. Section 2a(ii) has no other possible meaning. Like many an agreement resolving a spat, the Accord addressed a symptom rather than the problem. Options are only one among many instruments that can have attributes of futures contracts as well as securities. . . .

Which means that the dispute of 1980-82 about options will be played out – is being played out – about each new instrument. . . .

Unless Congress changes the allocation of jurisdiction between the agencies . . . a court must resolve[:] is . . . the instrument a futures contract? If yes, then the CFTC's jurisdiction is exclusive, unless it is also an option on a security, in which case the SEC's jurisdiction is exclusive. So long as an instrument is a futures contract (and not an option), whether it is also a "security" is neither here nor there.

The court in *Chicago Mercantile Exchange v. Securities and Exchange Commission* then engaged in a complicated analysis as to whether the instrument in the case was a security or a future. (It ultimately determined it was both and that the CFTC's "exclusive" jurisdiction over futures meant that the CFTC had jurisdiction.)

Dissatisfaction with the Shad-Johnson Accord reached its peak in 2000.

United States General Accounting Office, CTFC and SEC Issues Related to the Shad-Johnson Jurisdictional Accord

GAO/GGD-00-89 (April 6, 2000)

. . . In the United States, SEC has authority over securities trading and the securities markets, and CFTC has authority over futures trading and the futures markets. According to SEC and CFTC, three amendments to the [Commodity Exchange Act (the "CEA")] . . . in 1974 led to jurisdictional disputes over securities-based futures. First, the act was amended to expand the definition of a commodity to include virtually anything — tangible or intangible. Consequently, a security fell within the definition of a commodity. Second, the act was amended to provide CFTC with exclusive jurisdiction over all commodity futures transactions, including options on futures. Third, the act was amended to preserve SEC's preexisting authority over securities trading and the securities markets.

These three CEA amendments led to a dispute between SEC and CFTC that was eventually resolved through the Shad-Johnson Jurisdictional Accord. In 1975, CFTC approved a Chicago Board of Trade (CBT) application to trade futures on Government National Mortgage Association pass-through mortgage-backed certificates. In an exchange of letters, SEC asserted that the contracts were securities within its jurisdiction, and CFTC responded that they were futures within its exclusive jurisdiction. The dispute remained unresolved, and in 1981, SEC approved rule changes for the Chicago Board Options Exchange (CBOE) that allowed the exchange to trade options on the certificates. CBT petitioned the U.S. Seventh Circuit Court of Appeals to set aside the SEC order. The court prevented CBOE from trading the options until it could render its decision.[ii] Under these circumstances, SEC and CFTC reached the accord to

---

[ii] [N. 10] In *Board of Trade of the City of Chicago v. Securities and Exchange Commission*, 677 F. 2d 1137 (7th Cir. 1982), the Seventh Circuit Court of Appeals subsequently found that SEC lacked the authority to approve CBOE to trade the options, because the options fell within CFTC's exclusive jurisdiction.

clarify their respective jurisdictions over securities-based options and futures. In February 1982, they submitted the accord to Congress to be enacted into law. Congress codified the accord substantially as proposed in the federal securities laws as section 2 of the Securities Act of 1933 and section 3 of the Securities Exchange Act of 1934 and in the CEA as section 2(a)(1)(B).[iii]

The accord allocated jurisdiction between SEC and CFTC for, among other things, securities-based options and securities-based futures and options on futures.[iv] First, it provided SEC with jurisdiction over securities-based options, including stocks and stock indexes. Second, the accord prohibited futures (and options thereon) on single corporate and municipal securities. According to SEC and CFTC, the ban was intended to be temporary . . .

Finally, the accord provided CFTC with jurisdiction over futures (and options thereon) on exempted securities[v] (other than municipal securities) and stock indexes. . . .

Given the potential benefits of repealing the accord trading prohibitions and the potential for jurisdictional differences to continue to impede such efforts, we recommend that the Chairmen of SEC and CFTC (1) work together and with Congress to develop and implement an appropriate legal and regulatory framework for allowing the trading of futures on single stocks and all stock indexes, and (2) submit to Congress legislative proposals for repealing the accord trading prohibitions. . . .

Due to dissatisfaction with the Shad-Johnson Accord, as noted below in section E1, the General Accounting Office's recommendations were shortly followed by Congressional action in the form of the Commodity Futures Modernization Act of 2000, a sweeping liberalization of off-exchange derivatives trading. However, in the interim, an ever-more sophisticated and large market in derivatives traded off-exchange (interchangeably referred to as "over-the-counter," "OTC," or "off-exchange" derivatives) was developing.

[iii] [N. 11] The accord was codified in the Securities Act Amendments of 1982, which amended the federal securities laws, and the Futures Trading Act of 1982, which amended the CEA.

[iv] [N. 12] The accord also clarified SEC and CFTC jurisdiction over options and futures on, among other things, certificates of deposit and foreign currencies.

[v] [N. 13] Exempted securities include securities issued or guaranteed by the United States, the District of Columbia, or any U.S. state.

C. GROWTH IN THE OVER-THE-COUNTER DERIVATIVES MARKET

The modern over-the-counter swaps market is generally viewed as having begun in 1981 with a cross-currency interest rate swap brokered by Salomon Brothers between the World Bank and IBM.[23] Jon Rotenstreich, the partner at Salomon Brothers responsible for the IBM-World Bank swap noted that, at the time, "Nobody understood what the hell we were doing . . . We were just trying to hammer it out to get the damn thing done . . ."[24]

From such inauspicious beginnings, a substantial market developed with the first over-the-counter interest rate swap generally held as being transacted in 1982, the first over-the-counter commodity swap in 1986, and the first over-the-counter equity swap in 1989.[25] By the end of 1994, more than $10 billion in notional of over-the-counter interest rate derivatives and cross-currency swaps was estimated to be outstanding.[26] By 2008, that number exceeded $400 billion.[27]

An essential bridge between the IBM swap and a $400 billion marketplace in just over-the-counter interest rate derivatives and cross-currency swaps alone, was the development of standardized documentation for over-the-counter derivatives under the auspices of a newly formed trade association, the International Swap Dealers Association, today known as the International Swaps and Derivatives Association or "ISDA."

Sean M. Flanagan, The Rise of a Trade Association: Group Interactions Within the International Swaps and Derivatives Association

6 Harvard Negotiation Law Review 211 (Spring 2001)

. . . The International Swaps and Derivatives Association, Inc. ["ISDA"], is a trade association for OTC derivatives dealers and other market-participants. The majority of ISDA's activities focuses on the market for privately negotiated swaps contracts. . . .

ISDA began as an informal swap documentation project undertaken by eleven financial institutions in 1984. In the early 1980s, swaps were still a novelty. Banks received large fees and substantial spreads for arranging interest-rate and currency swaps between large corporations, banks, and government entities. As swap mechanics were improved and swap volume increased, the major financial institutions that handled swaps each developed their own standard form agreements. . . . Each swap dealer's standard contract, including the definitions of the terms used in the contract, was unique.

The result was that swaps with ostensibly identical terms differed depending on the individual who had negotiated the swap and the dealer from which they came. In addition, when dealers traded with one another, substantial effort was required to bridge the gaps between the two parties' forms and definitions. Negotiation over these contract terms consumed large amounts of time and effort. . . .

In 1984, Salomon Brothers contacted ten other institutions involved in the swaps market and arranged a meeting. The agenda was to discuss the development of documentation standards that would settle some of the issues that currently had to be negotiated – often at great expense – for each swap deal. An initial attempt to draft a standard form contract failed when parties involved in the process felt that the contract that was being developed too much resembled one participant's own standard form master agreement (most noticeably in typeface and layout). At this point, the group pooled its resources and retained the law firm Cravath, Swaine & Moore ("Cravath") to assist in drafting. Lawyers from Cravath attended the earliest meetings of the group. . . .

After the initial experience of failure, the parties generally assumed that the differences between the participants were too great for a consensus to be reached about what an actual standard form contract should look like. Instead, the group decided to focus on developing standard definitions for terms commonly used in swap agreements. These definitions included terms typically used in contracts and fallback provisions dictating actions in unforeseen circumstances.[vi] Initially, this goal was intended to be the full extent of the group's activities. . . .

A committee of about 25 representatives from the eleven institutions was formed to work on developing . . . [standardized] definitions [for use in over-the-counter derivatives documentation]. These representatives included bankers, traders, in-house counsel, and outside counsel.[vii] The mix of participants provided the diversity of financial, legal, and practical expertise essential to developing robust documentation that would withstand the scrutiny of courts and the market. At documentation committee meetings, generally held in the offices of member institutions or outside counsel, the members discussed each definition as a group, sharing their personal and institutional opinions regarding appropriate standards and their experience with the issues involved.

Generally, each point was discussed by the group until a consensus was reached. The Cravath lawyers would try to capture the consensus in a draft definition, which then would be circulated among the group members for comment and discussion before being redrafted. The discussion, draft,

---

[vi] [N. 124] An example of this type of term is the "fallback rate" for LIBOR, which dictates what rates, if any, should be used to calculate payments on an interest rate swap if the interest rate index chosen as the measure of LIBOR by the parties is unavailable on the day a payment is to be calculated. . . .

[vii] [N. 127] Lawyers from Sullivan & Cromwell, Davis Polk, and Cleary, Gottlieb, Steen & Hamilton represented some of the parties on the documentation committee.

comment, and redraft processes often were repeated several times for each definition. This openness was one of the keys to the success of the process. . . .

When significant differences of opinion existed on the committee and consensus was not readily reached, the issue would be left to "float" without a push for an immediate resolution. Rick Grove, the Executive Director of ISDA from 1997 to January 2001, notes that policy disagreements have always been common in the organization. Successful resolution of such disagreements has been one of ISDA's key functions. . . .

Issues that remained contentious often could be resolved at the drafting stage. The outside counsel facilitating the drafting process prepared a compromise definition that met each party's interests. Alternatively, the definition was structured such that it included a menu of alternate standard definitions from which the contracting parties could choose, thereby avoiding resolution of the issue but allowing contracting parties to select for themselves.

The process of negotiating and drafting standard documentation that the documentation committee developed as it created these definitions has become the standard documentation process for ISDA projects. . . .

As the definitions project neared completion, the members of the group decided that they wanted to copyright the definitions and needed some sort of official entity to release the document and hold the copyright. The result was ISDA, the International Swaps Dealers Association,[viii] which was formally created as a nonprofit corporation in 1985.

ISDA released the final definitions in 1985. While not technically a contract, the . . . [definitions, known as the "SWAPS Code,"] provided most of the key building blocks for a contract and ensured that swap dealers using it would be speaking the same language. For instance, parties could incorporate representations and warranties from the SWAPS Code wholesale by stipulating that they were incorporating them "as defined in the SWAPS Code" rather than negotiating and drafting them. The SWAPS Code was thus a great leap forward in standardization of the swaps market . . .

The initial membership of ISDA consisted of the eleven participants in the development of the SWAPS Code. The board comprised ten representatives from those institutions with the board chairman functioning as the chief executive officer of the organization.[ix] . . .

[viii] [N. 136] This name was changed in 1993 to the International Swaps and Derivatives Association to reflect the development of the industry and the expanding scope of ISDA's activities. . . . [T]he new name reflected a belief at the board level that ISDA's role was to represent the interests of the entire OTC derivatives industry, not just those of dealers.

[ix] [N. 139] . . . The initial directors were drawn from Shearson Lehman, Citibank, Bankers Trust, Morgan Guaranty, Salomon Brothers, Kleinworth Benson Cross Finance, Morgan Stanley, Merrill Lynch, First Boston and Goldman, Sachs.

Motivated both by interest in its activities from other market players and a desire to increase the revenue base of the organization, ISDA developed three membership categories. The first, Primary Membership, was open to the same types of entities that had initially been eligible for ISDA membership, dealers in swaps and other OTC derivatives. Only Primary Members have the right to be represented on the board of directors and to vote in board elections. Associate Membership, the first new membership category to be added, was designed for professional service firms, such as law firms, accounting firms, and consulting firms that participated in the OTC swaps and derivatives industry as service providers. In 1988, ISDA added the Subscriber membership category, targeted at end-users of swaps, such as corporations and governments. . . .

In the year following its formal creation, ISDA remained focused on standardizing terms and vocabulary, and it released an update of the SWAPS Code in 1986. In 1987, ISDA also published interest-rate and currency definitions. Like the original SWAPS Code, the development of these definitions was primarily done by ISDA members based in New York. During this period, some ISDA members in London, particularly Morgan Stanley's London office, began to push for the creation of a full, standardized master agreement.

Unlike the New York membership, which remained reluctant to attempt to develop a standard form contract for the industry, the London members saw a standardized master agreement as the logical next step. ISDA's board of directors agreed, and the London membership . . . took the lead role in the new documentation project. The end result was a pair of standard form master agreements, one for U.S.-dollar interest-rate swaps, and another for multicurrency interest-rate and currency swaps. Collectively, these two . . . agreements are referred to as the 1987 ISDA Master Agreement.

Major documentation accomplishments of ISDA during the early nineties included the re-drafting of the 1987 ISDA Master Agreement (resulting in the 1992 ISDA Master Agreement),[x] the development of the 1991 ISDA Definitions,[xi] the development of credit support and collateral documentation, and the development of definition booklets tailored to specific types of transactions. . . .

---

[x] [N. 178] The re-draft . . . of the 1987 ISDA Master Agreement was motivated by several factors. First, the market had developed new financial products. . . . [I]t became desirable to design a master agreement with maximum flexibility, adding provisions, for instance, for physical settlement. The earlier agreement only provided for cash payments. . . In addition, regulators were putting pressure on the industry to modify the close-out netting provisions in the agreement. In the 1987 Master Agreement close-out netting provisions (referred to in the industry as the "first method"), if the net value of transactions terminated upon default were calculated to be in favor of the defaulting party, no payment needed to be made by the non-defaulting party. . . . U.S. regulators preferred a system in which both parties, not just the defaulting party, were obligated to pay any net obligation to their counterparty. The 1992 ISDA Master Agreement was drafted so as to provide for this "second method" of close-out netting as an option . . .

[xi] [N. 179] These definitions centered around payment calculations . . .

Starting in the late 1980s, the scope of ISDA's activities began to expand beyond just documentation. ISDA became involved in discussions with regulators on behalf of the OTC derivatives industry. ISDA board members and representatives now regularly testify before congressional committees. It coordinated industry opposition to CFTC and SEC regulation, acting both as an advocate for the industry and as an instrument for its self-regulation. ISDA has also lobbied successfully to get legislation passed in the U.S. explicitly recognizing the validity of netting agreements for derivatives contracts in bankruptcy contexts. . . .

In 2002, ISDA developed a successor to the 1992 ISDA Master Agreement, known as the 2002 ISDA Master Agreement. Both the 1992 and the 2002 ISDA Master Agreement are commonly used by market participants. The documentation of off-exchange derivatives is discussed in more detail in Chapter 10.

The growth in the over-the-counter derivatives market was not without its setbacks. First, there was uncertainty in the marketplace as to whether these over-the-counter derivatives might be deemed to be off-exchange commodity futures or commodity options contracts in violation of the Commodity Exchange Act. Second, it also spurred litigation. We turn to both of these issues in the following section.

D. AN ERA OF DEREGULATION AND GROWTH, PART II 1992 – 1997

1. *Futures Trading Practices Act of 1992*

Prior to 1992, the CFTC had the authority to exempt commodity option contracts from regulation under the Commodity Exchange Act.[28] However, the CFTC lacked analogous authority to exempt commodity futures contracts from regulation under the Commodity Exchange Act. Therefore, even where the CFTC viewed a product as not necessitating regulation under the Commodity Exchange Act and the imposition of the Commodity Exchange Act's prohibition on off-exchange commodity futures, their only remedy was to issue an interpretation defining the scope of "contract for the sale of a commodity for future delivery."[29]

The perceived ambiguity of the Commodity Exchange Act was such that the Department of the Treasury advocated for a legislative solution instead of *ad hoc*, case-by-case issuances of exemptions or interpretations.[30] The inadequacy of this approach was further illustrated by *Transnor (Bermuda) Limited v. BP*

North America Petroleum, 738 F. Supp. 1472 (S.D.N.Y. 1990), in which a district court judge ruled that 15-day Brent futures contracts were contracts "for the sale of a commodity for future delivery" under the Commodity Exchange Act. With no explicit statutory exemptive authority, within six months of this ruling the CFTC issued an interpretation excluding such transactions from the scope of contracts "for the sale of a commodity for future delivery" in direct contradiction of the ruling in *Transnor*.[31] The contradiction between a judicial statutory interpretation and the CFTC's interpretation of the same subject matter led to market disruption.[32] It was unknown whether in litigation such contracts would be ruled unenforceable off-exchange commodity futures contracts.

Largely in response to the clamor for more regulatory certainty, Congress enacted the Futures Trading Practices Act of 1992 that, in addition to strengthening the CFTC's enforcement capability and attempting to rationalize the structure of the Commodity Exchange Act, amended § 4 of the Commodity Exchange Act to grant the CFTC broad exemptive authority.[33]

Almost immediately following passage of the Futures Trading Practices Act, the CFTC issued a broad exemption from the Commodity Exchange Act for swap agreements between "eligible swap participants" (i.e., regulated institutions or entities meeting specified asset thresholds),[34] referenced throughout as the "1993 CFTC Swap Exemption," and for the contracts that were the subject of *Transnor*.[35]

2. *Bankruptcy*

In addition to the other statutory developments described in this chapter, during this era there were also various modifications to the Bankruptcy Code to ensure the enforceability of certain provisions contained in standard over-the-counter derivatives transactions in the event of the bankruptcy of one of the parties. These are discussed in detail in Chapter 11.

3. *Bankers Trust Litigation*

The market certainty intended to be provided by the Futures Trading Practices Act of 1992 did not preclude litigation. There were open questions as to whether over-the-counter swaps could be construed as securities and what duty of care, if any, was owed by the seller of a derivative to a purchaser.

In the following case, the judge sought to address these questions. The backdrop to his ruling were the "Bankers Trust tapes" of employees of Bankers Trust, at the time one of the most prominent derivatives dealers, boasting of derivatives trading gains at the expense of their customers.[36] The tapes, mostly recorded trading lines, contained remarks such as:

- "Funny business, you know? Lure people into that calm and then totally [expletive] 'em."
- "They would never know . . . how much money was taken out of that . . . . That's the beauty of Bankers Trust."
- "[W]e set 'em up."
- "I mean we told him $8.1 million when the real number was 14. So now if the real number is 16, we'll tell him that it is 11. You know, just slowly chip away at that differential between what it really is and what we're telling him."
- "[A]s soon as we quit selling dynamite, maybe we'll have a good business."
- "Pad the numbers a little bit."
- "[T]hese guys have done some pretty wild stuff. And you know, they probably do not understand it quite as well as they should. I think that they have a pretty good understanding of it, but not perfect. And that's like perfect for us."
- "[W]hat Bankers Trust can do for Sony and IBM is get in the middle and rip them off – take a little money."[37]

Proctor & Gamble Company v. Bankers Trust Company

925 F. Supp. 1270 (S.D. Ohio 1996)

. . . Feikens, District Judge . . .

Plaintiff, The Procter & Gamble Company ("P & G"), is a publicly traded Ohio corporation. Defendant, Bankers Trust Company ("BT"), is a wholly-owned subsidiary of Bankers Trust New York Corporation ("BTNY"). BTNY is a state-chartered banking company. BT trades currencies, securities, commodities and derivatives. Defendant BT Securities, also a wholly-owned subsidiary of BTNY, is a registered broker-dealer. The defendants are referred to collectively as "BT" in this opinion.

P & G filed its Complaint . . . alleging fraud, misrepresentation, breach of fiduciary duty, negligent misrepresentation, and negligence in connection with an interest rate swap transaction it had entered with BT. . . . This swap, explained more fully below, was a leveraged derivatives transaction whose value was based on the yield of five-year Treasury notes and the price of thirty-year Treasury bonds ["the 5s/30s swap"). . . .

P & G [also added] . . . claims related to a second swap. . . . This second swap was also a leveraged derivatives transaction. Its value was based on the four-year German Deutschemark rate. . . .

This motion [to dismiss P & G's claims] involves questions of first impression whether the swap agreements fall within federal securities or commodities laws. . . .

I conclude that the 5s/30s and DM swap agreements are not securities as defined by the Securities Acts of 1933 and 1934 . . .; that these swap agreements are exempt from the Commodity Exchange Act ["CEA"]; [and] that there is no private right of action available to P & G under the antifraud provisions of that Act . . .

I conclude that as a counterparty to swap agreements, BT owed no fiduciary duty to P & G. . . .

One leading commentator describes two "visions" of the "explosive growth of the derivatives market." Hu, *Hedging Expectations: "Derivative Reality" and the Law and Finance of the Corporate Objective*, Vol. 73 Texas L. Rev. 985 (1995). One vision, that relied upon by derivatives dealers, is that of perfect hedges found in formal gardens. This vision portrays the order – the respite from an otherwise chaotic universe – made possible by financial science. Corporations are subject to volatile financial and commodities markets. Derivatives, by offering hedges against almost any kind of price risk, allow corporations to operate in a more ordered world.

The other vision is that of "science run amok, a financial Jurassic Park." . . .

Given the potential for a "financial Jurassic Park," the size of the derivatives market and the complexity of these financial instruments, it is not surprising that there is a demand for regulation and legislation. Several bills have been introduced in Congress to regulate derivatives.[xii] BT Securities has been investigated by the Securities and Exchange Commission ("SEC") and by the Commodity Futures Trading Commission ("CFTC") regarding a swap transaction with a party other than P & G. *In re BT Securities Corp.*, Release Nos. 33–7124, 34–35136 and CFTC Docket No. 95–3 (Dec. 22, 1994). Bankers Trust has agreed with the Federal Reserve Bank to a Consent Decree on its leveraged derivatives transactions.

At present, most derivatives transactions fall in "the common-law no-man's land beyond regulations . . ." Cohen, *The Challenge of Derivatives*, Vol. 63 Fordham L. Rev. at 2013. This is where the two highly specialized swap transactions involved in this case fall. . . .

[The P & G/BT Swap Agreements] are governed by . . . [a] standardized form, drafted by the International Swap Dealers Association, Inc. ("ISDA"), together with a customized Schedule and written Confirmations for each swap. . . .

P & G unwound both [the DM Swap and the 5s/30s Swap early] . . . as interest rates in both the United States and Germany took a significant turn upward, thus putting P & G in a negative position *vis-a-vis* its counterparty BT. BT now claims that it is owed over $200 million on the two swaps, while P & G claims the swaps were fraudulently induced and fraudulently executed, and seeks a declaratory verdict that it owes nothing. . . .

[xii] [N. 2] *See* H.R. 31, 104th Cong. 1st Sess. (1995); H.R. 20, 104th Cong. 1st Sess. (1995); H.R. 4745, 103rd Cong.2d Sess. (1994).

P & G asserts that the 5s/30s and DM swaps fall within any of the following portions of [the definition of "security" in the Securities Act of 1934 and the Securities Exchange Act of 1934]: 1) investment contracts; 2) notes; 3) evidence of indebtedness; 4) options on securities; and 5) instruments commonly known as securities. . . .

Economic reality is the guide for determining whether these swaps transactions that do not squarely fit within the statutory definition are, nevertheless, securities. . . .

While the swaps may meet certain elements of the . . . investment contract [test], what is missing is the element of a "common enterprise." P & G did not pool its money with that of any other company or person in a single business venture. . . . Furthermore, BT was not managing P & G's money; BT was a counterparty to the swaps, and the value of the swaps depended on market forces, not BT's entrepreneurial efforts. The swaps are not investment contracts. . . .

As with the test whether an instrument is an investment contract, these swap agreements bear some, but not all, of the earmarks of notes. At the outset, and perhaps most basic, the payments required in the swap agreements did not involve the payment or repayment of principal. . . .

Balancing all the . . . factors, I conclude that the 5s/30s and DM swaps are not notes for purposes of the Securities Acts.

P & G argues that if the swaps are not notes, they are evidence of indebtedness because they contain bilateral promises to pay money and they evidence debts between the parties. . . .

The test whether an instrument is within the category of "evidence of indebtedness" is essentially the same as whether an instrument is a note. . . .

I do not accept P & G's definition of "evidence of indebtedness" in large part because that definition omits an essential element of debt instruments – the payment or repayment of principal. Swap agreements do not involve the payment of principal; the notional amount never changes hands.[38] . . .

The definition of a "security" in the 1933 and 1934 Acts includes the parenthetical phrase "(including any interest therein or based on the value thereof)," which could lead to a reading of the statute to mean that an option based on the value of a security is a security. Legislative history, however, makes it clear that that reading was not intended. . . .

Two Orders by the Security and Exchange Commission must be considered. These rulings involve transactions between BT and Gibson Greetings, Inc. in swaps that have some similarities to the 5s/30s swap. *In re BT Securities Corp.*, Release Nos. 33–7124, 34–35136 (Dec. 22, 1994), and *In the Matter of Mitchell A. Vazquez*, Release Nos. 33–7269, 34–36909 (Feb. 29, 1996). In these cases, the SEC ruled that a "Treasury–Linked Swap" between BT and Gibson Greetings, Inc. was a security within the meaning of the federal securities laws. . . .

These SEC Orders were made pursuant to Offers of Settlement made by BT Securities and Vazquez. . . . They are not binding in this case . . . nor do they have collateral estoppel effect.

Even though both the Gibson Greetings, Inc. swap and the P & G 5s/30s swap derived their values from securities (Treasury notes), they were not options. . . .

Finally, P & G contends that both the 5s/30s and the DM swaps are securities simply because that is how these instruments were offered and how they have become known through a course of dealing. In support of this position, P & G points to the SEC Orders in the Gibson Greetings matter and asserts that BT labels leveraged derivatives as investments, speculative, and options; and that the financial markets and the media characterize derivatives as securities. . . .

[W]hen a party seeks to fit financial instruments into the non-specific categories of securities, those instruments must nevertheless . . . be a pooling of funds in a common enterprise. These swaps do not qualify as securities. . . .

Even if the 5s/30s and DM swaps are defined as . . . [commodity futures], swap agreements are exempt from all but the antifraud provisions of the CEA under the CFTC Swap Exemption. Title V of the Futures Trading Practices Act of 1992 granted the CFTC the authority to exempt certain swaps transactions from CEA coverage.

In response to this directive, on January 22, 1993, the CFTC . . . [provided] that swap agreements which [meet specified criteria, including that it is entered into between "eligible swap participants" are exempt from all but the anti-fraud provisions of the CEA.[39]]

The 5s/30s and DM swaps meet these criteria. . . .

P & G contends that a fiduciary relationship existed between it and BT. It argues that it agreed to the swap transactions because of a long relationship it had with BT and the trust that it had in BT, plus the assurance that BT would take on the responsibility of monitoring the transactions and that BT would look out for its interests. . . .

Even accepting these contentions as true, these contentions fail. . . .

P & G and BT were in a business relationship. They were counterparties. Even though, as I point out hereafter, BT had superior knowledge in the swaps transactions, that does not convert their business relationship into one in which fiduciary duties are imposed. . . .

[However,] New York caselaw establishes an implied contractual duty to disclose in business negotiations. Such a duty may arise where 1) a party has superior knowledge of certain information; 2) that information is not readily available to the other party; and 3) the first party knows that the second party is acting on the basis of mistaken knowledge. . . .

Thus, I conclude that defendants had a duty to disclose material information to plaintiff both before the parties entered into the swap transactions and in their performance, and also a duty to deal fairly and in good faith during the performance of the swap transactions. I confine these conclusions to the parameters outlined in this opinion. . . .

To summarize these rulings, I grant [BT's motions dismissing P & G's claims in which, though formally plaintiff, P & G asserted defenses to payment of $200 million which BT said was owed by P & G.]

But these rulings should not be misinterpreted. While they are required by the case management rules of civil procedure, plaintiff's case will proceed to trial [to adjudicate BT's $200 million claim against P & G.] . . .

The *Proctor & Gamble* case had a number of ramifications. A changing of the guard at Bankers Trust was considered to be primarily motivated by the associated scandal.[40] Bankers Trust ultimately accepted $35 million from Proctor & Gamble in lieu of the $200 million it claimed Proctor & Gamble was obligated to pay in settlement of its claims.[41] In total, due to derivatives disputes, Bankers Trust wrote off approximately $300 million in amounts it claimed it was otherwise owed.[42] There were allegations of improprieties with respect to nine customers in addition to Proctor & Gamble, including one based in Indonesia.[43] Bankers Trust settled related regulatory claims with the CFTC, SEC, and Federal Reserve.[44] Nor was Bankers Trust the only swap provider threatened with litigation with claims against, among others, Bear Stearns, Morgan Guaranty, and Solomon Brothers International Limited.[45]

In the over-the-counter derivatives market, it led to the market adoption of standardized "non-re iance" representations drafted by ISDA.[46]

The questions raised in *Proctor & Gamble* regarding the regulatory treatment for over-the-counter swaps – whether they should be deemed securities, commodities, or neither – were not resolved until the passage of the Commodity Futures Modernization Act of 2000 and, later, the Dodd-Frank Act.

E. AN ERA OF DEREGULATION AND GROWTH, PART II: 1998 – 2007

1. *Developments Leading to the Commodity Futures Modernization Act of 2000*

On May 6, 1998, the CFTC, chaired by President Clinton appointee Brooksley Born, issued a Concept Release on over-the-counter derivatives.[47] It was cast as a reexamination of the CFTC's approach to over-the-counter derivatives, triggered by market changes since 1993[48] and "a number of large, well-publicized, financial losses."[49] The CFTC specifically asked for public comment on

75 questions it posed on topics ranging from eligible products and participants to clearing, registration, capital, and reporting requirements.[50]

The Department of the Treasury, Federal Reserve Board, and SEC sent a joint letter to both houses of Congress within a month of the 1998 Concept Release condemning it and attaching proposed legislation pre-empting the CFTC from altering the *status quo ante* with respect to derivatives as of the 1993 CFTC Swap Exemption.[51]

The CFTC's claim to have "no preconceived result in mind"[52] was treated skeptically by the marketplace, particularly after the testimony of Chairman Born before the House Committee on Banking and Financial Services on July 24, 1998, in which she stated that "the OTC derivatives market is already subject to regulation by the Commission through the CEA's prohibition of OTC futures and option that are not exempted from the exchange-trading requirement . . ." and implied a looming rollback of some of the safe harbors for over-the-counter derivatives established in 1993.[53] Largely interpreted as presaging an initiative by the CFTC to regulate over-the-counter derivatives and being the cause of market uncertainty, the reaction of over-the-counter market participants to the 1998 Concept Release was uniformly hostile as shown in the following comments made to the Concept Release by market participants:

- "Swap transactions have not changed in any fundamental way since the CFTC adopted its Swap Exemption in 1993 . . . the CFTC's other justifications for its review . . . divert attention from what users of these transactions truly require: a clear declaration that swaps are not futures subject to the Commodity Exchange Act . . ."[54]
- "[The 1998 Concept Release] raises issues that may call into question the legal certainty and enforceability of OTC derivatives transactions."[55]
- "[A]ny actions taken by the Commission to implement the types of regulation contemplated by the Concept Release will serve only to foster uncertainty with respect to the enforceability and legal status of a wide variety of important financial transactions."[56]

The only (tepid) support the CFTC received on the initiative was from the two major futures exchanges.[57]

Bowing to the broad front arrayed against the CFTC, in October 1998 Congress enacted legislation substantially in the form proposed by the Treasury Department, Federal Reserve, and SEC prohibiting the CFTC from any regulatory initiatives on the matter until March 30, 1999.[58] The CFTC withdrew the Concept Release on November 17, 1999.[59] As one Commissioner noted:

> [The Concept Release] has been widely perceived, both within the derivatives industry and among other financial regulators, as indicating an intent to expand the Commission's regulatory reach with respect to OTC

> derivatives. In view of that perception and any legal uncertainty it may have created, I agree to withdrawal of the Concept Release.[60]

In opposing the 1998 Concept Release, a group of industry associations had stated:

> We are confident that Congress, drawing upon the experience and views of all interested parties, will take appropriate action to permit continued growth in the use of these important risk management tools and to protect the reputations of the United States as a safe environment for financial innovation and a major market for these transactions.[61]

Their confidence in Congress was well placed. On December 21, 2000, the Commodity Futures Modernization Act of 2000 was enacted into law.[62]

2. *The Commodity Futures Modernization Act of 2000*

Just over a year before passage of the Commodity Futures Modernization Act, the President's Working Group on Financial Markets issued a report outlining recommendations aimed at providing more flexibility, including by allowing for the establishment of trading facilities with a lower regulatory burden than that in place for designated contract markets where futures traditionally trade (*See* Chapter 4 for designated contract markets.) Note that the President's Working Group throughout uses the phrase "eligible swap participant" defined by the CFTC in the 1993 CFTC Swap Exemption for certain swaps, which was issued after passage of the Futures Trading Practices Act of 1992. The Commodity Futures Modernization Act, instead, used a new term, "eligible contract participant," which was more inclusive than "eligible swap participant." Therefore, references to "eligible swap participants" should be read as references to "eligible contract participants."

President's Working Group on Financial Markets,[63] Over-the-Counter Derivatives Markets and the Commodity Exchange Act

November 1999[64]

. . . The members of the Working Group agree that there is no compelling evidence of problems involving bilateral swap agreements that would warrant regulation under the CEA; accordingly, many types of swap agreements should be excluded from the CEA. The sophisticated counterparties that use OTC derivatives simply do not require the same protections under the CEA as those required by retail investors. In addition, most of the dealers in the swaps market are either affiliated with broker-dealers or FCMs that are regulated by the SEC or the CFTC or are financial institutions that are subject to supervision by bank regulatory agencies. . . .

Most OTC derivatives are not susceptible to manipulation. The vast majority of the contracts are settled in cash, based on a rate or price determined by a separate highly liquid market with a very large or virtually unlimited deliverable supply. Thus, for example, it is highly unlikely that interest rate swaps could be used to manipulate interest rates. Furthermore, prices established in OTC derivatives transactions do not serve a significant price discovery function.

Due to the characteristics of markets for non-financial commodities with finite supplies, however, the Working Group is unanimously recommending that the exclusion not be extended to agreements involving such commodities. For example, in the case of agricultural commodities, production is seasonal and volatile, and the underlying commodity is perishable, factors that make the markets for these products susceptible to supply and pricing distortions and to manipulation. There have also been several well-known efforts to manipulate the prices of certain metals by attempting to corner the cash or futures markets. Moreover, the cash market for many non-financial commodities is dependent on the futures market for price discovery. The CFTC should, however, retain its current authority to grant exemptions for derivatives involving non-financial commodities, as it did in 1993 for energy products, where exemptions are in the public interest and otherwise consistent with the CEA.

Accordingly, the Working Group unanimously makes the following recommendations:

- Bilateral swap agreements (including those that reference non-exempt securities) entered into by eligible swap participants, on a principal-to-principal basis, should be excluded from the CEA, provided that the transactions are not conducted on [a physical or electronic facility in which all market makers and other participants have the ability to execute transactions and bind both parties by accepting offers which are made by one member and open to all members of the facility]. . . . Certain types of electronic trading systems described below should, however, also be excluded from the CEA.

- Because the material economic terms of many swap agreements are similar, the requirement in the . . . [1993 CFTC Swap Exemption] that swap agreements not be standardized as to their material economic terms should be eliminated. Moreover, as discussed below, the Working Group is recommending that clearing of swap agreements be permitted, subject to appropriate regulatory oversight of the clearing function. Accordingly, insofar as transactions are subject to regulated clearing, the exclusion should not prohibit fungibility of contracts or require that creditworthiness be a material consideration.

- The exclusion should not extend to any swap agreement that involves a nonfinancial commodity with a finite supply.[65]

- The exclusion should only cover swaps between eligible swaps participants (defined in a manner similar to the definition in the current Swap Exemption). Thus, the exclusion should only be available for regulated financial institutions, business enterprises that meet certain tests relating to total assets or net worth, certain pension funds, state and local governments, and individuals with significant assets. . . .

- The CEA should be amended to clarify that a party to a transaction may not avoid performance of its obligations under, or recover losses incurred on, a transaction based solely on the failure of that party (or its counterparty) to comply with the terms of an exclusion or exemption under the CEA.

- To the extent that OTC derivatives transactions between eligible swap participants are excluded from the CEA, they should also be excluded from the coverage of certain state laws (such as laws designed to regulate gambling or bucket shops) that might be construed to prohibit or inappropriately regulate such transactions. . . .

The Working Group members agree that the introduction of electronic trading systems for OTC derivatives has the potential to promote efficiency and transparency, and, by enhancing liquidity and enabling firms that participate in the systems to impose more reliable internal controls on their traders, to reduce risks. Furthermore, there is not at this time a demonstrable need for regulation of systems with the characteristics described below. The method by which a transaction is executed has no obvious bearing on the need for regulation in markets, such as the markets for financial derivatives, that are not used for price discovery. Moreover, electronic trading systems for OTC derivatives have only just begun to emerge on a widespread basis, and such systems should be allowed to grow, unburdened by a new anticipatory statutory structure that could prove entirely inappropriate to their eventual evolution.

The Working Group has concluded, however, that a broad exclusion from the CEA should be available only for systems in which eligible swap participants trade for their own account. . . .

Accordingly, the Working Group unanimously recommends that Congress amend the CEA to clarify that entering into or trading excluded swap agreements (i.e., agreements between eligible swap participants that do not involve non-financial commodities with finite supplies) through electronic trading systems with certain characteristics does not affect the status of the agreements traded through the system and does not provide a basis for regulation of the system. . . .

The Working Group notes that its recommendation to exclude certain trading systems from the CEA should not be viewed as a determination that regulation of these systems may never be appropriate. Limited regulation aimed at enhancing market transparency and price discovery may become necessary under certain circumstances as electronic trading systems for OTC derivatives develop and grow, if problems of the sort that are appropriately addressed by regulation emerge. . . .

Clearing of OTC derivatives has the potential to reduce counterparty risks associated with such transactions through risk management techniques that may include mutualizing risks, facilitating offset, and netting. Clearing, however, tends to concentrate risks and certain responsibilities for risk management in a central counterparty or clearinghouse. Consequently, the effectiveness of the clearinghouse's operations and risk management systems is critical for the stability of the markets that it serves. For this reason, the Working Group unanimously recommends that Congress enact legislation to provide a clear basis for the regulation of clearing systems that may develop for OTC derivatives. . . .

The Working Group's recommendations with respect to electronic trading and clearing for OTC derivatives . . . are intended to remove legal obstacles to innovations that have the potential to increase efficiency, transparency, liquidity, and competition and to reduce systemic risk. Some market participants have argued, however, that U.S. futures exchanges are at a competitive disadvantage to OTC derivatives markets as the result of CEA regulation, and that the introduction of electronic trading and clearing for derivatives outside of the CEA has the potential to exacerbate the perceived imbalance.

The Working Group acknowledges that the . . . recommended [swap] exclusion would create differences in the level of regulation between OTC derivatives that are electronically traded and cleared and products offered by futures exchanges that may have some similar characteristics.

The difference would be mitigated to some extent if the Working Group's recommendations are adopted, because futures exchanges could establish electronic trading systems and clearing systems under the same conditions as their competitors. Floor-traded futures contracts with some economic characteristics similar to the derivatives for which electronic trading systems might develop would, however, face different levels or different forms of regulation.

Where regulation exists, it should serve valid public policy goals. The justifications generally cited for regulation of the futures markets include the goals of protecting retail customers from unfair practices, protecting the price discovery function, and guarding against manipulation. With similar policy goals in mind, the Working Group has recommended limiting the proposed exclusion for swap agreements to eligible swap participants . . .

Exchange trading should not be subject to regulations that do not have a public policy justification. Although specific recommendations about the regulatory structure applicable to exchange-traded futures are beyond the scope of this report, the CFTC is currently examining the CEA to determine the extent to which modifications of the status quo are necessary.

Although the CEA gives the CFTC broad authority to grant exemptive relief if it determines it is in the public interest, the CFTC notes that the Conference Report for the FTPA specifically stated that "[t]he goal of providing the Commission with broad exemptive authority is not to prompt a wide-scale deregulation of markets falling within the ambit of the [CEA]."[xiii] Accordingly, the CFTC believes that further Congressional direction is necessary. In deference to the CFTC's views, the Working Group as a whole believes that the enactment of its recommendations with respect to OTC derivatives should be accompanied by explicit authority for the CFTC to provide appropriate regulatory relief for exchange-traded financial futures if deemed by the CFTC to be consistent with the public interest. . . .

These recommendations of the President's Working Group were substantially embodied in the Commodity Futures Modernization Act.

The President's Working Group also recommended amendment of the Commodity Exchange Act to "provide that transactions in foreign currency futures and options are subject to . . . [the Commodity Exchange Act] if they are entered into between a retail customer and an entity that is neither regulated or supervised by the SEC or a federal banking regulator nor affiliated with such a regulated or supervised entity."[66] This was largely accomplished by the Commodity Futures Modernization Act's grant of jurisdiction to the CFTC over retail foreign exchange options and futures unless: (i) transacted on an SEC-regulated exchange; or (ii) one of the parties is a financial institution, broker-dealer, futures commission merchant, insurance company or affiliate, financial holding company, or "investment bank holding company," a now defunct category of SEC registration.[67]

The Commodity Futures Modernization Act overturned the prohibition in the Futures Trading Act of 1982 on security futures on other than a broad-based securities index and provided for the trading of a "security future," i.e., "a contract of sale for future delivery of a single security or of narrow-based security index . . ." by granting the CFTC and SEC joint jurisdiction over such products. The statute required facilities on which such products are traded to be

---

[xiii] [N. 45] H.R. Rep. 102-978, 102d Cong., 2d Sess. 81 (1992).

registered with the CFTC and SEC and intermediaries to be registered as broker-dealers and futures commission merchants.[68]

The Commodity Futures Modernization Act ultimately also blocked the SEC from "registering, or requiring, *recommending, or suggesting*" (emphasis added) registration of a security-based swap agreement traded between "eligible contract participants" as a security.[69]

This era of deregulation would prove to be short-lived.

E. THE SECOND ERA OF NATIONAL REGULATION

1. *Fraud in the Foreign Exchange Markets and the "Enron Loophole"*

As noted above, the Commodity Futures Modernization Act granted the CFTC jurisdiction over retail foreign exchange options and futures with exceptions if traded on a securities exchange or through specified entities already subject to regulation. Disputes arose as to the extent of that jurisdiction with two circuits narrowly construing the scope of "futures" and broadly construing what were deemed to be foreign exchange forwards outside of the CFTC's jurisdiction.[70]

Congress ultimately responded to these cases by including in the CFTC Reauthorization Act of 2008[71] amendments to the Commodity Exchange Act expanding the CFTC's jurisdiction to include retail foreign exchange when "offered, or entered into, on a leveraged or margined basis, or financed" by one of the parties.[72] An exception for spot contracts remained only to the extent that such a contract is a "contract of sale that . . . results in actual delivery within 2 days, or creates an enforceable obligation to deliver. . . ."[73] In 2010, the CFTC finalized rules establishing a new category of CFTC registrant, a "retail foreign exchange dealer."[74] We discuss the CFTC's regulation of foreign exchange in greater detail in Chapter 12.

The CFTC Reauthorization Act of 2008 also sought to address what was perceived as a lax regulatory regime established by the Commodity Futures Modernization Act for derivatives trading facilities other than designated contract markets, sometimes referred to as the "Enron loophole" after the energy trading firm that filed for bankruptcy in December 2001. The Act tightened the reporting and position limits requirements on derivatives trading facilities other than designated contract markets (which were always subject to the most regulatory oversight).[75] It turned out to be the opening salvo for regulation of the entire over-the-counter derivatives market.

2. *Financial Crisis of 2007-2009*

The Financial Crisis has been described as the "worst since the Great Depression"[76] and as "a once-in-a-century credit tsunami."[77]

Convention places the start of the Financial Crisis in the summer of 2007,[78] though, of course, its causes lay in preceding events, particularly with respect to the structure of the market for so-called sub-prime mortgages.[79]

In testimony before the House of Representatives Committee of Government Oversight and Reform, former Federal Reserve Chairman Greenspan summarized the causes of this breakdown in the sub-prime mortgage market:

> What went wrong with global economic policies that had worked so effectively for nearly four decades? The breakdown has been most apparent in the securitization of home mortgages. The evidence strongly suggests that without the excess demand from securitizers, subprime mortgage originations (undeniably the original source of crisis) would have been far smaller and defaults accordingly far fewer. But subprime mortgages pooled and sold as securities became subject to explosive demand from investors around the world. These mortgage backed securities being "subprime" were originally offered at what appeared to be exceptionally high risk-adjusted market interest rates. But with U.S. home prices still rising, delinquency and foreclosure rates were deceptively modest. Losses were minimal. To the most sophisticated investors in the world, they were wrongly viewed as a "steal."
>
> The consequent surge in global demand for U.S. subprime securities by banks, hedge, and pension funds supported by unrealistically positive rating designations by credit agencies was, in my judgment, the core of the problem. Demand became so aggressive that too many securitizers and lenders believed they were able to create and sell mortgage backed securities so quickly that they never put their shareholders' capital at risk and hence did not have the incentive to evaluate the credit quality of what they were selling. Pressures on lenders to supply more "paper" collapsed subprime underwriting standards from 2005 forward. Uncritical acceptance of credit ratings by purchasers of these toxic assets has led to huge losses.[80]

Losses in the sub-prime markets and the resultant economic malaise ultimately led to, in the U.S. alone:[81]

- The bankruptcy of Lehman Brothers.
- Placement of Fannie Mae and Freddie Mac into conservatorship.
- Bank of America's purchase of Countrywide Financial and Merrill Lynch.
- The acquisition of Wachovia by Wells Fargo.

- Washington Mutual's seizure by Federal regulators and subsequent sale of its assets to JPMorgan Chase.
- The U.S. government's investment in American International Group, commonly known as "AIG," preceded by its recordmaking $61.7 billion quarterly loss.
- JPMorgan's purchase of Bear Stearns.
- The placement of IndyMac Bank, FSB, into receivership by the Federal Deposit Insurance Corporation.
- The bankruptcy of sub-prime lenders New Century Financial Corporation and American Home Mortgage Investment Corporation.
- Purchases by the Department of the Treasury of preferred shares in many U.S. banks as part of effort to recapitalize banks.
- The bankruptcy of General Motors.
- The bankruptcy of CIT Corporation.

To bolster market confidence and increase liquidity, various emergency programs were sponsored by the Federal Reserve and the Department of the Treasury.

In the final report of the Financial Crisis Inquiry Commission investigating the causes of the Financial Crisis, credit default swaps were described as significant contributors.[82]

This led to a dissenting statement by Peter Wallison and Arthur F. Burns in which it was noted:

> Despite a diligent search, the FCIC never uncovered evidence that unregulated derivatives, and particularly credit default swaps (CDS), was a significant contributor to the financial crisis through "interconnections." The only company known to have failed because of its CDS obligations was AIG, and that firm appears to have been an outlier. Blaming CDS for the financial crisis because one company did not manage its risks properly is like blaming lending generally when a bank fails. Like everything else, derivatives can be misused, but there is no evidence that the "interconnections" among financial institutions alleged to have caused the crisis were significantly enhanced by CDS or derivatives generally. For example, Lehman Brothers was a major player in the derivatives market, but the Commission found no indication that Lehman's failure to meet its CDS and other derivatives obligations caused significant losses to any other firm, including those that had written CDS on Lehman itself.[83]

Title VII of The Dodd-Frank Wall Street Reform and Consumer Protection Act (the "Dodd-Frank Act"), enacted into law on July 21, 2010, imposed a new regulatory framework on over-the-counter derivatives.[84]

3. *The Dodd-Frank Act*

The Dodd-Frank Act unwound the broad exemption from derivatives regulation provided by the Commodity Futures Modernization Act. It substituted a complex regulatory framework. This framework was founded on a division of the derivatives market into "swaps" (to be primarily regulated by the Commodity Futures Trading Commission) and "security-based swaps" (to be primarily regulated by the Securities and Exchange Commission). New categories of registrants were created such as "swap dealers," "major swap participants," "security-based swap dealers," and "major security-based swap participants."

Prescriptive requirements were introduced regarding market operation with mandatory clearing requirements and requirements to trade on "swap execution facilities."

These changes, and the resultant present regulatory framework, are discussed in Chapters 7 through 10.

F. THE FUTURE OF DERIVATIVES REGULATION

It has been a regulatory rollercoaster for derivatives, going from regulation to near total deregulation (for off-exchange derivatives) to comprehensive re-regulation. An original motivation for derivatives regulation was protection of retail customers, just as a motivation for the Commodity Futures Modernization Act's deregulation was the lesser regulatory safeguards needed for a market comprised of non-retail parties (i.e., eligible contract participants).

The Dodd-Frank Act modified this calculus. With the Financial Crisis, a new perception took hold that institutions with large derivatives exposures could pose a systemic threat to the financial system. The focus, as reflected in the Dodd-Frank Act, shifted to regulating the largest market participants – the ones arguably least in need of regulatory protections – in the interest of the global economy.

Derivatives have been blamed for much of the Financial Crisis. Yet, they are an essential component of our financial system. The one certainty is that the effort to find the right regulatory balance will continue.

QUESTIONS AND COMMENTS

1. Should the economic derivative that Thales entered into be treated by the CFTC or SEC as a derivative for regulatory purposes? Why or why not?

2. Stout notes at 1204 of *Uncertainty, Dangerous Optimism, and Speculation: An Inquiry into some Limits of Democratic Governance* that "In 1888, an estimated 25 quadrillion bushels of wheat were traded through futures contracts, even though farmers harvested only 415 million actual bushels of wheat in the United States that year." Are the derivatives markets today different? What are some reasons why the amount traded as futures might be multiples larger than the amount harvested?
3. What is the difference between a derivative and a security? How do they overlap? This is a question that will continue to arise and will be further addressed in Chapter 3.
4. Why were bucket shops difficult to extinguish? What might have been the public policy rationale for eliminating them?
5. Brooksley Born, chairman of the CFTC from 1996 until 1999, advocated that the CFTC regulate all derivatives, including on-exchange derivatives. Was she correct as a public policy matter? Has her position been vindicated by the passage of the Dodd-Frank Act in 2010 and the resulting regulation of on-exchange derivatives?
6. Should the derivatives markets be regulated to protect society from the consequences of the misuse of derivatives or deregulated so the markets have the flexibility to evolve and adapt to new conditions? (This question is one that should be considered throughout this book and is a public policy question that arises in any regulatory context.)

CHAPTER 3
THE COMMODITY FUTURES TRADING COMMISSION

A. INTRODUCTION

The Commodity Futures Trading Commission Act of 1974 amended the Commodity Exchange Act to grant the CFTC broad jurisdiction. The exact extent of that jurisdiction has been the subject of challenges from other regulators and from private litigants. Some of these challenges have been resolved by statutory fixes or judicially. Others remain unresolved.

The disputes over the CFTC's jurisdiction are the result of efforts to navigate between two extremes – broad regulation that results in overlapping jurisdiction and narrow regulation that causes regulatory gaps. The process of charting this course is ongoing, with the Dodd-Frank Act being the most recent such effort.

In this chapter, we examine the extent of the CFTC's jurisdiction. Note that the CFTC's jurisdiction over foreign exchange and option transactions is discussed in detail in Chapter 12.

B. CFTC JURISDICTION OVER COMMODITY FUTURES

Section 2(a)(1)(A) of the Commodity Exchange Act provides that the CFTC:

> shall have exclusive jurisdiction . . . with respect to accounts, agreements (including any transaction which is of the character of, or is commonly known to the trade as, an "option," "privilege," "indemnity," "bid," "offer," "put," "call," "advance guaranty," or "decline guaranty"), and transactions involving . . . contracts of sale of a commodity for future delivery (including significant price discovery contracts), traded or executed on a contract

> market designated pursuant to section 7 of this title or a swap execution facility pursuant to section 7b-3 of this title or any other board of trade, exchange, or market . . .

To distill this even further, the CFTC is granted exclusive jurisdiction over "contracts of sale of a commodity for future delivery . . ." (Note: There are some exceptions; we will discuss them below.) We saw in Chapter 2 that the definition of "commodity" is so broad as to include nearly everything by stating that it applies to, in addition to a specifically enumerated list of commodities, "all other goods and articles . . . and all services, rights, and interests . . . in which contracts for future deliver are presently or in the future dealt in."

Figure 3-A: Definition of Commodity in Commodity Exchange Act § 1a(9)

Wheat, cotton, rice, corn, oats, barley, rye, flaxseed, grain sorghums, mill feeds, butter, eggs, Solanum tuberosum (Irish potatoes), wool, wool tops, fats and oils (including lard, tallow, cottonseed oil, peanut oil, soybean oil, and all other fats and oils), cottonseed meal, cottonseed, peanuts, soybeans, soybean meal, livestock, livestock products, and frozen concentrated orange juice, and all other goods and articles, except onions (as provided by section 13-1 of this title) and motion picture box office receipts (or any index, measure, value, or data related to such receipts), and all services, rights, and interests (except motion picture box office receipts, or any index, measure, value or data related to such receipts) in which contracts for future delivery are presently or in the future dealt in.

With such a broad definition of "commodity" in mind, we now look to the phrase "future delivery." Unfortunately, the phrase "future delivery" is defined in the negative by what § 1a(27) of the Commodity Exchange Act excludes: "The term 'future delivery' does not include any sale of any cash commodity for deferred shipment or delivery." It is not further defined by regulation.

This carve-out of any "cash commodity for deferred shipment or delivery," commonly known as the forward exemption, is, therefore, essential to understanding what is a contract for future delivery. Without this carve-out, something as prosaic as a magazine subscription could conceivably be a commodity future transaction subject to the CFTC's exclusive jurisdiction and, as we will discuss in Chapter 4, would be illegal unless transacted on a board of trade designated as a contract market.

Commodity Futures Trading Commission v. Co Petro Marketing Group, Inc.

680 F.2d 573 (9th Cir. 1982)

Canby, Circuit Judge:

Co Petro Marketing Group, Inc., and individual appellants, Harold Goldstein and Michael Krivacek, (Co Petro) appeal from an order of the district court permanently enjoining them from offering, selling, or otherwise engaging in futures contracts in petroleum products, in violation of . . . the Commodity Exchange Act . . . Co Petro contends that the contracts it sold were not subject to the Act. . . . We affirm the district court's judgment that Co Petro was offering and selling "contracts of sale of a commodity for future delivery" (futures contracts) within the meaning of . . . the Act. . . .

Co Petro is licensed by the State of California as a gasoline broker. It operated a chain of retail gasoline outlets and also acted as a broker of petroleum products, buying and reselling in the spot market several hundred thousand gallons of gasoline and diesel fuel monthly. While part of its business operations involved the direct sale of gasoline to industrial, commercial, and retail users of gasoline, Co Petro also offered and sold contracts for the future purchase of petroleum products pursuant to an "Agency Agreement for Purchase and Sale of Motor Vehicle Fuel" (Agency Agreement).

Under the Agency Agreement, the customer (1) appointed Co Petro as his agent to purchase a specified quantity and type of fuel at a fixed price for delivery at an agreed future date, and (2) paid a deposit based upon a fixed percentage of the purchase price. Co Petro, however, did not require its customer to take delivery of the fuel. Instead, at a later specified date the customer could appoint Co Petro to sell the fuel on his behalf. If the cash price had risen in the interim Co Petro was to (1) remit the difference between the original purchase price and the subsequent sale price, and (2) refund any remaining deposit. If the cash price had decreased, Co Petro was to (1) deduct from the deposit the difference between the purchase price and the subsequent sale price, and (2) remit the balance of the deposit to the customer. A liquidated damages clause provided that in no event would the customer lose more than 95% of his initial deposit.

Co Petro marketed these contracts extensively to the general public through newspaper advertisements, private seminars, commissioned telephone solicitors, and various other commissioned sales agents. The Commodity Futures Trading Commission brought this statutory injunctive action . . . seeking to enjoin Co Petro's sales of petroleum products pursuant to its Agency Agreements. . . .

Co Petro contends that the Commission lacks jurisdiction over transactions pursuant to its Agency Agreements because these agreements are "cash forward" contracts expressly excluded from regulation . . . While [the Act] . . . provides the Commission with regulatory jurisdiction over "contracts of sale of a commodity for future delivery," it further provides that the term *future delivery* "shall not include any sale of any cash commodity for deferred shipment or delivery." Cash commodity contracts for deferred shipment or delivery are commonly known as "cash forward" contracts, while contracts of sale of a commodity for future delivery are called "futures contracts". See H.R.Rep.No.93-975, 93d Cong., 2d Sess. 129-30 (1974). The Act, however, sets forth no further definitions of the term "future delivery" or of the phrase "cash commodity for deferred shipment or delivery." The statutory language, therefore, provides little guidance as to the distinctions between regulated futures contracts and excluded cash forward contracts and, to our knowledge, no other court has dealt with this question. . . . Our examination of the relevant legislative history leads us to conclude that the Co Petro's Agency Agreements are not cash forward contracts within the meaning of the Act.

The exclusion for cash forward contracts originated in the Future Trading Act, Pub.L.No.67-66, s 2, 42 Stat. 187 (1921). . . . There is no indication that Congress drew this exclusion otherwise than to meet a particular need such as that of a farmer to sell part of next season's harvest at a set price to a grain elevator or miller. These cash forward contracts guarantee the farmer a buyer for his crop and provide the buyer with an assured price. Most important, both parties to the contracts deal in and contemplate future delivery of the actual grain.

The exclusion was carried forward without change into the Grain Futures Act, Pub.L.No.67-331, s 2, 42 Stat. 998 (1922). In 1936, Congress enacted the Commodity Exchange Act, Pub.L.No.74-675, 49 Stat. 1491 (1936). This Act . . . reworded the exclusion to except "any cash commodity for deferred shipment or delivery." . . . Although the Act has been amended numerous times since 1936, the language excluding cash commodities for deferred shipment or delivery has remained the same. . . .

The situation for which the exclusion for cash forward contracts was designed is not present here. Co Petro's Agency Agreement customers were, for the most part, speculators from the general public. The underlying petroleum products had no inherent value to these speculators. They had neither the intention of taking delivery nor the capacity to do so. Yet it was to the general public that Co Petro made its strongest sales pitches. For example, in an advertisement in the Los Angeles Times under the headline "Invest in Gasoline," Co Petro stated: "The Sophisticated Small Investor Can Make Money Buying Gasoline. It's a high risk-high potential yield opportunity." . . .

There is nothing in the legislative history surrounding cash forward contracts to suggest that Congress intended the exclusion to encompass agreements for the future delivery of commodities sold merely for purposes of such speculation. . . .

Even though Co Petro's Agency Agreements do not fall within the exclusion for cash forward contracts, there remains the question whether they are "contracts of sale of a commodity for future delivery" (futures contracts) within the meaning of . . . the Act. Co Petro contends that its Agency Agreements cannot be futures contracts because they lack most of the common distinguishing features of futures contracts as they are known in the industry. Futures contracts traded on the designated markets have certain basic characteristics. Except for price, all the futures contracts for a specified commodity are identical in quantity and other terms. The fungible nature of these contracts facilitates offsetting transactions by which purchasers or sellers can liquidate their positions by forming opposite contracts. The price differential between the opposite contracts then determines the investor's profit or loss.

While contracts pursuant to Co Petro's Agency Agreements were not as rigidly standardized as futures contracts traded on licensed contract markets, neither were they individualized. . . .

Co Petro's customers, like customers who trade on organized futures exchanges, could deal in commodity futures without the forced burden of delivery. . . . We also reject Co Petro's final contention that, contrary to the practice in organized futures markets where price is established by public auction, it negotiated prices directly with its Agency Agreement customers. The evidence indicates that, for the most part, Co Petro unilaterally set prices for its products according to the then-prevailing market rates with the spot market determining resale prices to subsequent purchasers. Moreover, the fact that public auction did not determine Co Petro's prices is merely a result of Co Petro's failure to seek Commission licensing for organized exchange trading in petroleum futures.

In determining whether a particular contract is a contract of sale of a commodity for future delivery over which the Commission has regulatory jurisdiction . . . no bright-line definition or list of characterizing elements is determinative. The transaction must be viewed as a whole with a critical eye toward its underlying purpose.

The contracts here represent speculative ventures in commodity futures which were marketed to those for whom delivery was not an expectation. Addressing these circumstances in the light of the legislative history of the Act, we conclude that Co Petro's contracts are "contracts of sale of a commodity for future delivery." . . .

In the below case, the question of the distinction between a future and a cash commodity was analyzed in the context of foreign exchange transactions. Although, as is discussed in Chapter 12, this particular question was ultimately resolved in the context of foreign exchange transactions by statute in 2008, the analysis applies to any determination of whether a contract is for future delivery or is a contract involving a "cash commodity for deferred shipment or delivery."

Commodity Futures Trading Commission v. Erskine

512 F.3d 309 (6th Cir. 2008)

. . . We must next determine . . . what constitutes a "futures contract." Generally speaking, the [Commodity Exchange Act (the "CEA")] vests the CFTC with regulatory jurisdiction over "futures contracts" – putatively, "transactions involving contracts of sale of a commodity for future delivery." Expressly excluded from the term "future delivery," and therefore excluded from CFTC regulation, is "any sale of any cash commodity for deferred shipment or delivery," commonly referred to as a "forward contract." Drawing a distinction between futures contracts and forward contracts has proven difficult. The district court used the Seventh Circuit's "trade in the contract" test, *see* [*CFTC v. Zelener*, 373 F.3d 861 (7th Cir. 2004)] at 867, but the CFTC argues that it should have used a "totality of the circumstances" test, *see Andersons, Inc. v. Horton Farms, Inc.*, 166 F.3d 308, 317 (6th Cir. 1998). Based on the analysis and reasoning set forth below, we begin with the simplified distinction that a "futures contract" is a contract for a future transaction, while a "forward contract" is a contract for a present transaction with future delivery, and conclude with a specific definition for each. . . .

In 1995, the Ninth Circuit considered a claim by the CFTC that Nobel Metals was unlawfully engaging in "futures contracts," under which Nobel sold precious metals to customers who received title but directed that the actual metal be delivered to a third party. *CFTC v. Nobel Metals Int'l, Inc.*, 67 F.3d 766 (9th Cir. 1995). Relying on *Co Petro*, the court reasserted that the forward contract exclusion is unavailable for "contracts of sale for commodities sold merely for speculative purposes and which are not predicated upon the expectation that delivery of the actual commodity by the seller to the original contracting buyer will occur in the future." The court went on:

> To take advantage of the cash forward contract exclusion under the [CEA], the delivery requirement cannot be satisfied by the simple device of a transfer of title. As we said in *Co Petro*, "a cash forward contract is one in which the parties contemplate physical transfer of the actual commodity." If this were not so, the cash forward contract exception would quickly swallow the futures contract rule.

The court concluded that there was no legitimate expectation that the customers would take actual delivery of the purchased metals, and deemed the contracts futures contracts while dismissing as irrelevant the "self-serving labels" that the defendants had given the contracts.

In 1998, this Circuit considered claims by private parties, which turned on the question of whether certain grain contracts at issue were covered by the CEA and thereby subject to CFTC regulation. *Andersons*, 166 F.3d at 317. We explained:

> "Futures contracts" are governed by the CEA and concomitantly, subject to CFTC regulations. "Futures contracts" are contracts of sale of a commodity for future delivery. The term "future delivery," however, explicitly does not include any sale of any cash commodity for deferred shipment or delivery. Contracts falling under this latter definition are typically referred to as 'cash forward' contracts.
>
> The purpose of this "cash forward" exception is to permit those parties who contemplate physical transfer of the commodity to set up contracts that (1) defer shipment but guarantee to sellers that they will have buyers and visa versa [*sic*], and (2) reduce the risk of price fluctuations, without subjecting the parties to burdensome regulations. These contracts are not subject to the CFTC regulations because those regulations are intended to govern only speculative markets; they are not meant to cover contracts wherein the commodity in question has an "inherent value" to the transacting parties. We hold that in determining whether a particular commodities contract falls within the cash forward exception, courts must focus on whether there is a legitimate expectation that physical delivery of the actual commodity by the seller to the original contracting buyer will occur in the future.

. . . A "futures contract," or "future," never precisely defined by statute, nevertheless has an accepted meaning which brings it within the scope of transactions historically sought to be regulated by the CEA.

It is generally understood to be an executory, mutually binding agreement providing for the future delivery of a commodity on a date certain where the grade, quantity, and price at the time of delivery are fixed. To facilitate the development of a liquid market in these transactions, these contracts are standardized and transferrable. Trading in futures seldom results in physical delivery of the subject commodity, since the obligations are often extinguished by offsetting transactions that produce a net profit or loss. The main purpose realized by entering into futures transactions is to transfer price risks from suppliers, processors and distributors (hedgers) to those more willing to take the risk (speculators). Since the prices of futures are contingent on the vagaries of both the production of the commodity and the economics of the marketplace, they are particularly susceptible to manipulation and excessive speculation.

In contrast to the fungible quality of futures, cash forwards are generally individually negotiated sales of commodities between principals in which actual delivery of the commodity is anticipated, but is deferred for reasons of commercial convenience or necessity. These contracts are not readily transferable and therefore are usually entered into between parties able to make and receive physical delivery of the subject goods. . . .

Much has been made in the case law – and by the parties to this appeal – of Congress's failure to define a "futures contract" expressly, in either the original Commodity Exchange Act or its amendment, the Commodity Futures

Modernization Act of 2000. But, this does not mean that the term "futures contract" is undefined. On the contrary, many pertinent sources have defined "futures contract," in terms that investors and traders are expected to (and do) rely upon, and it is reasonable to surmise that regulators – other than the CFTC, apparently – would rely on similar definitions, even without express codification in a federal statute. Although each differs slightly from the others, the definitions, considered altogether, exhibit a consistent theme and typically include six common elements. Based on our consideration of these numerous lay definitions, we find that, in common parlance, "futures contract" means:

(1) the "contract" is standardized so that it can be traded on an exchange, and is
(2) a fungible agreement to buy or sell
(3) a stated unit quantity of
(4) a stated commodity
(5) at a stated unit price
(6) at or before a stated future time.

See, e.g., Merriam-Webster's Dictionary of Law (contract), available at http://dictionary.reference.com/browse/contract (last accessed Jan. 3, 2008). It is important to recognize that it is the agreement or contract that is traded on an exchange. It is unremarkable (though easily enough mistaken as relevant) that the underlying commodity is also traded on a market exchange.

The alternative concept, i.e., "forward contract," is also defined by numerous sources, often with an emphasis on distinguishing it from a "futures contract." A "forward contract" is:

(1) neither standardized nor traded on an exchange, and is
(2) an individual agreement to buy or sell
(3) some agreed-upon quantity of
(4) some commodity
(5) at some agreed-upon price
(6) at some agreed-upon time in the future.

See, e.g., Merriam-Webster's Dictionary of Law (contract), available at http://dictionary.reference.com/browse/contract (last accessed Jan. 3, 2008). Thus, with a "forward contract," the underlying commodity is typically traded on a market exchange (as it typically is with a "futures contract" as well), but the agreement or contract itself is neither standardized nor traded on an exchange.

Notably, none of these definitions/distinctions makes any mention of any anticipation of actual delivery (or lack thereof). This is simply not a practical distinction. Instead, the distinction – as commonly understood – turns on the standardization and fungibility of the contract, and as the Seventh Circuit suggested, whether there is "trading in the contract," rather than trading only in the underlying commodity. . . .

C. CFTC JURISDICTION OVER OFF-EXCHANGE OPTIONS AND SWAPS

1. Off-Exchange Options

Putting aside foreign exchange options, discussed in Chapter 12, the CFTC's 1974 jurisdictional grant, as modified by the Futures Trading Act of 1978, granted broad plenary authority over commodity options. The passage of the Commodity Futures Modernization Act of 2000, with respect to options, would appear to have permitted the CFTC to assert jurisdiction only over:

- Agricultural options;
- Retail transactions in other commodity options; and
- Fraud with respect to non-agricultural commodity options traded in the non-retail markets.

Nonetheless, though never subjected to judicial scrutiny, the CFTC maintained rules in Part 32 of the CFTC's regulations in relation to all commodity options transactions and claimed "plenary authority" over all commodity options.[1]

The Dodd-Frank Act removed ambiguity regarding the CFTC's jurisdiction over all commodity options, regardless of whether traded on or off-exchange and whether agricultural or non-agricultural. The CFTC harmonized its exiting regulatory regime for off-exchange agricultural commodity options with its regime for off-exchange swaps.[2]

We discuss the regulation of commodity options in more detail in Chapter 12.

2. Swaps

Whereas the Commodity Futures Modernization Act had placed non-agricultural off-exchange swaps between "eligible contract participants" largely outside of both SEC and CFTC jurisdiction, the Dodd-Frank Act divided these products into three regulatory categories: (1) swaps, (2) security-based swaps, and (3) mixed swaps.

The Commodity Exchange Act provides the CFTC broad jurisdiction over swaps. To understand the extent of that jurisdiction, we need to evaluate the definition of swap, including what is statutorily excluded from the definition of swap.

The statutory definition of a "swap" is comprised of a broad economic description of options and swaps, including a laundry list of products currently traded as swaps. The definition also includes a catch-all provision for unforeseen instruments that are developed in the future and will be considered swaps. Note that the statutory definition of swaps includes options whereas, economically, swaps and options are different.

The definition of swap includes:

Figure 3-B: Swap Definition	
Commodity Exchange Act § 1a(47)(A)	Commentary
[A]ny agreement, contract, or transaction-	
(i) that is a put, call, cap, floor, collar, or similar option of any kind that is for the purchase or sale, or based on the value, of 1 or more interest or other rates, currencies, commodities, securities, instruments of indebtedness, indices, quantitative measures, or other financial or economic interests or property of any kind; [or]	*This includes all options, including, apparently, securities options. As will be seen below, though, securities options are ultimately excluded from the definition.*
(ii) that provides for any purchase, sale, payment, or delivery (other than a dividend on an equity security) that is dependent on the occurrence, nonoccurrence, or the extent of the occurrence of an event or contingency associated with a potential financial, economic, or commercial consequence; [or]	*Note that this is so broadly worded as to potentially include insurance. Once more, it is necessary to see below what is excluded from the definition.*
(iii) that provides on an executory basis for the exchange, on a fixed or	*This describes what is traditionally within the economic definition of a*

contingent basis, of 1 or more payments based on the value or level of 1 or more interest or other rates, currencies, commodities, securities, instruments of indebtedness, indices, quantitative measures, or other financial or economic interests or property of any kind, or any interest therein or based on the value thereof, and that transfers, as between the parties to the transaction, in whole or in part, the financial risk associated with a future change in any such value or level without also conveying a current or future direct or indirect ownership interest in an asset (including any enterprise or investment pool) or liability that incorporates the financial risk so transferred, including any agreement, contract, or transaction commonly known as-	*swap.*
(I) an interest rate swap; **(II)** a rate floor; **(III)** a rate cap; **(IV)** a rate collar; **(V)** a cross-currency rate swap; **(VI)** a basis swap; **(VII)** a currency swap; **(VIII)** a foreign exchange swap; **(IX)** a total return swap; **(X)** an equity index swap; **(XI)** an equity swap; **(XII)** a debt index swap; **(XIII)** a debt swap; **(XIV)** a credit spread; **(XV)** a credit default swap; **(XVI)** a credit swap; **(XVII)** a weather swap; **(XVIII)** an energy swap; **(XIX)** a metal swap; **(XX)** an agricultural swap; **(XXI)** an emissions swap; and **(XXII)** a commodity swap; [or]	*This is a laundry list of transaction types that were in existence at the time of the definition and are deemed to be swaps.*
(iv) that is an agreement, contract, or transaction that is, or in the future becomes, commonly known to the trade as a swap; [or]	*This is a catch-all provision to incorporate future financial innovations.*

(v) including any security-based swap agreement which meets the definition of "swap agreement" as defined in section 206A of the Gramm-Leach-Bliley Act of which a material term is based on the price, yield, value, or volatility of any security or any group or index of securities, or any interest therein; or	*The Gramm-Leach-Bliley Act definition of swap agreement generally parallels the definition of swap. Note that security-based swaps are a subset of swaps. We will discuss them below.*
(vi) that is any combination or permutation of, or option on, any agreement, contract, or transaction described in any of clauses (i) through (v).	*This is to ensure that combinations of the foregoing fall within the definition of swap.*

The above definition is so broad that it could arguably include some securities transactions and insurance. It is, therefore, important to evaluate what is excluded from the definition. The definition of swap excludes:

Figure 3-C: Exclusions from Swap Definition	
Commodity Exchange Act § 1a(47)(B)	Commentary
(i) any contract of sale of a commodity for future delivery (or option on such a contract), [certain leveraged bullion contracts], security futures product, or agreement, contract, or [leveraged, financed or margined retail foreign exchange or commodity transactions]; [and]	*1. Commodity futures and options thereon are subject to a different CFTC regulatory regime than swaps (as discussed above in section B) and 2. security futures have a distinct regime as a result of the Commodity Futures Modernization Act.*
(ii) any sale of a nonfinancial commodity or security for deferred shipment or delivery, so long as the transaction is intended to be physically settled; [and]	*This is the so-called forward contract exemption, discussed above in section B.*
(iii) any put, call, straddle, option, or privilege on any security, certificate of deposit, or group or index of securities, including any interest	*This excludes securities options subject to SEC jurisdiction.*

therein or based on the value thereof, that is subject to- **(I)** the Securities Act of 1933; and **(II)** the Securities Exchange Act of 1934; [and]	
(iv) any put, call, straddle, option, or privilege relating to a foreign currency entered into on a national securities exchange registered pursuant to section 6(a) of the Securities Exchange Act of 1934; [and]	*Foreign currency options entered into on a securities exchange are excluded.*
(v) any agreement, contract, or transaction providing for the purchase or sale of 1 or more securities on a fixed basis that is subject to- **(I)** the Securities Act of 1933; and **(II)** the Securities Exchange Act of 1934; [and]	*This provides a general exclusion for securities purchases.*
(vi) any agreement, contract, or transaction providing for the purchase or sale of 1 or more securities on a contingent basis that is subject to the Securities Act of 1933 and the Securities Exchange Act of 1934, unless the agreement, contract, or transaction predicates the purchase or sale on the occurrence of a bona fide contingency that might reasonably be expected to affect or be affected by the creditworthiness of a party other than a party to the agreement, contract, or transaction; [and]	*A purchase or sale being subject to a contingency is not a swap unless the contingency is based on the creditworthiness of a third party, such as would be the case with a credit default swap.*
(vii) any note, bond, or evidence of indebtedness that is a security, as defined in section 2(a)(1) of the Securities Act of 1933; [and]	*Securities are not swaps even if they have economic features typically associated with swaps.*
(viii) any agreement, contract, or transaction that is- **(I)** based on a security; and	*This excludes agreements between securities underwriters and the issuer of securities.*

(II) entered into directly or through an underwriter (as defined in the Securities Act of 1933 § 2(a)(11)) by the issuer of such security for the purposes of raising capital, unless the agreement, contract, or transaction is entered into to manage a risk associated with capital raising;	
(ix) any agreement, contract, or transaction a counterparty of which is a Federal Reserve bank, the Federal Government, or a Federal agency that is expressly backed by the full faith and credit of the United States; and	*This clarifies that acts of the U.S. government or its agencies are not to be restrained by the swap regulatory regime.*
(x) any security-based swap, other than a . . . [mixed swap, discussed below in section D3.]	*Security-based swaps are discussed below in section D2.*

The Dodd-Frank Act required the CFTC and SEC to jointly define swap. Their definition expounds on the above and adds a safe harbor for insurance and reinsurance transactions, which might otherwise fall within the above definition. To satisfy the safe harbor test, the tests in "(A)" and "(B)" below must be met or the test in "(C)" must be met.

Insurance Safe Harbor from Swap Definition

17 C.F.R. § 1.3(xxx)(4)

. . . The terms swap as used in section 1a(47) of the Commodity Exchange Act and security-based swap as used in section 1a(42) of the Commodity Exchange Act do not include an agreement, contract, or transaction that:

(A) By its terms or by law, as a condition of performance on the agreement, contract, or transaction:
(1) Requires the beneficiary of the agreement, contract, or transaction to have an insurable interest . . . and thereby carry the risk of loss with respect to that interest . . .; [and]
(2) Requires that loss to occur and to be proved, and that any payment or indemnification therefor be limited to the value of the insurable interest; [and]
(3) Is not traded, separately from the insured interest, on an organized market or over-the-counter; . . . [and]

(B) Is provided:
(1)(i) By a person that is subject to supervision by the insurance commissioner (or similar official or agency) of any State or by the United States or an agency or instrumentality thereof; and (ii) Such agreement, contract, or transaction is regulated as insurance under applicable State law or the laws of the United States; [or]
(2) . . . Directly or indirectly by the United States, any State or any of their respective agencies or instrumentalities . . . [or] [p]ursuant to a statutorily authorized program thereof; or
(3) . . . [Reinsurance offered to a person meeting the criteria in sub-section (B) provided that the agreement meets the criteria in sub-section (A) or (C) or] . . .
(4) [Insurance provided by a non-admitted insurer] listed on the Quarterly Listing of Alien Insurers as maintained by the International Insurers Department of the National Association of Insurance Commissioners [or meeting state eligibility criteria for non-admitted insurers or] . . .

(C) Is provided in accordance with the conditions set forth in [B above] . . . and is one of the following types of products:
(1) Surety bond; (2) Fidelity bond; (3) Life insurance; (4) Health insurance; (5) Long term care insurance; (6) Title insurance; (7) Property and casualty insurance; (8) Annuity; (9) Disability insurance; (10) Insurance against default on individual residential mortgages; and (11) Reinsurance of any of the foregoing . . .

There is also a carve-out for certain foreign exchange transactions pursuant to a Department of the Treasury exemption and a definition of "mixed swap." We examine both of these below.

In short, among the products that are swaps, i.e., that aren't excluded from the definition, the CFTC has exclusive jurisdictional over all swaps save for: (1) security-based swaps, which are subject to SEC jurisdiction and described in section C2 below, (2) physically settled foreign exchange swaps and forwards over which it has a more limited jurisdiction discussed in further detail in Chapter 12, and (3) mixed swaps over which jurisdiction is shared with the SEC, discussed in section D3 below.

In an effort to resolve the jurisdictional battles in which the SEC and CFTC have historically engaged, the Dodd-Frank Act required the SEC and CFTC to jointly agree on a rule further defining the term "swap" and related definitions[3] or else the authority to decide between the SEC and CFTC or to select a compromise would fall to the Financial Stability Oversight Council.[4]

With the CFTC's jurisdiction outlined, in the following sections we analyze where the CFTC's jurisdiction overlaps or conflicts with other regulators in order to better understand the CFTC's exact jurisdictional limits.

D. THE CFTC AND THE SEC

In Chapter 2 we examined some of the historical jurisdictional conflicts between the CFTC and SEC. Sometimes, efforts to "split the baby" led to poor outcomes, such as the prohibition on single stock futures, only repealed in 2000 by the Commodity Futures Modernization Act. Other times, it has led to complicated tests, such as whether derivatives reference a "narrow-based security index" or not, discussed in section D2 below and "mixed swaps," discussed in section D3 below.

1. Dispute Over Securities Options and Futures

The Shad-Johnson Accord was revised in 2000 by the Commodity Futures Modernization Act to lift the Futures Trading Act of 1982's prohibition against listing single-stock futures. The prohibition was in place merely because the SEC and CFTC could not agree on which regulator was jurisdictionally responsible for the oversight of single-stock futures, not due to any specific concerns about the nature of the product.

The Commodity Futures Modernization Act granted the SEC jurisdiction over single stock futures or futures on a "narrow-based security index." The test for a narrow-based index is complicated. As a general matter, an index comprised of nine or fewer securities is a narrow-based security index (with some additional tests if there are exactly nine securities) and there are further exceptions based on the weighting and trading volume of the securities. Options on a security future,[5] including a narrow-based security index, are still banned by Commodity Exchange Act § 2(a)(1)(D)(iii)(II) in the absence of joint authorization by the CFTC and the SEC.

The Dodd-Frank Act, though modifying the jurisdictional boundaries between the SEC and CFTC in many areas, did not do so with respect to exchange-traded derivatives.

2. Security-Based Swaps

Security-based swaps are a subset of swaps. In other words, before a derivative can be a security-based swap, it must be a swap. In addition to having the characteristics of a swap, a security-based swap, must be based on:

> (I) an index that is a narrow-based security index, including any interest therein or on the value thereof;
> (II) a single security or loan, including any interest therein or on the value thereof; or
> (III) the occurrence, nonoccurrence, or extent of the occurrence of an event relating to a single issuer of a security or the issuers of securities in a

> narrow-based security index, provided that such event directly affects the financial statements, financial condition, or financial obligations of the issuer.[6]

The only categories of swaps that reference securities or loans, and therefore are security-based swaps, are equity swaps or, potentially, credit default swaps.

As noted above in section D1, the test for a narrow-based security index was initially devised to provide a dividing line for the listing of exchange-traded products and was added by the Commodity Futures Modernization Act. The listing process is one that typically takes months. Accordingly, there was significant time to apply these tests and conclusively determine whether a security index was a narrow-based one or not for the purposes of determining whether the product in question was subject to the SEC's or the CFTC's jurisdiction.

The Dodd-Frank Act directly utilized this historic definition in the very different context of off-exchange trading where parties enter into individual trades, often with little time to conduct an analysis of whether the traded product meets the narrow-based security index definition or not. This has implications because the determination of whether a product is a security-based swap also determines whether the SEC's or the CFTC's regulatory requirements must be satisfied.

Throughout, unless the context requires otherwise, we refer to a "swap" as a product regulated by the CFTC and a "security-based swap" as one regulated by the SEC.

3. Mixed Swaps

Some swaps may be difficult to characterize as exclusively a swap or security-based swap. Accordingly, the Dodd-Frank Act provided for "mixed swaps" that contain elements of both, defined at Commodity Exchange Act § 1a(47)(D) and Securities Exchange Act of 1934 § 3(a)(68)(D):[7]

> The term "[mixed swap]" includes any [security-based swap that is also] based on the value of 1 or more interest or other rates, currencies, commodities, instruments of indebtedness, indices, quantitative measures, other financial or economic interest or property of any kind (other than a single security or a narrow-based security index), or the occurrence, non-occurrence, or the extent of the occurrence of an event or contingency associated with a potential financial, economic, or commercial consequence (other than [the occurrence, nonoccurrence, or extent of the occurrence of an event relating to a single issuer of a security or the issuers of securities in a narrow-based security index, provided that such event

directly affects the financial statements, financial condition, or financial obligations of the issuer]).

The solution arrived at by the Dodd-Frank Act is to subject such products to regulation by both the SEC and the CFTC. The SEC and the CFTC have jointly stated that they "believe that the scope of mixed swaps is, and is intended to be, narrow."[8]

E. INSURANCE

The insurance safe harbor referenced above in section C protects against an insurance product being regulated as a swap. Traditionally, insurance regulation is within the province of the states.

Credit default swaps, discussed in Chapter 1, operate by providing "protection" to a buyer against specified "Credit Events" such as the bankruptcy of a third party. Superficially a credit default swap bears similarities to insurance. Unlike insurance, though, there is no insurable interest requirement and, instead of operating as an indemnity against a verified loss as is typically the case with insurance, the economic pay-off to the purchaser if a Credit Event occurs is hard-wired into the agreement regardless of whether the protection buyer suffers an actual economic loss.

The Dodd-Frank Act added § 12(h) to the Commodity Exchange Act that, in unequivocal form, likewise protects against a swap being regulated as insurance:

> A swap –
> (1) shall not be considered to be insurance; and
> (2) may not be regulated as an insurance contract under the law of any State.

One of the motivations for the Dodd-Frank Act's preemption of state regulation of swaps as insurance, was a September 2008 issuance, Circular Letter No. 19 (2008), from the New York State Insurance Department (now part of New York State's Department of Financial Services) that indicated that a seller of credit default swaps, despite a previous opinion to the contrary from the Insurance Department's General Counsel, might be engaged in an act requiring a license as an insurance company. Two months later, the Insurance Department revoked its Circular Letter through a First Supplement to Circular Letter No. 19 (2008).

Despite the revocation, the tangible possibility of state regulation of the credit default swap market as insurance was of great concern to financial market participants until the Dodd-Frank preempted such regulation.

F. FEDERAL ENERGY REGULATORY COMMISSION DISPUTE

The Energy Policy Act of 2005 granted the Federal Energy Regulatory Commission ("FERC") broader jurisdiction over the energy markets than FERC had enjoyed previously. In 2007 a trader at a large hedge fund was accused by FERC and the CFTC of manipulating the natural gas market via futures positions. FERC viewed its grant of authority as relating to *any* manipulation of the energy market, regardless of the means. FERC also believed that the Energy Policy Act of 2005 implicitly modified the Commodity Exchange Act's grant of exclusive jurisdiction over commodity futures. The CFTC, filing an *amicus* brief in support of the trader (note that the CFTC had already conducted its own civil enforcement proceedings against the trader), argued that FERC had no jurisdiction over commodity futures because of the exclusive jurisdiction over commodity futures conferred to the CFTC by the Commodity Exchange Act.

Hunter v. Federal Energy Regulatory Commission

711 F.3d 155 (D.C. Cir. 2013)

Tatel, Circuit Judge:

Pursuant to the Energy Policy Act of 2005, the Federal Energy Regulatory Commission fined petitioner $30 million for manipulating natural gas futures contracts. According to petitioner, FERC lacks authority to fine him because the Commodity Futures Trading Commission has exclusive jurisdiction over all transactions involving commodity futures contracts. Because manipulation of natural gas futures contracts falls within the CFTC's exclusive jurisdiction and because nothing in the Energy Policy Act clearly and manifestly repeals the CFTC's exclusive jurisdiction, we grant the petition for review.

According to FERC, Hunter sold a significant number of natural gas futures contracts during the February, March, and April 2006 settlement periods. During these settlement periods, Hunter's sales ranged from 14.4% to 19.4% of market volume. Given their volume and timing, Hunter's sales reduced the settlement price for natural gas. Hunter's portfolio benefited from these sales because he had positioned his assets in the natural gas market to capitalize on a price decrease – that is, he shorted the price for natural gas.

Hunter's trades caught the attention of federal regulators. On July 25, 2007, the CFTC filed a civil enforcement action against Hunter, alleging that he violated section 13(a)(2) of the Commodity Exchange Act by manipulating the price of natural gas futures contracts. The next day, FERC filed an administrative enforcement action against Hunter, alleging that he violated section 4A of the Natural Gas Act, which prohibits manipulation. FERC claimed that Hunter's manipulation of the settlement price affected the price of natural gas in FERC-regulated markets. Following a lengthy administrative process, FERC ruled against Hunter and imposed a $30 million fine.

Hunter [argues] . . . that FERC lacks jurisdiction to pursue this enforcement action. The CFTC has intervened in support of Hunter on this issue. . . .

Stated simply, Congress crafted CEA section 2(a)(1)(A) to give the CFTC exclusive jurisdiction over transactions conducted on futures markets like the NYMEX.

In response to the California energy crisis, Congress enacted the Energy Policy Act of 2005, which significantly expanded FERC's authority to regulate manipulation in energy markets. As codified at section 4A of the Natural Gas Act, the statute makes it

> unlawful for any entity, directly or indirectly, to use or employ, in connection with the purchase or sale of natural gas or the purchase or sale of transportation services subject to the jurisdiction of the Commission, any manipulative or deceptive device or contrivance . . . in contravention of such rules and regulations as the Commission may prescribe as necessary in the public interest or for the protection of natural gas ratepayers.

FERC subsequently promulgated regulations prohibiting manipulative trading in natural gas.

The Energy Policy Act contains only two references to the CFTC. . . .

[S]ection 23 requires FERC and the CFTC to enter into a memorandum of understanding about information sharing [and] provides that it has no effect on the CFTC's exclusive jurisdiction.

As we see it, this case reduces to two questions. First, does CEA section 2(a)(1)(A) encompass manipulation of natural gas futures contracts? If yes, then we need to answer the second question: did Congress clearly and manifestly intend to impliedly repeal CEA section 2(a)(1)(A) when it enacted the Energy Policy Act of 2005?

A quick glance at the statute's text answers the first question. . . . By CEA section 2(a)(1)(A)'s plain terms, the CFTC has exclusive jurisdiction over the manipulation of natural gas futures contracts.

Against the statute's plain text, FERC marshals two counterarguments. According to FERC, although it and the CFTC "each have exclusive jurisdiction over the day-to-day regulation of their respective physical energy and financial markets, where, as here, there is manipulation in one market that directly or indirectly affects the other market, both agencies have an enforcement role." But FERC's contention that the CFTC may exclusively regulate only day-to-day trading activities – not an overarching scheme like manipulation – finds no support in CEA section 2(a)(1)(A)'s text. . . .

FERC also relies on our decision in *FTC v. Ken Roberts Co.*, 276 F.3d 583 (D.C.Cir.2001). There, the FTC subpoenaed a company for information concerning its instructional courses about futures market trading. The company argued that the FTC had no jurisdiction to investigate instructional courses about futures markets because only the CFTC could regulate such activities. . . . Concluding that an instructional course about futures trading did not qualify as a contract, agreement, or transaction on a commodity futures market, we held that the CFTC lacked exclusive jurisdiction and the FTC's subpoena could be enforced. . . .

As we read *Ken Roberts*, the decision actually supports Hunter's position because it endorses a robust view of the CFTC's exclusive jurisdiction. For example, we remarked that the CFTC "was invested with exclusive jurisdiction over certain aspects of the futures trading market. The aim of [CEA section 2(a)(1)(A)], according to one of its chief sponsors, was to 'avoid unnecessary, overlapping and duplicative regulation,' especially as between the [SEC] and the new CFTC" [and] "[t]he word 'transactions,' " we further explained, "conveys a reciprocity, a mutual exchange, which seem[ed] absent from the allegedly deceptive advertising materials that the FTC [sought] to investigate." By contrast, Hunter's alleged manipulation scheme involved transacting in commodity futures contracts, thus falling on the other side of the *Ken Roberts* dividing line.

Because any infringement of the CFTC's exclusive jurisdiction would effectively repeal CEA section 2(a)(1)(A), we must next determine whether, as FERC insists, the Energy Policy Act constitutes a repeal by implication. On this front, FERC carries a heavy burden. . . .

"[A]bsent a clearly expressed congressional intention" to repeal CEA section 2(a)(1)(A), *Morton v. Mancari*, 417 U.S. 535, 551, 94 S. Ct. 2474, 41 L.Ed.2d 290 (1974), FERC cannot demonstrate that section 4A encroaches upon the CFTC's exclusive jurisdiction. Having failed to meet the high bar of showing an implied repeal, FERC lacks jurisdiction to charge Hunter with manipulation of natural gas futures contracts. . . .

For the foregoing reasons, we grant the petition for review.

The D.C. Circuit interpreted the grant of "exclusive" jurisdiction to the CFTC strictly. This has an antecedent in *Chicago Board of Trade v. Securities and Exchange Commission*, 677 F.2d 1137 (7th Cir. 1982),[9] in which the Seventh Circuit ruled in favor of the CFTC in the GNMA option dispute (discussed in Chapter 2) which led to the Shad-Johnson Accord. There, although superseded by the statutory codification of the jurisdictional divide between the SEC and

CFTC agreed by their respective Chairmen, Shad and Johnson, the Seventh Circuit also took a broad reading of the Commodity Exchange Act's grant of "exclusive" jurisdiction to the CFTC.

G. BANK REGULATORS

The Commodity Exchange Act is disapplied from, and the CFTC does not have jurisdiction over, "identified banking products" so long as "an appropriate banking agency certifies that the product has been commonly offered, entered into, or provided in the United States by any bank on or before December 5, 2000 . . ."[10] Included in "identified banking products" are deposit accounts, savings accounts, debit accounts, certificates of deposit, letters of credit, and loan participations.[11]

However, the CFTC can assert jurisdiction with respect to an identified bank product that:

> (1) is a product of a bank that is not under the regulatory jurisdiction of an appropriate Federal banking agency;
> (2) meets the definition of swap in section 1a(47) of the Commodity Exchange Act . . .; and
> (3) has become known to the trade as a swap . . ., or otherwise has been structured as an identified banking product for the purpose of evading the provisions of the Commodity Exchange Act (7 U.S.C. 1 et seq.) . . ."

Legal Certainty for Bank Products Act of 2000 § 403 as amended by Dodd-Frank Act § 725(g).

H. EXTRATERRITORIAL LIMITATIONS

The Commodity Exchange Act, rules promulgated by the CFTC thereunder, caselaw, and guidance issued by the CFTC together are sources that assist in determining the extent to which the CFTC's jurisdiction has extraterritorial reach. Chapter 15 examines the extraterritorial extent of the CFTC's regulation of derivatives.

I. JURISDICTION SHARED WITH STATES

In the Futures Trading Act of 1978, in order to permit any state to enforce a Commodity Exchange Act violation, a new section (§ 6d) was added to the Commodity Exchange Act. The passage of the Act was accompanied by the following Senate report summarizing the new grant of state jurisdiction.

Report of the Committee on Agriculture, Nutrition and Forestry on S. 2391

S. Rep. 95-850 (May 15, 1978)

Compounding [the problem of limited CFTC enforcement resources] was the reluctance of the states, whose regulatory authority had been preempted by the 1974 amendments, to bring *parens patriae* actions under the commodity exchange act or actions under their general antifraud statutes. . . .

The recent experience of the commission with commodity options transactions clearly demonstrates the need for the establishment of an effective working relationship between the commission and the states in order to ferret out and prosecute successfully commodities fraud. . . .

S.2391 adds a new Section 6d to the Commodity Exchange Act, authorizing states to institute actions seeking injunctive relief for violations of the Commodity Exchange Act, or Commission rules, regulations, or orders thereunder. The cause of action available to the states is derived directly from this Congressional enactment – not from common law principles and practice under the *parens patriae* doctrine. This new cause of action would not be subject to the possible limitation that the state, bringing an action *parens patriae*, may sue only to vindicate its quasi-sovereign interests. The Committee intends that the state may sue to enjoin acts and practices that, proceeding in violation of the Act, or rules, regulations, or orders thereunder, have injured, are injuring, or threaten to injure any resident of the state. . . .

This authority is subject to the qualification that such state actions may not be brought against a contract market or floor broker designated or registered as such with the Commission. The intent of the section is to provide states with the tools to combat fraudulent and other unlawful activity directed at their residents. Plenary authority to register, regulate, and discipline the contract markets and the 'locals' whose activities are generally of the character of pit trading rather than customer contact is reserved to the Commission. . . .

The statute on which all actions brought under this section is to be based is the Commodity Exchange Act. The states would not, in these actions, be involved in enforcement of their local laws. Consistent with the Commission's exclusive jurisdiction and preemption of state regulatory activity enacted in 1974, and with the present decision to make federal law the basis for all actions brought under this section, it was also determined to make the federal courts the exclusive forum for such actions. This is consistent with the pattern established in the Securities Exchange Act of 1934, which requires private actions brought under that statute to proceed in the federal courts. The vast body of decisional law relating to SEC Rule 10b-5 securities "fraud" has developed exclusively in the federal courts. In this way, it is believed, a readily available, coherent body of law is most likely to evolve, subject to review and correction within the single, unified system of federal courts, employing common procedures throughout the United States.

It is understood that some states may desire to bring emergency actions in their own courts, and may desire to seek relief other than injunctive relief. Notwithstanding the provisions of this section, it will remain possible, as it has been in the past, for an authorized state official to proceed in state court on the basis of an alleged violation of any general civil or criminal antifraud statute. . . .

To assure that the body of decisional law developed under this section would be coherent and consistent with national policy, new Section 6d provides that states, before instituting an action thereunder, must receive the prior approval of the Commission. State prosecutorial discretion would, therefore, be checked only to the degree that contemplated state prosecutions deviate from national policy established by the commission. . . .

The participation of the states in the enforcement of the Commodity Exchange Act is desirable. It is recognized that the widely available investigatory and prosecutorial capabilities of the states should be employed in the enforcement of the Commodity Exchange Act. Any state official who has investigative powers bestowed on his or her by state law is free, under new Section 6d, to exercise those powers in preparation for bringing any action under this section, or in determining whether such an action shall be instituted.

Each individual state remains free to allocate responsibilities internally. A state may authorize either its attorney general, or its securities administrator, or both or some other official or officials, to bring actions under this section and conduct investigations for the purpose of bringing such actions.

Prominent Practitioner Sidenote: William T. Bagley, Esq.

William Bagley was Chairman of the CFTC at its founding in 1975, six months after passage of the Commodity Futures Modernization Act of 1974. In law practice for more than 60 years, he is also a partner at the law firm of Nossaman LLP and a former California assemblyman and Regent of the University of California.

How did you end up in your role at the CFTC?

I ran for state comptroller in California in 1974. When, in October, President Ford pardoned Nixon, the polls were down massively and I was a Republican running for state comptroller, and the governor lost by 500,000 and I lost by 200,000.

I knew Rita Hauser, a very successful lawyer, close to Nelson Rockefeller, because I was a moderate/liberal Republican and traveled with Rockefeller in California in '64 all over the state as a volunteer [when he ran for the Republican presidential nomination against the more conservative Goldwater ticket]. Rita wrote me a little note before the November 1974 state comptroller election saying, "I know you want to win, but you're not going to." She added something to the effect of "maybe you ought to come to Washington?"

A month later, I am at Pat Brown's office, the former governor. His son has just been elected governor. He wanted me to join his law firm. While I'm at his office, I get a call from the White House Executive Office saying that they wanted me to come to Washington. Pat Brown says, "Yeah Bill, go ahead."

Rita hadn't told me this, but I knew that Rita had talked to either Donald Rumsfeld, who at the time was President Ford's chief of staff, or President Ford. Sometime in late December, I go to D.C. and meet with the head of appointments and they ask me to be chairman of the new Commodity Futures Trading Commission.

I had absolutely no knowledge of, or affinity with, the subject of the Commission. Never thought about futures in my life. I had educational credentials, though, and fit in as a moderate Republican. Also, they didn't want to appoint, in their words, a "commodity hack," someone too close to the industry.

What was the greatest challenge faced by the CFTC in its early years?

First of all, the Commission itself. Absolutely no commonality and no control. The one thing I could do to get a Commissioner's attention was to approve travel expenditures.

There were only six months from the passage of the Commodity Futures Trading Commission Act to when it took effect on April 21, 1975. The transition team paid someone $5,000 to design a seal. I thought that was ridiculous. I cut out a picture of a San Francisco sea lion and put it on my door. That was the Commission "seal."

The transition was supposed to occur over a period of months, and it occurred over a period of a week. We were not sworn in until Wednesday, April 16, six days before Monday, April 21.

There were two transition attorneys, loaned from the SEC to write some initial regulations. On Thursday we received the regulations. We passed them Friday morning. The attorneys got to the Federal Register by ten minutes to two on Friday. The regulations said that the CFTC's open for business and the markets could continue trading. It wasn't anything fancy, but they had to be published in the Federal Register on Monday otherwise the markets would have closed.

We were in the basement of the Department of Agriculture. [Prior to the CFTC, the Commodity Exchange Authority was a bureau of the Department of Agriculture.] And it was decrepit. They had intercom systems from the 1930s. You would push a button and it would buzz in the other guy's office. It was unbelievable. In the Chicago office of the CFTC they were renting the basement of the Chicago Board of Trade building! The Federal government was a tenant. We changed that.

Getting started was the second problem. There was no body of law. A massive nationwide commodity options fraud was underway. And here's the itch: When the Commodity Futures Trading Commission Act was written, it preempted 50 state corporation commissioners from regulating commodities. The CFTC Enforcement Division had at this time, I don't know, maybe 15 people maximum? We had no body of law. How's a judge going to stop someone from selling something like a phony commodity option? We couldn't get an injunction other than maybe six months later, but no such thing as a preliminary injunction, a preliminary restraining order, or anything else.

Looking at the regulatory landscape today, is there anything you would have done differently?

I don't think so. The leadership of the markets at that time was confused and suspicious. What are these CFTC guys going to do? They were afraid. So the best thing that I could have done, and I did it, was major cooperation. No sense to do something inordinate. So they were helpful, they were cooperative. Financial futures were a big one. They wanted financial futures. Within six months we instituted Ginnie Mae futures. We got threatened by the SEC.[12] Rod Hills was the SEC chairman. Rod had been an L.A. lawyer and I knew Rod (in fact he still owes me some money, said he was going to contribute to my campaign in '74 but he never did!) I called him and I told him, "Good God Rod, could you imagine anyone outside of the beltway hearing that two Federal agencies are suing each other. You can't do that." So that was fun.

Looking back at your career, what are you most proud of?

I stopped the repeal of fair housing in California. This is 1967; the Fair Housing Act in California passed in '63. Four Republicans voted for fair housing, including me. Fair housing was killed in a ballot initiative in 1964. The Supreme Court in California ruled the initiative unconstitutional because it not only repealed the act, it also violated the state constitution by stating that you could never pass the Fair Housing Act again, that is, it violated the state constitution's equal protection clause.

Ronald Reagan was running for governor, teeth grinding, table pounding, "Repeal the act!" The repeal passed in the state senate 25-5. It came to the state assembly and it got assigned to me. I put together a little compromise making a few exceptions to the repeal. Back to the state senate. You know the game. The senate would not confirm the assembly amendments. We had a conference committee and I was appointed chairman. Incidentally, I'm a Republican and I'm appointed chairman by the Democratic speaker because he knew what I was doing. I never called a meeting of the conference committee. So fair housing continues to exist. And because of that I'm very proud.

While Chairman of the CFTC you wrote that the "very structure of [the CFTC] is at fault when, by statute, the [CFTC] is the rule maker, the investigator, the prosecuting attorney, the grand jury – receiving evidence of an internal action – and then the judge and jury all in the same case over the same time period."[13] What would you propose as a solution to this lack of separation?

The American Bar Association in the 1930s had a proposal to create an independent bureau where your administrative law judges (ALJs) would all be. We have that in California now. The ALJs would not be assigned to the entity over which they were going to be ruling.

During a CFTC investigation – and the CFTC was a small entity at the time with just over 400 people, most of them in New York and Chicago, maybe 100 in Washington – we hear about this bad guy. By God, he's defrauding the world! There is a formal investigation and the Commission votes five to zero to bring an enforcement action. There were only three ALJs and they knew all of this is going on. Obviously, the case comes to one of the ALJs who has heard all of this noise about this terrible person, this commodity fraud trader. That's not due process.

It must have been controversial for the first Chairman of the CFTC to take such a critical position and it must have taken the courage of your convictions. What were some of the reactions you received?

None, there was nothing – Washington exists in its own world.

What advice would you offer for a lawyer entering into practice?

My answer in California and in the West is water law. Water is the oil of the twenty-first century. The other piece of advice relates to the relation between public service and my success in my law firm (and I've been there almost 25 years). I have originated business in half a dozen different arenas simply because of my stories here. I knew people in Washington. I knew half of the

California congressional delegation personally because I served with them in the legislature. All over California, I was known. Public service brought a very expansive arena for this lawyer (meaning myself) into play.

So public service for a young lawyer is a great way of establishing a reputation. And there's two ways of doing public service. One is to start in an impoverished arena and be successful. Another is to make yourself a couple of million dollars by the age of 40 and then go into public service as a major endeavor. We lawyers need to do that and I've done my share.

QUESTIONS AND COMMENTS

1. If you were Commissioners Shad or Johnson, what accord would you have reached? Why?
2. What might have been an alternative to banning trading in single stock futures and options on single stock futures?
3. Why might the definition of swap be so broad? What are the pros and cons of a broad definition compared to a more specific one?
4. The definition of "narrow-based security index," originally used to determine whether a product could be listed on a CFTC-regulated board of trade or an SEC-regulated exchange, was later applied to the off-exchange derivatives market. What were the consequences of doing so? What better approaches might there have been? Is there a less complicated definition that might allow for categorization to be automated?
5. Why can it sometimes be difficult to distinguish between a security and a future? What types of products are particularly hard to categorize?
6. Is the demarcation between insurance products and swaps clear? Can you think of any product that might challenge that demarcation?
7. Is there a way to more simply define a "narrow-based security index"? What might the reasoning be for the current definition?
8. Does subjecting a "mixed swap" to both SEC and CFTC regulation have a downside? What incentives might such regulatory treatment provide to market participants?
9. The Seventh Circuit is located in Chicago, the historical hub of the commodity futures industry. What advantages and disadvantages might this confer on the Seventh Circuit?
10. Do the jurisdictional boundaries make sense?
11. Some commentators have proposed a single "super regulator" with authority over all financial market activities. What are the pros and cons of this approach?
12. Can overlapping jurisdiction, such as between the CFTC and the states with respect to the Commodity Exchange Act have benefits?

CHAPTER 4
CONTRACT MARKETS

A. BACKGROUND

In Chapters 2 and 3 we have examined commodity futures and the CFTC's jurisdiction over commodity futures. A central pillar of the Commodity Exchange Act is the requirement that commodity futures be traded on a board of trade designated as a contract market.

Commodity Exchange Act § 4(a) reads:

> **[I]t shall be unlawful for any person** to offer to enter into, **to enter into**, to execute, to confirm the execution of, or to conduct any office or business anywhere in the United States, its territories or possessions, for the purpose of soliciting or accepting any order for, or otherwise dealing in, any transaction in, or in connection with, **a contract for the purchase or sale of a commodity for future delivery** (other than a contract which is made on or subject to the rules of a board of trade, exchange, or market located outside the United States, its territories or possessions) **unless** –
>
> (1) **such transaction is conducted on or subject to the rules of a board of trade which has been designated or registered by the Commission as a contract market . . . for such commodity;**
> (2) **such contract is executed or consummated by or through a contract market; and**
> (3) **such contract is evidenced by a record in writing which shows the date, the parties to such contract and their addresses, the property covered and its price, and the terms of delivery** . . .
> [emphasis added.]

In addition, Commodity Exchange Act § 5(d)(1)(A) reads:

> To be designated, and maintain a designation, as a contract market, a board of trade shall comply with –
> (i) any core principle described in this subsection; and
> (ii) any requirement that the Commission may impose . . .

Taken together then, it is unlawful to trade a commodity future other than on a board of trade designated as a contract market. The CFTC determines designation as a contract market and adherence with the "core principles" with which designated contract markets must comply.

Designated contract markets are markets that are potentially accessible to retail investors, through an introducing broker or futures commission merchant as intermediary. These two categories of CFTC registrants, introducing brokers and futures commission merchants, are the subject of Chapter 5.

B. BOARDS OF TRADE

To be "designated as a contract market," an entity first needs to meet the definition of a "board of trade." The term "board of trade" is an anachronistic one. Commodity Exchange Act § 1a(6) defines a "board of trade" as "any organized exchange or other trading facility." A "trading facility" (a term broader than "organized exchange" and, therefore, inclusive of an organized exchange) is defined in Commodity Exchange Act § 1(a)(51) as:

> [A] person or group of persons that constitutes, maintains, or provides a physical or electronic facility or system in which multiple participants have the ability to execute or trade agreements, contracts, or transactions –
>
> (i) by accepting bids or offers made by other participants that are open to multiple participants in the facility or system; or
> (ii) through the interaction of multiple bids or multiple offers within a system with a pre-determined non-discretionary automated trade matching and execution algorithm.

Described another way, a trading facility is a so-called multiple-to-multiple platform, i.e., it provides a facility (it can be electronic) for transactions between more than one offeror and more than one offeree.[14]

> Example 1: User-Friendly Bank, National Association wishes to establish a web portal for the convenience of its customers where its customers can access quotes from User-Friendly offering to trade various commodity futures.

This does not meet the definition of trading facility because it is a single (User-Friendly Bank) to multiple (its customers) platform, contract market designation would be unavailable to User-Friendly Bank's web portal, and any offers by User-Friendly Bank to trade commodity futures using the web portal (or any means other than via a designated contract market) would violate Commodity Exchange Act § 4(a). (*See* section A above.)

Example 2: The Acme Finance Company, Inc., proposes to establish an online page where it lists requests for quotations ("RFQs") for commodity futures it wishes to trade.

This is also not a trading facility and designation as a contract market would not be possible for its web page, because even though there are multiple offerors, there is only one offeree, Acme. As in Example 1, any RFQs by Acme Finance relating to commodity futures would violate Commodity Exchange Act § 4(a).

Example 3: The Silicon Valley MBA Co. designs a phone app that allows the listing of bids or offers for a variety of commodity futures. This meets the definition of "trading facility." Since commodity futures must be traded on a board of trade designated as a contract market, the Silicon Valley MBA Co. must receive CFTC designation of the phone app as a contract market before it goes live.

C. DESIGNATION AS A CONTRACT MARKET

The CFTC has broad authority to both designate boards of trade as contract markets and to establish the regulatory framework boards of trade must operate within.

American Board of Trade, Inc. v. Bagley

402 F. Supp. 974 (S.D.N.Y. 1975)

Werker, District Judge.

Plaintiff American Board of Trade, Inc. (ABT), has brought an action against the Chairman of the Commodity Futures Trading Commission (CFTC), several of its employees and the United States Department of Agriculture by complaint filed on August 26, 1975. The complaint prays for (1) an order enjoining the defendants from interfering with his (sic) business and dealing with him (sic) in an arbitrary and capricious manner and taking his (sic) property without due process of law, (2) the designation of the plaintiff as a contract market for transactions in commodity futures, and (3) compensatory and punitive damages aggregating $1,000,000.00. (The use of the male gender is presumably a reference to Arthur W. Economou, the president of ABT.) . . .

The statute creating the CFTC was signed into law on October 23, 1974 and became effective April 21, 1975. It amended the Commodity Exchange Act, created the Commission as an independent regulatory agency and assigned broad responsibility to the Commission for the regulation of transactions involving the sale of commodities for future delivery (commodity futures).

Section 4 of the Act makes it unlawful for any person to engage in transactions in any futures contract except through members of a "board of trade" that has been designated by the Commission as a "contract market." . . .

The Commission was authorized and directed under Section 5 of the Act to grant designation "when, and only when," a board of trade has met the conditions and requirements specified in the Act. The application for contract market designation must be accompanied by a showing that the board of trade complies with . . . [Commodity Exchange Act] requirements . . .

Although the Act became effective April 21, 1975 a majority of the Commission was not appointed and confirmed until April 10, 1975. Consequently Congress determined that there would not be sufficient time for the Commission to review applications for designation before April 21, 1975 and permitted the Commission to provisionally designate boards of trade for a period not to exceed 90 days after April 21, 1975.

At the first official meeting of the Commission held on April 15, 1975 the Commission considered a regulation for provisional designation of boards of trade as contract markets.

Mr. Economou, president of ABT, along with other applicants, was notified by letter dated April 16, 1975 that the Commission was adopting a provisional designation rule which required that the applicant demonstrate to the Commission's satisfaction that it was a board of trade within the meaning of the Act and that it actually was operating as a contract market on April 15, 1975. The object of the provisional designation rule was to prevent a disruption of the business of exchanges that were already in operation.

Applicants were instructed to file their applications by April 18, 1975, and also to file a list of their memberships, board of directors and officers and copies of their bylaws, rules, regulations and resolutions under which they operated. April 18 was the last business day before April 21, the effective date of the CFTC Act.

ABT submitted its application on April 18. The Commission considered the application on April 18 and 19 and denied provisional designation to ABT on April 19 because of the Commission's inability to determine from the information supplied whether ABT was a board of trade under the Act and the regulations.

The denial was made without prejudice to filing additional information and the decision was conveyed by telephone and telegram to Mr. Economou. ABT did not seek judicial review of that decision.

The Commission's concern was based in part on the fact that ABT did not have an exchange floor, on the uniqueness of some of the practices described in ABT's application and the uncertain impact of those practices and on the fact that the board of trade appeared to be nothing more than Mr. Economou, his wife and companies controlled by him. Seven members were listed in the application, all but one being residents of states or countries outside New York where the exchange is located.

On May 7, 1975 ABT by its attorney furnished additional information which it was informed on May 19, 1975 was inadequate. A further showing by on site inspection was requested and offered on May 20. This was resisted by Mr. Economou and his attorney. On May 22, 1975 the application of ABT again was considered by the Commission and denied. On that day Mr. Economou was again informed of the decision by letter which among other things informed ABT that it had concluded "that to be a board of trade transaction prices must be competitively determined."

The Chairman also wrote "only through a physical inspection of the trading facilities, a review of the transaction records and interviews can the Commission determine whether The American Board of Trade was a 'board of trade' and as such entitled to be considered for designation as a contract market." Further submission of written material, Mr. Economou was advised, would not significantly advance the application. . . .

On July 18, 1975 the Commission's power to grant provisional designation expired.

The Commission continued to process ABT's application as one for permanent designation after July 18, 1975. During the period April 21, 1975 through July 18, 1975 and thereafter the Commission processed in addition to ABT's application nine board of trade applications . . . The last was granted on September 11, 1975. In addition to these applications the Commission received and processed 18,000 applications for registration by various classes of persons including futures commission merchants, persons associated with futures commission merchants, floor brokers, commodity pool operators and commodity trading advisors.

Due to the number of applications, the Commission's limited manpower and the shortness of time, the Commission had to establish priorities. The application of ABT fell in a second level of priority due to the poorly organized and less complete application and the resistance of the ABT. . . .

Considering the facts as recited above the court has reached the conclusion that plaintiff has failed to show any possibility of success on the merits . . . and its motion for a preliminary injunction is therefore denied.

With respect to defendants' motions they are granted. It appears from the factual situation here that the delays in processing plaintiff's application for permanent designation as a board of trade and as such a contract market have been due in large part to ABT's failure to comply with the requirements of the Commission and the guidelines and regulations issued under the Act. These guidelines and regulations are demonstrably reasonable considering the economic and public interest to be protected. The charge of bias made by plaintiff is frivolous . . .

For the above reasons, I am dismissing the complaint herein. . . .

Note the reference in *American Board of Trade, Inc.* to the CFTC's concern that the American Board of Trade did not have an exchange floor. In light of modern trading norms, this should not be viewed as a CFTC requirement to have a ***physical*** exchange floor. Particularly since the Commodity Futures Modernization Act, the trend has strongly been toward electronic trading being the established norm.

As of June 2014 there were 16 designated contract markets, some of which are under common ownership.[15] By requiring commodity futures to be traded on designated contract markets, the Commodity Exchange Act establishes an oligopoly.[16]

As the following case illustrates, the CFTC's discretionary authority to approve designation as a contract market is as broad as its authority to deny designation as a contract market.

Board of Trade of the City of Chicago v. Commodity Futures Trading Commission

66 F. Supp. 2d 891 (N.D. Ill. 1999)

Bucklo, District Judge.

The Board of Trade of the City of Chicago, the Kansas City Board of Trade, and the Minneapolis Grain Exchange brought this action against the Commodity Futures Trading Commission (the "Commission"), seeking judicial review of the Commission's approval of the Cantor Financial Futures Exchange (the "Cantor Exchange") as a contract market. The Commission moves to dismiss for lack of subject matter jurisdiction and failure to state a claim [and] . . . has filed . . . for summary judgment. For the following reasons, the Commission's motions to dismiss are denied, and its motion for summary judgment is granted. . . .

In January 1998 the Cantor Exchange applied to the Commission for designation as a contract market for trading on certain United States Treasury futures contracts. On September 4, 1998, the Commission approved the Cantor Exchange's contract market designation application. Under 7 U.S.C. § 7, the Cantor Exchange, as an applicant exchange, was required to meet numerous requirements, including showing that its operations would not be "contrary to the public interest," before being approved as a contract market. The plaintiffs argue that the Commission never made the required finding on the public interest issue and other issues, that the Commission held the Cantor Exchange to a different, lower regulatory standard than other futures exchanges, that the Commission failed to address or respond to material public comments raised by the plaintiffs, and that the Commission failed to provide notice or an opportunity to comment on the Cantor Exchange's final application. . . .

Under the Commodity Exchange Act, futures contracts must be traded on exchanges, called boards of trade that have been approved by the Commission as "contract markets." 7 U.S.C. § 6(a). The approval process under which a board of trade is initially designated as a contract market is governed by 7 U.S.C. §§ 7 and 8. Section 7 provides that the Commission is authorized to designate a board of trade as a contract market when the board of trade complies with numerous statutory requirements . . . Section 8 . . . provides that if the Commission denies an application, it must state the reasons and give the board of trade an opportunity for a hearing before the Commission . . .

The Commission's argument is essentially that, by allowing boards of trade to seek judicial review of their designation denials in the courts of appeals, Congress has precluded competing boards of trade from seeking judicial review of designation approvals in the district courts. The plaintiffs respond that the statute is merely silent on the issue of judicial review of application approvals, and that the presumption favoring review is therefore controlling. I agree. Approval for designation as a contract market is a final agency action, which is presumptively reviewable under the Administrative Procedure Act. . . . [T]he Commodity Exchange Act provides for specific procedures – including an express authorization of who may seek judicial review – for one type of agency action, denials, and no procedures for another type of agency action, approvals. This legislative scheme leaves substantial doubt as to whether Congress intended entirely to preclude judicial review of approvals, and the strong presumption in favor of review accordingly applies. . . .

The plaintiffs argue that the Cantor Exchange's provision for "exclusive time trading" [a method of providing two principals the opportunity to directly trade for a limited period] is a deviation from "open and competitive trading," which is required . . . The Commission interpreted this regulation to include exclusive time trading as proposed by the Cantor Exchange application. . . . The interpretation is not plainly erroneous or inconsistent with the language of the regulation, which allows "other" competitive methods, and it is entitled to deference. . . .

The plaintiffs argue that the Cantor Group is a proven wrongdoer, and that it was arbitrary and capricious for the Commission not to respond to comments regarding the public interest issues raised by the Cantor Group's "control" of the Cantor Exchange.[i] In January 1997 the Commission found Cantor Fitzgerald &

[i] [N. 3] Commentators were concerned with the Cantor Group's ability to name eight of thirteen Cantor Exchange directors.

Co., the Cantor Group's futures commission merchant subsidiary, liable for fraud. . . . [I]ndividuals who commit disciplinary offenses [are prohibited by CFTC regulations] from serving on self-regulatory organization governing boards or committees. The Commission has interpreted this . . . to mean that only "natural persons who themselves commit disciplinary offenses" should be disqualified. . . .

The Commission . . . considered commentators' concerns about the Cantor Group's disciplinary history . . . and specifically addressed mechanisms that monitor the integrity of the Cantor Exchange Board. In light of this consideration, the plaintiffs have not shown that the Commission's approval order was arbitrary and capricious. . . .

The plaintiffs also have not shown that the Commission overlooked whether the Cantor Exchange will fragment treasury futures markets contrary to the public interest. The administrative record reveals that the Commission addressed concerns about market fragmentation, specifically including concerns raised by one of the plaintiffs, the Chicago Board of Trade. The plaintiffs are unsatisfied, arguing that the Commission should have spent more time addressing particular objections relating to market fragmentation . . . The Commission addressed the major issue of policy about which the commentators expressed concerns, market fragmentation, in a reasoned manner and based on factors that are not arbitrary and capricious. . . .

For the reasons discussed above, the Commission's motions to dismiss are denied, and its motion for summary judgment is granted. . . .

D. REGULATION OF DESIGNATED CONTRACT MARKETS

The operation of the commodity futures market is distinctive. Among other things, designated contract markets are required to adhere to established "core principles."[17]

The basic operation of designated contract markets were summarized by the Second Circuit in *In re Amaranth Natural Gas Commodities Litigation* in relation to an allegation that a hedge fund, Amaranth Advisors LLC, had exceeded position limits and otherwise had manipulated the natural gas market in relation to the same events described in *Hunter* in Chapter 3. Natural gas futures traders argued that the firm Amaranth used to clear its natural gas swaps and futures, J.P. Morgan Futures, Inc., was liable for aiding and abetting Amaranth in manipulating the natural gas futures market. The court ultimately found that the role of J.P. Morgan Futures as Amaranth's futures commission merchant responsible for providing clearing services for its trades was insufficient on its own to support an aiding and abetting allegation under the

Commodity Exchange Act. We revisit this case, focusing on the manipulation allegations, in Chapter 13.

For the purposes of this chapter, in addition to the description of how designated contract markets operate, note the contrast between the high level of regulation pertaining to a "designated contract market" and the lesser level of regulation applying to an "exempt commercial market," commonly known as an "ECM." As we discuss below, exempt commercial markets are one of a number of market categories created by the Commodity Futures Modernization Act and repealed by the Dodd-Frank Act due to concerns about the relatively light regulatory requirements applying to them.

In re Amaranth Natural Gas Commodities Litigation

730 F.3d 170 (2d Cir. 2013)

Debra Ann Livingston, Circuit Judge. . . .

[The New York Mecantile Exchange ("NYMEX")] is a futures and options exchange based in New York City. We have previously described the basic features of commodity futures trading:

> A commodities futures contract is an executory contract for the sale of a commodity executed at a specific point in time with delivery of the commodity postponed to a future date. Every commodities futures contract has a seller and a buyer. The seller, called a "short," agrees for a price, fixed at the time of contract, to deliver a specified quantity and grade of an identified commodity at a date in the future. The buyer, or "long," agrees to accept delivery at that future date at the price fixed in the contract. It is the rare case when buyers and sellers settle their obligations under futures contracts by actually delivering the commodity. Rather, they routinely take a short or long position in order to speculate on the future price of the commodity. Then sometime before delivery is due, they offset or liquidate their positions by entering the market again and purchasing an equal number of opposite contracts, i.e., a short buys long, a long buys short. In this way their obligations under the original liquidating contracts offset each other. The difference in price between the original contract and the offsetting contract determines the amount of money made or lost.

Strobl v. N.Y. Mercantile Exch., 768 F.2d 22, 24 (2d Cir.1985).

One type of futures contract traded on NYMEX is for the delivery of natural gas. In its standard form, this contract obligates the buyer to purchase 10,000 MMBtu[ii] of natural gas released during the contract's delivery month at the Henry Hub distribution facility in Erath, Louisiana. Trading on the future begins

---

[ii] [N. 2] 1 MMBtu is equal to 1 million BTU (British Thermal Unit).

five years before the delivery month and ends three business days before the first calendar day of the delivery month. To determine the future's final price, NYMEX uses a weighted average of the trades executed during the final half hour of trading – 2:00 to 2:30 P.M. – on the last trading day. This final half hour is referred to as the contract's "final settlement period," and final price as the "final settlement price."

NYMEX is a designated contract market, or "DCM." As a DCM, NYMEX may offer options and futures trading for any type of commodity, but is subject to extensive oversight from the Commodity Futures Trading Commission ("CFTC"). . . .

All trades on NYMEX must go through the exchange's clearinghouse. To finalize, or "clear," a trade, traders must transact with a NYMEX clearing member – a firm approved as a member of the clearinghouse. The seller's clearing firm will sell the contract to the clearinghouse, which then sells the contract to the buyer's clearing firm. Through this act of simultaneously buying and selling the contract, the clearinghouse guarantees both sides of the trade and ensures that neither buyer nor seller is exposed to any counterparty credit risk. The clearing firms, in turn, guarantee their clients' performance to the clearing-house.

To protect itself from risk of nonpayment, the NYMEX clearinghouse requires that its members deposit margin sufficient to cover any potential short-term losses on their clients' open positions. At the end of each trading day, the clearinghouse examines the change in value to these positions and determines whether the firm must post additional margin (generally the case if value has decreased) or receives payment on margin (generally the case if value has increased). This process is called "marking-to-market." Clearing firms engage in the same process with their customers, requiring an initial margin payment for any newly acquired position and conducting a daily recalculation of that margin requirement as the position changes in value.

In addition to clearing members, traders on NYMEX also interact with futures commissions [*sic*] merchants, or "FCMs." "An FCM is the commodity market's equivalent of a securities brokerage house, soliciting and accepting orders for futures contracts and accepting funds or extending credit in connection therewith." FCMs must register with the CFTC and are subject to numerous regulatory requirements. A firm may be both a clearing member and an FCM. Such dual status would enable it to both accept orders from clients and clear any resulting trades. . . .

ICE is an electronic commodity exchange based in Atlanta, Georgia. At the time of the events alleged in the amended complaint, ICE offered trading in natural gas swaps.[iii] Swaps, unlike futures contracts, do not contemplate

---

[iii] [N. 3] ICE has since stopped offering natural gas swaps for trading, and instead offers trading in natural gas futures and options. *See* Press Release, ICE Completes Transition of Energy Swaps to Futures (Oct. 16, 2012), http://ir.theice.com/releasedetail.cfm

delivery of the underlying commodity. Rather, in a typical commodity swap, the buyer agrees to pay the seller a fixed amount of money and the seller agrees to pay the buyer the price of an underlying commodity at the time the swap expires. For ICE's Natural Gas Henry Hub Swap, this "floating value" paid by the seller was the final settlement value of the NYMEX natural gas future for the corresponding month. Hence, if the final settlement value of the NYMEX natural gas future was above whatever price the buyer paid for the swap, the buyer would profit; if it was below, the seller would.

Since the settlement price of an ICE Henry Hub natural gas swap was pegged to the final settlement price of the corresponding NYMEX natural gas future, the two instruments were functionally identical for risk management purposes. Indeed, arbitrageurs ensured that their prices moved in virtual lockstep with one another. Whether a trader decided to transact in ICE swaps or in NYMEX futures often depended on factors such as which market had greater liquidity.

An important difference between the two instruments, however, was that ICE did not face the same level of regulatory oversight as did NYMEX. At the time of the events alleged in the amended complaint, ICE qualified as an "exempt commercial market," or "ECM," under the CEA.[iv] While this status limited both the type of instruments ICE could offer for trading and the parties that could trade them, it also exempted ICE from most of the regulatory obligations placed upon NYMEX. . . .

The case refers to "exempt commercial markets," established by the Commodity Futures Modernization Act as a low-regulation alternative to designated contract markets and that, as noted above, the Dodd-Frank Act unwound. The Dodd-Frank Act's rollback of this and other low regulation market categories are numerous:

?ReleaseID=713717 [as of June 7, 2014 this release is now available at http://ir.theice.com/investors-and-media/press/press-releases/press-release-details/2012/ICE-Completes-Transition-of-Energy-Swaps-to-Futures/default.aspx.]

[iv] [N. 4] In 2008, Congress increased the CFTC's oversight of any ECM that offered trading in products the CFTC deemed to be "significant price discovery contracts." *See* Food, Conservation, and Energy Act of 2008, Pub.L. No. 110–246, Tit. XIII, Sub. B, 124 Stat. 1651, 2197–2204. Two years later, the Dodd–Frank Wall Street Reform and Consumer Protection Act repealed the statutory basis for ECMs. *See* Dodd–Frank Act § 723, 123 Stat. at 1675 (repealing 7 U.S.C. § 2(h)(3)—(5)). The effective date of this repeal was July 16, 2011. *Id*. The CFTC, however, has conditionally exempted preexisting ECMs from compliance with the new laws as it works to implement Dodd–Frank's changes. *See* CFTC Letter No. 13–28, No–Action Letter (June 17, 2013) (providing conditional no-action relief until October 2, 2013).

> The exclusions or exemptions removed by Dodd–Frank included, *inter alia*, "transactions in excluded commodities between eligible contract participants and not executed or traded on a trading facility"; "principal-to-principal transactions in excluded commodities between certain eligible contract participants and executed or traded on an electronic trading facility"; "transactions subject to individual negotiation between eligible contract participants in commodities other than agricultural commodities and not executed or traded on a trading facility"; "transactions in exempt commodities between eligible contract participants and not entered into on a trading facility"; "principal-to-principal transactions in exempt commodities between eligible commercial entities . . . and executed or traded on an electronic trading facility (called exempt commercial markets . . .)"; and "transactions in commodities, among other things, having a nearly inexhaustible deliverable supply or no cash market, between eligible contract participants and traded on an [exempt boards of trade, or EBOT]."

Investment Company Institute v United States Commodity Futures Trading Commission, 891 F. Supp. 2d 162, 173 n.8 (2013), *citing Effective Date for Swap Regulation*, 76 Fed. Reg. 35372, 35375 (June 17, 2011).

The Commodity Exchange Act provides for 23 core principles by which designated contract markets must abide, each of which is subject to further elucidation by CFTC regulation. "Core principles" are intended to be less prescriptive than a laundry list of detailed rules and to provide "reasonable discretion" to the designated contract market.

Core Principles for Contract Markets

Commodity Exchange Act § 5(d) (emphasis added)

(d) Core principles for contract markets

(1) Designation as contract market

(A) . . . To be designated, and maintain a designation, as a contract market, a board of trade shall comply with . . . any core principle described in this subsection. . . .

(B) . . . Unless otherwise determined by the Commission by rule or regulation, a board of trade described in subparagraph (A) shall have reasonable discretion in establishing the manner in which the board of trade complies with the core principles . . .

(2) Compliance with rules

(A) . . . The board of trade shall establish, monitor, and enforce compliance with the rules of the contract market, including –

(i) access requirements;

(ii) the terms and conditions of any contracts to be traded on the contract market; and

(iii) rules prohibiting abusive trade practices on the contract market.

(B) . . . The board of trade shall have the capacity to detect, investigate, and apply appropriate sanctions to any person that violates any rule of the contract market. . . .

(3) Contracts not readily subject to manipulation

The board of trade shall list on the contract market only contracts that are not readily susceptible to manipulation.

(4) Prevention of market disruption

The board of trade shall have the capacity and responsibility to prevent manipulation, price distortion, and disruptions of the delivery or cash-settlement process through market surveillance, compliance, and enforcement practices and procedures, including –

(A) . . . [by] real-time monitoring of trading; and

(B) comprehensive and accurate trade reconstructions.

(5) Position limitations or accountability

(A) . . . To reduce the potential threat of market manipulation or congestion (especially during trading in the delivery month), the board of trade shall adopt for each contract of the board of trade, as is necessary and appropriate, position limitations or position accountability for speculators.

(B) . . . [T]he board of trade shall set the position limitation of the board of trade at a level not higher than [any] position limitation established by the Commission.

(6) Emergency authority

The board of trade . . . shall adopt rules to provide for the exercise of emergency authority, as is necessary and appropriate, including the authority –

(A) to liquidate or transfer open positions in any contract;

(B) to suspend or curtail trading in any contract; and

(C) to require market participants in any contract to meet special margin requirements.

(7) Availability of general information

The board of trade shall make available to market authorities, market participants, and the public accurate information concerning –

(A) the terms and conditions of the contracts of the contract market; and

(B)(i) the rules, regulations, and mechanisms for executing transactions on or through the facilities of the contract market; and (ii) the rules and specifications describing the operation of the contract market's –

(I) electronic matching platform; or

(II) trade execution facility.

(8) Daily publication of trading information

The board of trade shall make public daily information on settlement prices, volume, open interest, and opening and closing ranges for actively traded contracts on the contract market.

(9) Execution of transactions

(A) . . . .The board of trade shall provide a competitive, open, and efficient market and mechanism for executing transactions that protects the price discovery process of trading in the centralized market of the board of trade. . . .

(10) Trade information

The board of trade shall maintain rules and procedures to provide for the recording and safe storage of all identifying trade information in a manner that enables the contract market to use the information –

(A) to assist in the prevention of customer and market abuses; and

(B) to provide evidence of any violations of the rules of the contract market.

(11) Financial integrity of transactions

The board of trade shall establish and enforce –

(A) rules and procedures . . . ensuring the financial integrity of transactions entered into on or through the facilities of the contract market . . .; and

(B) rules to ensure –

(i) the financial integrity of any –

(I) futures commission merchant; and

(II) introducing broker; and

(ii) the protection of customer funds.

(12) Protection of markets and market participants

The board of trade shall establish and enforce rules –

(A) to protect markets and market participants from abusive practices committed by any party, including abusive practices committed by a party acting as an agent for a participant; and

(B) to promote fair and equitable trading on the contract market.

(13) Disciplinary procedures

The board of trade shall establish and enforce disciplinary procedures that authorize the board of trade to discipline, suspend, or expel members or market participants that violate the rules of the board of trade, or similar methods for performing the same functions, including delegation of the functions to third parties.

(14) Dispute resolution

The board of trade shall establish and enforce rules regarding, and provide facilities for alternative dispute resolution as appropriate for, market participants and any market intermediaries.

(15) Governance fitness standards

The board of trade shall establish and enforce appropriate fitness standards for directors, members of any disciplinary committee, members of the contract market, and any other person with direct access to the facility (including any party affiliated with any person described in this paragraph).

(16) Conflicts of interest

The board of trade shall establish and enforce rules –

(A) to minimize conflicts of interest in the decision-making process of the contract market; and

(B) to establish a process for resolving conflicts of interest . . .

(17) Composition of governing boards of contract markets

The governance arrangements of the board of trade shall be designed to permit consideration of the views of market participants.

(18) Recordkeeping

The board of trade shall maintain records of all activities relating to the business of the contract market –

(A) in a form and manner that is acceptable to the Commission; and

(B) for a period of at least 5 years.

(19) Antitrust considerations

Unless necessary or appropriate to achieve the purposes of this chapter, the board of trade shall not –

(A) adopt any rule or taking any action that results in any unreasonable restraint of trade; or

(B) impose any material anticompetitive burden on trading on the contract market.

(20) System safeguards

The board of trade shall –

(A) establish and maintain a program of risk analysis and oversight . . .;

(B) establish and maintain emergency procedures, backup facilities, and a plan for disaster recovery that allow for the timely recovery and resumption of operations and the fulfillment of the responsibilities and obligations of the board of trade; and

(C) periodically conduct tests to verify that backup resources are sufficient . . .

(21) Financial resources

(A) . . . The board of trade shall have adequate financial, operational, and managerial resources to discharge each responsibility of the board of trade.

(B) . . . The financial resources of the board of trade shall be considered to be adequate if the value of the financial resources exceeds the total amount that would enable the contract market to cover the operating costs of the contract market for a 1-year period, as calculated on a rolling basis.

(22) Diversity of board of directors

The board of trade, if a publicly traded company, shall endeavor to recruit individuals to serve on the board of directors and the other decision-making bodies (as determined by the Commission) of the board of trade from among, and to have the composition of the bodies reflect, a broad and culturally diverse pool of qualified candidates.

(23) Securities and Exchange Commission

The board of trade shall keep any such records relating to [security-based swaps] open to inspection and examination by the Securities and Exchange Commission.

E. DESIGNATED CONTRACT MARKETS AS SELF-REGULATORY ORGANIZATIONS

1. Generally

Boards of trade have a long history of requiring members to abide by internal rules. This is a double-edged sword for boards of trade designated as contract markets and their members. On the one hand, it allows for regulatory flexibility and self-policing. On the other hand, contract markets can be held liable for a failure to enforce their own rules. Courts have typically been deferential to the self-regulatory role of designated contract markets, including by requiring members to exhaust all procedural remedies provided for by the rules of the designated contract market before seeking judicial review.

Westheimer v. Commodity Exchange, Inc.

651 F. Supp. 364 (S.D.N.Y. 1987)

Leisure, District Judge . . .

Defendant Commodity Exchange, Inc. ("COMEX") is a duly designated contract market, pursuant to the Commodity Exchange Act, as amended (the "CEA"), and serves as a large market for the trading of precious metals futures contracts and options. COMEX is a not-for-profit corporation organized under the laws of the State of New York with its principal place of business in New York City. COMEX consists of institutional and individual members. It is a private self-regulatory organization that has been charged with law enforcement responsibilities by federal statute and regulation. . . .

Plaintiff Gerald Westheimer became a member of COMEX on June 19, 1968. Plaintiff Valerie Westheimer became a member of COMEX on July 27, 1984. The plaintiffs are married to each other.

During August 1984, an issue arose as to whether the gold option positions held by plaintiffs should be aggregated for the purposes of COMEX rules which limit the maximum number of contract positions in a particular commodity option that an individual or persons trading in common may hold. . . . COMEX's general counsel stated that plaintiffs' marital affiliation would not itself require aggregation and that COMEX did not presently intend to pursue the matter, but that "if circumstances change," COMEX might inquire further to determine whether its rules had been violated.

On March 18 and 19, 1985, plaintiffs and James R. Paruch ("Mr. Paruch") were unable to meet margin calls of approximately $26 million on gold futures options by Volume Investors Corporation ("Volume Investors"), where each of them maintained accounts for the purpose of clearing trades executed on COMEX. These and other related events resulted in the financial collapse of Volume Investors. On March 20, 1985, the COMEX Board of Governors, believing there was sufficient evidence of violations of COMEX's rules, suspended plaintiffs' membership in COMEX, pending a hearing. Specifically, the Board of Governors charged that plaintiffs failed to meet members' minimum financial requirements and failed to adhere to reporting obligations with respect to reductions in net current assets. . . .

COMEX's compliance department conducted an investigation of plaintiffs' trading activity and recommended that the COMEX Committee on Business Conduct (the "business conduct committee") issue a complaint against plaintiffs and Mr. Paruch. The business conduct committee, which is made up of COMEX members, issued a complaint on June 30, 1986, containing six counts against plaintiffs. The committee charged that plaintiffs: exceeded COMEX limits on short call gold and silver options; controlled uncovered short gold call options and uncovered short silver call options; submitted false affidavits to COMEX; and failed to notify COMEX that they were unable to fulfill trading obligations, pay debts and meet obligations to other members or member firms of COMEX.

COMEX's Supervisory Committee is scheduled to hold a disciplinary hearing based on these charges against plaintiffs. The Supervisory Committee is also scheduled to address the charges for which plaintiffs were suspended by COMEX's Board of Governors. . . . COMEX rules . . . provide parties to the hearing with the right to review the documentary evidence compiled against them, to appear in person, to call witnesses on their behalf, to cross-examine adverse witnesses, and to retain counsel to represent them.

After receiving all of the evidence, the disciplinary hearing panel must promptly deliver a written decision . . . and must set forth a summary of the evidence, a statement of findings and conclusions, and a declaration of any sanctions to be imposed. Upon an adverse decision, parties may request review by the Board of Governors, during which time the decision of the disciplinary panel may be stayed. The Board of Governors is required to issue a written decision of its findings and is empowered to order a new hearing. If a party is dissatisfied with the final determination by the Board of Governors, that party's appeal is to the CFTC. . . . [T]he Commission may affirm, modify, set aside or remand the action. Judicial review may be sought after the CFTC has taken action.

In addition to the action taken by COMEX with regard to the collapse of Volume Investors and plaintiffs' alleged conduct, the Commodity Futures Trading Commission (the "CFTC") has . . . issued a complaint . . . which names as defendants, among others, COMEX and plaintiffs. The complaint charges that COMEX violated the Commodity Exchange Act, as amended, by failing to take appropriate action to achieve compliance by plaintiffs with COMEX's rules limiting the number of contract positions in a particular commodity option that an individual or persons trading in common may hold. As to plaintiffs, the CFTC complaint charges that the Westheimers exceeded COMEX's limits on contract positions and, in turn, violated certain provisions of the CEA which refer to rules of contract markets, such as COMEX.

At the present time there is no date scheduled for the CFTC hearing. The COMEX disciplinary hearing . . . [has] been adjourned . . . due to ongoing settlement discussions with Mr. Paruch.

Plaintiffs state in their verified complaint (the "Complaint") that COMEX's disciplinary procedure is inherently biased against them. However, plaintiffs explain that the "primary reason" that COMEX "cannot provide plaintiffs with a fair, impartial and unbiased hearing" is the existence of the CFTC proceeding, in which COMEX is a co-defendant. Plaintiffs state that, in an attempt to "preview" plaintiffs' case before the CFTC, "COMEX has sought to force a quick trial" of its own disciplinary hearing. . . .

The doctrine of exhaustion of administrative remedies applies to the disciplinary proceedings of a private self-regulatory organization such as COMEX, which has been charged by federal statute and regulation with law enforcement responsibilities and which serves as an integral part of an overall enforcement scheme. . . .

The comprehensiveness of the procedure for review of a COMEX disciplinary hearing indicates a congressional intent that "self-regulation is the best 'first-line' defense against unethical or illegal" commodities practices, and application of the doctrine of exhaustion of administrative remedies prevents frustration of that intent. . . .

The charge that the COMEX hearing panel is biased or is seeking to preview plaintiffs' CFTC case provides no grounds for departure from the application of the exhaustion of remedies rule. . . .

Plaintiffs have not established the extreme circumstances necessary to justify application of an exception to the exhaustion doctrine, such as an agency's clear violation of a constitutional right or specific statutory provision, or an agency's action in gross excess of its power. Plaintiffs have also failed to demonstrate that irreparable harm will result from their exhaustion of administrative remedies. Plaintiffs' claim that defendant is seeking to preview plaintiffs' case before the CFTC rests on "too tenuous a string of possibilities" to serve as a foundation for a finding of immediate irreparable harm. . . .

Thus, the Court finds applicable the "general principle of administrative law that 'no one is entitled to judicial relief for a supposed or threatened injury until the prescribed administrative remedy has been exhausted.'" Plaintiffs' motion is denied.

---

2. Liability of Designated Contract Markets

a. CFTC Enforcement

Commodity Exchange Act § 6b makes it a violation of the Commodity Exchange Act if "[A]ny registered entity is not enforcing or has not enforced its rules of government made a condition of its designation or registration." Accordingly, a failure by a designated contract market to enforce its rules could lead to CFTC enforcement proceedings.

b. Private Right of Action

As will be discussed in Chapter 14, § 22 of the Commodity Exchange Act provides a statutory private right of action for certain violations of the Commodity Exchange Act. In its role as a self-regulatory organization, however, a private right of action against a designated contract market for a failure to enforce its rules is only available if it has acted in bad faith.

Grossman v. Citrus Association of the New York Cotton Exchange, Inc.

742 F. Supp. 843 (S.D.N.Y. 1990)

Haight, District Judge . . .

Plaintiff Gerald Grossman, d/b/a Commodity Traders Weather Service was at all times relevant to this litigation a commodities trading advisor. In short, Grossman "was at all relevant times engaged in the business of managing and investing customer funds on a discretionary basis in the commodities markets." . . .

Grossman took short positions in the [Frozen Concentrate Orange Juice, *i.e.* "FCOJ"] market on behalf of himself and his clients . . . on which he lost money. . . .

FCOJ futures contracts are regularly traded on the Citrus Associates of the New York Cotton Exchange, Inc. ("Citrus Exchange"). . . .

In terms of the factors which influence the price of FCOJ contracts, plaintiffs identify the following "four major ongoing fundamental statistics which affect the price of FCOJ futures contracts" on "information and belief":

> (i) the weather and temperatures in Florida, particularly in the months of December, January and February and especially U.S. government computer forecasts, as to whether there will be a winter "freeze" in Florida;
> (ii) the first of the month, FCOJ cold storage stocks in Florida;
> (iii) the average price and quantities of Brazilian imported FCOJ; and
> (iv) the weekly movement of FCOJ from the processors and distributors to the wholesale grocers, supermarkets, etc. . . .

During the relevant trading period, December 12, 1985 through December 17, 1985, the trading volume in the FCOJ market was heavy and the price changes extensive. Grossman attributes that situation to certain weather reports which erroneously predicted a freeze in southern Florida. . . .

Plaintiffs contend that the weather outlook for the subject time period was artificially dire, which resulted in unduly inflated prices on FCOJ contracts. Grossman was short FCOJ contracts from December 12, 1985 through December 17, 1985 over which time the price of the contracts rose. Hearing rumors of a freeze, William Mallers, the president of First American Discount Corporation ("First American"), both former defendants in this action, called Grossman on December 16, 1985. Mallers "demanded enough margin to cover two limit days beginning Tuesday morning [the morning of December 17, 1985]." Mallers further stated that even with this additional margin he would take off half of the Joint Account's position on the opening on Tuesday if the market opened above Monday's close. The market did open up on Tuesday, December 17, 1985, and as he said he would Mallers liquidated fourteen of the twenty-eight short positions . . .

[J]ust after the liquidation . . . Grossman put on stop limits . . . on all of his as well as his client's remaining accounts. The . . . orders were filled . . .

As a result of covering his short positions at prices higher than that at which he sold the contracts, Grossman lost his own money as well as that invested on behalf of his clients. . . .

The Citrus Exchange is both a board of trade and a licensed contract market . . .

The Citrus Exchange has its own by-laws to which it is clearly subject. . . . The portion of the by-laws relevant to the instant lawsuit is that covering "Emergency Action" [which permits the Citrus Exchange to take action in an "emergency" by, for example, limiting or halting trading]. . . .

In short, plaintiffs argue that the defendant Citrus Exchange improperly failed to take emergency action in the form of suspending or limiting trading in FCOJ contracts and that such failure caused them monetary loss.

The Act provides a remedy against an exchange defendant, such as the Citrus Exchange, whose actions or non-actions cause another financial loss. In addition to the causation element, plaintiffs must plead bad faith by the Citrus Exchange in order to defeat the instant motion. . . .

In evaluating bad faith allegations against an exchange for improper action or non-action, the Second Circuit has said that "when self-interest or other ulterior motive unrelated to proper regulatory concerns is alleged to constitute the sole or the dominant reason for the exchange action, a complaint is sufficient even though the action was not beyond the bounds of reason." *Sam Wong & Son, Inc. v. New York Mercantile Exch.,* 735 F.2d 653, 677 (2d Cir.1984). . . .

[P]laintiffs at bar allege that "[t]he sole or dominant reason for the failure of defendant, its Board of Directors and its Executive Committee to take necessary and appropriate emergency action under the these [*sic*] circumstances was to elevate its self-interest above proper regulatory concerns, thereby constituting bad faith . . .

At the heart of plaintiffs' complaint are the weather reports for the orange belt which came out during the December 12, 1985 through December 17, 1985 time period. . . . The trading that morning was hectic and the price high, in response, plaintiffs contend, to reports of a possible weekend freeze. Plaintiffs argue that these reports were unrealistic and there was no chance of a weekend freeze. With the benefit of hindsight plaintiffs were proved right as the weekend came and went with no freeze in the orange belt. The fact remains, however, that certain reputable weather forecasters were predicting a freeze, giving traders in the market who agreed with those predictions cause to purchase FCOJ contracts, thereby driving the price of the contracts up.

In essence, plaintiffs contend that someone was intentionally driving up the price of FCOJ contracts and using a deliberately false freeze prediction as their vehicle. However, the Citrus Exchange is not a weather forecaster and while it is charged with monitoring those factors which influence the price of the futures contracts traded on the exchange, it is not responsible for making decisions as to which of conflicting weather reports is correct and which way the market should be moving. It is precisely the fact that traders disagree over components which go into a price determination that makes the market work. . . . It is not the function of an exchange to allow the market to function only when there is no disagreement amongst traders, nor is it the function of an exchange to determine the ultimate "truth" in respect of whether prices should rise or fall. That truth is determined by the interrelationship between the buyers and sellers in the marketplace.

This is not a situation where the Citrus Exchange is alleged to have had anything to do with the publication of the allegedly false weather reports . . . Rather, this is a case where plaintiffs argue that the Citrus Exchange should have known that someone else was engaging in the intentional publication of false weather reports and that it should then have suspended trading on December 17, 1985, which would, in the plaintiffs' view, have prevented their losses. . . .

Unless the Citrus Exchange know of a price manipulation or consciously avoided acquiring such knowledge, it was under no obligation to take any corrective action and its failure to do so cannot be said to have been in bad faith. Indeed, the Second Circuit has held that "[a] claim of bad faith must be supported by two allegations: first, that the exchange acted or failed to act with knowledge; and second, that the exchange's action or inaction was the result of an ulterior motive." *Ryder Energy Distrib. v. Merrill Lynch Commod.,* 748 F.2d 774, 780 (2d Cir.1984) (citation omitted). The complaint at bar fails in its charge of bad faith because it does not sufficiently allege that the Citrus Exchange "failed to act with knowledge." . . .

If the Citrus Exchange were itself in on a plan to elevate the price of FCOJ contracts by the publication of deliberately false weather reports, or the allowance of trading based on what it knew to be intentionally fraudulent reports, or if there was no explanation at all for the heavy market activity of December 17, 1985, plaintiffs might have a claim, but as it is they do not. . . .

In *Grossman*, the plaintiff claimed that the designated contract market's rules required emergency action to be taken and that he had a private right of action against the contract market for failing to take such action. Sometimes a designated contract market when faced with a market "emergency" may have two unpalatable choices (and face litigation either way). As the court noted in a case brought by farmers alleging harm due to an emergency resolution by the Chicago Board of Trade requiring phased reductions in large soybean positions:

> Eleanor Roosevelt once said, "[d]o what you feel in your heart to be right – for you'll be criticized anyway. You'll be damned if you do, and damned if you don't." In this case, the Chicago Board of Trade "did," and as a result it has been "damned" with over ten years of litigation and the prospect of

> significant liability. However, we believed that had the Board not acted, it might have been "damned" anyway, as its inaction would have subjected it to claims . . .

Zimmerman v. Chicago Board of Trade, 360 F. 3d 612, 630 (7th Cir. 2004).

In *Sam Wong & Son, Inc. v. New York Mercantile Exchange*, 735 F.2d 653 (2d Cir. 1984), the Second Circuit was faced with two such opposing claims: one alleging that the New York Mercantile Exchange failed to take appropriate emergency action and one related to emergency action it ultimately took:

> Wong's complaint . . . was that, once the delivery problems [in Maine potatoes] had manifested itself . . . the NYME had failed to take proper action [and the] other was that the NYME had failed in a duty to revise the Maine round white potato futures contract so that it would be a better vehicle for hedging and less susceptible to the problem that had developed . . . [Spinale's] complaint, almost the exact opposite of Wong's, was that the Exchange should not have taken emergency action when it did, and alternatively that any action should have been less drastic . . .

Sam Wong & Son, Inc., 656-657.

The dismissal of Wong's claim was affirmed and Spinale's claim was remanded to the district court for further discovery on the question of whether the New York Mercantile Exchange acted in bad faith. It was ultimately dismissed.[18]

c. Antitrust Claims

Due to the availability of treble damages with respect to antitrust claims, the complaints of plaintiffs against designated contract markets often include antitrust claims.[19] Where the designated contract market is acting in compliance with the Commodity Exchange Act or a CFTC order, the designated contract market receives qualified immunity from antitrust claims. Where a designated contract market has discretion, it is difficult to find bad faith in a case where, as was the case in *Zimmerman*, there is "close involvement and informal approval of the CFTC . . ."[20]

American Agricultural Movements, Inc. v. Board of Trade of City of Chicago

977 F.2d 1147 (7th Cir. 1992)

Flaum, Circuit Judge. . . .

The American Agriculture Movement, a national organization representing the interests of farmers . . . brought this suit against the Chicago Board of Trade and 26 of its officers and employees (collectively "CBOT") under the Commodity Exchange Act (CEA), the Sherman Anti-trust Act and state common law. . . . The [district] court . . . granted the CBOT's motion for summary judgment . . . reasoning that the CEA . . . had impliedly repealed the Sherman Act . . . We . . . reverse the court's entry of summary judgment on the antitrust count . . .

The CEA governs the trading of commodity futures contracts, and grants to the Commodity Futures Trading Commission (CFTC or Commission) the authority, in large measure, to implement the regulatory regime established therein. The Commission, pursuant to that authority has designated the CBOT as a "contract market" on which investors may trade various commodity futures contracts. The CBOT's status as a contract market imposes upon it a duty of self-regulation, subject to the Commission's oversight. As part of its duties, the CBOT must enact and enforce rules to ensure fair and orderly trading, including rules designed to prevent price manipulation, cornering and other market disturbances. CEA § 5(d). In performing this particular self-regulatory function, the CBOT is required to monitor "market activity for indications of possible congestion or other market situations conducive to possible price distortion."

This case involves an emergency action taken by the CBOT in response to what it claims was the threat of such a distortion. In the summer of 1989, Ferruzzi Finanziaria, S.p.A., and others (Ferruzzi Group or Ferruzzi) attempted to execute a "squeeze" in the July 1989 soybean futures market. The CBOT's Business Conduct Committee (Committee), the body charged with monitoring the soybean futures markets, determined that the Ferruzzi Group held an unusually large, and dangerous, market position; it controlled nearly 60 percent of the long open interests in the futures market, as well as over 60 percent of the cash soybeans in deliverable locations. Moreover, Ferruzzi's futures position was more than four times larger than the deliverable soybean stocks available to other cash market participants. If Ferruzzi did not substantially liquidate its position prior to the delivery date of the July 1989 contracts, the stability of the soybean futures and cash markets could have been seriously compromised.

In late June and early July, the Committee repeatedly urged the Ferruzzi Group to reduce in an orderly manner its outstanding open futures position. Ferruzzi stonewalled and declared that it would maintain its position, and in response the Committee, on July 10, recommended that the CBOT's governing board (Board) take emergency action. The following day, the Board, by a 16 to 1 vote, issued an "Emergency Resolution" (Resolution) pursuant to its self-regulatory powers. The Resolution declared a market emergency, and ordered any person or group controlling gross long or short positions in excess of three million bushels to liquidate their positions by at least 20 percent daily. In addition, it ordered that no person or group could own contracts in excess of three million bushels on July 18, or in excess of one million bushels on July 20, the last trading day for July 1989 contracts. The Board . . . immediately made the Resolution public, and . . . informed the Commission of its action.

Not surprisingly, publication of the Resolution led to a price decline in the July 1989 futures market . . .

The Resolution no doubt restrained trade in the July 1989 soybean futures market, and for that reason would ordinarily fall within the purview of the antitrust laws. But this case is not ordinary, for here the CBOT was also subject to the dictates of the CEA and the regulatory regime established thereunder. That regime imposes upon the CBOT a duty of self-regulation, and upon the Commission the duty to oversee the CBOT's self-regulatory activities, and grants both a certain degree of flexibility when it comes to making judgment calls regarding the efficient operation and maintenance of the futures markets. Conflicts between antitrust law and the CEA, supposed or actual, are inevitable, as exchange activities that would be considered inappropriate under the antitrust laws might arguably be justified, or even required, under the CEA. *Ricci v. Chicago Mercantile Exch.*, 409 U.S. 289, 299–300, 306, 93 S. Ct. 573, 579–80, 582–83, 34 L.Ed.2d 525 (1973). The problem, then, arises "from the need to reconcile pursuit of the antitrust aim of eliminating restraints on competition with the effective operation of a public policy contemplating that [commodity] exchanges will engage in self-regulation which may well have anticompetitive effects in general and in specific application." *Silver v. New York Stock Exch.*, 373 U.S. 341, 349, 83 S. Ct. 1246, 1252–53, 10 L.Ed.2d 389 (1963).

Under certain circumstances, reconciling antitrust law with a regulatory regime compels the conclusion that Congress intended the latter to oust the former – that is, compels the conclusion that the regulatory regime has impliedly granted antitrust immunity to private parties operating under its rubric. Those circumstances, however, are rare. . . . As with all matters of statutory construction, the intent of Congress governs, but in order to find implied immunity that intent must be clear.

With these precepts in mind, we outline, in some detail, the regulatory environment in which the CBOT adopted, implemented and published the Resolution. As noted, self-regulating contract markets designated under CEA § 5 are required to adopt rules "for the prevention of the manipulation of prices and the cornering of any commodity." As a general matter, a market must gain the Commission's approval prior to implementing exchange rules of this nature, and the statute outlines the procedures under which the Commission may approve or disapprove such rules. The statute nonetheless carves an exception for "emergencies" requiring immediate action. Under such circumstances, an exchange, by a two-thirds vote of its governing board, may adopt and immediately implement a temporary emergency rule without prior Commission approval. In lieu of prior approval, the exchange must notify and provide the Commission with a complete explanation of both the emergency and the action it took in response.

Neither the statute nor the applicable regulations explicitly provide for Commission review of temporary emergency rules. Nonetheless, the Commission believes . . . that [the] CEA . . . empowers the Commission to overturn, modify or approve a rule after receiving notification from an exchange.

While the Commission has to power to take action . . . it need not do so, and oftentimes "simply [chooses] to refrain from acting." . . . [If] its Division of Trading and Markets . . . determines that a given temporary emergency rule was reasonable and enacted in good faith, the Commission may decide that further or formal action on its part is unnecessary.

That is precisely what happened in this case. . . .

Having examined the . . . Commission's actions in this case, we return to the principles of implied antitrust immunity. . . .

We can dispatch rather quickly with the CBOT's argument – echoing that made by the Commission, as amicus – that the CEA bestows "pervasive" implied immunity upon contract markets. At the outset, it is important to recognize that Congress did not intend the CEA to extend blanket immunity to the exchanges for their adoption and enforcement of exchange rules, emergency or otherwise. The Supreme Court, in 1973, recognized that the CEA did not "confer general antitrust immunity" on the exchanges and their members for conduct taken pursuant to a Commission regulation or exchange rule. *Ricci*, 409 U.S. at 302 n. 13, 93 S. Ct. at 580 n. 13. Shortly thereafter, during deliberations on the 1974 Act, the House Agriculture Committee considered and rejected a provision that would have shielded from antitrust attack any conduct of that nature. . . .

Congress' clear rejection of blanket immunity casts serious doubt upon the CBOT's contention that the Commission's regulation of exchange emergency actions . . . is so "pervasive" as to demand antitrust immunity. . . .

In the absence of a pervasive regulatory scheme, we may imply antitrust immunity in either one of two circumstances: first, where the challenged action was compelled by a statute, regulation, or agency, and, second, where the action was "scrutin[ized] and approv[ed]" by the appropriate agency. Had the Commission . . . ordered the CBOT to take emergency action in response to the impending Ferruzzi squeeze, or had it modified the action the CBOT took on its own, there can be no doubt as to the outcome of this case. Exposing the CBOT to potential antitrust liability under such circumstances would subject it to conflicting standards, leading to the inevitable conclusion that Congress intended to grant antitrust immunity. But the Commission did not compel the CBOT to do anything, so implied repealer cannot rest upon this ground.[v]

---

[v] [N. 9] Alternatively, the CBOT could argue that its action was compelled by a statute or regulation, namely [the requirement] . . . to enforce rules to ensure fair trading and

We must determine, then, whether the Commission's performance after receiving notification from the CBOT constitutes "scrutiny and approval" sufficient to warrant antitrust immunity. . . .

The fact that an agency let stand a practice voluntarily initiated by a regulated entity – even when it had the power to review, modify and overturn that practice – is not sufficient, in and of itself, to confer antitrust immunity. . . .

While the issue posed is admittedly a close one, we conclude that the regulatory supervision in this case was not sufficient to cloak the Resolution with similar immunity. . . . [The Commission's] "approval" of the Resolution was not the product of any affirmative action, but rather of acquiescence, or the failure to take action. . . .

Our holding is limited strictly to the issue of implied immunity, and does not in any way portend our view of the legal or factual merits of the . . . antitrust count. To ultimately prevail, the [plaintiffs] will have to demonstrate that the CBOT acted in bad faith . . .

Perhaps due to judicial recognition of the Hobbesian conundrum faced by designated contract markets when faced with market emergencies – historically a rich source of litigation for claims against designated contract markets – we have seen that the bar is high for private claims by traders. There would be no claims at all against the designated contract markets if the CFTC directly ordered emergency action as Commodity Exchange Act § 8a(9) permits. The CFTC has used these powers only four times since its formation, each noted in Figure 4-A below. Since 1980, the CFTC has not invoked these powers in *de facto* reliance on the designated contract markets themselves taking any emergency actions deemed to be necessary.

[that] . . . authorizes it to invoke emergency resolutions to prevent market disruption due to a threatened market cornering. This, however, is the essence of the suit: was the CBOT action taken pursuant to the statute and regulations, making it unassailable . . . or was the emergency resolution adopted in bad faith, not to prevent market disruption but to further private interests, and therefore outside the statutory authority and open to Sherman Act liability? . . . This issue was not addressed by the district court and remains open on remand.

Figure 4-A: The CFTC's Emergency Authority[21]			
Date	Commodity	Contract Market	Action
November 1976	Maine Potatoes	New York Mercantile Exchange	100% margins and only liquidation of positions permitted
December 1977	Coffee	New York Coffee and Sugar Exchange	Phased orderly liquidation
March 1979	Wheat	Chicago Board of Trade	Suspension of trading and mandatory settlement of positions
January 1980	Wheat, corn, oats, soybeans, soybean meal and soybean oil	All designated contract markets with contracts referencing the commodities subject to the emergency order	Two-day suspension

As discussed in Chapter 14, the bar to a private litigant is higher still – perhaps insuperably high – for all claims made against designated contract markets by market intermediaries, such as futures commission merchants, as opposed to parties directly engaged in trading and exposed to losses or gains on actual positions held.[22]

F. DERIVATIVES CLEARING ORGANIZATIONS

Designated contract markets are associated with clearing firms that clear trades on behalf of the markets. Whereas the designated contract market is where trades actually occur, the derivatives clearing organization, commonly known as

"DCO," is the actual central counterparty for the two parties entering into the trade. *See* Chapter 5 for a description of the operation of the market.

Although clearing organizations have an essential role in the operation of the marketplace, they were not regulated separate and apart from their associated designated contract market until the passage of the Commodity Futures Modernization Act of 2000. The Commodity Futures Modernization Act created a new registration category, derivatives clearing organizations.

We will revisit derivatives clearing organizations in Chapter 9 in the context of "swap execution facilities," i.e., trading venues for the formerly largely unregulated off-exchange derivatives market.

Commodity Futures Trading Commission, A New Regulatory Framework for Clearing Organizations

66 Fed. Reg. 24308-01 (May 14, 2001)

. . . Congress on December 15, 2000, passed, and the President on December 21, 2000, signed into law, the [Commodity Future Modernization Act "CFMA"], which substantially amended the Commodity Exchange Act ("Act"). New Section 5b(a) of the Act, added by the CFMA, requires that contracts of sale of a commodity for future delivery, options on such contracts, and options on a commodity be cleared only by a derivatives clearing organization ("DCO") registered with the Commission. . . .

To be registered as a DCO, an applicant must demonstrate that it complies with fourteen [now eighteen, *see* Commodity Exchange Act § 5b(c)(2)] core principles set forth in the CFMA. . . .

The Commission is now proposing rules [as 17 C.F.R. § 39] to implement section 5b of the Act. . . . Part 39 does not apply to the execution of transactions cleared by DCOs; its provisions apply specifically and only to the clearing of transactions by DCOs. . . .

If certain conditions were met, an organization would be deemed to be registered with the Commission as a DCO under part 39 . . . sixty days after receipt by the Commission of an application for registration, unless notified otherwise.[vi] This would include submission of the applicant's rules, a demonstration that the applicant satisfies the core principles of the Act, submission of any agreements with third parties that enable the applicant to meet one or more of the core principles, and descriptions of any system test procedures and results.

Appendix A to part 39 would provide guidance that applicants could use to meet the core principles. The CFMA provides that an applicant shall have reasonable discretion in establishing the manner in which it complies with the

---

[vi] [N. 9] The Act does not include an express time limit for Commission consideration of applications to become registered DCOs.

core principles. The guidance in proposed Appendix A is intended merely to illustrate the manner in which a clearing organization may meet a core principle and is not intended to be a mandatory checklist. . . .

An applicant may request that the Commission approve any of its rules . . . at the time it makes its initial application or thereafter.

New section 5b(d) of the Act provides that existing DCOs shall be deemed to be registered with the Commission to the extent that the DCO clears agreements, contracts, or transactions for a board of trade that has been designated by the Commission as a contract market for such agreements, contracts, or transactions prior to enactment of the CFMA. This provision captures all futures clearing organizations regulated by the Commission that have ever cleared any futures contracts for designated contract markets prior to December 21, 2000, the effective date of the CFMA. This language does not capture any organization approved to clear futures in connection with a pre-CFMA contract market designation which has not yet cleared any contracts. . . .

Under . . . part 39, a DCO and the clearing of transactions on a DCO are exempt from all Commission regulations except for . . . certain select regulations relating to, for example, the segregation of customer funds and recordkeeping. To maintain registration as a DCO, part 39 would require DCOs to remain in compliance at all times with the core principles. . . .

[Part 39] . . . also contains an antifraud provision. This provision would be specifically limited to prohibit fraudulent actions by persons in or in connection with the clearing of transactions on a DCO. . . .

[Part 39] provides that a contract or transaction cleared pursuant to the rules of a DCO shall not be void, voidable, subject to rescission, or otherwise invalidated or rendered unenforceable as a result of a violation by the DCO . . .

The Part 39 rules were finalized in substantially similar form to the proposed rules in August 2001.[23]

G. FOREIGN BOARDS OF TRADE

We discuss cross-border issues in Chapter 15. Of immediate relevance in the context of designated contract markets is the regulatory status of a foreign futures market that provides access to persons in the United States. Evaluated in light of the Commodity Exchange Act alone, such foreign futures market, which we will refer to as a "foreign board of trade," commonly known as an FBOT (pronounced, *f-bot*), would be required to register as a designated contract market.

Instead of requiring registration, though, historically the CFTC staff provided "no-action relief" on an individual basis to foreign boards of trade wishing to offer access to persons in the United States.[24] No-action relief is a statement by the staff of a government agency that the staff will not recommend an enforcement action to the governing body of the agency. Though the staff's position is not binding on the agency's governing body, it is highly unlikely in such circumstances that the governing body (for example the Commission) will not honor the position taken by the staff. No-action relief is not precedential and theoretically may be relied upon only by those to whom it is directly addressed. In the case of the no-action relief provided to foreign boards of trade offering access to persons in the United States, CFTC staff agreed not to require registration as a designated contract market provided that the foreign board of trade meet specified criteria.

In 2011, the CFTC revoked the various no-action letters and established registration requirements for foreign boards of trade wishing to provide access to persons in the United States.

Commodity Futures Trading Commission, Registration of Foreign Boards of Trade

76 Fed. Reg. 80674 (December 23, 2011)

. . . On July 21, 2010, President Obama signed the Dodd-Frank Act. . . .

Section 738 of the Dodd-Frank Act amended CEA section 4(b) to provide that the Commission may adopt rules and regulations requiring FBOTs that wish to provide their members or other participants located in the United States with direct access to the FBOT's electronic trading and order matching system to register with the Commission. Direct access is defined in the statute as an explicit grant of authority by an FBOT to an identified member or other participant located in the U.S. to enter trades directly into the FBOT's trade matching system.[vii] CEA section 4(b) also authorizes the Commission to promulgate rules and regulations prescribing procedures and requirements applicable to the registration of such FBOTs.

Accordingly, on November 19, 2010, the Commission published a notice of proposed rulemaking that set forth proposed regulations that would establish a registration requirement and related registration procedures and conditions applicable to FBOTs that wish to provide their members or other participants located in the United States with direct access to their electronic trading and order matching system (NPRM).[viii] . . . [T]he Commission has determined to issue these final rules which are substantially the same as those proposed . . .

Since 1996, FBOT requests to provide members and other participants that are located in the U.S. with direct access to their electronic trading and order matching systems have been addressed by Commission staff in accordance with

---

[vii] [N. 4] Direct access is defined in CEA section 4(b)(1)(A).

[viii] [N. 5] *See Registration of Foreign Boards of Trade*, 75 FR 70974 (November 19, 2010).

the no-action process set forth in Commission regulation 140.99.[ix] Specifically, such FBOTs seeking to provide direct access to members and participants located in the U.S. have requested, and, where appropriate, received from the relevant division of the Commission, a no-action letter in which division staff represents that, provided the FBOT satisfies the conditions set forth therein, the division will not recommend that the Commission institute enforcement action against the FBOT for failure to register as a designated contract market (DCM). . . . Since 1996, Commission staff has issued 24 direct access no-action relief letters (formerly referred to as foreign terminal no-action relief letters) to FBOTs, 20 of which remain active. . . .

While the no-action process has served a useful purpose, the Commission, given the new authority provided by Congress in the Dodd-Frank Act to promulgate registration requirements applicable to FBOTs that provide direct access, has determined to replace the staff no-action process with generally applicable Commission regulations. . . .

In determining to adopt formal registration rules for FBOTs, the Commission has also considered that the no-action process is generally better suited for discrete, unique factual circumstances and for situations where neither the CEA nor the Commission's regulations address the issue presented. The Commission has determined that, where the same type of relief is being granted on a regular and recurring basis, as it has been with respect to permitting FBOTs to provide direct access to their trading systems to specified members and other participants that are located in the U.S., it is no longer appropriate to handle requests for the relief through the no-action process. Rather, such matters should be addressed in generally applicable registration regulations.

By implementing uniform application procedures and registration requirements and conditions, the process by which FBOTs are permitted to provide members and other participants located in the United States with direct access to their trading systems will become more standardized and more transparent to both registration applicants and the general public and will promote fair and consistent treatment of all applicants. Further, generally applicable regulations will provide greater legal certainty for FBOTs providing direct access than the no-action relief process because no-action letters are issued by the staff and are not binding on the Commission. The Commission also notes that an FBOT registration regime will be more consistent with the statutory authority pursuant to which other countries, including the United

---

[ix] [N. 6] *See*, e.g., CFTC Letter No. 96-28 (February 29, 1996). Commission regulation 140.99 defines the term "no-action letter" as a written statement issued by the staff of a Division of the Commission or of the Office of the General Counsel that it will not recommend enforcement action to the Commission for failure to comply with a specific provision of the Act or of a Commission rule, regulation or order if a proposed transaction is completed or a proposed activity is conducted by the beneficiary.

Kingdom, Australia, Singapore, Japan and Germany, among others, permit U.S.-based DCMs to provide direct access internationally.

Accordingly, for the reasons noted above and pursuant to the new authority provided by amended CEA section 4(b), the Commission has determined to adopt FBOT registration regulations. The final rules will replace the existing policy of accepting and reviewing requests for no-action relief to permit an FBOT to provide for direct access to its trading system with a requirement that an FBOT seeking to provide such access must apply for and be granted registration with the Commission. . . .

Prominent Practitioner Sidenote: Richard A. Miller, Esq.

Richard Miller is vice president and corporate counsel at Prudential Insurance Company of America and a lecturer in law at Columbia University School of Law. He is the founder of the primary practitioners periodical in the field of derivatives law, the *Futures and Derivatives Law Report*. Before joining Prudential Insurance Company in 2002, Richard was in private practice and a staff member on the Presidential Task Force on Market Mechanisms, commonly known as the Brady Commission, formed to investigate and make recommendations regarding the 1987 stock market crash.

How did you end up practicing in derivatives law?

A few of my original clients in private practice in the late 1970s were futures commission merchants in New York. As I assessed the state of futures law at the time – shortly after the advent of the CFTC – I sensed that it was still in its very early, formative stages and would eventually develop like securities law (which likewise involved financial transactions and intermediation) into a robust area of legal specialization. I took a few CLE courses in the subject matter, started attending relevant conferences and meetings, and proceeded to develop a practice.

You are the founder and editor-in-chief of the primary law journal for derivatives lawyers, the *Futures and Derivatives Law Report*. How long has it been in print?

I launched the Futures and Derivatives Law Report (then called "Commodities Law Letter") in March 1981. The lead article discussed the split in the circuits over whether there was a private right of action under the Commodity Exchange Act. From the beginning we had the assistance of a volunteer board of editors that contributed their valuable expertise and articles to our efforts to spread knowledge of the subject matter. A year's subscription in 1981 was $144.

What led you start the *Futures and Derivatives Law Report*?

Similar to the decision to pursue this specialty, I noticed that at the same time that securities and most every other area of law had a number of well-received secondary sources (like treatises, journals, and newsletters) available to practitioners, there was absolutely nothing similar for futures (the terms "swap" and "derivative," in this context, did not exist yet.) So, as the saying goes, I saw an opportunity and I took it. Coincidentally, Robert Parker started the *Wine Advocate* at roughly the same moment in time. As it turns out, there are more subscribers to wine journals than law journals. But who knew?

You have been one of the most influential voices in derivatives law. What legal, regulatory, or policy issue are you most proud of having influenced?

I was fortunate to be chosen to serve on the staff of the Presidential Commission on Market Mechanisms (better known as the "Brady Commission") following the 1987 stock market crash. There I was principally responsible for researching and writing the portions of the final report devoted to problems that were encountered in connection with the futures clearing houses during the market break. That experience sparked my concern for systemic risks and I have always been pleased to have my name associated with the Brady Commission's well-received recommendations (like circuit breakers and better regulatory coordination) aimed at reducing systemic risk. Years later, when the Swaps Concept Release became the controversy of the day, but having learned something about the potential for risk from my Brady Commission experience, I testified in Congress that some objective, regulatory scrutiny of the swaps market was not a bad idea. Of course, the ideas behind the Concept Release were eventually rejected in 2000, only to be reintroduced a decade later by the Dodd-Frank Act.

More generally, looking back on your career, what gives you the most pride?

The legendary Simon Rifkind told young associates at his firm that you are not really a lawyer unless you have a client. I think that means that we are meant to be service providers, not navel gazers. So, in my career I am most proud of those times when I achieved something against the odds for my clients in private practice or corporate practice. Years ago, shortly after the CFTC adopted the procedure for "Wells" submissions, where you could argue that the staff should not pursue an enforcement case against a designated target, I was the first advocate who successfully persuaded the enforcement division to abandon its case, because I found a dispositive jurisdictional flaw in their case that the division had long overlooked. Later I argued and won a landmark case in the Second Circuit for an individual entrepreneur against well-financed, institutional adversaries. Also, I successfully formed for another creative client the first fully electronic exchange and clearing house to be approved by the CFTC immediately after enactment of the Commodity Futures Modernization Act. Unfortunately, the exchange, known as OnExchange, never developed any products to trade. More recently, I successfully advocated for a clearing exemption (embodied in CFTC Rule 50.52) for my company and others who use treasury or conduit affiliates to conduct their interaffiliate swap transactions, where each side of the transaction would be considered a financial entity and therefore otherwise be subject to the clearing mandate of Dodd-Frank. I am also grateful that for 14 years I have been able to teach derivatives law and regulation at Columbia School of Law, adding to the accumulation of collective knowledge and expertise in this subject matter.

Looking at the current state of derivatives law and regulation, what would you change, if anything?

While I have no doubt that over deregulation contributed to the Financial Crisis, I also believe that the Dodd-Frank Act and the resulting regulations are overly complex and burdensome. The weak regulatory conditions that led to the main act of the crises (which in my mind was AIG's insolvency and near collapse) might have been remedied more efficiently, in my opinion, by (a) compelling swaps between financial entities to be collateralized from a zero threshold of exposure or centrally cleared; (b) requiring swaps between financial entities to be centrally reported; and (c) increasing the capital requirements and reducing the leverage ratios of financial entities. The first step would have solved the enormous build-up of uncollateralized exposure and risk that AIG and others were allowed to experience to everyone's eventual detriment; the second step would empower regulators to see into a trading market that was opaque and impossible to decipher; and the third step would increase the shock absorbers of the financial system so that it can withstand more stress going forward. While the Dodd-Frank Act succeeds in all these respects, it also adds other unnecessary laws and regulations.

What advice would you offer for a lawyer entering into practice?

Be patient; find a mentor, if possible; live, breath, and immerse yourself in the law for the first few years of practice, when you will most likely develop the good instincts, habits, connections, and successes that will pay dividends over the years; and finally, try to find a specialty that fits your nature and is poised to grow, taking you along for the ride.

QUESTIONS AND COMMENTS

1. Contrast "core principles" with the regulatory construct applicable in other fields, such as securities law. Do "core principles" provide more or less latitude to a regulator such as the CFTC? Do they make it easier or more difficult for an entity subject to regulation to identify legal requirements?
2. What are the pros and cons of the Commodity Exchange Act's requirement that commodity futures be traded exclusively on designated contract markets?
3. In section D, there is a reference to the Dodd-Frank Act's removal of the exempt commercial market registration category. What are the benefits, if any, of a low regulation alternative to designated contract markets? If such an alternative existed once more, should retail investors be able to access it? Which of the designated contract market "core principles" should apply?
4. As the court in *American Agricultural Movements, Inc.* noted, immunity from antitrust claims is likely available to a designated contract market acting with the CFTC's explicit approval. Moreover, acting with the CFTC's informal approval is an indicium of good faith. Should the CFTC accordingly be more prescriptive?
5. What might the public policy rationale be for permitting foreign boards of trade to offer access to persons in the United States (and, similarly, for non-U.S. jurisdictions to allow designated contract markets in the United States to give their residents access)?

CHAPTER 5
MARKET INTERMEDIARIES

A. BACKGROUND

In the previous chapter we examined the direct regulation by the CFTC of the markets in which commodity options and futures trade. In addition to regulating the trading markets, the CFTC requires the registration of market intermediaries.

Market intermediaries are parties that act on behalf of third parties. In their role as intermediaries, they do not themselves take trading positions. They are akin to what, in securities regulation, are regulated as broker-dealers.

1. *Role of the National Futures Association*

The Commodity Futures Trading Commission Act of 1974, in addition to providing for the creation of the CFTC, also provided a framework for the formation of an industrywide self-regulatory organization. However, no such self-regulatory organization for the futures industry was formed until after the passage of the Futures Trading Act of 1978.

The Futures Trading Act of 1978 gave the CFTC the authority to require registrants to be members of a self-regulatory organization. The self-regulatory organization for the futures industry, the National Futures Association, commonly known as the "NFA," began operations in 1982, and membership of the National Futures Association is mandatory for futures commission merchants and is a practical necessity for introducing brokers, commodity pool operators, and commodity trading advisors.[1]

As a result, just as it is often necessary for performing a legal analysis with respect to designated contract markets to look to the intersection of the Commodity Exchange Act, CFTC rules, and the rules of the relevant designated contract market, for intermediaries and other registrants it is necessary to look to the Commodity Exchange Act, CFTC rules, and National Futures Association rules.

2. *The Operation of the Marketplace*

The designated contract markets we discussed in Chapter 4 have members. These members are bound to follow the rules of the designated contract market and accept the jurisdiction of the designated contract market as a self-regulatory organization with the ability to monitor and enforce rules. In return, members have the privilege to place trades through a floor trader directly on the designated contract market, with the derivatives clearing organization stepping in as the central counterparty. The member is required to adequately collateralize net positions with the designated contract market.

Intermediaries provide non-members of designated contract markets access to designated contract markets. There are three categories of intermediaries we examine in this chapter: futures commission merchants, introducing brokers, and floor brokers.

3. *Associated Persons*

Throughout this chapter (and Chapter 6) we will be examining futures commission merchants, introducing brokers and floor brokers (this chapter) and commodity pool operators and commodity trading advisors (Chapter 6), all of which are categories of market participants that require registration with the CFTC and, in most cases, the National Futures Association.

Additionally, other than with respect to floor brokers, each of their "associated persons" have registration obligations. An associated person is, in essence, a natural person, such as a partner, officer, or employee, whose function involves soliciting customer orders, funds, property, or discretionary account management, or a supervisor of any of the foregoing.[2]

B. FUTURES COMMISSION MERCHANTS

Futures Commission Merchants, commonly known as "FCMs," are central to the architecture of futures trading. Although having the privilege to trade on a designated contract market does not require registration as a futures commission merchant, futures commission merchants are permitted to hold customer funds as security in their role as intermediary and, therefore, provide a key to access of designated contract markets by non-members.

Let us say that Manhattan Poultry Feed Corporation produces poultry feed from a number of ingredients, including corn. They expect to need, in a year's time, 50,000 bushels of corn. Each corn contract on the Chicago Board of Trade, a designated contract market, is for 5,000 bushels of corn. Therefore, they wish to buy 10 such contracts with delivery in a year. How exactly do they go about doing that?

If, for example, they show up at the Chicago Board of Trade in person, they will be turned away by security. Instead, the Manhattan Poultry Feed Corporation will need to establish an account with a Chicago Board of Trade member who will enter into the trade on Chicago Board of Trade and take responsibility for the Manhattan Poultry Feed Corporation's contractual performance. The Chicago Board of Trade member will require margin – i.e., liquid collateral – from the Manhattan Poultry Feed Corporation based on the Manhattan Poultry Feed Corporation's potential liability. Figure 5-A provides an illustration:

Figure 5-A: Trading Futures with a Futures Commission Merchant as Intermediary

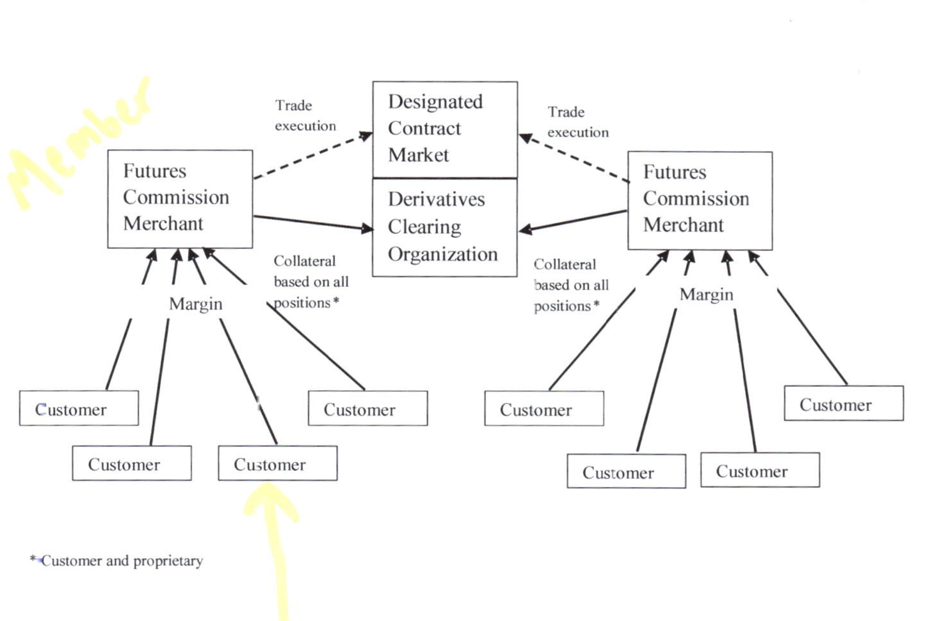

The Manhattan Poultry Feed Corporation is in the role of one of the customers, able to access the designated contract market through a futures commission merchant who is a member. The Manhattan Poultry Feed Corporation will agree to a customer agreement with its selected futures commission merchant and, provided there is sufficient margin in their account with the futures commission merchant, will be able to place the corn futures trade on Chicago Board of Trade through the futures commission merchant. The trade will be cleared by CME Clearing (a division of Chicago Mercantile Exchange, Inc.[3]), resulting in the futures commission merchant posting collateral to CME Clearing for all of its exposures, including the purchase of corn futures on behalf of the Manhattan Poultry Feed Corporation and, in return, requiring margin from the Manhattan Poultry Feed Corporation. The amount of margin required will fluctuate as the market price of the corn contract purchased by the Manhattan Poultry Feed Corporation changes.

Futures commission merchants obtain income by charging trade commissions and by reinvesting customers' margin. A more entertaining explanation is found in the movie *Trading Places* (1983), where Eddie Murphy's character Billy Ray offers the following analysis to the movie's antagonists, Mortimer and Randolph Duke, as they seek to explain the role of commodities brokers (in the context of the movie, he is probably referring to a futures commission merchant, though he could be referring to an introducing broker, discussed in section C below, or floor broker, discussed in section D below):

> Randolph Duke: . . . Now, some of our clients are speculating that the price of gold will rise in the future. And we have other clients who are speculating that the price of gold will fall. They place their orders with us, and we buy or sell their gold for them.
>
> Mortimer Duke: Tell him the good part.
>
> Randolph Duke: The good part, William, is that, no matter whether our clients make money or lose money, Duke & Duke get the commissions.
>
> Mortimer Duke: Well? What do you think . . .?
>
> Billy Ray: Sounds to me like you guys a couple of bookies.[4]

Marchese v. Shearson Hayden Stone, Inc.

644 F. Supp. 1381 (C.D. Cal. 1986)

Wm. Matthew Byrne, Jr., District Judge.

Plaintiff, Dominic Marchese, filed this action against Shearson Hayden Stone, Inc. (Shearson), a securities broker and futures commission merchant, seeking a declaratory judgment that "interest and increment" on margin funds maintained pursuant to . . . the Commodities [*sic*] Exchange Act (CEA) may not be retained by Shearson in excess of its lawful commission. The action is brought on behalf of a class consisting of all persons, who, within the relevant limitations period, gave money, securities, or property to Shearson to margin, guarantee or secure trades or contracts. . . .

The central issue presented by this motion is whether under section 4d of the CEA and its attendant regulations the interest and increment earned on margin funds is the property of the futures commission merchant. This Court finds that the futures commission merchant is entitled to retain all interest and increment on margin funds, and the motion to dismiss is granted. . . .

Investors enter into contracts of purchase or sale of commodities for future delivery as a means of speculating on the price changes in various commodities. The investors do not ordinarily anticipate taking delivery of the commodity, rather, they seek to enter into "offsetting" contracts prior to the delivery date, liquidate their obligations, and reap a profit should the market price move favorably. H.R. Rep. No. 93–975, 93rd Cong., 2d Sess. 1, 149, *reprinted in* 1974 U.S. Code Cong. & Ad. News 5843 (House Report) (only 3% of all futures contracts culminate in delivery). . . .

Futures trading occurs on exchanges designated as contract markets by the Commodities [*sic*] Futures Trading Commission (CFTC). Generally, an investor makes his futures trades through a Futures Commodities [*sic*] Merchant (FCM), who may be viewed as the commodities counterpart to a securities broker. In addition to the FCM's role in the exchange, each contract market has an affiliated clearing organization which is substituted as the buyer to every seller, and as the seller to every buyer. This substitution occurs at the end of each trading day; thereafter the contracting parties are obligated only to the clearing organization.

An investor must deposit a specified amount of money with the FCM when he enters into a futures transaction. This deposit, called "initial margin money" or "original margin" insures that the contract will be performed. The FCM, in turn, is required to deposit margin with the clearing organization to secure the investor's futures position.

Contract markets determine the minimum initial margin which must be deposited by the investor, as well as what form the margin may take (cash, Treasury bills or securities). The margin not only varies with each contract market, but with the underlying commodity itself. As the price of the futures contracts fluctuate, the investor may be required to make adjustments to the margin account. If the price moves adversely to the investor's position, his margin will be viewed as declining, and he will be required to deposit additional funds. This "margin call" is necessary to restore the margin account to the initial margin level. On the other hand, if the price moves favorably, the investor may be permitted to withdraw funds from the margin account. . . .

Prior to 1936, brokers commingled customer monies with their own, used customer monies as part of their own working capital, lent customer deposits to other customers, and used customer monies for their own speculative purposes. Similarly, banks holding customer funds commingled and used these funds as their own. And, in the event of the bankruptcy of a broker or bank, the customers ranked only as general creditors, and suffered considerable losses.

Congress responded by enacting the Commodities [*sic*] Exchange Act which broadened the scope of federal regulation to include other commodities, and set out several new requirements. Significant among the new requirements was . . . that FCMs treat funds and property received by them "to margin, guarantee, or secure" trades or contracts or accruing "as the result of such trades or contracts" as belonging to the customer [and] . . . that customer funds and property be separately accounted for; FCMs were prohibited from commingling customer funds with their own funds, or using customer funds to margin the trades of other customers. . . . [The CEA] authorized FCMs to continue investing customer monies, but carefully circumscribed the class of permissible investments. . . .

The statutory language does not express any intention by Congress that interest and increment gained on margin funds is the property of the customer. In fact, if any inference can be drawn from the text, it is that Congress intended that such interest and increment need not be treated as belonging to the customer. By its terms . . . [the CEA] provides that only two categories of funds, securities or property, be treated as belonging to the customer – those received by the FCM to margin, guarantee or secure trades or contracts, and those accruing to such customer as a result of trades or contracts. The . . . [CEA] specifically allows FCM's to invest margin funds in certain securities. If Congress intended that income gained as a result of the FCM's investment of the margin was to be treated as belonging to the customer, it could have included this . . .

While Congress has been silent or ambiguous in its statutory language on this issue, the regulatory body charged with implementing the statute has expressed itself clearly. Regulations 1.25 through 1.29, originally promulgated in 1937, deal specifically with the investment of customer funds, and the rights to resulting increment and interest.[i] Regulation 1.25 sets out those investments permitted . . . and requires that such investments be made through customer accounts, and that proceeds from the sale of the obligations be redeposited in such accounts. Regulation 1.29 specifically allows the FCM to retain the increment or interest resulting from investment of customer funds. . . .

Prior to the enactment of the CEA . . . futures commission merchants commingled customer funds with their own funds and used customer funds for their own business purposes. As a result, when commission firms went bankrupt customer funds were lost.[ii] The House version . . . attacked these abuses by prohibiting any investment of customer funds by the FCM. This blanket

---

[i] [N. 13] Regulations 1.25-1.29, 2 Fed. Reg. 1223-28 (1937), *currently,* 17 C.F.R. sections 1.25-1.29 (1984).

[ii] [N. 17] During the Senate debate . . . Senator Pope summarized the problem. He stated that customer margin deposits: "[h]ave been intermingled with the funds of these futures commission merchants, and have been used by them in the conduct of their own business. They have not been held intact for the benefit of the traders. It further appears that certain favored dealers have not been required actually to put up the money for margins, and have been extended credit in that respect. This gives these favored dealers an advantage. In some instances, large commission firms have become bankrupt and the funds placed with them by a large number of dealers were lost." 80 Cong. Rec. S6162 (1936).

prohibition was rejected by the Senate, which felt that FCMs should be able to invest customer funds in trustworthy securities. The Senate therefore introduced an amendment . . . which would allow FCMs to use margin funds for certain investments. The amendment accommodated the twin aims of the section, "to protect properly the margin of the customers and to provide some limitation under which the commission men may use that money to invest." 80 Cong. Rec. S7911 (1936) (Remarks of Senator Norris). The House later approved the bill as amended, and it was signed into law as the Commodity Exchange Act. Ch. 545, 49 Stat. 1491 (1936).

This legislative history illustrates that Congress could have completely prohibited FCMs from investing customer funds. Instead, it chose to curb the previous abuses by limiting the category of permissible investments, thereby allowing merchants to continue benefitting from the use of customer funds. The inference that Congress intended the FCMs to profit from investment of customer margin is strengthened by the fact that the FCMs are given discretion as to whether they will make such investments. FCMs would have little incentive to exercise their discretion to invest margin funds if they were unable to retain the interest and increment.[iii] . . .

Congress intended that futures commission merchants be entitled to retain any and all interest on their investment of customer margin funds. The motion to dismiss is granted.

In addition to the permissible investment limitations, other methods that the Commodity Exchange Act and CFTC rules use to mitigate customer risk are imposing minimum capital and recordkeeping requirements on futures commission merchants. Notwithstanding these safeguards, at least seven futures commission merchants have failed since the passage of the Commodity Futures Trading Commission Act of 1974: Chicago Discount Commodity Broker in 1980, Incomco in 1980, Volume Investors in 1985 (the subject of the litigation in *Westheimer v. Commodity Exchange, Inc.*, in Chapter 4 and *Comex Clearing Association, Inc. v. Flo-Arb Partners* excerpted further below) and, more recently, Refco, Inc., in 2005, Lehman Brothers, Inc., in 2008, MF Global in 2011, and Peregrine Financial Group in 2012 (the events underlying *Prestwick Capital Management, Ltd. v. Peregrine Financial Group, Inc.*, excerpted in section C below, and the criminal complaint in *United States v. Wasendorf*, excerpted in Chapter 13). The failure of MF Global and Peregrine Financial Group triggered renewed scrutiny of the protection of customer funds held by futures commission merchants. Largely due to the these events, the CFTC sought to

[iii] [N. 21] This is particularly true in light of the regulatory history of the section. The FCM must put his own funds in the customer account if the value of the investment declines. The FCM would have l ttle reason to take this risk without the prospect of realizing a profit on the investment.

strengthen customer protections by further limiting the investments that FCMs could make and adding new risk management and compliance requirements.

Commodity Futures Trading Commission, Enhancing Protections Afforded Customers and Customer Funds Held by Futures Commission Merchants and Derivatives Clearing Organizations

78 Fed. Reg. 68506-01 (November 13, 2013)

. . . The protection of customers – and the safeguarding of money, securities or other property deposited by customers with an FCM – is a fundamental component of the Commission's disclosure and financial responsibility framework. Section 4d(a)(2) of the Commodity Exchange Act ("the Act" or "the CEA") requires each FCM to segregate from its own assets all money, securities, and other property deposited by futures customers to margin, secure, or guarantee futures contracts and options on futures contracts traded on designated contract markets. Section 4d(a)(2) further requires an FCM to treat and deal with futures customer funds as belonging to the futures customer, and prohibits an FCM from using the funds deposited by a futures customer to margin or extend credit to any person other than the futures customer that deposited the funds. . . .

[CFTC] Regulation 1.20 requires each FCM and DCO to separately account for and to segregate from its own proprietary funds all money, securities, or other property deposited by futures customers for trading on designated contract markets. In addition, all futures customer funds must be separately accounted for, and may not be commingled with the money, securities or property of an FCM or of any other person, or be used to secure or guarantee the trades, contracts or commodity options, or to secure or extend the credit, of any person other than the one for whom the same are held. Regulation 1.20 also provides that an FCM or DCO may deposit futures customer funds only with a bank or trust company, and for FCMs only, a DCO or another FCM. The funds must be deposited under an account name that clearly identifies the funds as belonging to the futures customers of the FCM or DCO and further shows that the funds are segregated as required . . .

FCMs and DCOs also are restricted in their use of futures customer funds. Regulation 1.22 prohibits an FCM from using, or permitting the use of, the futures customer funds of one futures customer to purchase, margin, or settle the trades, contracts, or commodity options of, or to secure or extend the credit of, any person other than such futures customer. In addition, § 1.22 provides that futures customer funds may not be used to carry trades or positions of the same futures customer other than in commodities or commodity options traded through the facilities of a contract market. Under § 1.20, an FCM or DCO may, however, for convenience, commingle and hold funds deposited as margin by multiple futures customers in the same account or accounts with one of the recognized depositories. An FCM or DCO also may invest futures customer funds in certain permitted investments under § 1.25. . . .

FCMs also are subject to minimum net capital and financial reporting requirements that are intended to ensure that such firms meet their financial obligations in a regulated marketplace, including their financial obligations to customers and DCOs. Each FCM is required to maintain a minimum level of "adjusted net capital," which is generally defined under § 1.17 as the firm's net equity as computed under generally accepted accounting principles, less all of the firm's liabilities (except for certain qualifying subordinated debt) and further excluding all assets that are not liquid or readily marketable. Regulation 1.17(c)(5) further requires an FCM to impose capital charges (i.e., deductions) on certain of its liquid assets to protect against possible market risks in such assets.

FCMs also are subject to financial recordkeeping and reporting requirements. FCMs that carry customer accounts are required under § 1.32 to prepare a schedule each business day demonstrating their compliance with the segregation and secured amount requirements. Regulation 1.32 requires the calculation to be performed by noon each business day, reflecting the account balances and open positions as of the close of business on the previous business day.

Each FCM also is required by § 1.10 to file with the Commission and with its designated self-regulatory organization ("DSRO") monthly unaudited financial statements and an annual audited financial report.[iv] Regulation 1.12 requires an FCM to file a notice with the Commission and with the firm's DSRO whenever, among other things, the firm: (1) Fails to maintain compliance with the Commission's capital requirements; (2) fails to hold sufficient funds in segregated or secured amount accounts to meet its regulatory requirements; (3) fails to maintain current books and records; or (4) experiences a significant reduction in capital from the previous month-end. . . .

The statutory mandate to segregate customer funds – to treat them as belonging to the customer and not use the funds inappropriately – takes on greater meaning in light of the devastating events experienced over the last two years. Those events, which are discussed in greater detail below, demonstrate that the risks of misfeasance and malfeasance, and the risks of an FCM failing to maintain sufficient excess funds in segregation: (i) Put customer funds at risk; and (ii) are exacerbated by stresses on the business of the FCM. . . .

[iv] [N. 9] The term "self-regulatory organization" is defined by § 1.3 to mean a contract market, a swap execution facility, or a registered futures association [i.e. the National Futures Association]. A DSRO is the SRO that is appointed to be primarily responsible for conducting ongoing financial surveillance of an FCM that is a member of two or more SROs under a joint audit agreement submitted to and approved by the Commission under § 1.52.

The Commission's oversight structure provides that SROs are the frontline regulators of FCMs, introducing brokers ("IBs"), commodity pool operators, and commodity trading advisors. In 2000, Congress affirmed the Commission's reliance on SROs by amending section 3 of the Act to state: "It is the purpose of this Act to serve the public interests through a system of effective self-regulation of trading facilities, clearing systems, market participants and market professionals under the oversight of the Commission." . . .

The recent insolvencies of two FCMs demonstrate the need for revisions to the Commission's customer protection regime. On October 31, 2011, MF Global, Inc. ("MFGI"), which was dually-registered as an FCM with the Commission and as a securities broker-dealer ("BD") with the U.S. Securities and Exchange Commission ("SEC"), was placed into a liquidation proceeding under the Securities Investor Protection Act by the Securities Investor Protection Corporation ("SIPC").

The trustee appointed to oversee the liquidation of MFGI reported a potential $900 million shortfall of funds necessary to repay the account balances due to customers trading futures on designated contract markets, and an approximately $700 million shortfall in funds immediately available to repay the account balances of customers trading on foreign futures markets.[v] The shortfall in customer segregated accounts was attributed by the MFGI Trustee to significant transfers of funds out of the customer accounts that were used by MFGI for various purposes other than to meet obligations to or on behalf of customers.

In addition, the Commission filed a civil injunctive complaint in federal district court on July 10, 2012, against Peregrine Financial Group, Inc. ("PFGI"), a registered FCM and its Chief Executive Officer ("CEO") and sole owner, Russell R. Wasendorf, Sr., alleging that PFGI and Wasendorf, Sr., committed fraud by misappropriating customer funds, violated customer fund segregation laws, and made false statements regarding the amount of funds in customer segregated accounts in financial statements filed with the Commission. The complaint states that in July 2012 during an NFA examination PFGI falsely represented that it held in excess of $220 million of customer funds when in fact it held approximately $5.1 million.[vi] . . .

These recent incidents highlighted weaknesses in the customer protection regime prescribed in the Commission's regulations and through the self-

---

[v] [N. 10] *See* Report of the Trustee's Investigation and Recommendations, In re MF Global Inc., No. 11-2790 (MG) SIPA (Bankr. S.D.N.Y. June 4, 2012). [Note that customers ultimately received full restitution. *See Customers of MF Global Inc. to Begin Receiving Final Restitution Payments from MF Global*, CFTC Press Release PR6904-14, http://www.cftc.gov/PressRoom/PressReleases/pr6904-14 (accessed June 8, 2014).]

[vi] [N. 11] Complaint, *U.S. Commodity Futures Trading Commission v. Peregrine Financial Group, Inc.*, and Russell R. Wasendorf, Sr., No. 12-cv-5383 (N.D. Ill. July 10, 2012). A copy of the Commission's complaint has been posted to the Commission's Web site.

regulatory system. In particular, questions have arisen on the requirements surrounding the holding and investment of customer funds, including the ability of FCMs to withdraw funds from futures customer segregated accounts. . . . Additionally, the incidents have underscored the need for additional safeguards – such as robust risk management systems, strengthened early-warning systems surrounding margin and capital requirements, and enhanced public disclosures. . . .

In December 2011, the Commission adopted final rule amendments revising the types of investments that an FCM or DCO can make with customer funds under § 1.25, for the purpose of affording greater protection for such funds.[vii] Among other changes to §§ 1.25 and 30.7, the final rule amendments removed from the list of permitted investments: (1) Corporate debt obligations not guaranteed by the U.S. Government; (2) foreign sovereign debt; and (3) in-house and affiliate transactions.

In adopting the amendments to § 1.25, the Commission was mindful that customer segregated funds must be invested by FCMs and DCOs in a manner that minimizes their exposure to credit, liquidity, and market risks both to preserve their availability to customers and DCOs, and to enable investments to be quickly converted to cash at a predictable value in order to avoid systemic risk. The amendments are consistent with the general prudential standard contained in § 1.25, which provides that all permitted investments must be "consistent with the objectives of preserving principal and maintaining liquidity."

The Commission also approved final regulations that require DCOs to collect initial customer margin from FCMs on a gross basis.[viii] Under the final regulations, FCMs are no longer permitted to offset one customer's margin requirement against another customer's margin requirements and deposit only the net margin collateral with the DCO. As a result of the rule change, a greater portion of customer initial margin is posted by FCMs to the DCOs. . . .

The Commission also included customer protection enhancements in a final rulemaking for designated contract markets issued in June 2012. These enhancements codify into regulations staff guidance on minimum requirements for SROs regarding their financial surveillance of FCMs. The regulations require a DCM to have arrangements and resources for effective rule enforcement and trade and financial surveillance programs, including the authority to collect information and examine books and records of members and market participants. The regulations also establish minimum financial standards for both member FCMs and IBs and non-intermediated market participants. . . .

[vii] [N. 14] *See* Investment of Customer Funds and Funds Held in an Account for Foreign Futures and Foreign Options Transactions, 76 FR 78776 (Dec. 19, 2011).

[viii] [N. 15] *See* Commission Regulation 39.12(g)(8)(i) and Derivatives Clearing Organization General Provisions and Core Principles, 76 FR 69334 (Nov. 8, 2011).

In the futures trading model, customer funds are at risk in the case of a so-called double default, i.e., where a large customer defaults in making a margin payment and the futures commission merchant is unable to make up for the shortfall:

> Under the traditional futures model, DCOs hold an FCM's futures customers' funds on an omnibus basis in a futures customer account. In the event of a double default, which is a situation where a futures customer defaults on its obligation to its clearing FCM and the loss is so great that the clearing FCM defaults on its obligation to the DCO, the DCO is permitted to use the funds held in the [defaulting FCM's] futures customers' omnibus account to cover the loss of the defaulting futures customer before applying its own capital or the guaranty fund contributions of non-defaulting FCM members.

Enhancing Protections Afforded Customers and Customer Funds Held by Futures Commission Merchants and Derivatives Clearing Organizations, 78 Fed. Reg. 68506-01, 68510.

As we will see in Chapter 9, a different regime applies for swaps clearing where non-defaulting customers are protected against the "fellow customer" risk that arises in a double default scenario.

A "double default" occurred in the gold futures and options market in 1985 resulting in shortfalls to the clearinghouse being apportioned among all of the account balances of customers of the failed futures commission merchant. Innocent, non-defaulting customers of the defaulting futures commission merchant saw their accounts debited *pro rata* to pay the shortfalls owed by their futures commission merchant to the clearinghouse.

Comex Clearing Association, Inc. v. Flo-Arb Partners

711 F. Supp. 1169 (S.D.N.Y. 1989)

Kevin Thomas Duffy, District Judge . . .

This opinion will, I hope, conclude the story of the financial collapse of Volume Investors Corporation ("Volume"). At all pertinent times, Volume was a member of the Commodities Exchange, Inc. ("COMEX"), and the Comex Clearing Association ("CCA"). Volume was also a futures commission merchant ("FCM") registered with the Commodities [*sic*] Futures Trading Commission ("CFTC") . . . In its position as an FCM and as a member of COMEX and CCA, Volume handled accounts for members of the public and for other FCMs. . . .

Flo-Arb Partners ("Flo-Arb") was also an FCM duly registered and, through one of its partners, a member of COMEX. To clear its trades through CCA, Flo-

Arb put all of its accounts with Volume and was permitted to act as a floor broker on the Commodities Exchange by reason of a guarantee issued by Volume. Flo-Arb is made up of two general partners: Ronny Apfel and Abraham Goldstein. . . . [B]oth Apfel and Goldstein were quite knowledgeable about the futures market. . . .

On March 21, 1985, prior to the commencement of trading on COMEX, Frank H. Wohl was appointed Temporary Receiver of Volume. The appointment was made pursuant to an order of a judge of this court, on application of CFTC and on consent of Volume. At the same time Volume was suspended as a member of COMEX and of CCA. The Temporary Receiver undertook to liquidate the positions of Volume in an orderly manner and pursuant to the rules of CCA as approved by CFTC. Wohl effectively secured the records and property of Volume and worked out arrangements for the initial liquidation of the Volume account at CCA.

Shortly thereafter, I appointed John F. X. Peloso as the Receiver of the Estate of Volume. Peloso undertook the wind-up of the estate, including sales of property, renegotiation of leases, and payments to public customers of Volume. The claims of Flo-Arb against Volume and its successors, and the claims of Volume and the receivers against Flo-Arb are now the main barrier to completion of the wind-up. These claims were held aside to be resolved after all of the public was out of the picture and all of the din appurtenant thereto had quieted.

During the pendency of these actions, CCA paid out the purely public customer accounts, i.e., the non-members of COMEX, and became the successor to the receiver of Volume.[ix] . . .

Once before, in a dispute related to this matter, I set forth my views on the risks involved in trading on certain commodities and futures markets. I nonetheless believe it necessary to reiterate what I have said because much of it has apparently fallen on deaf ears.

Trading in gold options is a highly volatile market where fortunes can be made and lost in one day. This case should stand as a reminder that the fallout from an explosive day in the gold market can affect not only the traders in that market but can also have a detrimental effect on the market place, including the organized exchanges dealing in gold, the exchange clearing house, the members of the exchange, and the innocent public customers of member firms, which customers may not even be involved in the trading of gold or gold options. . . .

Apfel and Goldstein, were not "hedging" by their activities in the futures markets. They were pure speculators seeking to make money at the expense of others in the marketplace. . . .

[ix] [N. 2] The matters presently before the court involve only the claims between Flo–Arb Partners, Ronny Apfel and Abraham Goldstein, on the one hand and Volume Investors, Inc. and its successors in interest on the other hand.

Both Goldstein and Apfel were aware that the CCA viewed all of Volume's accounts (whether house accounts or for customers like Flo-Arb) as the accounts of one member. The CCA does not differentiate between the types of accounts held by any member, and Goldstein and Apfel had to be aware that there was a risk clearing through another FCM. Specifically, if the clearing FCM went broke, the accounts held would be netted by CCA with the possible result that the customers would lose everything. . . .

Volume permitted other customers, the Westheimers, and their agent to have a large number of gold futures contracts. Following a dramatic change in gold prices the Westheimers were caught short and were unable to come up with the amounts required to maintain their margin accounts. The amounts necessary were so enormous that Volume was also unable to meet the margin demands of CCA, which had netted all of the Volume accounts, including those of the Westheimers. Because of the Westheimers, Volume was broke and CCA sold out all the Volume accounts. In effect, everyone connected with Volume lost and the problem became how to spread the loss equitably among all of the victims. By this point this court was involved both directly and through its receiver. While there was no precedent on point that could guide me in this task, I decided that it would be most appropriate and fair to analogize this situation to the rule of "general average" found in the law of Admiralty.

"General average" is perhaps the oldest, still extant, doctrine of the law of Admiralty. It is used when a ship loses some of its cargo due to the perils of the sea. In that situation the remaining cargo is liquidated and each of the cargo owners, regardless of whose cargo was lost, and the ship owner share the monetary loss. Throughout history, beginning at least with the Greeks and the Phoenicians, this has been considered a fair and equitable method of resolving the problem. The liquidation and distribution of Volume was effected according to this time-honored principle and each step was taken with the approval of this court. . . .

No one has suggested that the collapse of Volume was caused by Flo-Arb. Indeed, it is irrelevant. Volume's accounts were not liquidated because of some fault on the part of Flo-Arb or its partners. Rather, they were liquidated because Volume could not meet the CCA's margin requirements. Flo-Arb in first entering its arrangements with Volume assumed that risk along with the sundry other risks that the futures markets entail. In speculating in the market, Flo-Arb accepted the risk of losing its money. If Flo-Arb's trading resulted in this loss, the loss would be assessed without regard to blame. So also, here, it is totally unnecessary to assess blame and the absence of "fault" (in that sense) is irrelevant. . . .

Flo-Arb has successfully delayed paying what it owes to the estate of Volume for redistribution to the truly innocent public customers. To obviate any bad public relations, CCA has already put up the money owed to public customers under the rule of general average. This permitted the public to be paid without delay arising from the arguments of Flo-Arb. By making the payment to the public customers, CCA has succeeded to their interests and now can collect from Flo-Arb through the estate of Volume. . . .

Regardless of whether registered or not, a person or entity that "is engaged in soliciting or in accepting orders for the purchase or sale of any commodity for future delivery [or] a commodity option authorized under [CEA] section 4c of the Act . . . and in connection with any of these activities accepts any money, securities, or property (or extends credit in lieu thereof) to margin, guarantee, or secure any trades or contracts that result or may result therefrom" is a futures commission merchant.[5] An important exception exists for entities that have only proprietary accounts, i.e., accounts of related entities, such as affiliates.[6]

Therefore, a person or entity meeting the definition of a futures commission merchant and not exempt from registration, will be held to the same requirements as a futures commission merchant, regardless of whether registered or not.

Ping He (Hai Nam) Co. Ltd. v. NonFerrous Metals (U.S.A.) Inc.

22 F. Supp. 2d 94 (S.D.N.Y. 1998)

Sotomayor, District Judge. . . .

The two instant actions arise from a dispute between plaintiff Ping He (Hai Nam) Company Limited ("Ping He") and defendant NonFerrous Metals (U.S.A.) Inc. ("NFM") over a commodity futures trading account opened by Ping He with NFM in 1993. Ping He moves for summary judgment . . . seeking the return of $350,000 it deposited into the account, on the grounds that NFM defrauded Ping He into opening the account, engaged in unauthorized trading, falsified an invoice, and misappropriated Ping He's funds. . . . In opposing the motion, NFM claims that Ping He owes it more than $650,000 in trading losses. . . .

The following facts are undisputed. Ping He and NFM are both entities owned by the People's Republic of China. Ping He is a foreign corporation with its principal place of business in China. NFM, although owned by the Chinese government, is a New York corporation with its principal place of business in Manhattan. NFM holds itself out as being in the business of soliciting orders for the purchase and sale of commodity futures. Once an order is placed with NFM, NFM arranges for the order to be executed on American and foreign markets through registered floor brokers. NFM, however, is not and has never been registered with the Commodity Future Trading Commission ("CFTC"), or with any federal or state regulatory body in the United States, in any capacity.

In or about April 1993, Ping He agreed to open a futures trading account with NFM. . . . [A]ll trades were to be non-discretionary, meaning that NFM was only authorized to execute trades for Ping He upon the express instructions of

Ping He or Ping He's designated agent. Toward that end, by letter dated April 27, 1993, Ping He advised NFM that it was authorizing Mr. Li Zheng of China National Metal Products Co. ("China Metals") to act as Ping He's agent in all matters relating to its futures trading account. . . .

Unfortunately, nearly all facts concerning what actually happened to Ping He's trading account after it was opened are in dispute, including: whether NFM conducted any trading for Ping He; when such trading began and ended; whether trades on Ping He's account were authorized or unauthorized; and whether trades conducted for Ping He resulted in profits or losses. The parties additionally dispute whether Ping He knew when it opened the account that NFM was not registered with the CFTC. . . .

China Metals sent NFM a fax suspending the account. The letter stated:

> We are very pleased to see that we have made a little profits [sic] through those deals done with your brokerage. . . . As a result of our internal arrangements, we would like to inform you that we have suspended our future trading account with your brokerage effective from today. . . .

China Metals' . . . letter also requested that NFM provide it with a list of all trades executed on the account, together with a list of all commissions charged.

Soon afterwards, NFM sent China Metals an account invoice . . . [which] stated that $344,893 was due on Ping He's account (not $800,000, as NFM had contended when it sought to draw upon the letters of credit). That figure consisted of $104,500 in alleged trading losses and $240,393 in commissions and interest, for trading activity . . . Several months later . . . Ping He wired NFM the sum of $300,000. . . .

Ping He brought the instant suit . . . claiming that NFM defrauded it at every step of their dealings. First, Ping He claims, NFM misrepresented itself as a registered commodity broker in order to induce Ping He to open an account with NFM. Ping He further claims that, after the account opened, neither it nor China Metals ever authorized NFM to execute trades on its behalf, but that NFM nevertheless improperly charged it for large trading losses. According to Ping He, NFM either engaged in unauthorized trading on Ping He's account, charged Ping He for fictitious trades, or fraudulently allocated to Ping He's account losing trades that had been undertaken for other customers. Whichever was the case, Ping He contends that NFM's fraudulent conduct is evinced by the fact that NFM has been unable to produce any records reflecting trades ordered by Ping He or China Metals, or showing that the losing trades charged to Ping He were in fact made for Ping He's account. . . .

NFM maintains that all of the trades it conducted for Ping He were authorized by NonFerrous B.M. Corp. ("B.M.Corp."), a private New Jersey corporation (unrelated to NFM and Ping He) that China Metals allegedly retained to give trading instructions for Ping He's account. In effect, NFM claims that a two-tiered agency structure existed: Ping He authorized China Metals to act as its agent, which in turn authorized B.M. Corp. to act as *its* agent. . . . Furthermore, NFM maintains that Ping He knew from the outset that NFM was not registered with the CFTC. According to NFM, it had no reason to misrepresent its registration status because it was at all times legally exempt from registration. . . .

Central to the regulatory scheme [of the Commodity Exchange Act (the "CEA")] are its registration requirements . . .

Because of their critical importance, the CEA's registration requirements apply to nearly every class of professionals who deal in commodities. Thus, under the Act, anyone who acts as a broker and executes sales of commodities on the trading floor of a contract market must be registered as a broker. . . . Futures commission merchants ("FCMs"), who do not trade themselves on the floor, but who, like NFM, solicit transactions which are then executed through brokers, must also register.[x] . . . Those who either fail to register or who misrepresent their registration status can be criminally prosecuted. . . .

[A] key purpose of the CEA is to protect customers against fraudulent and abusive trading practices by FCMs and other market participants. . . .

Also, . . . [the CEA] requires FCMs to maintain intelligible daily trading records for each customer, and to report to customers on their transactions, in the manner prescribed by the CFTC. In that regard, the CFTC has promulgated Rules 1.33 and 1.35, setting forth strict record-keeping and reporting requirements. . . .

Ping He seeks to recover $350,000 on the basis that NFM failed to register as an FCM. . . . However, Ping He offers no evidence or basis for believing that it incurred damages simply by dealing with an unregistered FCM. . . .

If Ping He can assert any damages claim based upon NFM's unregistered status, it is . . . on the grounds that NFM fraudulently induced it to open a futures trading account by misrepresenting or concealing its unregistered status. Cast as a fraudulent inducement claim, there is a causal link between NFM's alleged violation of the statute and Ping He's out-of-pocket losses because, the argument goes, "but for" NFM's misrepresentation or concealment of its unregistered status, a material fact, Ping He would not have opened the account with NFM and would not have incurred any losses. . . .

Rule 1.33 requires FCMs to send customers monthly statements setting forth, among other things, the profits or losses realized upon trades and all financial charges assessed a customer during the monthly reporting period. Here, there is no question that NFM violated Rule 1.33. NFM has not produced copies of any monthly reports it prepared for Ping He's account, nor does NFM maintain that it ever prepared such reports for Ping He, or Ping He's agent. . . . Nevertheless, Ping He's damages claim under Rule 1.33 must be dismissed

---

[x] [N. 2] It is evident that, at all relevant times, NFM operated as an FCM. By its own account, NFM solicited and accepted customer orders for futures trades, which it then placed through floor brokers. This squarely meets the CFTC's definition of an FCM . . .

because Ping He has never contended that NFM's failure to issue it monthly reports . . . is what caused its loss of $350,000. . . .

Ping He has, however, made a case for actual injury by NFM's violation of Rule 1.35. . . . Rule 1.35 imposes numerous record-keeping requirements upon FCMs. The requirements are intended to ensure the complete segregation of customer accounts, the correct attribution of trades to the customers who ordered them, and the maintenance of detailed records for every transaction relating to each customer account. Here, Ping He claims that NFM failed so miserably to comply with any of Rule 1.35's requirements, that any demand by NFM for the payment of trading losses was guaranteed to be false because NFM had no way of itself knowing or checking what trades had been done for Ping He, and whether those trades had produced profits or losses. Indeed, Ping He claims that NFM's violations of Rule 1.35 were so pervasive, as to suggest strongly the commission of fraud. . . .

Rule 1.55 prohibits any FCM from opening a commodity futures account for any customer unless the FCM has first provided the customer with a risk disclosure statement containing . . . prescribed language. . . . It is undisputed that NFM did not provide Ping He, or any agent of Ping He, with the required risk disclosure statement. . . .

[T]he CFTC has held in reparations proceedings that Rule 1.55 is so critical to protecting customers that, when an FCM violates the rule, a causal link between the customer's damages and the Rule 1.55 violation will be presumed. . . .

The Court now must turn to the factual record in this case, to determine whether Ping He is entitled to summary judgment for NFM's alleged unauthorized trading, invoice falsification, and record-keeping violations. . . .

Even a cursory review . . . makes it painfully obvious that the losses reported in the June 16 invoice were entirely falsified, and, furthermore, that NFM could not possibly have prepared an accurate invoice for any loss amount because NFM maintained no records indicating what trades were made on Ping He's behalf, and whether such trades resulted in profits or losses. . . .

Given the record in this case, there is no question that Ping He is entitled to summary judgment based upon [these] claims. . . . No rational juror could possibly find NFM innocent of violations under these statutory provisions. . . .

C. INTRODUCING BROKERS

1. Generally

Introducing broker is a category of registration created by the Futures Trading Act of 1982 and is, therefore, newer than the futures commission merchant or floor broker categories of registration discussed in section B above and section D below. Previously, a regulatory gap was perceived to exist for entities acting as agents of futures commission merchants who solicited or placed orders on behalf of customers through a futures commission merchant. These entities had no obligation to register as futures commission merchants because they never took custody of customer funds. The House of Representatives Committee on Agriculture, in reporting on the bill that was to become the Futures Trading Act of 1982, described the quandary it intended to address as follows:

> Although agents may perform the same functions as branch officers of futures commission merchants, agents generally are separately owned and run. Futures commission merchants frequently disavow any responsibility for sales abuses or other violations committed by these agents. The Committee believes that the best way to protect the public is to create a new and separate registration category for "agents" (e.g., as introducing brokers). Many of these "agents" are individuals or very small businesses. Activities of agents and those of commodity trading advisors or associated persons of futures commission merchants may be virtually identical, yet commodity trading advisors and such associated persons are registered and regulated under the Act while many agents are not.
>
> The new registration category of "introducing broker" would encompass persons who solicit or accept futures orders but who do not handle customer funds, and in the case of individuals, who elect to be registered as introducing brokers rather than associated persons [of a futures commission merchant]. The current ambiguity and the resulting uncertainties of the regulatory status of agents would thus be eliminated.

House Report 97-565 (May 17, 1982), p. 48.

By creating a new class of registrant, Congress took a path between, on the one hand, leaving these entities unregulated and, on the other hand, placing responsibility on the futures commission merchants for their acts.

Commodity Futures Trading Commission v. Mass Media Marketing, Inc.

156 F. Supp. 2d 1323 (S.D. Fla. 2001)

Graham, District Judge. . . .

Mass Media Marketing, Inc. ("Mass Media") and Commodity Referral Service, Inc. ("CRS") (collectively "Defendants") are Florida advertising, marketing, video production and syndication companies whose marketing services range from advertising Ginsu knives and exercise equipment to promoting culinary schools and private universities. Rolando Nanasca ("Nanasca") is the President of both companies.

In 1995, Defendants added commodity futures to their marketing curriculum. Commodity futures involve the purchase of an option to buy or sell a particular commodity, such as unleaded gasoline, at a predetermined price on or before a given date.[7] Defendants' marketing services entailed producing, directing and arranging for the broadcast of 60-second commercials and 30-minute long infomercials ("advertisements") touting the benefits of commodity futures investments. Each advertisement urged viewers, who had at least $5,000 to invest, to call a toll-free number featured in the advertisement to obtain information on how to profit from investments in commodity options. Once a viewer placed a call to the toll-free number, the answering service operator would ask what product or service the viewer was calling about. If the viewer was calling in reference to a commodities advertisement, the answering service operator would give the caller a short description of the product or service being offered and would try to obtain the callers [*sic*] name, address and telephone number in order to create a "lead."

Defendants marketed two forms of advertisements, sponsored and non-sponsored. Sponsored advertisements were advertisements that Defendants created and broadcasted on behalf of a commodity broker registered with the Commodity Futures Trading Commission ("CFTC"). A registered commodity broker, also known as an Introducing Broker, essentially operates as a brokerage firm that solicits potential investors to place orders on commodity options. An Introducing Broker would seek the marketing services of Defendants to produce an advertisement approved by the Introducing Broker and featuring the Introducing Broker's name. Defendants would agreed to sell a specified number of leads generated by the advertisement to the sponsoring Introducing Broker. Any excess leads would be sold to other Introducing Brokers whose names did not appear in the advertisement.

Non-sponsored ("blind") advertisements were not approved by an Introducing Broker and did not include the name of an Introducing Broker in the advertisement. The leads generated from blind advertisements were sold on a random basis to any interested Introducing Broker. The contents of blind advertisements were ultimately approved by Nanasca who is not registered as a commodity broker.

Sponsored and blind advertisements essentially claimed that existing supply and demand factors in the cash market for a particular product, such as unleaded gasoline or soy beans, make options on that product's futures contracts "predictable" and "logical" and an investor had a "legitimate chance of doubling, tripling, or even quadrupling" his money. One advertisement described the manner in which commodities trading function as follows:

> We're discussing some common-sense approaches for investing in the commodities futures market and how to know when to invest.
>
> One of the most direct approaches in determining your investment in commodities options is what is known as trends. If you analyze and act upon a sound trend, then the profits can be astounding.
>
> There are many reasons that trends develop in commodities, but one of the more common reasons are of the cyclical nature, commodities such as unleaded gasoline and heating oil, for example.
>
> There's a much larger demand for heating oil in the winter, for obvious reasons. And for unleaded gasoline, the demand increases in the summer when people drive the most. These are seasonal trends, where the movement in price becomes predictable.

The advertisements assured viewers that although investment in commodities "[is] not for everybody, and it does involve risk," such "risks are, in fact, predetermined" and "known."

Nanasca wrote most of the scripts for the advertisements produced by Defendants or had otherwise the "final say-so on the scripts." Nanasca never "really researched" the background of commodities trading or the "way that commodities markets actually work" prior to writing the scripts and airing the advertisements. Instead, Nanasca based the advertisements' contents primarily on radio advertisements which he thought "sounded exciting," though he never took any steps to verify the accuracy of such information. . . .

The marketing and advertising services provided by Defendants never required Defendants to enlist callers to become Introducing Brokers' customers or to collect any money from callers. Rather, any discussions with callers about commodity investments occurred once the Introducing Broker purchased the leads from Defendants and contacted the prospective customers.

The National Futures Association ("NFA") is the commodity futures and options industry's self-regulatory organization. In the early 1990's, the NFA determined that some Introducing Brokers provided prospective investors with misleading information about the seasonality trends of commodities when soliciting their orders. Most of these Introducing Brokers received severe monetary penalties or were otherwise subjected to disciplinary action. To remedy this situation . . . the NFA issued a notice stating that seasonality claims were a violation of its rules. In early 1997, Nanasca discovered that the NFA "frowned upon" blind advertisements because "someone's got to be responsible for the contents of those advertisements." Consequently, Nanasca voluntarily ceased to broadcast blind advertisements. . . .

Introducing Brokers form a category of commodity futures market participants created by Congress in 1982. Prior to 1982, Introducing Brokers acted as independently affiliated "agents" of Futures Commission Merchants ("FCM").[xi] The main function of such agents was to procure business for FCMs. These unregistered agents operated free from regulation due to a gap in the Act's registration requirement which precluded jurisdiction by the CFTC over such agents. In 1982, the CFTC advised Congress that the number of agents had increased significantly, and that FCMs who used their services "have often disavowed any responsibility for violations of the Act by these 'agents.'" To remedy the ambiguity and the resulting uncertainties of the agents' regulatory status, the CFTC proposed that "each 'agent' of a futures commission merchant be required to register as an associated person of that futures commission merchant."

Congress, however, opted to resolve the problem by amending the Act to require all persons who solicit or accept customer orders for FCMs to register either as "associated persons" of the FCMs, or as part of a new class of registrants called Introducing Brokers.[xii] Unlike associated persons of a FCM, Congress viewed Introducing Brokers as independent entities that solicited and accepted customer orders, but used the services of FCMs for clearing, record keeping and retaining customer funds. . . .

[T]he Act defines an Introducing Broker as:

> any person (except an individual who elects to be and is registered as an associated person of a futures commission merchant) . . . engaged in soliciting or in accepting orders for the purchase or sale of any commodity for future delivery [who] does not accept any money, securities or property (or extend credit in lieu thereof) to margin, guarantee, or secure any trades or contracts that result or may result therefrom.

In the instant case, the CFTC claims that by soliciting and referring prospective investors to Introducing Brokers, Defendants have themselves acted as unregistered Introducing Brokers in violation of the Act. The CFTC interprets

---

[xi] [N. 1] FCMs function as the commodity market's equivalent of a securities brokerage house, soliciting and accepting orders and funds for futures contracts and extending credit in connection therewith.

[xii] [N. 2] Like Introducing Brokers, Associated Persons of an FCM solicit futures orders and deal directly with the public, but do so under the supervision and control of the FCM that clear their orders.

the phrase "soliciting or in accepting orders" contained in the definition of an Introducing Broker as covering a whole range of conduct, including Defendants' solicitation to the public through television advertisements. In contrast, Defendants assert that the plain language of the Introducing Broker registration requirement excludes them from registration because they are advertising production companies that neither solicit orders, nor accept orders from customers. Defendants posit that the phrase "soliciting or in accepting orders" cannot conceivably cover general solicitation to the public through television advertisements, which neither invite nor accept the placement of an order. . . .

Giving the words used in the Act their ordinary meaning, the Court finds that the phrase "engaged in soliciting or in accepting orders" contained within the definition of an Introducing Broker is subject to several interpretations. The Court cannot naturally discern whether Congress intended the term "soliciting" to modify the term "order" or if Congress intended the term "soliciting" to remain open-ended. The Act does not define the term "soliciting" nor does it explain its application. Even assuming the Court were to accept either party's interpretation of the phrase, the Court is still unable to determine whether the definition applies to advertisers. Accordingly, the Court finds the phrase to be ambiguous. . . .

The CFTC interprets the phrase "engaged in soliciting or accepting orders" as covering customer "solicitation[ ] for compensated referral to other registrants so that a trading relationship can be initiated and the customer's orders executed." Based on this interpretation, the CFTC concludes that Defendants' activities fall within the Act because:

> Mass Media produces and arranges for the broadcast of its advertisements and infomercials for the sole purpose of obtaining the names, phone numbers and addresses of individuals who may be interested in purchasing options. Mass Media's entire activities are tied to the number of leads that they generate. It is compensated on a per-lead basis by the IBs to which the leads are sold and it pays, in some cases, for television air time on a per-lead basis as well. It also licenses these leads to IBs and attempts to relicense these leads to other IBs after a period of time. . . .

[T]he Court cannot conclude that the CFTC's interpretation of the phrase "engaged in soliciting or in accepting orders" is a permissible interpretation of the Act.

First, Defendant advertisers' primary goal is to obtain leads, not orders for commodity futures. The CFTC's expert opines that Defendants' "entire activities are tied to the number of leads that they generate" and Defendants conduct their advertisements "for the sole purpose of obtaining the names, phone numbers and addresses of individuals who may be interested in purchasing options." Defendants never collected any money from viewers of the advertisements and never received compensation for the number of callers who subsequently opened accounts through an Introducing Broker. Accordingly, the Court finds that Defendants' main objective in broadcasting the advertisements was to facilitate the collection of leads, not to facilitate the purchases of orders for futures contracts.

Second, Defendants have a "good reason" to conduct their advertising activities that is not entirely ancillary to requesting purchases. Through their advertisements, Defendants find individuals who may become prospective commodity customers. As such, Defendants' activities are better characterized as those of a customer finder rather than an Introducing Broker. The Act, however, does not require a person who acts as a customer finder to register as an Introducing Broker. Moreover, unlike Introducing Brokers, whose compensation is commensurate with the orders obtained, Defendants receive compensation for the leads regardless of the Introducing Broker's success in soliciting, accepting or introducing an order to an FCM. Hence, Defendants have a "good reason" for conducting their solicitation activities that is not ancillary to requesting purchases. Accordingly, the Court finds that Defendants' activities . . . do not amount to "solicitation of orders"

Other factors similarly fail to support the CFTC's interpretation of the Introducing Broker registration requirement. First, the CFTC's prior understanding of the objective behind the 1982 Introducing Broker registration requirement cannot be reconciled with the CFTC's current interpretation. In its Rules and Regulations, passed shortly after the 1982 amendments, the CFTC expressed its understanding of Congress' intent "to require registration as Introducing Brokers those persons who were formerly agents of FCMs" or who "performed the types of activities traditionally engaged in by agents." . . . The CFTC expressed no concern about advertisers or entities who simply generate and sell leads to Introducing Brokers. The Court finds this factor to be specifically relevant because[,] based on the CFTC's prior interpretation of the Introducing Broker requirement, Defendants would not be required to register under the Act.

Second, the Act's legislative history, which delineates the underlying purpose of the Introducing Broker registration requirement, makes not a single reference to advertisers or an intent by Congress to regulate as Introducing Brokers entities who neither invite, nor accept the placement of an order. . . .

[I]n the instant case, Defendants never introduced an account to an FCM or any registered entity. Defendants' general solicitation through their advertisements never involved the making of an offer to enter into a commodity transaction or assisting customers in carrying out such transactions. . . .

[T]he CFTC has introduced no evidence to establish that Defendants' advertisements have caused commodity investors the type of harm Congress intended to prevent by enacting the Introducing Broker registration requirement. On the contrary, the record shows that the CFTC is effectively protecting the public by imposing strict solicitation guidelines on Introducing Brokers. The CFTC's expert confirms that the NFA has taken "several disciplinary actions against Members [Introducing Brokers] for the foregoing promotional practices." Moreover, Introducing Brokers are subject to serious monetary penalties, including customer restitution, if they fail to fully disclose to prospective investors the risks involved in commodity investments, especially when the investor's interest in commodities stems from television advertisements. *See Scheufler v. Stuart,* 1997 WL 599871 (C.F.T.C.) (Introducing Broker held liable for failure to fully disclose realistic profit and risk information to infomercial viewer). Hence, the evidence before the Court supports the view that the "simple act of referral does not directly jeopardize the interests of the investing public." After examining these relevant factors . . . the Court finds no permissible basis that would justify the CFTC's expansive interpretation of the Act's Introducing Broker registration requirement.

Congress has ample authority to expand the Act's registration requirement to include advertisers, such as Defendants. Congress, however, has not done so. . . .

Having determined that the Act's registration requirement is inapplicable to Defendants as advertisers, the Court's next inquiry is whether the CFTC may still enforce its anti-fraud regulations against Defendants. The CFTC contends that it has the authority to impose anti-fraud regulations on Defendants, even if Defendants do not meet the Introducing Broker registration requirement. Defendants contend that the CFTC's anti-fraud regulations, to the extent the CFTC seeks to enforce them against Defendants, are invalid because they enlarge the CFTC's jurisdiction beyond the authority granted to the CFTC by Congress. . . .

According to the CFTC, Defendants "fall squarely" within its anti-fraud regulations because through their advertisements they engaged in fraud, "directly or indirectly" "in connection with" commodity options "by any means whatsoever." . . .

The CFTC has cited to no portion of the Act or the Act's legislative history that confers the CFTC with the authority to impose its anti-fraud rules and regulations on entities who do not participate in commodity trading transactions.

The CFTC has likewise identified no legal authority which would support a federal agency's imposition of its rules and regulations on entities who neither are, nor should be governed by the statute. Instead, the cases cited by the CFTC involved entities who, although unregistered, had direct participation in the commodity market or were otherwise required to be registered with the CFTC, and all involved alleged violations of the Act's anti-fraud provision, not the CFTC's anti-fraud regulations. The CFTC, however, does not contend that Defendants violated the Act's anti-fraud provision, which is narrower in jurisdictional scope than the CFTC's anti-fraud regulations. . . .

[T]he Court finds that while the CFTC may liberally choose how to promulgate its rules, the CFTC cannot choose to impose them on entities who the Act clearly excludes. The CFTC's anti-fraud regulations are therefore inapplicable to Defendants. . . .

---

2. Guaranteed Introducing Brokers

The creation of the introducing broker registration was partially intended to put to rest the question of whether a futures commission merchant is liable for the acts of an introducing broker with which it has a relationship. It clarified that futures commission merchants are not ordinarily liable for the acts of an introducing broker with which it transacts and established an introducing broker registration regime intended to provide some safeguards for the public.

The CFTC, however, leaves open the possibility of a futures commission merchant voluntarily guaranteeing the obligations of an introducing broker and allows for, in such circumstances, relief from some regulatory responsibilities for the introducing broker.

To the extent a futures commission merchant can revoke such a guarantee at will, it might allow the introducing broker and futures commission merchant to "have their cake and eat it too," since the futures commission merchant could reduce its exposure to the introducing broker by revoking the guarantee at will – and, until such revocation – the introducing broker could have reduced regulatory responsibilities. The customer of the formerly guaranteed introducing broker may not be aware that the introducing broker is no longer guaranteed and that the customer no longer has the protections originally in place. This, indeed, was the fact-pattern in the below case.

Prestwick Capital Management, Ltd. v. Peregrine Financial Group, Inc.

727 F.3d 646 (7th Cir. 2013)

Barker, District Judge. . . .

[T]he instant lawsuit requires us to clarify the scope of a futures trading "guarantee gone wrong." . . .

In 2009, Prestwick Capital Management Ltd., Prestwick Capital Management 2 Ltd., and Prestwick Capital Management 3 Ltd. (collectively, "Prestwick") sued Peregrine Financial Group, Inc. ("PFG"), Acuvest Inc., Acuvest Brokers, LLC, and two of Acuvest's principals (John Caiazzo and Philip Grey), alleging violations of the Commodity Exchange Act ("CEA"). Prestwick asserted . . . a guarantor liability claim against PFG. After the district court awarded summary judgment to PFG in August 2011, Prestwick moved to dismiss the remaining defendants with prejudice in order to pursue its appeal of right against PFG. . . .

This commodities fraud lawsuit presents a corporation's attempt to recoup investments allegedly depleted during commerce involving an underfunded trading pool. . . .

In August 1983, the CFTC promulgated a final rule setting forth minimum financial benchmarks for [introducing brokers, hereafter "IBs"] . . . [of] $20,000 and permitted IBs to credit toward this balance 50 percent of guarantee or security deposits maintained with FCMs. The current requisite minimum adjusted net capital is $45,000 or "[t]he amount of adjusted net capital required by a registered futures association of which [an IB] is a member." . . . However, an IB "shall be deemed to meet the adjusted net capital requirement" if it is a party to a binding guarantee agreement. . . . A guaranteed IB, in other words, is not subject to the same reporting requirements imposed on an IB that has assumed an independent status. According to the CFTC, this dispensation is appropriate because "the guarantee agreement provides that the FCM . . . will guarantee performance by the [IB] of its obligations under the Act and the rules, regulations, and order thereunder . . . [and] is an alternative means for an [IB] to satisfy the [CFTC's] standards of financial responsibility." . . .

In the case before us, the plaintiff, Prestwick, is a conglomerate of Canadian investment companies. . . . The defendant, PFG, is an Iowa corporation with its principal place of business in Chicago, Illinois; it also conducts business in New York as an active foreign corporation. Importantly, PFG is registered with the CFTC as an FCM that guarantees compliance with the CEA by certain registered IBs, including two of the Acuvest defendants (Acuvest Inc. and Acuvest Brokers, LLC). . . .

In 2004, pursuant to the CFTC regulations discussed *supra*, Acuvest and PFG executed a guarantee agreement ("the 2004 Guarantee Agreement"). The portion of their 2004 Guarantee Agreement that is the focus of this lawsuit provided, in relevant part, as follows:

> PFG guarantees performance by [Acuvest] . . . of, and shall be jointly and severally liable for, all obligations of the IB . . . with respect to the solicitation of and transactions involving all commodity customer, option customer, foreign futures customer, and foreign options customer accounts of the IB entered into on or after the effective date of this Agreement.

Thus, the arrangement between PFG and Acuvest contemplated (1) Acuvest's solicitation of customers and subsequent engagement with customers for business dealings, and (2) PFG's willingness to assure Acuvest's customers that Acuvest would conform its conduct to the mandates of the CEA. Further, as the district court noted, this provision made PFG responsible for any fraudulent conduct engaged in by Acuvest.

Two years later, PFG's compliance director, Susan O'Meara, sent a memorandum to the NFA to inform the NFA of a change in PFG's relationship with Acuvest. This correspondence, titled "Guaranteed IB Termination," was dated August 25, 2006 and advised, "As of August 24, 2006, [PFG] will terminate its guarantee agreement with Acuvest. . . . This termination has been done by mutual consent."

Acuvest and PFG executed an agreement of a slightly different nature the very same month – a "Clearing Agreement for Independent Introducing Broker" ("the 2006 IIB Agreement"). . . . [T]he 2006 IIB Agreement stated that this contract "supersede[d] and replace[d] any and all previous agreements between [Acuvest] and PFG." Under the new arrangement, PFG agreed to "execute[,] buy [,] and sell orders and perform settlement and accounting services for and on behalf of [c]ustomers introduced by [Acuvest]." . . . Acuvest, by contrast, assumed significantly more responsibilities to PFG and its customers. Notably, Acuvest's signature on the 2006 IIB Agreement evinced its consent to:

> comply with the rules and regulations of all relevant regulatory entities, exchanges[,] and self-regulatory organizations related to the purchase and sale of [f]utures [i]nvestments. . . .

This adjustment was consistent with the CFTC's official differentiation between guaranteed and independent IBs: "By entering into the agreement, the [guaranteed IB] is relieved from the necessity of raising its own capital to satisfy minimum financial requirements. In contrast, an independent [IB] must raise its own capital to meet minimum financial requirements."[xiii] Here, Acuvest was accountable for all customer losses, charges, and deficiencies. . . . Acuvest also accepted absolute financial responsibility for its own actions and pledged to indemnify PFG from any harm resulting therefrom. Perhaps the most salient feature of the 2006 IIB Agreement was its treatment of guarantees. As an independent IB, Acuvest was bound by a new indemnification provision: "[Acuvest] guarantees all the financial obligations of the [c]ustomer accounts of [c]ustomers serviced by [Acuvest] and/or carried on the equity run reports produced by PFG for [Acuvest]."

PFG and Acuvest . . . [entered] into yet another agreement ("the 2008 Guarantee Agreement"). As was true of the 2006 IIB Agreement, this contract superseded all previous agreements between Acuvest and PFG. However, the new arrangement restored Acuvest to its prior status as a guaranteed IB. . . . Acuvest's role as an IB eventually intersected with Prestwick. The Acuvest–Prestwick business relationship arose when Acuvest advised Prestwick to become a limited partner in Maxie Partners L.P. ("Maxie"), a New York commodity trading pool. . . . For purposes of the instant litigation, Acuvest was the IB for all of Maxie's accounts. Prestwick elected to join the Maxie trading pool and invested approximately $7,000,000 in that fund. . . . During this time

---

[xiii] U.S. COMMODITY FUTURES TRADING COMM'N, CFTC GLOSSARY, http://www.cftc .gov/consumerprotection/educationcenter/cftc glossary/glossary_ g (last visited July 15, 2013).

period, the Acuvest defendants assumed full responsibility for Maxie's management and investment decisions regarding the account holding Prestwick's funds and maintained open lines of communication with Prestwick.

In April 2007, Prestwick informed Grey (one of Acuvest's executive vice presidents) of its intent to redeem Prestwick's limited partnership interest in Maxie. . . . Believing that Maxie's assets were valued at approximately $20,000,000, Prestwick was understandably alarmed to learn . . . that much of its $7,000,000 investment in Maxie was unavailable. . . .

Ultimately, Prestwick's notice of redemption did not generate the anticipated payout. Prestwick claims to have received only two disbursements of its original investment in the pool – one in August 2007, and the other in October 2007 – totaling approximately $3,000,000. . . . Prestwick's efforts to collect the remaining balance since October 2007 have been wholly unsuccessful. . . .

Prestwick raises . . . for our review . . . whether termination of PFG's guarantee of Acuvest's obligations under the CEA also terminated such protection "for existing accounts opened during the term of the guarantee," a result Prestwick vehemently repudiates. . . .

Prestwick's challenge to the district court's decision regarding the temporal scope of the 2004 Guarantee Agreement is threefold. First . . . Prestwick's suggested construction of the 2004 Guarantee Agreement would render PFG liable for Acuvest's obligations concerning any account opened with PFG "during the term of" that agreement – no matter when any subsequent wrongdoing related to such account occurred. Second . . . [a]ccording to Prestwick, the parties did not intend the 2006 IIB Agreement to end PFG's guarantee of Acuvest's obligations for accounts predating its execution. Third, Prestwick argues that the district court's ruling contravenes significant consumer protection policies underlying the CFTC's regulatory scheme for guaranteed IBs. . . .

The CFTC explicitly addressed the contours of termination in its final rule on "Registration and Other Regulatory Requirements" for IBs, dated August 3, 1983, as follows:

> If [a] guarantee agreement does not expire or is not terminated in accordance with the provisions of § 1.10(j) . . . , it shall remain in effect indefinitely. The [CFTC] wishes to make clear that the termination of a guarantee agreement by an FCM or by an introducing broker, or the expiration of such an agreement, does not relieve any party from any liability or obligation arising from acts or omissions which occurred during the term of the agreement.

48 Fed. Reg. 35,248, 35,265 (citation omitted). This rule corresponds to Title 17, Section 1.10(j) of the Code of Federal Regulations, which provides the protocol for ending a guaranteed IB relationship. Termination of a guarantee agreement may take place at any time during its effective term . . .

[T]he 2006 agreement unequivocally states: "[t]his Agreement supersedes and replaces any and all previous agreements between IB [Acuvest] and PFG." It is difficult to imagine a clearer way in which the parties could have terminated the 2004 agreement. . . .

[R]ecords of the NFA – the organization vested with IB registration authority – verify PFG's status as Acuvest's designated guarantor from June 26, 2004 until August 24, 2006. The same records demonstrate that between August 24, 2006 and July 8, 2008 (one day prior to the "start date" of the 2008 Guarantee Agreement), Acuvest was not a party to any guarantee agreement with a FCM. Without a legally binding agreement establishing such a relationship, Acuvest was not a guaranteed IB from August 24, 2006 until July 9, 2008. The corollary to this historical recitation must be, and is, that in July 2007, when the misconduct of which Prestwick complains allegedly occurred, Acuvest was not a guaranteed IB.

Nonetheless, according to Prestwick, the foregoing records have no bearing on PFG's contractual duties to Acuvest. . . .

[W]e . . . find Prestwick's position perplexing. Nothing within the governing regulations or the "four corners of the contract" remotely indicates that . . . [the 2004 Guarantee Agreement] was to continue in full force with respect to "existing accounts." That Prestwick asks us to impute this intent into the 2004 Guarantee Agreement (or, for that matter, any of the operative documents) is contrary to time-honored principles of contract interpretation. . . . Despite Prestwick's ardent pronouncements that it does not consider the 2004 Guarantee Agreement a perpetual guarantee, we fail to see how else to credit Prestwick's interpretation. . . .

Equally untenable is Prestwick's argument that . . . the 2004 Guarantee Agreement was not terminated. . . . Prestwick asserts that the parties did not intend the 2006 IIB Agreement to end PFG's guarantee of Acuvest's obligations regarding Prestwick's Maxie account because the contract (1) defines "customer" as an entity that opens a "new" account with PFG or transfers an existing account from another FCM to PFG, and (2) "does not mention existing accounts." . . . The fact that the 2006 IIB Agreement covered new accounts does not prompt the inference that the 2004 Guarantee Agreement was not terminated. . . .

Prestwick's third argument regarding termination of the 2004 Guarantee Agreement implicates our understanding of public policy in the area of consumer protection. Prestwick apparently believes that CFTC regulations – and guarantee agreements executed thereunder – have different meanings based on brokers' actions after such agreements are terminated. It is unclear to us why Prestwick would consider this fair or sound policy. . . . [Congress has] expressly disapproved of "impos[ing] vicarious liability on a futures commission merchant for the actions of an in-dependent [broker]." S.REP. NO. 97–384, at 41. . . .

According to PFG, [NFA rules] give FCMs "the responsibility, and hence the authority, to supervise" the guaranteed IB, but "[o]nce the guarantee agreement has been terminated, the FCM no longer has the authority to force this independent legal entity to conform its conduct to the FCM's requirements." Prestwick's most compelling rejoinder is that this argument undercuts a major goal of the CEA and its attendant rules: protecting IBs' customers. . . . We are, of course, sympathetic to the plight of investors, like Prestwick, who may have no idea when a guarantee relationship is severed. Although some due diligence must be expected, we understand that a few weeks may elapse after guarantee termination wherein investors cannot protect themselves from the actions of unguaranteed brokers. This can certainly be an unfortunate result, but it does not authorize us – or even permit us – to require FCMs to close all accounts opened during the term of a severed guarantee agreement with an IB and then reopen those accounts if a new guarantee arises. There is simply no evidence that Congress, through the CEA, intended to place such a burden on FCMs. Thus, despite our sense that the well-being of investors ought to be considered in some fashion in these cases, perhaps by recognizing a right to notice of the end of the guarantee agreement (which would enable the investor to take appropriate self-protective steps), the courts are not the proper place to impose new regulatory requirements.

No policy arguments can overcome the simple fact that the contracts at issue in this lawsuit are definitive. . . . Fairness aside, we are unwilling to resolve a legislative issue through a ruling that would contravene the CEA and established common-law contract rules. Guarantee agreements would simply make no sense if they required parties to look back in time for some FCM that might well be insolvent or no longer in existence. Prestwick's policy arguments, therefore, are untenable in our current legislative and regulatory atmosphere. Although Prestwick may have legitimate grounds to challenge this framework, the place to do so is not before the courts. . . .

D. FLOOR BROKERS

Floor traders, referenced in section A2 above, have privileges to place trades as principal on the trading floor of a designated contract market (physical or virtual, in the case of electronic trading) of a designated contract market. Floor brokers, on the other hand, have privileges to place trades directly on the trading floor of a designated contract market as agent for third party customers.

United States v. Sanders

688 F. Supp. 367 (N.D. Ill. 1988)

Aspen, District Judge:

Currently before this Court is defendant Thompson Sanders' motion to dismiss the indictment. For the reasons stated below, that motion is denied. . . .

The indictment sets forth a scheme in which Sanders and his three co-defendants engaged in fraudulent trading on the Chicago Board of Trade ("CBT"). . . . Sanders and his co-defendants devised a scheme wherein . . . utilizing stolen, bogus and counterfeit CBT trading jackets and identification credentials and with the help of wigs and make-up, the conspirators made risk-free trades on the floor of the CBT. . . .

Proper commodity trading on the floor of the CBT proceeds in the following manner. In order to enter into a trading contract, one must open and maintain a margin account with a Futures Commission Merchant ("FCM"). A FCM is a corporation which accepts orders for the purchase of commodities for future delivery. Margin is money or other property of value which a customer is required to deposit into a commodity trading account as earnest money to demonstrate their good faith that they will pay any losses incurred as a result of entering into commodity futures trades and to ensure future performance on commodity futures trades by customers.

All commodity trading at the CBT is done in a restricted trading area which is closed to the public. [Today, there is also electronic trading which has cryptographic access restrictions.] Access to this area is restricted by CBT rules to authorized CBT members and employees. Trading on the floor of the CBT is conducted by floor brokers who execute trades on behalf of their customers. When a floor broker enters into a contract to buy or sell a particular commodity with another floor broker, the brokers must record the transaction on a trading card or endorse an order listing certain information material to the trade such as the commodity traded, the trading price, the time of the trade, the name of the opposite broker and his member firm. After the brokers fill out the trading cards, the cards are delivered to the brokerage firms employing the respective brokers.

After receiving the trading cards, the information listed by the floor brokers on the cards is entered into the computer records of the clearing house for the CBT. At the end of the trading day, the clearing house for the CBT matches up various buy and sell commodity trades for that day based upon the information initially listed by the floor brokers on the trading cards and subsequently entered into the computer records of the clearing house.

After the clearing house has finished matching up trades, the brokerage firms receive from the clearing house a record of that day's trading activity involving that firm. Based upon this record, the brokerage firm will determine whether to issue a margin call to a customer, that is, a request that the customer deposit additional money into the margin account due to trading losses sustained or trading positions assumed by the customer during that trading day. . . .

It is charged in sum that beginning in May 1986, Sanders and his three co-defendants hatched a plan to fraudulently engage in "risk-free" trading on the CBT. Defendants Sanders and David Pelleu did "steal, obtain and create false, bogus and counterfeit" CBT trading jackets and identification credentials. These items were used by defendants Daniel Dewey and Daniel Kolton to enter restricted CBT trading areas. Dewey would also wear wigs and cosmetic make-up to alter his physical appearance. Dewey would enter the trading area in disguise with bogus identification and trading jackets and would then place orders to buy or sell Treasury Bond commodities with various floor brokers. Dewey would then transfer the trading cards for the trades to Sanders.

Sanders and the others would then determine whether the trades had been profitable or whether there had been a loss. If the trades placed by Dewey turned out to be profitable, the defendants would claim the trade and take the profits. But if the trades lost money, the defendants would not claim the trade. Because these trades had been executed with bogus credentials and while in disguises, the losing commodity trades placed by this conspiracy could not be traced. Thus, the government charges that defendants created a way to engage in truly risk-free trading, only at the expense of the other floor broker's customers. . .

[The Commodity Exchange Act (the "CEA")] makes it a felony for any person to misrepresent himself as a member of a contract market in "handling" or "soliciting" a futures contract order. 7 U.S.C. § 6h states . . .

> It shall be unlawful for any person falsely to represent such person to be a member of a contract market [now this provision applies to all "registered entities," i.e. contract markets, derivatives clearing organizations and swap execution facilities] or the representative or agent of such member, or to be a registrant under this chapter or the representative or agent of any registrant, in soliciting or handling any order or contract for the purchase or sale of any commodity in interstate commerce or for future delivery, or falsely to represent in connection with the handling of any such order or contract that the same is to be or has been executed on, or by or through a member of, any contract market.

Sanders contends that this section, *unambiguously,* makes it only unlawful to defraud *public customers* in the "solicitation" and "handling" of their futures contract orders and not the defrauding of commodity traders and brokers as is alleged in the indictment. The government agrees that the statute is unambiguous, but finds Sanders' interpretation "narrow and misguided." The government fails to read any limitation . . . to prohibit misrepresentations only to public customers. We agree with the government. . . .

[E]ven if there were such a limitation, it would be satisfied in this case. The misrepresentation charged in the indictment occurred when Daniel Dewey, falsely dressed and bearing identification as a floor broker, executed trades on the floor of the CBT with a legitimate floor broker who was led to believe the disguised Dewey was also a legitimate floor broker. . . . [A] floor broker is merely a conduit for a customer. Therefore, when Dewey falsely pretended to be a legitimate floor broker, he was in essence falsely representing himself to the customer upon whose behalf the duped floor broker made the trade. Accordingly, even if we found that § 6h was limited to a situation where the false representation is made to a "*customer,*" we would conclude that the indictment makes such an allegation. . . .

Accordingly, Sanders' motion to dismiss the indictment is denied. It is so ordered.

In the late 1980s the Chicago Board of Trade was rocked by another scandal. An agricultural services company, Archer Daniels Midland, complained about fraud at the Chicago Board of Trade and cooperated with the FBI.[8] At least 4 FBI agents infiltrated the Chicago Board of Trade, pretending to be floor traders or floor brokers and renting apartments in a glitzy Chicago neighborhood, one agent going so far as to wear a gold Rolex and drive a Mercedes-Benz.[9]

Ultimately, a 534–count indictment was brought against 19 defendants.[10] One court described the wrongdoing:

> The defendants consist of two types of floor traders: "locals," who trade on their own accounts [i.e., floor traders], and brokers who execute orders from customers who may be CBOT members, but usually are members of the public trading through brokerage firms [i.e., floor brokers]. The defendants, as well as numerous other traders, both indicted and unindicted, traded contracts for soybeans futures. . . .
>
> At trial, the government presented hundreds of allegedly fraudulent trades executed by the various defendants. The core of the charged crimes involved brokers surreptitiously avoiding . . . [competitively executing trades and, instead, arranging them directly with floor traders, i.e.,] locals at selected prices. These arranged trades, determined without the usual open . . . bid or offer in the market, guaranteed profits to the local [at the expense of the floor broker's customer]. The local would then do one of three things (or some combination) with these profits: he might keep the profits as repayment . . . [to set-off a debt] with the broker; he might hold the profits from the arranged trade as a credit against future . . . [debts]; or he might pass the profits back to the broker who had arranged the trade in

> the first place (i.e., a kickback) or to another trader to whom the broker owed money. . . .

United States v. Ashman, 979 F.2d 469, 475-477 (7th Cir. 1992).

As with the other categories of registrants, the CFTC has broad discretion as to whether or not a party may be registered as a floor broker.

Hirschberg v. Commodity Futures Trading Commission

414 F.3d 679 (7th Cir. 2005)

Kanne, Circuit Judge.

Judd Hirschberg's floor broker registration was revoked after he was convicted of mail fraud in 1991. In 2000, he received a presidential pardon for that conviction, but the Commodity Futures Trading Commission ("CFTC") nevertheless denied his post-pardon application for floor broker registration. Because a pardon does not eliminate the legal determination that Hirschberg was guilty of the crime of which he was convicted, and the crime was properly considered in the CFTC's application process, we affirm the decision of the CFTC and deny Hirschberg's petition for review. . . .

Hirschberg became a registered floor broker in 1985. According to the Commodities [*sic*] Exchange Act, floor brokers buy and sell futures contracts for others on an exchange floor such as that of the Chicago Mercantile Exchange ("CME"), where Hirschberg worked. Floor brokers commonly act as fiduciaries in conducting transactions. They are required to register with the CFTC, which has delegated most of the registration process to the National Futures Association ("NFA"). The CFTC also has the power to revoke registration from floor brokers who violate CFTC or NFA rules.

The CFTC initiated revocation proceedings against Hirschberg in 1991, alleging disqualification under Sections 8(a)(2) (conviction of a felony involving fraud) and 8(a)(3) (for good cause) of the Commodities [*sic*] Exchange Act. Hirschberg had indeed been convicted in federal court on four felony counts of mail fraud and two felony counts of tampering with vehicle identification numbers. These 1991 convictions stemmed from an insurance fraud scheme that took place in 1984, when Hirschberg reported that his car had been stolen and then collected $43,300 from his insurance company. Several years later, evidence was discovered suggesting that Hirschberg had voluntarily transferred the car to a friend and altered its vehicle identification number to hide the crime. On appeal, this court found insufficient evidence to uphold the conviction for identification number tampering, but affirmed the conviction for mail fraud. Hirschberg was ordered to serve three years of probation and pay $40,000 in restitution.

The CFTC proceedings ultimately led to revocation of Hirschberg's registration in 1994. The Administrative Law Judge ("ALJ") presiding over the hearing did not find sufficient evidence of mitigation or rehabilitation to justify Hirschberg keeping his registration. Weighing against Hirschberg was evidence of disciplinary proceedings brought against him by the CME – several years after the 1984 insurance fraud, Hirschberg was disciplined for engaging in pre-arranged trading in violation of CME rules. Hirschberg has made his living since 1994 (earning substantially less than he did as a floor broker) by consulting for trading houses and training young traders.

In 1998, Hirschberg applied for a presidential pardon of his mail fraud conviction, which was granted by President Clinton in 2000. Pardon in hand, he applied to the NFA for registration as a floor broker in July 2001. After a designated subcommittee conducted a hearing, the NFA denied Hirschberg's application. The subcommittee found that Hirschberg's conviction and subsequent revocation of registration subjected him to a Section 8a(2)(A) disqualification based on his prior revocation. Although this merely created a rebuttable presumption that he was unfit for registration, the subcommittee did not find that Hirschberg presented enough mitigating evidence to rebut the presumption of unfitness. The CFTC affirmed the denial of registration in 2004. Hirschberg appeals the denial on the grounds that the CFTC's decision violates the Pardon Clause, due process, and his statutory rights under the Commodities [*sic*] Exchange Act. . . .

[T]he legal effect of a presidential pardon is to preclude further punishment for the crime, but not to wipe out the fact of conviction. The CFTC did not violate the pardon clause by considering the conduct underlying Hirschberg's conviction in determining whether he was qualified to do business as a floor trader, because its decision was grounded in protection of the public rather than in punishing Hirschberg as a convicted felon. Hirschberg's due process and statutory rights arguments also do not justify reversal of the decision to deny his application for registration. . . .

The CFTC denied Hirschberg's 2001 application for registration based on Section 8a(2)(A) of the Commodities [*sic*] Exchange Act, which . . . allows the CFTC to revoke or deny registration of any person "if a prior registration of such person in any capacity has been suspended . . . or has been revoked[.]" The revocation underlying this statutory disqualification was, of course, based on Hirschberg's 1991 conviction for mail fraud. Hirschberg asserts that, because he received a full and unconditional pardon for that conviction, the CFTC's denial unconstitutionally interferes with the presidential pardon power. . . .

The Constitution gives the President "Power to grant Reprieves and Pardons for Offences against the United States, except in cases of impeachment." U.S. Const. art. II § 2. . . .

A pardon in no way reverses the legal conclusion of the courts . . . The effect of a pardon is not to prohibit all *consequences* of a pardoned conviction, but rather to preclude future *punishment* for the conviction. The question we must answer, then, is whether the CFTC's denial of Hirschberg's registration is impermissible punitive action or simply a consequence of the conduct underlying the conviction that the pardon could not erase.

The answer turns on whether the conduct for which Hirschberg was convicted has any bearing on his ability to work as a floor broker. Government licensing agencies may consider conduct underlying a pardoned conviction – without improperly "punishing" the pardoned individual – so long as that conduct is relevant to an individual's qualifications for the licensed position. . . . In cases where governmental action has been held to violate the pardon clause, on the other hand, the pardoned individual is stripped of his rights based not on the conduct underlying the conviction, but on the fact of conviction alone. . . .

The statutory disqualification scheme under which Hirschberg's registration was revoked in 1994 and then denied in 2004 was enacted with the Futures Trading Act of 1982. It was designed to "streamline and simplify the [former] registration procedures to enable the [CFTC] to register fit persons more expeditiously and to remove unfit persons from the industry more promptly." H.R. Rep. No. 97–565, pt. 1, at 50 (1982). Given the fiduciary nature of most of the transactions engaged in by a floor broker, there can be no serious doubt that honesty and integrity are legitimate qualifications for the job. Engaging in fraudulent behavior (such as an insurance scam) demonstrates a serious lack of these qualities. In revoking Hirschberg's original registration, the CFTC was allowed to use the conviction as an authoritative source on whether the fraudulent conduct occurred, theoretically improving efficiency and "freeing resources for the performance of its other important regulatory and oversight functions." That revocation served as presumptive evidence that Hirschberg was unfit to be a floor broker when he reapplied for registration, again eliminating the need for the CFTC to spend time and money determining whether Hirschberg had engaged in fraudulent conduct. Convictions for fraud play into the CFTC's registration process because the conduct underlying such convictions *is* relevant to the business of floor trading, not because the CFTC is interested in further punishing convicted felons. This enables the CFTC to protect the public from unfit floor brokers and to register fit applicants more efficiently.

Further evidence of the CFTC's non-punitive purpose in denying Hirschberg's application is the fact that the conduct underlying Hirschberg's mail fraud conviction would be cause for denial even if he had not been criminally convicted for it. Fraud can be grounds for statutory disqualification when it is the subject of an injunction or of a civil court or administrative ruling in a case to which a government agency is a party. CFTC may also revoke registration "for good cause" . . . which includes any conduct demonstrating moral turpitude, lack of honesty, or financial irresponsibility, with no prior formal proceedings. Hirschberg's registration in 1991 was not revoked because he was a convict per se, but because he engaged in fraudulent conduct that demonstrated the lack of qualities necessary to be a floor broker. He would have met with the same consequences (the 1994 revocation and the 2004 denial of registration) had the fraudulent conduct been proven independent of a criminal conviction.

One further element convinces us that the CFTC was not impermissibly punishing Hirschberg for his pardoned conviction: Hirschberg was given a chance to rebut the presumption that he was unfit to be a floor broker. Hirschberg would have obtained registration in 2004 if he had been able to demonstrate that he would not pose a significant risk to the public. Unfortunately, Hirschberg did not offer enough evidence in mitigation or of rehabilitation to overcome the presumption that he was unfit for floor broker registration – to the contrary, the evidence of CME disciplinary action bolstered the presumption. The fact that the CFTC's procedural scheme provides an applicant with the opportunity to rebut a presumption of unfitness shows that the relevant consideration is not the conviction itself, but the conduct underlying it.

Given the fiduciary nature of transactions made by a floor trader, the CFTC's reasons for denying Hirschberg's application were both prudent and within the law of presidential pardon. The decision was based on concern for protecting the public in an efficient manner rather than on the desire to punish Hirschberg for his criminal conviction. The denial of floor broker registration based on fraudulent conduct underlying a pardoned criminal conviction does not constitute a violation of the pardon clause. . . .

The CFTC's denial of Hirschberg's registration was based on Section 8a(2)(A) of the Commodities [sic] Exchange Act, which states: "[T]he Commission is authorized . . . to refuse to register . . . any person and with such a hearing as may be appropriate to revoke the registration of any person – if a prior registration of such person in any capacity has been suspended . . . or has been revoked[.]" . . . [T]he plain language of this provision does not contain a time limit for underlying suspensions or revocations. Hirschberg argues that the ten-year time limit from Section 8a(2)(D),[xiv] the provision on which his 1994 revocation was based, should be incorporated into Section 8a(2)(A). Because he was convicted in 1991, more than ten years prior to filing his current application, this incorporated time limit would make Section 8a(2)(A) inapplicable to Hirschberg. . . .

Limitations periods are favored in connection with lawsuits to encourage prompt resolution of claims and to prevent a party from being prosecuted or sued after witnesses have become incapacitated due to faded memory or death. Neither these policy reasons nor the tradition of inferring a time limitation are present in the context of disciplinary actions.

[xiv] [N. 1] This provision . . . allows the CFTC to revoke or deny registration to a person who "has been convicted *within ten years* preceding the filing of the application for registration or at any time thereafter of any felony that . . . (iv) involves the violation of section . . . 1341 . . . of Title 18 [mail fraud]." (emphasis added).

Looking at Section 8a as a whole reinforces the notion that a time limitation should not be inferred in Section 8a(2)(A). While the plain language of that provision contains no time limit, some of the other twenty-two subsections laying out grounds for disqualification in Sections 8a(2) and 8a(3) do. This suggests a conscious choice by Congress to require that a person who has lost his registration once must affirmatively show rehabilitation before again obtaining registration, regardless of when the conduct underlying the revocation occurred. . . .

The CFTC violated neither the pardon clause nor principles of due process, because it did not seek to punish Hirschberg for his pardoned federal conviction. The CFTC permissibly and rationally considered the conduct underlying Hirschberg's conviction in ascertaining whether he would be fit to act as a floor broker. Also, we are not compelled to infer a time limitation on the statutory disqualification relied upon by the CFTC. We therefore AFFIRM the decision of the CFTC and deny Hirschberg's petition.

QUESTIONS AND COMMENTS

1. In the wake of the failure of MF Global and Peregrine, the CFTC enacted rules adding further restrictions on the use of customer funds by FCMs. Do you think these efforts will be successful? How can outright fraud, such as occurred with Peregrine, be addressed by regulators?
2. The decision in *Prestwick v. Peregrine* appears to allow for cancellation of a guarantee of an introducing broker by an FCM without notice to customers of the introducing broker. What are ways of allowing FCMs the freedom to cancel contractual relationships while protecting customers of introducing brokers who may not be aware that a guarantee has been cancelled?
3. Customers of securities broker-dealers may be able to avail of Securities Investor Protection Corporation protection and customers of banks may be able to avail of Federal Deposit Insurance Corporation protection. Should a similar regime exist with respect to customer funds held by futures commission merchants?
4. The court in *Prestwick v. Peregrine* notes that "Although Prestwick may have legitimate grounds to challenge this framework, the place to do so is not before the courts." What might the court be suggesting?
5. In *United States v. Sanders* the nation's commodity markets were infiltrated by fraudsters armed with wigs, stolen jackets, and a lot of chutzpah. Is electronic trading more or less susceptible to fraud?

CHAPTER 6 COMMODITY POOL OPERATORS AND COMMODITY TRADING ADVISORS

A. BACKGROUND

As we have seen in the preceding chapters, the CFTC regulates the markets on which commodity futures trade and the intermediaries that operate in those markets. The CFTC also regulates the derivatives investment industry, the subject of this chapter.

It is natural to seek parallels between the SEC's regulation of the securities investment industry and the CFTC's regulation of the derivatives investment industry. However, the SEC's two categories of securities investment registrants, investment advisers and investment companies, are not directly analogous to the two categories of commodities investment registrants, commodity pool operators and commodity trading advisors, despite superficial similarities. While the securities law term "investment adviser" and the derivatives law term "commodity trading advisor" may seem similar, they possess important distinctions. Therefore, practitioners who possess a background in securities law must take care to look at the regulation of the commodities investment industry apart from pre-existing understandings of the securities investment industry's regulatory regime.

In this chapter, first we will evaluate the CFTC's regulation of commodity pool operators. Equally important, particularly for the private fund industry, are commodity pool operators' ability to meet the criteria for several exemptions from CFTC registration requirements.

Second, we will examine the CFTC's regulation of commodity trading advisors and the exemptions that sometimes allow a person otherwise engaged in commodity trading advisory activities to lawfully avoid registration, in addition to other requirements that would otherwise apply.

B. COMMODITY POOLS AND COMMODITY POOL OPERATORS

Unlike investment companies, the closest counterpart to commodity pools under the securities laws, commodity pools do not have a registration obligation. The registration and regulatory burdens are, instead, placed on the operators of commodity pools. The Commodity Exchange Act defines a commodity pool operator as a person "engaged in a business that is of the nature of a commodity pool, investment trust, syndicate, or similar form of enterprise, and who, in connection therewith, solicits, accepts, or receives from others, funds, securities, or property, either directly or through capital contributions, the sale of stock or other forms of securities, or otherwise, for the purpose of trading in commodity interests . . ."[1]

1. Commodity Pools

To understand whether a person is a "commodity pool operator," one must first understand the meaning of a "commodity pool." The Commodity Exchange Act defines a commodity pool as ". . . any investment trust, syndicate, or similar form of enterprise operated for the purpose of trading in commodity interests. . . ."[2] The extent to which the commodity pool must engage in actual trading activities has been a source of controversy.

Lopez v. Dean Witter Reynolds, Inc.

805 F.2d 880 (9th Cir. 1986)

Nelson, Circuit Judge:

Alfred D. Lopez ("Lopez") and Jeanie Reitzell ("Reitzell") appeal the district court dismissal of their claims for violations of the Securities Act of 1933 and the Commodity Exchange Act against Dean Witter Reynolds Inc. ("Dean Witter"). They argue that the district court erred in dismissing these claims because the account in which Reitzell invested was one in which commodities futures contracts were purchased and sold, and therefore constituted both a commodity pool and a security. . . .

This action arose as a result of losses sustained by Lopez and Reitzell in investments which they made through Dean Witter. . . .

[A]ppellants . . . [claimed] that churning[i] by Dean Witter of their investment accounts, constituted a violation of the Securities and Exchange Act of 1934 and

---

[i] [N. 1] Churning is defined to occur "when a broker, exercising control over the volume and frequency of trades, abuses his customer's confidence for personal gain by initiating

Rule 10b–5 promulgated thereunder. In addition, Lopez and Reitzell charged Dean Witter with violating Section 10(b) and Rule 10b–5 by entering into transactions unsuitable to their investment accounts, and they also raised several common law and constructive fraud claims and breach of contract claims.

Reitzell, individually, charged Dean Witter with violating the Commodity Exchange Act by inducing her to invest in its Commodity Guided Account Program ("CGAP").[ii] She also alleged that Dean Witter engaged in mishandling of her CGAP account in violation of the Securities Act of 1933. It is these claims which are the subject of this appeal. . . .

The two issues presented for our review are:

> (1) Whether the district court erred in dismissing appellant's claim alleging a violation of the Commodity Exchange Act, finding that the program in which appellant had invested was not a commodity pool subject to the provisions of the Act; and
>
> (2) Whether the district court erred in dismissing appellant's claim alleging a violation of the Securities Act of 1933, finding that the program in which appellant had invested was not a security subject to the provisions of the Act. . . .

In order to determine whether the commodity accounts which Appellants held with Dean Witter were subject to the provisions of the . . . [Commodity Exchange Act], our first inquiry must be whether Dean Witter was running a commodity pool subject to the requirements of the Commodity Exchange Act. A commodity pool operator ("CPO") . . . is one who is engaged in a business "of the nature of investment trust, syndicate, or *similar* form of enterprise." (emphasis supplied). The Commodity Futures Trading Commission ("CFTC") regulations track the statute. However, no authority binding on us has spelled out the definition more precisely. . . .

Dean Witter argues that in order to constitute a commodity pool, there must be a pro rata sharing by the participants of profits and losses, and since here, there was no such sharing, there was no pool.

---

transactions that are excessive in view of the character of account and the customer's objectives as expressed to the broker."

[ii] [N. 2] The CGAP in which Reitzell invested . . .was a program in which . . . twenty percent [of a customer's deposit was] placed in an account, along with funds from other participants in the CGAP. It was from these combined funds that commodities futures contracts were purchased and sold. However, each investor had separate accounts to which individual account numbers were assigned, and an individual's ability to engage in any purchases or trades of a particular commodity was dependent upon the minimum equity level in that individual's account. Thus, not all accounts traded the same contracts . . .

Appellants on the other hand, argue that at the crucial moment when a trade was executed, it was executed for the combined account, not for any individual customer. Thereafter, the contracts were allocated to individual accounts, and this allocation of contracts performed a function similar, although not identical, to a pro rata division of the profits and losses.

Those courts which have raised the issue require the following factors to be present in a commodity pool: (1) an investment organization in which the funds of various investors are solicited and combined into a single account for the purpose of investing in commodity futures contracts; (2) common funds used to execute transactions on behalf of the *entire* account; (3) participants share pro rata in accrued profits or losses from the commodity futures trading; and (4) the transactions are traded by a commodity pool operator in the name of the pool rather than in the name of any individual investor. . . .

Applying the above requirements to Dean Witter's CGAP, we find that the program did not have the necessary characteristics to constitute a pool. There was a disparity in investment in the individual accounts, and because of the equity level required to engage in certain purchases and trades, not all accounts traded the same contracts. Therefore, not all accounts shared a pro rata profit or loss.

Although the CGAP possessed some of the requirements which have been deemed necessary to constitute a commodity pool . . . the CGAP's characteristics are sufficient to distinguish it from a commodity pool. Furthermore, while we recognize that the speculative commodities market requires strict regulation, we do not find the CGAP to be the type of account which Congress intended to constitute a commodity pool subject to the registration, reporting requirements of the Commodity Futures Exchange Act.

We hold, therefore, that because the CGAP was not a commodity pool, the district court was correct in its finding and grant of summary judgment on this claim. . . .

Reitzell argues that the CGAP constitutes an investment contract and is therefore a security subject to the registration requirement of section 5 of the Securities Act of 1933. . . .

We have previously held that a discretionary commodities trading account, such as the CGAP, is not an investment contract . . .

While we recognize a need for added investor protection, under current case law and the law of this circuit, the district court properly granted summary judgment in favor of Dean Witter. . . .

The court in *Lopez* laid out a four-part test for identifying a commodity pool, stating that a commodity pool is:

> (1) an investment organization in which the funds of various investors are solicited and combined into a single account for the purpose of investing in commodity futures contracts;
> (2) common funds used to execute transactions on behalf of the *entire* account;
> (3) participants share pro rata in accrued profits or losses from the commodity futures trading; and
> (4) the transactions are traded by a commodity pool operator in the name of the pool rather than in the name of any individual investor.

Lopez, 805 F.2d 880, 884 (9th Cir. 1986).

This test implied that a prerequisite to commodity pool status is the existence of actual commodity futures trades.[3] Subsequent courts took up the question of whether, for a commodity pool to exist, actual trading in commodity futures must occur or whether the mere solicitation of funds for that purpose is sufficient. This is an important question for determining the CFTC's enforcement authority with respect to frauds where customer funds are solicited for an ostensible "commodity pool" and, instead, personally appropriated by the party making the solicitation.

Commodity Futures Trading Commission v. Williams D. Perkins

385 Fed. Appx. 251 (3d Cir. 2010)

Barry, Circuit Judge.

This is the second of two actions brought by the Commodity Futures Trading Commission ("CFTC") in response to a multi-million dollar investment fraud scheme involving commodity futures trading. In the first case, we affirmed the judgment entered against the manager of an investment vehicle called Shasta Capital Associates ("Shasta"), holding that Shasta's manager, Equity Financial Group LLC ("Equity Group"), was a "commodity pool operator" ("CPO") for purposes of the Commodity Exchange Act even though Shasta did not actually execute any futures trades and instead forwarded money to another fund – Tech Traders – which executed trades. *Commodity Futures Trading Comm'n v. Equity Fin. Group LLC,* 572 F.3d 150 (3d Cir.2009) ("*Equity*"), cert. denied, *Shimer v. Commodity Futures Trading Comm'n,* 559 U.S. 991, 130 S. Ct. 1737, 176 L.Ed.2d 212 (2010). We consider here whether appellant William Perkins ("Perkins"), the manager of another investment vehicle, Universe Capital Appreciation, LLC ("Universe"), which also did not execute futures trades, and instead forwarded investment funds to Shasta (which in turn forwarded the funds to Tech Traders), was a CPO.

The issue before us is essentially identical to the one we considered in *Equity,* and we respectfully decline Perkins's emphatic invitation to revisit our recently-established precedent. The District Court determined that Perkins acted as a CPO. We agree, and will affirm. . . .

Perkins argues that he was not acting as a CPO because Universe did not participate in "the actual trading itself . . . in the name of the pool entity from a commodity futures trading account that has been opened at a futures commission merchant . . . in the name of the pool." That argument is unavailing in light of our opinion in *Equity,* in which we explained that

> the statute does not require a commodity pool operator to execute commodity futures transactions. The language of the definition lacks an explicit trading requirement, and the remedial purposes of the statute would be thwarted if the operator of a fund could avoid the regulatory scheme simply by investing in another pool rather than trading. If an entity is engaged in a business in the nature of an investment trust, syndicate, or similar form of enterprise, and it solicits, accepts, or receives funds for the purpose of trading, it is a commodity pool operator. The actual trading of commodity futures is not required.

572 F.3d at 158.

Perkins offers numerous reasons why he believes we should revisit *Equity* and follow *Lopez v. Dean Witter Reynolds, Inc.,* 805 F. 2d 880 (9th Cir. 1986), which he insists imposes a trading requirement. In *Equity,* we quoted *Lopez's* four-part test (for determining whether an entity is a commodity pool) and wrote that "[t]he *Lopez* court confronted . . . a different legal question" and "did not address whether a commodity pool operator must itself execute commodity futures transactions." 572 F.3d at 158. Thus, we have already considered the specific arguments Perkins raises, and rejected them.

Perkins nevertheless suggests that we might benefit from "a competent analysis of the legislative history of the . . . [Commodity Exchange Act (the "CEA")] and the expectation of Congress about the direct involvement in commodity futures trading activity by CPO's [sic]." We think our legislative history analysis in *Equity* was more than satisfactory. There, we determined that "[t]he absence of a trading requirement is consistent with the purposes of the" CEA, explaining that "when Congress defined commodity pool operator, it sought to regulate the solicitation of funds from customers and potential customers. And it intended to protect them from harmful conduct, especially fraudulent solicitation. The statute would be undermined if one entity could escape regulation merely by having another execute its trades." *Equity,* 572 F.3d at 157.

Perkins posits that the District Court's analysis of *Lopez* is "a stunning example of why appellate review is . . . necessary," arguing that Universe could not have been a commodity pool because the Universe funds did not remain "combined" in "a single account," but were instead "periodically transferred from time to time over a period of more than two years to . . . Shasta which, in turn, periodically wired the funds . . . to . . . Tech [Traders]." (emphasis omitted.) This argument is without merit. Similar fund transfers took place in *Equity,* and we made clear that such transfers do not offend the definition of "commodity pool." Allowing an investment manager to circumvent regulation merely by transferring funds from one account to another does not comport with Congress's aim of protecting investors.

In his reply brief, Perkins cites thirty-eight provisions of the CFTC regulations and argues that our holding in *Equity* is "in direct conflict with all thirty-eight!"[iii] The cited provisions unsurprisingly require CPOs to provide commodity pool participants with extensive information about the commodity futures trades involving their money. Perkins reads those provisions as signaling that the CFTC itself interprets the terms "commodity pool" and "CPO" more narrowly than we did in *Equity.* However, as we pointed out in *Equity,* other CFTC regulations suggest just the opposite. 572 F.3d at 157 n. 13. The conflicting language of those regulations does not change our conclusion that Congress intended broad definitions of "commodity pool" and "CPO."

Perkins also contends that Universe is distinguishable from Equity Group in that Universe was further from the actual trading (twice removed, instead of just once), and so did not have the character of a commodity pool. Our holding in *Equity* makes clear that the proximity to trading is not an important factor. If the pool is established with the purpose of trading in commodity futures, then the pool is a commodity pool for CEA purposes. *See Equity,* 572 F.3d at 158.

We reject the other arguments made by Perkins and the Tax Accounting Office, Inc., without further discussion. We will affirm the judgment of the District Court.

If the *Lopez* four-part test is adopted *verbatim* it would mean, as one court noted, the exemption of "pool operators who receive investors' money 'for the purpose of trading in any commodity for future delivery,' but simply misappropriate the entire fund without trading in any commodities futures at all."[4] Moreover, it is difficult to reconcile an actual trading requirement with the statutory language defining a commodity pool as "any investment trust,

---

[iii] [N. 2] For example, Perkins quotes regulations requiring that CPOs provide pool participants with certain information which only the trader is likely to know, like the "commodity interest positions liquidated," "unrealized gain or loss in which the pool engaged," and the "total amount of all brokerage commissions during the reporting period." (emphasis omitted.)

syndicate, or similar form of enterprise *operated for the purpose of trading* in commodity interests. . . ." (emphasis added).[5]

On the other hand, another way to look at the *Lopez/CFTC v. Perkins* circuit split is as a narrow versus broad construction of the Commodity Exchange Act's grant of jurisdiction to the CFTC over pooled investments. In the context of fraud, a court might feel compelled to take a broad view of CFTC jurisdiction so that the fraud is addressed. However, it is important to remember that the CFTC is not the only means to address fraud. For example, state prosecutors often have the option of pursuing common law fraud claims. *See Commodity Futures Trading Commission v. R.J. Fitzgerald & Co., Inc.,* 310 F.3d 1321 (11th Cir. 2002).

2. *Commodity Pool Operators*

In the following case related to *CFTC v. Perkins*, the court, building on a finding by a trial court that the trading pool at issue was a commodity pool (ultimately upheld by the Third Circuit in *CFTC v. Perkins*[6]), examined the question of whether parties were commodity pool operators or, alternatively, "associated persons" of a commodity pool operator (for a discussion on associated persons generally, *see* Chapter 5) and, therefore, liable for either failure to register as a commodity pool operator or as associated persons of a commodity pool operator. Additionally – in what should be a salutary caution to lawyers – the internal counsel for the putative commodity pool, was charged with aiding and abetting the failure to register by the operators of the commodity pool.

Commodity Futures Trading Commission v. Equity Financial Group, LLC

2006 WL 3751911 (D.N.J. Dec. 18, 2006)

Kugler, United States District Judge.

Before the Court is a motion by Plaintiff Commodity Futures Trading Commission for partial summary judgment against Defendants Equity Financial Group, Robert W. Shimer and Vincent J. Firth with respect to charges that they violated . . . the Commodities [*sic*] Exchange Act . . . In addition, Plaintiff moves for summary judgment with respect to the charge that Defendant Shimer aided and abetted . . . [Commodity Exchange Act violations]. For the reasons provided below, Plaintiff's motion will be granted in part and denied in part. . . .

The motions presently before the Court relate to the role of Robert W. Shimer ("Shimer"), Vincent J. Firth ("Firth") and Equity Financial Group, LLC ("Equity"), (collectively "Equity Defendants"), in a multi-million dollar commodity fraud operated by Defendants Tech Traders and its president Coyt Murray ("Murray"). Between June 2001 and April 2004, Tech Traders allegedly solicited over $47 million in investments by claiming to employ a portfolio trading system that guaranteed significant annual returns. While Tech Traders and its supposedly independent certified public accountant ("CPA"), Defendant J. Vernon Abernethy ("Abernethy"), reported substantial monthly and quarterly gains, Tech Traders was actually hemorrhaging money at a remarkable rate, resulting in losses in excess of $20 million. Tech Traders lost at least $7 million in trading commodity futures contracts, and unlawfully appropriated investors' funds to pay salaries, expenses, and make disbursements under the guise of profit.

The Equity Defendants' liability arises from their control and operation of a related investment group, Shasta Capital Associates, LLC ("Shasta"), which was essentially a feeder fund for Tech Traders. The Commodity Futures Trading Commission ("CFTC" or "Plaintiff") alleges that the Equity Defendants solicited approximately $15 million from 74 investors between June 2001 and March 2004, for the purpose of investing in Tech Traders. . . . Upon receipt, investor funds were deposited into Shimer's attorney escrow account and then transmitted to Tech Traders. . . .

Plaintiff CFTC alleges that because Equity failed to register with CFTC as a Commodity Pool Operator ("CPO"), Equity violated 7 U.S.C. § 6m(1) when it allegedly used instrumentalities of interstate commerce, such as the telephone and the mail, in connection with its business as a CPO. Equity Defendants do not directly address this count in their opposition papers. Rather, they continue to insist that Shasta is not a "commodity pool," the threshold issue for bringing this action under the jurisdiction of the CFTC. . . .

This Court previously held that Shasta constituted a commodity pool. *See Commodity Futures Trading Comm'n v. Equity Fin. Group,* No. 04-1512, 2006 WL 3359418 (D.N.J. Nov. 16, 2006); *see also Commodity Futures Trading Comm'n v. Equity Fin. Group,* No. 04-1512, 2005 WL 2864784 (D.N.J. Oct. 4, 2005). Likewise, the Court concludes that Equity is the CPO for Shasta, because Equity solicited funds from investors, pooled those funds, and invested them in futures trading through Tech Traders. . . .

The question now before the Court is whether Equity used the mails and other instrumentalities of interstate commerce in connection with its business as a CPO. . . .

The evidence demonstrates that Equity, acting as an unregistered CPO, used instrumentalities of interstate commerce, i.e., the telephone, in connection with its business. Therefore, the Court . . . grants Plaintiff's motion for summary judgment with regard to this count. . . .

Plaintiff also moves for summary judgment on the charge that Defendant Shimer aided and abetted Equity's failure to register as a CPO.

The Act provides that:

> Any person who commits, or who willfully aids, abets, counsels, commands, induces, or procures the commission of, a violation of any of the provisions of this chapter, or any of the rules, regulations, or orders issued pursuant to this

> chapter, or who acts in combination or concert with any other person in any such violation, or who willfully causes an act to be done or omitted which if directly performed or omitted by him or another would be a violation of the provisions of this chapter or any of such rules, regulations, or orders may be held responsible for such violation as a principal.

7 U.S.C. § 13c(a).

Plaintiff asserts that Defendant Shimer "had the requisite knowledge that Equity was a CPO . . . because he was a lawyer . . . and [had] been registered as an [Associated Person] of a CPO before." Although the evidence supports Plaintiff's assertions regarding Shimer's status as a lawyer and as a registered Associated Person of another CPO, the evidence does not conclusively establish that Defendant Shimer acted willfully. In his deposition testimony, Defendant Firth stated that Defendant Shimer researched whether Shasta, Equity, or any individuals needed to register with CFTC. Firth further testified that Shimer concluded that registration was not required, and his findings were subsequently verified by a "firm." Given this evidence, there is a genuine issue of material fact as to whether Defendant Shimer willfully violated the Act by failing to register Equity as a CPO. Therefore, Plaintiff's motion for summary judgment on the aiding abetting count associated with 7 U.S.C. § 6m(1) is denied. . . .

Plaintiff CFTC [also] alleges that Defendants Firth and Shimer violated 7 U.S.C. § 6k(2) of the Act by failing to register as Associated Persons ("APs") of the CPO. . . .

The question now before the Court is whether Defendants Shimer and Firth are APs under the Act, and if so, whether they registered with CFTC. Courts define an AP as someone who "engage[s] in the solicitation of customers' orders." *Miller v. Commodities Future Trading Comm'n,* 197 F.3d 1227, 1229 (9th Cir. 1999); *see also Commodities* [*sic*] *Future Trading Comm'n v. Sidoti,* 178 F.3d 1132, 1134 (11th Cir. 1999) (defining APs as "salespeople" for the brokerage house).

The record demonstrates that Shimer and Firth acted as APs for Equity. . . . [T]he deposition testimony of Defendant Firth, as well as Nicholas Stevenson, referenced telephone conversations during which Defendant Firth solicited prospective investors. Stevenson further elaborated that his understanding was that Defendant Firth was the "marketing sales guy" for the CPO, and that Defendant Shimer was not only the "legal representative" for Shasta, but that he also played a "meaningful role getting investors" because he was an attorney, and his credentials made potential investors more comfortable because the investors assumed that Shimer, as member of the bar, performed the proper due diligence. In addition, the record demonstrates that Defendant Shimer personally referred potential investors to Shasta.

Finally, the record demonstrates that neither Defendant Firth, nor Defendant Shimer, were registered as APs for Equity. . . .

This Court previously held that Defendant Shimer acted as an AP for Shasta, a CPO. . . . [T]he next inquiry is whether Shimer used the "mails or any means or instrumentality of interstate commerce" to "engage[ ] in any transaction, practice or course of business which operate[d] as a fraud or deceit on any client or participant or prospective client or participant."

CFTC offers uncontroverted evidence that Shimer drafted the [private placement memorandum] which touted the Tech Traders' system and performance . . .

In addition, there were signs throughout the relationship with Murray and Tech Traders that there was a problem. . . .

Because Shimer, who had a fiduciary relationship to Shasta's investors, intentionally ignored the numerous and varied warning signs regarding Tech Traders and Murray, his lack of action had the effect of perpetrating a fraud on Shasta's investors. In addition, Shimer used the internet to post . . . [the private placement memorandum] on the Shasta website, and he communicated with the CPAs, potential investors, and Murray via e-mail. . . .

Note that in *CFTC v. Equity Financial Group* at issue were also allegations that Equity failed to register as a commodity trading advisor, discussed below in section C. The court ruled in favor of the defendants and then, on a subsequent motion for reconsideration filed by the CFTC, found a violation of a failure to register as a commodity trading advisor by Tech Trader, Inc., and aiding and abetting liability for the attorney, Robert Shimer.[7] The Third Circuit subsequently affirmed the district court's rulings.[8]

C. COMMODITY TRADING ADVISORS

1. Background

The Commodity Exchange Act regulates as a commodity trading advisor, with some exceptions described below herein and in section D, any person who "for compensation or profit, engages in the business of advising others, either directly or through publications, writings, or electronic media, as to the value of or the advisability of trading in [among others] any contract of sale of a commodity for future delivery [or] for compensation or profit, and as part of a regular business, issues or promulgates analyses or reports concerning [among others] any contract of sale of a commodity for future delivery."[9]

The following are excluded from the definition of commodity trading advisor so long as "the furnishing of such services . . . is solely incidental to the conduct of their business or profession"[10]:

> (i) any bank or trust company or any person acting as an employee thereof;
> (ii) any news reporter, news columnist, or news editor of the print or electronic media, or any lawyer, accountant, or teacher;
> (iii) any floor broker or futures commission merchant;
> (iv) the publisher or producer of any print or electronic data of general and regular dissemination, including its employees;
> (v) the fiduciary of any defined benefit plan that is subject to the Employee Retirement Income Security Act of 1974 (29 U.S.C. 1001 et seq.); [and]
> (vi) any contract market. . . .

Commodity Exchange Act § 1a(12)(B).

The CFTC also has the authority to broaden this exemption by rule, which it has done. We will analyze the CFTC's regulatory exemptions in section D below.

2. *Constitutional Issues*

The provision of advice, whether "directly or through publications, writings, or electronic media" or otherwise, is a speech activity. The requirement to register as a commodity trading advisor restricts speech, thereby potentially conflicting with the First Amendment's imperative that "Congress shall make no law respecting an establishment of religion, or prohibiting the free exercise thereof; or abridging the freedom of speech, or of the press . . ."[11] The Supreme Court has visited this question in the context of the Securities and Exchange Commission's regulation of securities investment advisors. Though the Supreme Court ultimately decided the case on narrower grounds without the need to address the constitutional issues, the *obiter* analysis is instructive, as is the separate opinion of Justice White (with Chief Justice Rehnquist's concurrence), which is grounded in the First Amendment.

The free speech questions stemming from the regulation of financial advisory activities are nearly identical whether applied to securities or derivatives, despite the otherwise distinct regimes for regulating securities investment advisors and commodity trading advisors.

Lowe v. Securities and Exchange Commission

472 U.S. 181 (1985)

Justice Stevens delivered the opinion of the Court.

The question is whether petitioners may be permanently enjoined from publishing nonpersonalized investment advice and commentary in securities newsletters because they are not registered as investment advisers under . . . the Investment Advisers Act of 1940 (Act).

Christopher Lowe is the president and principal shareholder of Lowe Management Corporation. From 1974 until 1981, the corporation was registered as an investment adviser under the Act. During that period Lowe was convicted of misappropriating funds of an investment client, of engaging in business as an investment adviser without filing a registration application with New York's Department of Law, of tampering with evidence to cover up fraud of an investment client, and of stealing from a bank. Consequently, on May 11, 1981, the Securities and Exchange Commission (Commission), after a full hearing before an Administrative Law Judge, entered an order revoking the registration of the Lowe Management Corporation, and ordering Lowe not to associate thereafter with any investment adviser.

In fashioning its remedy, the Commission took into account the fact that petitioners "are now solely engaged in the business of publishing advisory publications." The Commission noted that unless the registration was revoked, petitioners would be "free to engage in all aspects of the advisory business" and that even their publishing activities afforded them "opportunities for dishonesty and self-dealing."

A little over a year later, the Commission commenced this action by filing a complaint in the United States District Court for the Eastern District of New York, alleging that Lowe, the Lowe Management Corporation, and two other [related] corporations, were violating the Act, and that Lowe was violating the Commission's order. The principal charge in the complaint was that Lowe and the three corporations (petitioners) were publishing two investment newsletters and soliciting subscriptions for a stock-chart service. The complaint alleged that, through those publications, the petitioners were engaged in the business of advising others. . . .

Although three publications are involved in this litigation, only one need be described. A typical issue of the Lowe Investment and Financial Letter contained general commentary about the securities and bullion markets, reviews of market indicators and investment strategies, and specific recommendations for buying, selling, or holding stocks and bullion. The newsletter advertised a "telephone hotline" over which subscribers could call to get current information. The number of subscribers to the newsletter ranged from 3,000 to 19,000. It was advertised as a semimonthly publication, but only eight issues were published in the 15 months after the entry of the 1981 order.

Subscribers who testified at the trial criticized the lack of regularity of publication, but no adverse evidence concerning the quality of the publications was offered. There was no evidence that Lowe's criminal convictions were related to the publications; no evidence that Lowe had engaged in any trading activity in any securities that were the subject of advice or comment in the publications; and no contention that any of the information published in the advisory services had been false or materially misleading. . . .

A splintered panel of the Court of Appeals for the Second Circuit . . . held that petitioners were engaged in business as "investment advisers" within the meaning of the Act. It concluded that the Act does not distinguish between person-to-person advice and impersonal advice given in printed publications. . . .

[T]he Court of Appeals rejected petitioners' constitutional claim, reasoning that this case involves "precisely the kind of regulation of commercial activity permissible under the First Amendment."

In order to evaluate the parties' constitutional arguments, it is obviously necessary first to understand, as precisely as possible, the extent to which the Act was intended to regulate the publication of investment advice. . . . Moreover, in view of the fact that we should "not decide a constitutional question if there is some other ground upon which to dispose of the case," and the further fact that the District Court and the dissenting judge in the Court of Appeals both believed that the case should be decided on statutory grounds, a careful study of the statute may either eliminate, or narrowly limit, the constitutional question that we must confront. . . .

One of the statutory exclusions [in the Act] is for "the publisher of any bona fide newspaper, news magazine or business or financial publication of general and regular circulation."[12] Although neither the text of the Act nor its legislative history defines the precise scope of this exclusion, two points seem tolerably clear. Congress did not intend to exclude publications that are distributed by investment advisers as a normal part of the business of servicing their clients. . . . Congress, plainly sensitive to First Amendment concerns, wanted to make clear that it did not seek to regulate the press through the licensing of nonpersonalized publishing activities. . . .

The exclusion itself uses extremely broad language that encompasses any newspaper, business publication, or financial publication provided that two conditions are met. The publication must be "bona fide," and it must be "of regular and general circulation." Neither of these conditions is defined, but the two qualifications precisely differentiate "hit and run tipsters" and "touts" from genuine publishers. Presumably a "bona fide" publication would be genuine in the sense that it would contain disinterested commentary and analysis as opposed to promotional material disseminated by a "tout." Moreover, publications with a "general and regular" circulation would not include "people who send out bulletins from time to time on the advisability of buying and selling stocks" or "hit and run tipsters." Because the content of petitioners' newsletters was completely disinterested, and because they were offered to the general public on a regular schedule, they are described by the plain language of the exclusion. . . .

The Act was designed to apply to those persons engaged in the investment-advisory profession – those who provide personalized advice attuned to a client's concerns, whether by written or verbal communication. The mere fact that a publication contains advice and comment about specific securities does not give it the personalized character that identifies a professional investment adviser. Thus, petitioners' publications do not fit within the central purpose of the Act because they do not offer individualized advice attuned to any specific portfolio or to any client's particular needs. On the contrary, they circulate for sale to the public at large in a free, open market-a public forum in which typically anyone may express his views.

The language of the exclusion, read literally, seems to describe petitioners' newsletters. Petitioners are "publishers of any bona fide newspaper, news magazine or business or financial publication." The only modifier that might arguably disqualify the newsletters are the words "bona fide." Notably, however, those words describe the publication rather than the character of the publisher; hence Lowe's unsavory history does not prevent his newsletters from being "bona fide." . . . Moreover, there is no suggestion that they contained any false or misleading information, or that they were designed to tout any security in which petitioners had an interest. Further, petitioners' publications are "of general and regular circulation." Although the publications have not been "regular" in the sense of consistent circulation, the publications have been "regular" in the sense important to the securities market: there is no indication that they have been timed to specific market activity, or to events affecting or having the ability to affect the securities industry. . . .

We therefore conclude that petitioners' publications fall within the statutory exclusion for bona fide publications and that none of the petitioners is an "investment adviser" as defined in the Act. It follows that neither their unregistered status, nor the Commission order barring Lowe from associating with an investment adviser, provides a justification for restraining the future publication of their newsletters. It also follows that we need not specifically address the constitutional question we granted certiorari to decide. . . .

Justice White, with whom the Chief Justice and Justice Rehnquist join, concurring in the result.

The issue in this case is whether the Securities and Exchange Commission may invoke the injunctive remedies of the Investment Advisers Act to prevent an unregistered adviser from publishing newsletters containing investment advice that is not specifically tailored to the needs of individual clients. The Court holds that it may not because the activities of petitioner Lowe (hereafter petitioner) do not make him an investment adviser covered by the Act. For the reasons that follow, I disagree with this improvident construction of the statute. In my view, petitioner is an investment adviser subject to regulation and sanction under the Act. I concur in the judgment, however, because to prevent petitioner from publishing at all is inconsistent with the First Amendment. . . .

[O]ur duty to avoid constitutional questions through statutory construction is not unlimited: it is subject to the condition that the construction adopted be "fairly possible." As Chief Justice Taft warned, "amendment may not be substituted for construction, and . . . a court may not exercise legislative functions to save the law from conflict with constitutional limitation." *Yu Cong Eng v. Trinidad,* 271 U.S. 500, 518, 46 S. Ct. 619, 623, 70 L. Ed. 1059 (1926). . . .

When the choice facing a court is between finding a particular application of a statute unconstitutional and adopting a construction of the statute that avoids the difficulty but at the same time materially deviates from the legislative plan and frustrates permissible applications, the choice of constitutional adjudication may well be preferable. . . .

Although petitioner does not offer his subscribers investment advice specifically tailored to their individual needs and engages in no direct communications with them, he undeniably "engages in the business of advising others . . . through publications . . . as to the value of securities" and "issues or promulgates analyses or reports concerning securities." Thus, he falls outside the definition of an "investment adviser" only if each of his publications qualifies as a "bona fide newspaper, news magazine or business or financial publication of general and regular circulation." The question is whether the "bona fide publications" exception is to be construed so broadly as to exclude from the definition all persons whose advisory activities are carried out solely through publications offering impersonal investment advice to their subscribers. . . .

If the [bona fide publications] exception is expanded to include more than just publications that are not primarily vehicles for distributing investment advice, it is difficult to imagine any workable definition that does not sweep in all publications that are not personally tailored to individual clients. . . .

The aim of the Act is the protection of the investing public against fraud or manipulation on the part of advisers. Viewed in light of this purpose, a publication that is no more than a vehicle for investment advice is an obvious target for regulatory measures: it makes sense to treat the entire publication as an adviser and to impose liability on the publication itself in the case of fraud or manipulation. On the other hand, the publisher of a publication that presents diverse forms of information and is not narrowly focused on the provision of investment advice is not so likely to engage in abusive practices. . . .

Nothing in the legislative history of the statute supports a construction of "investment adviser" that would exclude persons who offer investment advice only through such publications as newsletters and reports. . . .

The question is whether the First Amendment permits the Federal Government so to prohibit petitioner's publication of investment advice. . . .

This issue involves a collision between the power of government to license and regulate those who would pursue a profession or vocation and the rights of freedom of speech and of the press guaranteed by the First Amendment. . . . Regulations on entry into a profession, as a general matter, are constitutional if they "have a rational connection with the applicant's fitness or capacity to practice" the profession. *Schware v. Board of Bar Examiners,* 353 U.S. 232, 239, 77 S. Ct. 752, 756, 1 L.Ed.2d 796 (1957).

The power of government to regulate the professions is not lost whenever the practice of a profession entails speech. . . .

Perhaps the most obvious example of a "speaking profession" that is subject to governmental licensing is the legal profession. Although a lawyer's work is almost entirely devoted to the sort of communicative acts that, viewed in isolation, fall within the First Amendment's protection, we have never doubted that "[a] State can require high standards of qualification, such as good moral character or proficiency in its law, before it admits an applicant to the bar. . . ." *Schware v. Board of Bar Examiners, supra,* 353 U.S. at 239, 77 S. Ct., at 756. . . .

The Government's position is that these same principles support the legitimacy of its regulation of the investment advisory profession, whether conducted through publications or through personal client-adviser relationships. . . .

But the principle that the government may restrict entry into professions and vocations through licensing schemes has never been extended to encompass the licensing of speech *per se* or of the press. At some point, a measure is no longer a regulation of a profession but a regulation of speech or of the press . . .

One who takes the affairs of a client personally in hand and purports to exercise judgment on behalf of the client in the light of the client's individual needs and circumstances is properly viewed as engaging in the practice of a profession. . . . Where the personal nexus between professional and client does not exist, and a speaker does not purport to be exercising judgment on behalf of any particular individual with whose circumstances he is directly acquainted, government regulation ceases to function as legitimate regulation of professional practice with only incidental impact on speech; it becomes regulation of speaking or publishing as such, subject to the First Amendment's command that "Congress shall make no law . . . abridging the freedom of speech, or of the press." . . .

The application of the Act's enforcement provisions to prevent unregistered persons from engaging in the business of publishing investment advice for the benefit of any who would purchase their publications, however, is a direct restraint on freedom of speech and of the press . . .

Not all restrictions on speech are impermissible. . . . Under the commercial speech doctrine, restrictions on commercial speech that directly advance a substantial governmental interest may be upheld. . . .

I do not believe it is necessary to the resolution of this case to determine whether petitioner's newsletters contain fully protected speech or commercial speech. The Act purports to make it unlawful for petitioner to publish newsletters containing investment advice and to authorize an injunction against such publication. The ban extends as well to legitimate, disinterested advice as to advice that is fraudulent, deceptive, or manipulative. Such a flat prohibition or prior restraint on speech is, as applied to fully protected speech, presumptively invalid and may be sustained only under the most extraordinary circumstances. . . .

But even where mere "commercial speech" is concerned, the First Amendment permits restraints on speech only when they are narrowly tailored to advance a legitimate governmental interest. The interest here is certainly legitimate: the Government wants to prevent investors from falling into the hands of scoundrels and swindlers. The means chosen, however, is extreme. . . . Accordingly, I would hold that the Act, as applied to prevent petitioner from publishing investment advice altogether, is too blunt an instrument to survive even the reduced level of scrutiny called for by restrictions on commercial speech. . . .

The Second, Fifth, and Seventh Circuits have, in the context of the CFTC's regulation of commodity trading advisors, examined the First Amendment questions raised by *Lowe v. SEC.*[13] Moreover, in the case below, these First Amendment questions have arisen in the context of a non-traditional medium, a computer program and the advertisements touting the computer program.

Commodity Futures Trading Commission v. Vartuli

228 F.3d 94 (2d Cir. 2000)

Sack, Circuit Judge:

The Commodity Futures Trading Commission (the "Commission" or the "CFTC"), an independent federal regulatory agency charged with the administration and enforcement of the Commodity Exchange Act (the "CEA"), and the regulations promulgated thereunder brought a civil enforcement action . . . against defendants AVCO Financial Corp., Anthony Vartuli and J. Michael Gent. In its complaint, the Commission claimed that the defendants had violated the CEA by manufacturing, selling and advertising a computer program called "Recurrence," which the defendants fraudulently claimed provided profitable trading opportunities for its purchasers and users in the market for currency futures. . . .

The district court . . .conducted a bench trial [and] entered judgment against AVCO and Vartuli . . . *See CFTC v. Avco Fin. Corp.,* 28 F.Supp.2d 104, 122 (S.D.N.Y.1998) (*"Avco II"*). The complaint against Gent was dismissed in its entirety. The court issued a permanent injunction against AVCO and Vartuli and ordered the disgorgement of the profits that they had garnered from the sale of Recurrence. . . .

Because we agree that AVCO and Vartuli violated the CEA, we affirm the district court's holding to that effect, although on somewhat different grounds. Because the conduct enjoined by the district court included the dissemination of Recurrence as speech and the district court did not first engage in prior restraint analysis, however, we conclude that the injunctive relief granted by the district court is in part unconstitutional, and to that extent we reverse and remand for the injunction to be modified. . . .

In 1989 AVCO, of which Vartuli was the sole shareholder, began marketing a set of materials called the "Recurrence" system, which Vartuli had developed with defendant Gent. Five versions of Recurrence were eventually produced (Recurrence I–V), the first two in book form and the latter three as computer software on disk. In this appeal, we are concerned principally with the computerized versions.

AVCO told its customers to obtain a market reporting service to feed current market prices for Swiss franc future contracts (or, for Recurrence V, Japanese yen future contracts) into a computer loaded with the Recurrence program. Recurrence would then analyze the transactions taking place in the futures market and give the user instantaneous "buy" or "sell" signals. AVCO claimed that following these signals would enable Recurrence users to trade futures contracts profitably. . . .

In addition to selling the system, AVCO gave occasional supplemental advice to Recurrence users by telephone. It also provided customers with a list of "authorized brokers" who were willing to trade for the account of an AVCO customer using the Recurrence system if the purchaser of the system did not want to order each specific transaction him or herself. . . .

The advertising made clear that Recurrence was being sold as a system for trading commodities futures, and that for the system to function properly its commands were to be followed explicitly. . . .

AVCO advertised that "Recurrence III makes money automatically," "the system turned a $10,000 trading account into a $544,704 fortune – a return of 833% per year." . . . But AVCO's claims were based on computer-generated hypothetical use of the system rather than actual trades. . . .

The results of actual trading using the Recurrence system did not live up to AVCO's promotional claims. The district court found that trading as directed by the Recurrence system, whether conducted by individuals or "authorized broker[s]," resulted in substantial losses. . . .

[T]he [district] court found that AVCO's representations about the Recurrence system's level of risk and past performance were material, false, misleading, and made with scienter [and] . . . that AVCO was in fact a CTA even though it had never registered as one, and that AVCO's actions were therefore subject to the regulations governing CTA conduct. . . .

Because the district court concluded that AVCO was a CTA and AVCO concededly never registered with the Commission, the district court held that AVCO was liable . . . [for] failure to register as a CTA. . . .

[T]he court permanently enjoined AVCO and Vartuli from acting as CTAs, trading in commodities, and soliciting customers for commodities trading. . . .

On appeal, Vartuli argues that . . . a software publisher such as AVCO does not fall within the statutory definition of a CTA; that if software publishers are CTAs then the CEA licensing scheme violates the First Amendment; [and] that AVCO's customers were not "clients." . . .

We conclude that AVCO meets the statutory definition of a CTA and affirm the district court's holding that AVCO violated the fraud provisions applicable to CTAs. Those provisions apply to CTAs irrespective of whether they are "exempt from registration under the Act," so the question of whether the CEA's registration requirement would be unconstitutional as applied to AVCO is independent from the question of whether AVCO is a CTA for purposes of the remainder of the Act. . . .

[T]he term "commodity trading advisor" [as defined by the CEA] means any person who –

> (i) for compensation or profit, engages in the business of advising others, either directly or through publications, writings, or electronic media, as to the value of or the advisability of trading in –
> (I) any contract of sale of a commodity for future delivery made or to be made on or subject to the rules of a contract market; . . . or
> (ii) for compensation or profit, and as part of a regular business, issues or promulgates analyses or reports concerning any of the activities referred to in clause (i).

[The definition of commodity trading advisor excludes] certain classes of people and entities from this definition, however. Relevant for our purposes, they exclude both "any news reporter, news columnist, or news editor of the print or electronic media," and "the publisher or producer of any print or electronic data of general and regular dissemination, including its employees," provided that "the furnishing of such [advisory services as described] . . . is solely incidental to the conduct of their business or profession."

There is no dispute that as the district court found, AVCO advised others through the electronic media, for profit, as to "the value or the advisability of trading in" futures contracts for Swiss francs and Japanese yen. . . .

The question thus becomes whether AVCO fits within the relevant CEA exclusions from the definition of CTA. Based upon the plain language of the statute it does not. The electronic data it produced were not "general[ly] and regular[ly] disseminat[ed]." And the information about the currency futures markets provided by Recurrence was not "solely incidental" to the conduct of AVCO's business; it *was* AVCO's business.

Vartuli relies on *Lowe v. SEC,* 472 U.S. 181, 105 S. Ct. 2557, 86 L.Ed.2d 130 (1985), to argue that one of the exclusions must nonetheless apply.

Because the *Lowe* court, in order to avoid the First Amendment issue, read the Investment Advisers Act's registration provision to apply only to personalized communications, Vartuli would have us read *Lowe* to state, by implication, that we must construe the CEA's general definition of CTA to include only those who engage in personalized communications. To do otherwise, he argues, would render the CEA, or at least its registration provision . . ., unconstitutional.

But *Lowe* was decided on the basis of the language and history of the Investment Advisers Act. The *Lowe* court . . . refused to reach the constitutional question. Thus *Lowe* provides us with neither a binding interpretation of the CEA, which was not the subject of the litigation before the Court, nor a constitutional analysis of the Investment Advisers Act.

We are thus left where we began, with the statutory language of the CEA. First, to fit within the exclusion, AVCO's data had to be "of general and regular dissemination." . . . [As] the Supreme Court reasoned when analyzing the identical phrase in the Investment Advisers Act, regular dissemination requires that there be " . . . no indication that [dissemination] ha[s] been timed to specific market activity." In this case, the petitioners' recommendations were provided by software that was programmed to "speak" only when certain market conditions were met. Thus, the petitioners' recommendations were timed to particular market activity and not "regularly" disseminated.

Second, whereas the Investment Advisers Act excluded from its registration requirement "the publisher of any bona fide newspaper, news magazine or business or financial publication of general and regular circulation," the CEA exclusion from its definition of a CTA applies to publishers and disseminators of information only if "the furnishing of such services . . . is solely incidental to the conduct of their business or profession." The publishing of Recurrence was AVCO's primary business. The exclusion therefore does not cover AVCO, and for purposes of . . . the complaint AVCO was a CTA. . . .

[Vartuli] argues, however, that AVCO did not violate the . . . [Commodity Exchange Act and CFTC rules] because those provisions apply only to frauds committed by a CTA upon a "client or participant or prospective client or participant." . . .

One would not ordinarily think of a purchaser of software as a "client" of the seller of the software, even if the purpose of the software was to tell the purchaser when to buy and sell futures contracts or other securities. . . .

The Commission has suggested to us that [this] issue was not raised in the district court, and Vartuli has not established that it was. . . .

The district court was right to ignore the issue if it was not litigated before the court. . . . We therefore decline to reach this question, at least at this time. . . .

The district court concluded that treating AVCO as a CTA, and therefore enjoining and sanctioning the defendants . . . for the fraud in which the defendants engaged, avoided constitutional infirmity because Recurrence "constituted personalized investment advice." *AVCO II,* 28 F.Supp.2d at 119. The emphasis on "personal" advice comes from *Lowe.* 472 U.S. at 191–96, 105 S. Ct. 2557. *Lowe*'s holding was based on the Investment Advisers Act, not the Constitution. It therefore does not provide a framework for analysis of the constitutional issues raised on this appeal.

We are also not as certain as was the district court that AVCO provided "personalized investment advice." The advice was not personal in the sense that the defendants learned about the needs, resources and sophistication of individual clients and gave individualized advice based upon that information. . . .

But we agree with the district court nonetheless that there are no constitutional impediments to the court's judgment in this respect. . . . [T]he district court found, and we agree, that the defendants "made false and misleading representations to customers regarding the past profitability and track record of Recurrence in an effort to induce customers to purchase the program and follow Recurrence's recommendations." *Avco II,* 28 F. Supp. 2d at 119. It has long been understood that such "[f]rauds may be denounced as offenses and punished by law."

Moreover, . . . [t]he speech [at issue] . . . is . . . not statements made *by* Recurrence, but those made in the advertisements *for* Recurrence. These communications about Recurrence did "no more than propose a commercial transaction," between AVCO and its prospective customers. They were, therefore, commercial speech . . . It has long been firmly established that "[f]or commercial speech to come within [the protection of the First Amendment], it at least must . . . not be misleading." The misleading statements that were the subject of the CFTC's attack . . . were therefore not protected by the First Amendment. . . .

[W]e agree with the district court that AVCO acted as a CTA. By the terms of the statute, it was therefore required to register as one. But the CEA's registration requirements insofar as they are a prerequisite for constitutionally protected speech are a quintessential form of prior restraint. . . .

We note in this connection that the electronic form in which Recurrence supplies information does not affect the constitutional analysis. *Leaves of Grass* is protected speech irrespective of whether it is communicated by print on leather-bound pages or by electrons translated to words and read from a cathode-ray tube. A prior restraint against speech is no less suspect because the speech is conveyed electronically. . . .

The First Amendment issues arise, however, only if AVCO is being sanctioned for having engaged in or is being prevented from freely engaging in constitutionally protected speech. The First Amendment prohibits governmental abridgement of "the freedom of speech." We do not think that Recurrence in the form it was sold and marketed by the defendants was "speech" of the sort thus protected.

AVCO sold Recurrence not as a learning program, or an editorial, or an informational newsletter, but as a "system" and "trading program." "The system [was] automatic," with "NO complicated rules to follow. NO calculations to make. NO fundamentals to analyze. And NOTHING to interpret." Users were told they must "follow the signals with no second-guessing." When Recurrence displayed a "sell" signal, the customer was supposed to sell; when it flashed "buy" the customer was supposed to buy. He or she was expected to make no decision of his or her own. The system was advertised and marketed on the basis that it was to be trusted implicitly and followed explicitly. The customer or "client" was to be an automaton, mechanically following Recurrence's commands. . . .

In selling Recurrence in the manner in which it was sold, as an automatic trading system, AVCO acted as a CTA without engaging in constitutionally protected speech. For that it could, consistent with the First Amendment, be required to register, and its failure to do so can constitutionally be punished. The defendants are of course entitled to constitutional protection, but the applicable protection is that which would protect AVCO, Vartuli and their non-speech behavior from overreaching by the government, under the Due Process Clause of the Fifth Amendment, for example, not that which would protect their speech under the First Amendment. . . .

As part of the relief granted to the Commission, however, the district court permanently enjoined AVCO and Vartuli from "[a]cting as [ ] commodity trading advisor[s] . . . and from using the mails or any means or instrumentality of interstate commerce in connection with activity as [ ] CTA [s] unless registered with the Commodity Futures Trading Commission." . . . [I]t is clear that publishing Recurrence alone – i.e., not as an automatic trading system – would qualify as "acting as a commodity trading advisor." The district court enjoined the defendants from acting as such unless they registered with the CFTC. Under the injunction as it currently stands, therefore, the defendants would be required to register with the Commission to publish Recurrence even if it were being used solely as speech, if for example it were being advertised, sold and used as an academic commentary on the commodities markets. Thus formulated, the injunction together with the registration requirement may act as a prior restraint on constitutionally protected speech for which the district court did not perform any constitutional analysis. We therefore remand for the district court to limit the injunction to the dissemination of systems for the automatic trading of futures contracts. . . .

In 2000, the CFTC added a new exemption from commodity trading advisor registration, Rule 4.14(a)(9) (17 C.F.R. § 4.14(a)(9)), discussed in *S & A Farms, Inc. v. Farms.com, Inc.,* below. Exempt is any commodity trading advisor that "does not engage in . . . [d]irecting client accounts; or [p]roviding commodity trading advice based on, or tailored to, the commodity interest or cash market positions or other circumstances or characteristics of particular clients."[14] The new provision was promulgated to address the "uncertainty" caused by the litigation at the time.[15]

As noted above, the Fifth and Seventh Circuits, within the same year *CFTC v. Vartuli* was decided, reached similar decisions to the *Vartuli* court, distinguishing *Lowe v. SEC* and determining that the Commodity Exchange Act's regime for the regulation of commodity trading advisors was more inclusive than the SEC's regime for investment advisors. In the Seventh Circuit case, *Commodity Trend Service, Inc. v. Commodity Futures Trading Commission*, 233 F.3d 981 (7th Cir. 2000), the court ruled that the First Amendment questions arising in light of *Lowe v. SEC* (i.e., that the Commodity Exchange Act may impose an unconstitutional registration requirement for engaging in protected speech activities) were mooted by the CFTC's rulemaking.

3. Private Right of Action for Failure to Register as a CTA

The Commodity Exchange Act § 22 provides a private right of action, which will be discussed in more detail in Chapter 14. The following case evaluated whether the Commodity Exchange Act's private right of action could provide a claim against a commodity trading advisor for failing to register as such.

S & A Farms, Inc. v. Farms.com, Inc.

678 F.3d 949 (8th Cir. 2012)

Smith, Circuit Judge.

S & A Farms, Inc. ("S & A") sued Farms.com Risk Management, Limited ("Farms.com"), alleging that Farms.com violated the Commodity Exchange Act (CEA) . . .

S & A is an Iowa corporation that produces soybeans, hogs, and corn and sells soybeans and hogs. Scout Renaud ("Renaud") and Abbie Renaud are S & A's sole officers, directors, and shareholders. Renaud is S & A's sole employee.

Farms.com is a Canadian corporation that advises producers in the marketing and selling of crops and hogs.

In September 2007, based on a friend's recommendation, Renaud met with Victor Aideyan, a Senior Risk Management Consultant for Farms.com. At this meeting, Renaud sought risk-management advice for his corn and hog operations. On September 17, 2007, Aideyan and Renaud executed a Price Risk Management Service Letter. This letter obligated Farms.com to provide consulting services for S & A's corn inputs and hog outputs and obligated S & A to pay for these services.

After the September 2007 meeting, Renaud opened a commodities-trading account with MF Global, Inc. Although the account only authorized Renaud to make trades, he typically did so after consulting Aideyan. On some occasions, Aideyan would contact MF Global in advance or participate in conference calls with Renaud and MF Global to ensure that Renaud accurately communicated the trades as Aideyan advised. In September 2008, Aideyan left his employment at Farms.com. Maurizo Agostino replaced Aideyan as Renaud's investment advisor.

Between September 20, 2007, and February 24, 2009, Renaud made all of the trades reflected on his MF Global account, except for one, based on Aideyan's or Agostino's advice. During this time, Renaud's MF Global account lost a net value of $1,040,958.75. On February 24, 2009, S & A unilaterally liquidated its positions and stopped obtaining advice from Farms.com.

On December 8, 2009, S & A sued Farms.com, alleging . . . that it violated the Commodity Exchange Act . . . by failing to register with the Commodity Futures Trading Commission (CFTC). . . .

Because S & A could not show that Farms.com's unregistered status – the alleged CEA violation – proximately caused S & A's harm, the district court granted summary judgment in favor of Farms.com. . . .

S & A argues that the district court erred in granting summary judgment for Farms.com on its fraud claim [due to the failure of Farms.com to register as a commodity trading advisor]. Specifically, S & A argues that the district court applied an incorrect standard of causation in analyzing its fraud claim. Farms.com counters, arguing that . . . S & A adduced no evidence that Farms.com's unregistered status proximately caused S & A's damages. . . .

A party may recover damages for CEA violations under 7 U.S.C. § 25(a)(1), which provides:

> Any person (other than a registered entity or registered futures association) who violates this chapter or who willfully aids, abets, counsels, induces, or procures the commission of a violation of this chapter shall be liable for actual damages resulting from one or more of the transactions referred to in subparagraphs (A) through (D) of this paragraph. . . .

The district court interpreted this language to require a plaintiff to show damages caused by the alleged CEA violation. We agree. . . . Thus, it is not enough for a plaintiff to show a CEA violation and damages, rather a plaintiff must show that the CEA violation *proximately caused* the damages for which the plaintiff seeks relief. . . .

Here, S & A's complaint . . . does not allege that Farms.com's failure to register caused its damages. . . .

S & A also argues that the district court erred in granting summary judgment to Farms.com on its breach-of-fiduciary-duty claim. In response, Farms.com argues that S & A presented no evidence establishing a commodity investment advisor's standard of care or showing that Farms.com breached that standard of care. . . .

In response to Farms.com's motion for summary judgment, S & A asserted that . . . [the report of Nicholas Zagotta, their expert] set forth the standard of care for commodity-trading advisors and also showed that Farms.com breached that standard. Zagotta opined:

> [T]he strategy of [Farms.com] was not an effective, efficient or legitimate strategy. It was not effective in that S & A lost $1,040,958.75 in its implementations, it was not efficient in that it would have and should have been much simpler and much smaller. . . . It was not a legitimate hedge strategy because the ratio of cash to derivatives was so much greater than 1:1 and because the S & A's purchases of cash corn obviated the need to hedge a large portion of the cash short.

Viewing the record, we find that S & A presented no evidence describing a commodity trading advisor's standard of care or how Farms.com breached that standard of care. Zagotta's opinion failed to set forth a standard of care for commodity trading advisors. Zagotta also did not state that Farms.com, as an investment trading advisor, breached its standard of care. Zagotta only faulted Farms.com's strategy as a poor hedge strategy. But nowhere in the record does S & A provide evidence that a commodity investment advisor must always recommend a proper hedge strategy when advising investors. . . .

Accordingly, we affirm the district court's grant of Farms.com's motion for summary judgment on S & A's claims.

D. PRIVATE FUNDS AND EXEMPTIONS TO REGISTRATION AS COMMODITY POOL OPERATORS AND COMMODITY TRADING ADVISORS

1. *Private Funds*

In general, a private fund is an investment vehicle that operates within a variety of regulatory exemptions from the rules that would apply to an investment vehicle offered to the general public. Examples of such a fund might be a so-called hedge fund or private equity fund.

Many private funds invest only in securities and, therefore, need only be concerned with the relevant securities law regulations and exemptions. A large portion of private funds invest in both commodities and securities and, therefore, may need to be mindful of both regulatory regimes. Others invest exclusively in commodities. Any investment in "commodity interests," i.e., a product subject to CFTC jurisdiction, could exposes an investment vehicle's management or principals to the requirement to register as a CPO or CTA.

Regulations applying to CPOs and CTAs apply when there is a requirement to register, regardless of whether an entity is actually registered as a CPO or CTA. Therefore, the determination of registration obligation exists or not has substantial ramifications.

Figure 6-A: Summary of Primary CPO and CTA Exclusions and Exemptions

Regulatory Basis	Primary Basis in Commodity Exchange Act	Exclusion or Exemption?	Applies to CPOs or CTAs?	Summary of Relief
17 C.F.R. § 4.5	§ 1a(11)	Exclusion	CPOs	Exclusion from definition for certain already regulated entities.
17 C.F.R. § 4.7	§ 4n	Exemption	CPOs & CTAs	Exemption from some of the requirements that would apply to a commodity pool offered to the public at large.
17 C.F.R. § 4.12(b)	§ 8a(5)	Exemption	CPOs	Exemption from some of the requirements that would apply with respect to pools primarily trading

				securities and engaged in *de minimis* trading of products subject to CFTC jurisdiction.
17 C.F.R. § 4.13	§ 1a(11)	Exemption	CPOs	Various exemptions from registration based on limited scope of CPO activities.
17 C.F.R. § 4.14(a)(10)	§ 4m(1)	Exemption	CTAs	Exemption from registration for commodity trading advisors with activities limited in scope.
17 C.F.R. § 4.14(a)(8)	§ 4m(3)	Exemption	CTAs	Exemption from registration for SEC-registered investment advisers with limited commodity trading advisor activities.
17 C.F.R. § 4.14(a)(1-7 & 9)	§ 8a(5)	Exemption	CTAs	Variety of exemptions from registration.

2. CFTC Rule 4.5

Formally, CFTC Rule 4.5 (17 C.F.R. § 4.5) is an *exclusion* not an exemption since entities that fall within its parameters are completely excluded from the definition of commodity pool operator and its application. The relevant *exemptions* evaluated further below, on the other hand, recognize that the entities fall within the definition of commodity pool operator or commodity trading advisor and, nonetheless, relieve such entities from some or all of the law and regulation that might otherwise apply.

Rule 4.5 is based on the Commodity Exchange Act's definition of commodity pool operator that allows for the CFTC to provide for exclusions consistent with "effectuat[ing] the purposes of the statute."[16] The CFTC has accordingly provided relief for investment companies registered under the Investment Company Act of 1940 (17 C.F.R. § 4.5(a)(1)), insurance companies (17 C.F.R. § 4.5(a)(2)), banks (17 C.F.R. § 4.5(a)(3)) and pension funds (17 C.F.R. § 4.5(a)(4)), requiring only a filing with the NFA (17 C.F.R. § 4.5(c)). Before 2003, the CFTC also required that all trading of commodity interests be for *bona fide* hedging purposes save for a *de minimis* amount of up to 5% in margin amount of the investment vehicle's liquidation value that could be for speculative purposes.[17] In 2003, the CFTC abolished this requirement[18] only to restore it in 2012 solely for registered investment companies while leaving it abolished for insurance companies, banks and pension funds.[19] This disparity in regulatory treatment led the primary industry association for investment companies to challenge the rule.

Investment Company Institute v. Commodity Futures Trading Commission

720 F.3d 370 (D.C. Cir. 2013)

Sentelle, Senior Circuit Judge:

The Investment Company Institute and the Chamber of Commerce of the United States brought this action against the Commodity Futures Trading Commission (CFTC), seeking a declaratory judgment that recently adopted regulations of the Commission regarding derivatives trading were unlawfully adopted and invalid, and seeking to vacate and set aside those regulations and to enjoin their enforcement. . . .

Under . . . [the Commodity Exchange Act ("CEA" or "Act")], the Commission has regulatory jurisdiction over a wide variety of markets in futures and derivatives. . . . [T]he CEA also directly imposes certain duties on regulated entities. As relevant here, the Act requires that Commodity Pool Operators (CPOs) register with CFTC and adhere to regulatory requirements related to such issues as investor disclosures, recordkeeping, and reporting. . . . The CEA, however, empowers CFTC to exclude an entity from regulation as a CPO if CFTC determines that the exclusion "will effectuate the purposes of" the statute.

Since 1985, the Commission has exercised its authority to exclude "otherwise regulated" entities through § 4.5 of its regulations. *See* Commodity Pool Operators, 50 Fed. Reg. 15,868 (Apr. 23, 1985) (codified at 17 C.F.R. § 4.5). Under the version of § 4.5 that applied before amendments of 2003, otherwise regulated entities could claim exclusion by meeting certain regulatory conditions. These conditions included that the entity:

> (i) Will use commodity futures or commodity options contracts solely for bona fide hedging purposes . . . [;] (ii) Will not enter into commodity futures and commodity options contracts for which the aggregate initial margin and premiums exceed 5 percent of the fair market value of the entity's assets . . . [;] (iii) Will not be, and has not been, marketing participations to the public as or in a commodity pool or otherwise as or in a vehicle for trading in the commodity futures or commodity options markets; [and,] (iv) Will disclose in writing to each

prospective participant the purpose of and the limitations on the scope of the commodity futures and commodity options trading in which the entity intends to engage[.]

These conditions were amended slightly in 1993, when CFTC promulgated a rule removing the bona fide hedging requirement and excluding bona fide hedging from the trading threshold. Commodity Pool Operators, 58 Fed. Reg. 6,371, 6,372 (Jan. 28, 1993). Under these conditions, there was no automatic exclusion for registered investment companies, or "RICs," regulated by the Securities and Exchange Commission pursuant to the Investment Company Act of 1940. Therefore, a commodity pool operator that was also a registered investment company was included within CFTC's regulatory definition of CPOs unless it met all of the § 4.5 requirements for exclusion. . . .

[T]he Commission [subsequently] amended its requirements for exclusion to eliminate the five percent ceiling. *See* Additional Registration and Other Regulatory Relief for Commodity Pool Operators and Commodity Trading Advisors, 68 Fed. Reg. 47,221, 47,224 (Aug. 8, 2003). These 2003 amendments "effectively excluded RICs from the CPO definition," freeing registered investment companies from most CFTC CPO regulations. . . .

In 2010, the Commission began shifting back to a more stringent regulatory framework. This shift came in the wake of the 2007-2008 financial crisis . . . As relevant here, Dodd-Frank repealed several statutory provisions that had excluded certain commodities transactions from CFTC oversight. Dodd-Frank also gave CFTC regulatory authority over swaps, and amended the statutory definition of commodity pool operators to include entities that trade swaps. Dodd-Frank, however, did not affect CFTC's authority to set exclusion requirements for CPOs. . . .

After Congress passed Dodd-Frank, the National Futures Association (NFA), to which all CPOs must belong, filed a petition of rulemaking with CFTC requesting that CFTC amend § 4.5 to limit the scope of its exclusion for registered investment companies. *See* Petition of the National Futures Association, 75 Fed. Reg. 56,997 (Sept. 17, 2010). In NFA's view, mutual funds were using the relaxed § 4.5 standards to evade CFTC oversight of their derivative operations, reducing transparency and potentially harming the public because no other regulator had rules equivalent to CFTC's. . . . In essence, NFA sought a return to the pre-2003 regulatory framework, but only for registered investment companies.

On February 11, 2011, CFTC proposed new regulations that would amend § 4.5 "to reinstate the pre-2003 operating criteria" for all registered investment companies. Commodity Pool Operators and Commodity Trading Advisors: Amendments to Compliance Obligations, 76 Fed. Reg. 7,976, 7,984 (Feb. 11, 2011). One notable difference from the 2003 framework is that because of Dodd-Frank's extension of CFTC authority to swaps, the regulations proposed that swaps be included in the trading thresholds. *See id.* at 7,989. . . . CFTC provided four explanations for these proposed regulations: First, the regulations would align CFTC's regulatory framework "with the stated purposes of the Dodd-Frank Act." Second, they would "encourage more congruent and consistent regulation of similarly situated entities among Federal financial regulatory agencies." Third, they would "improve accountability and increase transparency of the activities of CPOs" and commodity pools. Fourth, they would make it easier to collect data for the Financial Stability Oversight Council ("FSOC"), a new body created by Dodd-Frank charged with "identify[ing] risks to the financial stability of the United States." . . .

CFTC promulgated a Final Rule amending § 4.5 . . . largely as proposed. *See* Commodity Pool Operators and Commodity Trading Advisors: Compliance Obligations, 77 Fed. Reg. 11,252 (Feb. 24, 2012), as corrected due to Fed. Reg. errors in its original publication, 77 Fed. Reg. 17,328 (Mar. 26, 2012). . . .

In its Final Rule, CFTC justified its decision to return to the pre-2003 regulatory framework on the basis of "changed circumstances [that] warrant revisions to these rules." According to CFTC, the 2003 "system of exemptions was appropriate because [registered investment companies] engaged in relatively little derivatives trading." Since the 2003 amendments, however, such companies have engaged in "increased derivatives trading activities" and "now offer[ ] services substantially identical to those of registered entities [that] are not subject to the same regulatory oversight." Given this changed circumstance, and Dodd-Frank's "more robust mandate to manage systemic risk and to ensure safe trading practices by entities involved in the derivatives markets," CFTC considered it necessary to narrow the exclusions from its derivatives regulation. Following this rule change, RICs that do not satisfy the exclusion requirements must register with CFTC per § 4.5. . . .

Appellants contend that CFTC violated the [Administrative Procedures Act (the "APA")] . . . in its rulemaking by: (1) failing to address its own 2003 rationales for broadening CPO exemptions; (2) failing to comply with the Commodity Exchange Act and offering an inadequate evaluation of the rule's costs and benefits; (3) including swaps in the trading threshold, restricting its definition of bona fide hedging, and failing to justify the five percent threshold; and, (4) failing to provide an adequate opportunity for notice and comment. We address each contention in turn. . . .

The appellants first contend that CFTC failed to explain why it changed from its more generous exemption requirements that had existed since 2003 to the more stringent requirements contained in the Final Rule. Though it is true that the Final Rule stated that investment companies are increasing their participation in derivatives markets, the 2003 rule was explicitly designed to promote liquidity in the commodities markets by making it easier for registered investment companies to participate in derivatives markets. CFTC, according to the appellants, completely failed to address the liquidity issue, and therefore its change in position was arbitrary and capricious.

We disagree. An agency changing course "need not demonstrate to a court's satisfaction that the reasons for the new policy are *better* than the reasons for the old one; it suffices that the new policy is permissible under the statute, that there are good reasons for it, and that the agency *believes* it to be better." . . . So long as CFTC provided a reasoned explanation for its regulation, and the reviewing court can "reasonably . . . discern[ ]" the agency's path, we must uphold the regulation, even if the agency's decision has "less than ideal clarity."

CFTC's regulation clears this low bar. CFTC explicitly acknowledged that it was changing its position from its 2003 rulemaking. The Final Rule detailed the changed circumstances that prompted CFTC to amend the rule, including increased derivatives trading by investment companies (an issue inherently tied to liquidity) and a perceived lack of market transparency that could lead to a buildup of systemic risk. It is clear that the Commission, in adopting the changes and the rule, was attempting to respond to those changed circumstances by adding registration and reporting requirements. . . . Such reasoned decisionmaking is an acceptable way to change CFTC's past rules the appellants' policy disagreements with CFTC notwithstanding. . . .

Appellants next contend that CFTC failed to adequately consider the costs and benefits of the rule. The Commodity Exchange Act requires that CFTC "consider the costs and benefits" of its actions and "evaluate[ ]" those costs and benefits "in light of" five factors: "(A) considerations of protection of market participants and the public; (B) considerations of the efficiency, competitiveness, and financial integrity of futures markets; (C) considerations of price discovery; (D) considerations of sound risk management practices; and (E) other public interest considerations." . . .

Appellants point to two recent cases in which we vacated SEC regulations because SEC had failed to address existing regulatory requirements to determine whether sufficient protections were already present. *See Business Roundtable v. SEC,* 647 F.3d 1144, 1154 (D.C.Cir.2011); *American Equity Inv. Life Ins. Co. v. SEC,* 613 F.3d 166, 179 (D.C.Cir.2010). According to the appellants, CFTC similarly failed to consider whether existing regulations made its proposed regulation unnecessary.

We are unconvinced. In its Final Rule, CFTC explicitly discussed SEC's oversight in the derivatives markets. . . . We hold that CFTC's consideration and evaluation of the rule's costs and benefits was not arbitrary or capricious. . . .

The appellants challenge three particular aspects of the Final Rule. The first is CFTC's decision to include swap transactions in the registration threshold, which has the effect of requiring more investment companies to register pursuant to § 4.5. The appellants claim that this decision was arbitrary and capricious because Dodd-Frank implemented a separate reporting framework with regard to swaps. . . .

CFTC gave sufficient . . . explanations for including swap trades in the § 4.5 trading threshold that we can "reasonably . . . discern[ ]" its rationale. . . .

The second aspect of the rule challenged by the appellants is its definition of bona fide hedging transactions, a definition that the appellants claim is too narrow and should encompass risk management strategies in financial markets. This argument amounts to nothing more than another policy disagreement with CFTC, so we must reject it. . . .

The third and final particular aspect of the rule challenged by the appellants is the five percent registration threshold for § 4.5, which the appellants argue is too low. . . . We defer to CFTC's judgment and hold that adopting the five percent threshold was neither arbitrary nor capricious. . . .

Finally, appellants contend that CFTC failed to provide adequate opportunity for notice and comment. . . . We disagree. The APA requires "reference to the legal authority under which the rule is proposed" and "either the terms or substance of the proposed rule or a description of the subjects and issues involved." 5 U.S.C. § 553(b). The proposed rule included a separate section entitled "Cost-Benefit Analysis" that gave adequate notice of CFTC's approach to the cost-benefit analysis by setting forth the factors that CFTC would consider and summarizing expected costs and benefits. . . .

For the foregoing reasons, the decision of the district court is Affirmed.

---

3. *CFTC Rules 4.7 and 4.12*

a. Generally

CFTC Rules 4.7 (17 C.F.R. § 4.7) and 4.12 (17 C.F.R. § 4.12) provide relief from a variety of requirements, particularly disclosure requirements, which would otherwise be imposed on registered commodity pool operators. For instance, commodity pools operators have to deliver disclosure documents regarding the commodity pool (17 C.F.R. § 4.21), risk statements, and information regarding the type of commodities to be traded and conflicts of interest, fees, and expenses (17 C.F.R. § 4.24), monthly statements regarding the performance of the commodity pool (17 C.F.R. § 4.25), and account statements and annual reports for the commodity pool (17 C.F.R. § 4.26).

Both the Rule 4.7 and Rule 4.12 exemptions require a filing with the National Futures Association.[20]

b. Rule 4.7

Rule 4.7 applies to commodity pools offered solely to "qualified eligible persons," commonly known as "QEPs" or to commodity trading advisors advising a qualified eligible person. Generally, a qualified eligible person must either have $5 million in assets, be a natural person qualifying as an "accredited investor" under the SEC's Regulation D,[21] a non-U.S. person, or be one of the regulated entities listed in the rule.[22] In order to be deemed a qualified eligible person, some entities have the additional requirement of satisfying a "portfolio requirement" of having $2,000,000 invested in securities, $200,000 on margin for futures and options trading with a futures commission merchant or a combination thereof, such as $1,000,000 in securities and $100,000 on margin for futures and options trading.[23]

c. Rule 4.12

To satisfy the requirements of Rule 4.12, the relevant commodity pool must "trade . . . commodity interests in a manner solely incidental to . . . securities trading activities" with margins on commodity transactions not exceeding 10% of the pool's fair market value or be registered under the Securities Act of 1933 or the Investment Company Act of 1940.[24]

4. *CFTC Rule 4.13*

The relief in CFTC Rules 4.7 and 4.12 is available only to registered commodity pool operators or commodity trading advisors. CFTC Rule 4.13, on the other hand, provides an exemption from registration for a commodity pool operator operating commodity pools if it files a notification with the National Futures Association, notifies potential participants of its registration exemption, and meets any of the following tests:

> (i) It does not receive any compensation . . . for operating the pool, except reimbursement for the ordinary administrative expenses of operating the pool;
> (ii) It operates only one commodity pool at any time;
> (iii) It is not otherwise required to register with the [CFTC or affiliated with someone who does]; and
> (iv) . . . does [no] advertising in connection with the pool. . . .

17 C.F.R. § 4.13(a)(1).

> (i) None of the pools operated by it has more than 15 participants at any time; and
> (ii) The total gross capital contributions it receives for units of participation in all of the pools it operates or that it intends to operate do not in the aggregate exceed $400,000 [excluding principals and their near relatives].

17 C.F.R. § 4.13(a)(2).

> (i) Interests in the pool are exempt from registration [as securities and] offered and sold without marketing to the public in the United States;
> (ii) . . . [each pool either does not exceed a *de minimis* amount of trading with margining of more than 5% of its liquidation value in commodity interests or notional amounts equal to 100% of its liquidation value];
> (iii) . . . at the time of investment . . . each person who participates in the pool is [an accredited investor or qualified eligible person]; and
> (iv) Participations in the pool are not marketed as or in a vehicle for trading in the commodity futures or commodity options markets. . . .

17 C.F.R. § 4.13(a)(3).

One of the primary exemptions relied upon by hedge funds, Rule 4.13(a)(4) was repealed in 2012 by the CFTC.[25] The CFTC had also considered repealing Rule 4.13(a)(3).[26] The CFTC decided against repealing 4.13(a)(3) after receiving comments mostly critical of the proposal. The CFTC's reasoning for repealing Rule 4.13(a)(4) (17 C.F.R. § 4.13(a)(4)) and for considering repeal of Rule 4.13(a)(3) is outlined in the 2011 proposal.

Commodity Futures Trading Commission, Commodity Pool Operators and Commodity Trading Advisors: Amendments to Compliance Obligations

76 Fed. Reg. 7976-01 (February 11, 2011)

. . . On July 21, 2010, President Obama signed the Dodd-Frank Wall Street Reform and Consumer Protection Act ("Dodd-Frank Act"). The legislation was enacted to reduce risk, increase transparency, and promote market integrity within the financial system by, inter alia, enhancing the Commodity Futures Trading Commission's (the "Commission" or "CFTC") rulemaking and enforcement authorities with respect to all registered entities and intermediaries subject to the Commission's oversight. . . .

The Commodity Exchange Act ("CEA") empowers the Commission with the authority to register Commodity Pool Operators ("CPOs") and Commodity Trading Advisors ("CTAs"), exclude any entity from registration as a CPO or CTA,[iv] and to require "[e]very commodity trading advisor and commodity pool operator registered under [the CEA to] maintain books and records and file such reports in such form and manner as may be prescribed by the Commission."[v]

[iv] [N. 5] 7 U.S.C. 1a(11) and 1a(12).

[v] [N. 6] 7 U.S.C. 6n(3)(A). Under part 4 of the Commission's regulations, entities registered as CPOs have reporting obligations with respect to their operated pools. *See*

The Commission also has the power to "make and promulgate such rules and regulations as, in the judgment of the Commission, are reasonably necessary to effectuate the provisions or to accomplish any of the purposes of [the CEA]."[vi] The Commission's discretionary power to exclude or exempt persons from registration was intended to be exercised "to exempt from registration those persons who otherwise meet the criteria for registration . . . if, in the opinion of the Commission, there is no substantial public interest to be served by the registration."[vii] It is pursuant to this authority that the Commission has promulgated the various exemptions from registration as a CPO that are enumerated in § 4.13 of its regulations as well as the exclusions from the definition of CPO that are delineated in § 4.5.

Following the recent economic turmoil, and consistent with the tenor of the provisions of the Dodd-Frank Act, the Commission has reconsidered the level of regulation that it believes is appropriate with respect to entities participating in the commodity futures and derivatives markets. The Commission believes that it is necessary to rescind or modify several of its exemptions and exclusions to more effectively oversee its market participants and manage the risks that such participants pose to the markets. . . .

Title IV of the Dodd-Frank Act requires advisers to large private funds[viii] to register with the SEC.[ix] Through this registration requirement, Congress sought

---

17 C.F.R. 4.22. Although CTAs have recordkeeping obligations under part 4, the Commission has not required reporting by CTAs, *See* [*sic*] *generally*, 17 C.F.R. part 4.

[vi] [N. 7] 7 U.S.C. 12a(5).

[vii] [N. 8] *See* H.R. Rep. No. 93-975, 93d Cong., 2d Sess. (1974), p. 20.

[viii] [N. 14] Section 202(a)(29) of the Investment Advisers Act of 1940 ("Investment Advisers Act") defines the term "private fund" as "an issuer that would be an investment company, as defined in section 3 of the Investment Company Act of 1940 (15 U.S.C. 80a-3), but for section 3(c)(1) or 3(c)(7) of that Act." 15 U.S.C. 80a-3(c)(1), 80a-3(c)(7). Section 3(c)(1) of the Investment Company Act provides an exclusion from the definition of "investment company" for any "issuer whose outstanding securities (other than short term paper) are beneficially owned by not more than one hundred persons and which is not making and does not presently propose to make a public offering of its securities." 15 U.S.C. 80a-3(c)(1). Section 3(c)(7) of the Investment Company Act provides an exclusion from the definition of "investment company" for any "issuer, the outstanding securities of which are owned exclusively by persons who, at the time of acquisition of such securities, are qualified purchasers, and which is not making and does not at that time propose to make a public offering of such securities." 15 U.S.C. 80a-3(c)(7). The term "qualified purchaser" is defined in section 2(a)(51) of the Investment Company Act. *See* 15 U.S.C. 80a-2(a)(51).

[ix] [N. 15] The Dodd-Frank Act requires private fund adviser registration by amending section 203(b)(3) of the Advisers Act to repeal the exemption from registration for any adviser that during the course of the preceding 12 months had fewer than 15 clients and neither held itself out to the public as an investment adviser nor advised any registered investment company or business development company. See section 403 of the Dodd-

to make available to the SEC "information regarding [the] size, strategies and positions" of large private funds, which Congress believed "could be crucial to regulatory attempts to deal with a future crisis." In section 404 of the Dodd-Frank Act, Congress amended section 204(b) of the Investment Advisers Act to direct the SEC to require private fund advisers registered solely with the SEC[x] to file reports containing such information as is deemed necessary and appropriate in the public interest and for investor protection or for the assessment of systemic risk. These reports and records must include a description of certain prescribed information, such as the amount of assets under management, use of leverage, counterparty credit risk exposure, and trading and investment positions for each private fund advised by the adviser. . . .

In order to ensure that the Commission can adequately oversee the commodities and derivatives markets and assess market risk associated with pooled investment vehicles under its jurisdiction, the Commission is re-evaluating its regulation of CPOs and CTAs. Additionally, the Commission does not want its registration and reporting regime for pooled investment vehicles and their operators and/or advisors to be incongruent with the registration and reporting regimes of other regulators, such as that of the SEC for investment advisers under the Dodd-Frank Act. . . .

The Commission's proposed amendments are designed to (1) bring the Commission's CPO and CTA regulatory structure into alignment with the stated purposes of the Dodd-Frank Act; (2) encourage more congruent and consistent regulation of similarly situated entities among Federal financial regulatory agencies; (3) improve accountability and increase transparency of the activities of CPOs, CTAs, and the commodity pools that they operate or advise; and (4) facilitate a collection of data that will assist the FSOC [the Financial Stability Oversight Council established by the Dodd-Frank Act], acting within the scope of its jurisdiction, in the event that the FSOC requests and the Commission provides such data. The proposed amendments will also allow the Commission to more effectively oversee its market participants and manage the risks posed by the commodities and derivatives markets. To those ends, the [proposed]

Frank Act. There are exemptions from this registration requirement for advisers to venture capital funds and advisers to private funds with less than $150 million in assets under management in the United States. There also is an exemption for foreign advisers with less than $25 million in assets under management from the United States and fewer than 15 U.S. clients and private fund investors. See sections 402, 407 and 408 of the Dodd-Frank Act.

[x] [N. 17] In this release, the term "private fund adviser" means any investment adviser that is (i) registered or required to be registered with the SEC (including any investment adviser that is also registered or required to be registered with the CFTC as a CPO or CTA) and (ii) advises one or more private funds (including any commodity pools that satisfy the definition of "private fund").

amendments [, among other things,] rescind the exemptions from registration under §§ 4.13(a)(3) and (a)(4). . . .

Section 4.13(a)(3) of the Commission's regulations currently provides that a person is exempt from registration as a CPO if the interests in the pool are exempt from registration under the Securities Act of 1933 and offered only to QEPs, accredited investors, or knowledgeable employees, and the pool's aggregate initial margin and premiums attributable to commodity interests do not exceed five percent of the liquidation value of the pool's portfolio. Section 4.13(a)(4) of the Commission's regulations provides that a person is exempt from registration as a CPO if the interests in the pool are exempt from registration under the Securities Act of 1933 and the operator reasonably believes that the participants are all QEPs.

As a result of the creation of exemptions from registration as a CPO under §§ 4.13(a)(3) and (a)(4), a large group of market participants have fallen outside of the oversight of regulators (i.e., there is very little if any transparency or accountability over the activities of these participants). The Commission has concluded that continuing to grant an exemption from registration and reporting obligations for these market participants is outweighed by the Commission's concerns of regulatory arbitrage.

Indeed, the Commission believes that it is possible for a commodity pool to have a portfolio that is sizeable enough that even if just five percent of the pool's portfolio were committed to margin for futures, the pool's portfolio could be so significant that the commodity pool would constitute a major participant in the futures market.

In addition, the Commission proposes to eliminate the exemption in § 4.13(a)(4) because there are no limits on the amount of commodity interest trading in which pools operating under this regulation can engage. That is, it is possible that a commodity pool that is exempted from registration under § 4.13(a)(4) could be invested solely in commodities. . . .

The Commission's proposal seeks to eliminate the exemptions under §§ 4.13(a)(3) and (4) for operators of pools that are similarly situated to private funds that previously relied on the exemptions under §§ 3(c)(1) and (7) of the Investment Company Act and § 203(b)(3) of the Investment Advisers Act. [Note: for an explanation of these references to the Investment Company Act and the Investment Advisers Act, *see* above within this excerpt, n. 14 and 17.] It is the Commission's view that the operators of these pools should be subject to similar regulatory obligations . . . in order to provide improved transparency and increased accountability with respect to these pools. The Commission has determined that it is appropriate to limit regulatory arbitrage . . . so that operators of such pools will not be able to avoid oversight by either the Commission or the SEC through claims of exemption under the Commission's regulations. . . .

As noted above, the CFTC ultimately decided to retain the Rule 4.13(a)(3) exemption reasoning that maintaining a *de minimis* exemption was preferable because "overseeing entities with less than five percent exposure to commodity interests is not the best use of the Commission's limited resources."[27] The lack of a *de minimis* limit underlay the CFTC's elimination of the Rule 4.13(a)(4) exemption:

> [A]s stated in the proposal, there are no limits on the amount of commodity interest trading in which pools operating under this regulation can engage. That is, it is possible that a commodity pool that is exempted from registration under § 4.13(a)(4) could be invested solely in commodities, which, in the Commission's view, necessitates Commission oversight to ensure adequate customer protection and market oversight. Therefore, the Commission adopts the rescission of § 4.13(a)(4) as proposed.

Commodity Pool Operators and Commodity Trading Advisors: Compliance Obligations (February 24, 2012), 11265.

5. *Commodity Exchange Act §§ 4m(1) and (3)*

An exception to a commodity trading advisor's obligation to register with the CFTC is for a commodity trading advisor "who, during the course of the preceding twelve months, has not furnished commodity trading advice to more than fifteen persons and who does not hold himself out generally to the public as a commodity trading advisor. . . ."[28] Another exception applies to a commodity trading advisor who is registered with the SEC as an investment adviser and "whose business does not consist primarily of acting as a commodity trading advisor . . . and that does not act as a commodity trading advisor to any commodity pool that is engaged primarily in trading commodity interests.[29] CFTC Rules 4.14(a)(10) and (8), both cited below, implement these two statutory exemptions.

6. *CFTC Rule 4.14*

CFTC Rule 4.14 is a catch-all provision, exempting entities that are not intended to be captured by the commodity trading advisor registration requirements from registration.

Exemption from Registration as a Commodity Trading Advisor

17 C.F.R. § 4.14

(a) A person is not required to register under the Act as a commodity trading advisor if:

(1) It is a dealer, processor, broker, or seller in cash market transactions of any commodity (or product thereof) and the person's commodity trading advice is solely incidental to the conduct of its cash market business;

(2) It is a non-profit, voluntary membership, trade association or farm organization and the person's commodity trading advice is solely incidental to the conduct of its business as such association or organization;

(3) It is registered under the Act as an associated person and the person's commodity trading advice is issued solely in connection with its employment as an associated person;

(4) It is registered under the Act as a commodity pool operator and the person's commodity trading advice is directed solely to, and for the sole use of, the pool or pools for which it is so registered;

(5) It is exempt from registration as a commodity pool operator and the person's commodity trading advice is directed solely to, and for the sole use of, the pool or pools for which it is so exempt;

(6) It is registered under the Act as an introducing broker and the person's trading advice is solely in connection with its business as an introducing broker;

(7) . . . It is registered under the Act as a leverage transaction merchant [or a] a retail foreign exchange dealer and the person's trading advice is solely in connection with its business as a [leverage transaction merchant or] retail foreign exchange dealer[, as applicable].

(8) It is registered as an investment adviser under the Investment Advisers Act of 1940 or with the applicable securities regulatory agency of any State, or it is exempt from such registration, or it is excluded from the definition of the term "investment adviser" pursuant to the provisions of sections 202(a)(2) and 202(a)(11) of the Investment Advisers Act of 1940, Provided, That . . . commodity interest trading advice is directed solely to, and for the sole use of, one or more of the following[:] . . .

[A] [Entities eligible for a Rule 4.5 exclusion]; . . .

[B] [Certain pension plans]; . . .

[C] Commodity pools that are organized [and marketed] . . . outside of the United States . . . where . . .[t]he commodity pool operator of each such pool has not so organized and is not so operating the pool for the purpose of avoiding commodity pool operator registration . . . [and no U.S. persons will invest other than] the pool's operator, advisor and their principals. . . . Provided, That units of participation in the pool held by [U.S.] persons [which are not] . . . qualified eligible persons represent . . . less than 10 percent of . . . the pool; . . .

[D] A commodity pool operator who has claimed an exemption from registration under § 4.13(a)(3) . . . and [p]rovides commodity interest trading advice solely incidental to its business of providing securities or other investment advice [and] . . . [i]s not otherwise holding itself out as a commodity trading advisor [so long as notice to the NFA is provided and there is compliance with recordkeeping requirements] . . .

(9) It does not engage in . . . [d]irecting client accounts; or . . . [p]roviding commodity trading advice based on, or tailored to, the commodity interest or cash market positions or other circumstances or characteristics of particular clients; or

(10) If . . . during the course of the preceding 12 months, it has not furnished commodity trading advice to more than 15 persons and it does not hold itself out generally to the public as a commodity trading advisor . . .

QUESTIONS AND COMMENTS

1. Why regulate commodity pool operators instead of the commodity pools themselves?
2. In light of *Lowe v. SEC*, was the Commodity Exchange Act's definition of commodity trading advisor, as implemented by the CFTC, unconstitutionally overbroad before it added the exemption contained in Rule 4.14(a)(9) (17 C.F.R. § 4.14(a)(9)) and discussed in section C2 above?
3. What about after the addition of Rule 4.14(a)(9)? Could a claim be made that it violates the First Amendment?
4. What is the public policy underlying the regulation of private funds that limit investors to ultra-high net worth entities and individuals? Surely not investor protection, along with market manipulation, one of the original impetuses for the regulation of the securities and commodities investment industries. What, today, might be additional drivers for the regulation of investment industries?

5. As discussed in section D2 above, exemptions added to CFTC Rule 4.5 in 2003 were repealed in 2012. When implementing a regulatory reversal of this nature what are some of the factors for which a regulator should account? How do such policy changes impact market parties relying on the previous regime? Are there ways, such as long transition periods or grandfathering (i.e., allowing entities relying on the old regime to continue to do so), to soften the transition?

CHAPTER 7
PROHIBITED SWAP TRANSACTIONS

A. INTRODUCTORY NOTES

We are now making a significant transition from examining the CFTC's well-established regime for the regulation of commodity futures to its ongoing establishment of a regulatory regime for swaps, as mandated by the Dodd-Frank Act. In this chapter and Chapters 8, 9, and 10, we examine the CFTC's regime for the regulation of swaps.

The Dodd-Frank Act also charged the SEC with the establishment of a regulatory regime for security-based swaps (*see* Chapter 3). The SEC has taken only preliminary steps toward its implementation and, therefore, it is not covered herein.

The historical antecedents to the CFTC's swaps regulatory regime and the impetus for its establishment provided by the Financial Crisis beginning in 2007 were discussed in Chapter 2 and are further discussed in section B below.

Since the swaps regulatory regime is a new one, instituted by the Dodd-Frank Act in 2010 and rolled out incrementally over the following years, caselaw is less available as a resource for understanding the law. We are forced to rely more on regulatory releases, analogy to other better-established areas of law, such as for the regulation of commodity futures, and ancillary materials, such as Congressional reports. The one area where significant caselaw related to swaps has developed is with respect to interpretation of Bankruptcy Code provisions specific to swaps. In Chapter 11 we examine those cases.

The focus of this chapter is on categories of swap transactions that are prohibited. Since these prohibitions were all put in place by the Dodd-Frank Act, we first look at the events that underlay its enactment.

B. IMPETUS FOR THE DODD-FRANK ACT'S REGULATION OF SWAPS

1. Background

In Chapter 2 we listed significant financial institution failures and "fire sale" acquisitions occurring during the peak of the Financial Crisis. Household names such as Wachovia, Bear Stearns, Lehman Brothers, and Washington Mutual seemingly disappeared overnight.

Figure 7-A: FDIC-Insured Bank Failures 2000-2014*

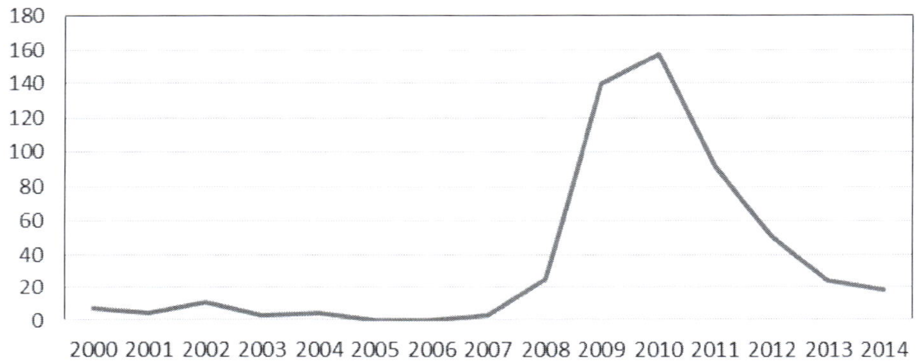

* *Failed Bank List*, Federal Deposit Insurance Corporation, available at http://www.fdic.gov/bank/individual/failed/banklist.html (accessed June 14, 2014). 2014 data is annualized based on failures as of June 1, 2014

However, it was not derivatives exposures that caused these institutions or the banks insured by the Federal Deposit Insurance Corporation referenced in Figure 7-A to fail.[1] Instead, for many of these institutions, it was a result of excessive exposures to real estate, which saw increasing borrower defaults amidst declining values:

> While the vulnerabilities that created the potential for crisis were years in the making, it was the collapse of the housing bubble – fueled by low interest rates, easy and available credit, scant regulation, and toxic mortgages – that was the spark that ignited a string of events, which led to a full-blown crisis in the fall of 2008. Trillions of dollars in risky mortgages had become embedded throughout the financial system, as mortgage-related securities were packaged, repackaged, and sold to investors around the world. When the bubble burst, hundreds of billions of dollars in losses in mortgages and mortgage-related securities shook markets as well as

> financial institutions that had significant exposures to those mortgages and had borrowed heavily against them.

The Financial Crisis Inquiry Report, xvi.

Only one major financial entity, American International Group, discussed in section B2 below, was felled primarily by exposure to derivatives.

2. Derivatives and the Financial Crisis

If the Financial Crisis was the result of the collapse of a real estate bubble, why then were formerly off-exchange "over-the-counter" derivatives heavily regulated subsequent to the Financial Crisis? It is impossible to parse out every motivation for regulating the industry. For example, as we saw in Chapter 2, efforts to regulate the off-exchange derivatives industry such as that spurred by former CFTC Chairman Brooksley Born preceded the Financial Crisis by a decade. It could have been that the moment was right for those who were already in favor of derivatives regulation to get broad congressional support. Alternatively, whereas Federal Reserve provision of bank depository institutions has historically been tolerated, support of this nature going to American International Group, a non-bank, with respect to its derivatives exposures was undoubtedly also a significant motivation. As the Congressional Oversight Committee noted, the bailout of American International Group "undermined the credibility of . . . America's system of financial regulation."[2]

Indeed, whatever the true motivation for each proponent of the regulation of off-exchange derivatives, the match that lit the fire was the taxpayer-funded bailout of American International Group.

The Congressional Oversight Panel was an office within the Department of the Treasury's Office of Financial Stability. The Panel was created in 2008 to "review the current state of the financial markets and the regulatory system" in light of the Financial Crisis and submit various reports to Congress.[3] It was bipartisan, constituted by five appointees selected by congressional leadership.[4] The Congressional Oversight Panel was terminated in April 2011. In its March Oversight Report – its final report – it described the extent of government-assistance provided to the finance and auto industries.[5]

<u>Congressional Oversight Panel, March Oversight Report</u>

Available at http://www.gpo.gov/fdsys/pkg/CHRG-112shrg64832/pdf/CHRG-112shrg64832.pdf (accessed June 15, 2014)

. . . The first tremors of the impending financial crisis and the severe recession that followed were seen in the American housing market. . . . The rapid appreciation in home prices . . . helped fuel housing speculation and a boom in mortgage refinancing and home equity loans. . . .

In late 2006, home prices began to decline and delinquencies on home mortgages . . . began to rise. . . .

Bear Stearns closed two mortgage-backed securities (MBS) focused hedge funds, and two of the largest subprime mortgage originators and securitizers – New Century Financial and American Home Mortgage – filed for bankruptcy. On August 9, 2007, BNP Paribas, the largest bank in France, suspended redemptions in three investment funds due to their exposure to the U.S. subprime mortgage market. . . .

As housing fundamentals continued to weaken and financial fear spread, some of the nation's largest financial firms began to teeter on the edge of failure. On January 11, 2008, Bank of America announced its purchase of a major mortgage originator, Countrywide Financial. Then on March 14, the Federal Reserve intervened to rescue Bear Stearns by helping to arrange for and assisting with its purchase by JPMorgan. . . . The nation's gross domestic product . . . contracted for four consecutive quarters through June 2009. . . .

[U]nemployment rose sharply in 2008 and early 2009. . . .

As the effects of the crisis spread to the wider market . . . IndyMac Bank, one of the nation's largest savings and loans and the second largest mortgage lender in the country, came under pressure as fear spread about its potential insolvency. Over an eleven-day period, depositors withdrew over $1.3 billion of the $19 billion it held in deposits and the institution was subsequently taken over by the Federal Deposit Insurance Corporation (FDIC). . . .

In September, the housing bubble, the liquidity crunch, and the financial crisis culminated in a string of unprecedented events and government interventions that took place over a 19-day stretch. During this period, Fannie Mae and Freddie Mac were placed into conservatorship, Lehman Brothers filed for bankruptcy, the Federal Reserve initiated an $85 billion government rescue of American International Group (AIG), Treasury announced a temporary guarantee of the $3.7 trillion money market funds (MMFs), and the FDIC steered Washington Mutual through the largest bank failure in U.S. history. By the beginning of October 2008, the value of the stock market had declined by nearly 20 percent from its level in January of that year, losing 10 percent in September alone. . . .

As a result of these events . . . Chairman of the Board of Governors of the Federal Reserve System Ben S. Bernanke and Secretary of the Treasury Henry M. Paulson, Jr. concluded . . . that their only realistic option to contain the rapidly spreading financial crisis was to convince Congress to authorize an overwhelming fiscal response by the federal government. . . .

[Congress] authorized the Treasury Secretary to purchase not only mortgage-related securities under the [troubled asset relief program, commonly known as "TARP," a Federal program allowing for purchases of mortgage-related securities from financial institutions,] but also "any other financial instrument" the purchase of which the Secretary determined to be "necessary to promote financial market stability." . . . Although the federal government has intervened to rescue financial institutions . . . on several previous occasions in U.S. history, the scale and breadth of the financial rescue . . . was unprecedented. . . .

On October 14, 2008, Secretary Paulson met with the heads of the nine largest U.S. banks . . . and told them that Treasury would instead make direct capital injections into each of their institutions [instead of purchasing troubled assets directly].

The nine institutions . . . included the four largest U.S. commercial banks (JPMorgan, Bank of America, Citigroup, and Wells Fargo), the three largest investment banks (Goldman Sachs, Morgan Stanley, and Merrill Lynch), and the two largest custodian banks (State Street and BNY Mellon). At that time, these banks held $10.3 trillion in assets, representing more than 75 percent of all the assets in the American banking system. . . .

In addition to the initial capital investments made in the nation's largest banks, Treasury undertook additional steps to ensure the stability of Citigroup and Bank of America in November and December 2008 by purchasing an additional $20 billion of preferred shares from both institutions. . . . Furthermore, in November, Treasury, in conjunction with the Federal Reserve and the FDIC, put together a hastily crafted $301 billion guarantee of Citigroup assets. . . .

Also in November, the federal government supplemented the original $85 billion loan to AIG and initiated a second round of assistance to AIG in which the TARP purchased $40 billion of preferred equity and the Federal Reserve provided $44 billion to create two special purpose vehicles (SPVs) to take ownership of certain AIG financial assets. Treasury also made its first investments in the automotive industry in late 2008 with loans and preferred stock purchases for General Motors, GMAC, Chrysler, and Chrysler Financial. By the end of January 2009, TARP assistance outstanding amounted to $301 billion with over 75 percent having been provided to only a few firms: the nation's biggest banks, the automotive industry, and AIG. . . .

By providing a complete bailout that called for no shared sacrifice among AIG and its creditors, FRBNY and Treasury fundamentally changed the rules of America's financial marketplace.

U.S. policy has long drawn a distinction between two different types of investments. The first type is safe products, such as checking accounts, which are highly regulated and are intended to be accessible and relatively risk free to even unsophisticated investors. Banks that offer checking accounts must accept a substantial degree of regulatory scrutiny, offer standardized features, and pay for FDIC insurance on their deposits. In return, the bank and its customers benefit from an explicit government guarantee: within certain limitations, no checking account in the United States will be allowed to lose even a penny of value.

By contrast, risky products, which are more loosely regulated, are aimed at more sophisticated players. These products often offer much higher profit margins for banks and much higher potential returns to investors, but they have never benefited from any government guarantee.

Before the AIG bailout, the derivatives market appeared to fall cleanly in the second category. Yet by bailing out AIG and its counterparties, the federal government signaled that the entire derivatives market – which had been explicitly and completely deregulated by Congress through the Commodities [*sic*] Futures Modernization Act – would now benefit from the same government safety net provided to fully regulated financial products. In essence, the government distorted the marketplace by transforming highly risky derivative bets into fully guaranteed transactions, with the American taxpayer standing as guarantor.

The Panel believes that the moral hazard problem unleashed by making whole AIG's counterparties in unregulated, unguaranteed transactions undermined the credibility of specific efforts at addressing the financial crisis that followed, including the entirety of the TARP, as well as America's system of financial regulation. . . .

In the following two sections, C and D, we evaluate the Dodd-Frank Act § 716 (the swap push-out rule) and Dodd-Frank Act § 619 (the Volcker Rule). It is important to be mindful that they overlap. Conduct might be permissible under the Volcker Rule, yet require foregoing Federal assistance due to the swap push-out rule. On the other hand, the same activity (for example, a commodity swap entered into for short-term trading gain) may violate both Volcker and be precluded by the swap push-out rule. Therefore, any analysis of an activity needs to examine its treatment under the Volcker Rule and § 716's swap push-out provisions.

C. SWAP PUSH-OUT

The Dodd-Frank Act specifically addressed the public policy concerns regarding taxpayer-funded bailouts being triggered by the derivatives activities of financial institutions.

Dodd-Frank Act § 716 requires financial institutions that significantly participate in the off-exchange derivatives markets and are, therefore, required to register with the CFTC in one of the primary swap market registrant categories[6] (all of which we discuss in Chapter 8) to, with some exceptions, forgo Federal assistance, such as the bailouts that occurred during the Financial Crisis. It is referred to as "swap push-out" since it pushes many derivatives activities out of banks and into their affiliates. Although not strictly a prohibition, it operates as one. Banks are unwilling to relinquish the Federal assistance referenced in § 716 since it is one of the perquisites of a banking charter.

Federal assistance is defined to include access to the Fed discount window, through which banks can pledge assets to receive cash, and Federal deposit insurance, without which retail deposit-taking is prohibited. Therefore, foregoing Federal assistance is not a realistic option for banks, and complying with the swap push-out rule is a necessity.

Recognizing that some derivatives activities are integral to banking, there are exceptions. Federal assistance is *not* forfeited if a bank receiving FDIC insurance or a U.S. branch or agency of a foreign bank[7] engages in swaps to hedge risk, interest rate swaps (including foreign exchange), or swaps referencing assets in which bank regulations already permit banks to invest (other than credit default swaps that are not centrally cleared[8]). Provided that an insured depository institution or U.S. branch or agency of a foreign bank complies with the limitations on inter-affiliate activities that already apply to most such entities (generally, these limitations require transactions to be arm's length and greatly limit the responsibility of the bank party for its affiliate[9]), § 716 does not limit the swaps activities of bank affiliates that do not and will not receive Federal assistance.[10]

As originally proposed, § 716 precluded even bank affiliates from engaging in many derivatives activities. A major factor in adding an exception for affiliates was the input of the banking industry and its primary regulators.

Letter from Sheila Bair, President, Federal Deposit Insurance Corporation to Senators Dodd and Lincoln

156 Cong. Rec. S3069 (daily ed. May 4, 2010)

Federal Deposit Insurance Corporation, Washington, DC, April 30, 2010.

Hon. Christopher J. Dodd, Chairman, Committee on Banking, Housing, and Urban Affairs, U.S. Senate, Washington, DC.

Hon. Blanche L. Lincoln, Chairman, Committee on Agriculture, Nutrition and Forestry, U.S. Senate, Washington, DC.

Dear Chairman Dodd and Chairman Lincoln: Thank you for reaching out to the Federal Deposit Insurance Corporation for our views on Title VII of the "Wall Street Transparency and Accountability Act" contained in S. 3217, the "Restoring American Financial Stability Act of 2010" [i.e. the Senate version of what was to become the Dodd-Frank Act]. . . .

I would like to share some concerns with respect to section 716 of S. 3217, which would require most derivatives activities to be conducted outside of banks and bank holding companies. If enacted, this provision would require that some $294 trillion in notional amount of derivatives be moved outside of banks or from bank holding companies that own insured depository institutions, presumably to nonbank financial firms such as hedge funds and futures commission merchants, or to foreign banking organizations beyond the reach of federal regulation. I would note that credit derivatives – the riskiest – held by banks and bank holding companies (when measured by notional amount) total $25.5 trillion, or slightly less than nine percent of the total derivatives held by these entities.

At the same time, it needs to be pointed out that the vast majority of banks that use OTC derivatives confine their activity to hedging interest rate risk with straightforward interest rate derivatives. Given the continuing uncertainty surrounding future movements in interest rates and the detrimental effects that these could have on unhedged banks, I encourage you to adopt an approach that would allow banks to easily hedge with OTC derivatives. . . .

In addition, I urge you to carefully consider the underlying premise of this provision – that the best way to protect the deposit insurance fund is to push higher risk activities into the so-called shadow sector. To be sure, there are certain activities, such as speculative derivatives trading, that should have no place in banks or bank holding companies. We believe the Volcker rule addresses that issue and indeed would be happy to work with you on a total ban on speculative trading, at least in the CDS market. At the same time, other types of derivatives such as customized interest rate swaps and even some CDS do have legitimate and important functions as risk management tools, and insured banks play an essential role in providing market-making functions for these products. . . .

If all derivatives market-making activities were moved outside of bank holding companies, most of the activity would no doubt continue, but in less regulated and more highly leveraged venues. . . .

We hope that a compromise can be achieved by perhaps moving some derivatives activity into affiliates, so long as capital standards remain as strict as they are for insured depositories and banks continue to be able to fully utilize derivatives for appropriate hedging activities. . . .

D. THE VOLCKER RULE

The Dodd-Frank Act § 619 is commonly known as the "Volcker Rule." It is named after Paul Volcker, former chairman of the Federal Reserve Board. It prohibits banks from engaging in "proprietary trading," i.e., speculative trading in, among other financial products, derivatives. The concept was originally publicized before the July 21, 2010 enactment of the Dodd-Frank Act by President Obama who, in a press conference on January 21, 2010, said:

> I'm proposing a simple and common-sense reform, which we're calling the "Volcker Rule." . . . Banks will no longer be allowed to own, invest, or sponsor hedge funds, private equity funds, or proprietary trading operations for their own profit, unrelated to serving their customers. If financial firms want to trade for profit, that's something they're free to do. Indeed, doing so – responsibly – is a good thing for the markets and the economy. But these firms should not be allowed to run these hedge funds and private equities funds while running a bank backed by the American people.

Remarks by the President on Financial Reform (Jan. 21, 2010), available at http://www.whitehouse.gov/the-press-office/remarks-president-financial-reform (accessed June 15, 2014).

Paul Volcker's first public remarks on the proposal were in a *New York Times* op-ed piece[11] just over a week later, followed by his testimony to the Senate in which he explained the public policy basis for the Volcker Rule.

Hearing Before the Committee on Banking, Housing and Urban Affairs, Prohibiting Certain High-Risk Investment Activities by Banks and Bank Holding Companies: Statement of Paul Volcker

S. Hrg. 11-771 (Feb. 2, 2010)

Mr. Chairman, Members of the Banking Committee . . .

I appreciate the opportunity today to discuss with you one key element in the reform effort that President Obama set out so forcibly a few days ago.

That proposal, if enacted, would restrict commercial banking organizations from certain proprietary and more speculative activities. . . . It is particularly designed to help deal with the problem of "too big to fail" and the related moral hazard that looms so large as an aftermath of the emergency rescues of financial institutions, bank and non-bank, in the midst of crises. . . .

The basic point is that there has been, and remains, a strong public interest in providing a "safety net" – in particular, deposit insurance and the provision of liquidity in emergencies – for commercial banks carrying out essential services. There is not, however, a similar rationale for public funds – taxpayer funds – protecting and supporting essentially proprietary and speculative activities. Hedge funds, private equity funds, and trading activities unrelated to customer needs and continuing banking relationships should stand on their own, without the subsidies implied by public support for depository institutions. . . .

A number of the most prominent of [investment banks], each heavily engaged in trading and other proprietary activity, failed or were forced into publicly-assisted mergers under the pressure of the crisis. It also became

> necessary to provide public support via the Federal Reserve, The Federal Deposit Insurance Corporation, or the Treasury to the largest remaining American investment banks [i.e., Goldman Sachs and Morgan Stanley[12]], both of which assumed the cloak of a banking license to facilitate the assistance. The world's largest insurance company [i.e., American International Group], caught up in a huge portfolio of credit default swaps quite apart from its basic business, was rescued only by the injection of many tens of billions of dollars of public loans and equity capital. . . .
>
> It is critically important that those institutions . . . do not assume a public rescue will be forthcoming in time of pressure. . . .
>
> [E]very banker I speak with knows very well what "proprietary trading" means and implies. My understanding is that only a handful of large commercial banks – maybe four or five in the United States and perhaps a couple of dozen worldwide – are now engaged in this activity in volume. In the past, they have sometimes explicitly labeled a trading affiliate or division as "proprietary," with the connotation that the activity is, or should be, insulated from customer relations.
>
> Most of those institutions and many others are engaged in meeting customer needs to buy or sell . . . stocks or bonds, derivatives, various commodities or other investments. Those activities may involve taking temporary positions. In the process, there will be temptations to speculate by aggressive, highly remunerated traders. . . .
>
> [P]atterns of exceptionally large gains and losses over a period of time in the "trading book" should raise [a bank] examiner's eyebrows. Persisting over time, the result should be not just raised eyebrows but substantially raised capital requirements.
>
> Third, I want to note the strong conflicts of interest inherent in the participation of commercial banking organizations in proprietary or private investment activity. . . . When the bank itself is a "customer", i.e., it is trading for its own account, it will almost inevitably find itself, consciously or inadvertently, acting at cross purposes to the interests of an unrelated commercial customer of a bank. . . . More generally, proprietary trading activity should not be able to profit from knowledge of customer trades. . . .
>
> What we can do, what we should do, is recognize that curbing the proprietary interests of commercial banks is in the interest of fair and open competition as well as protecting the provision of essential financial services. . . .
>
> By appropriately defining the business of commercial banks . . . we can go a long way toward promoting the combination of competition, innovation, and underlying stability that we seek.

The Volcker Rule ultimately embodied in § 619 of the Dodd-Frank Act required regulatory rulemaking for its implementation. On December 10, 2013, four of the five agencies charged with coordinating in finalizing the implementing rules (the Federal Reserve Board, the Federal Deposit Insurance Corporation, the Office of the Comptroller of the Currency, and the SEC), issued the final rulemaking with the CFTC's nearly identical release occurring simultaneously.[13] Illustrating the complexity and scope of the subject matter underlying the final rule, the release accompanying it contains 2,826 footnotes (2,833 in the CFTC version).[14]

The two Volcker Rule prohibitions are, at first glance, straightforward. There are bans on banking entities (1) engaging in short-term speculative trading, and (2) investing in hedge funds or private equity funds. However, the ban on short-term speculative trading, known as proprietary trading, the focus of our analysis, is replete with many exceptions that, in the aggregate, make the Volcker Rule especially complex.

Note that our analysis does not focus on the ban on banking entities investing in hedge funds or private equity funds since this is outside of the field of derivatives law and better covered in the fields of banking or securities regulation. It is also worth keeping in mind that, in evaluating the derivatives activities of banks, both Dodd-Frank Act § 716 and the Volcker Rule need to be consulted.

Prohibitions and Restrictions on Proprietary Trading and Certain Interests in, and Relationships with, Hedge Funds and Private Equity Funds

79 Fed. Reg. 5536 (January 31, 2014)[15]

. . . Section 13(a)(1)(A) of the [Bank Holding Company Act ("BHC Act")] prohibits a banking entity from engaging in proprietary trading unless otherwise permitted in section 13. . . . Section 13(h)(4) of the BHC Act defines proprietary trading, in relevant part, as engaging as principal for the trading account of the banking entity in any transaction to purchase or sell, or otherwise acquire or dispose of, a security, derivative, contract of sale of a commodity for future delivery, or other financial instrument that the Agencies include by rule. . . .

[T]he Agencies are defining proprietary trading as engaging as principal for the trading account of the banking entity in any purchase or sale of one or more financial instruments. . . .

A number of commenters expressed concern that, as a whole, the proposed rule may result in certain negative economic impacts, including: (i) reduced market liquidity; (ii) wider spreads or otherwise increased trading costs; (iii) higher borrowing costs for businesses or increased cost of capital; and/or (iv) greater market volatility. . . . [T]he termination of . . . proprietary trading activities of banking entities may lead to some general reductions in liquidity of certain asset classes. Although the Agencies cannot say with any certainty, there is good reason to believe that to a significant extent the liquidity reductions of this type may be temporary since the statute does not restrict proprietary trading activities of other market participants [and] over time, non-banking entities may provide much of the liquidity that is lost by restrictions on banking entities' trading activities. If so, eventually, the detrimental effects of increased trading costs, higher costs of capital, and greater market volatility should be mitigated. . . .

Definition of "Trading Account" . . .

Section 13(h)(6) of the BHC Act defines trading account as any account used for acquiring or taking positions in financial instruments principally for the purpose of selling in the near-term (or otherwise with the intent to resell in order to profit from short-term price movements). . . .

The proposed rule defined trading account to include three separate accounts.

First, the proposed definition of trading account included . . . any account that is used by a banking entity to acquire or take one or more covered financial positions for short-term trading purposes (the "short-term trading account"). The proposed rule identified four purposes that would indicate short-term trading intent: (i) short-term resale; (ii) benefitting from actual or expected short-term price movements; (iii) realizing short-term arbitrage profits; or (iv) hedging one or more positions described in (i), (ii) or (iii). . . .

Second, the proposed definition of trading account included any account that contains positions that qualify for trading book capital treatment under the banking agencies' market risk capital rules other than positions that are foreign exchange derivatives, commodity derivatives or contracts of sale of a commodity for delivery (the "market risk rule trading account"). . . .

Third, the proposed definition of trading account included any account used by a banking entity that is a securities dealer, swap dealer, or security-based swap dealer to acquire or take positions in connection with its dealing activities (the "dealer trading account"). . . .

After carefully reviewing the comments, the Agencies have determined to [generally] retain in the final rule the proposed approach for defining trading account that includes the short-term, market risk rule, and dealer trading accounts . . .

Rebuttable Presumption for the Short-Term Trading Account . . .

[T]he proposed rule provided that an account would be presumed to be a short-term trading account if it was used to acquire or take a covered financial position that the banking entity held for a period of 60 days or less. . . .

Based on their supervisory experience, the Agencies find that 60 days is an appropriate cut off for a regulatory presumption [of short-term trading]. . . . The Agencies are not providing a safe harbor or a reverse presumption (i.e., a presumption for positions that are outside of the trading account), as suggested by some commenters, in recognition that some proprietary trading could occur outside of the 60 day period. . . .

<u>Definition of "Financial Instrument"</u>

Under the final rule, a financial instrument is defined [with some exclusions, such as for loans and purchases or sales of physical commodities] as: (i) a security, including an option on a security; (ii) a derivative, including an option on a derivative; or (iii) a contract of sale of a commodity for future delivery, or option on a contract of sale of a commodity for future delivery. . . .

[T]he Agencies note that to the extent a banking entity purchases or sells a foreign exchange forward or swap, or any other financial instrument, in a manner that meets an exclusion from proprietary trading [such as] the purchase or sale of a financial instrument by a banking entity acting solely as agent [it is not subject to the ban] . . .

<u>Proprietary Trading Exclusions</u> . . .

[T]he final rule provides exclusions [1] . . . [for] repurchase and reverse repurchase agreements and securities lending agreements; [2] for bona fide liquidity management purposes; [3] [for trades] by . . . clearing agencies, derivatives clearing organizations in connection with clearing activities; [4] [for trades] by a member of a clearing agency, derivatives clearing organization, or designated financial market utility engaged in excluded clearing activities; [5] to satisfy existing delivery obligations; [6] to satisfy an obligation of the banking entity in connection with a judicial, administrative, self-regulatory organization, or arbitration proceeding; [7] [for acting] solely as broker, agent, or custodian; [8] [trades] through a deferred compensation or similar plan; and [9] to satisfy a debt previously contracted. . . .

<u>Section 75.4(b): Market-Making Exemption</u> . . .

Section 13(d)(1)(B) of the BHC Act provides an exemption from the prohibition on proprietary trading for the purchase, sale, acquisition, or disposition of securities, derivatives, contracts of sale of a commodity for future delivery, and options on any of the foregoing in connection with market making-related activities. . . .

[T]he final rule focuses on providing a framework for assessing whether trading activities are consistent with market making. . . . [W]hile a bright-line or safe harbor based approach would generally provide a high degree of certainty about whether an activity qualifies for the market-making exemption, it would also provide less flexibility . . . [and] would be more likely to be subject to gaming and avoidance as new products and types of trading activities are developed. . . .

[T]he final rule has been crafted around the overall market making-related activities of individual trading desks, with various requirements that these activities be demonstrably related to satisfying reasonably expected near term customer demands and other market-making activities. . . . Thus, banking entities will be able to continue to engage in market making-related activities across markets and asset classes . . .

Section 75.5: Permitted Risk-Mitigating Hedging Activities . . .

Section 13(d)(1)(C) [of the BHC Act] provides an exemption for risk-mitigating hedging activities [(the "hedging exemption")]. . . .

The final rule provides a multi-faceted approach . . . intended to permit hedging activities that are risk-mitigating and to limit potential abuse of the hedging exemption. . . .

[T]he final hedging exemption . . . permits risk-mitigating hedging activities . . . while requiring a robust compliance program and other internal controls to help ensure that only genuine risk-mitigating hedges can be used in reliance on the exemption. . . .

[T]he final rule requires that the hedging activity at inception of the hedging activity, including, without limitation, any adjustments to the hedging activity, be designed to reduce or otherwise significantly mitigate . . . one or more specific, identifiable risks, including market risk, counterparty or other credit risk, currency or foreign exchange risk, interest rate risk, commodity price risk, basis risk, or similar risks, arising in connection with and related to identified individual or aggregated positions, contracts, or other holdings of the banking entity. . . .

[T]he final rule [requires] that the compensation arrangements of persons performing risk-mitigating hedging activities be designed not to reward prohibited proprietary trading. The final rule [makes] clear that rewarding or incentivizing profit making from prohibited proprietary trading is not permitted. . . .

The final rule [requires] enhanced documentation for hedging activity conducted under the hedging exemption if the hedging is not conducted by the specific trading desk . . . responsible for the underlying positions, contracts, or other holdings, the risks of which the hedging activity is designed to reduce. . . .

Section 75.6(a)-(b): Permitted Trading in Certain Government and Municipal Obligations . . .

Section 13(d)(1)(A) permits [proprietary] trading in various U.S. government, U.S. agency and municipal securities. . . .

The final rule [does not] permit a banking entity to engage in proprietary trading of derivatives on U.S. government and agency obligations. . . .

[T]he final rule will permit banking entities to participate fully in these cash markets. In addition, the final rule permits banking entities to make a market in U.S. government securities and in derivatives on those securities. Moreover, the final rule allows banking entities to continue to use U.S. government obligations and derivatives on those obligations in risk-mitigating hedging activities permitted by the rule. . . .

[T]he Agencies have determined not to provide an exemption for proprietary trading in municipal securities, beyond the underwriting, market-making, hedging and other exemptions provided generally in the rule. . . .

Section 75.6(c): Permitted Trading on Behalf of Customers

Section 13(d)(1)(D) of the BHC Act provides an exemption from the prohibition on proprietary trading for the purchase, sale, acquisition, or disposition of financial instruments on behalf of customers. The statute does not define when a transaction or activity is conducted "on behalf of customers." . . .

The final rule . . . permits transactions in any financial instrument, including derivatives such as foreign exchange forwards, so long as those transactions are on behalf of customers. . . .

Section 75.6(e): Permitted Trading Activities of a Foreign Banking Entity

Section 13(d)(1)(H) of the BHC Act permits certain foreign banking entities to engage in proprietary trading that occurs solely outside of the United States (the "foreign trading exemption"). The statute does not define when a foreign banking entity's trading occurs solely outside of the United States. . . .

[T]he final rule provides that the exemption for the proprietary trading activity of a foreign banking entity is available only if:

- The banking entity engaging as principal in the purchase or sale (including any personnel of the banking entity or its affiliate that arrange, negotiate or execute such purchase or sale) is not located in the United States or organized under the laws of the United States or of any State; . . .
- The purchase or sale, including any transaction arising from risk-mitigating hedging related to the instruments purchased or sold, is not accounted for as principal directly or on a consolidated basis by any branch or affiliate that is located in the United States or organized under the laws of the United States or of any State;
- No financing for the banking entity's purchase or sale is provided . . . by any branch or affiliate . . . located in the United States . . . ;

- The purchase or sale is not conducted with or through any U.S. entity, other than [a] purchase or sale with the foreign operations of a U.S. entity, if no personnel of such U.S. entity . . . are involved. . . .

The Agencies believe it is appropriate to exercise their exemptive authority under section 13(d)(1)(J) to also allow . . . the following types of purchases or sales conducted with a U.S. entity:

- A purchase or sale with an unaffiliated market intermediary acting as principal, provided the purchase or sale is promptly cleared and settled through a clearing agency or derivatives clearing organization acting as a central counterparty; or
- A purchase or sale through an unaffiliated market intermediary, provided the purchase or sale is conducted anonymously . . . on an exchange or similar trading facility and promptly cleared and settled through a clearing agency or derivatives clearing organization acting as a central counterparty. . . .

Section 75.7: Limitations on Permitted Trading Activities

. . . [S]ection 13(d)(2) of the BHC Act . . . provides that a banking entity may not engage in certain exempt activities (e.g., permitted market making-related activities, risk-mitigating hedging, etc.) if the activity [1] would involve or result in a material conflict of interest between the banking entity and its clients, customers, or counterparties; [2] result, directly or indirectly, in a material exposure by the banking entity to a high-risk asset or a high-risk trading strategy; [3] or pose a threat to the safety and soundness of the banking entity or U.S. financial stability. . . .

The Volcker Rule, as can be seen from the above, is extremely complicated and presents a substantial departure from pre-existing market practices. The costs of the Volcker Rule have been estimated by the Office of the Comptroller of the Currency, primary regulator of many of the affected banks, as between \$412 million and \$4.3 billion upon implementation and up to \$550 million in annual compliance costs.[16]

E. RETAIL SWAPS PROHIBITION

The final transactional prohibition imposed by the Dodd-Frank Act is a prohibition on retail swaps, other than if traded on designated contract markets. As we know from Chapter 4, designated contract markets are markets historically regulated by the CFTC where commodity futures and options contracts are traded.

The prohibition in Commodity Exchange Act § 2(e) operates by requiring all swaps traded on other than a designated contract market to be between "eligible contract participants." As we will see, eligible contract participants are, by definition, entities which are non-retail.

1. *Historical Function of Eligible Contract Participant Definition*

The definition of "eligible contract participant" first appeared in the Commodity Futures Modernization Act (though its predecessor, "eligible swap participant," first appeared in CFTC regulations in 1993).[17] Its original purpose was to denote categories of derivatives transactions for which the CFTC's and SEC's oversight was limited to fraud prevention.[18] As we will see below in section E2, the Dodd-Frank Act changed the function of the definition dramatically from its pre-Dodd-Frank function.

The pre-Dodd-Frank allowed a largely unregulated market in swaps between financially sophisticated entities to flourish, as described in Chapter 2. Swaps between eligible contract participants were generally "unregulated" by the CFTC or SEC.

2. *Eligible Contract Participants*

Swaps post-Dodd-Frank Act are not only heavily regulated, as we will see in the forthcoming chapters, they are also illegal *unless* between eligible contract participants or on a designated contract market. This reflects a substantial retreat from deregulation of transactions between sophisticated counterparties. This operates by way of amendment to the Commodity Exchange Act made by the Dodd-Frank Act:

> It shall be unlawful for any person, other than an eligible contract participant, to enter into a swap unless the swap is entered into on . . . a board of trade designated as a contract market. . . ."

Commodity Exchange Act § 2(e) (as amended by Dodd-Frank Act § 723(a)(2)).

The definition of eligible contract participant, since it determines who may participate in the non-retail swaps market, is of critical importance.

Definition of Eligible Contract Participant

Commodity Exchange Act § 1a(18)

The term "eligible contract participant" means –

(A) acting for its own account –

(i) a financial institution;

(ii) an insurance company . . . including a regulated subsidiary or affiliate . . . ;

(iii) an investment company . . . or a foreign person performing a similar role or function subject as such to foreign regulation (regardless of whether each investor . . . is itself an eligible contract participant);

(iv) a commodity pool that –

(I) has total assets exceeding $5,000,000; and

(II) is formed and operated by a [commodity pool operator registered with the CFTC or exempt from registration] . . . provided, however, that . . . the term "eligible contract participant" shall not include a commodity pool in which any participant is not otherwise an eligible contract participant;

(v) a corporation, partnership, proprietorship, organization, trust, or other entity –

(I) that has total assets exceeding $10,000,000;

(II) the obligations of which under an agreement . . . are guaranteed . . . by an entity [with assets exceeding $10,000,000, meeting any of the foregoing tests or a government entity]; or

(III) that –

(aa) has a net worth exceeding $1,000,000; and

(bb) enters into an agreement . . . in connection with the conduct of the entity's business or to [hedge risk];

(vi) an employee benefit plan –

(I) that has total assets exceeding $5,000,000; or

(II) the investment decisions of which are made by –

(aa) an investment adviser or commodity trading advisor . . . ;

(bb) a foreign person performing a similar role . . . subject . . . to foreign regulation;

(cc) a financial institution; or

(dd) an insurance company . . . or a regulated subsidiary or affiliate . . . ;

(vii) [governmental and quasi-governmental entities]

(I) a governmental entity . . . ;

(II) a multinational or supranational government entity; or

(III) an instrumentality, agency, or department of [either of the foregoing meeting additional financial criteria] . . .

(viii) [securities brokers and holding companies]

(I) a broker or dealer . . . or a foreign person performing a similar role . . . subject . . . to foreign regulation . . . [unless] a natural person or proprietorship . . . ;

(II) an associated person of a registered broker or dealer . . . ;

(III) an investment bank holding company . . . ;

(ix) a futures commission merchant . . . or a foreign person performing a similar role . . . subject . . . to foreign regulation . . . [unless] a natural person or proprietorship . . . ;

(x) a floor broker or floor trader . . . ; or

(xi) an individual who has amounts invested on a discretionary basis . . . in excess of –

(I) $10,000,000; or

(II) $5,000,000 and who enters into the agreement . . . [to hedge risk];

(B) [Acting as agent –]

(i) a person . . . [itself meeting certain of the eligible contract participant categories] acting as broker . . . ; or

(ii) an investment adviser . . . , a commodity trading advisor . . . , a foreign person performing a similar role . . . subject . . . to foreign regulation, or a person . . . [meeting certain of the eligible contract participant categories] acting as investment manager or fiduciary . . . ; or

(C) any other person that the Commission determines to be eligible . . .

Although the definition of eligible contract participant has multi-faceted tests applying to some entities, the definition is straightforward for the preponderance of potential parties to a swap which are corporations or natural persons. For corporations, this means a $10,000,000 net worth test (or $1,000,000 if the swap relates to its business or is for risk hedging) and, for individuals, this means a person investing $10,000,000 on a discretionary basis (or $5,000,000 if the swap is for risk hedging).

The CFTC, by rulemaking, has made minor additions to the list of entities qualifying as eligible contract participants.[19]

In addition to the outright prohibitions on swap activities enacted in Dodd-Frank Act §§ 619 and 716 and Commodity Exchange Act § 2(a)(1), the Dodd-Frank Act also instituted a comprehensive regulatory regime that, though influenced by the existing regulatory regime for commodity futures and options, was nonetheless new. This regulatory regime is the subject of Chapter 8 through 10.

QUESTIONS AND COMMENTS

1. Why was the bailout of American International Group such a dramatic event? What is the difference in public policy concerns, if any, between the bailout of a insured depository bank and an entity such as American International Group?
2. How did the Financial Crisis affect you, if at all? What were your views at the time and have they changed?
3. Enumerate some of the functions of derivatives (Chapter 1 provides some refreshment on this topic). To the extent the swap push-out rule displaces traditional bank participants in the derivatives area, how should the gap be filled?
4. The Volcker Rule has been criticized for its complexity. Much of the complexity, however, lies in its exemptions. If you were charged with implementing the policy goals of the Volcker Rule (i.e., limiting commercial deposit banks to their traditional lending-focused activities), how would you implement them?
5. The prohibition on non-eligible contract participants trading swaps is motivated, to a large extent, by a view that non-eligible contract participants lack the economic sophistication and financial risk-taking means, to trade swaps. This is similar to the rationale underlying, among others, the securities "accredited investor" regime that allows broad participation in private securities offerings only by "accredited investors." Is it appropriate for government to allow only some (wealthier) persons to participate in these activities? Should a *caveat emptor* approach apply, just as it does with most other economic sectors?

CHAPTER 8 SWAP MARKET REGISTRANTS

A. BACKGROUND

1. *Newly Created CFTC Registration Categories*

The Dodd-Frank Act imposed a new regulatory regime for the swaps market and its participants, which has been jointly summarized by the CFTC and SEC as:

> a statutory framework to reduce risk, increase transparency, and promote market integrity within the financial system by, among other things: (i) providing for the registration and regulation of swap dealers and major swap participants; (ii) imposing clearing and trade execution requirements on standardized derivative products; (iii) creating recordkeeping and real-time reporting regimes; and (iv) enhancing the [CFTC's and SEC's] rulemaking and enforcement authorities with respect to all registered entities and intermediaries subject to [their] oversight.

Further Definition of "Swap Dealer," "Security-Based Swap Dealer," "Major Swap Participant," "Major Security-Based Swap Participant" and "Eligible Contract Participant", 77 Fed. Reg. 30596 (May 23, 2012), 30596.

This chapter focuses on the first item enumerated in the above list, i.e., the main categories of swaps market registrants required to register with the CFTC, swaps dealers and major swap participants. The other new categories of CFTC registrants, swap execution facilities and swap data repositories, are discussed in Chapter 9, where we also revisit derivatives clearing organizations and clearing and trade execution requirements. Reporting requirements are addressed in Chapter 9 with respect to cleared swap transaction and Chapter 10 with respect to uncleared swap transaction.

2. Treatment of Existing CFTC Registration Categories

For decades before the Dodd-Frank Act, the CFTC operated a regulatory regime for the commodity futures and options markets, the focus of our discussions in Chapters 4 through 6. Accordingly, the CFTC bears primary responsibility (shared with the National Futures Association) for the registration and regulation of futures commission merchants, introducing brokers, commodity pool operators, and commodity trading advisors.

The Dodd-Frank Act augmented this regime in two particularly significant ways.

First, swaps activities can provide a basis to register as a futures commission merchant, introducing broker, commodity pool operator, or commodity trading advisor, just as commodity futures and options activities did historically.

> Example 1: Hot Swap Trades, LLC, accepts money from a broad base of investors, which it will pool in an entity it manages titled Swaps Only Return Pool and seek to obtain a return for the investors solely by entering into swaps.
>
> Before the Dodd-Frank Act, Swaps Only Return Pool would not meet the definition of commodity pool (for a discussion on commodity pools, commodity pool operators, and commodity trading advisors generally, *see* Chapter 6) because the moneys were not pooled for the purposes of investing in commodity futures or option transactions. Without Swaps Only Return Pool meeting the definition of commodity pool, Hot Swap Trades, LLC, would not have an obligation to register with the CFTC as a commodity pool operator. Due to the Dodd-Frank Act, though, swaps trading activities are now included as one of the activities of a pool that would cause it, subject to the exceptions discussed in Chapter 6, to be deemed a commodity pool, therefore requiring Hot Swap Trades, LLC, subject again to the exceptions discussed in Chapter 6, to register with the CFTC as a commodity pool operator.
>
> Example 2: The Cutting Edge Swap Advisory Company has a business where, for a percentage of market returns, it will provide customized advice to customers as to how to make money in the swap markets. The business is very successful, with over 30 customers.
>
> Before the Dodd-Frank Act, the Cutting Edge Swap Advisory Company would not have an obligation to register as a commodity trading advisor with the CFTC because its advisory role did not relate to commodity futures or options transactions. Due to the Dodd-Frank Act, the Cutting Edge Swap Advisory Company would now be required to register with the CFTC as a

commodity trading advisory because swaps advisory activities now also potentially trigger register.

Second, the CFTC now has explicit oversight of the swaps activities of existing futures commission merchant, introducing broker, commodity pool operator, and commodity trading advisor registrants.

B. HISTORICAL MARKET PRACTICES

As discussed throughout, most activities in the off-exchange swaps market had no CFTC regulatory implications before passage of the Dodd-Frank Act. This is no longer the case, and the primary focus of this chapter is the registration and related regulatory requirements for the primary participants in the swaps market.

Additionally, before the Dodd-Frank Act, the swaps market was predominantly comprised of parties bilaterally negotiating and entering into transactions. These were typically off-exchange and without any centralized clearing.

Today this is not the case for many categories of counterparties and transactions because of the mandatory clearing and on-facility trading requirements we discuss in Chapter 9. For some counterparty and transaction types, though, the swaps market still operates such that parties bilaterally negotiate and enter into transactions that are off-exchange and not centrally cleared. We discuss this in greater detail in Chapter 10.

The below case describes the participants in the historical off-exchange swaps market. An understanding of the historical off-exchange swaps market is relevant to understanding the residual portion of the swaps market that still operates on this model, as well as the regulatory framework that, in many cases, replaced it.

Bank One Corporation v. Commissioner of Internal Revenue

120 T.C. 174 (Tax 2003)

. . . Those who use financial derivatives in general can identify, isolate, and manage separately the fundamental risks and other characteristics which are bound together in traditional financial instruments. In addition to increasing the range of financial products available, financial derivatives have fostered more precise ways of understanding, quantifying, and managing financial risk. Most institutional borrowers and investors . . . use financial derivatives. Many of these entities also act as intermediaries dealing in those financial products. . . .

Interest rate swaps generally require that the parties thereto negotiate and agree upon several economic terms. These terms generally include (1) a notional amount, (2) a fixed interest rate, (3) a floating interest rate index, (4) a duration (term or tenor) of the contract, (5) an effective date of the contract, and (6) a payment schedule. The parties to an interest rate swap also must negotiate a particular country's currency (or countries' currencies) in which a swap is denominated. . . .

The main participants in the interest rate swaps market are end users, dealers, and brokers. . . .

End users are typically major corporations, government or governmental-related entities, investment funds, or other financial institutions. These end-users typically use . . . swaps to combat interest rate movements, express market preferences through position taking, and/or reduce their cost of funding. . . .

Since at least 1992, the swaps market has been almost entirely intermediated by institutions acting as dealers. Swaps dealers are generally major financial institutions (e.g., securities firms and banks . . .) which hold themselves out as market-makers; i.e., entities ready and willing to take either side of a swap transaction for the purpose of earning a profit by originating new swaps. On some occasions, these institutions enter into swaps in their capacity as swaps dealers. On other occasions, these institutions enter into swaps in their capacity as end users to manage the overall structure of their portfolios to minimize the net exposure to interest rate movements. Swaps dealers trade with both end-users and other dealers. . . .

Swaps dealers maintain a portfolio of swaps on their books and usually attempt to maintain a neutral, hedged position in the market. Swaps dealers attempt to maintain a neutral, hedged position either by: (1) Serving as a counterparty to opposite sides of two matching swaps or (2) managing the overall structure of the portfolio so as to minimize the net exposure to interest rate movements. . . .

When the swaps market first began, every swap generally was facilitated by a dealer. The dealer was not a party to the transaction but, generally for a fee, arranged the swap by introducing the counterparties to each other and helping them to effect the mechanics of the transaction. With the evolution of the market, dealers became parties to each swap. In the early years of the market's evolution, a dealer would effect a swap transaction by warehousing the swap (i.e., entering into the swap without having entered into a matching swap but with the expectation of hedging the entered-into swap either through a matching swap or a portfolio of swaps or temporarily in the cash, securities, or futures market) until the dealer could arrange an offsetting swap with another counterparty (i.e., match a book). In the later years of the market's evolution, the dealer would simply accept a position opposite the counterparty without expecting to locate another counterparty transaction to match the first transaction. . . .

Swap brokers do not take a position or act as a principal in a swap transaction, and they do not maintain any exposure with respect to a swap. Swap brokers simply arrange for dealers to enter into interdealer swaps by matching dealers who want to effect a particular swap with other dealers who want to effect a similar swap. . . . A swap broker is paid a standard fee for its services based on a percentage of the notional principal amount. . . .

As we examine the CFTC's swap market registration categories, we should evaluate how these categories match the categories described at the time of *Bank One Corporation*. For example, the swap dealer category the case describes has a direct analogue in the CFTC "swap dealer" registration. Swap brokers are required to register with the CFTC as futures commission merchants or introducing brokers. In Chapter 9, though, we will see that the swap dealer's former role as acting as direct principal to its customer has changed in fundamental ways due to the Dodd-Frank Act's clearing and on-facility trading requirements.

What about the end-user entities *Bank One Corporation* references that are neither swap dealers nor swap brokers? In rare cases, these entities are now required to register with the CFTC as "major swap participants," a previously undefined community of non-dealers engaged in significant speculative swaps trading activities.

In many cases, the obligations of swap dealers and major swap participants are identical. Swap dealers, however, can engage in customer dealing activities. This may partially explain why, as noted below in section D2, only two entities are registered as major swap participants. If the regulatory requirements are similar, why not choose the swap dealer registration category that offers more versatility?

This chapter and Chapters 9 and 10 will primarily focus on the regulatory regime imposed on swap dealers. Major swap participants will be directly addressed below in section D and otherwise by describing the swap dealer regime and noting where the regime for major swap participants differs.

In the context of clearing and swap execution facility trading requirements discussed in Chapter 9, we will also account for a category of end-user non-registrant, known as financial end-users. These entities, though not subject to any CFTC registration obligation, have some clearing and on-facility trading obligations.

C. SWAP DEALERS

Swap dealers, functionally described in *Bank One Corporation*, now are defined by the Commodity Exchange Act and CFTC regulation. Swap dealers are required to register with the CFTC. The Commodity Exchange Act defines a swap dealer as any person who:

> (i) holds itself out as a dealer in swaps;
> (ii) makes a market in swaps;
> (iii) regularly enters into swaps with counterparties as an ordinary course of business for its own account; or
> (iv) engages in any activity causing the person to be commonly known in the trade as a dealer or market maker in swaps, provided however, in no event shall an insured depository institution be considered to be a swap dealer to the extent it offers to enter into a swap with a customer in connection with originating a loan with that customer.

Commodity Exchange Act § 1a(49).

The CFTC and SEC were tasked by Congress to jointly formulate rules further defining "swap dealer."[1] Instead of providing a codification of the statutory provisions, the rules provide broad guidance that, arguably, raises as many, if not more, interpretative questions than the statute. Of particular note, is the extraordinary – and by the CFTC unprecedented – deference to the body of law and administrative materials regarding securities dealing as being highly influential in identifying swap dealing activities.

Further Definition of "Swap Dealer," "Security-Based Swap Dealer," "Major Swap Participant," "Major Security-Based Swap Participant" and "Eligible Contract Participant"

77 Fed. Reg. 30596-01 (May 23, 2012)

. . . The Dodd-Frank Act contains a comprehensive definition of the term "swap dealer," based upon types of activities. . . . [W]e are adopting a final rule under the CEA that . . . defines the term "swap dealer" using terms from the four statutory tests. . . .

The rule provides that certain swaps are not considered in the determination of whether a person is a swap dealer. In particular, swaps entered into by an insured depository institution with a customer in connection with originating a loan with that customer, swaps between majority-owned affiliates, swaps entered into by a cooperative with its members, swaps entered into for hedging physical positions as defined in the rule, and certain swaps entered into by registered floor traders are excluded from the swap dealer determination.

If . . . [a] person determines that it is engaged in swap dealing activity, the next step is to determine if the person is engaged in more than a *de minimis* quantity of swap dealing. If so, the person is a swap dealer. . . .

This guidance separately addresses the following: application of the dealer-trader framework; the "holding out" and "commonly known" criteria; market making; the not part of "a regular business" exception; the exclusion of swaps entered into for hedging physical positions as defined in the rule; and the overall interpretive approach to the definition.

a. Use of the Dealer-Trader Distinction

We believe that the dealer-trader distinction – which already forms a basis for identifying which persons fall within the longstanding [Securities Exchange Act of 1934] definition of "dealer" – in general provides an appropriate framework for interpreting the statutory definition of the term "swap dealer." While there are differences in the structure of those two statutory definitions,[i] we believe that their parallels – particularly their exclusions for activities that are "not part of a regular business" – warrant analogous interpretive approaches for distinguishing dealers from non-dealers. Thus, the dealer-trader distinction forms the basis for a framework that appropriately distinguishes between persons who should be regulated as swap dealers and those who should not. We also believe that the distinction affords an appropriate degree of flexibility to the analysis, and that it would not be appropriate to seek to codify the distinction in rule text.

The Commissions recognize that the dealer-trader distinction needs to be adapted to apply to swap activities in light of the special characteristics of swaps and the differences between the "dealer" definition, on the one hand, and the "swap dealer" definition, on the other. Relevant differences between the swap market and the markets for securities (other than security-based swaps) include:

> Level of activity – Swap markets are marked by less activity than markets involving certain types of securities . . . [I]n the swap context, concepts of "regularity" should account for a participant's level of activity in the market relative to the total size of the market.

---

[i] [N. 174] For example, while the "dealer" definition encompasses certain persons in the business of "buying and selling" securities, the "swap dealer" definition does not address either "buying" or "selling." We also note that the "dealer" definition requires the conjunctive "buying and selling" – which connotes a degree of offsetting two-sided activity. In contrast, the swap dealer definition (particularly the "regularly enters into" swaps language of the definition's third prong) lacks that conjunctive terminology.

> No separate issuer – Each counterparty to a swap in essence is the "issuer'' of that instrument; in contrast, dealers in cash market securities generally transact in securities issued by another party. This distinction suggests that the concept of maintaining an "inventory" of securities is inapposite in the context of swaps. . . .
>
> Predominance of over-the-counter and non-standardized instruments – Swaps . . . thus far are not significantly traded on exchanges or other trading systems. . . .[ii]
>
> Mutuality of obligations and significance to "customer" relationship – In contrast to a . . . securities . . . purchase or sale transaction . . . , the parties to a swap often will have an ongoing obligation to exchange cash flows over the life of the agreement. . . .

[T]he following activities are indicative that a person is acting as a swap dealer: (i) Providing liquidity by accommodating demand for or facilitating interest in . . . [a swap,] holding oneself out as willing to enter into swaps . . . or being known in the industry as being available to accommodate demand for swaps; (ii) advising a counterparty as to how to use swaps to meet the counterparty's hedging goals, or structuring swaps on behalf of a counterparty; (iii) having a regular clientele and actively advertising or soliciting clients in connection with swaps; (iv) acting in a market maker capacity on an organized exchange or trading system for swaps; and (v) helping to set the prices offered in the market (such as by acting as a market maker) rather than taking those prices . . .

The Commissions further note that the following . . . [elements apply to the] swap dealer definition . . . : (i) A willingness to enter into swaps on either side of the market is not a prerequisite to swap dealer status; (ii) the swap dealer analysis does not turn on whether a person's swap dealing activity constitutes that person's sole or predominant business; (iii) a customer relationship is not a prerequisite to swap dealer status; and (iv) in general, entering into a swap for the purpose of hedging, absent other activity, is unlikely to be indicative of dealing. . . .

Prior interpretations and future developments in the law . . . regarding securities . . . may inform the interpretation of the swap dealer definition, but will not be dispositive in identifying dealers in the swap markets.[iii]

[ii] [N. 177] Even though we expect trading of swaps on exchanges following the implementation of Title VII [of the Dodd-Frank Act], we expect there to remain a significant amount of over-the-counter activity involving swaps.

[iii] [N. 185] In interpreting the term "swap dealer," we intend to consider, but do not formally adopt, the body of court decisions, SEC releases, and SEC staff no-action letters that have interpreted the dealer-trader distinction.

b. Indicia of Holding Oneself Out as a Dealer in Swaps or Being Commonly Known in the Trade as a Dealer in Swaps . . .

[T]he term [swap dealer] includes a person that is holding itself out as a dealer in swaps or is engaging in any activity causing it to be commonly known in the trade as a dealer or market maker in swaps. . . . [A] number of factors . . . [are] indicia of "hold[ing] itself out as a dealer in swaps" and "engag[ing] in any activity causing [itself] to be commonly known in the trade as a dealer or market maker in swaps."[iv] . . .

Because of the flexibility – including the consideration of applicable facts and circumstances – needed for such an analysis, we do not believe that it is appropriate to codify this guidance in rule text. . . .

c. Market Making . . .

The final rule defining "swap dealer" includes the provision from the proposed rule which incorporates the statutory requirement that this term include a person that "makes a market in swaps." . . .

[W]e clarify that making a market in swaps is appropriately described as routinely standing ready to enter into swaps at the request or demand of a counterparty. In this regard, "routinely" means that the person must do so more frequently than occasionally, but there is no requirement that the person do so continuously. . . .

Such activities include routinely: (i) Quoting bid or offer prices, rates or other financial terms for swaps on an exchange; (ii) responding to requests made directly, or indirectly through an interdealer broker, by potential counterparties for bid or offer prices, rates or other similar terms for bilaterally negotiated swaps; (iii) placing limit orders for swaps; or (iv) receiving compensation for acting in a market maker capacity on an organized exchange or trading system for swaps. . . .

In determining whether a person's routine presence in the market constitutes market making under these four factors, the dealer-trader interpretative framework may be usefully applied. . . .

[iv] . . . [The relevant] factors are as follows: Contacting potential counterparties to solicit interest; developing new types of swaps . . . and informing potential counterparties of their availability and of the person's willingness to enter into the swap . . . ; membership in a swap association [such as the International Swaps and Derivatives Association, also known as "ISDA"] in a category reserved for dealers; providing marketing materials describing the type of swaps . . . the party is willing to enter into; and generally expressing a willingness to offer or provide a range of products or services that include swaps. . . .

d. Exception for Activities Not Part of "a Regular Business"

The final rule includes the provisions . . . of the statutory definition regarding activities that are not part of "a regular business" of entering into swaps. One provision states that the term "swap dealer" includes a person that "regularly enters into swaps with counterparties as an ordinary course of business for its own account"; the other provision states that the term "swap dealer" does not include a person that "enters into swaps for such person's own account, either individually or in a fiduciary capacity, but not as a part of a regular business." . . .

[A]ny one of the following activities would generally constitute both entering into swaps "as an ordinary course of business" and "as a part of a regular business": (i) Entering into swaps with the purpose of satisfying the business or risk management needs of the counterparty (as opposed to entering into swaps to accommodate one's own demand or desire to participate in a particular market); (ii) maintaining a separate profit and loss statement reflecting the results of swap activity or treating swap activity as a separate profit center; or (iii) having staff and resources allocated to dealer-type activities with counterparties, including activities relating to credit analysis, customer onboarding, document negotiation, confirmation generation, requests for novations and amendments, exposure monitoring and collateral calls, covenant monitoring, and reconciliation. . . .

e. . . . Swaps Entered Into for Hedging Physical Positions . . .

[T]he statutory definition leaves the treatment of hedging swaps to the CFTC's discretion . . .

In general, entering into a swap for the purpose of hedging is inconsistent with swap dealing. The practical difficulty lies in determining when a person has entered into a swap for the purpose of hedging, as opposed to other purposes . . .

Specifically, the CFTC . . . will not consider a swap that the person enters into, if:

> (i) The person enters into the swap for the purpose of . . . mitigating the person's price risks that arise from the potential change in the value of one or several (a) assets that the person owns . . . or anticipates owning . . . ; (b) liabilities that the person owns or anticipates incurring; or (c) services that the person provides, purchases, or anticipates providing or purchasing;
>
> (ii) the swap represents a substitute for transactions made or to be made . . . in a physical marketing channel;

(iii) the swap is economically appropriate to the reduction of the person's risks in the conduct and management of a commercial enterprise;

(iv) the swap is entered into in accordance with sound commercial practices; and

(v) the person does not enter into the swap in connection with activity structured to evade designation as a swap dealer.[v] . . .

[T]here may be circumstances where a person's activity of entering into swaps is encompassed by the statutory definition of the term "swap dealer," notwithstanding that the swaps have the effect of hedging or mitigating the person's commercial risk. . . .

The CFTC believes that since the over-the-counter swap markets have operated largely without regulatory oversight and encompass swaps used for a wide variety of commercial purposes, no method has yet been developed to reliably distinguish, through a per se rule, between: (i) Swaps that are entered into for the purpose of hedging or mitigating commercial risk; and (ii) swaps that are entered into for the purpose of accommodating the counterparty's needs or demands or otherwise constitute swap dealing activity, but which also have a hedging consequence. . . .

f. Swaps Entered Into by Persons Registered as Floor Traders . . .

[T]he CFTC believes that it would lead to potentially duplicative regulation if floor traders engaging in swaps in their capacity as floor traders were also required to register as swap dealers. . . .

There is also a *de minimis* exception to swap dealer registration.[2] Swap dealer registration is not required if the sum of the notional of all of the swaps entered into through swap dealing activities over any preceding 12-month period for the party and any affiliates (i.e., entities "controlling, controlled by or under common control"[3]) is below $8 billion or, with respect to "special entities" (a regulatory category discussed in Chapter 10) $25 million. The CFTC has the authority to drop the $8 billion notional test down to $3 billion. The CFTC has proposed to exclude special entities that are public utilities from the $25 million *de minimis* sub-limit applicable to special entities and instead to treat such swaps as ordinary trades subject to the $8 billion *de minimis* limit.[4]

As of June 16, 2014, 102 swap dealers have provisionally registered with the CFTC.[5]

---

[v] [N. 215] All five requirements set forth in the regulation must be met . . . for the swap to be excluded from the swap dealer determination . . .

D. MAJOR SWAP PARTICIPANTS

1. *Regulatory Motivation*

Whereas significant numbers of market parties have registered with the CFTC as swap dealers, only two have registered as major swap participants, and none have done so since March 1, 2013.[6] The "major swap participant" category was intended to encompass hedge funds and other non-dealers acquiring significant exposures to swaps on a speculative basis. The bailout of American International Group, discussed in Chapter 7, provided the primary motivation for the creation of this category of registrant.

Unlike the term "swap dealer," which existed prior to the swap dealer registrant category, the term "major swap participant" is an invention of the Dodd-Frank Act. In the following Senate hearing, during a discussion on a proposal by the Department of the Treasury, which formed the backbone of the bill that later became the Dodd-Frank Act, the new term "major swap participant" was discussed. The participants are the former chair of the Senate Agriculture Committee, Senator Blanche Lincoln, and Gary Gensler, a significant proponent of the Dodd-Frank Act and, at the time, chairman of the CFTC.

Senate Committee on Agriculture, Nutrition and Forestry, *Reforming U.S. Financial Market Regulation*

S. Hrg. 11-799 (November 18, 2009)

. . . LINCOLN: A major swap participant is defined in the Treasury proposal as a non-dealer who maintains substantial net positions in outstanding swaps. For the purpose other than to create and maintain an effective hedge . . . I understand that some of the players want a limited . . . definition of the MSP so that, not to kind of get pulled into that category. . . .

Are you comfortable with the Treasury's definition of major swap participants? . . . Is a substantial net position standard workable and is it going to capture all the institutions that pave the kind of systemic risk that we're trying to get at?

GENSLER: What we're trying to do in the legislation is ensure that there's two complementary regimes: that the dealers are regulated, they have to register and be regulated, have capital and business conduct [standards]; and then that the markets themselves have these clearing and trading requirements.

"Major swap participant" is a term that nine months ago none of us knew. It was just created in the legislative language. But what it's really trying to address is the next AIG or the near-dealers, something that is not quite a financial institution, but it holds itself out to the public as a substantial net swaps business. There are many counterparties that would be at risk if it failed.

And I don't know it's [a] broad category. It's not meant to pick up the thousands of end-users or even the hundreds of end-users. It's supposed to – I believe it should be a category that is included, that we not just bring this regulation to the five or six large financial institutions. There are some, sort of, the next AIG or the next swap dealer category. . . .

It is an understatement to note that the events related to American International Group provided the primary motivation for the major swap participant registration category. The following quotes from the above hearing help to illustrate the centrality of American International Group in the discussion.

> GENSLER [speaking to Senator Stabenow of Michigan]: I think that every manufacturer in your state and all of the states suffered greatly when AIG went asunder and $180 billion of our taxpayer money. I mean roughly $3.5 billion per state. . . . And so, that's the risk we're trying to protect against – that large financial institutions aren't so interconnected with the economy at large and that we try to move these transactions over to these well regulated clearinghouses. . . .[7]
>
> [Senator] CONRAD: I remember, very well, Senator [Lincoln], several years ago Warren Buffett called derivatives a "nuclear time bomb." And we saw the bomb go off. I will never forget, as long as I live, being called after one of our group of 10 meetings, Senator Chambliss, being called to the leader's office and I got there and there were the leaders, Republican and Democrat of Congress, and the chairman of the Federal Reserve and the secretary of treasury, and they were telling us they were taking over AIG the next day. They weren't there to ask us. They were there to inform us. And they told us, in no uncertain terms they believed if it was not done, there would be a global financial collapse. Now that's about as stark as anything can be.
>
> So, already just on the AIG debacle, we've seen taxpayers saddled with $180 billion of debt. We must act to prevent that from ever happening again. . . .
>
> [I]n that meeting when I described where we were told the government was going to take over AIG because there would be a global financial collapse if it was not done, what became clear is that AIG had written insurance contracts and they didn't have the capital to back up the commitment. And somehow, we have got an absolute obligation to make sure that can't happen again. . . . It would be unthinkable if we were to permit that same circumstance to occur again.[8]

> [Senator] CHAMBLISS: If we have had had total transparency, if AIG had been required to report to . . . the CFTC . . . the details of all of their transactions, would not that have put not only CFTC in a better position, but the potential buyers of AIG products or investors in AIG products in a much better position to look at them and say: Wow, they've got all these transactions out there, and all these obligations out there, but they don't [have] the capital. And aren't these sophisticated traders just that. They are so sophisticated that they would have known that AIG was not capable of delivering on the products that they were selling or that their capital was so low that there was no way they could meet those commitments, and they wouldn't have made the investment if there had been total transparency at that time. . . .[9]
>
> [Senator] CONRAD: What strikes me about this conversation is transparency as I see it is necessary, but not sufficient. In the case of AIG, as my memory serves me, one of the big financial houses wanted to go from 10-to-one leverage to 30-to-one leverage. They knew there was inherent risk in moving to that kind of leverage. If everything is going well, you make a lot more money. If things are not going well, you lose a lot more money.
>
> And so they recognized the need for an insurance product and they went to AIG and convinced them to write such insurance products, and AIG saw a gift horse and said, "Oh, yes, we can make a lot of money on this deal." What they forgot about is having the resources to cover against the downside risk of these transactions. And when the downside risk occurred, here we go. Taxpayers were the ultimate funder of the liability. That we cannot permit to happen again. . . .[10]

2. *Definition*

a. Generally

A major swap participant is defined in 17 C.F.R. § 1.3(hhh) as any entity that is not a swap dealer and either maintains a "substantial position" in swaps that are not for hedging purposes (i.e., are speculative in nature) or whose swaps exposure to counterparties "could have serious adverse effects on the financial stability of the United States banking system or financial markets." A second definition, also contained in 17 C.F.R. § 1.3(hhh) applies solely to "financial entities" that maintain a "substantial position" in swaps, *including swaps for hedging purposes*, and is "highly leveraged relative to the amount of capital such entity holds and that is not subject to capital requirements established by an appropriate Federal banking agency. . . ." The term "highly leveraged" is defined as a ratio of liabilities to equity exceeding 12 to 1.[11]

The analysis of whether or not a party is a major swap participant is conducted by category of swaps (rates, credit, equity, and other commodity swaps[12]) so that, theoretically, a major swap participant could be a major swap participant for one category of swaps and not for another. However, the two current major swap participant registrants are registrants with respect to all swap categories.

b. Substantial Position

"Substantial position" is defined as positions meeting *either* Test #1 or Test #2 in the table in Figure 8-A, below. A position that "could have serious adverse effects on the financial stability of the United States banking system or financial markets," referred to as the "serious adverse affects" test, is summarized in the final row.[13] It is important to remember that the substantial position test excludes hedging swaps, except in the case of highly leveraged financial entities:

Figure 8-A: "Substantial Position" and "Serious Adverse Affects" Tests (Rates, Credit, Equity, and Other Commodity Rows Reflect "Substantial Position" Test and the All Swaps Row Reflects the "Serious Adverse Effects" Test)

Category of Swaps	Test #1: Daily Average Aggregate Uncollateralized Mark-to-Market Exposure Equals or Exceeds	Test #2: Amount in Test #1 Plus Daily Average Aggregate Outward Exposure
Rates	$3 billion	$6 billion
Credit	$1 billion	$2 billion
Equity	$1 billion	$2 billion
Other Commodity	$1 billion	$2 billion
All Swaps	$5 billion	$8 billion

As with swap dealers, there is a *de minimis* exception. The exception, however, is comparatively complicated. It exempts any entity that meets *all* of the following criteria:

Figure 8-B: *De Minimis* Exception for Major Swap Participants		
Applies if any of these tests are satisfied	Required Element #1	Required Element #2
Test #1	Total uncollateralized exposure to all counterparties does not exceed $100 million due to express terms of all agreements [note, most swaps are collateralized]	No more than: (1) $2 billion in total notional in any category of swaps; (2) or $4 billion notional in all categories
Test #2	Total uncollateralized exposure to all counterparties cannot exceed $200 million due toexpress terms of all agreements [note, most swaps are collateralized]	Monthly calculations applying "substantial position" and on whether "substantial counterparty exposure that could have serious adverse effects on the financial stability of the United States banking system or financial markets" have results less than or equal to: (1) $1 billion in aggregate uncollateralized outward mark-to-market swap exposure plus aggregate potential outward exposure in any swap category excluding hedging swaps (unless it is a financial entity "highly leveraged relative to the amount of capital such entity holds and that is not subject to capital requirements established by an appropriate Federal banking agency" in which case hedging swaps are included); or (2) $2 billion in aggregate uncollateralized outward mark-to-market swap exposure plus aggregate potential outward exposure

Test #3	At the end of each month, aggregate uncollateralized outward mark-to-market exposure with respect to swap positions in each major swap category is less than \$1.5 billion with respect to rate swaps and less than \$500 million with respect to each of the other major swap categories	If: (1) the sum of the following is less than \$3 billion with respect to rate swaps and \$1 billion with respect to any other category: (a) the amount in "Requirement #1"; and (b) total notional of swaps multiplied by multipliers, based on type of swap and its duration, spanning from 0 for interest rate swaps maturing in a year or less to 0.15 for commodity swaps other than foreign exchange or precious metals maturing in more than 5 years[14]; or (2) if (a) aggregate uncollateralized mark-to-market swap exposure is less than \$500 million; and (b) the amount in "Requirement #1" plus the total notional of all swaps multiplied by 0.15 is less than \$1 billion

E. ENTITY LEVEL OBLIGATIONS OF REGISTRANTS

1. *Introduction*

The requirements applicable to swap dealers and major swap participants can be divided into "entity level" requirements (i.e., requirements such as capital, annual chief compliance officer reports, risk management, and recordkeeping) and "transaction level" requirements (i.e., requirements that pertain to actual swap transactions such as clearing, margin, and segregation requirements for uncleared swaps; swap trading relationship documentation requirements; portfolio reconciliation and compression; swap trade reporting; trade confirmation; and external business conduct[15]).

Though the entity level requirements are the same regardless of how a swap is executed, the transaction level requirements differ depending on whether the swap is centrally cleared or not. In Chapter 9 we focus on the regime applicable to swaps required to be centrally cleared and, in most cases, also required to be executed on a swap execution facility (or designated contract market, in which case, our analysis of designated contracts markets in Chapter 4 applies). We will find that these cleared swaps are the most similar to the regime for commodity futures with which we already familiarized ourselves in Chapters 4 and 5. In Chapter 10 we look at the transaction level requirements that apply to uncleared swaps.

2. *Capital*

Whereas the CFTC's jurisdiction is nearly plenary with respect to most aspects of swap regulation, capital (and margin) provide an exception. An entity regulated by a "prudential regulator," i.e., the Federal Reserve Board, Office of the Comptroller of the Currency, Federal Deposit Insurance Corporation, Farm Credit Administration, or Federal Housing Finance Agency,[16] is required to follow their regulator's capital requirements instead of the CFTC's capital requirements.[17]

Though the Federal Reserve Board regulates non-bank subsidiaries of bank holding companies (i.e., entities that own banks), such non-bank subsidiaries are subject to CFTC capital rules.[18] However, the CFTC has proposed to permit such entities to follow capital requirements already established by the Federal Reserve Board.[19]

Both the CFTC and the prudential regulators have proposed capital rules.[20] The CFTC proposal is based on an "adjusted net capital" concept whereby, in short, certain assets deemed to be risky are discounted or disallowed and all other assets are set off against liabilities.[21] The remaining amount is the "net capital," which the CFTC has proposed be a minimum of $20 million.[22]

The prudential regulators' proposed approach to swap dealer and major swap participant capital is different and reflective of the model commonly applied to banks. In this model, an entity must hold equity or subordinated debt equal to a specified percentage of assets, often weighted by risk.[23] The amount of such capital and the forms that it can take differ depending on the current regulatory status of the entity.[24]

3. *Chief Compliance Officer*

In addition to other compliance and oversight roles, the chief compliance officer of a swap dealer or major swap participant is required to submit an annual report to the CFTC describing internal policies and every requirement to which the registrant is subject under the Commodity Exchange Act or CFTC regulations; provide an assessment on the effectiveness of the policies, including what can be improved; and disclose any material noncompliance and any action taken in association therewith.[25] It puts the chief compliance officer in the difficult role of affirmatively disclosing to the CFTC every material violation of the Commodity Exchange Act or CFTC rules. It also raises ethical questions for any lawyer appointed as a chief compliance officer who as an attorney is bound to preserve client confidences if the client swap dealer or major swap participant does not agree to disclosure, but who is simultaneously mandated to affirmatively disclose noncompliance with applicable law or regulation to the CFTC.

In other compelled disclosure contexts, such as with a lawyer representing a natural person, such conflicts and questions would not arise to the same extent due to the application of the client's Fifth Amendment right against self-incrimination.[26] However, the Fifth Amendment has been found not to apply to corporations. Moreover, questions arise as to in what form an assertion of the right against self-incrimination could be asserted by a chief compliance officer *in personam* and what impact such an assertion would have on the required annual report.

United States v. Kordel

397 U.S. 1 (1970)

Mr. Justice Stewart delivered the opinion of the Court.

The respondents . . . were convicted . . .along with [Detroit Vital Foods, Inc.] for violations of the Federal Food, Drug, and Cosmetic Act. The Court of Appeals for the Sixth Circuit reversed the respondent's convictions on the ground that the Government's use of interrogatories to obtain evidence from the respondents in a nearly contemporaneous civil condemnation proceeding operated to violate their Fifth Amendment privilege against compulsory self-incrimination. . . .

[T]he . . . Food and Drug Administration (hereafter FDA) instructed the agency's Detroit office to investigate the respondents' possible violations of the Food, Drug, and Cosmetic Act. . . . [C]ivil seizure of two of the respondents' products . . . was recommended. . . . The [FDA's] General Counsel requested . . . [commencement of] an in rem action against these products of the corporation, and the United States Attorney filed a libel three days later. The corporation, appearing as the claimant answered the libel. . . . An FDA official . . . prepared extensive interrogatories to be served on the corporation. . . .

[T]he FDA serve[d] upon the corporation and the respondents a notice that the agency contemplated a criminal proceeding against them with respect to the transactions that were the subject of the civil action. . . .

[T]he corporation . . . moved to stay further proceedings in the civil action or, in the alternative, to extend the time to answer the interrogatories until after disposition of the criminal proceeding. . . . The moving papers urged the District Court to act "in the interest of substantial justice." . . . Permitting the Government to obtain proof of violations of the Act by resort to civil discovery procedures, the movant urged, would be "improper" and would "work a grave injustice against the claimant." . . . Counsel expressly disavowed any "issue of a self-incrimination privilege in favor of the claimant corporation." And nowhere in the moving papers did counsel raise a claim of the Fifth Amendment privilege against compulsory self-incrimination with respect to the respondents.

[T]he District Court denied the motion. . . . The court reasoned that the . . . notice did not conclusively indicate the Government would institute a criminal proceeding, that six to 12 months could elapse from the service of the statutory notice to initiation of a criminal prosecution, and that the Government could obtain data for a prosecution from the testimony in the civil action or by subpoenaing the books and records of the corporation. Accordingly, the court concluded, the interests of justice did not require that the Government be denied the information it wanted simply because it had sought it by way of civil discovery procedures. . . . [I]n compliance with the court's directive, the corporation, through the respondent Feldten, answered the Government's interrogatories. . . .

The civil case, still pending in the District Court, proceeded to settlement by way of a consent decree . . . and eight months later the Government obtained the indictment underlying the present judgments of conviction. . . .

[W]e assume that the information Feldten supplied the Government in his answers to the interrogatories . . . provided evidence or leads useful to the Government. However, the record amply supports . . . that the Government did not act in bad faith in filing the interrogatories. . . .

The Court of Appeals thought the answers to the interrogatories were involuntarily given. The District Judge's order denying the corporation's motion to defer the answers to the interrogatories, reasoned the court, left the respondents with three choices: they could have refused to answer, thereby forfeiting the corporation's property that was the subject of the libel; they could have given false answers to the interrogatories, thereby subjecting themselves to the risk of a prosecution for perjury; or they could have done just what they did – disclose the requested information, thereby supplying the Government with evidence and leads helpful in securing their indictment and conviction. . . .

[W]e think the Court of Appeals erred. For Feldten need not have answered the interrogatories. Without question he could have invoked his Fifth Amendment privilege against compulsory self-incrimination. Surely Feldten was not barred from asserting his privilege simply because the corporation had no privilege of its own,[vi] or because the proceeding in which the Government sought information was civil rather than criminal in character.

To be sure, service of the interrogatories obliged the corporation to "appoint an agent who could, without fear of self-incrimination, furnish such requested information as was available to the corporation." The corporation could not satisfy its obligation . . . by pointing to an agent about to invoke his constitutional privilege. "It would indeed be incongruous to permit a

---

[vi] [N. 9] That the corporation has no privilege is of course long established, and not disputed here.

corporation to select an individual to verify the corporation's answers, who because he fears self-incrimination may thus secure for the corporation the benefits of a privilege it does not have." Such a result would effectively permit the corporation to assert on its own behalf the personal privilege of its individual agents.

The respondents press upon us the situation where no one can answer the interrogatories addressed to the corporation without subjecting himself to a "real and appreciable" risk of self-incrimination. For present purposes we may assume that in such a case the appropriate remedy would be a protective order . . . postponing civil discovery until termination of the criminal action. But we need not decide this troublesome question. For the record before us makes clear that even though the respondents had the burden of showing that the Government's interrogatories were improper, they never even asserted . . . that there was no authorized person who could answer the interrogatories without the possibility of compulsory self-incrimination. To the contrary, the record shows that nobody associated with the corporation asserted his privilege at all. . . . His failure at any time to assert the constitutional privilege leaves him in no position to complain now that he was compelled to give testimony against himself. . . .

---

4. Risk Management

Swap dealers and major swap participants are required to establish risk management programs, accounting for, among others, market, credit, liquidity, foreign currency, legal, operation, and settlement risks.[27] The risk management program must include regular monitoring and trading limits. The risk management function must be staffed by a risk management unit independent of the trading function. New products require a special risk assessment and a business continuity/disaster recovery plan needs to be in place.

Quarterly reports on the above risks, including recommended changes and the status of items previously recommended but not yet acted upon, must be provided to management and the CFTC. The risk management policies and procedures must be internally examined and tested at least once a year.

5. Recordkeeping

All categories of records of a swap dealer or major swap participant that are required to be retained are open to inspection by the CFTC, Department of Justice, or any "prudential regulator."[28] Records generally need to be kept for five years and be "readily accessible" for two.

Swaps and related transactions, however, must be kept for five years after the transaction ends and be "readily accessible" for the first two. An exception exists for "records of oral communications," which can be kept for one year only.

The categories of records required to be maintained are:

- Transaction and position records of all swaps "including, but not limited to, records of all orders (filled, unfilled, or cancelled); correspondence; journals; memoranda; ledgers; confirmations; risk disclosure documents; statements of purchase and sale; contracts; invoices; warehouse receipts; [and] documents of title . . . " and records of every position identified as "long" or "short" and whether or not it is cleared.

- Business records such a governance documents, organizational charts, biographies, and job descriptions of senior personnel, audit reports, financial records, customer complaints, including the resolution thereof, and marketing and sales materials.

- Daily trading records such as original records of transactions, swap trade information sufficient to allow a "comprehensive and accurate trade reconstruction," searchable by transaction and counterparty, pre-trade communications, and post-trade events.

QUESTIONS AND COMMENTS

1. In *Bank One Corporation*, the swaps market is described as historically having operated as follows:

> When the swaps market first began, every swap generally was facilitated by a dealer. The dealer was not a party to the transaction but, generally for a fee, arranged the swap by introducing the counterparties to each other and helping them to effect the mechanics of the transaction. With the evolution of the market, dealers became parties to each swap. In the early years of the market's evolution, a dealer would effect a swap transaction by warehousing the swap (i.e., entering into the swap without having entered into a matching swap but with the expectation of hedging the entered-into swap either through a matching swap or a portfolio of swaps or temporarily in the cash, securities, or futures market) until the dealer could arrange an offsetting swap with another counterparty (i.e., match a book). In the later years of the market's evolution, the dealer would simply accept a position opposite the counterparty without expecting to locate another counterparty transaction to match the first transaction.

120 T.C. 174, 196 (Tax 2003).

Evaluate the potential benefits and shortcomings of each of these paradigms: one in which the swap dealer facilitates a transaction between two parties transacting with each other, and one in which the swap dealer acts as counterparty with one of those parties. Now contrast these with a model in which there is a central intermediary, such as with commodity futures as has been mandated for some categories of swaps (*see* Chapter 9).

2. The release accompanying the final definition of swap dealer, jointly agreed by the CFTC and the SEC, states: "We also believe that the [trader/dealer] distinction affords an appropriate degree of flexibility to the analysis, and that it would not be appropriate to seek to codify the distinction in rule text."[29] What are the positives associated with the regulators retaining "flexibility" in how a term such as "swap dealer" will be defined? What impact does this have on market participants seeking to prospectively plan?
3. Was the creation of the "major swap participant" category of registration driven too singularly by one event, the bailout of American International Group? Or was that the "shot across the bow" that the regulators addressed before it could reoccur?
4. We will evaluate "special entities" in Chapter 10. Begin to consider why there might be a special *de minimis* sub-limit for transactions with special entities.
5. Can an attorney act as chief compliance officer? If so, what safeguards, if any, might be necessary?

CHAPTER 9
REGULATION OF CLEARED SWAPS

A. BACKGROUND

The Dodd-Frank Act requires a category of swaps to be cleared if either the CFTC determines that it should be cleared, or a derivatives clearing organization plans to clear it.[1] There are two processes for determining that a category of swap is required to be cleared. They differ only in whether the CFTC or a derivatives clearing organization initiates the clearing determination.

One is initiated by the CFTC if the CFTC determines, after allowing for at least a 30-day public comment period, that a category of swaps should be cleared.[2] The other is initiated by any derivatives clearing organization that intends to clear a category of swap.[3] The CFTC must review the submission of the derivatives clearing organization and provide a 30-day public comment period before making a determination.[4]

Swaps that are required to be cleared are also required to be traded on a designated contract market or swap execution facility, if determined to be "available to trade."[5] Below we will also examine this process. Generally, swaps that are required to be cleared are coterminous with swaps that are required to be traded on a facility, i.e., traded on a designated contract market or swap execution facility.

Certain counterparty types, however, as detailed below in section B3, have the option of not having their swaps cleared.[6] In such cases, neither mandatory clearing nor mandatory on-facility trading apply.

Although the "entity level" requirements we discussed in Chapter 8 apply to swap dealers and major swap participants regardless of whether or not a transaction is cleared, many of the "transaction level" requirements, i.e., requirements that pertain to actual swap transactions such as clearing, margin, and segregation requirements for uncleared swaps, swap trading relationship documentation, portfolio reconciliation and compression, swap trade reporting, trade confirmation, and external business conduct, do not apply to swaps that are required to be cleared. These, therefore, are the subject of Chapter 10.

In this chapter we will examine, among other concepts: (1) registration requirements for derivatives clearing organizations and the clearing requirement, (2) registration requirements for swap execution facilities and the on-facility trading requirement, and (3) registration requirements for swap data repositories and reporting.

B. DERIVATIVES CLEARING ORGANIZATIONS AND THE CLEARING REQUIREMENT

1. Derivatives Clearing Organizations

As discussed in Chapter 4, derivatives clearing organizations are a creation of the Commodity Futures Modernization Act. Entities must be registered as derivatives clearing organizations in order to clear swaps.[7] Swaps clear similarly to futures.

For example, let us assume that two parties are each customers of futures commission merchants. (In reality, instead of being a customer of a futures commission merchant, either or both could instead themselves be a registered futures commission merchant or, even if unregistered, be a "self-clearing" member of a derivatives clearing organization.) The derivatives clearing organization would step between the two parties and be counterparty to each, with futures commission merchants that are members of the derivatives clearing organization, guaranteeing each of their customer's positions to the derivatives clearing organization. Each party would post margin to its futures commission merchant and each futures commission merchant would post collateral to the derivatives clearing organization. For more details on the process and a diagrammatic explanation, *see* Chapter 5.

In the context of swaps only, derivatives clearing organizations are additionally required to abide by "open access" requirements and, therefore:

> [P]rovide for non-discriminatory clearing of a swap . . . executed bilaterally or on or through the rules of an unaffiliated designated contract market or swap execution facility.

Commodity Exchange Act § 2(h)(1)(B).

2. *Clearing Requirement*

The Dodd-Frank Act added a new § 2(h) to the Commodity Exchange Act that makes it "unlawful for any person to engage in a swap unless that person submits such swap for clearing to a derivatives clearing organization . . . if the swap is required to be cleared." The Commodity Exchange Act, CFTC rules, and a CFTC no-action letter together combine to provide some counterparty types, at their option, an exception from clearing.[8]

The definitive questions, then, are: (1) whether a swap is required to be cleared, and (2) if so, whether the counterparty in question benefits from an exception from clearing. Question (1) we examine now, and question (2) we examine below in section B3.

There are two methods by which a category of swaps can be required to be cleared. Regardless of which is undertaken, the following must be evaluated:

> [1] The existence of significant outstanding notional exposures, trading liquidity, and adequate pricing data.
>
> [2] The availability of [a] rule framework, capacity, operational expertise and resources, and credit support infrastructure to clear the contract on terms that are consistent with the material terms and trading conventions on which the contract is then traded.
>
> [3] The effect on the mitigation of systemic risk, taking into account the size of the market for such contract and the resources of the derivatives clearing organization available to clear the contract.
>
> [4] The effect on competition, including appropriate fees and charges applied to clearing.
>
> [5] The existence of reasonable legal certainty in the event of the insolvency of the relevant derivatives clearing organization or 1 or more of its clearing members with regard to the treatment of customer and swap counterparty positions, funds, and property.

Commodity Exchange Act § 2(h)(2)(D).

The first four statutory factors that must be accounted for are specific to the relevant category of swaps subject to the determination. The fifth applies to derivatives clearing organizations and their futures commission merchant members generally. The CFTC, in its first clearing determination, discussed further below, in section B2(a) concluded that the fifth statutory factor applies generally for U.S. derivatives clearing organizations (for one non-U.S. derivatives clearing organization, the CFTC relied on an opinion of external counsel), noting that:

> [N]either a clearing member's bankruptcy nor any order of a bankruptcy court could prevent [a U.S. derivatives clearing organization] from closing out/liquidating [swap] positions. . . . [C]ustomers of clearing members would have priority over all other claimants with respect to customer funds that had been held by the defaulting clearing member to margin swaps . . .
>
> Similarly, [the Bankruptcy Code and CFTC rules] would govern the bankruptcy of a [derivatives clearing organization] . . . providing for the termination of outstanding contracts and/or return of remaining clearing member and customer property to clearing members.

Clearing Requirement Determination Under Section 2(h) of the CEA, 77 FR 74284-01 (December 13, 2012), 74299.

We examined bankruptcy issues generally in Chapter 10.

a. CFTC Initiated Clearing Determination

The Commodity Exchange Act requires the CFTC to "on an ongoing basis" make a determination as to whether any category of swaps should be cleared.[9] If the CFTC concludes that a clearing determination may be merited, it must provide at least a 30-day comment period.[10]

To date, the CFTC has issued one clearing determination, requiring the clearing of nearly all interest rate swaps denominated in U.S. dollars, euro, sterling or yen and specific credit default swaps referencing commonly used indices.[11]

b. Derivatives Clearing Organization Initiated Clearing Determination

A derivatives clearing organization can submit to the CFTC notice of any category of swaps it intends to accept for clearing.[12] The CFTC is required to review this submission, release it for a minimum 30-day comment period[13] and has 90 days to make its determination.[14]

To date, no submissions have been made using this method.

3. *Clearing Exceptions*

a. Generally

Even if a category of swaps is subject to clearing, there are exceptions. These exceptions provide certain types of entities the option of whether to have their trades cleared or not. The four entity types exempt from clearing are:

- A non-financial end-user regardless of the entity type with which it is trading so long as it is hedging commercial risk and reports certain information related to its use of the clearing exception, such as how it generally meets its obligations in association with uncleared swaps, to a swap data repository or the CFTC.[15]

- An affiliate of a non-financial end-user regardless of the entity with which it is trading so long as it is hedging commercial risk acting as an agent or on behalf of such entity (or as principal subject to a few additional restrictions that are not relevant herein[16]) so long as the affiliate is not a swap dealer, security-based swap dealer, major swap participant, major security-based swap participant, commodity pool, hedge fund or private equity fund, or bank holding company with over $50 billion in assets.[17]

- A cooperative whose members are all non-financial end-users regardless of the entity type with which it is trading is exempt from clearing, even if the cooperative itself is a financial end-user, so long as the swap is in connection with loans to members and reports certain information related to its use of the clearing exception, such as how it generally meets its obligations in association with uncleared swaps, to a swap data repository or the CFTC.[18]

- If two entities are affiliated with one another (i.e., one owns the other, directly or indirectly, or are under common control) and report their financial statements on a consolidated basis and the trades are documented, subject to a centralized risk management program and reports certain information related to its use of the clearing exception, such as how it generally meets its obligations in association with uncleared swaps, to a swap data repository or the CFTC.[19]

Three of the four exceptions require determination of what is a non-financial end-user. A non-financial end-user is merely any end-user that is not a financial end-user. Therefore, to answer what a non-financial end-user is, it is necessary to understand what a financial end-user is.

b. End-Users and Financial Entities

An end-user is any entity that is not a swap or security-based swap market registrant, i.e., any entity other than a swap dealer, security-based swap dealer, major swap participant, or major security-based swap participant. Entities other than the foregoing registrants are typically referred to as "end-users" and further sub-divided into financial and non-financial end-users.

A financial end-user is an end-user that is a financial entity. As seen from the preceding section, the definition of financial entity is of central importance in most cases in determining whether an exception from clearing is available. A financial entity is any of:

- Certain SEC or CFTC Registrants: A swap dealer, security-based swap dealer, major swap participant, major security-based swap participant, or commodity pool.[20]

- Certain Funds: A hedge fund, private equity fund, or pension plan.[21]

- Banks: Any entity primarily engaged in banking except for a bank, farm credit system institution, or a credit union with total assets of less than $10 billion.[22]

- An Entity Primarily Engaged in Activities "Financial in Nature": "Financial in nature" includes lending, investing for others, safeguarding money or securities, insurance activities, financial advisory activities, issuing interests in certain assets, underwriting, dealing or market making in securities, merchant banking activities and acting as a "finder" in securities transactions.[23]

In addition to non-financial end-users being able to avail of the non-financial end-user exceptions from clearing, end-users generally have a right to require clearing when trading with swap market registrants, such as swap dealers, even for swaps that are not subject to a mandatory clearing requirement.[24]

c. Application of the Clearing Exception

Let us evaluate the non-financial end-user exception in light of the following three examples.

> Example A: The Law School Brewing Company is borrower under a loan facility where the interest rate is "floating" and, therefore, changes from month-to-month. The Law School Brewing Company approaches Mega Bank to enter into an interest rate swap to hedge its loan exposure. The

interest rate swap is subject to a clearing determination, requiring it to be cleared, unless there is an exception to clearing. The Law School Brewing Company informs Mega Bank that it would like the swap to be uncleared.

Result: This is permissible because the Law School Brewing Company is a non-financial end-user hedging risk and has elected to use the clearing exception. Either the Law School Brewing Company or Mega Bank will have to report required information to the CFTC related to the Law School Brewing Company's status as a non-financial end-user.

Example B: Suppose the same facts as in Example A except that the Law School Brewing Company expresses no view on whether it would like the swap to be cleared or uncleared. Instead, the swap trader from Mega Bank informs her counterpart at the Law School Brewing Company that Mega Bank will trade the swap without clearing it.

This violates the Commodity Exchange Act and CFTC rules because the non-financial end-user exception is only available if elected by the non-financial end-user.

Example C: A trader from the Law School Brewing Company decides that entering into an interest rate swap that takes the position that interest rates will increase would be a good idea in the current economic climate. He calls his colleague at Mega Bank and says that he elects to not clear the swap since Law School Brewing Company is a non-financial end-user.

Result: This violates the Commodity Exchange Act and CFTC rules because the non-financial end-user, Law School Brewing Company, is not entering into the swap to hedge risk.

In order to determine whether a counterparty claiming eligibility to use an exception from clearing is indeed eligible, swap dealers and major swap participants rely on direct representations from the end-user counterparty, usually in questionnaire form. These can be exchanged directly or, more commonly, are exchanged automatically through an online system operated by Markit (a financial information platform) known as "ISDA Amend."[25] We discuss this in detail in Chapter 10.

4. Public Policy Motivations

With centralized clearing, the risk of a counterparty default, inherent to uncleared swaps, is replaced by the risk of a default by the derivatives clearing organization. The latter is much less likely to occur because the derivatives clearing organization is capitalized, the obligations of the derivatives clearing organization are guaranteed by its members, and members are required to collateralize exposures the derivatives clearing organization has to them.

However, centralized clearing also has risks, as noted in the below speech given by Federal Reserve Board Chairman Ben S. Bernanke.

Ben S. Bernanke, Clearinghouses, Financial Stability, and Financial Reform

2011 Financial Markets Conference, Stone Mountain, Georgia (April 4, 2011) available at http://www.federalreserve.gov/newsevents/speech/bernanke20110404a.htm (accessed June 20, 2014)

I am pleased to speak once again at the Federal Reserve Bank of Atlanta's Financial Markets Conference. . . .

Tonight I would like to discuss post-crisis reform as it relates to a prominent part of our financial market infrastructure--namely, clearinghouses for payments, securities, and derivatives transactions. . . . Because clearinghouses and other parts of the financial infrastructure fared relatively well during the crisis – despite moments of significant stress – the public debate on financial reform has understandably focused on the risks posed by so-called too-big-to-fail financial firms, whose dramatic failures or near failures put our financial system and economy in dire jeopardy. . . .

[V]irtually all clearinghouses perform certain basic functions. Notably, by centralizing and standardizing specific classes of financial transactions, clearinghouses reduce the costs and operational risks of clearing and settlement among multiple market participants. In many cases they also act as a guarantor of transactions – the counterparty to every trade – thereby helping to reduce counterparty credit and liquidity risks. However, the flip side of the centralization of clearing and settlement activities in clearinghouses is the concentration of substantial financial and operational risk in a small number of organizations, a development with potentially important systemic implications. Because the failure of, or loss of confidence in, a major clearinghouse would create enormous uncertainty about the status of initiated transactions and, consequently, about the financial positions of clearinghouse participants and their customers, strong risk management at these organizations as well as effective prudential oversight is essential. . . .

The first important clearinghouse in the United States . . . was founded by New York City's commercial banks in 1853 to streamline the clearing and settling of checks. . . . By the late 19th century, check clearinghouses had been established across the United States. . . . In the years prior to the establishment of the Federal Reserve, to increase public confidence in banks, clearinghouse associations at times took on quasi-governmental supervisory functions – for example, by examining the financial condition of members rumored to be experiencing difficulties – and even served at times as lender of last resort to individual clearinghouse members.

In the securities and derivatives markets, the story unfolded a bit later and was more complex than in the case of checks. . . . In 1892 . . . the New York Stock Exchange . . . [created] a clearinghouse for limited types of brokers' trades. . . . [T]he New York Stock Exchange took a further step in 1920 by establishing the Stock Clearing Corporation. . . .

It was not until the dramatic increase in equity trading volumes in the late 1960s, however, that backlogs of trading tickets, confirmations, and delivery instructions caused the infamous "paperwork crisis" that led the exchange to curtail trading hours and close on Wednesdays for six months in order to manage the situation.[i] . . . Unprocessed instructions and delivery failures . . . increased the financial risks faced by many firms. . . .

Pressed by the Congress and regulators, the industry began . . . to establish central securities depositories and central counterparties (CCPs) to immobilize paper certificates, encourage multilateral netting of trades, reduce pre-settlement risk through the guarantee of trades, and conduct securities settlements through "book entries" to electronic records. . . .

In the case of exchange-traded derivatives, the significant benefits of clearinghouses likewise became apparent over time. The Chicago Board of Trade (CBOT), now part of the CME Group, was established in 1848. After various experiments to manage the paperwork associated with growing trading volumes, the CBOT established a clearinghouse in 1883. Although the role of the clearinghouse was initially limited, it significantly reduced back-office work and the amount of funds and credit needed by its members.[ii] In 1925, the members of the CBOT set up a full-fledged and independent central counterparty – The Board of Trade Clearing Corporation, now called The Clearing Corporation – to provide the guarantee and settlement functions that are familiar today. . . .

As clearinghouses developed, their resilience – in particular, their ability to manage their liquidity and ensure the integrity of transactions under stressed conditions – was tested by financial shocks and crises. . . . [T]hese episodes warn us to remain vigilant and to guard against complacency; complexity and change in the financial system will continue to present new challenges to stability, as they have in the past. . . .

Overall, the historical record shows that clearinghouse arrangements have generally withstood even severe crises. This solid performance reflects good planning and sound institutional structures but also some degree of good luck . .

---

[i] [N. 6] *See* U.S. Securities and Exchange Commission (1971), *Study of Unsafe and Unsound Practices of Brokers and Dealers: Report and Recommendations (Pursuant to section 11 (h) of the Securities Investor Protection Act of 1970)* (Washington: Government Printing Office), pp. 13-14.

[ii] [N. 7] *See* The Clearing Corporation (2011), *A History: Trusting, Growing, Leading, Clearing Leaving the Board* (Chicago: Board of Trade Clearing Corporation).

. Clearly, if we do not want to put all our trust in continued good fortune, we will have to continue to be proactive in identifying and remedying weaknesses in these critical infrastructures. . . .

Broadly speaking, the recent financial reform legislation bears on the future structure and role of clearinghouses in two different ways. First, it aims to increase the resilience of these critical institutions against severe financial shocks, the issue that I have emphasized thus far. Second, it also encourages the greater development and use of clearinghouses to address weaknesses identified in other parts of the financial system. Of course, increased reliance on clearinghouses to address problems in other parts of the system increases further the need to ensure the safety of clearinghouses themselves. As Mark Twain's character Pudd'nhead Wilson once opined, if you put all your eggs in one basket, you better watch that basket.

The theme of expanded use of clearinghouses as a tool to address other problems in the system is perhaps best illustrated by the derivatives provisions of the Dodd-Frank Act. Prior to the crisis, some of the same economic forces that had led to the development of clearinghouses for other instruments were already pushing industry participants toward greater use of clearinghouses for OTC derivatives transactions. For example, as one response to the growth of the market for interest rate swaps in the early 1990s, a clearinghouse was created in London in 1999 that, by the onset of the financial crisis, was handling a major portion of interdealer activity in those swaps. Also, in the years leading up to the crisis, the Federal Reserve Bank of New York initiated joint efforts with other regulators and market participants to improve clearing arrangements for credit default swaps. However, for several reasons, the willingness of market participants to move all derivatives transactions to clearinghouses was limited. Notably, many believed that the standardization of derivatives contracts that is needed for multilateral clearing imposed too high a cost on end users with needs for customized arrangements. Market participants also were concerned that the establishment of clearinghouse guarantees might require implicit subsidies from clearinghouse members with stronger credit to those with weaker credit.

These calculations, however, were substantially changed by the galvanizing events of 2008, notably the development of large and uncertain counterparty credit risks in many bilateral derivatives agreements. On the heels of the crisis, the Group of Twenty countries endorsed a policy of mandatory central clearing for standardized OTC derivatives. The aim was to reduce systemic risk in the financial system more broadly as well as to improve the transparency of the OTC derivatives markets. In the United States, title 7 of the Dodd-Frank Act incorporated a mandatory clearing policy for standardized derivatives. Other major countries are following suit. In the spirit of keeping a close eye on the basket, as dependence on clearinghouses grows, private-sector participants and regulators will need to review risk-management and member-default procedures for financial market utilities to ensure that they meet high standards of safety. . . .

What was once a landscape of numerous, separate clearinghouses that operated largely independently from one another has now become dominated by fewer and larger clearinghouses supporting more integrated markets and consolidated, global financial firms. Moreover, the same globally active banks participate in all of the major clearinghouses, and the major clearinghouses often rely on similar sets of banks for payment services, funding, settlement, and emergency liquidity. In such a world, problems at one clearinghouse could have significant effects on others, even in the absence of explicit operational links. The need for strong risk management and oversight will only increase as we go forward. . . .

Given the growing interdependencies among clearinghouses, along with the new mandates for central clearing, now is a good time to reflect on the lessons of the recent crisis and consider whether further improvements are possible.

For more than a century, financial stability has depended on the resilience under stress of clearinghouses and other parts of the financial infrastructure. As we rely even more heavily on these institutions in the United States and around the world, we must do all that we can to ensure their resilience, even as our financial system continues to evolve rapidly and in ways that we cannot fully predict. In short, I think Pudd'nhead Wilson would agree that that is one important basket.

C. SWAP EXECUTION FACILITIES AND THE ON-FACILITY TRADING REQUIREMENT

Commodity Exchange Act § 2(h)(8) requires that all swaps that are required to be cleared to be traded on a designated contract market or swap execution facility *unless* neither "makes the swap available to trade. . . ." However, before we assess how it is determined whether or not a swap is made available to trade, it is important to examine swap execution facilities.

1. Swap Execution Facilities

The requirement in Commodity Exchange Act § 2(h)(8) is satisfied if a swap is traded on a designated contract market or a swap execution facility. We are familiar with designated contract markets from Chapter 4. Swap execution facilities are a creation of the Dodd-Frank Act.

a. Definition

A swap execution facility is defined in the Commodity Exchange Act as a "trading system or platform in which multiple participants have the ability to execute or trade swaps by accepting bids and offers made by multiple participants in the facility or system. . . ."[26] The central feature, then, is the "multiple-to-multiple" nature of the facility. We discussed this concept in Chapter 4 in the context of what constitutes a trading facility. We revisit it here with some new examples.

Example A: The Law School Brewing Company sends out a request-for-quotes using an online system that shows selected dealers the swaps in which the Law School Brewing Company would like bids.

This is not a "multiple-to-multiple" facility because, even though it is available to multiple offerors, the dealers, it only has one offeree, the Law School Brewing Company.

Example B: Mega Bank decides to give its customers access to an online system whereby they can see what Mega Bank's bid or offer is for particular swaps.

This is not a "multiple-to-multiple" facility because, even though it has multiple offerees, the customers, it has only one offeror, Mega Bank.

Example C: Mega Bank and Wonder Bank decide that their customers will be better served if they jointly develop a platform to provide access to customers to see both of their bids and offers on swaps.

Result: Although this may indeed better serve their customers, Mega Bank and Wonder Bank would be required to register their platform as a swap execution facility. This is because there are two offerors, Mega Bank and Wonder Bank, using the platform to potentially enter into swaps with multiple offerees, their combined customers.

b. Swap Execution Facility Core Principles

Just as designated contract markets must comply with the "core principles" outlined in Chapter 4, so must swap execution facilities. The core principles are similar in many respects. One major difference worth highlighting, though, relates to access to swap execution facilities. Though, just as with designated contract markets, there is a requirement to provide "impartial access,"[27] with swap execution facilities such access must be limited to "eligible contract participants," a definitional category discussed in Chapter 7.[28]

2. *On-Facility Trading Requirement*

Whereas the CFTC or a derivatives clearing organization can initiate a mandatory clearing requirement, only a designated contract market or swap execution facility can initiate a determination that a swap that is subject to mandatory clearing is also "available to trade" and, therefore, pursuant to Commodity Exchange Act § 2(h)(8), must trade on a designated contract market or swap execution facility.[29] The factors that must be considered are designed with similar objectives – namely that there is a liquid available market – to those that must be considered before making a determination that a category of swaps is required to be cleared. The factors are:

(1) Whether there are ready and willing buyers and sellers;
(2) The frequency or size of transactions;
(3) The trading volume;
(4) The number and types of market participants;
(5) The bid/ask spread; or
(6) The usual number of resting firm or indicative bids and offers.

17 C.F.R. § 37.10(b) and § 38.12(b).

There are two methods for a designated contract market or swap execution facility to make an "available to trade" determination.

The first is to self-certify that a category of swaps are available to trade. If pre-conditions are met, such as having already vetted the proposal to market participants, the self-certification is effective 10 business days after submission to the CFTC unless the CFTC issues a 90-day stay to solicit comments from the public.[30]

The second is to submit the proposal to the CFTC without certifying that the proposal has already been vetted with market participants. The CFTC has 45 days to review it, extendable in some circumstances for an additional 45 days.[31]

Regardless of the method chosen, once the submission is approved, the determination is effective 30 days later.[32]

Though swaps that are required to be traded on a facility are by definition a sub-set of swaps that are required to be mandatorily cleared (since the on-facility trading requirement only applies to swaps that must be cleared), because swap execution facilities have successfully submitted broad "available to trade" determinations, the set of swaps that must be cleared is the same as those that must be traded on-facility, with minor exceptions.

3. *Statutory Intent*

As with much of the Dodd-Frank swaps regulatory regime, a paramount principle of the on-facility trading requirement is to obtain greater market transparency.

Remarks of Chairman Gary Gensler at Swap Execution Facility Conference: Bringing Transparency and Access to Markets

Available at http://www.cftc.gov/pressroom/speechestestimony/opagensler-152 (accessed June 19, 2014)

. . . For the first time, all swaps market participants have access to compete. For the first time, all – and that means dealers and non-dealers alike – benefit from transparency.

Since the time of Adam Smith and The Wealth of Nations, economists have consistently written that transparency and open access to markets benefits the broad public and the overall economy.

When markets are open and transparent, markets are more efficient, competitive, and liquid, and costs are lowered for companies and their customers.

President Roosevelt understood this when he asked Congress during the Great Depression to bring transparency, access and competition to the commodities and securities markets. . . .

The swaps market emerged nearly 50 years later, but remained dark and closed until just last year. Lacking transparency and common-sense rules of the road, the swaps market contributed to the 2008 crisis. . . .

Bright lights now are shining on the swaps market. Transparency is shining both prior to and after a trade. . . .

The playing field has been leveled through transparency, impartial access, central clearing and straight-through processing. Asset managers, pension funds, insurance companies, community banks and all market participants are gaining benefits that until recently only swap dealers had. . . .

Congress said that SEFs are to provide market participants with impartial access to the market.

Consistent with Congress' direction, the Commission's final SEF rules, completed six months ago, are clear. Impartial access is about allowing market participants to "compete on a level playing field." . . .

[T]he Commission's regulations require SEFs to provide all its market participants – dealers and non-dealers alike – with the ability to fully interact on order books or request-for-quote (RFQ) systems.

SEFs are required to provide dealers and non-dealers alike the ability to view, place or respond to all indicative or firm bids and offers, as well as to place, receive, and respond to RFQs. . . .

Further, SEFs must provide to all eligible contract participants (ECPs) market services, including quote screens and similar pricing data displays. . . .

Dodd-Frank reforms truly are about bringing greater access to these markets. Reforms really are about allowing multiple market participants to meet and transact with multiple market participants. . . .

Congress was also clear that transparency must shine on the swaps market both before and after a trade.

When light shines on a market, the economy and public benefit. . . .

The price and volume of each swap transaction can be seen as it occurs. This post-trade transparency spans the entire market, regardless of product, counterparty, or whether it's a standardized or customized transaction.

This information is available, free of charge, to everyone in the public. The data is listed in real time – like a modern-day tickertape – on the websites of each of the three swap data repositories.

Regulators also gained transparency into the details on each of the 1.8 million transactions and positions now in data repositories. The data repositories, swap dealers and SEFs, though, need to do more to ensure that the data flowing into the data repositories is accurate; consistent; and able to be readily sorted, filtered, and aggregated. . . .

To benefit the public, broaden competition, and promote transparency, Congress required that certain standardized swaps must be executed on a SEF or designated contract market (DCM). The trade execution requirement covers all swaps that are subject to mandatory clearing and made available to trade. . . .

Requiring trading platforms to be registered and overseen by regulators was central to the swaps market reform President Obama and Congress included in the Dodd-Frank Act. They expressly repealed exemptions, such as the so-called "Enron Loophole," for unregistered, multilateral swap trading platforms. . . .

D. TREATMENT OF SWAPS COMPARED TO TREATMENT OF FUTURES

1. *Futurization*

With the Dodd-Frank Act's swaps regulatory regime largely influenced by the existing regulatory regime for futures, questions have arisen as to what extent the CFTC is seeking to "futurize" swaps, i.e., have swaps trade as futures or in circumstances where a substantially similar regulatory structure and trading methodology exists.

Bloomberg L.P. v. Commodity Futures Trading Commission

949 F. Supp. 2d 91 (D.D.C. 2013)

Beryl A. Howell, District Judge.

This is a challenge to a regulation . . . by the . . . CFTC . . . which sets minimum liquidation times for swaps and futures contracts. The plaintiff Bloomberg L.P. ("Bloomberg") . . . alleges that, unless immediately enjoined, the Commission's regulation prescribing minimum liquidation times, when combined with other regulatory and market forces, will encourage the plaintiff's subscribers to migrate permanently to competitors' trading venues. . . . [A]s discussed below, the Court denies the plaintiff's application for preliminary injunctive relief and dismisses this case for lack of standing. . . .

This case is about how the CFTC regulates the trading of derivatives. . . . Although derivatives can come in many forms, there are two categories of derivatives implicated in this lawsuit: "swaps" and "futures." . . .

[The Commodity Exchange Act (the "CEA") requires] futures to be traded on centralized exchanges known as "designated contract markets" ("DCMs") which are subject to a variety of regulatory requirements that ensure transparency and prudent risk management. For example, a DCM is required to "make public daily information on settlement prices, volume, open interest, and opening and closing ranges for actively traded contracts on the contract market." 7 U.S.C. § 7(d)(8). Specifically, DCMs are required to make information on prices, trading volume, and other trading information "readily available to the news media and the general public without charge, in a format that readily enables the consideration of such data, no later than the business day following the day to which the information pertains." 17 C.F.R. §§ 16.01(e), 38.451. Additionally, every transaction executed on a DCM must be "cleared" through an entity called a "derivatives clearing organization" ("DCO"). . . .

[The] Dodd–Frank [Act] generally requires that all cleared swaps be traded on either a DCM or a new entity called a "swap execution facility" ("SEF"). Since the CFTC's rules regarding mandatory clearing and SEFs are still being phased in, however, large swaths of swaps continue to be traded OTC. . . .

A transaction is "cleared" when a member of a DCO uses a novation to interpose itself between the two original counterparties to the derivatives contract, thereby assuming the credit risk of both counterparties. . . .

DCO members are generally large financial institutions who "invest capital that the clearinghouse can use to cover default losses," and in this way a DCO is "analogous to a mutual insurance company." Unlike a mutual insurance company, however, which charges premiums to the customers it insures, DCOs require their members to post a "margin" or a "performance bond," which acts as collateral against the possibility of default. When a trade is first cleared, the DCO collects an initial margin payment based on the amount of default risk assumed by the DCO, and then periodically (usually twice per day), the DCO will "mark positions to market" to ensure that "collateral reflects current market conditions." For example, if the price of a commodity goes down during the trading day, the buyer of a futures contract would be required to post additional margin "to offset the risk that a buyer might walk away from a futures contract in which the agreed-upon price now seems too high." . . .

Pursuant to . . . the rulemaking authority delegated by Congress in the CEA, the Commission published a Notice of Proposed Rulemaking ("NPRM") . . . DCOs to use liquidation times for this margin model that were: (1) "a minimum of five business days for cleared swaps that are not executed on a DCM," and (2) "a minimum of one business day for all other products that it clears." . . .

After considering this diverse array of public comments, the Commission published its final rule regarding minimum liquidation times . . . *See* Derivatives Clearing Organization General Provisions and Core Principles ("Final Rule"), 76 Fed. Reg. 69,334 (Nov. 8, 2011) (codified at 17 C.F.R. pt. 39). This Final Rule . . . requires . . . that a DCO must use (A) "[a] minimum liquidation time that is one day for futures and options," (B) "[a] minimum liquidation time that is one day for swaps on agricultural commodities, energy commodities, and metals," (C) "[a] minimum liquidation time that is five days for all other swaps," or (D) "[s]uch longer liquidation time as is appropriate based on the specific characteristics of a particular product or portfolio." . . .

As to the benefits of the Final Rule with regard to protection of market participants and the public, the Commission stated that the five-day and one-day minimum liquidation times were "consistent with existing requirements" and "reflect the risk assessments DCOs have made." In the Commission's opinion, the DCOs' determination that "these are the appropriate standards for these instruments" was "a reasonable and prudent judgment." At the same time, however, the Commission stated that "[a] minimum standard is designed to prevent DCOs from competing by offering lower margin requirements than other DCOs and, as a result, taking on more risk than is prudent." Related to this concern about a "race to the bottom," the Commission was also "concerned that a DCO may misjudge the appropriate liquidation time frame because of limited experience with clearing and managing the risks of financial swaps" in particular. In sum, prescribing minimum liquidation times was intended to "prevent DCOs from taking on too much risk." . . .

The Commission's Final Rule regarding minimum liquidation times went into effect on January 9, 2012. . . . On December 13, 2012, the Commission published a final rule regarding the categories of swaps that would be required to be cleared. . . .

A month and a half after this clearing requirement was published – and over fourteen months after the minimum-liquidation-time rule was published – the plaintiff sent a letter to the Commission, which raised "a serious concern . . . with the [Final Rule], and more specifically, with regulation 39.13(g)(2)(ii) [sic] which sets out the minimum liquidation time for financial futures and financial swaps." The plaintiff was interested in the Final Rule because it "operates the BLOOMBERG PROFESSIONAL® service, a leading privately held electronic service that, among other things, facilitates the trading and processing of swaps [OTC]." Bloomberg generates revenue from its swap trading platform by charging a monthly fee to those who subscribe to its BLOOMBERG PROFESSIONAL® service (also known as "Bloomberg terminals"), and thus Bloomberg does not generate revenue on a per-trade basis. In addition, Bloomberg "intends to operate a SEF in order to facilitate trading in the swaps market" and, to that end, "has already created a subsidiary that will operate the SEF, has drafted a rulebook for that SEF . . . , and has taken substantial steps toward creating the technological infrastructure for operating the SEF."

In its January 30, 2013 letter to the Commission, Bloomberg raised a number of objections to the minimum-liquidation-time rule, most of which focused on the so-called "futurization of swaps." Futurization, according to the plaintiff, refers to "a phenomenon by which futures products are designed to mimic the essential characteristics of a swap." More specifically, a swap can be "futurized" by "preassembling strips of futures contracts with aggregate cash flows that resemble swaps with the same size, tenor, and reset characteristics." The resulting financial product is often referred to as a "swap future." Bloomberg contended in its January 30, 2013 letter that the Commission's minimum-liquidation-time rule "on its face will be the strongest driver of the forced 'futurization' of economically equivalent financial swaps."

A major premise of this concern was that so-called "swap futures" have "the same risk characteristics as a swap," and thus, by the plaintiff's logic "[e]ither the swap executed on a SEF or futures exchange is being 'over-margined' by a factor of five, or the futures contract executed on a futures exchange is being 'under-margined' by a factor of five." The plaintiff was concerned that this scenario "could lead to clearinghouses absorbing more risk than they otherwise would have if they were permitted to margin cleared financial products that are economically equivalent using an appropriate risk-based metric regardless of the formal label given to the product." . . . Since Bloomberg believed "futurization" generally was "exactly the type of situation the Commission had in mind when it approved this language," Bloomberg "formally request[ed] that the Commission adopt an order that requires DCOs to impose the same margin requirements for financial swaps as they impose on financial futures that are economically equivalent and have a comparable risk profile."

On March 11, 2013, Bloomberg sent a second letter to the Commission – this time through counsel – which laid out its objections to the minimum-liquidation-time rule in more detail and stated for the first time that the Final Rule "threatens significant adverse effects for Bloomberg" that would be "irreversible." In its March 11, 2013 letter Bloomberg also sought more far-reaching relief from the Commission, requesting "that the Commission promptly take all steps necessary to stay the five-day minimum liquidation period for financial swaps, so that the same one-day minimum period applies to all cleared swaps and futures." Two days later, on March 13, 2013, Ananda Radhakrishnan, the Commission's Director of the Division of Clearing and Risk, responded by letter to Bloomberg. In that letter, Mr. Radhakrishnan stated that Bloomberg's January and March 2013 letters "have been referred to the Division of Clearing and Risk for consideration." After explaining the Commission's rationale for adopting the minimum-liquidation-time rule, Mr. Radhakrishnan concluded that Bloomberg's requests "will be given prompt and careful consideration," though "[t]o assist the Commission staff in considering them," Mr. Radhakrishnan requested that Bloomberg "provide any data, studies, or other supporting information" by March 29, 2013.

In response to the Commission's request, Bloomberg sent a third letter, through counsel, to the Commission on March 29, 2013, which attached "two sets of data for each trading day in February 2013." . . . Bloomberg concluded by stating that, since it had not received a response to its March 11, 2013 letter by March 19, 2013, as requested, it had "proceeded with preparing a federal court complaint, which [it] expect[ed] to file shortly."

Bloomberg filed its Complaint in the instant action eighteen days later on April 16, 2013 . . .

[O]n April 25, 2013, the Commission sent a letter responding to the data submitted by Bloomberg in its March 29 letter. In that letter, Mr. Radhakrishnan stated that the Division of Clearing and Risk had "identified a number of questions which require further data and analysis" before the Commission could come to a conclusion regarding Bloomberg's request to stay the five-day minimum liquidation rule. . . .

To summarize, the plaintiff's chain of injury goes as follows: (1) at least some DCOs will set lower liquidation times for financial swap futures than for financial swaps; (2) this lower liquidation time will result in lower margin requirements for financial swap futures than for financial swaps; (3) . . . entities will trade financial swap futures on DCMs rather than trading financial swaps on Bloomberg's trading platform; and, thus (4) at least some . . . [entities] will stop subscribing to Bloomberg's trading platform, causing Bloomberg to lose revenue. The actualization of this chain of events, however, depends on several assumptions about the behavior of third parties who are not before the Court. Most fundamentally, Bloomberg's injury rises or falls with the behavior of third-party DCOs, who are the entities actually regulated by the minimum-liquidation-time rule and are the ones who actually decide what liquidation times to set and how much margin to collect. Yet, inexplicably, Bloomberg has not put forth a single factual allegation that any DCO has set or intends to set liquidation times for financial swap futures at a level lower than that set for financial swaps. Instead, Bloomberg . . . simply assume the worst-case scenario – DCOs will set liquidation times for financial swap futures at the minimum of one day, and will set liquidation times for financial swaps at the minimum of five days – without grounding their assumption in the actual behavior of DCOs. . . .

Due to the absence of any factual allegation that DCOs are setting or are imminently likely to set liquidation times for financial swap futures at a level lower than that for financial swaps, the plaintiff cannot establish a " 'substantial probability' of injury as a result of the rule." . . .

[T]he Court concludes that the plaintiff lacks standing to assert its claims. . . .

---

2. *Derivatives Clearing Organization Selection*

In the futures trading model, as noted in Chapter 5, the clearing function is embedded in the designated contract market because clearing is provided via either a division of the designated contract market or an affiliate of the designated contract market. With the regulatory model for swaps, the parties choose the derivatives clearing organization, regardless of the swap execution facility on which the trade occurs. In cases where one party is a swap dealer or major swap participant, and the other party is neither, i.e., is an end-user, the end-user chooses the derivatives clearing organization.[33]

E. REPORTING REQUIREMENTS AND SWAP DATA REPOSITORIES

1. *Reporting Requirements*

There are a number of reporting requirements for swaps cleared and traded on swap execution facilities. The objective of these reporting requirements is "to enhance transparency and price discovery."[34] Below we analyze the reporting requirements for swaps that are cleared and traded on a swap execution facility. In Chapter 10, we evaluate reporting requirements for such swaps when uncleared and not traded on a swap execution facility.

a. Real-Time Public Reporting

Swap execution facilities are required to report swap transaction and pricing data to a swap data repository for dissemination to the public "as soon as technologically feasible."[35] The public reports contain the pricing and volume of each trade and exclude the names of the parties, so that parties may maintain anonymity.[36] For trades exceeding certain established notional thresholds, time reporting delays are permitted.[37]

b. Regulatory Reporting Requirements

There is other information that, though not publicly reportable, the CFTC receives in its role as regulator. As with the real-time public reporting requirements, parties are required to report this information to a swap data repository, which then holds the data to which the CFTC has access.

Three categories of data must be reported:

1. Primary economic terms. These are the basic economic terms of the transaction. They must be reported by the swap execution facility "as soon as technologically feasible" in a combined report with the "confirmation data" referenced below.[38]

2. Confirmation data. These are all of the relevant terms agreed by the parties. As with the primary economic terms, these must be reported by the swap execution facility "as soon as technologically feasible" in a combined report with the "primary economic terms" referenced above.[39] Additionally, the derivatives clearing organization must report all of the confirmation data as soon as technologically feasible after clearing occurs.[40]

3. Continuation data. Continuation data requires reporting of life cycle events, i.e., changes to the previously reported primary economic terms and valuation data. The life cycle events are required to be reported to a swap data repository by the derivatives clearing organization and the valuation data is required to be reported to a swap data repository by both the derivatives clearing organization and, if any of the parties to the trade is a swap dealer or major swap participant, then one such party must also report the valuation data.[41] Which party depends on the application of a reporting hierarchy in CFTC Rule 45.8 (17 C.F.R. § 45.8).

2. Swap Data Repositories

Swap data repositories are a category of registrant created by the Dodd-Frank Act. Perhaps an oddity of swap reporting is that different parties report different sets of data to a swap data repository. A dispute has arisen over whether such swap data repository should, regardless of the reporting party, be whichever swap data repository the swaps were originally reported to or whether each reporting party should be able to choose the swap data repository to which it reports required data.

DTCC Data Repository (U.S.) LLC v. Commodity Futures Trading Commission

2014 WL 905810 (D.D.C. March 10, 2014)

Amy Berman Jackson, United States District Judge . . .

Plaintiffs, The Depository Trust & Clearing Corporation ("DTCC") and DTCC Data Repository (U.S.) LLC ("DDR"), challenge three separate but interrelated actions taken by the Commission, all of which relate to the Commission's new requirements for swaps. Defendants have moved to dismiss all but one count of the amended complaint. . . .

[The] Dodd-Frank [Act] requires that most swaps be "cleared" by a derivatives clearing organization ("DCO"). DCOs are regulated by the Commission. In the clearing process, a DCO substitutes its own credit for the credit of the original parties to a swap, thereby reducing risk and assuring the financial integrity of a swap transaction. To that end, the Commission requires DCOs to maintain significant financial resources. The Commission also oversees DCOs in a variety of other ways, including by requiring them to submit changes to their internal rules for review.

Dodd-Frank also requires that data about swaps be reported to new entities called "registered swap data repositories" ("SDRs"), which are also regulated by the Commission. This reporting requirement is intended to increase transparency by providing data both to the public and to regulators. The data to be reported includes data about the creation and confirmation of swaps. It also includes "continuation" data, which encompasses any changes made to the terms of a swap over its lifetime, including clearance by a DCO. . . .

According to the amended complaint, plaintiff DDR is the only SDR that is not affiliated with a derivatives clearing organization, or DCO.

This litigation centers on the question of whether it is lawful for the Commission to permit DCOs to require that cleared swap data be reported to their affiliated, or "captive," SDRs. Plaintiffs believe that the Commission has violated the letter and spirit of Dodd-Frank and its own regulations by failing to prohibit what they characterize as "anticompetitive tying arrangements" between DCOs and their captive SDRs. Plaintiffs allege that these arrangements elbow any independent SDRs (that is, plaintiff DDR) out of the marketplace and reduce market participant choice. Plaintiffs also claim that permitting DCOs to require that cleared swap data be reported to their affiliated SDRs injures the public interest by imposing increased costs on market participants and by causing "duplication and fragmentation of swap data" that "[has] the potential to create significant systemic risk to the market as a whole." Finally, plaintiffs allege that the Commission has unlawfully reversed course, and that until November 2012, it had clearly expressed that it would not permit DCOs to require that cleared swap data be reported to their captive SDRs.

Plaintiffs allege that the CFTC violated the Administrative Procedure Act ("APA") and the Commodity Exchange Act in three separate ways in connection with its regulation of swaps. First, in Count I, plaintiffs challenge the revisions of the Commission's published answers to Frequently Asked Questions ("FAQs") that originally indicated that DCOs would be prohibited from requiring that cleared swaps data be reported to their captive SDRs. The three FAQs in question were withdrawn on November 28, 2012.[iii] Plaintiffs claim that the withdrawal of the FAQs was the first step in the Commission's reversal of its position regarding the relationship between DCOs and SDRs.

Second, in Counts II and III, plaintiffs object to the Commission's approval of a new rule submitted by a DCO, the Chicago Mercantile Exchange, Inc. ("CME"), that would require that cleared swaps be reported to CME's captive SDR. CME is a wholly-owned subsidiary of the CME Group, a prominent derivatives marketplace. . . .

Third, in Counts IV and V, plaintiffs challenge the self-certification of a substantially similar rule by ICE Clear Credit ("ICE"), another DCO. . . . Like [the] CME Rule . . . [the] ICE Rule . . . provides that all swaps cleared by ICE must be reported to ICE's SDR. . . .

The Commission's withdrawal of three Frequently Asked Questions six weeks after issuing them is not a reviewable final agency action. At the outset, it is not clear that the withdrawal of the FAQs constitutes "agency action" at all, since "[a]n agency action is not final if it is only 'the ruling of a subordinate official.'" The FAQs plainly state that they reflect the views of Commission staff, not of the Commission itself. And the Commission asserts that its staff, not the Commission, made the decision to withdraw the FAQs at issue here. But the Court need not decide this issue because even if the withdrawal of FAQs could be considered an "agency action," it was not a "final" action, and therefore it is not reviewable.

To be final, an agency action must not be "tentative or interlocutory," and must "be [an action] from which 'rights or obligations have been determined' or from which 'legal consequences will flow.'" The withdrawal of the FAQs did not determine any rights or obligations, nor was it the culmination of a Commission decision-making process. Rather, the Commission or its staff withdrew the advice it had been posting online about a particular question, leaving that question open for later decision by the Commission.[iv] Indeed, the Commission's subsequent approval of [the] CME Rule . . . , which, as plaintiffs point out, expressly "supersede[d]" any prior conflicting guidance, underscores the fact

---

[iii] [N. 1] Plaintiffs characterize the withdrawal of the FAQs as an action of the Commission itself, but the Commission insists that the withdrawal was a decision made by its staff.

[iv] [N. 2] Plaintiffs assert that until the withdrawal of the FAQs, the Commission had "repeatedly affirmed" that it would not allow a DCO to require that data be reported to its captive SDR. Even if true, this would not transform the withdrawal of the FAQs into a final agency action, because the withdrawal, on its own, was not a repudiation of the Commission's alleged prior statements.

that the withdrawal of the FAQs was not a final agency action. The withdrawal of the FAQs was merely "tentative or interlocutory," and is therefore not final agency action subject to APA review. . . .

Counts IV and V challenge the Commission's tacit approval of [the] ICE Rule . . . But that rule was approved by operation of law, and therefore the Court finds that Counts IV and V do not present any agency action or "failure to act" that would be subject to review under the APA. If Congress has "spelled out the legal effect" of agency inaction without articulating any limiting principle, that inaction is typically unreviewable. . . .

[T]he Court finds that since Congress has not articulated a limitation on the approval by operation of law of a rule like [the] ICE Rule . . . , there is no "discrete" agency action to review, and the self-certification . . . is not a reviewable "failure to act." . . .

The Court will grant defendant's motion to dismiss Counts I, IV, and V for failure to state a claim because plaintiffs have failed to allege any final agency action that would be reviewable under the APA. The Court will deny defendant's motion to dismiss Count III because it advances a unique legal theory and is not duplicative of Count II. Defendants do not challenge Count II in this motion, and so Counts II and III will remain in this case.

F. EXTERNAL BUSINESS CONDUCT REQUIREMENTS FOR SWAP DEALERS AND MAJOR SWAP PARTICIPANTS

In Chapter 10, we will examine the external business conduct requirements, i.e., requirements with respect to swap activities with third parties that apply to swap dealers and major swap participants.

When trades are conducted anonymously using a swap execution facility, most of these requirements do not apply. Additionally, for swaps traded non-anonymously through a swap execution facility that are intended to be cleared, the CFTC staff has provided no-action relief from many of the external business conduct requirements.[42]

QUESTIONS AND COMMENTS

1. Is centralized clearing a public good and does it reduce risk? What risks might it reduce and to what risks might the economic system be exposed by centralized clearing?

2. Examining the exceptions from clearing, what might be the public policy motivations for providing them? If clearing is a public good and reduces risk, why is it not applied to all counterparties?
3. Trades on designated contract markets are cleared using a derivatives clearing organization associated with the designated contract market. Trades on swap execution facilities use a different model in which the derivatives clearing organization is selected by the parties to the trade. Why might the Dodd-Frank Act have implemented this model instead of the pre-existing "captive" model used by designated contract markets?
4. Does the Dodd-Frank tend to incentivize futures trading on designated contract markets over trading on swap execution facilities as alleged in *Bloomberg v. CFTC*?
5. What are the public policy benefits to having the swap data repository where a trade was initially reported continue to be the swap data repository throughout such trade's life? What are the benefits to ensuring that swap data is "portable" among swap data repositories?

CHAPTER 10 REGULATION AND DOCUMENTATION OF UNCLEARED SWAPS

A. BACKGROUND

In this section we examine the regulatory regime that applies to swaps that are not cleared and are traded off-facility. As discussed in Chapter 9, if a swap is not required to be cleared, it will also not be required to be traded on a facility, i.e., a designated contract market or swap execution facility.

A swap is not required to be cleared if: (1) it is not subject to a clearing determination, or (2) at least one party to the swap is an end-user who has the option of claiming one of the exceptions from clearing discussed in Chapter 9.

When swaps are traded off-facility and uncleared, swap dealers and major swap participants have enhanced regulatory obligations. In particular, we will focus on the requirements relating to: (1) external business conduct, (2) margin, including margin segregation, (3) reporting, (4) portfolio reconciliation and compression, and (5) documentation, including trade confirmations.

As we will see below in section F, it is important to keep in mind that many of these requirements allow for compliance using written disclosures or other efficient means, such as the multilateral electronic system sponsored by the International Swaps and Derivatives Association and Markit described below.

B. EXTERNAL BUSINESS CONDUCT REQUIREMENTS WITH ALL COUNTERPARTIES

External business conduct requirements are the requirements that apply when a swap dealer or major swap participant interacts with a third party regarding a swap transaction. As we will see, one standard applies to ordinary counterparties (all of whom must be eligible contract participants, *see* Chapter 7) and a stricter standard applies to "special entities," defined below in section C.

1. Verification of Counterparty Status

Swap dealers and major swap participants are required to affirmatively verify whether counterparties are eligible contract participants and special entities.[1]

2. Disclosures and Communications to Counterparties

With respect to any particular swap, swap dealers and major swap participants must disclose to any end-user counterparty the material risks (such as market, credit, liquidity, foreign currency, legal, and operation risks), characteristics, and any incentives or conflicts of interest the swap dealer or major swap participant might have.[2] Part of a disclosure of "incentives" is informing the end-user what the "mid-market" is of the proposed swap.[3] The mid-market shows the price without the additional amounts that the end-user counterparty is paying, thereby allowing the end-user counterparty to see the potential profits of the swap dealer or major swap participant. In addition to disclosing the mid-market before the swap, such mid-market mark must be provided daily thereafter along with associated disclosures on the methodology and limitations of the daily mid-market mark.[4]

Moreover, on the request of any end-user counterparty, a swap dealer or major swap participant is required, before entering into a swap, to collaborate with the end-user counterparty in preparing a "a scenario analysis to allow the counterparty to assess its potential exposure in connection with the swap. . . ."[5]

In all communications to counterparties (whether end-users or not), swap dealers and major swap participants must "communicate in a fair and balanced manner based on principles of fair dealing and good faith."[6]

One might ask, though, what, in the context of swaps, constitutes "fair dealing"? It is a concept that existed prior to the CFTC rule in the form of the rules of self-regulatory organizations, i.e., private organizations in the securities and futures industries that are run by the relevant industry as a self-policing tool operating in cooperation with government regulators.[7] It is intended to be flexible and adaptable, as the CFTC notes below.

Business Conduct Standards for Swap Dealers and Major Swap Participants With Counterparties

77 Fed. Reg. 9734 (February 17, 2012)

. . . [T]he Commission is providing the following guidance regarding the . . . fair dealing rule. . . . [T]he fair dealing rule works . . . to ensure that counterparties receive material information that is balanced and fair at all times. The Commission intends . . . [the rule] to address . . . concerns raised . . . regarding transactions . . . [involving] structured CDOs, [that] were problematic because they were designed to fail and the disclosures omitted and/or misrepresented the material risks, characteristics, incentives and conflicts of interest. . . . [T]he Commission's fair dealing rule . . . operate[s] as an independent basis for enforcement proceedings.

The fair dealing rule . . . is principles based and applies flexibly based on the facts and circumstances of a particular swap. For example, when addressing the risks and characteristics of a swap with features . . . that increase its complexity, the fair dealing rule requires the swap dealer or major swap participant to provide a sound basis for the counterparty to assess how those features would impact the value of the swap under various market conditions during the life of the swap. In a complex swap, where the risks and characteristics associated with an underlying asset are not readily discoverable by the counterparty upon the exercise of reasonable diligence, the swap dealer or major swap participant is expected, under both the disclosure rule and fair dealing rule, to provide a sound basis for the counterparty to assess the swap by providing information about the risks and characteristics of the underlying asset. The fair dealing rule also will supplement requirements to inform counterparties of material incentives and conflicts of interest that would tend to be adverse to the interests of a counterparty in connection with a swap . . . In this regard, a swap dealer or major swap participant will have to follow policies and procedures reasonably designed to ensure that the content and context of its disclosures are fair and complete to allow the counterparty to protect itself and make an informed decision.

In addition . . . the Commission is confirming that it will look to [National Futures Association] guidance when interpreting [this requirement] and, as appropriate, will consider providing further guidance, if necessary . . . The Commission concludes that the futures and securities industry familiarity with these precedents considerably mitigates concerns about legal certainty as a result of the principles based rule. Also, in the absence of fraud, the Commission will consider good faith compliance with policies and procedures reasonably designed to comply with the business conduct standards rules as a mitigating factor when exercising its prosecutorial discretion in connection with a violation of the rules. . . .

---

3. *Recommendations and Suitability*

Swap dealers only (not major swap participants), when making a recommendation to an end-user, are required to "[u]ndertake reasonable diligence to understand the potential risks and rewards associated with the recommended swap . . . and [h]ave a reasonable basis to believe that the recommended swap . . . is suitable for the counterparty."[8]

C. EXTERNAL BUSINESS CONDUCT REQUIREMENTS WITH SPECIAL ENTITIES

1. *Background*

Special entities are defined as being:

(1) A Federal agency;

(2) A State, State agency, city, county, municipality, other political subdivision of a State, or any instrumentality, department, or a corporation of or established by a State or political subdivision of a State;

(3) Any . . . employee benefit plan . . . subject to . . . the Employee Retirement Income Security Act of 1974;

(4) Any governmental [benefit plan] . . .;

(5) Any endowment, including an endowment that is an organization described in Section 501(c)(3) of the Internal Revenue Code of 1986 . . .; or

(6) Any [other] employee benefit plan defined in . . . the Employee Retirement Income Security Act of 1974 . . . that elects to be a Special Entity by notifying a swap dealer or major swap participant of its election prior to entering into a swap with the particular swap dealer or major swap participant.[9]

Additional (and arguably onerous) external business conduct requirements apply to special entities based on a perception that special entities require additional protections. This perception is partially grounded on a number of derivatives losses associated with special entities occurring over the last 25 years and that special entities require special protections for which the law did not, as the below case demonstrates, previously allow.[10]

St. Matthew's Baptist Church v. Wachovia Bank National Association

2005 WL 1199045 (D.N.J. May 18, 2005)

Wolfson, J. . . .

In 1997, Plaintiff St. Matthews's Baptist Church ("St. Matthew's") decided to construct a new administrative wing and community development center. Plaintiff received a short term construction loan for $3,172,000.00 from Wachovia, f/d/b/a CoreStates Bank and First Union National Bank ("Wachovia"), to finance construction of the expansion.

Because of the high interest rate associated with the Short Term Loan, Plaintiff sought to refinance its existing debt by converting the Short Term Loan into a permanent five-year long term loan in the amount of $5,055,048.97. When the Church met with Wachovia in February, 2000 to discuss approval for the Long Term Loan, it requested a fixed interest rate loan, feeling that it "would not be able to meet its debt service obligations with a high fluctuating interest rate." The Church alleges that Wachovia informed it that it did not qualify for a fixed interest rate. Instead, Wachovia suggested and that the Church should consider using a floating loan with a fixed rate hedge that would protect the Church against the risk of rising interest rates, also known as an "interest rate swap agreement." The Church and Wachovia entered into this Interest Rate Swap Agreement ("Swap Agreement"). . . .

Pursuant to the Swap Agreement, the Church agreed to pay a fixed rate of 9.13% over a term of five years in exchange for Wachovia's payment of a rate equal to LIBOR plus 1.5%. The notional amount was the amount of the loan, $5,055,048.97. . . .

[O]n April 20, 2000, the parties executed a Promissory Note ("Note"), under which Wachovia agreed to loan $5,055,048.97 to the Church. The floating interest rate on the Note was calculated "at a rate equal to 1-month LIBOR plus one hundred fifty percent (150%) per annum."

Approximately two years later, after making twenty-four 24 monthly payments, the Church considered pre-paying its loan to Wachovia in order to refinance with another lender and receive a more favorable interest rate. The Church alleges that it then learned, for the first time, that if it chose to pre-pay the Note and terminate the Swap Agreement, the Church would have to pay a "termination fee," or pre-payment penalty. The Church alleges that Wachovia represented in February 2000 that the Swap Agreement would provide benefits not available with a fixed rate loan, and that in the event that the Church cancelled the Swap, the Church may have to pay an "unwind fee," which would be smaller than a standard prepayment penalty on a fixed rate bank loan. It further alleges that it was never disclosed that the Church would incur any fee or penalty if it opted to prepay the amount owed under the Swap Agreement, or the manner in which any prepayment penalty would be calculated and assessed by Wachovia. . . .

[U]nder both New York and New Jersey law, the plaintiff is required to allege reasonable reliance on the alleged misrepresentation in order to state a claim for either fraudulent or negligent misrepresentation. Defendant argues that the Swap Agreement and Note both contain merger and integration clauses that prevent Plaintiff from demonstrating reliance.[i] Plaintiff contends, in response, that courts will routinely refuse to dismiss claims that written agreements were fraudulently induced, even where merger and integration clauses are included in the agreements.

The Note also contains an integration clause, stating that "this Note and the other Loan Documents constitute the sole agreement of the parties with respect to the transaction contemplated hereby and supersede all oral negotiations and prior writings with respect thereto."

General merger and integration clauses and disclaimers of reliance are insufficient to prevent the introduction of parol evidence of misrepresentations . . . The Court finds that the merger and integration clauses in the Swap Agreement would be characterized as general, and would not alone suffice to prevent evidence of allegedly fraudulent representations. . . .

[H]owever, alleged misrepresentations that contradict the express words of a written instrument are inadmissible to avoid an obligation knowingly assumed.

Here, Plaintiff alleges that "with respect to the Church's possible cancellation of the agreement, Wachovia instructed the Church that, in the event that the Church would cancel the Swap, the Church might, at worst, have to pay an 'unwind fee' which, according to Wachovia would be smaller than a standard prepayment penalty on a fixed rate bank loan." . . .

Plaintiff's arguments are expressly contradicted by the terms of the governing documents of the [Swap] Agreement . . . and the Note. . . .

[T]he . . . [Swap Agreement] clearly contemplate[s] the requirement that the borrower make payments on the specified due dates according to the agreement regardless of whether or not there exists any continued commitment for financing, including repayment prior to the Effective Date.

In addition, the Note contains a provision addressed to the Church's obligations under the Swap Agreement in the event of pre-payment:

> PREPAYMENT. The Loan may be prepaid, in whole or in part, at any time and from time to time . . . Nothing herein shall be deemed to alter or affect any obligations that Borrower may have to Bank under any interest rate swap agreements.

---

[i] [N. 2] The Swap Agreement itself provides that it "constitutes the entire agreement and understanding of the parties with respect to its subject matter and supersedes all oral communication and prior writings with respect thereto." In addition, [it contains representations that neither party is relying on advice from the other party] . . .

This provision also clearly contemplates that even if the Note was repaid in advance of the Termination date, obligations that the Borrower has to the Bank under interest rate swap agreements would still remain.

Plaintiff's decision to "prepay the note and terminate the Long Term Loan," thereby failing to make continued payments as specified by the Agreement, thus constituted an Event of Default . . .

Thus, the alleged misrepresentations are inadmissible because they are expressly contradicted by the terms of the Agreement. As such, Plaintiff is unable to demonstrate reliance upon these representations, a necessary element of claims for fraudulent and negligent misrepresentation. . . .

Defendant also moves to dismiss Plaintiff's unjust enrichment claim based on the existence of a valid express contract between the parties. Where there is an express contract covering the identical subject matter of the claim, plaintiff cannot pursue a quasi-contractual claim for unjust enrichment.

Plaintiff argues that its unjust enrichment claim should not be dismissed because it alleges that none of the contractual documents make reference to any prepayment penalty. . . .

[T]he Swap Agreement clearly contemplates that Plaintiff was liable for payments for the duration of the Agreement, regardless of the existence or amount of the principal amount of financing. It further contemplates that Plaintiff's failure to continue making payments according to the terms of the agreement would constitute an Event of Default, and specifies how payments are to be calculated upon such an occurrence. . . . [A]lthough the documents do not reference a prepayment fee, *per se*, the Court finds that the Agreement explicitly addresses Plaintiff's claims. . . .

Defendant also moves to dismiss Plaintiff's claim for breach of fiduciary duty, arguing that Plaintiff is unable to establish that Defendant was acting as a fiduciary when Plaintiff entered into the Swap Agreement. . . .

It is well-settled that the relationship between a bank and its customer is a debtor-creditor relationship that does not ordinarily give rise to a fiduciary duty. . . .

Thus, banks and other lending institutions have been held liable to their customers only "for gross acts of misconduct and deceit," or where "the lender encouraged the borrower to repose special trust or confidence in its advice, thereby inducing the borrower's reliance." . . .

Plaintiff argues that its allegations in the Complaint suffice to establish a fiduciary relationship because (1) Wachovia possessed highly specialized knowledge with respect to swap agreements; (2) the Church was an unsophisticated borrower that relied on this expertise; and (3) the Church placed its trust and confidence in Wachovia. Plaintiff's allegations are insufficient to establish that its relationship with the Bank was outside the realm of the normal debtor-creditor relationship. First, the Complaint does not sufficiently allege grossly unequal bargaining power. Although Plaintiff submits that its counsel in the instant lawsuit did not represent the Church in connection with the execution of the Note and the Swap Agreement, it does not submit that it did not retain counsel that had familiarity with swap agreements to advise the Church, or that it was unable to do so. Plaintiff similarly does not allege facts demonstrating that the Bank was in a position to exercise control over the Church's decision to enter into the agreement, or any other facts that distinguish the instant case from the normal debtor-creditor relationship. . . .

The Court therefore finds that no fiduciary relationship existed between Wachovia and the Church. Moreover, the Schedule to the Swap Agreement specifically disclaims the existence of a fiduciary relationship. . . .

[A] covenant of good faith and fair dealing is implied in every contract. . . .

Plaintiff's good faith and fair dealing claim is based on the alleged inconsistency of the termination fee with the terms of the Agreement and Note. . . . [T]he Court finds that Defendant was entitled to continued payments under the Agreement, regardless of whether or not there was a continued loan in effect, and the implied duty of good faith and fair dealing thus may not be invoked to prevent Defendant from exercising the right to receive payments as specified in the Agreement. . . .

Plaintiff also alleges violations of Section 10(b) of the Securities Exchange Act of 1934 (the "Exchange Act"), 15 U.S.C. § 78j(b), and Rule 10b-5 promulgated thereunder, 17 C.F.R. § 240.10b. To state a claim under § 10(b) and Rule 10b-5, plaintiffs are required to plead that a particular defendant: (1) made a misstatement or an omission of a material fact (2) with scienter (3) in connection with the purchase or sale of a security (4) upon which the plaintiff reasonably relied and (5) that the plaintiff's reliance was the proximate cause of his or her injury. . . .

Defendant moves to dismiss Plaintiff's federal securities claims because of Plaintiff's failure to allege that fraud was committed "in connection with the purchase or sale of any security." Congress specifically addressed the general confusion regarding whether swap agreements were to be considered securities for the purpose of the Exchange Act in passing the [Commodity Futures Modernization Act]. . . .

Plaintiff has not alleged facts demonstrating that [Rule 10b-5 applies to] the Swap Agreement here . . . [and] Plaintiff's claims under the Exchange Act must be dismissed. . . .

---

2. Requirements When Acting as Counterparty to a Special Entity

a. Representative Requirement

A swap dealer or major swap participant needs to have a "reasonable basis to believe" that the special entity has a representative that, among other things, has "sufficient knowledge to evaluate the transaction and risks," acts in the best interest of the special entity, "[m]akes appropriate and timely disclosures to the Special Entity," and "[e]valuates, consistent with any guidelines provided by the Special Entity, fair pricing and the appropriateness of the swap. . . ."[11] The special entity's representative also must be "independent" of any swap dealer or major swap participant with which it transacts a swap.

The requirement that the representative be "independent," is a multi-faceted requirement. It precludes any transaction between a special entity and a swap dealer or major swap participant if the representative of the special entity:

- Has, in the preceding year, worked for the swap dealer or major swap participant in anything other than a clerical or ministerial function;

- Is directly or indirectly affiliated with the swap dealer or major swap participant;

- Was recommended or introduced to the special entity during the past year by the swap dealer or major swap participant; and

- Has not disclosed to the special entity all material conflicts of interest which could affect its independence or has not complied with policies and procedures designed to mitigate such conflicts.[12]

Note that the first three items are within the knowledge of a swap dealer or major swap participant and, therefore, easily determined by the swap dealer or major swap participant. The fourth, whether or not the special entity's representative has made the required disclosures to the special entity, is likely not known to the swap dealer or major swap participant. This reaffirms the importance of written disclosures and representations by the special entity or its representative as a means to satisfy many of these requirements.

In addition to the requirements pertaining to a special entity's representative, swap dealers and major swap participants must disclose the capacity in which it is acting with respect to the swap and, if it is acting in more than one capacity (for example, arranging a competitive bid for the swap and acting as a competitor), it must disclose those capacities and their differences.[13]

b. Limitation on Political Contributions

Swap dealers may not offer to enter into a swap with a governmental special entity, i.e., a special entity in the second or fourth category of the definition of special entity in section C1 above, if the swap dealer, its senior management, its employees who solicit swaps with governmental special entities, or the supervisors of such employees have made any contribution to an official of such special entity within the last two years.[14]

There is an exception for an up to $350 limit per official per election for management or employees who are entitled to vote for the official or $150 limit per official per election for management or employees not entitled to vote for the official and for contributions made by management or employees, other than those soliciting swaps with governmental entities, more than six months before being employed by the swap dealer.[15] The CFTC also provides a process for petitioning the CFTC for relief from the two-year ban in individual cases.[16]

The political contribution limitations do not apply to major swap participants. At the time the rule was issued, the CFTC reasoned:

> [T]he Commission decided to exclude major swap participants from the pay-to-play prohibition [i.e., the limitations on political contributions] because major swap participants, as defined, do not "solicit" swap transaction business within the meaning of the final rule and, as such, the Commission does not expect that major swap participants will assume a dealer-type role in the swap market.

Business Conduct Standards for Swap Dealers and Major Swap Participants With Counterparties, 77 Fed. Reg. 9734 (February 17, 2012), 9800.

Limitations on political contributions raise First Amendment questions. Similar limitations were upheld in the context of a rule issued by the Municipal Securities Rulemaking Board related to soliciting municipalities in relation to securities activities, such as bond issuances.

Blount v. Securities and Exchange Commission

61 F.3d 938 (D.C. Cir. 1995)

Stephen F. Williams, Circuit Judge:

In late 1993, regulators of the municipal securities markets began to investigate reports that brokers and dealers were engaging in a variety of ethically questionable practices in order to secure underwriting contracts. These practices, often lumped together under the label "pay to play", include as a paradigmatic example the making of political contributions to state and local officials who may influence the choice of underwriter. Concerned that such practices were becoming more prevalent and were undermining the integrity of the $250 billion municipal securities market, the Municipal Securities Rulemaking Board ("MSRB" or "Board") drafted several new rules, which were then approved by the Securities and Exchange Commission. Among these was Rule G-37, the rule challenged in this case.

The two principal sections of Rule G-37, (b) and (c), together restrict the ability of municipal securities professionals to contribute and to solicit contributions to the political campaigns of state officials from whom they obtain business. Section (d) serves as a loophole-closer, prohibiting indirect violations of the restrictions in (b) or (c). . . .

The petitioner, William B. Blount, is the chairman of the Alabama Democratic Party and a registered broker and dealer of municipal securities. He challenges the SEC's order approving Rule G-37, claiming that each of the three sections of the rule we have described impermissibly infringes his First Amendment rights; that section (d) is, in addition, unconstitutionally vague; and that the rule as a whole violates the Tenth Amendment. The SEC rebuts each of these claims, and the MSRB, as intervenor, raises two defenses not urged by the SEC: that Blount does not have standing under the Exchange Act to pursue his claim and that the rule is not the product of government action and thus cannot violate either the First or Tenth Amendments. We find that Blount has standing to sue and that Rule G-37 is government action. We therefore meet all of Blount's arguments on the merits, though ultimately we reject them and deny the petition for review. . . .

We turn now to the central issue in this case, petitioner's claim that Rule G-37 violates his First Amendment rights to free speech and free association. . . .

All three sections of Rule G-37 at issue here infringe speech. Giving money is one method of indicating one's devotion to a cause; hence the familiar challenge, "Put your money where your mouth is." The Supreme Court has characterized the campaign contribution as a "symbolic act" that "serves as a general expression of support for the candidate and his views", though noting at the same time that the contribution does not indicate the basis for the support and that a limit on contributions does not "infringe the contributor's freedom to discuss candidates and issues." *Buckley v. Valeo*, 424 U.S. 1, 21, 96 S. Ct. 612, 636, 46 L.Ed.2d 659 (1976) (*per curiam*). Solicitation of campaign funds, the target of sections (c) and (d), is close to the core of protected speech, as it is "characteristically intertwined" with both information and advocacy and essential to the continued flow of both. . . .

The intensity with which we scrutinize Rule G-37 depends on whether the rule is content-based, eliciting "strict" scrutiny, or content-neutral, eliciting only "intermediate" scrutiny. The proper categorization of Rule G-37 is not clear-cut. As petitioner points out, under the everyday meaning of the word "content", the rule appears to be content-based, as it restricts only messages that concern one "topic", specifically, financial contributions to political campaigns. But the Supreme Court does not regard a rule's use of subject-based categories as automatically establishing it as content-based. The critical issue is whether the state's justification for the distinction is the "content" of the speech itself or some other concern . . .

If the rule can withstand strict scrutiny there is no need to decide the issue. Accordingly we turn to applying such scrutiny and ask . . . whether the rule is narrowly tailored to serve a compelling government interest. . . .

The Commission claims that Rule G-37 supports two interests . . . : (1) protecting investors in municipal bonds from fraud and (2) protecting underwriters of municipal bonds from unfair, corrupt market practices. Both of these interests are not only substantial . . . but, we think, compelling. . . .

[P]etitioner claims there is no support for the Commission's finding that pay-to-play practices are prevalent in the negotiated municipal bond business, because the record contains no evidence of specific instances of *quid pro quos*. But underwriters' campaign contributions self-evidently create a conflict of interest in state and local officials who have power over municipal securities contracts and a risk that they will award the contracts on the basis of benefit to their campaign chests rather than to the governmental entity. Petitioner himself remarked on national radio that "most likely [state and local officials] are gonna call somebody who has been a political contributor" and, at least in close cases, award contracts to "friends" who have contributed. Morning Edition (National Public Radio, June 1, 1994), available in LEXIS, News Library, Transcript No. 1358-9. While the risk of corruption is obvious and substantial, actors in this field are presumably shrewd enough to structure their relations rather indirectly – indeed, the phrase "pay to play" suggests that a contribution brings the donor merely a chance to be seriously considered, not the assurance of a contract. . . . Although the record contains only allegations, no smoking gun is needed where, as here, the conflict of interest is apparent, the likelihood of stealth great, and the legislative purpose prophylactic. . . .

Even assuming the prevalence of *quid pro quos*, Blount maintains, the Commission has not demonstrated that eliminating such activity advances the asserted interests in protecting investors and promoting just and equitable principles of trade. As to the harm to investors, we tend to share the petitioner's skepticism. . . .

On the other hand, the link between eliminating pay-to-play practices and the Commission's goals of "perfecting the mechanism of a free and open market" and promoting "just and equitable principles of trade" is self-evident. . . .

Blount asserts that Rule G-37 is too broad, arguing that the Commission could have achieved its goal with less restrictive means. . . .

[T]he regulation is "closely drawn" and thus "avoid[s] unnecessary abridgement" of First Amendment rights, *Buckley v. Valeo*, 424 U.S. at 25, 96 S. Ct. at 638. Rule G-37 constrains relations only between the two potential parties to a *quid pro quo*: the underwriters and their municipal finance employees on the one hand, and officials who might influence the award of negotiated municipal bond underwriting contracts on the other. Even then, the rule restricts a narrow range of their activities for a relatively short period of time. The underwriter is barred from engaging in business with the particular issuer for only two years after it makes a contribution, and it is barred from soliciting contributions only during the time that it is engaged in or seeking business with the issuer associated with the donee. A municipal finance professional may contribute [a limited amount] per election to each official for whom he or she is entitled to vote, without triggering the business bar. Furthermore, as the Commission interprets the rule, municipal finance professionals are not in any way restricted from engaging in the vast majority of political activities, including making direct expenditures for the expression of their views, giving speeches, soliciting votes, writing books, or appearing at fundraising events. . . .

Because Rule G-37 withstands all of Blount's challenges, the petition for review is Denied.

Blount v. SEC was decided before the Supreme Court ruled, in *Citizens United v. FEC*, 558 U.S. 310 (2010), that the First Amendment applies to corporations. The SEC has subsequently issued Rule 206(4)-5 (17 C.F.R. § 275.206(4)-5), which limits political contributions by regulated investment advisers in a similar fashion to MSRB Rule G-37's limitations on securities broker-dealers and the CFTC's limitations on swap dealers. The SEC sought to distinguish *Citizens United* by arguing that "*Citizens United* deals with certain independent expenditures (rather than contributions to candidates), which are not implicated by our rule."[17]

No agency or court has yet determined what impact the Supreme Court's abolition of individual campaign contribution limits in *McCutcheon v. Federal Election Commission*, 134 S. Ct. 1434 (2014) will have, if any, on limitations on political contributions by registered entities such as swap dealers.

3. Requirements When Acting as Advisor to a Special Entity

Additional requirements are imposed on a swap dealer (not a major swap participant) acting as an advisor to a special entity in relation to swaps.[18] The general duty imposed is to make a "reasonable determination" that any recommended swap is in the "best interests" of the special entity.[19]

The CFTC has affirmed that, despite this standard bearing similarity to a fiduciary's duty of care, these requirements do not impose a fiduciary relationship between a swap dealer and a special entity.

Business Conduct Standards for Swap Dealers and Major Swap Participants with Counterparties

77 Fed. Reg. 9734 (February 17, 2012)

. . . The Commission has determined not to define the term ''best interests,'' but rather to provide further guidance as to the meaning of the term and the scope of the duty.

The Commission has considered commenters' views and the legislative history in regard to whether [Commodity Exchange Act] Section 4s(h)(4) [the statutory provision on which the rule is based] imposes a fiduciary duty. The Commission has determined that the "best interests" duty under Section 4s(h)(4) is not a fiduciary duty. Additionally, the Commission does not view the business conduct standards statutory provisions or rules . . . [as imposing] a fiduciary duty on a swap dealer with respect to any other party.

Whether a recommended swap is in the "best interests" of the Special Entity will turn on the facts and circumstances of the particular recommendation and particular Special Entity. However, the Commission will consider a swap dealer that "acts as an advisor to a Special Entity" to have complied with its duty . . . where the swap dealer (1) . . . [makes] a reasonable effort to obtain necessary information [for making a recommendation], (2) acts in good faith and makes full and fair disclosure of all material facts and conflicts of interest with respect to the recommended swap, and (3) employs reasonable care that any recommendation made to a Special Entity is designed to further the Special Entity's stated objectives.

For a recommendation of a swap to be in the best interests of the Special Entity, the swap does not need to be the "best" of all possible alternatives that might hypothetically exist, but should be assessed in comparison to other swaps, such as swaps offered by the swap dealer or "made available for trading" on a SEF or DCM. To be in the best interests of a Special Entity, the recommended bespoke swap would have to further the Special Entity's hedging, investing or other stated objectives. Additionally, whether a recommended swap is in the best interests of the Special Entity will be analyzed based on information known to the swap dealer (after it has employed its reasonable efforts [as] required . . .) at the time the recommendation is made. The "best interests" duty does not prohibit a swap dealer from negotiating swap terms in its own interests, nor does it prohibit a swap dealer from making a reasonable profit from a recommended transaction. Depending on the facts and circumstances, the "best interests" duty also does not require an ongoing obligation to act in the best interests of the Special Entity. For example, a swap dealer would be able to exercise its rights under the terms and conditions of the swap when determining whether to make additional collateral calls in response to the Special Entity's deteriorating credit rating, whether or not such collateral calls would be, from the Special Entity's perspective, in the Special Entity's "best interests." . . .

D. REGULATIONS APPLYING TO UNCLEARED SWAPS OTHER THAN EXTERNAL BUSINESS CONDUCT OR DOCUMENTATION REQUIREMENTS

1. Margin

As is also the case with capital requirements, discussed in Chapter 8, the regulator responsible for imposing margin requirements on swaps entered into by swap dealers and major swap participants will not necessarily be the CFTC. An entity regulated by a "prudential regulator," i.e., the Federal Reserve Board, Office of the Comptroller of the Currency, Federal Deposit Insurance Corporation, Farm Credit Administration or Federal Housing Finance Agency,[20] is required to follow its regulator's margin requirements instead of the CFTC's margin requirements.[21]

The CFTC and prudential regulators have each proposed margin rules providing for different margin requirements to be applied on a trade-by-trade basis depending on whether the counterparty to the trade is also a swap dealer or major swap participant or, alternatively, a financial end-user or non-financial end-user.[22]

Margin can be divided into two concepts, initial margin and variation margin, both of which the CFTC asserts are necessary elements of risk management.

<u>Margin Requirements for Uncleared Swaps for Swap Dealers and Major Swap Participants</u>

76 Fed. Reg. 23732 (April 28, 2011)

. . . During the recent financial crisis, derivatives clearing organizations ("DCOs") met all their obligations without any financial infusions from the government. By contrast, significant sums were expended as the result of losses incurred in connection with uncleared swaps, most notably at AIG. A key reason for this difference is that DCOs all use variation margin and initial margin as the centerpiece of their risk management programs while these tools were often not used in connection with uncleared swaps. Consequently, in designing the proposed margin rules for uncleared swaps, the Commission has built upon the sound practices for risk management employed by central counterparties for decades.

Variation margin entails marking open positions to their current market value each day and transferring funds between the parties to reflect any change in value since the previous time the positions were marked. This process prevents losses from accumulating over time and thereby reduces both the chance of default and the size of any default should one occur.

Initial margin serves as a performance bond against potential future losses. If a party fails to meet its obligation to pay variation margin, resulting in a default, the other party may use initial margin to cover most or all of any loss based on the need to replace the open position.

More formally, the CFTC defines "initial margin" as "money, securities, or property posted by a party to a swap as performance bond to cover potential future exposures arising from changes in the market value of the position" and "variation margin" as "a payment made by or collateral posted by a party to a swap to cover the current exposure arising from changes in the market value of the position since the trade was executed or the previous time the position was marked to market."[23]

Historically, initial margin has not been frequently required in off-facility swap transactions, whereas variation margin is the norm. The Dodd-Frank Act requires that end-user counterparties of swap dealers or major swap participants be granted the right to require segregation of any initial margin, i.e., to have the margin held in a separate account by an unaffiliated third party. This requirement does not apply to variation margin.[24]

2. *Reporting*

Swap dealers and major swap participants (and, potentially, U.S. end-users, as noted below), must perform the trade reporting responsibilities that are otherwise undertaken by swap execution facilities for swaps that are not traded on a swap execution facility. For a description of the real-time and regulatory trade reporting responsibilities, *see* Chapter 9.

Only one party to a trade must report the trade. The relevant party is determined by a "reporting hierarchy" that specifies which party is required to report a particular trade. The reporting hierarchy differs depending on whether the trade reporting is the real-time or regulatory reporting. Figure 10-A summarizes this reporting hierarchy.

Figure 10-A: Reporting Hierarchy for Real-time and Regulatory Trade Reporting

Real-Time Trade Reporting	Regulatory Trade Reporting
If a swap dealer is a party to the trade, the swap dealer is always required to be the reporting party (if both parties are swap dealers, they must agree as to which is the reporting party)	Same as for real-time reporting
If no swap dealer is a party to the transaction, a major swap participant is required to be the reporting party (if both parties are major swap participants, they must agree as to which is the reporting party)	Same as for real-time reporting
If no swap dealer or major swap participant is a party to the transaction then the parties must agree on the reporting party[25]	If no swap dealer or major swap participant is a party to the transaction, the end-user that is a U.S. person is required to be the reporting party
Not applicable	If both end-users are U.S. persons, the financial end-user is the reporting party (if both parties are financial end-users, they must agree as to which is the reporting party)
Not applicable	If both end-users are non-financial end-users they must agree as to which is the reporting party

Note that, if both parties are non-U.S. persons trading outside the United States, CFTC jurisdiction normally would not apply and, therefore, there would be no CFTC reporting requirements.

3. Portfolio Reconciliation and Compression

As a risk management function, swap dealers and major swap participants are required to periodically ensure agreement with counterparties on their relevant positions, including the market value of those positions, and to engage in exercises to reduce duplicative exposures.[26] If there are material discrepancies in each party's view of the market value of their positions, such discrepancies must be resolved or reported to the CFTC. Figure 10-B summarizes the requirements.

Figure 10-B: Portfolio Reconciliation Obligations for Swap Dealers and Major Swap Participants					
Counter-party Type	Size of Swap Portfolio	Frequency	Time Period for Resolving Material Difference in Terms Applying to Swap	Time Period for Resolving Material Difference (10% or more) in Portfolio Valuation	Timing of Report to CFTC of Valuation Dispute in Excess of $20 MM
Swap dealer or major swap participant	>500	Daily	Immediate	5 business days	3 business days
Swap dealer or major swap participant	>50 <500	Weekly	Immediate	5 business days	3 business days
Swap dealer or major swap participant	≤ 50	Quarterly	Immediate	5 business days	3 business days
All others types	>100	Quarterly	"timely fashion"	"timely fashion"	5 business days
All other types	≤ 100	Annually	"timely fashion"	"timely fashion"	5 business days

E. DOCUMENTATION REQUIREMENTS

1. *Regulatory Requirements*

Swap trading relationship documentation are the agreements governing swap transactions between parties. The CFTC has implemented rules with highly prescriptive requirements for what such documentation must contain in circumstances where at least one of the parties is a swap dealer or major swap participant. It must be in writing and minimally contain, among others:

> [A]ll terms governing the trading relationship . . . including, without limitation, terms addressing payment obligations, netting of payments, events of default or other termination events, calculation and netting of obligations upon termination, transfer of rights and obligations, governing law, valuation, and dispute resolution . . . all confirmations of swap transactions . . . .credit support arrangements, which shall contain, in accordance with applicable requirements under Commission regulations or regulations adopted by prudential regulators . . . [i]nitial and variation margin requirements, if any . . . assets that may be used as margin and asset valuation haircuts, if any . . . [i]nvestment and rehypothecation terms for assets used as margin for uncleared swaps, if any [and] [c]ustodial arrangements for margin assets, including whether margin assets are to be segregated with an independent third party . . . [and upon request by a non-financial end-user and automatically with respect to all other parties] . . . written documentation in which the parties agree on the process, which may include any agreed upon methods, procedures, rules, and inputs, for determining the value of each swap at any time from execution to the termination, maturity, or expiration of such swap for the purposes of complying with . . . margin requirements . . . [and] risk management requirements . . .

17 C.F.R. § 23.504(b).

Most of these requirements are already met by the industry-standard documentation used to agree to swap transactions, the ISDA Master Agreement (it has a 1992 and a 2002 version), prepared by the primary industry association for the swaps industry, the International Swaps and Derivatives Association, more commonly referred to as "ISDA" (*iz-də*) and, where the swaps between the parties are collateralized, the 1994 Credit Support Annex, also prepared by the International Swaps and Derivatives Association. The CFTC, while recognizing that the ISDA Master Agreement and Credit Support Annex together satisfy many of the documentation requirements, also noted shortfalls at the time it released the swap trading relationship documentation rule.

Confirmation, Portfolio Reconciliation, Portfolio Compression, and Swap Trading Relationship Documentation Requirements for Swap Dealers and Major Swap Participants

77 Fed. Reg. 55904 (September 11, 2012)

. . . Several commenters requested that the Commission clarify the standing under the rules of the ISDA Master Agreement and Credit Support Annex (the ISDA Agreements), which are prevalent in the swaps market [and] . . . requested that the Commission acknowledge the general adequacy of the ISDA Agreements for purposes of the rule. . . . Similarly, . . . [a commentator] argued that many end users have already negotiated existing documentation under the ISDA architecture and thus requested that the Commission make clear that: (1) ISDA Agreements or any substantially similar master agreements satisfy the documentation requirements of the final rules; (2) in accordance with the ISDA Agreements and applicable state law, swaps are binding when made orally; and (3) long-form confirmations that contain all requisite legal terms to establish a binding agreement also satisfy the requirements of the rules. . . . [Another commentator] also recommended that the Commission expressly state that the ISDA Agreements satisfy the documentation requirements of the final rules or state how the ISDA Agreements are deficient to eliminate any confusion. Finally, the Coalition for Derivatives End-Users argued that, given that the ISDA Agreements are used by nearly all end users and that such documentation substantially complies with the proposed rules, the Commission should expressly state that the ISDA Agreements satisfy the documentation requirements of the rules.

On the other hand, the Committee on the Investment of Employee Benefit Assets (CIEBA) anticipates that ISDA may initiate a uniform protocol to conform existing ISDA Agreements to the requirements of the rules. In this regard, CIEBA stated that ISDA protocols, which in the past have typically been developed by dealer-dominated ISDA committees, are not form documents that can be revised by the parties. Rather, CIEBA argues, end users may only adopt these protocols on a ‘‘take it or leave it’’ basis, which may not be in their best interests.

Accordingly, CIEBA recommended that the Commission not, either explicitly or implicitly, require market participants to consent to ISDA protocols in order to comply with the Dodd-Frank Act or the Commission's regulations.

The Commission notes that many comments received with respect to this and other rulemakings stated that swaps are privately negotiated bilateral contracts. Although the Commission recognizes that the ISDA Agreements in their pre-printed form as published by ISDA are capable of compliance with the rules, such agreements are subject to customization by counterparties. In addition, the Commission notes that while the pre-printed form of the ISDA Master Agreement is capable of addressing the requirements . . . it is not possible to determine if the pre-printed form of the ISDA Credit Support Annex will comply . . . because . . . [the documentation rule] requires that the documentation include credit support arrangements that comply with the Commission's rules regarding initial and variation margin and custodial arrangements, which have been proposed but not yet finalized. Further, the Commission does not believe that the standard ISDA Agreements address the swap valuation requirements . . . [or] orderly liquidation termination provisions. . . . Given the foregoing, the Commission declines to endorse the ISDA Agreements as meeting the requirements of the rules in all instances.

Whereas the ISDA Master Agreement and Credit Support Annex may not fully satisfy the CFTC's documentation rules, they satisfy most of the requirements. Where there are shortfalls ISDA has established a process, known as the "Dodd-Frank Protocols" and described further below in section F, intended to plug the gaps by facilitating necessary amendments to ISDA Master Agreements already in place between parties (as well as satisfy many of the other requirements pertaining to uncleared swaps.)

2. ISDA Documentation and the Negotiation Thereof

Because of their prevalence, it is important to have a basic understanding of ISDA Master Agreements, including the basics of its negotiation.

Gary E. Kalbaugh and Richard A. Miller, Master Agreements for OTC Derivatives

In *Commercial Contracts: Strategies for Drafting and Negotiation* (Vladimir R. Rossman & Morton Moskin, eds., 3d ed., Aspen Publishers 2014)

. . . Frequently, a dealer or "end-user" of derivatives may enter into many derivatives of different types contemporaneously. To avoid individually negotiating the legal terms to apply to each such transaction, and to ensure that each transaction can be viewed as forming one single agreement,[ii] widely used "master agreements" have been created for documenting derivatives transactions.

This chapter describes the . . . 2002 Master Agreement published by the International Swaps and Derivatives Association, Inc. (ISDA)[iii] and discusses the

---

[ii] [N. 5] *See* Netting at *infra* [A].

[iii] [N. 6] . . . Also commonly used for over-the-counter derivatives transactions is the Multicurrency-Cross Border version of the 1992 Master Agreement. Due to the similarity of the 1992 and 2002 agreements, much of the discussion herein with respect to the 2002 agreement applies equally to the 1992 agreement. Where there are significant divergences between the two, they are noted.

most important terms that are negotiated in connection with this agreement. Consideration is also given to the reasons for choosing among the pre-listed elections made available under the master agreement and to the special provisions that are most commonly added to ISDA master agreements to customize coverage to the special circumstances of the parties. . . .

[T]he form used most commonly for documenting OTC derivatives is the form entitled "2002 ISDA Master Agreement" which was released in 2002[iv] (hereinafter referred to as the "ISDA Master," or the "Master"). Documentation for OTC transactions of types that can be covered by an ISDA Master generally consists of the Master Agreement, a Schedule to the ISDA Master and one or more Confirmations memorializing particular transactions.

The ISDA Master comprises 28 pages and 14 paragraphs that are never altered by interlineating or physical mark-up. All elections under, or modifications to, the Master are included in the Schedule or, in some cases, one or more Confirmations. The ISDA Master by its terms provides that provisions in the Schedule supersede any inconsistent provisions in the Master, and any provisions in Confirmations supersede any inconsistent provisions in the Schedule. The Master covers the broad, substantive terms of the parties' agreement and its operation. The Master has a well-recognized status as an agreement that can provide for netting of payments on an ongoing basis (payment netting) and upon termination of the Master (close-out netting) that is considered enforceable in accordance with its terms in a great many jurisdictions.[v]

The Master, Schedule, and Confirmation should be read in conjunction with a number of other ISDA-published documents which are incorporated either by specific reference or by industry practice. Which documents are relevant will depend upon the type of transaction involved[vi] but, at a minimum, the 2006 ISDA Definitions and the User's Guide to the 2002 ISDA Master Agreement are generally relevant. Very broadly speaking, the ISDA Master includes:

[iv] [N. 46] The earliest official version of the ISDA Master Agreement was entitled the 1987 Interest Rate & Currency Exchange Agreement. It was superseded by the 1992 ISDA Master Agreement. The 2002 ISDA Master Agreement, based on the structure of the 1992 ISDA, is now generally the market standard though the 1992 ISDA Master Agreement is still in circulation.

[v] [N. 48] ISDA has obtained opinions of counsel or memoranda in many jurisdictions analyzing the application of bankruptcy laws to transactions documented under ISDA Master Agreements. . . .

[vi] [N. 49] For example, there are ISDA-specified definitions and user's guides for foreign currency transactions, equity derivatives, credit derivatives, and commodity transactions. In each instance, the definitions are an effort to incorporate market-standard practices that will provide conformity and certainty to the parties' dealings. These definitions and guides are available from ISDA.

(a) Representations made by each party to the other, some of which have been the subject of dispute and litigation in the past, including regarding a party's power to enter into derivative transactions and the resulting enforceability of derivative agreements;[vii]

(b) Conditions precedent to each party's payment to the other . . .

(c) Agreements by the parties to furnish certain information to each other;

(d) Events that would constitute "Events of Default," giving the nondefaulting party the right to close out all (but not less than all) of the transactions entered into under the ISDA Master. Such Events of Default include failure to make a payment, failure to comply with or perform an obligation under the ISDA Master, misrepresentations, Default under Specified Transactions (*see infra* [C][4]), Cross-Default (*see infra* [C][5]), bankruptcy, and merger of a party with another entity where the resulting entity fails to assume the obligations of the party under the ISDA Master.

(e) "Termination Events," which are "no-fault" events which give one or both parties (depending on the applicable Termination Event)[viii] the right to close out all "affected" transactions under the ISDA Master, but which (unlike Events of Default) provide, in the case of some Termination Events, some time for the other party to cure the Termination Event by transferring transactions to an Affiliate, and also provide, when there are two "Affected Parties," for pricing closed-out transactions based on the average of each parties' estimate, ensuring that neither party is disadvantaged as they might be in circumstances where one party makes the sole determination of the payment due or owed as a result of termination.[ix] The ISDA Master's standard Termination Events include changes in law that make a previously lawful transaction unlawful, force majeure,[x] tax events (including as the result of a merger), and Credit Event Upon Merger (*see infra* [C][6]).

[vii] [N. 52] *See, e.g., Lehman Bros. Commercial Corp. v. Minmetals Int'l Non-Ferrous Metal Trading Co.*, 2001 WL 423031 (S.D.N.Y. Apr. 25, 2001) and *Borough of Hammersmith & Fulham v. Hazell* 2 A.C.1 (1992).

[viii] [N. 55] Somewhat confusingly, this could be the "Non-affected party" in a Credit Event Upon Merger, the "Burdened Party" in the case of a Tax Event Upon Merger and the "Affected Party" in case of any of the other Termination Events.

[ix] [N. 56] . . . The 1992 ISDA had different calculation methodologies. Notwithstanding, it was also structured to provide a calculation methodology which limits disadvantage to a particular party in the event of their being two "Affected Parties."

[x] [N. 57] The 2002 ISDA Master Agreement is the first to contain a force majeure event. All preceding ISDA Master Agreements, including the 1992 ISDA Master Agreement, did

(f) Rights and procedures to terminate transactions upon an Event of Default or Termination Event, including methodologies for calculating amounts due from one party to the other on a net basis (*see infra* [B]).

In addition, one or both of the parties may require "up-front" or "mark-to-market" collateral to be posted to support a party's exposure from transactions under the Master. ISDA has issued a form of collateral agreement, called the Credit Support Annex that sets forth standard terms for the posting of collateral and, like the Schedule to an ISDA Master, permits the parties to make various elections, in this case about their collateral arrangements.[xi] . . .

A party to an agreement or transaction is sometimes referred to herein as a "Party" or "Counterparty."

[A] Netting

Derivatives frequently represent a bilateral commitment between the parties to exchange payments based upon the price movement of the underlying interest rate, currency, security, commodity or other reference. For example, in a typical interest rate swap, one party will agree to pay to its counterparty an amount equal to a quarterly fixed percentage (e.g., 5.75 percent) of a "notional" sum (e.g., 100 million dollars) on a periodic basis, for a designated period of time. In return, the counterparty agrees to pay the first party an amount equal to a variable percentage (e.g., the prevailing U.S. Treasury bill yield plus 25 basis points (i.e., 0.25 percent)) on the agreed-upon payment dates. Only the amounts calculated by multiplying the percentage rate by the notional amount are exchanged. The notional amounts themselves are not exchanged or paid. Thus, the parties are "swapping" fixed versus floating obligations and will calculate the payments required by their agreement on each payment date. However, instead of making two separate payments (one fixed and one floating), the Master permits the parties to net their obligations so that the party with the greater payment obligation will pay the net difference between the gross payment calculations to the other party. The Master also permits the parties to elect, in the Schedule, to net obligations across different transactions entered into under the Master.

Similarly, the Master provides that if one party elects to terminate the Master, and all transactions outstanding that were entered into under the Master, early (because, for example, an Event of Default or Termination Event –

---

not contain such a clause though such clauses were sometimes negotiated by the parties.

[xi] [N. 58] The current Credit Support Annex most commonly in use in New York law transactions dates from 1994. On June 7, 2013 ISDA issued a new Credit Support Annex, known as the 2013 Standard Credit Support Annex. *See* "ISDA Publishes 2013 Standard Credit Support Annex (SCSA)," ISDA News Release (June 7, 2013). An analysis of the CSA is outside the scope of this chapter.

both of which are discussed below – has occurred with respect to the other party), the parties' obligations will be closed out and netted, even when one of the parties is bankrupt. Because swap transactions are so integral to the ebb and flow of finance, international regulators and legislators have enacted laws and regulations consistent with this close-out and netting regime. In the United States, these initiatives have included . . . Bankruptcy Code provisions . . ., federal banking laws, and the New York State banking law.

ISDA has obtained numerous memorandum opinions supporting the view that the termination and close-out netting provisions of an ISDA Master will be enforced under the laws of a variety of jurisdictions. . . .

[B] Termination and Calculation Methodology

The 1992 ISDA Master permitted the parties to elect among calculation methodologies for determining amounts due or owed as a result of a termination of an ISDA Master.[xii] The 2002 ISDA uses one calculation methodology, comprised of the sum of (a) the present value of future payments under the transactions underlying the agreement, known as "Close-out Amount"; and (b) the aggregate of payments due, payable and unpaid, known as "Unpaid Amounts."

It is important to note that, pursuant to the 2002 ISDA, even if this calculation results in an amount payable to the defaulting party, the nondefaulting party is obligated to pay such amount, even though the defaulting party's default is the cause of the termination.[xiii]

[xii] [N. 62] Under the 1992 ISDA Master, the Parties were required to decide between "Market Quotation" or "Loss" as the means of measuring the value of the Terminated Transactions as of the Early Termination Date. Market Quotation provided that the value of the Transactions would be set by obtaining price quotations from leading dealers in the relevant derivatives. The Market Quotation would be for the replacement cost of the particular Terminated Transaction(s). However, if fewer than three quotations were obtained – for example, because of chaotic market conditions or because there were few dealers who deal in particular types of illiquid transactions – or if a Market Quotation would not (in the reasonable belief of the Party making the determination) produce a commercially reasonable result, the 1992 ISDA Master's form language stated that Loss would apply in respect of the relevant Terminated Transaction(s). "Loss," the alternative in the 1992 ISDA Master to Market Quotation, was a general indemnification provision and the 1992 ISDA Master defined it as a payment measure by which a party reasonably determines in good faith its total losses and gains in connection with the Terminated Transactions. Although a party could determine its Loss based upon quotations obtained from third parties, there was no requirement that the determining party obtain such quotations. . . .

[xiii] [N. 63] This was not necessarily the case under the 1992 ISDA Master where the parties could choose between a "First Method" and "Second Method." The "First Method," sometimes referred to as a "walkaway" or "walk away" provision, provided that if the party that has defaulted is owed money, the nondefaulting out-of-the-money party is allowed to "walk away" from its payment obligation because of the default. This

Close-out Amount is calculated, when termination is triggered by an Event of Default, by the nondefaulting party or, depending on the trigger for the Termination Event, one or both parties. The party calculating the Close-out Amount is known as the "Determining Party." If there are two Affected Parties, both parties make a calculation of close-out amount which is then averaged.

The Determining Party is required to calculate the present "economic equivalent" of the transactions documented under the ISDA Master and state this net amount as a loss (*i.e.* a negative amount, signaling an amount owed to it by the other party) or a gain (*i.e.* a positive amount signaling an amount it owes to the other party). The amount must be calculated in "good faith" using "commercially reasonable procedures in order to produce a commercially reasonable result." Further limiting the discretion of the Determining Party is the requirement that, unless reasonably believing in good faith that market quotations from third parties or other market data are not readily available or would not provide for a commercially reasonable result, the Determining Party must consider such sources in calculating Close-out Amount.

The ISDA Master also provides that a nondefaulting party or the party not affected by the termination event may set-off amounts that it owes to the other party against any amounts due from the other party under any other agreements.[xiv] When these amounts are denominated in different currencies, the party exercising the set-off may convert the other currency using "the rate of exchange at which such party would be able, in good faith and using commercially reasonable procedures, to purchase the relevant amount of such currency."

[C] Negotiating an ISDA Schedule

As noted above, modifications and alterations to an ISDA Master Agreement are documented in an attached Schedule. The preprinted Schedule includes a number of provisions that require an election to be made (or, in some cases, if an election is not made, a standard term of the ISDA Master will apply) and allows the parties to make further additions. In the following sections we will review the elections that are in the preprinted Schedule and touch upon others that may be, and often are, added. Readers may also consult the above-referenced ISDA user's guides, particularly the User's Guide to the 2002 ISDA Master Agreements.

[1] Choosing an "as of" Date. . . .

The "as of" date will normally, but is not required to be, the date of execution.

---

clause triggered significant regulatory opposition [and litigation] . . . [F]ar more common in 1992 ISDA Master's is the election of the Second Method which operates so that a Party receives any Termination Amount it is owed, even if it is the Defaulting Party.

[xiv] [N. 66] The 1992 ISDA did not have a built-in set-off provision. However, parties frequently included one in the schedule based on the User's Guide to the ISDA 1992 Master Agreement.

[2] Naming the Parties

Customarily, the party drafting the Schedule and generating confirmations, which is frequently a derivatives dealer, will designate itself as "Party A." The other party will be "Party B." Each party will thereinafter be referred to as a "Party" or "Counterparty," as applicable. In accordance with market practice, and (if agreed upon) unless there is an event of default or potential event of default with respect to Party A, Party A is typically also the party selected to act as "Calculation Agent," calculating the amounts due to it or Party B, as the case may be, on the designated payment dates.[xv] . . .

[3] Choice of a "Specified Entity"

Part 1 of the Schedule allows each party to name one or more entities as a "Specified Entity" with respect to four substantive provisions of the Master. These provisions govern Default under Specified Transactions (Section 5(a)(v) of the Master; *see infra* [C][4]), Cross-Default (Section 5(a)(vi) of the Master; *see infra* [C][5]), Bankruptcy (Section 5(a)(vii) of the Master) and Credit Event Upon Merger (Section 5(b)(v) of the Master[xvi]; *see infra* [C][6]), all of which are capable of triggering a default or being deemed a Termination Event, as the case may be, under the Master.

If no "Specified Entity" is named, the four provisions listed above will apply only to the named parties to the Master. By naming, for example, the parent of a party as a "Specified Entity" with respect to any or all of such provisions, an adverse event that affects the parent of a party may also trigger a default or termination under such party's Master. Similarly, other of the party's "Affiliates" may be included as "Specified Entities" of the party. If a party anticipates that credit weakness in its counterparty's corporate family could endanger the counterparty's ability to perform on transactions under the Master, "Affiliates" is often an election in the Schedule defining what are "Specified Entities" for this purpose.

[4] Defining a "Specified Transaction"

The Master includes a definition of "Specified Transaction" that incorporates a broad array of derivatives, repurchase and similar transactions when entered into between the parties to the Master. Under the Master, a default by a party (or a Specified Entity of the party) under any Specified Transaction with the counterparty (or a Specified Entity of the counterparty) will trigger an Event of Default under the Master. Whether the pre-printed definition of a "Specified Transaction" is too broad will depend upon the types of transactions between the parties. The definition in the Master of "Specified Transaction" may be fine-tuned in the Schedule if the parties want to exclude certain types of transactions.[xvii]

[xv] [N. 68] For the role of Calculation Agent, *see infra* [C][16].

[xvi] [N. 69] Section 5(b)(iv) under the 1992 ISDA Master Agreement.

[xvii] [N. 71] Under the 1992 ISDA Master, however, credit derivatives are not specifically included, although the phrase "any other similar transaction" in the Master's standard

It is also common for parties to modify the Master by providing that a default caused by administrative circumstances, such as communications breakdowns and clerical errors, will not constitute a default with respect to a Specified Transaction, provided the funds necessary to performance were available at the time of the "default" and the administrative default is promptly cured.[xviii]

[5] "Cross-Default," "Specified Indebtedness," and "Threshold Amount"

As discussed above, a party's default with respect to "Specified Transactions" with a third party can trigger an Event of Default under the subject Master if the parties elect to include third-party transactions. Similarly, if the appropriate elections are made in the Schedule, a party's default with respect to any indebtedness (to any person, not just the counterparty) may also trigger an Event of Default. For it to do so, a party will require that "Cross-Default" (as defined in the Master) shall apply to that counterparty. Under the Master, a Cross-Default is triggered by a party's default, event of default or other similar conditions or events with respect to Specified Indebtedness, where the sum in default is not less than a specified Threshold Amount for that party. Specified Indebtedness is defined as any "obligation . . . in respect of borrowed money." However, there are other transactions that are similar to "obligations in respect of borrowed money" that might also be included by modification in the Schedule. These could include, for example, collateral payments under margining agreements and capital leases. Again, however, the parties may wish to excuse mere administrative and clerical defaults if timely cured.

The Threshold Amount may be specified in the Schedule and is often expressed as a percentage of shareholders' equity, in the case of large public companies, or in absolute dollar terms for smaller entities.[xix] Parties sometimes specify a "zero" threshold with respect to indebtedness between the immediate parties and their Affiliates. What is appropriate for particular counterparties will depend upon their respective financial circumstances and relative creditworthiness.

The Cross-Default provision, unmodified, applies to defaults which in the aggregate, if made due and payable immediately or, if capable of being made due and payable immediately, will exceed the threshold. However, it is common to modify the provision by removing the words ", or becoming capable at such time of being declared," so that, with respect to non-payment defaults, only an

---

definition may be construed to include such transactions. Forward contracts (other than forward rate agreements), repurchase agreements and securities lending agreements are also not included in the standard definition in the 1992 ISDA Master.

[xviii] [N. 72] This is also a commonly negotiated change to Section 5(a)(i) (the "Failure to Pay" Event of Default) itself.

[xix] [N. 73] The 1992 ISDA Master is similar except that payment defaults and other events of default are not aggregated for the purposes of determining whether the default in question exceeds the threshold.

actual amount being due and payable as a result of the default in question will apply to the threshold. This is known, in industry parlance, as a replacement of the "cross-default" provision with a "cross-acceleration" clause.

[6] "Credit Event Upon Merger"

The parties may elect to have "Credit Event Upon Merger" (as defined in Section 5(b)(v) of the Master) apply to one or both parties. If elected, a merger of a party, comparable asset transfer by a party or change of control or substantial change in capital structure of a party will be a Termination Event (rather than an Event of Default) if the creditworthiness of the resulting, surviving, or transferee entity is materially weaker than that of such party prior to the occurrence of the event.[xx] This provision, like the other credit-sensitive provisions included in the Schedule, may also be made to apply to a party's Credit Support Provider (as that term is specified in the Schedule) and/or its Specified Entities. Parties may wish to define "materially weaker" for purposes of this provision, and often substitute external credit rating criteria for this general term.

[7] "Automatic Early Termination"

Ordinarily, a Master Agreement, and all Transactions thereunder, will terminate after the occurrence of an Event of Default or Termination Event and upon the nondefaulting party providing the requisite notice to the Defaulting Party designating an Early Termination Date. Alternatively, the parties may elect to have Automatic Early Termination (AET) apply.

When AET applies, the Master should be construed to read that the Master, and all Transactions thereunder, constructively terminate immediately prior to certain bankruptcy or insolvency events. In jurisdictions where the insolvency laws are less favorable to netting agreements than, for example the United States, AET may be an appropriate election.[xxi] However, it should be noted that its primary disadvantage is that an AET would, as its definition says, occur automatically. This may happen without the knowledge of the non-defaulting party, and before the nondefaulting party becomes aware of the termination, the relevant market could have moved significantly. In these circumstances, the nondefaulting party may be out-of-pocket on its hedge positions. For these reasons, the User's Guide advises practitioners to exercise caution when deciding to elect AET.

[8] Choice of "Termination Currency"

[xx] [N. 74] The 1992 ISDA Master has a more limited scope, covering only a merger or comparable asset transfer.

[xxi] [N. 75] . . . [P]arties do not typically elect to have Automatic Early Termination apply in Masters where both parties are domiciled in the United States and are subject to the Bankruptcy Code. On the other hand, AET remains a useful alternative for cross-border swaps, where one or more of the parties is domiciled in a jurisdiction that has not endorsed the enforceability of netting agreements. . . .

The parties may choose a "Termination Currency" in the Schedule. If so specified and provided, all Terminated Transactions will be converted to the selected currency. If no election is made, or if the elected currency is not freely available, U.S. dollars are selected by operation of the Schedule.[xxii]

[9] Specification of "Additional Termination Events"

The parties may provide for Additional Termination Events at Part 1(g) of the Schedule. Examples of Additional Termination Events include, where cross-default might not be applicable, a narrower cross-default applying only to a specified loan facility, a ratings downgrade below a specified level, the death, disability, or end of association with a party of an important individual or material officer, or the failure to maintain a certain specified level of capitalization or assets.

[10] "Tax Representations"

As stated above, the Master Agreement and Schedule include representations that each party makes to the other. Specifically, the Schedule allows each party to make certain tax representations to the other party consisting of "Payer Tax Representations" and "Payee Tax Representations." The tax representations are ongoing until termination of the Master Agreement and, in general, enable each party to determine whether any withholding taxes should be imposed with respect to any payments made under a Transaction, and whether information reporting may be required.

Each party should make the Payer Tax Representations. Under the Payer Tax Representations, each party typically represents that it is not required, under current law, to make any deduction or withholding for any taxes of the "Relevant Jurisdiction"[xxiii] from any payment made by it to the counterparty (excluding certain payments of interest made under the Agreement). In addition, the Payer Tax Representations generally specify that the party making the Payer Tax Representations may rely on (i) the Payee Tax Representations made by the counterparty, (ii) the delivery by the counterparty of properly completed tax forms and documents as specified in the Schedule,[xxiv] and (iii) the counterparty's agreement to give timely notification that a Payee Tax Representation is not accurate and true.

Each party should request that the counterparty make certain Payee Tax Representations. The Payee Tax Representations generally relate to a counterparty's tax status with respect to a specific tax jurisdiction and often

---

[xxii] [N. 78] Or Euro if the agreement is subject to English Law.

[xxiii] [N. 79] With respect to a "Payer," a relevant jurisdiction is generally a jurisdiction (i) where the Payer is incorporated, organized, managed or controlled, (ii) where the office through which the Payer is acting for purposes of the Master Agreement is located, (iii) where the Party executes the agreements; and (iv) from or through which the Payer makes such payment.

[xxiv] [N. 80] An exception to this requirement is with respect to certain documents that might materially prejudice the delivering party's "legal or commercial position."

establish whether the counterparty is eligible for an exemption from any withholding taxes or reporting requirements imposed by the specific tax jurisdiction. In addition, as noted above, the Payee Tax Representations interact with the Payer Tax Representations. For example, if the counterparty is a U.S. corporation, for U.S. withholding tax and information reporting purposes, the counterparty may be requested to represent that (i) it is a corporation and (ii) it is a U.S. person for U.S. federal tax purposes.

If the counterparty is a foreign corporation and has no connection with the U.S., for U.S. withholding tax and information reporting purposes, the counterparty may be requested to represent that (i) it is a foreign person for U.S. federal tax purposes, (ii) it is a corporation, and (iii) no part of any payment received or to be received by it is attributable to a trade or business carried on by it in the United States. Alternatively, if the counterparty is a foreign corporation and may act through a U.S. branch or a non-U.S. branch, for U.S. withholding tax and information reporting purposes, the counterparty may be requested to represent that (i) it is a foreign person for U.S. federal tax purposes, (ii) it is a corporation, (iii) for each payment received by its U.S. branch, the payment will be effectively connected with its conduct of a trade or business in the United States, and (iv) for each payment it receives that is not attributable to its U.S. branch, the payment will be attributable to a foreign person or a non-U.S. branch of a foreign person. In addition, if benefits are available under an income tax treaty, a counterparty that is a foreign corporation may be requested to represent that it is eligible to receive benefits under the treaty.

[11] Agreement to Deliver Documents

The parties may specify in the Schedule various forms, documents or certificates to be delivered. Such forms often include requisite tax forms (*e.g.*, U.S. IRS Form W-8BEN, Form W-8ECI or Form W-9), incumbency certificates, formation and operative documents and annual or quarterly audited or unaudited financial reports. A party may sometimes request a legal opinion from the counterparty's counsel as to the corporate power of the counterparty to enter into the Master, Schedule and/or a Confirmation, the enforceability of such agreements or other matters.

[12] Addresses for Notices

This provides for the address at which notices should be delivered to a party. Notices pursuant to the termination provisions of the ISDA Master, *i.e.*, Sections 5 and 6 thereof, may not be sent by e-mail or by electronic messaging system, despite the Schedule having line items for e-mail and electronic messaging system. Other notices under the agreement, such as change of account information, can be sent by e-mail or electronic messaging system.

[13] Process Agent

If a party is not located in the jurisdiction in which the agreement is to be enforced it is advisable to have the party appoint a process agent so that, to the extent there is a dispute and service of process is required, process can be served on such party.

[14] Offices

The parties can elect to have Section 10(a) of the ISDA Master apply or not apply. Section 10(a) provides that all obligations of a branch or office entering into the transaction will be deemed to be obligations of the head or home office.[xxv] It is common to have this election apply and, because serious economic consequences may result from not receiving such a representation and then having recourse to only a local branch or office, in the authors' experience disapplication of this clause is extremely uncommon.

[15] Multibranch Party

The Schedule allows bank counterparties to indicate whether they intend to enter into transactions through specific branches (as opposed to just their head office or the branch which is signing the ISDA Master) and, if so, to specify which branches.

[16] Calculation Agent

The term "Calculation Agent" is defined in the 2006 ISDA Definitions. It is the party responsible for calculating ordinary payments. The Schedule allows the parties to select which party will be the Calculation Agent though, in cases where one party is a dealer counterparty and the other is not, it is usually the dealer counterparty.

[17] Credit Support Document

The parties should insert into this section clear and identifiable descriptions of any guarantees or other types of credit support (including a Credit Support Annex which, without being defined as a Credit Support Document only receives a portion of the protections the ISDA Master provides to Credit Support Documents). By doing so, among others, the representations and other agreements made in the ISDA Master apply, in addition to the ISDA Master, to the Credit Support Document. Moreover, it allows for application of a unique Event of Default, Section 5(a)(iii) of the ISDA Master, "Credit Support Default".

[18] Credit Support Provider

For the same reasons applying to Credit Support Document . . . the parties should insert into this section clear and identifiable descriptions of any guarantor or provider of credit support in order to assure the application of certain representations and other agreements made in the ISDA Master to the Credit Support Provider and to benefit from the entirety of the protections in-built into Section 5(a)(iii) of the ISDA Master, "Credit Support Default".

[19] Governing Law

The Schedule is structured to provide for English or New York law.[xxvi] The choice of law election also determines the applicable jurisdiction, *i.e.* the

---

[xxv] [N. 82] Banks often act through local branches or representative offices.

[xxvi] [N. 84] Though the scope of this chapter is limited to analysis of New York law, since this is an explicit Schedule election, we have included its analysis herein.

exclusive or non-exclusive jurisdiction of the English courts[xxvii] or the non-exclusive jurisdiction of the courts of the State of New York and the United States District Court located in Manhattan.

[20] Netting of Payments

The general standard in Section 2(c) of the ISDA Master is that payments between parties denominated in the same currency and due on the same date with respect to the same transaction should be netted. However, the Schedule provides the opportunity to the parties to apply "Multiple Transaction Payment Netting" which would net all transactions subject to the ISDA Master between the parties, or a specified group of such transactions, so long as they are denominated in the same currency and due on the same day.

[21] Affiliate

The Schedule provides the parties a line item for re-defining the term "Affiliate," otherwise defined in Section 14 of the ISDA Master. It is important to emphasize that Part 5 of the Schedule provides the opportunity to the parties to amend any provisions of the ISDA Master which they wish to amend. Therefore, though the Schedule explicitly contemplates amendment of the "Affiliate" definition, it is not intended to exclude other possible definitional amendments.

[22] Absence of Litigation

One of the representations made by the parties and their Credit Support Providers is that there is no pending or actual litigation or similar proceedings "likely to affect the legality, validity or enforceability" of the ISDA Master or any Credit Support Document or obligations under either. The parties can also elect to include "Specified Entities" in the Schedule with respect to which the relevant party will also be deemed to make this representation.[xxviii]

[23] No Agency

Each party represents, pursuant to Section 3(g) of the ISDA Master that "It is entering into this Agreement, including each Transaction, as principal and not as agent of any person or entity."[xxix] The Schedule explicitly provides the option of applying or disapplying this representation if, for example, one of the parties is acting as agent for a third-party.

[24] Additional Representations

[xxvii] [N. 85] Whether it is the exclusive or non-exclusive jurisdiction of the English courts depends on whether the matter involves a "Convention Court" in which case the jurisdiction of the English courts is exclusive. A "Convention Court" is defined in Section 14 of the ISDA Master as "any court which is bound to apply to the Proceedings either Article 17 of the 1968 Brussels Convention on Jurisdiction and the Enforcement of Judgments in Civil and Commercial Matters or Article 17 of the 1988 Lugano Convention on Jurisdiction and the Enforcement of Judgments in Civil and Commercial Matters." Note that, under the 1992 ISDA, a selection of English governing law resulted in the exclusive jurisdiction of the English courts.

[xxviii] [N. 88] The 1992 ISDA automatically included all "Affiliates" in the representation.

[xxix] [N. 89] The 1992 ISDA did not have this representation, though many parties included a similar one via the Schedule.

In addition to the standard representations built into Section 3 of the ISDA Master, the Schedule contains an election to include three additional representations, namely that each party has made an independent decision to enter into the transaction without reliance on the other party for a recommendation investment advice, that it is capable of understanding and assuming the risks of each transaction and it is not acting as a fiduciary for or advisor to the other party.[xxx] It is uncommon for these representations not to be made.

[25] Recording of Conversations

New York State's General Obligations Law, in § 5-701 thereof, provides that certain categories of agreements, including those which by their terms are "not to be performed within one year from the making thereof . . ." are void "unless it or some note or memorandum thereof be in writing, and subscribed the party to be charged therewith, or by his lawful agent. . . ."

An exception, however, is provided for a "qualified financial contract" a definition capturing most, if not all, commonly traded over-the-counter derivatives so long as there is "sufficient evidence to indicate that a contract has been made . . ." One of the categories defined as "sufficient evidence" is "evidence of electronic communication (including without limitation, the *recording of a telephone call* or the tangible written text produced by computer retrieval), admissible in evidence under the laws of this state, sufficient to indicate that in such communication a contract was made between the parties."

Since recorded calls . . . [are] a common method by which over-the-counter derivatives trade (to be subsequently documented by a Confirmation signed by the parties), the Schedule provides elective language providing for the consent of each party to the recording of calls,[xxxi] the agreement to provide personnel appropriate notices or to obtain appropriate personnel consents and the

---

[xxx] [N. 90] Though these representations were not in the 1992 ISDA or form of Schedule, they are commonly included by parties using a 1992 ISDA. Such representations became common following *Procter & Gamble Co. v. Bankers Trust Co. & BT Sec. Corp.*, 925 F. Supp. 1270 (S.D. Ohio 1996) in which ultimately unsuccessful claims were made that the bank defendant, although a counterparty to an ISDA Master with a corporation, also acted as an advisor to the corporation on complex derivative transactions for purposes of federal securities and commodities laws and acted inappropriately in that capacity.

[xxxi] It is also a requirement for swap dealer's and major swap participant's registered with the Commission. *See* 17 C.F.R. § 23.202(a)(1). Under the laws of some states, the recording of a call without the consent of the other party may be deemed a wiretapping offence. "Currently . . . California, Connecticut, Florida, Illinois, Maryland, Massachusetts, Michigan, Montana, Nevada, New Hampshire, Pennsylvania and Washington require the consent of both, or all, parties to a conversation." Jasmine McNealy, *Balancing Statutory Privacy and the Public Interest: A Review of State Wiretap Laws as Applied to the Press*, Law Tech., First Quarter 2011, Vol. 44, at 1, 2. See also Charles H. Kennedy & Peter P. Swire, *State Wiretaps and Electronic Surveillance After September 11*, 54 Hastings L.J. 971 (Apr. 2003).

agreement that, to the extent permitted by law, recordings may be submitted in evidence in any dispute.

[26] Other Provisions . . .

[T]he parties may choose to add any other provisions to the Master in the Schedule. The following are some common additional provisions that parties may put in the Schedule:

[a] "Eligible Contract Participant"
In light of the basic requirement that parties to a swap not traded on a Designated Contract Market must be Eligible Contract Participants, it is industry practice to include mutual representations to this effect.

[b] Set-off
The standard set-off provision in the ISDA Master does not include set-off of amounts due or from affiliates of either party. Consideration should be paid as to whether, via the Schedule, to modify the standard set-off provision to provide for such rights.[xxxii]

[c] ERISA Representations
A party may request additional representations to be made by the other party relating to compliance with applicable law. For example, particular representations related to ERISA, as amended, may be required of a party that is a "plan" under ERISA, so that the transactions contemplated by the Master are not considered "prohibited transactions" under ERISA.

[d] Dodd-Frank Provisions
The Dodd-Frank Act and Commission regulations, known as the "external business conduct" requirements, impose disclosure and communications obligations on swap dealers and major swap participants, an obligation to "know your counterparty" and an obligation to verify its Eligible Contract Participant status. Moreover, any recommendations must meet a suitability standard. The Dodd-Frank Act and Commission regulations also impose swap trading relationship documentation, portfolio reconciliation and confirmation process requirements.

To facilitate compliance with . . . [the Dodd-Frank requirements], ISDA has prepared two "DF Protocols" by which parties can augment their contractual documentation to implement representations and covenants that assist with

---

[xxxii] [N. 98] However, note that there is caselaw indicating that such "triangular" set-off rights are not enforceable in bankruptcy. See *In re Lehman Bros. Inc.*, 2011 WL 4553015 (Bankr. S.D.N.Y. 2011) and *In re SemCrude, L.P.*, 399 B.R. 388 (Bankr. D. Del. 2009), aff'd, 428 B.R. 590 (D. Del. 2010).

complying with the Dodd-Frank Act and Commission rules and the exchange of questionnaires satisfying the aforementioned requirements.

---

3. *Confirmations*

The ISDA Master Agreement is the most common method of documenting derivatives agreements between parties for trades that will be uncleared and not traded on a facility, such as a swap execution facility. However, the ISDA Master Agreement is a framework agreement the parties put in place before trading. It does not contain the specific economics of a particular swap transaction.

To reflect the economic terms of each swap entered into by the parties, one of the parties will issue a trade confirmation to the other, reflecting in writing the specific terms of a swap trade that the parties have already recently transacted.

The CFTC has noted:

> Confirmation [of a swap] has been recognized as an important post-trade processing mechanism for reducing risk and improving operational efficiency by both market participants and their regulators. Prudent practice requires that, after coming to an agreement on the terms of a transaction, parties document the transaction in a complete and definitive written record so there is legal certainty about the terms of their agreement.
>
> Over the past several years, OTC derivatives market participants and their regulators have paid particular attention to the timely confirmation of swaps. . . . If transactions . . . are left unconfirmed, there is no definitive written record of the contract terms. Thus, in the event of a dispute, the terms of the agreement must be reconstructed from other evidence, such as email trails or recorded trader conversations. This process is cumbersome and may not be wholly accurate. . . ."

Confirmation, Portfolio Reconciliation, Portfolio Compression, and Swap Trading Relationship Documentation Requirements for Swap Dealers and Major Swap Participants, 77 Fed. Reg. 55904 (September 11, 2012), 55917.

The CFTC has imposed timing requirements for confirmations to be executed by both parties to a trade where one of the parties is a swap dealer or major swap participant. These are summarized in Figure 10-C below with "t" representing the time of trade and the number following the "+" symbol representing the number of business days remaining in which the confirmation must be fully executed by both parties.

Figure 10-C: Confirmation Obligations for Swap Dealers and Major Swap Participants

Counterparty Type	Type of Swap	Latest Permitted Timing
Another swap dealer or major swap participant	Interest rate and credit default swaps	Executed confirmation t+1
Another swap dealer or major swap participant	Equity, foreign exchange and commodity swaps	Executed confirmation t+1
Financial end-user	Interest rate and credit default swaps	Acknowledgment t+1, policies and procedures designed to ensure executed confirmation t+1
Financial end-user	Equity, foreign exchange and commodity swaps	Acknowledgment t+1, policies and procedures designed to ensure executed confirmation t+1
Non-financial end-user	Interest rate and credit default swaps	Acknowledgment t+1, policies and procedures designed to ensure executed confirmation t+2
Non-financial end-user	Equity, foreign exchange and commodity swaps	Acknowledgment t+1, policies and procedures designed to ensure executed confirmation t+2

F. ROLE OF INTERNATIONAL SWAPS AND DERIVATIVES ASSOCIATION DODD-FRANK PROTOCOLS

The Dodd-Frank Protocols provide a means by which parties can make required amendments to their ISDA Master Agreements to conform to CFTC requirements; to exchange questionnaires containing representations that satisfy many of the CFTC requirements such as those relating to eligible contract participant verification, status of the "representative" of a special entity, and eligibility of a counterparty for a clearing exception; and for swap dealers and major swap participants to provide required disclosure documentation.[27] The amendments are effected by each party adhering to an adherence letter to the International Swaps and Derivatives Association and paying a fee. This is a more convenient way to amend existing documentation than multiple bilateral exchanges organized by each pair of parties with existing swap documentation.

Moreover, instead of bilaterally exchanging questionnaires, parties can do so *en mass* using an online service provided jointly by the International Swaps and Derivatives Association and Markit (a financial information platform) where parties post their questionnaires, agree to "match," and automatically exchange questionnaires.[28]

Prominent Practitioner Sidenote: Robert G. Pickel, Esq.

Robert G. Pickel, Esq. began his practice at the law firm of Cravath, Swaine & Moore, LLP. He was general counsel of the International Swaps and Derivatives Association ("ISDA") from 1997 until 2001, chief executive officer from 2001 until 2009, executive vice-chairman from 2009 until 2011, and chief executive officer once more from 2011 to 2014.

What led you to choose to become a lawyer?

In a broad sense what attracted me to becoming a lawyer was an appreciation for the rule of law and the rigor that the study and practice of law requires. More specifically, my involvement in corporate law and eventually focusing on derivatives comes from an interest in bringing parties together to achieve a common goal. At ISDA, that often requires me to play the role of diplomat as much as advocate in order to achieve consensus among many parties with diverse views.

What career path led you to become the chief executive officer of ISDA?

I got involved in derivatives pretty much from the start of my legal career. The law firm I worked for, Cravath, Swaine & Moore, represented several dealers and also represented ISDA for many years. I worked on swap contracts, both ISDA and pre-ISDA versions, and also worked on other early documentation projects. Many people I worked with at Cravath remained actively involved in derivatives. One of those, my predecessor as CEO, hired me as general counsel of ISDA. When he left in early 2001, I took over the CEO role.

Having joined ISDA in 1997 as its general counsel, what have been the most significant developments you have subsequently seen in the derivatives market?

The globalization of managing risks of all types using derivatives, the expansion of central clearing of OTC derivatives, and the regulatory reform brought on by the Financial Crisis are the most significant developments. Products have evolved to allow management of all types of market risk (rates, equity prices, commodity prices) as well as credit risk, and more and more markets have made these products available. Clearing grew significantly between dealers and more recently has expanded to customers. Regulatory reform has fundamentally changed the way derivatives are executed and managed, but it remains to be seen whether the touted benefits will justify the enormous costs.

How would you describe the role of industry associations in the derivatives market?

I can only comment on the role of ISDA, which I believe has been unique. From its formation, ISDA has focused on providing a degree of standardization and consistency that facilitates the use of derivatives and empowers users of derivatives to effectively manage their risk. Industry associations often focus on erecting barriers to entry or barriers to competition, but at ISDA we have always been of the view that barriers ultimately are not good for the market or for the ability to manage risk in the most cost-effective way.

If the Financial Crisis was a test of the then prevailing model for swaps (i.e., bilaterally negotiated off-exchange derivatives agreements), was the model a success? What were its strengths and what were its weaknesses?

By and large, I believe the model worked – not perfectly, but pretty well given the magnitude of the crisis. Cleared trades between Lehman and dealers were handled smoothly. Lehman's uncleared trades were closed out and parties were able to re-hedge if needed. Of course, those claims needed to go through the bankruptcy process, but the important thing was to be able to move quickly and re-hedge.

There were, though, questions about the bilateral model. Some people suggest that a bank's uncertainty about its counterparty's derivative exposure exacerbated the crisis. It's true that better transparency of exposures would have been a good thing at the time, and a lot of improvement has been made in this area. It's also true that for anyone using collateral – and the majority of people used collateral – much of that exposure was mitigated. And there were also serious questions about whether a bank was going to be saved (Bear Stearns and AIG) or allowed to fail (Lehman).

There is no denying that AIG's extensive use of credit derivatives was a weakness. But that weakness was not a function of the product. Banks buying protection against exposure to real estate made a lot of sense and AIG was all too willing to sell protection. Worse, they relied on their AAA credit and refused to provide collateral (or only to do so if they were downgraded). It was the nature of their collateral arrangements (or lack thereof) that created the liquidity crunch they faced in September 2008.

Looking back on your career, what gives you the most pride?

The growth of ISDA as an organization – measured by the number of members, the number of skilled and capable employees, and its influence in debates around the world – is what I am most proud of.

Surveying the current state of derivatives law and regulation, what would you change, if anything?

I would change the highly prescriptive nature of regulation and focus more on supervisors actively understanding the businesses of their regulated institutions. Banking regulators have taken this approach in the past, but to be successful it requires active, informed regulators engaging with entities who understand the value that strong supervision provides. We had achieved that in the period immediately prior to the Financial Crisis by engaging in a collaborative dialogue with supervisors around the world responsible for derivatives oversight. The fact is that derivatives were actively overseen through the supervisory oversight provided by regulators around the world. They weren't the unregulated world that critics allege. Now firms are swimming in detailed rules and regulations and it is not clear that the result will be a safer, sounder system.

What advice would you offer for a lawyer entering into practice?

I would suggest that a young lawyer give careful consideration to who could serve as a mentor for them. I was fortunate in working with people early in my career who took me under their wing. That is one thing that will never change about the legal profession.

What is changing is the role of technology. Young lawyers entering the profession these days are well-versed in technology and are better able to consider how it can make them effective lawyers. They should think creatively.

QUESTIONS AND COMMENTS

1. The fair dealing rule is described by the CFTC as "principles based and . . . applied flexibly based on the facts and circumstances of a particular swap."[29] Does the CFTC thereby grant itself too much discretion? Should the rule's parameters be more clearly delineated at the expense of the CFTC's flexibility? Or would more prescriptive rules be unwieldy and ill-adapted to the facts and circumstances of individual cases?
2. Could heightened regulatory requirements applicable to special entities have unintended consequences? For example, do they incentivize some swap dealers and major swap participants to not transact with special entities? Might those who continue to transact with special entities charge more as compensation for the increased risk and obligations?
3. The public policy rationale underlying the enhanced regulatory regime applying to swaps transactions with special entities is spurred by a perception that mistakes regarding derivatives transactions have historically been a significant source of problems to municipalities. Even accepting this view uncritically, if the enhanced regulation causes costs to increase for all special entities, well-managed or otherwise, does this operate as a subsidy from well-managed special entities that do not need the increased protections of the special entity rules to the handful that do? Does the fact that many special entities, such as municipalities, are funded by taxpayers make this more or less palatable?
4. Evaluate the advantages and disadvantages of standardized documentation such as the ISDA Master Agreement.

CHAPTER 11 DERIVATIVES AND BANKRUPTCY

A. BACKGROUND

When a party is unable to make its payments, bankruptcy often results. Therefore, it is essential to consider what implications bankruptcy will have on derivatives.

We will first assess how the obligations of parties in futures and cleared swaps are treated in bankruptcy. Then we will assess their treatment in the context of uncleared swaps. As we will see, there are many special provisions in the Bankruptcy Code in relation to uncleared swap arrangements.

B. FUTURES AND CLEARED SWAPS

Two different models apply to futures and to cleared swaps, even though the transactional mechanics are similar in that, as discussed in Chapters 5 and 9, both utilize central clearing through futures commission merchants that are members of a derivatives clearing organization.

1. Futures

Suppose that a fictional registered futures commission merchant, Midwest Futures, is a member of a fictional registered derivatives clearing organization, the Topeka Clearinghouse. Midwest Futures has dozens of customers who enter into trades cleared by the Topeka Clearinghouse due to a guarantee to the Topeka Clearinghouse from Midwest Futures, one of its members. Midwest Futures collateralizes its net positions to the Topeka Clearinghouse and, in turn, requires initial margin for each contract from its customers (which it passes on to the Topeka Clearinghouse *in toto*) and variation margin, which it retains. Initial margin represents a fixed amount of margin that must be provided for each contract and variation margin is correlated to, and varies with, the market value of the customer's position.

The biggest customer of Midwest Futures, Mega Speculator, sees its positions overnight get a lot worse due to market movements. As a result, the next morning, Midwest Futures demands millions of dollars in additional margin. Mega Speculator cannot make the margin call. What happens now?

Regardless of whether Mega Speculator has posted the additional variation margin demanded by Midwest Futures, Midwest Futures ultimately has an obligation to the Topeka Clearinghouse. Midwest Futures will close out Mega Speculator's positions (in case they worsen more!) and liquidate whatever margin Mega Speculator has already provided to Midwest Futures. Midwest Futures will then have an obligation to pay any shortfall to the Topeka Clearinghouse, i.e., guarantee its customer's payment obligations.

To the extent Midwest Futures has insufficient funds to do so, the Topeka Clearinghouse has recourse to the margin of customers of Midwest Futures who are not defaulting. Those customers then, take the risk of a "double default," i.e., a default of their futures commission merchant's customer and a default of the futures commission merchant itself.

One real-life example of where such a default occurred is Volume Investors, the subject of the litigation in *Westheimer v. Commodity Exchange, Inc.*, discussed in Chapter 4, and *Comex Clearing Association, Inc. v. Flo-Arb Partners*, discussed in Chapter 5. In such a "double default" circumstance, non-defaulting customers of the futures commission merchant could have their margins reduced *pro rata* to make up for the loss. More likely, though, is that the position would be transferred. While a double default is rare, futures commission merchants do fail, often without losses to non-defaulting customers. (Some examples of futures commission merchant failures are discussed in Chapter 5.)

Futures commission merchants re-invest margin posted by customers. Even outside of a so-called double default circumstance, this puts the customers' money at risk to the extent the futures commission is unable to repay the money to the customer when due, whether because of, for example, honest investment losses or fraud by the futures commission merchant. The former event (i.e., investment losses leading to an inability to repay customers) occurred with respect to MF Global in 2011.

2. *Cleared Swaps*

The primary difference between the model for cleared swaps and the model for futures is that in the "double default" circumstance described above in section B1, the derivatives clearing organization could only use the margin of a defaulting customer to try to recover any shortfalls. Non-defaulting customers would be able to transfer their positions to a solvent futures commission merchant. This model is referred to as "legally segregated with operational commingling" or "LSOC" model.

It is important to note that, though the "legally segregated" aspect of the model protects non-defaulting customers in a "double default" scenario, customer monies are subject to "operational commingling," which means that they can be commingled and aggregated for investment purposes and, to the extent there is an investment loss situation (such as that which occurred in the futures context with respect to MF Global), those losses will be shared *pro rata* across all customers. CFTC rules however, discussed in Chapter 5, constrain the type of investments that can be lawfully made with customer margin monies to those that are considered minimally risky.

3. *Market Impact*

The futures model discussed in section B1 above indirectly imposes liability on non-defaulting customers of a futures commission merchant for what could be imprudent speculation of defaulting customers of a futures commission merchant. This risk-sharing imposes a potential cost on prudent customers while reducing the derivatives clearing organization's risk since it has recourse to more parties than it has under the "LSOC" model discussed in section B2 above. Perhaps the lowered risk to the derivatives clearing organization is reflected in better pricing for all market participants.

On the other hand, the LSOC model results in fewer parties to which a derivatives clearing organization has recourse and, therefore, that risk could be reflected in higher pricing to all parties. (The model is too new to determine this.) On the other hand, a prudent customer benefits from its prudence and is not required to indirectly assume the risk of other customers.

In both models, customers are exposed to the risk of fraud or investment losses by a futures commission merchant.

C. BANKRUPTCY CODE PROVISIONS APPLICABLE TO FUTURES AND SWAPS

A number of Bankruptcy Code provisions have direct relevance to a claim against a bankrupt debtor related to derivatives. Some of these provisions have direct application to futures and cleared swaps and nearly all of these provisions have direct application to a bankruptcy claim involving an uncleared swap. The provisions in the Bankruptcy Code that benefit uncleared swap claims against bankrupt debtors are, in the aggregate, commonly known as the "swap safe harbor."

1. *Automatic Stay*

Section 362(a) of the Bankruptcy Code (11 U.S.C. § 362(a)) imposes a stay on termination of agreements, collection of liabilities, or any other proceedings against a bankrupt debtor.[1] Exceptions are provided for futures and cleared swaps[2] (note that futures and cleared swaps are treated the same for Bankruptcy Code purposes)[3] and swaps.[4]

The swaps exception provides that the automatic stay does not apply to:

> [T]he exercise . . . of any contractual right . . . under any security agreement or arrangement or other credit enhancement forming a part of or related to any swap agreement, or of any contractual right . . . to offset or net out any termination value . . .

11 U.S.C. § 362(b)(17).

2. *"Ipso Facto" Clause*

Ipso facto is Latin for "by the fact itself." In the context of bankruptcy it refers to a statutory provision, 11 U.S.C. § 365(e)(1), disallowing any termination or modification of a contract due to the mere fact of a party being in bankruptcy.

Here again, the Bankruptcy Code provides an exception for parties to a future or a swap transaction. The following is the statutory provision applying to swaps (the one applying to futures, found in 11 U.S.C. § 556, is substantially similar):

> The exercise of any contractual right of any [party to a] swap . . . to cause the liquidation, termination, or acceleration of one or more swap agreements because of a condition of the kind specified in [11 U.S.C. §] 365(e)(1) . . . or to offset or net out any termination values or payment amounts arising under or in connection with the termination, liquidation,

> or acceleration of one or more swap agreements shall not be stayed, avoided, or otherwise limited. . . .

11 U.S.C. § 560.

In other words, a swap contract providing for "liquidation, termination or acceleration" due to the bankruptcy of one of the agreement's parties, is not a prohibited *ipso facto* provision. As we will see in section D below, the scope of this relief from the *ipso facto* prohibition has been disputed.

3. Payment Clawbacks

The Bankruptcy Code generally requires that payments made by the bankrupt debtor within 90 days of its bankruptcy be returned to the debtors' estate for distribution to the creditors (i.e., "clawed back") in accordance with the bankruptcy process.[5] This is extended to 1 year in the case of payments made to insiders of the debtor[6] and 2 years if there is "intent to hinder, delay, or defraud" or there is "less than a reasonably equivalent value" in exchange for such payment and the debtor at such time was nearly insolvent or insolvent.[7]

Parties to futures and swaps are exempt from this requirement so long as payments made are pursuant to the relevant agreement.[8]

> Example A: The Western Pacific Oil Company enters into an energy swap with the Great Northern Swap Corporation with payments due by the out-of-the-money party to the in-the-money party on the fifth calendar day of each month. (*See* Chapter 1 for how "in-the-money" and "out-of-the-money" are determined.) On June 5, July 5, and August 5, the Great Northern Swap Corporation is out-of-the money and makes the appropriate payments to the Western Pacific Oil Company. On August 10, the Great Northern Swap Corporation acknowledges that it's been insolvent for half a year and files for bankruptcy.
>
> Although generally such payments made by the Great Northern Swap Corporation within 90 days of its bankruptcy would need to be returned, this is not the case here since they were payments made in due course under the swap agreement between the parties.
>
> Example B: Let us assume the same facts as in Example A except that the Great Northern Swap Corporation doubles the required payments in June, July, and August because the Western Pacific Oil Company "has been a good customer all these years."
>
> Result: These amounts would be required to be "clawed back" and returned to Great Northern Swap Corporation's bankruptcy estate, to the

> extent they exceed what was provided for in the swap agreement, for distribution to creditors in accordance with the bankruptcy process.

4. Set-offs

In Chapters 1 and 10, we saw how a central feature of swap transactions is close-out netting. Close-out netting is where all payments streams that are the subject of a particular agreement are given a present value and netted against each other resulting in one amount due or payable from one party to another.

Set-off differs in that it represents netting an amount due or payable under one agreement with an amount due or payable under another agreement.

> Example: At the time the Great Northern Swap Corporation files for bankruptcy, the Western Pacific Oil Company and the Great Northern Swap Corporation have 10 swap transactions in place documented under a single ISDA Master Agreement. These transactions are terminated by the Western Pacific Oil Company resulting in a net payment of $500,000 due from the Great Northern Swap Corporation to the Western Pacific Oil Company. Under a separate agreement, the Great Northern Swap Corporation has lent $700,000 to the Western Pacific Oil Company. Were Western Pacific Oil Company able to legally "set-off" the $500,000 due from the Great Northern Swap Corporation as a result of the close-out netting process under the swap agreement against the $700,000 they owe under the loan, they could reduce their loan obligation to the Great Northern Swap Corporation from $700,000 to $200,000 and the $500,000 owed by the Great Northern Swap Corporation would be deemed paid. Whereas other creditors of the Great Northern Swap Corporation may only receive a portion of what is owed by the Great Northern Swap Corporation, due to the Western Pacific Oil Company's set-off, the Western Pacific Oil Company in effect received 100% of what was owed to it by the Great Northern Swap Corporation.

The Bankruptcy Code § 553(a), protects any set-off right a party validly has at the time of the bankruptcy.

D. BANKRUPTCY DISPUTES RELATING TO THE SWAP SAFE HARBOR

Beginning in the 2000s, a number of disputes arose as to the extent of the protection afforded by the bankruptcy "safe harbors" for swap providers. The preponderance of these cases related to the failure of Lehman Brothers.

1. *Disputes Alleging "Ipso Facto" Clauses*

In the below case, a district court faced a motion for an order granting leave to appeal a decision of a bankruptcy court. The underlying questions that were the subject of the litigation were (1) whether a contractual provision in a swap agreement subordinating a defaulting party in priority of payment as a result of its bankruptcy filing was within the scope of Bankruptcy Code § 560's carve out for swap agreements from the *ipso facto* clause, and (2) whether the *ipso facto* clause is triggered at all where a swap agreement provides that the bankruptcy of the parent of a party (and provider of a guarantee of the party's obligations) allows for subordinating the party when the parent files for bankruptcy first, followed weeks later by its affiliate, the actual party to the swap agreement.

The below case outlines the legal controversy, with the court recognizing the uncertain state of the law and granting the leave for appeal. Though the leave to appeal was granted, the actual appeal was never decided because the parties settled out of court, leaving this area of law unresolved.

Lehman Brothers Special Financing Inc. v. BNY Corporate Trustee Services Limited (In re Lehman Brothers Holdings Inc.)

2010 WL 10078354 (S.D.N.Y. Sept. 23, 2010)

McMahon, District Judge . . .

On September 18, 2008, Lehman Brothers Holdings Inc. ("LBHI"), one of the largest investment banks in the U.S. at the time, filed for chapter 11 bankruptcy protection in the Bankruptcy Court. Eighteen days later, on October 3, 2008, LBSF, an LBHI subsidiary, filed its chapter 11 petition in the Bankruptcy Court.

On May 20, 2009, LBSF initiated this adversary proceeding (the "Adversary Proceeding") against [BNY Corporate Trustee Services Limited "BNY"]. The Adversary Proceeding arises out of a complex series of synthetic collateralized debt obligations ("CDOs") and related credit default swaps, and has been further complicated by the pendency of parallel and potentially conflicting legal proceedings in the United Kingdom (the "English Litigation"). . . .

The Adversary Proceeding involves two series of credit-linked synthetic portfolio notes (the "Notes") that are now held by non-party Perpetual Trustee Company Limited ("Perpetual"), an Australian company. The Notes were secured by various assets and certain secured obligations (the "Collateral"), including credit default swap transactions between LBSF and the issuer of the Notes (a special-purpose vehicle created by Lehman Brothers International (Europe) called Saphir Finance Public Limited Co. ("Saphir")). The Collateral was held by BNY in trust for creditors of Saphir, including LBSF (as swap counterparty) and Perpetual (as the noteholder). LBHI . . . [guaranteed] LBSF's payment obligations under the swap agreements.

Pursuant to the terms of the Transaction Documents, LBSF's interest in the Collateral ordinarily takes priority over Perpetual's interest – this is called "Swap Counterparty Priority." However, in the event of a default by LBSF under a swap agreement, the Transaction Documents provide for a "flip" from Swap Counterparty Priority to "Noteholder Priority," such that Perpetual receives payments before LBSF. Among the events of default under each of the swap agreements are a filing in bankruptcy of any party to the transaction, including LBSF or LBHI.

On December 1, 2008, after LBHI and LBSF had separately filed for bankruptcy, Saphir exercised its right to terminate the swap agreements. . . . The question in this Adversary Proceeding is whether the Swap Counterparty Priority or Noteholder Priority distribution scheme applies – i.e., whether Perpetual or LBSF has priority in the payment of proceeds to satisfy Saphir's obligations. BNY holds the Collateral that is subject to these competing claims. . . .

LBSF initiated the instant Adversary Proceeding against BNY. Count I of LBSF's two-count Complaint seeks a declaratory judgment that the contractual provisions modifying LBSF's payment priority upon an event of default "constitute unenforceable *ipso facto* clauses" that violate the Bankruptcy Code, 11 U.S.C. §§ 365(e)(1) . . .and that, as a result, "LBSF is entitled to payment under Swap Counterparty Priority." Count II seeks a declaratory judgment that any action to enforce such provisions "constitutes a willful violation of the automatic stay under [Bankruptcy Code] section 362(a)(3)." . . .

On January 25, 2010, the Bankruptcy Court issued a "Memorandum Decision Granting Motion for Summary Judgment and Declaring Applicable Payment Priorities." Judge Peck's opinion granted summary judgment to LBSF, holding that "the provisions in the Transaction Documents purporting to modify LBSF's right to a priority distribution solely as a result of a chapter 11 filing constitute unenforceable *ipso facto* clauses" under 11 U.S.C. §§ 365(e)(1) . . . and that "any attempt to enforce such provisions would violate the automatic stay" under § 362(a). . . .

[T]he *ipso facto* protections . . . of the Bankruptcy Code . . . prohibit the modification of a debtor's right solely because of a provision in an agreement conditioned on "the commencement of a case under this title."

Relying on his interpretation of the legislative history and "plain meaning" of these *ipso facto* provisions, Judge Peck held that they apply to contract terms conditioned on the commencement of "presumably any [bankruptcy] case that is related in some appropriate manner to the contracting parties." Judge Peck acknowledged that this interpretation was unprecedented, stating that, "No case has ever declared that the operative bankruptcy filing is not limited to the commencement of a bankruptcy case by the debtor-counterparty itself but may be a case filed by a related entity." He further admitted that his interpretation of the Bankruptcy Code's *ipso facto* provisions as applying "to cases filed by debtors other than the counterparty itself has the potential of opening up a proverbial 'can of worms' that may lead to speculation as to the nature and degree of the relationship between debtors that is needed in order to properly apply the provision."

Judge Peck then applied his novel statutory interpretation to the circumstances at hand, and concluded that the separate bankruptcy filings of LBHI and its affiliates, including LBSF, constituted "a singular event" for *ipso facto* purposes – but not for purposes of "any other legal determination that may relate to the date of commencement of a case." Accordingly, Judge Peck held that LBHI's petition "entitled LBSF, consistent with the statutory language, fairly read, to claim the protections of the *ipso facto* provisions of the Bankruptcy Code because its ultimate corporate parent and credit support provider, at a time of extraordinary panic in the global markets, had filed a case under the Bankruptcy Code." . . .

Judge Peck entered an Order granting LBSF's motion for summary judgment and ordering that:

> the contractual provisions . . . that purport to modify LBSF's payment priority as a result of its chapter 11 filing and the chapter 11 filing of LBSF's corporate parent, [LBHI], are unenforceable *ipso facto* clauses . . . and any action to enforce such provisions is prohibited by the automatic stay under Bankruptcy Code section 362(a). . . .

[I]t is readily apparent that the Order satisfies the requirements for granting an interlocutory appeal. Accordingly, the Court grants BNY's motion for leave to appeal. . . .

Judge Peck's decision resolved a difficult, dispositive legal question of first impression. He forthrightly acknowledged that his unprecedented ruling – which he predicted would be "controversial" – was the "first such interpretation of the *ipso facto* language" in the Bankruptcy Code. He stated that he was not aware of any case that "has ever declared that the operative bankruptcy filing is not limited to the commencement of a bankruptcy case by the debtor-counterparty itself." Indeed, prior cases in this and other circuits appear to assume – albeit in circumstances that are factually distinguishable – that the Bankruptcy Code's *ipso facto* provisions invalidate clauses that condition an event of default on the contracting party's own bankruptcy filing. . . .

Furthermore, BNY has pointed to numerous legal and other commentaries questioning the correctness of Judge Peck's ruling. . . .

LBSF meekly responds, citing a single article, that the commentary on the Bankruptcy Court's decision has, in fact, been "mixed." But even that lone article, which predicts that Judge Peck's decision will be upheld on appeal, supports BNY's position that an interlocutory appeal is warranted – it highlights the "groundbreaking nature" of Judge Peck's ruling, and warns of the possibility that "savvy guarantors will soon begin to use the 'related entity bankruptcy' ploy as a means of invalidating ipso facto cross-corporate default provisions."

Dan Schechter, *Debtor's Prepetition Loss of Priority Under Springing Subordination Agreement Triggered by Parent Corporation's Bankruptcy Filing Is Unenforceable Ipso Facto Provision*, 2010 Com. Fin. Newsl. 16 (2010). Moreover, even if LBSF were correct that mainstream views are "mixed," that is consistent with the conclusion that "substantial ground for difference of opinion" exists. . . .

Note the references to the critical commentary the bankruptcy court decision in this case received, an indication that the decision in the bankruptcy court may not be the last conclusion on this topic.

A related issue arose in a case in which an ISDA Master Agreement entered into by Lehman Brothers Special Financing had a provision that ensured that a party who defaulted and was owed a termination payment under an ISDA Master Agreement would be paid after nearly all other creditors of the non-defaulting party were paid.

In this case, the non-defaulting party was a special purpose vehicle and the result of subordinating payment to the defaulting party was to, in effect, not pay the defaulting party to the extent the defaulting party was otherwise owed a termination amount. The special purpose vehicle was a collateralized debt obligation, commonly known as a "CDO." Its income, revenue from asset-backed securities, was finely tuned to bring slightly more revenue each month than its liabilities, generally payments on notes issued by the vehicle.

Because the revenue in these structures was finely tuned to the liabilities, rating agencies were concerned about the effect of a sudden liability on the vehicle, such as if Lehman Brothers Special Financing defaulted when the vehicle was out-of-the-money resulting in a large one-time termination payment payable by the vehicle to Lehman Brothers Special Financing. Therefore, at the time the vehicle was structured, rating agencies required that, if such an event occurred, the termination payment would be deeply subordinated so that it was only payable after the noteholders and other creditors were fully repaid and, in addition, capped at $30,000.

The question before the court was whether such an arrangement hinged on an unenforceable *ipso facto* clause.

Lehman Brothers Special Financing Inc. v. Ballyrock ABS CDO 2007-1 Limited (In re Lehman Brothers Holdings Inc.)

452 B.R. 31 (Bankr. S.D.N.Y. 2011)

James M. Peck, Bankruptcy Judge. . . .

This decision addresses a motion to dismiss filed by defendant Ballyrock ABS CDO 2007-1 Limited ("Ballyrock ") in an adversary proceeding [(the

"Adversary Proceeding")] commenced by Lehman Brothers Special Financing Inc. ("LBSF ").

The Adversary Proceeding raises questions relating to the enforceability in bankruptcy of a contractual provision triggered by the default and early termination of certain transactions under a swap agreement between LBSF and Ballyrock. . . .

At the time of termination, LBSF was in-the-money and entitled to a termination payment based on the cost of replacing each terminated transaction. Notably, the swap agreement contains a provision that effectively would deprive LBSF of its right to collect the termination payment on account of . . . [Lehman Brothers Holdings Inc.'s ("LBHI's")] bankruptcy. Thus, the motion to dismiss raises a controlling legal issue – i.e., whether a provision in the documentation that adversely impacts a debtor's right to property upon the filing of a chapter 11 petition may constitute an unenforceable *ipso facto* clause.

As discussed below, the contractual provision at issue appears to function as an unenforceable *ipso facto* clause that deprives LBSF of the benefit of its in-the-money position as a direct consequence of the commencement of a bankruptcy case by LBHI. For this reason, the LBSF complaint against Ballyrock (the "Complaint ") states a claim upon which relief may be granted and will survive the motion to dismiss. . . .

On July 12, 2007, LBSF and Ballyrock entered into an ISDA master agreement. The Ballyrock Master Agreement was modified and supplemented by a schedule (the "Schedule "), which included a guarantee from LBHI [as Credit Support Provider] . . .

Ballyrock, in turn, entered into an indenture with Wells Fargo Bank, N.A. (the "Trustee ") on July 12, 2007. Pursuant to the Indenture, Ballyrock issued several classes of notes to investors.[i] The Indenture requires that all disbursements by the Trustee be made in conformity with a specified priority of payments (the "Waterfall "). The Waterfall requires payment in full to the holders of higher priority notes before any distributions may be made to holders of notes with a lower priority.

The Ballyrock Master Agreement and Indenture thus established the terms that governed the transactions entered into between Ballyrock and LBSF [(each a "Transaction")] . . .

The Ballyrock Master Agreement specifies several "Events of Default," including the bankruptcy of a party or Credit Support Provider . . .

The Ballyrock Master Agreement further provides that, upon the designation of an Early Termination Date, the party that is the out-of-the-money party shall make a termination payment to the party that is in the money. . . .

With limited exceptions, an unpaid termination payment is given a high priority within the Waterfall and ordinarily would be paid before any

---

[i] [N. 5] The holders of all but the Subordinated Notes, as defined in the Indenture, are referred to herein as the "Senior Noteholders." . . .

distributions are made to the Senior Noteholders. One specified category of termination payment, however, is singled out for particularly harsh treatment under the Waterfall. A termination payment arising as a result of a default by LBSF or LBHI is defined as a "Defaulted Synthetic Termination Payment" and is excluded from the high priority afforded to other unpaid termination payments, subordinated to the Senior Noteholders, and capped in the amount of $30,000. Therefore, a termination payment due to LBSF can rank as high as the third-priority position or drop precipitously in rank to nineteenth place in the Waterfall if LBSF is the defaulting party.

The material shift in priority of this termination payment is at the core of the dispute between LBSF and Ballyrock. The right to receive payment of the remaining $137 million from Ballyrock depends on the determination of whether LBSF is entitled to a high-priority termination payment or a deeply subordinated and capped Defaulted Synthetic Termination Payment (The provisions in the Indenture describing the subordinated Defaulted Synthetic Termination Payment are defined for purposes of this decision as the "Defaulted Synthetic Termination Payment Clause").

Following the bankruptcy of LBHI on September 15, 2008, Ballyrock gave notice to LBSF that LBHI's bankruptcy filing constituted an Event of Default and designated September 16, 2008 as the Early Termination Date in respect of all outstanding Transactions under the Ballyrock Master Agreement. The Trustee then gave notice that Ballyrock owed LBSF a termination payment of approximately $404 million. Thereafter, Ballyrock liquidated its assets, generating approximately $326 million. On November 6, 2008, the Trustee disbursed approximately $189 million of this amount to the Senior Noteholders pursuant to the payment priority scheme of the Waterfall. The Trustee also announced its intent to distribute the remaining $137 million to the Senior Noteholders on the next scheduled distribution date (the "Proposed Distribution").

In response to the Trustee's announcement of the Proposed Distribution, LBSF filed the Complaint against Ballyrock on February 3, 2009 seeking . . . a declaratory judgment that the Proposed Distribution would violate applicable . . . bankruptcy law . . .

It is now axiomatic that ipso facto clauses are unenforceable in bankruptcy. . . .

[The Bankruptcy Code] prohibits modification of a debtor's right solely because of a provision in an agreement conditioned upon "the commencement of *a case* under this title." (emphasis added). Importantly, the language used is not limited to the commencement of a case *by or against the debtor*. . . .

The safe harbor provisions of Section 560 of the Bankruptcy Code were enacted to protect a non-defaulting swap participant's contractual rights to . . . liquidate, terminate or accelerate "one or more swap agreements because of a condition of the kind specified in section 365(e)(1)" of the Bankruptcy Code . . .

Courts have refrained from interpreting the language of section 560 beyond the plain meaning of the words "liquidation, termination, or acceleration".

The operative language of the Defaulted Synthetic Termination Payment Clause does not fall within the safe harbor protections of section 560. As alleged in the Complaint, this clause operates to deprive LBSF of valuable property rights upon designation by the non-debtor counterparty of an Early Termination Date. The provisions governing a Defaulted Synthetic Termination Payment purport to substantially lower the priority of payment within the Waterfall, thereby effectively nullifying any entitlement of LBSF to a termination payment that would have been payable were it not for the bankruptcy filing of LBHI. . . .

The Court concludes that the provisions governing the Defaulted Synthetic Termination Payment are susceptible to the interpretation that they function as an unenforceable *ipso facto* clause because they effectively eliminate the right to receive a termination payment due to commencement of the LBHI bankruptcy. . . .

Note that, unlike in *BNY Corporate Trustee Services Limited*, no leave to appeal was granted by the district court.[9]

Additionally, it is important to note that this structure bears much similarity to a so-called walk away clause that allows a non-defaulting party to a swap to recuse itself from all obligations. Such "walk away" clauses are statutorily unenforceable against most types of financial institutions in the event of such institution's conservatorship or receivership.[10] Since no statutory prohibition in effect at the time applied to Lehman Brothers Special Financing, the question before the court was whether such an arrangement functioned as an unenforceable *ipso facto* clause.[11]

Outside of a bankruptcy context, at least two district courts have found that a walk away clause is enforceable. One of the decisions was in 1992 when a district court ruled that a swap agreement allowing for the non-defaulting party to "walk away" from its obligations was "a valid liquidated damages clause and is, therefore, enforceable. . . ."[12] The other was in 2010 and found that a clause allowing one party to walk away from a swap agreement due to the insolvency of the other party was not an unenforceable penalty provision.[13]

In the case below, Judge James Peck, the same bankruptcy judge whose decision was the subject of the appeal in *BNY Corporate Trustee Services Limited* and who decided *Ballyrock*, evaluated the breadth of the safe harbor for derivatives providers allowing "termination, liquidation, or acceleration" of a swap agreement even where it is triggered by the bankruptcy of one of the parties. The dispute centered on whether the safe harbor protected a valuation methodology based on quotations from swap dealers indicating the price they would pay to assume the swap (which includes a "bid" or "offer" spread) instead of using "mid-market," which does not include such spreads.

In many ways, the dispute appeared similar to *BNY Corporate Trustee Services Limited* and *Ballyrock* leading to Judge Peck's effort to distinguish his arguably contradictory decision in the below case.

Michigan State Housing Development Authority v. Lehman Brothers Derivatives Products Inc. (In re Lehman Brothers Holdings Inc.)

502 B.R. 383 (Bankr. S.D.N.Y. 2013)

James M. Peck, United States Bankruptcy Judge

Lehman in its heyday structured and engaged in a dizzying array of sophisticated financial transactions using swaps. . . . As a consequence of that vast and varied prepetition activity in the derivatives markets, these bankruptcy cases have turned out to be a proving ground for interpreting, applying and testing the boundaries of the safe harbor provisions of the United States Bankruptcy Code (the "Bankruptcy Code").

This decision is the latest to consider the scope of the safe harbor for liquidating, terminating and accelerating swap agreements. . . . The question goes to the heart of this safe harbor: if the exercise of a contractual right to cause the liquidation of a swap agreement is protected, are the contractually specified means for conducting that liquidation so connected to the very concept of liquidation that they are also protected?

LBSF says no, arguing that the less favorable procedures triggered by a bankruptcy default are ineffective *ipso facto* alterations of a debtor's rights, and so do not fall within the safe harbor. Michigan State Housing Development Authority ("MSHDA") . . . [argues] that the protected right to liquidate cannot be viewed as an isolated right and necessarily includes those contractual provisions that provide needed guidance for liquidating and closing out the swap agreement. . . .

As explained in this decision, the Court has concluded that the protected right to liquidate must include a way to execute the liquidation in order to infuse the safe harbored right with meaning. . . .

This right of the non-defaulting party to rely upon contractual norms for disposing of collateral is an integrated aspect of what it means to cause the liquidation of a swap agreement and necessarily is protected by the language of Section 560 of the Bankruptcy Code. To rule otherwise . . . would strip away the defining characteristics of a contractual right to liquidation that by statute may not be limited in any manner. . . .

At an earlier stage in these bankruptcy cases, the Court decided that the safe harbor provisions of Section 560 of the Bankruptcy Code do not extend to a bargained for change in the priority of distributions between LBSF as swap counterparty and certain investors in notes issued by a special purpose vehicle. That dispute dealt with the issue of whether a so-called "flip clause" triggered by a bankruptcy default is an ineffective *ipso facto* provision. . . .

Despite the superficial similarity of the issues, the earlier determinations made with respect to impermissible changes to distribution priorities are not controlling. Here the question is more nuanced and closer to the statutory core of Section 560, leading to an examination of whether the methodology for conducting an indisputably exempt liquidation is also exempt. . . .

Notwithstanding the argument of LBSF that a liquidation methodology triggered by bankruptcy that generates a smaller termination payment for the defaulting party is comparable to a "flip clause," the Court concludes otherwise. There is a significant difference between the reordering of priorities within a hierarchy of distributions (an *ipso facto* contractual term that is not mentioned in Section 560) and selecting which method to use when disposing and valuing collateral in connection with liquidating a terminated swap agreement. The choice of an accepted and contractually specified method to liquidate, even if it produces a less desirable result from the point of view of the debtor, is consistent with full implementation of the exemption that is codified in Section 560. . . .

Accordingly . . . the alternative approach to liquidation of collateral used by MSHDA is effective even though it is contained in an *ipso facto* provision because that alternative is protected by the safe harbor of Section 560 and, as a consequence, is not subject to Section 365(e)(1). . . .

Though the Bankruptcy Code protects the right of a party to a swap agreement to terminate the agreement even if triggered by the bankruptcy of the other party to the agreement, it does not explicitly limit the period in which the non-defaulting party can elect to terminate the agreement. The question of whether such a time period should be imputed has arisen.

In re Mirant Corporation

314 B.R. 347 (Bankr. N.D. Tex. 2004)

Dennis Michael Lynn, Bankruptcy Judge.

Before the court is Debtors' Motion for the Entry of an Order (i) Enforcing the Automatic Stay Prohibiting MediaNews Group, Inc. ["MNG"] from Terminating its Swap Agreement with the Debtors, (ii) Holding MediaNews in Civil Contempt of the Automatic Stay, (iii) Assessing Sanctions, and (iv) Granting Related Relief (the "Motion"). . . .

Debtors' business is principally the production, purchase, sale and trading of energy products. Debtors conduct their trading and marketing activities through Mirant Americas Energy Marketing, L.P. ("MAEM"). Besides participating in the energy markets, MAEM has from time to time traded for profit various non-energy commodity derivatives including swap agreements.

In the course of that business, on March 17, 1998, MAEM and MNG entered into an International Swap Dealers Association Master Agreement (the "Swap Agreement") by which MAEM and MNG agreed to exchange quarterly cash flows for a period beginning May 1, 1998 and running through April, 2005 based on the pricing of 48.8 gram newsprint. Under the Swap Agreement, MAEM effectively guaranteed MNG a fixed price for newsprint. In other words, if the market price for 48.8 gram newsprint in a given quarter was higher than the price fixed pursuant to the Swap Agreement Schedules, MAEM would be liable to MNG for the difference; if the fixed price exceeded market, MNG would pay MAEM. At all times pertinent to resolution of the Motion, MAEM was "in the money," i.e., the market price of 48.8 gram newsprint was less than the fixed price established by the Swap Agreement.

On July 14, 2003, MAEM filed for relief under chapter 11 of the Bankruptcy Code (the "Code"). . . .

On July 15, 2003, MNG learned of Debtors' chapter 11 cases. . . .

[After negotiations between the parties regarding the Swap Agreement], MNG determined it would exercise its right under section 560 of the Code to terminate the Swap Agreement. On September 4, 2003, . . . [MNG] sent a letter to MAEM advising of the termination, and on September 16, 2003 . . . [MNG] sent a second letter to MAEM . . . [which] advised that MNG had calculated net amounts due to MAEM under the terminated Swap Agreement at $1,135,578. . . .

It is Debtors' position that MNG's termination of the Swap Agreement violated the automatic stay of section 362(a) of the Code. Although sections 362(b)(17) and 560 of the Code exempt from the automatic stay actions taken by a swap participant to terminate or settle a swap agreement, Debtors argue that those provisions are applicable only if the swap participant is terminating and settling the swap agreement in response to a bankruptcy filing. As MNG waited seven weeks after MAEM's case was commenced before terminating the Swap Agreement, Debtors argue MNG was unable to take advantage of sections 362(b)(17) and 560.

Alternatively Debtors insist that MNG "waived" its termination rights by its actions . . . [negotiating with MAEN] between July 15, 2003 and September 4, 2003. . . .

The court does not find merit in either of these arguments. MNG quite reasonably thought it was protected as a Counterparty under . . . [an] Interim Order [issued by the judge]. . . . Only on September 4, 2003 did MNG learn Debtors contested its right to invoke the Interim Order (and . . . [a] Final Order [subsequently issued]). When MNG learned . . . [this] it determined that it should terminate the Swap Agreement because of Debtors' chapter 11 cases. Debtors urge that MNG's motives were economic: it would be cheaper for MNG to terminate than to continue the Swap Agreement, as MNG was "out of the money." That may be so, but it would be inequitable to allow Debtors now to spring a trap on MNG. Having on July 15, Debtors' first day in chapter 11, given

MNG good reason to believe it was covered by the Interim Order and then, on September 4, having refused to acknowledge that coverage, Debtors would be enjoying their cake and yet keeping it whole if the court were to hold that through the passage of time MNG lost its right under Code § 560 to terminate. . . .

It has often been said that the automatic stay of section 362(a) is a shield for a debtor, not a sword to be used offensively. . . . [I]n the case at bar, Debtors appear to be attempting to use the automatic stay and this court's orders in a pincer attack on MNG. Even if MNG had technically violated the automatic stay, the court would not find it equitable to penalize MNG on these facts.

However, MNG did not violate the stay. It was a swap participant that was party to a swap agreement. By reason of MAEM's bankruptcy MNG invoked its rights under Code §§ 362(b)(17) and 560 to terminate the Swap Agreement. It did not waive those rights. Therefore MNG's actions were authorized under section 362(b)(17) and 560 of the Code and the orders entered by this court. . . .

For the foregoing reasons, the Motion must be, and is, DENIED. Any court costs shall be charged to Debtors. Counsel for Debtors shall prepare and submit to the court an order consistent with this opinion.

In *Mirant*, at issue was a seven-week delay that the judge attributed to a large extent to the debtor. In another bankruptcy case, *In re Enron Corporation*, a one-year delay after the bankruptcy of a debtor in terminating a swap agreement was found to result in forfeiture of the safe harbor protections:

> In essence, the Claimant is seeking to achieve, through equity, the statutory protections Congress limited to, among others, a participant in a swap agreement who, based upon the bankruptcy, elects to terminate the swap agreement as provided under section 560 of the Bankruptcy Code. To avail itself of the "safe harbor" provisions of the Bankruptcy Code, however, the swap participant must opt for the early termination of the swap agreement based upon one of the reasons enumerated in section 365(e)(1) of the Bankruptcy Code and if based upon the bankruptcy filing, the election to terminate must be made fairly contemporaneously with the bankruptcy filing. Here, [Claimant] could not have opted for the safe harbor protection when the rejection notice was provided because it was more than one year after the bankruptcy filing and therefore any termination would not be because of a condition of the kind specified in section 365(e)(1) [of] the Bankruptcy Code. Further, the record supports a finding that the termination was not prompted by the financial condition of the debtor since such condition was present for nearly two years and [Claimant] never took any action to terminate the contract such as, for example, availing itself of the Early Termination provisions.

In re Enron Corp., 2005 WL 3874285, at *4 (Bankr. S.D.N.Y Oct. 5, 2005).

Similarly, a party forbearing from terminating a swap agreement with a bankrupt debtor in order to benefit from a provision that allowed it to indefinitely suspend its performance (a result, since it was out-of-the-money, that was superior to terminating the agreement and being required to pay the net termination amount), was found to have waived the benefits of the safe harbor provisions.

In re Lehman Brothers Holdings, Inc.

No. 08-13555 (JMP) (Bankr. S.D.N.Y Sept. 15, 2009)

[Lehman Brothers Special Financing Inc. ("LBSF")] requests that the Court compel [Metavante Corporation ("Metavante") to perform its obligations under that certain 1992 ISDA Master Agreement dated as of November 20, 2007, defined as the "Master Agreement". And that certain trade confirmation dated December 4, 2007, defined as the "Confirmation", and together with the Master Agreement, the "Agreement." . . .

[T]he value of LBSF's position under the Agreement has increased. As of May 2009, under the payment terms of the Agreement, Metavante owed LBSF in excess of 6 million dollars. . . .

Metavante has refused to make any payments to LBSF. In fact, it has refused to perform its obligations under the Agreement . . . Instead, Metavante claims that LBSF and LBHI, via the filing of their respective Chapter 11 cases, each caused an event of default under the Agreement.

Metavante argues that due to such events of default it has the right, but not the obligation, under the safe harbor provisions of the Bankruptcy Code, to terminate all outstanding derivative transactions under the Agreement. Metavante also maintains that it is not otherwise required to perform under the Agreement. . . .

In the instant case Metavante has refused to perform under the Agreement on account of the event of default that has occurred, and is continuing, on account of the bankruptcies of LBSF and LBHI. Metavante has not, however, attempted to terminate the Agreement. . . .

The safe harbor provisions permit qualifying non-debtor counterparties to derivative contracts to exercise certain limited contractual rights triggered by, among other things, a Chapter 11 filing. They're available, however, only to the extent that a counterparty seeks to one, liquidate, terminate or accelerate its contracts or two, net out its positions. All other uses of *ipso facto* provisions remain unenforceable under the Bankruptcy Code.

Notably, Metavante does not dispute that it has failed to perform under the Agreement. . . . Metavante emphasizes the term, quote, "condition precedent" set forth in Sections [2(a)(i) and (iii)] of the Agreement, which subject payment obligations to the condition precedent that no event of default with respect to the party has occurred and is continuing.

Metavante argues that under New York State contract law a failure of a condition precedent excuses a party's obligation to perform. Metavante states that its unequivocal right to suspend payments until the termination of the Agreement is fundamental to the manner in which swap parties government themselves. . . .

[T]he safe harbor provisions . . . protect a non-defaulting swap counterparty's contractual rights solely to liquidate, terminate or accelerate one or more swap agreements because of a condition of the kind specified in Section 365(e) (1) . . .

In the instant matter Metavante has attempted neither to liquidate, terminate or accelerate the Agreement . . . Metavante simply is withholding performance, relying on the conditions precedent language in Sections 2(a)(i) and (iii) under the Agreement. . . .

The Court finds that Metavante's window to act promptly under the safe harbor provisions has passed, and while it may not have had the obligation to terminate immediately upon the filing of LBHI or LBSF, its failure to do so, at this juncture, constitutes a waiver of that right at this point. . . .

The court followed up two days later with an order requiring Metavante to perform under the agreement and to pay default interest for the missed payments.[14]

The decision has illuminated an apparent split between the U.S. and U.K. approach to the same issue with the United Kingdom ruling that a party using Section 2(a)(iii) of the ISDA Master Agreement to suspend performance due to the default of a counterparty can do so (though the obligation will revive if the default is cured).[15]

2. Disputes Regarding Set-off Rights

Whereas the previously examined "safe harbors" only benefit parties to specified transaction types, such as futures or swaps, the Bankruptcy Code's set-off provisions protect any party's valid set-off right.

Whether a set-off right is valid or not is a question of applicable state law. Additionally, the Bankruptcy Code imposes an obligation of mutuality that caselaw has helped delineate.

Though the following case does not involve futures or swaps, the principles are equally applicable. The question that arose in the following case is whether a so-called triangular set-off meets the Bankruptcy Code's mutuality requirement. In this case, Chevron was the creditor and its contracts for the purchase or sale of petroleum products with three related bankrupt debtors represented the obligations that Chevron sought to set-off against one another.

In re Semcrude, L.P.

399 B.R. 388 (Bankr. D. Del. 2009)

Brendan Linehan Shannon, Bankruptcy Judge.

Before the Court is the motion (the "Motion") . . . of Chevron Products Company, a division of Chevron USA, Inc. ("Chevron") seeking relief from the automatic stay to effect a "triangular setoff" of certain debts that are owed or owing between it and three separate debtors in these jointly administered cases. For the following reasons, the Court will deny the Motion. . . .

On July 22, 2008 (the "Petition Date"), SemGroup, L.P. ("SemGroup"), and certain direct and indirect subsidiaries (each a "Debtor" and collectively referred to hereinafter as the "Debtors"), including SemCrude, L.P. ("SemCrude"), SemFuel, L.P. ("SemFuel"), and SemStream, L.P. ("SemStream"), each filed a voluntary petition for relief under Chapter 11 of the Bankruptcy Code (the "Code"). The Debtors' Chapter 11 cases have been consolidated for procedural purposes. . . .

In the course of its business, Chevron entered into contracts with three of the Debtors: SemCrude, SemFuel, and SemStream. Chevron contracted with these entities for the sale or purchase of crude oil, regular unleaded gasoline, and/or butane, isobutene and propane, respectively. . . .

Additionally, SemGroup executed a continuing parent guaranty of any indebtedness incurred by SemCrude, SemStream, SemMaterials, L.P., and SemFuel in favor of Chevron (the "Continuing Guaranty"). . . .

Prior to the Debtors' bankruptcy filings, Chevron and the Debtors entered into a number of transactions pursuant to these contracts. As of the Petition Date, these transactions resulted in Chevron owing a balance of $1,405,878.40 to SemCrude. Chevron is owed $10,228,439.34 by SemFuel, however, and is owed an additional $3,302,806.03 by SemStream.

Claiming that the amounts owed under these balances can be setoff against each other pursuant to the contract terms discussed above, Chevron filed the Motion on August 21, 2008 for the purpose of obtaining leave from the automatic stay so that it could effect such a setoff. The Debtors . . . and a host of the Debtors' creditors each filed timely objections . . . [which] took issue with Chevron's argument that the Code allows for parties to contract around the Code's requirement in section 553 that debts be "mutual" in order to be setoff. The objectors contend that triangular setoff is impermissible, even if contemplated by a valid, pre-petition contract. Alternatively, the objectors argue that even if there is such a contract exception to the mutuality requirement, the contracts in the instant case fail to effect such a result. . . .

Chevron asserts that the terms of its contracts with the Debtors permit it to setoff the debt it owes to one corporation, SemCrude, against the debt owed to it by two other corporations, SemFuel and SemStream, thus effecting a "triangular setoff." The Court does not need to determine whether the specific terms of these various contracts grant SemCrude this right, however. Instead, the Court holds that Chevron is not permitted to effect such a setoff against the Debtors in this case because section 553 of the Code prohibits a triangular setoff of debts against one or more debtors in bankruptcy as a matter of law due to lack of mutuality. . . .

The Code section that governs setoff in bankruptcy, section 553, does not create a right of setoff . . . Rather, section 553 "preserves for the creditor's benefit any setoff right that it may have under applicable nonbankruptcy law," and "imposes additional restrictions on a creditor seeking setoff" that must be met to impose a setoff against a debtor in bankruptcy. Thus, setoff is appropriate in bankruptcy only when a creditor both enjoys an independent right of setoff under applicable non-bankruptcy law, and meets the further Code-imposed requirements and limitations set forth in section 553. . . .

In order to effect a setoff in bankruptcy, courts construing the Code have long held that the debts to be offset must be mutual, prepetition debts.

The authorities are also clear that debts are considered "mutual" only when "they are due to and from the same persons in the same capacity." . . . [B]ecause each corporation is a separate entity from its sister corporations absent a piercing of the corporate veil, "a subsidiary's debt may not be set off against the credit of a parent or other subsidiary, or vice versa, because no mutuality exists under the circumstances." Allowing a creditor to offset a debt it owes to one corporation against funds owed to it by another corporation – even a wholly-owned subsidiary – would thus constitute an improper triangular setoff under the Code.

Chevron asserts that an exception to the Code's mutuality requirement exists. It contends that a valid, pre-petition contract—executed by a creditor, a debtor, and one or more third parties—either satisfies the mutuality requirement or allows the parties to contract around the mutuality requirement found in section 553(a) if the contract provides that one or more parties to the agreement can elect to setoff any debt it owes to one of the other parties against an amount owed to it by a different party to the agreement. . . .

Chevron's Motion claims that the setoff it seeks is one of "mutual obligations." More specifically, it contends that this "multi-party mutuality is created" by the contracts discussed above. But Chevron also argues that triangular setoffs "are enforceable as an exception to the mutuality requirement" when contemplated by a valid contract. Although Chevron appears to take these positions as part of a single argument, and not as alternative arguments, the Court finds these propositions to be mutually exclusive.[ii] If a debt is mutual one, then the rule of mutuality is, by definition, satisfied without the need for an exception to the rule. For a setoff to be

---

[ii] [N. 6] No pun intended.

enforceable as an "exception" to the mutuality requirement, however, the mutuality requirement itself must not have been satisfied.

Therefore, in the complete absence of controlling or persuasive published caselaw on the issue, the Court is faced with two distinct questions. First, may debts owing among different parties be considered "mutual" when there are contractual netting provisions governing all parties' business relationship? If the answer is "no," then the second question is whether a "contractual exception" exists to section 553's mutuality requirement. . . .

As is made clear by the express language of the section 553, and the numerous decisions interpreting it, the Code only allows for setoff of "mutual debts" in bankruptcy. No mention is made in the statute of allowing setoff of non-mutual debts, thus a debt must be mutual in order to be setoff under section 553. On this general rule, the courts are in unanimous agreement. . . .

[T]he Court concludes that mutuality cannot be supplied by a multi-party agreement contemplating a triangular setoff. Unlike a guarantee of debt, where the guarantor is liable for making a payment on the debt it has guaranteed payment of, an agreement to setoff funds does not create an indebtedness from one party to another.[iii] An agreement to setoff funds, such as the one claimed by Chevron in this case, does not give rise to a debt that is "due to" Chevron and "due from" SemCrude. A party such as SemCrude does not have to actually pay anything to a creditor such as Chevron under a tripartite setoff agreement; rather, it only sees one of its receivables reduced in size or eliminated. SemCrude does not owe anything to Chevron, thus there are no debts in this dispute owed between the "same persons in the same capacity."

Likewise, Chevron does not have a "right to collect" against SemCrude under the agreement in this case. At most, the agreement of the parties would give Chevron a "right to offset" – a right to pay less than it would otherwise have to pay to the extent of the setoff. The agreement does not call for SemCrude to make a payment to Chevron, however. Consequently, the agreement does not call for Chevron to "collect" anything from SemCrude. Chevron is thus without a "right to collect" from SemCrude. At bottom, Chevron may enjoy privity of contract with each of the relevant Debtors, but it lacks the mutuality required by the plain language of section 553. . . .

Accordingly, the Court holds that non-mutual debts cannot be transformed into a "mutual debt" under section 553 simply because a multi-party agreement allows for setoff of non-mutual debts between the parties to the agreement. . . .

[iii] [N. 7] This is not to say that setoff would necessarily be appropriate against SemCrude if it were a guarantor of SemStream or SemFuel's debt, however. The Court notes that a split of authority exists regarding the issue of whether an unpaid guarantee can create mutuality for purposes of section 553. The Court does not reach this issue in this case because the only guarantor in this matter is SemGroup, an entity that is not owed a debt by Chevron.

The Court now turns to the question of whether there is a "contract exception" to the requirement of mutuality under section 553. . . .

The Court finds nothing in the language of the Code upon which to base a conclusion that there is a contractual exception to the "mutual debt" requirement. Absent a clear indication from the text of the Code that such an exception exists, the Court deems it improper to recognize one. . . .

Although dictated by the plain language of section 553, the Court's holding also is consistent with the purpose of section 553 and the broader policies of the Code. One of the primary goals – if not the primary goal – of the Code is to ensure that similarly-situated creditors are treated fairly and enjoy an equality of distribution from a debtor absent a compelling reason to depart from this principle. By allowing parties to contract around the mutuality requirement of section 553, one creditor or a handful of creditors could unfairly obtain payment from a debtor at the expense of the debtor's other creditors, thereby upsetting the priority scheme of the Code and reducing the amount available for distribution to all creditors. . . .

For the foregoing reasons, the Court finds that Chevron is not entitled to enact a triangular setoff of the amounts owed between it and the Debtors. Accordingly, the Court will deny the Motion. . . .

Whereas in *Semcrude* the facts of the triangular set-off involved multiple related bankrupt debtors and one creditor, what if, instead, multiple related creditors sought to exercise a set-off with respect to obligations with a single bankrupt debtor? Such facts occurred in the Lehman bankruptcy where UBS AG held excess collateral that it sought to set-off against amounts owed by Lehman Brothers, Inc., to affiliates of UBS AG.[16] The bankruptcy court, citing to *Semcrude*, decided that mutuality did not exist and, therefore, the set-off was impermissible.[17]

The mutuality requirement was even more narrowly construed in the following case, which decided that mutuality did not exist between a single creditor seeking to set-off obligations accrued before the debtor's bankruptcy petition against obligations incurred after the debtor's bankruptcy petition.

Swedbank AB (PUBL) v. Lehman Brothers Holdings Inc. (In re Lehman Bros. Holdings Inc.)

445 B.R. 130 (S.D.N.Y. 2011)

Naomi Reice Buchwald, District Judge.

Appellant Swedbank AB (publ.) ("Swedbank") appeals from . . . an order . . . compelling Swedbank to return post-petition funds to [Lehman Brothers Holdings Inc. ("LBHI")]. . . .

For the reasons stated herein, the decision below is affirmed. . . .

Swedbank and the Lehman Debtors had a multifaceted relationship that long predated the Lehman Debtors' Chapter 11 case. For example, LBHI was a party to an International Swaps and Derivatives Association ("ISDA") Master Agreement between LBHI and Swedbank, dated November 29, 2004 ("LBHI Master Agreement"). Additionally, between 1996 and 2004, Swedbank and certain LBHI affiliates entered into other ISDA Master Agreements. LBHI was a guarantor with respect to this latter set of agreements (together with the LBHI Master Agreement, the "Master Agreements"). Finally, LBHI maintained a general deposit account with Swedbank in Stockholm, Sweden ("Swedbank Account"). . . .

The Master Agreements include certain provisions that are relevant to this dispute. Specifically, the Master Agreements define a voluntary or involuntary bankruptcy filing as an "Event of Default." The Master Agreements further provide that an Event of Default: (1) triggers the early termination of the Master Agreements; and (2) grants the non-defaulting party a right of setoff. . . .

Following . . . [LBHI's] bankruptcy filing, Swedbank placed an administrative freeze on the Swedbank Account. As a result of the freeze, LBHI could not withdraw funds but was able to make deposits or wire transfers into the account. In the days and weeks to follow, LBHI and others deposited an additional SEK 82,765,466.45 (approximately $11.7 million) into the Swedbank Account.

On November 27, 2008, Swedbank informed LBHI that it intended to setoff LBHI's pre-petition debts, which arose under the Master Agreements, against the funds in the Swedbank Account, including the SEK 82.7 million that was deposited post-petition. Although LBHI contested Swedbank's right to take such action, Swedbank reaffirmed its position in a letter dated January 30, 2009. . . .

The issues presented on appeal are: (1) whether Swedbank's proposed setoff of LBHI's pre-petition obligations against LBHI's post-petition deposits was prohibited by section 553 of the Bankruptcy Code, which permits the offset of "mutual" pre-petition obligations; (2) whether Swedbank's proposed setoff was permissible under sections 560 and 561 of the Bankruptcy Code ("Safe Harbor Provisions"), which govern the right to liquidate, terminate, or accelerate swap agreements and master netting agreements; and (3) whether the Bankruptcy Court correctly ruled that Swedbank violated the automatic stay by placing a freeze on LBHI's post-petition funds. . . .

Swedbank's arguments turn on the relationship among section 553 [a concept in existence for over a century] and the later-enacted Safe Harbor Provisions [i.e. section 560, enacted in 1990 and section 561, enacted in 2005]. . . .

Congress legislates in light of the legal principles in existence at the time. As is relevant to this dispute, the mutuality requirement has existed for more than a century.

When a party argues that Congress has made a fundamental change to a well-settled legal principle, courts often look to legislative history. . . . Thus, if

Congress had intended to eliminate the fundamental principle of mutuality, we would expect some discussion of this change in the legislative history. . . .

On appeal, Swedbank concedes that but for the Safe Harbor Provisions, its actions would be unauthorized. Swedbank also admits that the post-petition deposits into the Swedbank Account were made fortuitously and were not required by the terms of the Master Agreements. However, Swedbank contends that sections 560 and 561 specifically authorize the offset of LBHI's pre-petition debts against the post-petition funds in the Swedbank Account. According to Swedbank, the legislative history of the Safe Harbor Provisions demonstrates that Congress intended to grant "special treatment" to swap agreements to prevent disruption to the capital markets. Thus, Swedbank continues, Congress must have intended to permit a creditor to satisfy its claims under a pre-petition swap agreement by offsetting such claims against a debtor's post-petition deposits. . . .

The legislative history of the Safe Harbor Provisions reveals three related themes, all of which focus narrowly on swap transactions and the swap market. First, the legislative history reflects that Congress intended to permit swap participants to terminate swap agreements. According to House Report 101-484:

> The new section 560 makes clear that a swap participant may exercise any contractual rights to terminate and net out a swap agreement in the event the other party files a bankruptcy petition, notwithstanding the automatic stay and trustee avoidance provisions of the Bankruptcy Code. . . . The intent of this provision is to permit either the non-debtor swap participant or the trustee to terminate a swap agreement, so that a swap agreement may continue after the bankruptcy petition is filed only by mutual consent of both the non-debtor swap participant and the trustee.

H.R. Rep. No. 101–484 (1990), reprinted in 1990 U.S.C.C.A.N. 223, 228, available at 1990 WL 92539.

In other words, Congress intended that section 560 would enable parties to swap agreements to terminate those transactions; neither the statute nor the legislative history extends the application of section 560 to the general commercial obligations of parties to swap agreements.

Second, the legislative history reflects a concern for the stability of the often-volatile swap market. Consequently, Congress emphasized that the Safe Harbor Provisions permit immediate termination of swap transactions in order to minimize the non-bankrupt counterparty's exposure to such unpredictability. For example, House Report 101-484 introduces the legislation in the following terms:

> U.S. bankruptcy law has long accorded special treatment to transactions involving financial markets, to minimize volatility. Because financial markets can change significantly in a matter of days, or even hours, a non-bankrupt party to ongoing securities and other financial transactions could face heavy losses unless the transactions are resolved promptly and with finality.

H.R. Rep. No. 101-484, 1990 U.S.C.C.A.N. at p. 224. . . .

Third, the legislative history addresses the need for swap participants to be able to close out existing transactions without fear that: (1) closing out swaps would violate the stay; (2) a debtor would opportunistically reject unfavorable swaps and assume favorable ones; or (3) the transactions would be challenged as voidable preferences. According to House Report 101-484:

> [u]nder the "avoidance" provisions in current bankruptcy law, if a swap agreement was in effect at the time one of the parties filed a bankruptcy petition, the fund transfer from the debtor to the other party might be "avoidable" by the trustee, while the transfer from the other party to the debtor would not be. Concerns have been raised that under current bankruptcy law, termination and setoff of a swap agreement would be automatically stayed when one of the parties files a bankruptcy petition, whereupon the trustee, after indefinitely postponing termination of the swap agreement, could refuse setoff and unfairly "cherry pick" only the portions of the agreement advantageous to the debtor, while rejecting the portions unfavorable to the debtor.

H.R. Rep. No. 101–484, 1990 U.S.C.C.A.N. at p. 225. . . .

Accordingly, Congress was further motivated by the fairness considerations that support the even-handed netting of favorable transactions against unfavorable ones to determine a single net termination value. . . .

In sum, the legislative history plainly supports the argument that Swedbank was entitled to terminate the Master Agreements and to determine a single net termination value. However, it does not support Swedbank's position that the Safe Harbor Provisions permit setoff against LBHI's post-petition assets, which were fortuitously deposited in the Swedbank Account and which have no connection to the underlying swaps. . .

For the foregoing reasons, the Bankruptcy Court's decision is affirmed.

E. CROSS-BORDER ISSUES IN BANKRUPTCY DISPUTES RELATING TO SWAPS

Although swaps may benefit from the safe harbor provisions where bankruptcy proceedings occur in the United States, this is not necessarily the case where bankruptcy proceedings occur outside the United States. To provide more certainty on the question of whether swap transactions are protected by provisions akin to the safe harbor provisions, the International Swaps and Derivatives Association commissions legal opinions in various jurisdictions globally.

Section 304 of the Bankruptcy Code provided a mechanism for a non-U.S. debtor to bring ancillary proceedings in the United States whereby U.S. courts provide assistance with the foreign jurisdiction's insolvency process. In 2005, it was replaced by new provisions contained in Chapter 15 of the Bankruptcy Code.[18]

The standards in both are similar in that where a request is contrary to public policy, the U.S. court does not have to enforce it. Lack of safe harbor provisions has not been found to be repugnant to U.S. public policy.

In re Petition of the Board of Directors of Compañia General de Combustibles S.A.

269 B.R. 104 (Bankr. S.D.N.Y. 2011)

Burton R. Lifland, Bankruptcy Judge.

The Petitioners, the Boards of Directors of Sociedad Comercial del Plata, S.A. ("SCP") and Compañía General de Combustibles, S.A. ("CGC" and together with SCP, the "Debtors"), as the representatives of SCP and CGC in "Concursos Preventivos," or reorganization proceedings (the "CGC Concursos"), pending in the Federal Commercial Trial Court No. 15 in and for the City of Buenos Aires, Argentina (the "Argentine Court"), seek a continuation of the preliminary injunction granted by this [Court] . . . Reef Exploration, Inc. ("Reef") and Hess Energy Trading Company LLC ("Hess" and together with Reef, the "Objectors") object to the continuation of the injunction as to their claims. . . .

SCP is a holding company organized under the laws of Argentina. Among other things, it owns CGC, an oil company, and Tren de la Costca ("TDC"), a transportation and entertainment company. On September 8, 2000, SCP, CGC, TDC and Solfina, S.A. ("Solfina") filed voluntary petitions (the "CGC Concursos") for the commencement of Concurso Preventivos in the Federal Commercial Trial Court (the "Argentine Court") in Buenos Aires, Argentina. By order dated November 2, 2000, the Argentine Court granted the order for relief for all four debtors. The CGC Concursos is the largest reorganization proceeding in Argentine history. On December 28, 2000, the Petitioners commenced this ancillary case under Section 304 of title 11 of the United States Code (the "Bankruptcy Code") and moved this court for an order enjoining all persons from continuing or commencing any action against SCP or CGC or their property in the United States. The motion was opposed by several creditors. . . .

[T]his Court signed an order granting a preliminary injunction over the objections. . . .

A Concursos Preventivos under Argentine law is similar to a Chapter 11 reorganization. Upon the filing of a petition, an automatic statutory stay is in place which prohibits creditors from taking actions against the debtor or its assets or from pursuing claims against the debtor outside the reorganization proceedings. A creditors committee, made up of the debtor's largest unsecured creditors, is appointed. . . . The judge also appointed three independent accounting firms to assist in the reorganization proceedings. One functions as a "Receiver," who monitors and supervises the finances of the businesses and two others, called Allowing Trustees or "Sindicos," handle claims administration and review the companies' claims. . . .

In the CGC Concursos, alleged creditors, including Reef and Hess, submitted proofs of claim to the Síndico for review as part of the claims verification process. CGC filed objections to claims of certain creditors, including Reef and Hess. . . .

The Argentine Court ruled that it could not admit Reef's claim without the presentation of evidence on the merits of its claim. The Argentine Court admitted a portion of Hess's claim but ruled that a disputed portion of the claim could not be determined absent an evidentiary hearing. . . .

Both Reef and Hess argue that . . . section 304(c) . . . prohibits the continuation of the preliminary injunction. In particular, the parties assert that because they will not receive a distribution of proceeds of CGC's estate substantially in accordance with section 304(c)(4)of the United States Bankruptcy Code, this court should not extend comity to the foreign proceeding. . . .

Reef and Hess . . . essentially take the position that they must be given identical treatment in the allowance of claims and distribution of proceeds of the estate in order for this court to find that the section 304(c)(4) requirement has been met. Although there are differences in the laws of Argentina and the United States that may effect the distribution that Reef and Hess ultimately receive, this alone cannot be grounds for a denial of the relief requested. . . .

Hess argues that because Argentine bankruptcy law does not provide special provisions for swap agreements as is found in section 560 of the Bankruptcy Code, its claim will not receive substantially similar treatment as required by section 304(c)(4). Section 560 preserves the right of a party to a swap agreement to terminate the agreement pursuant to a condition based on, *inter alia*, the filing of a bankruptcy petition by the debtor. These conditions, commonly known as *ipso facto* clauses, would otherwise be nullified by section 365(e) of the Bankruptcy Code. Argentine bankruptcy law does not have an analogous provision to section 560 regarding the swap agreement, and does not distinguish such agreements from other types of executory contracts. Under Argentine bankruptcy law, the debtor has a thirty-day period to decide whether to assume executory contacts before a creditor under such contract may exercise its contractual rights to terminate, and the incurrence of penalties by the debtor is prohibited during such time. It is therefore clear that with respect to the issue of termination provisions under swap agreements, there are differences between Argentine and United States bankruptcy law.

Section 304(c)(4) does not require that the foreign bankruptcy law provide identical treatment of a claim to that treatment provided under United States law in order to extend comity. . . . [T]his extreme approach would effectively end cooperation among countries because special interest priority schemes vary greatly around the world.

Moreover, there is no basis for Hess's arguments that the provisions of our domestic Bankruptcy Code dealing with swap agreements must be imported into the bankruptcy laws of foreign jurisdictions and that the provisions of Argentine bankruptcy law providing for a 30-day period in which the debtor may assume swap agreements and prohibiting "penalties" as a result of the filing of a Concursos are fundamentally unfair. The policy underlying the swap transaction provisions of the Bankruptcy Code is not to protect the rights of United States creditors entering into swap transactions with foreign corporations, but rather those of creditors (including foreign creditors) of United States counterparties that may be subject to the United States bankruptcy laws. Congress saw the need to ensure the ability of United States corporations to take advantage of the swap market by reducing the uncertainty about the potential impact of a bankruptcy filing in the United States of a U.S. party to such a swap agreement. This certainty, in turn, was expected to "help American businesses compete effectively in [the swap market]." Congress was not seeking to protect a fundamental right of swap participants, but was seeking to ensure access to the swap market for United States borrowers and stabilize United States domestic markets.

Argentine bankruptcy law provides a debtor thirty days following the granting of an order for relief to request authorization from the bankruptcy court to continue an executory contract. After such time the creditor may exercise its rights under the contract if a decision to continue has not been communicated by the debtor. Under the Bankruptcy Code, absent a specific provision, a debtor has until confirmation of a plan, and in some cases beyond to either assume or reject an executory contract. During such time a creditor is ordinarily barred by the automatic stay from terminating the contract. Therefore, Argentine bankruptcy law actually provides greater protection to the non-debtor party to an executory contract, because such party is not forced to continue to perform and instead may act on their contractual rights, in the absence of an assumption by the debtor, after thirty days. Certainly, the

Argentine law provides sufficient procedural safeguards so that the foreign proceedings are not "repugnant to American laws and policies." . . .

QUESTIONS AND COMMENTS

1. The "futures" model and "LSOC" model are each discussed in section B above. Is one model more fair to customers? Is one model an example of better public policy? Why have two different models?
2. Why treat claims relating to derivatives differently than other claims in bankruptcy?
3. Similarly, why allow parties to reap the benefits of set-off rights related to debt incurred pre-bankruptcy petition?
4. Can the different results in *Lehman Brothers Special Financing Inc. v. Ballyrock ABS CDO 2007-1 Limited* and *Michigan State Housing Authority* be reconciled? Both had termination methodologies that changed to the detriment of Lehman Brothers Special Financing due to the bankruptcy of its parent. Were there differences justifying the contradictory outcomes?
5. The Bankruptcy Code does not provide a specific time period for when termination of a swap agreement must be exercised, leading courts to try to devise one. How would you resolve such a claim before you if you were a judge deciding this issue?

CHAPTER 12
FOREIGN EXCHANGE TRANSACTIONS AND COMMODITY OPTIONS

A. BACKGROUND

In this chapter, we evaluate the regulatory status of foreign exchange transactions and commodity options.

Foreign exchange transactions and commodity options are different both economically and in their regulatory treatment. However, they share in common regulatory regimes that are distinct in some ways from the regulatory regime for futures and swaps and, therefore, are examined in this chapter together.

1. Foreign Exchange Transactions

Foreign exchange transactions can generally be divided into the following economic classifications: (1) spot transactions, i.e., an exchange of currencies settled on a market basis that, except for exotic currencies, means settlement within two days after the exchange is agreed, (2) forwards, i.e., an agreement to exchange currencies at a pre-agreed fixed price at some point more than two days after agreement, (3) options, i.e., agreements by which one party grants the other the right, though not the obligation, to exchange currency at a specified price on a specified date, and (4) swaps, i.e., pre-agreed multiple exchanges of currency at specified dates in the future.

From a regulatory standpoint, the status of foreign exchange transactions vary, depending on factors enumerated below. For example, in some cases and contexts, they are treated as swaps. In other contexts, though not treated as swaps, they are nonetheless subject to CFTC regulation or comparable regulation by banking or securities regulators. Finally, the most basic spot transactions are unregulated or, for participants in the business of making such exchanges, minimally regulated at the state and Federal level.

The primary reason for this varied regulatory treatment is that the foreign exchange regulatory regimes in existence today are a result of an evolutionary process, instead of the imposition of a comprehensive regulatory structure.

2. *Commodity Options*

Commodity options (including foreign exchange options) generally have the same regulatory treatment as swaps unless traded on a designated contract market. When traded on a designated contract market commodity options are treated nearly identically to commodity futures. The means by which this became the case, though, is non-linear. This chapter examines the development of the regulatory regime for commodity options and highlights where, in the case of commodity options traded off-exchange (i.e., on other than a designated contract market), the regulatory treatment of commodity options differs from the regulatory treatment of swaps.

B. EVOLUTION OF FOREIGN EXCHANGE TRANSACTIONS

1. *The Treasury Amendment*

The history of foreign exchange transaction regulation was discussed in Chapter 2. As discussed therein, the Commodity Futures Trading Commission Act of 1974 explicitly excluded "transactions in foreign currencies" from the otherwise broad jurisdiction over commodities provided to the CFTC unless they were traded on a board of trade.[1] This occurred through an amendment to the predecessor bill through what is today referred to as the "Treasury Amendment" due to the Department of the Treasury's advocacy for the exclusion.[2]

Though the Treasury Amendment excluded all "transactions in foreign currencies" from the CFTC's jurisdiction, the CFTC argued that foreign currency options were not part of this exclusion and that the CFTC could regulate them.

Dunn v. Commodity Futures Trading Commission

519 U.S. 465 (1997)

Justice Stevens delivered the opinion of the Court.

The question presented is whether Congress has authorized the Commodity Futures Trading Commission (CFTC or Commission) to regulate "off-exchange" trading in options to buy or sell foreign currency.

The CFTC brought this action in 1994, alleging that, beginning in 1992, petitioners solicited investments in and operated a fraudulent scheme in violation of the Commodity Exchange Act (CEA) and CFTC regulations.[i] The CFTC's complaint, affidavits, and declarations . . . indicate that customers were told their funds would be invested using complex strategies involving options to purchase or sell various foreign currencies. Petitioners apparently did in fact engage in many such transactions. To do so, they contracted directly with international banks and others without making use of any regulated exchange or board of trade. In the parlance of the business, petitioners traded in the "off-exchange" or "over-the-counter" (OTC) market. No options were ever sold directly to petitioners' customers. However, their positions were tracked through internal accounts, and investors were provided weekly reports showing the putative status of their holdings. Petitioners and their customers suffered heavy losses. Subsequently, the CFTC commenced these proceedings. . . .

The outcome of this case is dictated by the so-called "Treasury Amendment" to the CEA. . . . As a part of the 1974 amendments that created the CFTC and dramatically expanded the coverage of the statute to include nonagricultural commodities "in which contracts for future delivery are presently or in the future dealt in," Congress enacted the . . . exemption, which has come to be known as the "Treasury Amendment." . . .

The CFTC argues . . . that an option is not itself a transaction "in" foreign currency, but rather is just a contract right to engage in such a transaction at a future date. Hence, the Commission submits that the term "transactions in foreign currency" includes only the "actual exercise of an option (i.e., the actual purchase or sale of foreign currency)" but not the purchase or sale of an option

---

[i] [N. 2] . . . [T]he CFTC calls our attention to statements in the legislative history of a 1982 amendment to the CEA indicating that the drafters of that amendment believed that the CFTC had the authority to regulate foreign currency options "when they are traded other than on a national securities exchange." *See* S.Rep. No. 97–384, p. 22 (1982). Those statements, at best, might be described as "legislative *dicta*" because the 1982 amendment itself merely resolved a conflict between the Securities Exchange Commission and the CFTC concerning their respective authority to regulate transactions on an exchange. The amendment made no change in the law applicable to off-exchange trading. Although these "*dicta*" are consistent with the position that the CFTC advocates, they shed no light on the intent of the authors of the Treasury Amendment that had been adopted eight years earlier.

itself. That reading of the text seems quite unnatural to us, and we decline to adopt it. . . .

We think it . . . plain as a matter of ordinary meaning that . . . [a foreign exchange] option is a transaction "in" foreign currency for purposes of the Treasury Amendment.

Indeed, adopting the Commission's reading would deprive the exemption of the principal effect Congress intended. The CFTC acknowledges that futures contracts fall squarely within the Treasury Amendment's exemption, and there is no question that the exemption of off-exchange foreign currency futures from CFTC regulation was one of Congress' primary goals. Yet on the CFTC's reasoning the exemption's application to futures contracts could not be sustained.

A futures contract is no more a transaction "in" foreign currency as the Commission understands the term than an option. The Commission argues that because a futures contract creates a legal obligation to purchase or sell currency on a particular date, it is somehow more clearly a transaction "in" the underlying currencies than an option, which generates only the right to engage in a transaction. This reasoning is wholly unpersuasive. No currency changes hands at the time a futures contract is made. And, the existence of a futures contract does not guarantee that currency will actually be exchanged. Indeed, the Commission concedes that, in most cases, futures contracts are "extinguished before delivery by entry into an offsetting futures contract." Adopting the CFTC's reading would therefore place both futures and options outside the exemption, in clear contravention of Congress' intent.

Furthermore, this interpretation would leave the Treasury Amendment's exemption for "transactions in foreign currency" without any significant effect at all, because it would limit the scope of the exemption to "forward contracts" (agreements that anticipate the actual delivery of a commodity on a specified future date) and "spot transactions" (agreements for purchase and sale of commodities that anticipate near-term delivery). Both are transactions "in" a commodity as the CFTC would have us understand the term. But neither type of transaction for any commodity was subject to intensive regulation under the CEA at the time of the Treasury Amendment's passage. Our reading of the exemption is therefore also consonant with the doctrine that legislative enactments should not be construed to render their provisions mere surplusage.

Finally, including options in the exemption is consistent with Congress' purpose in enacting the Treasury Amendment. Although at the time the Treasury Amendment was drafted a thriving off-exchange market in foreign currency futures was in place, the closely related options market at issue here had not yet developed. The CFTC therefore suggests that Congress could not have intended to exempt foreign currency options from the CEA's coverage. The legislative history strongly suggests to the contrary that Congress' broad purpose in enacting the Treasury Amendment was to provide a general exemption from CFTC regulation for sophisticated off-exchange foreign currency trading, which had previously developed entirely free from supervision under the commodities laws. . . .

Although the OTC market for foreign currency options had not yet developed in 1974, the reasons underlying the Treasury Department's express desire at that time to exempt off-exchange commodity futures trading from CFTC regulation apply with equal force to options today.

The judgment of the Court of Appeals is reversed, and the case is remanded for further proceedings consistent with this opinion. . . .

Note that the Treasury Amendment's exclusion did not extend to transactions traded on a board of trade. Such transactions could be regulated by the CFTC pursuant to its authority to regulate contract markets. Similarly, foreign exchange transactions carried out on a securities exchange were within the SEC's jurisdiction.

2. *Limited Authority over Retail Foreign Exchange*

The CFTC obtained expanded authority over retail foreign exchange futures and options as a result of the Commodity Futures Modernization Act of 2000. Unless traded through a financial institution,[3] any such foreign exchange transactions with a retail counterparty (a retail counterparty being any party that was not an "eligible contract participant"; *see* Chapter 7) was subject to CFTC regulation.[4]

A dispute arose as to the extent of the CFTC's new jurisdiction with respect to "rolling" cash-settled foreign exchange spot transactions, i.e., transactions that, though nominally settled within two days of being agreed, are habitually renewed for another two days just before settlement would otherwise have been required and are ultimately cash-settled.

Commodity Futures Trading Commission v. Zelener

373 F.3d 861 (7th Cir. 2004)

Easterbrook, Circuit Judge.

This appeal presents the question whether speculative transactions in foreign currency are "contracts of sale of a commodity for future delivery" regulated by the Commodity Futures Trading Commission. Until recently almost all trading related to foreign currency was outside the CFTC's remit . . . [b]ut Congress modified the Treasury Amendment as part of the Commodity Futures Modernization Act of 2000, and today the . . . [CFTC has jurisdiction] unless the parties to the contract are "eligible contract participants". "Eligible contract participants" under the Commodity Exchange Act are the equivalent of "accredited investors" in securities markets: . . . persons who can look out for themselves . . . Defendants, which sold foreign currency to casual speculators rather than "eligible contract participants," are not protected by the Treasury Amendment except to the extent that it permits them to deal over-the-counter. . . .

The . . . [CFTC] believes that some of the defendants deceived some of their customers. . . . This allegation (whose accuracy has not been tested) makes it vital to know whether the contracts are within the CFTC's regulatory authority.

AlaronFX deals in foreign currency. Two corporations doing business as "British Capital Group" or BCG solicited customers' orders for foreign currency. (Michael Zelener, the first-named defendant, is the principal owner and manager of these two firms.) Each customer opened an account with BCG and another with AlaronFX; the documents made it clear that AlaronFX would be the source of all currency bought or sold through BCG in this program, and that AlaronFX would act as a principal. A customer could purchase (go long) or sell (short) any currency. . . . The customer specified the desired quantity, with a minimum order size of $5,000; the contract called for settlement within 48 hours. It is agreed, however, that few of BCG's customers paid in full within that time, and that none took delivery. AlaronFX could have reversed the transactions and charged (or credited) customers with the difference in price across those two days. Instead, however, AlaronFX rolled the transactions forward two days at a time – as the AlaronFX contract permits, and as BCG told the customers would occur. Successive extensions meant that a customer had an open position in foreign currency. If the dollar appreciated relative to that currency, the customer could close the position and reap the profit in one of two ways: take delivery of the currency . . . or sell an equal amount of currency back to AlaronFX. If, however, the dollar fell relative to the other currency, then the client suffered a loss when the position was closed by selling currency back to AlaronFX.

The CFTC believes that three principal features make these arrangements "contracts of sale of a commodity for future delivery": first, the positions were held open indefinitely, so that the customers' gains and losses depended on price movements in the future; second, the customers were amateurs who did not need foreign currency for business endeavors; third, none of the customers took delivery of any currency, so the sales could not be called forward contracts, which are exempt from regulation. . . .

These transactions could not be futures contracts . . . because the customer buys foreign currency immediately rather than as of a defined future date, and because the deals lack standard terms. AlaronFX buys and sells as a principal; transactions differ in size, price, and settlement date. The contracts are not fungible and thus could not be traded on an exchange. The CFTC replies that because AlaronFX rolls forward the settlement times, the transactions are for future delivery in practice even though not in form; and the . . . [CFTC] insists that fixed expiration dates and fungibility are irrelevant. It favors a multi-factor inquiry with heavy weight on whether the customer is financially sophisticated, able to bear risk, and intended to take or make delivery of the commodity. . . .

In organized futures markets, people buy and sell contracts, not commodities. Terms are standardized, and each party's obligation runs to an intermediary, the clearing corporation. Clearing houses eliminate counterparty credit risk. Standard terms and an absence of counterparty-specific risk make the contracts fungible, which in turn makes it possible to close a position by buying an offsetting contract. All contracts that expire in a given month are identical; each calls for delivery of the same commodity in the same place at the same time. Forward and spot contracts, by contrast, call for sale of the commodity; no one deals "in the contract"; it is not possible to close a position by buying a traded offset, because promises are not fungible; delivery is idiosyncratic rather than centralized. . . .

It is essential to know beforehand whether a contract is a future or a forward. The answer determines who, if anyone, may enter into such a contract, and where trading may occur. Contracts allocate price risk, and they fail in that office if it can't be known until years after the fact whether a given contract was lawful. Nothing is worse than an approach that asks what the parties "intended" or that scrutinizes the percentage of contracts that led to delivery *ex post.* What sense would it make – either business sense, or statutory-interpretation sense – to say that the same contract is either a future or not depending on whether the person obliged to deliver keeps his promise? That would leave people adrift and make it difficult, if not impossible, for dealers (technically, futures commission merchants) to know their legal duties in advance. . . .

These transactions were, in form, spot sales for delivery within 48 hours. Rollover, and the magnification of gain or loss over a longer period, does not turn sales into futures contracts. . . .

C. RETAIL FOREIGN EXCHANGE TRANSACTIONS

The *Zelener* decision was perceived by some, including the CFTC, as creating a regulatory gap in the retail foreign exchange market.

Written Testimony of CFTC Acting Chairman Walter Lukken

U.S. House of Representatives Committee on Agriculture (October 24, 2007), available at http://www.cftc.gov/ucm/groups/public/@newsroom/documents/speechandtestimony/opalukken-29.pdf (accessed June 22, 2014)

Good afternoon Chairman Etheridge, Ranking Member Moran and Members of the Subcommittee. I am pleased to appear on behalf of the Commodity Futures Trading Commission (Commission or CFTC) to discuss the important issues surrounding the reauthorization of the Commodity Exchange Act (CEA), the Commission's governing statute. . . .

In our commitment to protecting market participants and market integrity, I want to turn to the issue of retail fraud in foreign currency trading. In 2004, the Seventh Circuit Court of Appeals curtailed the Commission's ability to combat retail off-exchange foreign currency (forex) fraud. In the *Zelener* case, the court held that the contracts at issue were not futures contracts, but rather a type of spot contract that could not be the basis for a CFTC fraud action. This has provided a potential road map to scam artists as to how to deceive innocent retail customers while evading enforcement by the CFTC.

The CFTC believes that the *Zelener* case and others that have followed it were incorrectly decided and that the contracts at issue are futures contracts. Rather than continue to expend scarce Commission resources litigating this issue, however, we present to Congress the opportunity to restore legal certainty by clarifying the CFTC's jurisdiction in this area. . . .

[B]ecause of the *Zelener* decision and its progeny, the Commission has lost some key forex cases and now finds it is more difficult to prosecute forex actions. Unless Congress clarifies the Commission's jurisdiction over off-exchange forex transactions, a large sector of retail fraud will remain effectively outside of the prosecutorial authority of the CFTC. . . .

Congress heeded CFTC Chairman Lukken's call by enacting the CFTC Reauthorization Act of 2008,[5] which amended Commodity Exchange Act § 2(c)(2)(C) to grant the CFTC jurisdiction for off-exchange foreign exchange transactions sold to retail investors on a leveraged or margined basis or financed by the offeror, the counterparty, or someone working with either and created a new category of registrant, "retail foreign exchange dealers."[6]

Regulation of Off-Exchange Retail Foreign Exchange Transactions and Intermediaries

75 Fed. Reg. 3282 (January 20, 2010)

. . . The Commodity Futures Trading Commission Reauthorization Act of 2008 . . . [the "CRA"] was intended, among other things, to further clarify the Commission's jurisdiction in the area of retail forex, particularly in light of the proliferation of look-alike forex transactions such as those in the *Zelener* and *Erskine* cases, and to give the Commission additional authority to regulate retail forex transactions and to register persons involved in intermediating these products with members of the public. To remedy the large number of fraud cases where jurisdiction had been questioned, the CRA gave the Commission jurisdiction over certain leveraged retail foreign exchange contracts without regard to whether it could prove the contracts were off-exchange futures contracts. The CRA thus grants the Commission anti-fraud authority in leveraged retail forex transactions even if the transactions at issue are not futures or options. This allows the Commission to protect the public from fraud and provides a workable solution to the split in the decisions in the Federal appellate courts regarding when a so-called "spot" contract is a futures contract.

The CRA also created a new category of registrant, the retail foreign exchange dealer, or "RFED," and gave the Commission rulemaking authority over, and required registration of, intermediaries engaging in retail forex. The CRA provided that RFEDs and these other intermediaries must be NFA members and must register with the Commission subject to such terms as the Commission may prescribe. Among other requirements, the CRA established a $20 million minimum capital requirement for RFEDs and FCMs that offer retail forex.

The grant of authority over look-alike forex contracts is very broad and is intended to encompass transactions that do not result in actual delivery, or for which no legitimate business purpose exists for the customer to enter into the transaction. It is not intended to interfere with the large, sophisticated interbank market or to place additional requirements on businesses with a need to engage in forex transactions in connection with their legitimate business activities.

The CRA further provides that look-alike forex contracts are subject to the CFTC's authority if they are offered on a leveraged or margined basis, or financed by the offeror, counterparty, or someone acting with the offeror or counterparty. The Commission's authority, however, does not extend to securities, or to contracts that result in actual delivery within two days or that create an enforceable obligation to deliver between buyer and seller that have the ability to deliver or accept delivery in connection with their line of business. Thus, the CRA charges the Commission with regulating speculative forms of retail forex trading, but excludes from the Commission's purview true spot transactions that have a legitimate business purpose or that result in actual delivery. . . .

In the nine years since the passage of the [Commodity Futures Modernization Act], the Commission has observed a number of improper practices that have raised concern, among them solicitation fraud, a lack of transparency in the pricing and execution of transactions, unresponsiveness to customer complaints, and the targeting of unsophisticated, elderly, low net worth and other vulnerable individuals.[ii]

[ii] [N. 44] Between December 2000 and September 2009, the Commission has filed 114 forex-related enforcement actions on behalf of more than 26,000 customers. Those efforts have thus far resulted in the award of approximately $476 million in restitution

In addition to the regulations explicitly mandated by the CRA – including new registration requirements and enhanced financial requirements – the proposed regulations will require forex registrants to maintain records of customer complaints; require forex counterparties to guarantee the performance of all persons who introduce accounts to the counterparty; require counterparties to disclose, with the Risk Disclosure Statement, the percentage of profitable nondiscretionary forex customer accounts; and require forex counterparties to designate a chief compliance officer to be responsible for development and implementation of customer protection policies and procedures.

As noted above, the Commission believes that these additional requirements are militated both by the essential differences between on-exchange transactions and off-exchange retail forex transactions, and the history of fraudulent practices in this sector of the forex market. . . .

The CFTC ultimately finalized regulations reflecting the outline in their proposal.[7]

Exempted from registration as retail foreign exchange dealers are futures commission merchants, banks and bank holding companies, insurance companies and SEC-registered broker-dealers.[8]

Outside of the scope of CFTC regulation completely are spot foreign exchange transactions that do not use leverage or margin and are not financed by the offeror, the counterparty, or someone working with either, regardless of whether or not they are transacted in the retail market. What would be an example of such a transaction? An example would include an exchange of currency at, for example, an airport kiosk. The retail buyer or seller of currency does not maintain an account with the kiosk merchant and the kiosk merchant does not extend credit to the customer.

These transactions are not derivatives in an economic sense, either. They are not futures, options, or swaps. (*See* Chapter 1.) Though these transactions are outside the subject of this book, it should be noted that they are generally subject to Federal registration with the Financial Crimes Enforcement Network (commonly known as "FinCEN"), a bureau of the Department of the Treasury responsible for combatting money laundering.

---

and disgorgement, and $576 million in civil monetary penalties. An overwhelming majority of these cases have involved solicitation fraud.

D. FOREIGN EXCHANGE TRANSACTIONS AND REGULATION AS SWAPS

Before the passage of the Dodd-Frank Act, off-exchange foreign exchange transactions between eligible contract participants were not subject to CFTC or SEC regulation. The Dodd-Frank Act, however, brought any transaction falling within the CFTC's definition of swap within the CFTC's jurisdiction. Included in the Dodd-Frank Act's definition of "a swap" were currency options[9] and "currency swaps" and "foreign exchange swaps."[10]

However, the secretary of the treasury was vested with (and as we will see, exercised) the authority to limit the CFTC's jurisdiction:

> (i) . . . Foreign exchange swaps and foreign exchange forwards shall be considered swaps under this paragraph unless the Secretary [of the Treasury] makes a written determination . . . that either foreign exchange swaps or foreign exchange forwards or both . . .
> (I) should not be regulated as swaps . . . ; and
> (II) are not structured to evade the Dodd-Frank [Act] . . .
> (iii) Reporting
> Notwithstanding a written determination by the Secretary . . . all foreign exchange swaps and foreign exchange forwards shall be reported [in the same way as other products that qualify as swaps with the exception of real-time reporting] . . .
> (iv) Business standards
> Notwithstanding a written determination by the Secretary . . . any party to a foreign exchange swap or forward that is a swap dealer or major swap participant shall conform to . . . business conduct standards [applicable to swap dealers or major swap participants in other swap transactions] . . .

Commodity Exchange Act § 1a(47)(E).

In other words, if the secretary of the treasury determines that foreign exchange swaps and forwards are not swaps, then neither contribute to an assessment of whether registration as a swap dealer or major swap participant is required nor are subject to clearing and on-facility trading requirements. However, foreign exchange swaps and foreign exchange forwards would still be subject to reporting requirements (other than real-time reporting) and, if a party to a foreign exchange swap or foreign exchange forward were a registered swap dealer or major swap participant, it would still abide by the business conduct requirements applicable to swap dealers and major swap participants. For a description of these requirements, *see* Chapters 8 and 10.

A "foreign exchange swap" is defined as:

> [A] transaction that solely involves . . . an exchange of 2 different currencies on a specific date at a fixed rate that is agreed upon on the inception of the contract covering the exchange . . . [and] a reverse exchange of [those two currencies] at a later date and at a fixed rate that is agreed upon on the inception of the contract covering the exchange.

Commodity Exchange Act § 1a(25).

A "foreign exchange forward" is defined as:

> [A] transaction that solely involves the exchange of 2 different currencies on a specific future date at a fixed rate agreed upon on the inception of the contract covering the exchange.

Commodity Exchange Act § 1a(24).

What foreign exchange transactions are not foreign exchange swaps or foreign exchange forwards? Namely, currency or foreign exchange options; interest rate swaps with two currencies, known as "cross-currency swaps"; and cash-settled foreign exchange transactions, known as "non-deliverable forwards or "NDFs." All of these transaction types have the same regulatory treatment as swaps.

On November 20, 2012, Secretary of the Treasury Timothy Geithner determined to exempt foreign exchange swaps and forwards as authorized by the Dodd-Frank Act.

Determination of Foreign Exchange Swaps and Foreign Exchange Forwards Under the Commodity Exchange Act

77 Fed. Reg. 69694 (November 20, 2012)

. . . In general, swaps, including foreign exchange derivatives, carry three types of risks: (i) Counterparty credit risk prior to settlement; (ii) market risk; and (iii) settlement risk. Counterparty credit risk prior to settlement is the risk that a party to the transaction potentially could default prior to the settlement date, which could result in the non-defaulting party suffering an economic loss associated with having to replace the defaulted contract with another transaction at the then-current terms. Market risk is the risk that the value of the contract changes over the term of the transaction. In this context, market risk is intertwined with counterparty credit risk prior to settlement because the non-defaulting party (who thus bears the credit risk) also bears the risk that the value of the prior contract might have declined when that party seeks to replace the defaulted contract with another transaction. Settlement risk, particularly in the context of a foreign exchange swap or forward transaction, is the risk that the contract will not be settled in accordance with the initial terms, including when one party to the transaction delivers the currency it owes the counterparty, but does not receive the other currency from that counterparty. . . .

Settlement of most types of swaps and derivatives involves only payments of net amounts that are based on the changes in the value of the variables underlying the derivatives contracts. Given the features of most swaps and derivatives, including some types of foreign exchange derivatives, the clearing and exchange-trading requirements under the CEA, where applicable, would mitigate the relevant risks, notably counterparty credit risks prior to settlement.

By contrast, foreign exchange swap and forward participants know their own and their counterparties' payment obligations and the full extent of their exposures at settlement throughout the life of the contract. Thus, while the mark-to-market value of a position in a foreign exchange swap or forward may vary based on changes in the exchange rate or interest rates, the actual settlement amounts do not.

Under the regulatory regime enacted by the Dodd-Frank Act, foreign exchange swaps and forwards generally are subject to the requirements of the CEA and, in particular, would be subject to central clearing and exchange trading, unless the Secretary determines that foreign exchange swaps and forwards "(I) should not be regulated as swaps under [the CEA]; and (II) are not structured to evade [the Dodd-Frank Act] in violation of any rules promulgated by the [CFTC] pursuant to section 721(c) of the [Dodd-Frank Act]." . . .

The Secretary's authority to issue a determination is limited to foreign exchange swaps and forwards and does not extend to other foreign exchange derivatives. Foreign exchange options, currency swaps, and [non-deliverable forwards (NDFs)] . . . may not be exempted from the CEA's definition of "swap" because they do not satisfy the statutory definitions of a foreign exchange swap or forward. . . .

[T]he Secretary is issuing this determination to exempt foreign exchange swaps and forwards because of the distinctive characteristics of these instruments. Unlike most other swaps, foreign exchange swaps and forwards have fixed payment obligations, are settled by the exchange of actual currency, and are predominantly short-term instruments.

Counterparty credit risk prior to settlement is significantly reduced by the structure of a foreign exchange swap or forward transaction, particularly because the term for each type of transaction generally is very short. For the vast majority of foreign exchange swap or forward contracts, the risk profile is centered on settlement risk. Settlement risk often is addressed in foreign exchange swaps and forwards through the use of payment-versus-payment ("PVP") settlement arrangements,[iii] particularly with large financial institutions.

Treasury believes . . . that requiring central clearing and trading under the CEA on foreign exchange swaps and forwards would potentially introduce operational risks and challenges to the current settlement process. If central clearing were to be required, the central clearing facility would be effectively guaranteeing both settlement and market exposure to replacement cost. As a result, combining clearing and settlement in a market that involves settlement of the full principal amounts of the contracts would require capital backing, in a very large number of currencies, well in excess of what will be required for swaps that are settled on a "net" basis. Treasury believes that requiring foreign exchange swaps and forwards to be cleared and settled through the use of new systems and technologies could introduce new, unforeseen risks in this market. . . .

The Secretary's determination that foreign exchange swaps and forwards should not be regulated as "swaps" under the CEA does not affect the application of relevant provisions of the CEA that are designed to prevent evasion and improve market transparency. . . . [A]ll foreign exchange transactions would remain subject to the CFTC's new trade-reporting (but not the real-time reporting) requirements, enhanced anti-evasion authority, and . . . business-conduct standards. . . .

Unlike other types of swaps, foreign exchange swaps and forwards are distinct because, as defined by the CEA, these transactions must (1) involve the exchange of the principal amounts of the two currencies exchanged, as opposed to a set of cash flows based upon some floating reference rate, and (2) be settled on a physical basis.[iv]

A "swap" regulated under the CEA, such as a currency swap, interest rate swap, or other derivative, generally involves a periodic exchange of a floating amount of cash flows between the counterparties based on the value of the underlying variable(s) on which the derivative contract is based. In contrast, a foreign exchange swap (which will be exempt from the definition of "swap" under this determination) involves a simple exchange of principal at one point in time and a reversal of that exchange at some later date. For example, a user of a currency swap could seek funding advantages by obtaining financing in a foreign currency and swapping those cash flows back to the user's locally denominated currency. This would then entail paying or receiving a series of floating interest rate payments (i.e., based on prevailing interest rates) over the life of the transaction. This ability to receive periodic payments during the term of a

---

[iii] [N. 12] PVP settlement arrangements permit the final transfer of one currency to take place only if the final transfer of the other currency also takes place, thereby virtually eliminating settlement risk.

[iv] [N. 74] In this regard, Treasury notes that, in other swaps transactions, the parties may, by agreement, physically settle their obligations.

transaction is a significant feature of "swaps" that will be regulated under the CEA, which is absent from a foreign exchange swap or foreign exchange forward. . . .

Timothy F. Geithner, Secretary.

The CFTC, expressing concern about parties evading regulatory requirements, has noted that it:

> [Does] not want to enable market participants simply to label as 'spot' foreign exchange transactions that regularly settle after the relevant foreign exchange spot market settlement deadline, or with respect to which the parties intentionally delay settlement, both of which would be properly categorized as foreign exchange forwards, . . . in order to avoid applicable foreign exchange regulatory requirements."

Further Definition of "Swap," "Security-Based Swap," and "Security-Based Swap Agreement"; Mixed Swaps; Security-Based Swap Agreement Recordkeeping, 77 Fed. Reg. 48208 (August 13, 2012), 48257.

E. COMMODITY OPTIONS

Commodity options traded on a designated contract market are generally treated equivalently to commodity futures.

On the other hand, though in most cases commodity options traded outside of a designated contract market have the same treatment as other swaps, there is a significant exception for agricultural options. Agricultural options are in some cases exempt from nearly the entirety of the swaps regulatory regime. Their evolution to get to that point has been unique and irregular.

Gary E. Kalbaugh, The Erratic Journey of U.S. Commodity Options Regulation

33 No. 10 Futures & Derivatives L. Rep. 1 (Nov. 2013)

. . . The regulatory history of commodity options has been . . . circuitous. It includes moments of prohibition; forays into regulated exchange-traded and off-exchange commodity options; retrenchments into prohibitions; differing treatments for agricultural commodity options, options for physical delivery of non-agricultural products and options on non-agricultural futures; the inclusion of options for physical delivery of non-agricultural products and options on non-agricultural futures in the same framework for regulation of other derivatives; and, little more than a year ago, the convergence of treatment of options on agricultural commodities with other derivatives along with an exemption for commercial interests. . . .

The General Prohibition on Commodity Options

Prior to Federal regulation of commodity options, their status frequently varied. The Chicago Board of Trade prohibited them in 1865, before permitting them in 1869. Ruling in a bankruptcy case in 1874, a Federal court concluded that cash-settled options were prohibited under Illinois law as contracts which "partake of all of the characteristics of a wager" the effect of which "is to beget wild speculations, to derange prices, to make prices artificially high or low . . . thereby tending to destroy healthy business and unsettle legitimate commerce . . ." That same year the Illinois legislature banned grain options. . . . From 1906-1913 the Chicago Board of Trade permitted "indemnities" which, although economically identical to options, were characterized as being akin to insurance. In 1913, the Illinois legislature amended the 1874 legislation to narrow the prohibition on options only to those that were intended to be cash-settled. . . .

By 1932, the House of Representatives Committee on Agriculture had reported a bill prohibiting options on grain and additional commodities as "gambling transactions . . . objectionable also because they burden interstate commerce in that they lend themselves to improper uses by professional speculators and short sellers." . . .

[T]he Commodity Exchange Act of 1936 simply prohibited outright any options on the commodities subject to the statute . . .

The commodities subject to the Commodity Exchange Act were broader than the grains defined in the Grain Futures Act and ultimately included "wheat, cotton, rice, corn, oats, barley, rye, flaxseed, grain sorghums, mill feeds, butter, eggs, Solanum tuberosum (Irish potatoes), wool, wool tops, fats and oils (including lard, tallow, cottonseed oil, peanut oil, soybean oil and all other fats and oils), cottonseed meal, cottonseed, peanuts, soybeans, soybean meal, livestock, livestock products, and frozen concentrated orange juice." These commodities will be referred to herein as the "Enumerated Commodities" since, as a category, they continued until recently to have significant regulatory relevance.

Fraud in Options on Non-Enumerated Commodities

Although options on Enumerated Commodities were forbidden, the statutory prohibition did not apply to options on non-Enumerated Commodities . . . [T]hey seemingly fell into a regulatory lacuna between the Securities and Exchange Commission and the Commodity Exchange Commission, the body established by the Commodity Exchange Act to administer the act. Numerous commodity option firm failures occurred, in many cases amidst allegations of fraud. The most notorious one, Goldstein, Samuelson, Inc., parlayed $800 in capital into an investment empire selling $88 million in options and that eventually resulted in $70 million in customer losses.

Divided Statutory Treatment for Agricultural and non-Agricultural Commodities

To remedy the unregulated status of non-Enumerated Commodity futures and options, the Commodity Futures Trading Commission Act of 1974 . . . expanded [the definition of "commodity"] to include, in addition to the Enumerated Commodities, "all other goods and articles . . . and all services, rights, and interests in which contracts for future delivery are presently or in the future dealt in . . ." The Commodity Futures Trading Commission Act . . . maintained the Commodity Exchange Act's prohibition on options trading in Enumerated Commodities . . . [and] prohibited any options on non-Enumerated Commodities unless explicitly permitted under regulations of the newly formed Commodity Futures Trading Commission . . .

The First Attempt to Regulate Off-Exchange Options

. . . [A]fter evaluating the possible prohibition of options on non-Enumerated Commodities to parallel the one in place via statute with respect to Enumerated Commodities, the CFTC instead proposed a regulatory plan for options on non-Enumerated Commodities comprised of two phases. . . . The regulatory framework for the first phase was . . . comprised of a general prohibition on all trading of options on Enumerated Commodities combined with two exemptions which, in recognizable forms, survive in some way to the present. . . .

The first exemption was an exemption which required any person "soliciting or accepting orders for the purchase or sale of commodity options," or supervising any such person, to register as an associated person of a futures commission merchant. Futures commission merchants engaged in commodity option transactions were required to have more capital than futures commission merchants who limited their business to futures transactions. . . . This exemption existed to accommodate participation by speculators and non-speculator alike in the retail market in so-called "London options," i.e. options bought and sold on well-established options exchanges in London on precious metals and "world commodities" such as coffee and cocoa, and options on precious metals offered directly by domestic dealers. . . .

The other exemption was the so-called "trade option" exemption which allowed a commodity option to be offered without the dealer option requirements outlined above so long as the offeree had "a reasonable basis to believe that the option is offered to a producer, processor, or commercial user of, or a merchant handling, the commodity which is the subject of the commodity options transaction" and that the offeree entered "into the commodity option transaction solely for purposes related to its business as such." This exemption existed to accommodate commercial interests trading in commodity options for non-speculative purposes, such as hedging. . . .

[C]iting "fraudulent and other unlawful and unsound practices" in commodity options sales activities "[d]espite implementation and enforcement of the Commission's interim commodity option regulations" the CFTC . . . [declared a suspension of] all commodity option trading, including dealer options, other than option sales relying on the trade option exemption . . . effective . . . June 1, 1978. . . . Motivation for the ban was provided by the continuation of commodity option fraud on a par with that which existed before the Commodity Futures Trading Commission Act established CFTC jurisdiction. In one particularly egregious fraud, Alan Abrahams, an escaped convict going by the name of James A. Carr, established Lloyd Carr & Co. in July 1976 just one month after a spree of wrongdoing including an escape from a New Jersey prison farm in 1974, an arrest in Montreal and a disappearance before his deportation hearing, another arrest in Nassau where he apparently convinced the U.S. Consul to front his bail before fleeing, and a third arrest in California after floating a bad check to buy a used car. Annual sales at Lloyd Carr & Co. peaked at $50 million, despite operating in an environment where "some salesmen regularly made trips to the lavatory to smoke marijuana." . . .

On May 11, 1978, innocents expected to be harmed by the approaching ban petitioned the CFTC to disapply the ban to parties currently utilizing the dealer exemption and otherwise in good standing. . . . The CFTC relented and, just before the June 1 deadline for the effective date of the ban, provided that the dealer exemption would remain available for entities which, on May 1, 1978, were "both in the business of granting options on a physical commodity and in the business of buying, selling, producing, or otherwise utilizing that commodity" so long as net worth and other criteria aimed at customer protection were met. . . .

[T]he Futures Trading Act of 1978 codified many of the CFTC's recent actions with respect to commodity options. . . .

Following passage of the Futures Trading Act, the CFTC implemented a final rule restating much of the dealer option exemption regime . . . [without a] notice of proposed rulemaking. . . .

[T]he rule was withdrawn and re-proposed in substantially similar form one month later. The rule was re-re-proposed in a substantially modified form again over two years later in April 1981 presumably spurred by an industry campaign to roll-back the options prohibition to allow non-grandfathered entities to trade dealer options and then was the subject of an advanced notice of a proposed rulemaking in March 1985. It was never finalized, leaving the prohibition on off-exchange options trading intact until the passage of the Commodity Futures Modernization Act of 2000, save for grandfathered dealers relying on the dealer option exemption as of May 1, 1978 and for parties relying on the trade option exemption. . . .

A Renewed Effort for Exchange-Traded Commodity Options

The early 1980s saw a renewed drive to establish exchange-traded commodity options trading. . . .

Congress' passage of the Futures Trading Act of 1982 allowed for the possibility, with CFTC assent, of trading options on Enumerated Commodities. . . .

[B]y January 1987, the exchange trading of commodity options – without further distinction between options on non-Enumerated Commodity futures, non-Enumerated Commodity physicals or Enumerated Commodities – was permanently established. . . .

Commodity Futures Modernization Act of 2000

The impact of the Commodity Futures Modernization Act was as sweeping with respect to commodity options as it was for other derivatives. Other than with regard to "agricultural commodities" and fraud, the CFTC's jurisdiction over off-exchange derivatives transactions between "eligible contract participants," i.e. high net worth entities or persons, was eviscerated. In a way, the clock was wound back to 1975. Just like in 1975, the CFTC had anti-fraud jurisdiction over all commodity options. The primary differences were that now: (1) exchange-traded options were permissible; and (2) instead of off-exchange options on Enumerated Commodities being prohibited, the CFTC's regulations now only applied to the "agricultural commodities," a category comprised of, at a minimum, the Enumerated Commodities.

The Dodd-Frank Act

The interlude of deregulation of most commodity options – and most derivatives for that matter – was to last less than a decade. In 2010, the Dodd-Frank Wall Street Reform and Consumer Protection Act, known as the Dodd-Frank Act, granted the CFTC jurisdiction over nearly all swaps, with "swaps" defined to clearly include all commodity options other than exchange-traded options on futures over which the CFTC maintained its pre-Dodd-Frank Act jurisdiction. The Dodd-Frank Act also imposed an intricate regulatory apparatus with respect to swaps activities.

Options on "agricultural commodities," having remained subject to CFTC regulation even after the passage of the CFMA, continued to be subject to CFTC regulation (along with agricultural swaps). To harmonize the nascent regulatory regime for swaps with that for options on "agricultural commodities" and agricultural swaps, the CFTC proposed merging the pre-existing regulatory regime for agricultural options and swaps into Dodd-Frank's regulatory regime for all other swaps. The final rules provide for this absorption of the agricultural swaps and options regime into the Dodd-Frank regulatory regime for swaps while re-instating a trade option exemption covering non-financial commodities (including agricultural options).

The trade option exemption itself requires that the offeree be a "producer, processor, or commercial user of, or a merchant handling the commodity that is the subject of the commodity option transaction, or the products or by-products thereof, and such offeree is offered or entering into the commodity option transaction solely for purposes related to its business as such" and that the offeror either meet the preceding criteria or be an eligible contract participant. Additionally, the offeror must have a "reasonable basis to believe" that the offeree meets the trade option criteria and there must be an intent to physically deliver the commodity underlying the option. Trade options are generally exempt "from the rules otherwise applicable to other swaps (i.e., the Dodd-Frank swaps regime)." Compliance obligations for non-CFTC registrants are limited to recordkeeping and reporting. CFTC-registered swap dealers and major swap participants must comply with risk management, capital and margin requirements in addition to recordkeeping and reporting requirements.

Options on agricultural commodities had evolved from being prohibited outright to being, in the context of trade options, the least regulated derivative under the CFTC's jurisdiction. . . .

QUESTIONS AND COMMENTS

1. What may have been some of the motivations underlying the Department of the Treasury's lobbying for the "Treasury Amendment" in the time period immediately preceding passage of the Commodity Futures Trading Commission Act of 1974?
2. Why did the Dodd-Frank Act, with respect to foreign exchange swaps and foreign exchange forwards, maintain the regulatory tradition of treating foreign exchange transactions distinctly?
3. Consider why Congress in passing the Dodd-Frank Act only allowed limited foreign exchange exemptions from the Dodd-Frank Act and only with respect to foreign exchange swaps and foreign exchange forwards. In what ways do these merit distinct regulatory treatment from, say, a cross-currency swap, currency option, or non-deliverable foreign exchange forward?
4. What are some more examples of transaction that would be exempt from regulation as non-margined spot foreign exchange transactions? What about transactions that would be considered swaps because they do not fall within the CFTC's definition of a spot foreign exchange transaction?

5. Historically, the CFTC has struggled to regulate commodity options, even resorting to nearly entirely prohibiting them. Is there a reason options might raise public policy concerns not arising with futures?

CHAPTER 13
PUBLIC ENFORCEMENT

A. BACKGROUND

It has been noted that "[f]raud is as varied as the ingenuity of man."[1] A large motivation for the regulation of marketplaces is the prevention of fraud. Fraud has many guises. It can be as straightforward as embezzlement, predatory as so-called Ponzi schemes,[2] or as broad-scaled as manipulations of the market.

Market manipulation itself takes many forms, some of which we will examine. We will also examine the CFTC's authority to prevent market manipulation and the role of position limits in combatting market manipulations such as "market corners."

The Dodd-Frank Act greatly expanded the CFTC's enforcement authority by broadening the scope of conduct that could result in CFTC enforcement actions and by including swaps within the scope of the entire range of the CFTC's enforcement authority, instead of just its anti-fraud authority. We will examine the CFTC's authority, as expanded. Though some of the cases we look at are pre-Dodd-Frank Act, these represent the baseline for the CFTC's authority since they occurred before it was expanded.

This expansion in authority tracks a similar expansion in CFTC enforcement volume and awards, shown in Figure 13-A below.[3]

In addition to the enforcement powers granted to the CFTC, the Commodity Exchange Act and CFTC rules directly or indirectly provide various means for private enforcement of the Act through court proceedings or in reparations proceedings before the CFTC. We examine these in Chapter 14.

FIGURE 13-A: CFTC ENFORCEMENT ACTIVITY: 2002-2013

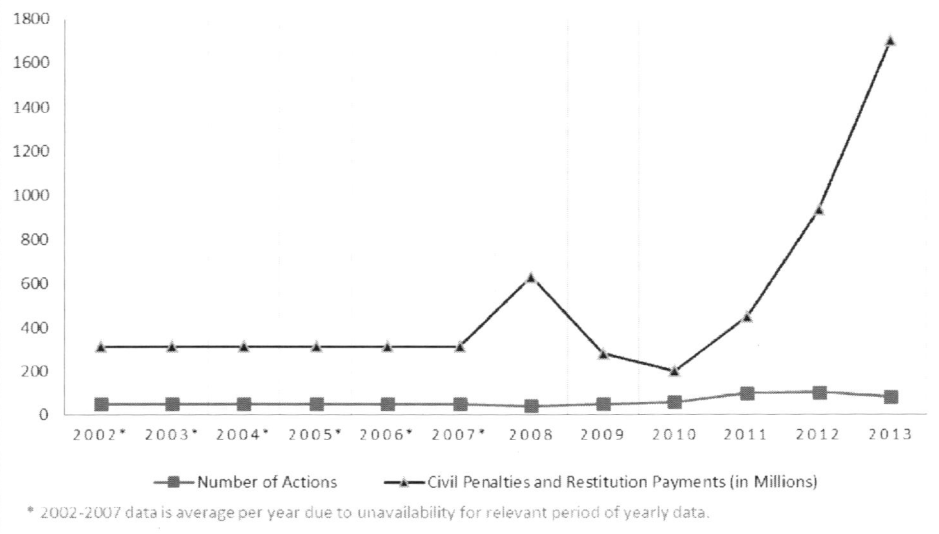

B. GENERAL FRAUD PROHIBITIONS

The Commodity Exchange Act has specific provisions intended to combat market manipulation. These need to be examined in light of provisions that prohibit fraud generally.

1. *Civil Proceedings*

a. Prohibitions

The Commodity Exchange Act makes it unlawful in connection with a commodity future or swap:

> . . . (A) to cheat or defraud or attempt to cheat or defraud the other [party to the transaction or potential transaction]; (B) willfully to make or cause to be made to the other person any false report[,] . . . statement or . . . record; [or] (C) willfully to deceive or attempt to deceive the other person by any means whatsoever in regard to any order or contract. . . .

Commodity Exchange Act § 4b(a).

With respect to swaps particularly, the Commodity Exchange Act also imposes liability on a party entering into a swap for fraud on the part of its counterparty by prohibiting entering:

> into a swap knowing, or acting in reckless disregard of the fact, that its counterparty will use the swap as part of a device, scheme, or artifice to defraud any third party. . . .

Commodity Exchange Act § 4c(a)(7).

This swap-specific provision exists because many categories of swaps are bilaterally negotiated, making substantive contacts between the parties on the subject of the swap possible, unlike the designated contract market for commodity futures where contracts are standardized and counterparties are anonymous.

Finally, CFTC Rule 180.1(a) (17 C.F.R. § 180.1(a)) imposes a recklessness standard by making it unlawful:

> in connection with any swap, or contract of sale of any commodity in interstate commerce, or contract for future delivery on or subject to the rules of any [designated contract market, swap execution facility, derivatives clearing organization, or swap data repository], to intentionally or recklessly:
>
> (1) Use or employ, or attempt to use or employ, any manipulative device, scheme, or artifice to defraud;
>
> (2) Make, or attempt to make, any untrue or misleading statement of a material fact or to omit to state a material fact necessary in order to make the statements made not untrue or misleading; [or]
>
> (3) Engage, or attempt to engage, in any act, practice, or course of business, which operates or would operate as a fraud or deceit upon any person . . .

CFTC Rule 180.1 (17 C.F.R. § 180.1).

b. Sanctions

The CFTC has the authority, pursuant to Commodity Exchange Act § 6(c)(4), to initiate and conduct a civil enforcement hearing for violation of the Commodity Exchange Act or any CFTC rule and may impose:

- A prohibition on trading on a designated contract market or swap execution facility[4];
- Suspension of the registration of any CFTC registrant[5];
- Penalties of up to the greater of $140,000 (or $1,000,000 for certain market manipulation offenses) or triple the monetary gain from the violation[6]; and
- Restitution for any customer losses caused by the violation.[7]

2. *Criminal Proceedings*

If a violation of the Commodity Exchange Act or a CFTC rule is wilful, then pursuant to Commodity Exchange Act § 9(a)(5), such violation is a felony, punishable by a $1,000,000 fine plus costs of prosecution and imprisonment of up to 10 years (with an exception, solely for imprisonment, which provides that a person cannot be imprisoned for a violation of this section if she proves that she had no "knowledge of such rule or regulation. . . ."[8]

It is also a felony knowingly:

> [T]o make, or cause to be made, any statement in any application, report, or document required to be filed under [the Commodity Exchange Act] . . . or any [CFTC] rule . . . which statement was false or misleading with respect to any material fact, or knowingly to omit any material fact required to be stated therein or necessary to make the statements therein not misleading . . . [or to willfully] falsify, conceal, or cover up by any trick, scheme, or artifice a material fact, make any false, fictitious, or fraudulent statements or representations, or make or use any false writing or document knowing the same to contain any false, fictitious, or fraudulent statement or entry to . . . [a board of trade, a swap execution facility, a derivatives clearing organization, a swap data repository, or the National Futures Association].

Commodity Exchange Act §§ 9(a)(3) and (4).

As described above in section B1, the CFTC has broad scope to bring civil enforcement hearings. It does not have the authority to bring a criminal complaint and is dependent upon the Department of Justice to actually prosecute criminal violations. In practice, the prosecution of a common fraud committed by a CFTC registrant is typically based on both the relevant

Commodity Exchange Act provision and the Federal mail and wire fraud statutes, which prohibit fraud generally.[9]

Not long after passage of the Commodity Futures Trading Commission Act of 1974 questions arose as to the extent to which Congress intended to permit usage of Federal statutes criminalizing fraud generally in the context of commodities fraud.

United States v. Abrahams

493 F. Supp. 296 (S.D.N.Y. 1980)

Conner, District Judge:

Defendant Alan Herbert Abrahams ("Abrahams") is charged with one count of violating the conspiracy statute and forty-nine counts of violating the mail fraud and wire fraud statutes, 18 U.S.C. ss 1341 and 1343, respectively. The charges arise out of his operation, between July 1, 1976 and January 15, 1978, of Lloyd, Carr & Company, which was in the business of offering to the public options to purchase or sell futures contracts on commodities traded on markets in London, England. . . . [T]he Government charges that Abrahams knowingly engaged in a conspiracy to obtain money by means of a scheme to defraud investors by employing such techniques as . . . representing to customers that Lloyd, Carr & Company would purchase options for them when in fact such options were never purchased; disseminating false and misleading recommendations respecting commodity options to the public; and employing unskilled salespersons who were encouraged to use high pressure techniques to sell options to the public. . . . [The Government also] charge[s] defendant with mail fraud or wire fraud:[i] the Government alleges that having devised the scheme to defraud the public . . . defendant then utilized the mails and the wires to send confirmations of purchases of options to customers and to place orders for the purchase of options for Lloyd, Carr & Company customers.

Abrahams moves to dismiss the indictment on several grounds [including]: (1) that he is being prosecuted under the wrong criminal statute; [and] (2) that he is being selectively prosecuted. . . .

Abrahams contends that for federal prosecutions for mail and wire fraud involving commodity options, the exclusive vehicle is the . . . [Commodity Exchange Act] ("the Act") . . . ; that by its enactment Congress intended that commodity options would be regulated solely under the Act; and that Congress implicitly repealed those provisions of other, more general statutes, including the mail and wire fraud statutes, imposing penalties for conduct now proscribed as criminal under the Act. . . .

---

[i] [N. 4] The wire fraud statute, 18 U.S.C. s 1343, is modeled after the mail fraud statute, 18 U.S.C. s 1341. The Court will discuss them collectively as the mail fraud statute.

Abrahams further contends that . . . [section] of the Act . . . which prohibits the use of the United States mails or any means of interstate commerce to perpetuate fraudulent schemes involving commodity options, was intended by Congress to be the sole means by which fraudulent conduct in the commodities field, including such conduct as is alleged in the instant indictment, should be prosecuted, even if that conduct violates the mail fraud statute as well.

The Government argues that neither the express wording of the Act nor its legislative history offers any support for defendant's theory that the Government is prohibited from prosecuting fraudulent schemes involving commodity options under the general criminal antifraud statutes, such as the mail fraud statute. The Government's position is that the mail fraud statute serves as a useful supplement to the criminal antifraud sanctions provided by Congress in the Act and that the two statutes . . . work in harmony in attempting to prevent fraud and misrepresentation in the commodities field. For the reasons that follow, this Court shares the Government's view. . . .

Defendant contends that by enacting the . . . [Commodity Futures Trading Commission Act of 1974,] a comprehensive statutory scheme to regulate trading in futures[,] Congress intended to repeal, by implication, the more general mail fraud statute insofar as it relates to schemes to defraud involving futures.

Whether the passage of a specific law precludes prosecution under a more general law covering the same offense is a question of legislative intent. The law is well settled, however, that repeal by implication is not favored and that it follows only where the later act is clearly intended to be in substitution for the earlier act.

In order to determine whether the Act's specific antifraud provision should be deemed to have repealed the mail fraud statute, this Court must first examine the legislative history of the Act to determine whether Congress expressed an intent partially to repeal the mail fraud statute and, second, must examine the two statutes to determine whether there is a repugnancy in the subject matter of the two statutes which would justify an implication of repeal. . . .

A review of the legislative history of the Act establishes that Congress intended to vest the Commodity Futures Trading Commission ("the Commission") with exclusive jurisdiction over the regulation of commodity futures; however, the legislative history does not support defendant's view that Congress, by the "exclusive jurisdiction" language, intended that prosecutions for fraudulent schemes involving commodity options would lie solely under the Act.

Prior to the enactment of the 1974 Act . . . a regulatory gap . . . existed and some forms of futures went unregulated. . . . [Accordingly,] Congress created a single federal agency equipped with broad authority to regulate futures trading and exchange activities. . . .

In addition to broad rule-making authority, the Commission was equipped with significant enforcement powers, including the authority to conduct investigations; to issue cease and desist orders; to obtain court-ordered injunctions; and to punish specified fraudulent conduct with fines . . . or imprisonment. . . .

The legislative history makes clear that Congress intended the Commission to exercise sole jurisdiction over the regulation of futures contracts. . . .

Although Congress equipped the Commission with the power to prosecute violations of the Act by including civil and criminal sanctions in the Act, there is no indication in the legislative history of a Congressional intent to make the criminal sanction provisions of the Act the sole vehicle for prosecuting fraud in the sale of futures. The various House, Senate, and Conference Reports make no reference to the general federal criminal statutes, except for the antitrust statutes, or the potential impact of the Act on those general statutes.

The little evidence relevant to this issue in the legislative history supports the Government's view that Congress contemplated that both the Act and the general criminal antifraud statutes would be utilized to punish fraud in futures markets. . . .

[I]n introducing the 1974 Act to the Senate for consideration, Senator Talmadge, Chairman of the Senate Committee on Agriculture and Forestry, stated:

> "In establishing this Commission, it is the committee's intent to give it exclusive jurisdiction over those areas delineated in the act. This will assure that the affected entities-exchanges, traders, customers, et cetera will not be subject to conflicting agency rulings. However, it is not the intent of the committee to exempt persons in the futures trading industry from existing laws or regulations such as the antitrust laws . . . ." 120 Cong. Rec. S. 30459 (Sept. 9, 1974).

In summary, there is no indication in the legislative history that, with the passage of the Act, Congress intended to repeal the general federal criminal antifraud statutes insofar as they relate to commodity futures. The Court must next determine whether there is a repugnancy in the subject matter of the two statutes which would justify an implication of repeal. . . .

The language of the mail fraud statute is broad: it condemns any scheme to defraud in which the mails are employed . . . And even where Congress has enacted comprehensive legislation, including criminal sanctions, to govern conduct in a particular field, the courts have very often held that the mail fraud statute continues in force. . . .

Despite the pervasive Government regulation of the drug industry, postal fraud statutes still play an important role in controlling the solicitation of mail-order purchases by drug distributors based upon fraudulent misrepresentations. . . .

The mail fraud statute and the criminal provisions of the Act are not in conflict; instead, they complement each other. The Court concludes that there is no conflict between the two statutory provisions which would justify an implication of repeal.

For the foregoing reasons, the Court concludes that the mail fraud statute has not been implicitly repealed by . . . the Act. Defendant's motion to dismiss on the ground that the exclusive jurisdiction for prosecuting defendant lies under the Act is denied. . . .

Defendant moves to dismiss the indictment in the instant matter on the ground that this is a selective prosecution.

Defendant alleges that in the past eight years, the Commodity Futures Trading Commission has instituted a criminal proceeding against an individual for the type of violations alleged herein on only one other occasion, while defendant's review of reported decisions reveals that the Commission has instituted civil proceedings against commodity trading houses for violations similar to those charged in the instant indictment in more than two hundred instances. Defendant contends that the Commission's institution of criminal, as contrasted with civil, proceedings in only 1% of the cases demonstrates that the agency has singled him out for criminal prosecution. The Government disputes the accuracy of defendant's figures.

Defendant contends that he has been singled out for criminal prosecution because he was actively involved in opposing the new rules and regulations concerning the commodity trading industry proposed by the Commission. Defendant's company was a plaintiff in an action instituted against the Commission which sought to enjoin the agency from implementing these new rules. He also voiced his opposition to the new rules and regulations at hearings held before the United States Congress. Defendant alleges that on three occasions agents of the Commission informed him that his activities would "cost him his business." . . .

A defendant is entitled to an evidentiary hearing on a claim of selective prosecution where he has made an initial showing that there is a colorable basis for his contention.

Abrahams has not supported his contentions with any evidentiary matter; he has not submitted any documentary evidence or affidavits to the Court. Accordingly, the Court will deny Abrahams' request for an evidentiary hearing without prejudice to renewal of the motion at a later date if a proper evidentiary basis for the motion is laid. . . .

A person making a materially false statement to the Federal government could have criminal liability.[10] This has the potential to arise with persons registered with the CFTC if, for example, reports to the CFTC are falsified. This, and the process by which a fraud is addressed by Federal authorities, is illustrated by the prosecution of the decades-long customer fraud that occurred at Peregrine Financial Group, Inc., formerly a CFTC-registered futures commission merchant.

United States v. Wasendorf

2012 WL 4052834 (N.D. Iowa Sept. 13, 2012)

Jon Stuart Scoles, United States Chief Magistrate Judge. . . .

On the 11th day of September 2012, this matter came on for hearing to determine whether Defendant Russell R. Wasendorf, Sr. should be detained pending further proceedings. . . .

On July 11, 2012, Defendant was charged by criminal complaint with making and using false statements in a matter within the jurisdiction of the Government of the United States, in violation of 18 U.S.C. § 1001(a)(1) and (3).

On August 13, 2012, Defendant was charged in the instant action with 31 counts of making and using false documents in violation of 18 U.S.C. § 1001(a)(3). Defendant was arraigned on August 17, and trial was scheduled for October 15. On September 7, the Court was advised that Defendant was asking for a detention hearing. The hearing was . . . scheduled for September 11. . . .

On Monday, July 9, 2012, Black Hawk County sheriff's deputies responded to a call of a suspicious vehicle outside the offices of Peregrine Financial Group, Inc. in Cedar Falls, Iowa. Deputies found Defendant unconscious inside the vehicle, with a hose connected to the exhaust pipe cut into the convertible roof. A bottle of vodka was found in the car and authorities later learned that Defendant had taken sleeping pills which he had "stockpiled" during the previous two months. Defendant was transported to the University of Iowa Hospitals in Iowa City, where he remained until he was arrested four days later. . . .

Defendant is the chairman and CEO of Peregrine Financial Group, Inc. ("PFG"). Found in the car was a four-page typed note in which Defendant admits committing fraud in connection with the business.

> Through a scheme of using false bank statements I have been able to embezzle millions of dollars from customer accounts at Peregrine Financial Group, Inc. The forgeries started nearly twenty years ago and have gone undetected until now.

Note of Russell R. Wasendorf, Sr.

According to Defendant's note, "[m]ost of the misappropriated funds went to maintain the increasing levels of Regulatory Capital to keep PFG in business and to pay business loses [*sic*], with a portion being used to build the office building at One Peregrine Way." In his note, Defendant states that "I am ready to die. I guess this is the only way out of a business I hate so much."

At the hearing, Special Agent William Langdon of the Federal Bureau of Investigation provided details regarding Defendant's criminal activity. Briefly stated, Defendant diverted funds from a bank account, which was intended to hold segregated customer funds, to his own uses. For example, customer funds were used to support a restaurant ("My Verona") owned by Defendant in Cedar

Falls, and a construction and development company in Romania, partially owned by Defendant.

Defendant concealed his illegal activity by falsifying bank statements. For example, a fake bank statement prepared by Defendant for the period ending May 31, 2012 shows a balance in the customer's segregated account of $224,830,835.85. The true balance in the account at that time was $5,446,891,086 [*sic*; presumably, $5,446,891.86 is intended]. . . . Defendant also filed false statements with the Commodity Futures Trading Commission ("CFTC"). . . .

The parties have entered into a plea agreement, which was signed by Defendant and his attorney on September 7 and by the prosecutors on September 11. According to the agreement, Defendant will waive indictment and plead guilty to a four-count Information charging him with mail fraud, embezzlement of customer funds by a person registered under the Commodity Exchange Act, making false statements to the Commodity Futures Trading Commission, and making false statements to a futures association registered under the Commodity Exchange Act. Collectively, the charges carry a maximum prison term of 50 years.

In the plea agreement, Defendant stipulates to facts supporting the charges. Specifically, Defendant admits that beginning in the early 1990s, he "fraudulently obtained and misappropriated for his own use customer funds that were supposed to be maintained by PFG for the benefit of and use by such customers to margin, guarantee, or secure commodities futures and options trades." The full amount of the loss is undetermined, but Defendant admits that he "embezzled and otherwise misappropriated in excess of $100,000,000 in PFG customer funds." Defendant also admits making false reports to the CFTC and the National Futures Association ("NFA"), a not-for-profit industry membership corporation operated under the supervision of the CFTC.

Special Agent Langdon testified that Defendant has been cooperative with law enforcement authorities, and with a court appointed receiver, in attempting to locate and recover assets. On July 27 – just two weeks after he was arrested – Defendant met for approximately six hours with two FBI agents, two assistant United States attorneys, the receiver from Chicago, and the receiver's attorney. One month later, on August 27, Defendant met again for approximately six hours with an FBI agent, an assistant United States attorney, a postal inspector, the bankruptcy trustee, the receiver, and two or three CFTC attorneys. Langdon acknowledged that one of the CFTC attorneys was "aggressive" in his questioning, including raising his voice, but Defendant continued to cooperate and did not "lose his cool." According to Langdon, Defendant attempted to answer all of the questions put to him, and is willing to cooperate further. Letters from AUSA Deegan to Defendant's counsel confirm that Defendant "has not requested a proffer agreement or any other protection" with regard to the interviews. . . .

On July 10, 2012 – the day after Defendant's attempted suicide – the CFTC filed an action against PFG and Defendant in the United States District Court for the Northern District of Illinois. As part of that action, a receiver was appointed to "[t]ake exclusive custody, control, and possession of all funds, property, and other assets in the possession, ownership, or control" of Defendant and any of his businesses, wherever situated, including property held jointly by Defendant and others. Also on July 10, PFG filed a Chapter 7 bankruptcy petition in the United States Bankruptcy Court for the Northern District of Illinois. Special Agent Langdon testified at the instant hearing that either the receiver, the bankruptcy trustee, or the FBI have taken possession of, or restrained, all of Defendant's known assets, with the exception of those in Romania. . . .

On September 10 . . . the receiver filed a 29-page First Report . . . [which] describes Defendant's assets.

- My Verona, the restaurant owned by Defendant in Cedar Falls, "never generated a profit" and has ceased operating.

- Wasendorf & Associates, Inc. is a publishing business which includes an online bookstore and an online magazine geared toward futures trading. The receiver . . . is attempting to sell the assets.

- Wasendorf Construction, LLC . . . owns several buildings used by Defendant's other businesses, including the PFG corporate headquarters in Cedar Falls.

- Wasendorf Air, LLC . . . [owns] a Hawker Beechcraft model 400A. . . .

- Rhombus Asset Management, Inc. is a company owned by Defendant and others to invest in Romanian real estate and related ventures. . . .

- Peregrine Charities is a 501(c)(3) corporation founded by Defendant and organized for charitable purposes. . . .

- The receiver also identified and has preserved various bank accounts held by Defendant or his businesses.

- Defendant owns his personal residence in Cedar Falls, another home in Cedar Falls used by PFG as a "corporate residence" for visiting staff and corporate guests, and a condominium in Chicago. . . .

- The receiver has surrendered a life insurance policy which had a cash surrender value of $1,287,339.55. . . .

- The receiver is making arrangements to sell Defendant's personal property, including a wine collection, motor vehicles, and boats. . . .

In an additional ironic twist, just months before the Peregrine fraud was uncovered, Peregrine had commissioned a white paper on protecting customer funds entitled "Commodity Customer Protections and Regulations: History and Potential Solutions for the Future 1938-2012" for the Commodity Customer Coalition, a not-for-profit group formed in the wake of the MF Global failure.[11]

C. MARKET MANIPULATION GENERALLY

Fraud of the Peregrine variant, where funds of third parties are embezzled, can be found in many contexts, including outside of the derivatives markets. Market manipulation is a specific type of fraud in which, instead of directly stealing customer funds (as, for example, occurred with Peregrine), the integrity of the market is compromised for the benefit of the perpetrator of the manipulation. This type of fraud requires the existence of an established market, such as the derivatives or securities markets.

The Commodity Exchange Act has a number of provisions specific to market manipulation. Some of these ban market manipulation generically and others ban particular types of market manipulation. We will examine the generic statutory prohibitions here. The statutory provisions focusing on particular types of manipulation are examined below in section D under the heading for each such type of manipulation.

1. *Civil Prohibitions on Market Manipulation*

Commodity Exchange Act § 6(c)

Prohibition regarding manipulation and false information

(1) Prohibition against manipulation

It shall be unlawful for any person . . . to use or employ, or attempt to use or employ, in connection with any swap, or a contract of sale of any commodity in interstate commerce, or for future delivery on or subject to the rules of any registered entity, any manipulative or deceptive device or contrivance . . .

(A) Special provision for manipulation by false reporting

Unlawful manipulation for purposes of this paragraph shall include, but not be limited to, delivering, or causing to be delivered . . . a false or misleading or inaccurate report concerning crop or market information or conditions that affect or tend to affect the price of any commodity in interstate commerce, knowing, or acting in reckless disregard of the fact that such report is false, misleading or inaccurate. . . .

(C) Good faith mistakes

Mistakenly transmitting, in good faith, false or misleading or inaccurate information to a price reporting service would not be sufficient to violate paragraph (1)(A). . . .

(3) Other manipulation . . .

[I]t shall be unlawful for any person, directly or indirectly, to manipulate or attempt to manipulate the price of any swap, or of any commodity in interstate commerce, or for future delivery on or subject to the rules of any . . . [designated contract market, swap execution facility, derivatives clearing organization or swap data repository].

Above, in section B, we examined the civil and criminal general anti-fraud provisions of the Commodity Exchange Act. The civil sanctions for market manipulation are the same, save that the potential civil penalty is up to the greater of $1,000,000 (instead of $140,000 for violations of the Commodity Exchange Act and CFTC rules generally) or triple the monetary gain from the violation.

In 2012, JPMorgan suffered a more than $6 billion loss due to the trading activities of a London-based trader taking very large positions in the credit default swap market who was known to the marketplace as the "London Whale."

In the Matter of JPMorgan Chase Bank, N.A.

CFTC Docket No. 14-01 (Oct. 16, 2013)

ORDER INSTITUTING PROCEEDINGS PURSUANT TO SECTIONS 6(c) AND 6(d) OF THE COMMODITY EXCHANGE ACT, MAKING FINDINGS AND IMPOSING REMEDIAL SANCTIONS . . .

The Commodity Futures Trading Commission ("Commission") has reason to believe that JPMorgan Chase Bank, N.A. ("JPMorgan") violated the Commodity Exchange Act ("Act") and Commission Regulations ("Regulations"). Therefore, the Commission deems it appropriate and in the public interest that public administrative proceedings be, and hereby are, instituted to determine whether JPMorgan has engaged in the violations as set forth herein and to determine whether any order should be issued imposing remedial sanctions. . . .

In anticipation of the institution of this administrative proceeding, JPMorgan has submitted an Offer of Settlement ("Offer"), which the Commission has determined to accept. . . .

The credit default swap ("CDS") market comprises globally traded credit derivatives used by various market participants to speculate on and hedge against credit defaults, and, as a result of the Dodd-Frank Wall Street Reform and Consumer Protection Act of 2010 ("Dodd-Frank Act"), the market for CDS that reference broad-based credit indices is subject to the Commission's jurisdiction. Tens of trillions of dollars in notional value of CDS instruments are traded and held by market participants seeking to transfer risk of credit defaults by companies in the United States and around the world. As such, the CDS market is an important aspect of the global economy. Market participants are entitled to rely on the notion that CDS prices are established based on legitimate forces of supply and demand. However, on February 29, 2012, JPMorgan traders acted recklessly with respect to this fundamental precept by employing an aggressive trading strategy concerning a particular type of CDS known as "CDX."

From approximately 2007 through 2011, a JPMorgan unit, the Chief Investment Office ("CIO"), operating through a trading desk in a JPMorgan branch in London, purchased and sold default protection in a portfolio of CDX and other credit default indices. As of the end of 2011, the CIO held a substantial position in CDX and other credit default indices, with a net notional value of more than $51 billion, including $217 billion in long risk positions and $166 billion in short risk positions. At the end of each trading day, traders in the CIO "marked" the positions in this swaps portfolio "to market," assigning a value to the portfolio's positions using various measures including market prices for the credit default index positions. The traders' marks were used to calculate profits and losses ("P&L").

Although previously quite profitable, as early as late January 2012 the portfolio's value had taken a serious turn for the worse. In February 2012, daily losses were large and growing, and by February 29 the traders believed the portfolio's situation was grave. Just ahead of critical February month-end internal portfolio valuations that would be distributed widely within JPMorgan through the P&L statement, the traders in the CIO, who wanted to reduce mark-to-market losses, recklessly employed an aggressive trading strategy on February 29 in connection with one particular CDX, the CDX.NA.IG.9 10 year index ("IG9 10Y"). In particular, as the value of the portfolio stood to benefit as the IG9 l0Y market price dropped, on February 29, the CIO sold on net more than $7 billion of IG9 l0Y, a staggering, record-setting, volume, $4.6 billion of which was sold during a three hour period as that day drew to a close. The February 29 trading followed sales of protection of more than $3 billion of this index in the previous two days. To put the quantity sold by the CIO into perspective, the net volume sold by the CIO over those three days amounted to roughly one-third of the volume traded for the entire month of February by all other market participants. During this same period at month-end, the market price on IG9 10Y dropped substantially and the CIO was selling at generally declining prices. The value of the position that the CIO held benefited on a mark-to-market basis from the declining market prices.[ii]

JPMorgan's controls and supervision over the CIO did not prevent the CIO from first accumulating the massive portfolio of positions in certain CDX and other credit default indices, and then from taking the steps to conceal the losses. In July 2012, JPMorgan's parent company disclosed that it had lost confidence in the integrity of the traders' marks and acknowledged that it ultimately lost more than $6 billion in 2012 in connection with the CIO's CDS index trading. . . .

The Act, as modified by the Dodd-Frank Act, provides the Commission with exclusive jurisdiction over accounts, agreements and transactions involving swaps, except to the extent otherwise provided by the Dodd-Frank Act . . .

Section 6(c)(1) of the Act provides, among other things, that it is unlawful for any person "to employ, or attempt to use or employ, in connection with any swap . . . any manipulative or deceptive device or contrivance, in contravention of [Commission rules and regulations]." Commission Regulation 180.1(a), 17 C.F.R. §180.1 (2012), which became effective on August 15, 2011, in relevant part, makes it unlawful for any person:

> in connection with any swap . . . to intentionally or recklessly: (1) Use or employ, or attempt to use or employ, any manipulative device, scheme, or artifice to defraud; (2) Make, or attempt to make, any untrue or misleading statement of a material fact or to omit to state a material fact necessary in order to make the statements made not untrue or misleading; (3) Engage, or attempt to engage, in any act, practice, or course of business, which operates or would operate as a fraud or deceit upon any person. . . .

[ii] [N. 3] Two now former JPMorgan traders have been accused of concealing trading losses from others at JPMorgan by using deceptive practices in how they marked the portfolio to market. These two traders' alleged deceptive practices are the subject of criminal charges brought against them by the United States Attorney for the Southern District of New York . . . *See U.S. v. Martin-Artajo*, No. 1:13-MJ-1975 (S.D.N.Y., filed Aug. 9, 2013) . . . [and] *U.S. v. Grout*, No. 1:13-MJ-1976 (S.D.N.Y., filed Aug. 9, 2013 . . . The facts alleged in these two sets of fraud charges also provide a basis for the Commission to charge the two traders with violations of Section 6(c)(1) of the Act and Regulation 180.1, 17 C.F.R. § 180.1 (2012), which prohibit, among other things, "any act, practice, or course of business, which operates or would operate as a fraud or deceit upon any person" "in connection with any swap." Nevertheless, . . . based on the facts and circumstances presented here as well as resource constraints faced by the Commission, the Division of Enforcement has determined not to recommend . . . virtually identical U.S. fraud charges against these two individuals at this time.

By way of background, under long-standing Commission precedent, manipulation was historically described as

> any and every operation or transaction or practice, the purpose of which is not primarily to facilitate the movement of the commodity at prices freely responsive to the forces of supply and demand; but, on the contrary, is calculated to produce a price distortion of any kind in any market either in itself or in its relation to other markets. If a firm is engaged in manipulation it will be found using devices by which the prices of contracts for some one month in some one market may be higher than they would be if only the forces of supply and demand were operative. . . . Any and every operation, transaction, device, employed to produce those abnormalities of price relationship in the futures markets, is manipulation.

. . . Under this standard, any device intentionally employed to distort pricing relationships may be manipulative. . . .

Section 6(c)(1) and Commission Regulation 180.1, because of their relatively recent enactment, have not been interpreted in this context by any court. Precedent applying very similar provisions in the SEC regime, however, provides guidance: "The language of CEA section 6(c)(1), particularly the operative phrase 'manipulative or deceptive device or contrivance,' is virtually identical to the terms used in section l0(b) of the Securities Exchange Act of 1934 ("Exchange Act")." Indeed, when the Commission promulgated Rule 180.1, the Commission observed that "[g]iven the similarities between CEA section 6(c)(1) and Exchange Act section 10(b), the Commission deems it appropriate and in the public interest to model final Rule 180.1 on SEC Rule l0b-5." . . . Accordingly, case law developed under Section l0(b) of the Exchange Act and SEC Rule 10b-5 is instructive in construing CEA Section 6(c)(1) and Commission Regulation 180.1(a).

It is well-settled that prohibitions on manipulative devices are designed to protect the market from devices that could interfere with legitimate pricing forces. . . .

In a properly functioning market, prices reflect the competing judgments of buyers and sellers as to the fair price of a commodity or, in this instance, swaps. Here, acting on behalf of JPMorgan, the . . . traders' activities . . . constituted a manipulative device in connection with swaps because they sold enormous volumes of the IG9 10Y in a very short period of time. . . .

Consistent with long-standing precedent under the commodities and securities laws, the Commission defines recklessness as an act or omission that "departs so far from the standards of ordinary care that it is very difficult to believe the actor was not aware of what he or she was doing." *Drexel Burnham Lambert Inc. v. CFTC*, 850 F.2d 742, 748 (D.C. Cir. 1988). Under this standard, the Commission need not prove that the defendant's motive or primary motive was to interfere with the forces of supply and demand. For example, even if a trader were motivated by a desire to obtain compensation rather than by a desire to affect a market price, if the trader recklessly effected the manipulative trades, he will be held liable.

The . . . traders here acted recklessly. Operating out of desperation to avoid further losses, they developed a resolve to "defend the position" . . ., i.e., protect its value . . . predicated, at least in part, on the market price. Recognizing that the sheer size of the . . . position in IG9 10Y had the potential to affect or influence the market, they recklessly sold massive amounts of protection on the IG9 10Y during a concentrated period . . .

Such activity designed to "defend" the position or "fight" other market participants, whether through concentrated month-end trading or otherwise, falls squarely within the prohibitions of Section 6(c)(1) of the Act and Commission Regulation 180.1(a). . . .

JPMorgan has submitted the Offer in which it . . . [c]onsents, solely on the basis of the Offer, to the Commission's entry of this Order that:

1. makes findings by the Commission that JPMorgan violated Section 6(c)(1) of the Act and Regulation 180.1, 17 C.F.R. §180.1 (2012), when it recklessly used or employed manipulative devices and contrivances in connection with swaps;

2. orders JPMorgan to cease and desist from violating Section 6(c)(1) of the Act and Regulation 180.1, 17 C.F.R. §180.1 (2012); [and]

3. orders JPMorgan to pay a civil monetary penalty in the amount of one hundred million dollars ($100,000,000) within ten (10) days of the date of entry of this Order, plus post-judgment interest. . . .

The enforcement action against JPMorgan was the CFTC's first use of its new authority, as promulgated in CFTC Rule 180.1(a)(1), making it unlawful to intentionally or recklessly "[u]se or employ, or attempt to use or employ, any manipulative device, scheme, or artifice to defraud." One of the CFTC commissioners, Scott D. O'Malia dissented from the CFTC's decision, stating:

> Because the settlement Order does not allege that JPMorgan engaged in manipulative or fraudulent conduct, I believe the Commission needs to do a better job of explaining why the company's aggressive trading strategy constitutes a "manipulative device."
>
> Regrettably, neither the CEA nor Commission regulations define a "manipulative device." This lack of a legal standard makes it even more difficult to determine whether JPMorgan engaged in a reckless behavior that put the company at risk or whether such behavior constitutes a "manipulative device."

> Although, some case law supports the Commission's conclusion that any device that is intentionally employed to distort a pricing relationship may be manipulative, the Commission has failed to produce data or conduct a more careful evaluation of the actual price to determine whether JPMorgan's conduct distorted the price of certain CDX indices. This problem is compounded even more by the fact that the allegations in the settlement Order center on bilateral or over-the-counter trading. Given this trading environment, I am not clear how the Commission can distinguish between "real" and "distorted" prices if the trades were executed through bilateral negotiations.

Statement of Commissioner Scott D. O'Malia Regarding JPMorgan's Use of Manipulative Device (October 15, 2013), available at http://www.cftc.gov/PressRoom/PressReleases/omaliastatement101613 (accessed June 26, 2014).

2. *Criminal Prohibition on Market Manipulation*

Similar to the wilful violations of the Commodity Exchange Act or CFTC rules we discussed above in section B2, a criminal manipulation is a felony punishable by up to 10 years in prison and a $1,000,000 fine, plus costs of prosecution. But unlike the civil burden of proof for proving market manipulations, the standard for proving a criminal charge requires knowledge, not mere recklessness.

United States v. Reliant Energy

420 F. Supp. 2d 1043 (N.D. Cal. 2006)

Walker, Chief Judge.

The United States has filed criminal charges against Reliant Energy Services, Inc. ("Reliant") and four Reliant employees: Jackie Thomas, Reginald Howard, Lisa Flowers and Kevin Frankeny (collectively "defendants"). The indictment charges each defendant with one count of commodities price manipulation in violation of § 9(a)(2) of the Commodity Exchange Act (CEA), four counts of wire fraud in violation of 18 U.S.C. § 1343 and one count of conspiracy in violation of 18 U.S.C. § 371. Defendants jointly moved to dismiss the original indictment on vagueness and other grounds. . . .

This case arises from California's electricity "crisis" in summer 2000. In 1996, California created two new non-governmental entities to orchestrate the transmission and sale of electricity: the California Independent System Operator ("CAISO") and the California Power Exchange ("CalPX") . . . CalPX was a crucial hub of the electricity generation market, overseeing an auction system for the sale and purchase of electricity . . . CalPX would determine, on an hourly basis, a single "market clearing price" which all electricity wholesalers would be paid based on short-term supply and demand bids submitted by all CalPX participants ("spot market"). In addition, CalPX operated a block forward market by matching supply and demand bids for long-term electricity contracts ("term market").

Responsibility for the efficient functioning of the high-voltage transmission grid fell to CAISO and, to that end, it ran the spot market for electricity. During the time period in question in this case, if consumer demands were not met by scheduled supplies into CalPX or other sources, CAISO was required to procure additional electricity to serve consumers' requirements and maintain the stability of the grid. To facilitate this, CAISO purchased reserve capacity from wholesalers. . . . The CAISO-operated market was called the "real time" or "imbalance" market. . . .

Reliant, based in Houston, Texas, owns five generation plants in southern California. According to the indictment, in early June 2000, defendant Flowers (on behalf of Reliant) entered into long-term trading contracts for electricity delivery for the third quarter of 2000 and 2001, expecting that electricity prices would increase. On June 19, 2000, however, the spot market price for electricity unexpectedly fell. Based upon the trading contracts entered into by Flowers and the sharply decreased market price, defendants determined that Reliant was facing a multi-million dollar loss. To avoid this loss, the indictment alleges that defendants conspired to manipulate (and did manipulate) the California electricity market to increase the price of electricity.

Specifically, the government asserts that defendants manipulated the market by creating a false and misleading appearance of an electricity supply shortage to CalPX, CAISO and other market participants. Defendants were able to create this illusion of a supply shortage by (1) shutting down some of Reliant's generation plants, (2) physically withholding electricity from the spot market, (3) submitting supply bids at inflated prices to ensure that the bids were not accepted and (4) disseminating false and misleading rumors and information to CAISO, brokers and other traders regarding the availability and maintenance status of, and environmental limitations on, Reliant's southern California generation plants.

The government asserts that defendants' scheme was successful; by June 21, 2000, the purported electricity supply shortage had caused the spot market price of electricity to soar. The indictment alleges that defendants took advantage of the artificial price they had created by selling large amounts of electricity at this inflated price. Ultimately, the government alleges, instead of suffering a loss, Reliant made millions in profits and that California electricity purchasers overpaid by as much as $32 million.

Based upon defendants' alleged conspiracy, scheme to defraud and manipulation . . . the government filed the criminal charges at issue here . . . (hereinafter the "criminal manipulation provision"). . . .

It is appropriate to address first defendants' . . . [allegation] that the criminal manipulation provision is unconstitutionally vague on its face and as applied to the case at hand. . . .

Defendants make much of the fact that, "[i]n the 68 years since commodity 'manipulation' was made a crime, there has never been a reported criminal prosecution" – until now. Yet, as Judge Selya stated when presented with this argument by a criminal defendant: "There is a first time for everything." *United States v. Nippon Paper Industries Co., Ltd.*, 109 F.3d 1, 6 (1st Cir.1997). There had to be a first time a defendant was prosecuted for price fixing under the Sherman Act. There had to be a first time a defendant was charged with illegal dumping under the Clean Water Act. The fact that this might be the government's premiere criminal prosecution under the criminal manipulation provision does not itself answer the court's inquiry whether the statute is unconstitutionally vague.

To be sure, a gap of two generations between enactment of a statute and prosecution under that statute is certainly a surprise. If commodities price manipulation were sufficiently harmful to society to require a criminal prohibition, it seems strange that it would take the government this long to get around to enforcing the statute. Surely, if there is such a thing as criminal market manipulation, the California energy crisis in the early 21st century cannot be the first instance of such conduct. Perhaps, the government has been able to deal with market manipulation through other criminal laws. If so, one wonders what a prosecution under the CEA adds to the government's law enforcement arsenal? But the absence of prior prosecutions is not enough to support dismissal of the indictment. . . .

Next, defendants argue that the CEA's criminal manipulation provision is void for vagueness on its face. . . .

Defendants argue that the criminal manipulation provision is unconstitutionally vague as applied for three reasons: (1) the term "manipulate" has no ordinary or plain meaning, (2) judicial explication has not remedied the term's ambiguity and (3) the legislative history of the CEA fails to evidence a sufficient definition of the term. . . .

As mentioned above, when a term lacks a statutory definition, the court will normally construe the term in accord with its ordinary meaning. This canon of construction begins by examining the term's dictionary definition.

As pertinent here, one modern dictionary defines "manipulate" as "to control, manage or play upon by artful, unfair or insidious means[;] esp. to one's own advantage." Webster's Third New Int'l Dictionary 1376 (1981); *see also* The Oxford American Dictionary and Language Guide 604 (1999) (defining manipulate as to "manage (a person, situation, *etc.*) to one's own advantage, esp. unfairly or unscrupulously"). Based on this definition, a person who "manages, controls or plays upon" the price of a commodity in interstate commerce by "artful, unfair or unscrupulous means" may be liable for criminal price manipulation under the CEA. Defendants characterize this ordinary meaning as full of "vague and subjective concepts." The court shares defendants' concern to some extent. Terms such as "unfairly," "unscrupulously" and the like are too subjective to afford a determinable legal standard by which criminal liability may be imposed.

Because a term's ordinary meaning should be assessed as of the time Congress enacted the provision at issue, dictionary definitions contemporaneous with enactment are most useful. Congress enacted § 9(a)(2) in 1936. At that time, Webster defined "manipulate" as "to manage or treat artfully or fraudulently." To the extent § 9(a)(2) of the CEA makes it a crime to "manage" the price of a commodity in interstate commerce by "fraudulent" means, the court is less inclined to agree that the term "manipulate" provides too vague a standard. . . .

Any uncertainty surrounding the term "manipulation" has been to an extent clarified by judicial explication. As defendants observe, the term "manipulation," like any term left to judicial interpretation, did not have a fixed meaning at the CEA's incipiency or during its adolescence.

In more recent times, . . . the courts and the CFTC have adopted four necessary elements an accuser must prove to prevail on a manipulation claim: (1) the defendants possessed the ability to influence prices, (2) an artificial price existed, (3) the defendant caused the artificial price and (4) the defendant specifically intended to cause the artificial price. . . .

Perhaps realizing that the judicial explication of the term "manipulate" is in line with the term's ordinary meaning, defendants' reply memorandum singles out a different term – "artificial price" – and attempts to demonstrate why this term's proposed definition is unconstitutionally vague. . . .

[D]efendants posit that criminalizing conduct undertaken with the intent to create a price that does not reflect the basic forces of supply and demand would "require businesses to guess what the 'reasonable' or 'real' value of a good was in order to conform their conduct to the law." In other words, defendants argue that the criminal manipulation provision requires them first to guess what the price of a commodity would be if the forces of supply and demand were uninhibited (i.e., guess what the "reasonable" or "real" price would be) and then avoid conduct that would cause the price of the commodity to deviate from this reasonable price. . . .

To avoid liability, defendants are not required to guess what the reasonable price of electricity is and then conform their conduct so as to create this price or sell at this price. The criminal manipulation provision does not criminalize the selling of a product at an unreasonable price. Rather, the criminal manipulation provision prohibits defendants from engaging in intentional conduct aimed at preventing the basic forces of supply and demand from operating properly. Thus, the criminal manipulation provision is concerned less with the price itself than it is with the process by which the price is set. . . .

The dissemination of false information into a commodities market has long been recognized as a form of price manipulation.

This is as it should be. Fraud and deceit are not legitimate market forces. Fundamentally, markets are information processing systems. The market price is only as "real" as the data that inform the process of price discovery. By the same token, the market price is "artificial" when the market is misinformed. Just as price artificiality implies misinformation, a specific intent to create an artificial price implies fraud or deceit. . . .

Putting aside the theoretical question whether a person of ordinary intelligence would understand that defendants' conduct was prohibited, it is sufficiently clear that defendants themselves knew their conduct was prohibited. Because all parties are familiar with them and in the interest of protecting the confidentiality of these criminal proceedings, the court will not recite portions of the taped telephone conversations offered by the government. It should suffice to say that one defendant actually uses the phrase "market manipulation" to explain why one of Reliant's generating facilities was idle. . . .

While the court does not afford much, if any, weight to these calls in addressing defendants' vagueness challenge, these telephone calls certainly do not add credibility to defendants' claims that they were unaware that their conduct in June 2000 was illegal.

Accordingly, defendants' motion to dismiss [the CEA market manipulation] count . . . of the indictment on vagueness grounds is DENIED. . . .

[D]efendants [also] argue that the "alleged conduct is not 'manipulation' as a matter of law." Specifically, defendants contend that unilateral supply decisions cannot constitute commodities price manipulation. As the court has already explained, if [the indictment] . . . were predicated solely upon defendants' unilateral supply decisions, "this would be a very different motion." But the indictment alleges that artificial prices were effected through the illusion of a supply shortage, which was created by the interplay between defendants' supply and bidding practices and the false and misleading rumors and information they allegedly disseminated into the market. . . .

Although *United States v. Reliant* established the viability of a criminal prosecution for market manipulation under the Commodity Exchange Act, it resulted in a settlement in which the defendants consented to a two-year deferred prosecution agreement (i.e., if, after two years, the defendants engaged in no unlawful behavior, the charges would be dropped) and a $22.2 million fine with no admission of wrongdoing by the defendants.[12]

D. TYPES OF MARKET MANIPULATION

1. Introduction

The types of market manipulation are varied and will always evolve as the markets evolve. Just as with fraud generally, one court has noted "[w]e think the test of manipulation must largely be a practical one if the purposes of the Commodity Exchange Act are to be accomplished [because the] methods and techniques of manipulation are limited only by the ingenuity of man."[13]

Therefore, in addition to the more general prohibitions of market manipulation described above in section C, certain types of market manipulation have been specifically identified and prohibited by the Commodity Exchange Act.

2. Order Bucketing, Wash Sales, and Fictitious Trades

The Commodity Exchange Act makes it unlawful to:

> (i) . . . bucket an order if the order is either represented by the person as an order to be executed, or is required to be executed, on or subject to the rules of a designated contract market; or (ii) to fill an order by offset against the order or orders of any other person, or willfully and knowingly and without the prior consent of the other person to become the buyer in respect to any selling order of the other person, or become the seller in respect to any buying order of the other person, if the order is either represented by the person as an order to be executed, or is required to be executed, on or subject to the rules of a designated contract market unless the order is executed in accordance with the rules of the designated contract market. . . .[14]

Commodity Exchange Act § 4b(a)(2)(D).

The Commodity Exchange Act also prohibits:

> a transaction that [is] . . . or is commonly known to the trade as, a "wash sale" or "accommodation trade"; or . . . is a fictitious sale; or . . . is used to cause any price to be reported, registered, or recorded that is not a true and bona fide price. . . .

Commodity Exchange Act § 4c(a)(2).

The following case centered around an allegation of engaging in "wash sales." The backdrop was a manipulation of the potato market that occurred in

1976 and resulted in a large default on delivery obligations required by parties holding a short position in the May 1976 Maine potato futures contracts.[15]

If the trades are *bona fide*, it follows that they are not "wash sales."

Stoller v. Commodity Futures Trading Commission

834 F.2d 262 (2d Cir. 1987)

Pierce, Circuit Judge:

Manning Stoller ("Stoller"), a registered account executive with a commodities brokerage firm, petitions for review of a decision and order entered in an administrative enforcement proceeding before the Commodity Futures Trading Commission (the "Commission"). The administrative complaint charged Stoller and others with engaging in "wash sales" in violation of section 4c(a)(A) of the Commodity Exchange Act (the "Act"). The Commission found that Stoller had engaged in prohibited transactions . . . For the reasons stated below, we grant Stoller's petition and reverse the Commission's order. . . .

This case concerns trading practices on the New York Mercantile Exchange (the "NYMEX") relating to May 1976 Maine potato futures contracts (the "Contracts"). . . .

[T]he market price of potato futures was being artificially depressed . . . by an illegal conspiracy. The conspirators planned to reap large profits when the May potato crop proved to be less plentiful than they were leading the market to believe, thereby causing the price of the futures contracts to rise. In the end, holders of many Contracts failed to deliver potatoes on the specified dates, "resulting in the largest default in the history of commodities futures trading in this country." . . .

In early May 1976, however, the details of this fraudulent scheme were still unknown. It apparently is clear that Stoller sensed that artificial forces were being brought to bear upon the market and recognized that the market price of the Contracts was below the level that would otherwise be indicated by an anticipated short supply of potatoes. Further, it appears that Stoller consequently believed that the artificial depression of the market would cease, either through official intervention or by investors' realization that the potato crop would be small. Futures prices would then rise, thereby creating a profit for those holding fixed-price "long" contracts to receive delivery of potatoes in May 1976.

NYMEX regulations specified that commodity deliveries were to be made first to those who had held their futures contracts the longest, with holders of the most recently acquired contracts receiving their deliveries last. Thus, when the price of the cash crop is expected to rise during the period when deliveries are made, it likely would be profitable to acquire long contracts very shortly before the close of trading in order to "get behind [i.e., get at the end of] the delivery line." Those like Stoller who already owned Contracts, and who therefore expected to have to take early delivery of potatoes, probably in mid-May, would likely prefer to sell their existing Contracts and to acquire newer ones, which would entitle them to take delivery instead in late May or early June, when the value of the commodity was expected to be higher. Stoller claims that this "rollover" or "roll forward" was a commonly-used practice in Maine potato futures.

On May 5 and 6, 1976, Stoller placed orders with floor brokers to sell existing Contracts, which carried early delivery dates because of the length of time for which they had been held, and to replace them one-for-one with other Contracts at a price as near as possible to the price for which the old ones were sold. . . .

The Commission brought a three count enforcement proceeding against Stoller in June 1977, alleging, inter alia, that these virtually simultaneous sale and repurchase transactions at substantially the same price constituted "wash sales" within the prohibitory language of section 4c(a)(A) of the Act. . . .

In August 1979, the administrative law judge ("ALJ") granted summary disposition in favor of Stoller on the ground that he had demonstrated a legitimate market purpose to the transactions, thereby excluding them from the intended scope of the "wash sales" prohibition. . . . [T]he Division of Enforcement appealed to the Commission from the ALJ's order with respect to the wash sale allegations, and in April 1986, almost ten years after the trades in question were executed, the Commission reversed the ALJ's decision and entered judgment against Stoller. In its decision, it said, "We infer from his conduct that [Stoller] initiated transactions with the intent to create the appearance of genuine purchases and sales while avoiding any *bona fide* market transaction."

The Chicago Mercantile Exchange requested a clarification of this decision on the ground that [it] . . . seemed to prohibit transactions in which the parties seek to minimize market risk. The Commission modified its holding and explained that it only sought to prohibit transactions that did not expose the principals to any risk of market price fluctuation. Nevertheless, it reaffirmed its decision that Stoller had violated this prohibition. This case never progressed beyond the stage of summary disposition; and no factual hearing was ever held at which Stoller would have had the opportunity to establish his defense that he did not have the requisite intent to avoid a bona fide market transaction. . . .

Stoller's . . . claims that the Commission did not provide adequate prior notice to the commodities industry and the public that the conduct in question would be considered to constitute prohibited "wash sales." . . .

The term "wash sale" is not defined in the Act itself, in any applicable regulations, or in any interpretive releases. The Commodity Exchange Authority (the "CEA"), the predecessor organization to the Commission, had advised commodities merchants and floor brokers by memorandum in 1948 that it considered trading to "get behind the delivery line" to constitute a "wash sale." However, this document was not published as an interpretive release. . . . In

1959, in another unpublished memorandum to the brokers, the CEA repeated this position. The CEA took the same position with respect to "roll forward" trading in an internal 1955 memorandum and in a 1971 letter to the Chicago Mercantile Exchange. However, we do not consider these documents to be sufficient to apprise the public at large of the rule interpretation, particularly when the policy apparently remained unenforced for years and the allegedly proscribed conduct apparently remained commonplace, as is asserted in this case.

An agency is free, of course, to interpret its governing statute case by case through adjudicatory proceedings rather than by rulemaking. However, if the Commission suddenly changes its view, as we discuss below, with respect to what transactions are "*bona fide* trading transactions," it may not charge a knowing violation of that revised standard and thereby cause undue prejudice to a litigant who may have relied on the agency's prior policy or interpretation.

Like the ALJ, we are unaware of any prior instances in which the Commission had sought sanctions against anyone who engaged in futures trading that accomplished only a modification of the delivery date of the commodity. The 1948 and 1959 memoranda from the CEA to floor brokers and the 1955 internal CEA memorandum were not generally available to the public; nor does the Commission assert that they were well-known to the commodity futures community. The 1971 letter to the Chicago Mercantile Exchange was sent to an exchange other than the one on which Stoller's alleged trading violations occurred. None of these documents was formally promulgated as an administrative interpretation or incorporated in adjudicative decisions. Thus, even if Stoller had investigated the Commission's view of "roll forward" trading, it seems unlikely that he would have been able to tell from that inquiry alone that such action was impermissible. . . .

The various prior decisions on the subject of "wash sales" had concerned transactions that were virtually risk-free, often prearranged, and intentionally designed to mislead or to serve other illicit purposes. The transactions in this case, by contrast, are claimed to have been designed only to minimize risk and to fulfill a purpose generally considered legitimate in the industry. . . .

At oral argument before this Court, counsel for the Commission conceded that a market sale followed by instructions to repurchase the same quantity at the closest possible price would not constitute a "wash sale" because the individual would be exposed to the risk of market fluctuation between the trades. . . . The Commission contends, however, that the preceding scenario is inapplicable to this case because Stoller's . . . instruction somehow operated to negate the risk entirely. . . .

The Commission first held that all "transactions which give the appearance of a *bona fide* purchase and sale, while avoiding any actual change in ownership" are illegal. It then revised its interpretation, claiming that the statute only prohibits transactions that negate market risk. The fact that the Commission abruptly changed its own interpretation in the middle of the proceedings in our judgment further demonstrates the need both for a clearer and more explicit interpretation and for appropriate notice thereof to the public as to what conduct is permissible. Because we find that the public was not adequately apprised that the Commission views "roll forward" trading to be encompassed within the "wash sale" prohibition, we conclude that Stoller may not be held liable under that interpretation for his alleged violations with respect to the Contracts at issue herein.

The petition for review is granted and the Commission's order is reversed.

As discussed in Chapter 2, order bucketing was one of the impetuses for the initial Federal regulation of derivatives. The following case centers on allegations of wash sales and order bucketing.

Reddy v. Commodity Futures Trading Commission

191 F.3d 109 (2d Cir. 1999)

Winter, Chief Judge:

Steven F. Reddy and John W. Sorkvist petition for review of an order of the Commodity Futures Trading Commission which found them guilty of several violations of the Commodity Exchange Act ("CEA") . . . Solomon Mayer ("SMayer"), Barry Mayer ("BMayer"), SHB Commodities, Inc. ("SHB"), Maye Commodities Corp. ("MCC"), and Steven Gelbstein petition for review of a similar order. Because of the similarity of issues, we heard these petitions together. . . .

In April 1992, the Enforcement Division of the Commission ("Division") filed an eight-count complaint against petitioners Reddy and Sorkvist, along with two other traders, accusing them of multiple violations of the CEA and the Commission's Rules in connection with their trading activities in the sugar pit of the Coffee, Sugar & Cocoa Exchange ("CSCE"). The complaint alleged that from June 29 through October 31, 1988, and during March 1989, Reddy and Sorkvist – both "dual traders"[iii] – had engaged in fraudulent executions of customer orders and had accommodated each other in such transactions. Specifically, the complaint alleged that Reddy had engaged in 35 trade-practice violations, including indirect "bucketing" of customers' orders and "wash trades." The complaint also alleged that Sorkvist had engaged in 19 trade-practice violations, primarily "accommodation" trades.

A broker buckets a customer's order by trading opposite the order for the broker's own account or for an account in which the broker has an interest. "Indirect bucketing" occurs when a broker, aided by an accommodating trader,

---

[iii] [N. 2] "Dual traders" are "floor brokers" who trade for customers and for their own accounts. . . .

trades opposite his own customer while appearing to trade opposite the accommodator.[iv] For example, if a customer directs a broker to buy five contracts, the broker can trade against the customer by buying the five contracts for the customer from a trader while selling five identical contracts from the broker's personal account to the same trader. A broker can profit from bucketing by obtaining a better price than available through open outcry or by trading ahead of the customer and reaping the difference between the price of the early trade and the predetermined price for the customer.

A wash trade is a transaction made without an intent to take a genuine, *bona fide* position in the market, such as a simultaneous purchase and sale designed to negate each other so that there is no change in financial position. Wash trades may be used, *inter alia*, to avoid margin requirements, to rearrange gains and loss for tax purposes, or to manipulate prices.

On November 2, 1995, the Administrative Law Judge ("ALJ") found Reddy liable for CEA violations in 35 trade sequences and Sorkvist liable in 16 trade sequences. Based on these findings, the ALJ imposed the following sanctions: cease and desist orders against both petitioners; revocation of their floor broker registrations; imposition of a ten-year trading ban on Reddy and a five-year trading ban on Sorkvist; and a $300,000 civil penalty on Reddy and a $150,000 penalty on Sorkvist. On February 4, 1998, the Commission affirmed both the ALJ's liability findings and the imposition of sanctions. . . .

In April 1992, petitioners SMayer, BMayer, SHB, MCC, and Gelbstein were, along with other traders, charged in a 23-count complaint of multiple recordkeeping and trade practice violations in connection with futures trading in the heating oil pit of the New York Mercantile Exchange ("NYMEX") from 1987 through mid-1989. With respect to the trade practice violations, the complaint alleged that: (i) SMayer, BMayer, SHB, and MCC knowingly engaged in noncompetitive trades to achieve wash results by trading the SHB and MCC accounts opposite each other . . . ; (ii) SMayer, SHB, and MCC knowingly engaged in noncompetitive trades and Gelbstein accommodated them . . . ; (iii) SMayer bucketed his customers' orders and Gelbstein accommodated him . . . ; and (iv) SMayer bucketed his customers' orders and Gelbstein accommodated him. . . .

On May 15, 1996, the ALJ found petitioners liable on 22 of the 23 counts alleged in the complaint and imposed sanctions. SMayer, BMayer, SHB, MCC, and Gelbstein were ordered to cease and desist from violating the CEA and the Commission's Rules; the registrations of SMayer, BMayer, and SHB were revoked; SMayer, BMayer, and SHB were prohibited from trading on, or subject to the rules of, any contract market for five years; Gelbstein was prohibited from doing the same for 30 days; and a civil monetary penalty of $200,000 was

---

[iv] [N. 3] An "accommodator" is a trader who enters into noncompetitive trading to assist others with illegal trades.

assessed against SMayer, $100,000 each against BMayer, SHB, and MCC, and $25,000 against Gelbstein.

Petitioners appealed the ALJ's decision to the Commission. . . .

[The Commission] affirmed the ALJ's imposition of cease and desist orders against all petitioners and affirmed the revocation of SMayer's, BMayer's, and SHB's registrations. Instead of the five-year trading ban imposed by the ALJ on SMayer and SHB, however, the Commission permanently banned them from trading. It also ordered a permanent trading ban against MCC, although the ALJ had imposed no ban. And, instead of the five-year trading ban imposed by the ALJ on BMayer and the thirty-day ban imposed upon Gelbstein, the Commission imposed ten-year bans upon each of them. . . .

The Commission's liability findings are conclusive if supported by the weight – or preponderance – of the evidence. However, our role in reviewing the Commission finding of preponderance is narrow. We will not "mechanically reweigh[ ] the evidence to ascertain in which direction it preponderates. . . ." Rather, we review the record only for the "purpose of determining whether the finder of [ ] fact was *justified, i.e., acted* reasonably, in concluding that the evidence, including the demeanor of the witnesses, the reasonable inferences drawn therefrom and other pertinent circumstances, supported [its] findings." . . .

With regard to Reddy and Sorkvist, the evidence was as follows. The Division's expert, Martha Kozlowski, examined thousands of trading cards and identified transactions in which a broker had simultaneously bought and sold identical sugar futures contracts in identical, or nearly so, quantities at or about the same price opposite the same trader. In the transactions pertinent to Reddy and Sorkvist, the broker's trades were both for a customer and for the broker's personal account. The accommodating trader bought and sold only for his personal account.

Kozlowski testified that trading with those characteristics – principally simultaneous trades of the same contracts, at the same price, in the same quantity, and between the same broker and trader – is unlikely to occur in a competitive open outcry. In her view, such trades exhibited the characteristics of indirect bucketing.

Petitioners countered this evidence with expert and other testimony that such trading configurations can just as plausibly involve lawful dual trading, in particular a practice known as "scalping." Scalping involves the buying and selling of the same contracts within a very short period of time on small market fluctuations, and sometimes, if the attempt to profit fails, buying and selling at the same price. Based on the existence of lawful practices that might result in similar trading configurations, petitioners argue that the evidence against them is no better than in equipoise and cannot as a matter of law support a more-probably-than-not finding of a violation. We disagree.

The Commission had a not unreasonable skepticism about viewing the transactions in question as lawful . . . The Commission noted that the transactions occurred when the market was unusually volatile and the immediate turn-arounds prevented any hope of gain as well as avoiding any loss . . . [and] found such risk-adverseness implausible. The Commission also noted that some of the trades occurred early in the day and were therefore not designed to end the day without margin fees. . . .

Moreover . . . Petitioners were required to record the terms and times of trades on trading cards [and] . . . [t]he cards reflecting the trades described above showed . . . irregularities . . .

Given the evidence, we cannot overturn the Commission's finding of liability. . . .

Sorkvist, whose only proven roles were as a money-passer or accommodating trader, argues that the Division failed to establish that he had a motive to participate in noncompetitive trading and thereby failed to prove scienter. He correctly argues that proof of participation in noncompetitive trades alone is not a sufficient basis for inferring knowing participation in trades. However, Sorkvist confuses intent with motive.

It is true that the Division must prove intent to establish a violation of either Section 4b or 4c of the CEA. *See CFTC v. Savage*, 611 F.2d at 284 ("One cannot have an 'accommodation' sale or a 'fictitious' transaction if one in fact believes he is bargaining faithfully and intends to effect a *bona fide* trade."). However, scienter may be inferred from . . . evidence other than motive. . . .

In addition to the evidence of a recurring pattern of noncompetitive trading, the audit trail irregularities suggested artificial trading in every trade sequence for which charges were brought. These irregularities, in conjunction with the suspicious pattern of trading, are highly probative evidence that Sorkvist knowingly assisted others in illegal transactions. . . .

SMayer, BMayer, SHB, and MCC claim that the Commission erred as a matter of law by finding that . . . [their] trades constituted illegal wash sales. These trades were between various accounts alleged by the division to be controlled jointly by SMayer and BMayer, and, if so, all gains were offset by all losses among the same parties. Petitioners argue that there is legally insufficient evidence of either common control of the accounts or identity of control of the trading. We disagree.

Although SMayer denied any ownership interest in MCC, he reported capital gains from MCC in an amount equal to that of his mother, the avowed owner, and the Commission quite plausibly found that he had such an interest. It further found that: SMayer, who together with BMayer owned two-thirds of SHB, "managed and controlled the operations of SHB"; "[f]unds were transferred between [MCC and SHB] without documentation of any underlying obligation"; "witnesses were unable to explain the reasons for various transfers"; and "all family members had authority to withdraw funds from the accounts at their own discretion." . . .

Petitioners claim that even if the trades were wash sales, there was legally insufficient evidence that their participation in such transactions was knowing. This claim is entirely meritless. . . .

The Commission based its finding on several compelling factors. SMayer was in the heating oil pit daily while BMayer entered the heating oil pit only rarely and sometimes only long enough to execute a single trade. For example, . . . [evidence] shows that on more than one occasion, BMayer executed trades in both the heating oil pit and the platinum and palladium pit during the same minute. It is also highly significant that although BMayer rarely executed heating oil trades, a substantial percentage of those trades were with SMayer on the other side. . . .

We agree with the Commission that the purpose of sanctions under the CEA is twofold: "to further the [CEA]'s remedial policies and to deter others in the industry from committing similar violations." *In re Miller*, No. 92–4, Comm. Fut. L. Rep. (CCH) ¶ 27,297, 1998 WL 107577, at *6 (C.F.T.C. Mar. 12, 1998). . . .

[W]e note that the transgressions here are extremely serious. Artificial trades, such as wash transactions or bucketing, have no purpose save to avoid some legal, statutory, regulatory, or contractual obligation or to manipulate the market. They are used, for example, to avoid margin requirements, or taxes, to defraud customers, or to manipulate prices. That is reason enough to impose meaningful sanctions. But artificial trading also strikes at the core purpose of exchanges – efficient y establishing accurate prices for futures contracts. More is at stake, therefore, than loss of revenue to the government or faithlessness to contractual or fiduciary obligations to customers.

We also note that, while artificial trading can over time be profitable, it is also difficult to detect. Because the gains available from artificial trading can be great and the danger of detection may seem low, the temptation to engage in such practices may be great. If deterrence is to be achieved, substantial penalties may be necessary. . . .

The petitions for review are therefore denied.

---

3. *Disruptive Practices*

The Commodity Exchange Act prohibits "disruptive practices," i.e.:

> [engaging] in any trading, practice, or conduct on or subject to the rules of a designated contract market or swap execution facility that – (A) violates bids or offers; (B) demonstrates intentional or reckless disregard for the orderly execution of transactions during the closing period [known as "banging the close"]; or (C) is, is of the character of, or is commonly known to the trade as, "spoofing" (bidding or offering with the intent to cancel the bid or offer before execution). . . .

Commodity Exchange Act § 4c(a)(5).

This is a new authority, granted to the CFTC by amendments to the Commodity Exchange Act by way of the Dodd-Frank Act.

Antidisruptive Practices Authority

78 Fed. Reg. 31890 (May 28, 2013)

. . . Section 747 of the Dodd-Frank Act amends section 4c(a) of the [Commodity Exchange Act (the "CEA") ("Prohibited Transactions") to add a new section entitled "Disruptive Practices." . . .

Dodd-Frank Act section 747 also amends section 4c(a) of the CEA by granting the Commission authority under new section 4c(a)(6) of the CEA to promulgate such "rules and regulations as, in the judgment of the Commission, are reasonably necessary to prohibit the trading practices" enumerated therein "and any other trading practice that is disruptive of fair and equitable trading."

The Commission is issuing this interpretive guidance and policy statement ("interpretive statement") to provide market participants and the public with guidance on the manner in which it intends to apply the [three new] statutory prohibitions set forth in section 4c(a)(5) of the CEA [i.e., prohibitions on violating bids and offers, "banging the close" and spoofing]. . . .

Violating Bids and Offers . . .

The Commission declines requests to interpret CEA section 4c(a)(5)(A) as applying only where a person intends to disrupt fair and equitable trading. The Commission interprets CEA section 4c(a)(5)(A) as a *per se* offense. Congress did not include an intent requirement in CEA section 4c(a)(5)(A) as it did in both CEA sections 4c(a)(5)(B) and 4c(a)(5)(C). Therefore, the Commission does not interpret CEA section 4c(a)(5)(A) as requiring the Commission to show that a person acted with scienter in violating bids and offers (e.g., that a person acted with either the intent to disrupt fair and equitable trading or with the intent to violate bids and offers). . . . While the Commission's determination of whether to bring an enforcement action depends on facts and circumstances, the Commission does not, for example, intend to exercise its discretion to bring an enforcement action against an individual who, purely by accident, makes a one-off trade in violation of CEA section 4c(a)(5)(A). . . .

The Commission agrees with commenters that parties trading non-cleared swaps may take into consideration factors other than price, such as counterparty risk, when determining how to best execute their trades. Therefore, the Commission interprets CEA section 4c(a)(5)(A) as not applying to non-cleared swap transactions, even if they are transacted on or through a registered entity. In such swap transactions, the credit considerations of the counterparties are important components of choosing which bid or offer to accept. . . .

Therefore, the Commission interprets CEA section 4(c)(a)(5)(A) as prohibiting a person from buying a contract on a registered entity at a price that is higher than the lowest available price offered for such contract or selling a contract on a registered entity at a price that is lower than the highest available price bid for such contract subject to the situations described above. Such conduct, regardless of intent, disrupts fair and equitable trading by damaging the price discovery function of CFTC-regulated markets. By adopting a policy that market participants cannot execute trades at prices that do not accurately reflect the best price for such contracts, this interpretive statement furthers the CEA's purpose of ensuring the integrity of the price discovery process by helping ensure that the prices disseminated to market users and the public reflect *bona fide* prices that accurately reflect the normal forces of supply and demand. . . .

Disregard for the Orderly Execution of Transactions During the Closing Period . . .

The Commission interprets Congress's inclusion of a scienter requirement in CEA section 4c(a)(5)(B) as meaning that accidental, or even negligent, trading, practices, or conduct will not be a sufficient basis for the Commission to claim a violation under CEA section 4c(a)(5)(B). The Commission interprets CEA section 4c(a)(5)(B) as requiring a market participant to at least act recklessly to violate CEA section 4c(a)(5)(B). The Commission declines to interpret CEA section 4c(a)(5)(B) to include either an extreme recklessness standard or a manipulative intent requirement because this modification would alter the scienter standard mandated by the statute, which prohibits conduct that demonstrates "intentional or reckless disregard for the orderly execution of transactions during the closing period." Recklessness is a well-established scienter standard, which has consistently been defined as conduct that "departs so far from the standards of ordinary care that it is very difficult to believe the actor was not aware of what he or she was doing." Consistent with long-standing precedent under commodities and securities law, the Commission intends to apply this commonly-known definition of recklessness to CEA section 4c(a)(5)(B). A person with manipulative intent, such as one attempting to "bang" or "mark the close" may also intend to disrupt the orderly execution of transactions during the closing period, but the finding of a manipulative intent is not a prerequisite for a finding of a violation of CEA section 4c(a)(5)(B).

The Commission interprets the prohibition in CEA section 4c(a)(5)(B) to apply to any trading, conduct, or practices occurring within the closing period that demonstrates an intentional or reckless disregard for the orderly execution of transactions during the closing period. The Commission interprets the closing period to be defined generally as the period in the contract or trade when the settlement price is determined under the rules of a trading facility such as a DCM or SEF. . . . Additionally, the Commission's policy is that conduct outside the closing period may also disrupt the orderly execution of transactions during the closing period and may thus form the basis of a violation under CEA section 4c(a)(5)(B) and any other applicable CEA sections. . . .

The Commission interprets CEA section 4c(a)(5)(B) violations as including not only executed orders by market participants that disrupt the orderly execution of transactions during the closing period, but also any bids and offers submitted by market participants that disrupt the orderly execution of transactions during the closing period. . . .

"Spoofing" . . .

The Commission interprets a CEA section 4c(a)(5)(C) violation as requiring a market participant to act with some degree of intent, or scienter, beyond recklessness to engage in the "spoofing" trading practices prohibited by CEA section 4c(a)(5)(C). Because CEA section 4c(a)(5)(C) requires that a person intend to cancel a bid or offer before execution, the Commission does not interpret reckless trading, practices, or conduct as constituting a "spoofing" violation. Additionally, the Commission interprets that a spoofing violation will not occur when the person's intent when cancelling a bid or offer before execution was to cancel such bid or offer as part of a legitimate, good-faith attempt to consummate a trade. Thus, the Commission interprets the statute to mean that a legitimate, good-faith cancellation or modification of orders (e.g., partially filled orders or properly placed stop-loss orders) would not violate section CEA 4c(a)(5)(C). However, the Commission does not interpret a partial fill as automatically exempt from being classified as "spoofing" and violating CEA section 4c(a)(5)(C).

When distinguishing between legitimate trading (such as trading involving partial executions) and "spoofing," the Commission intends to evaluate the market context, the person's pattern of trading activity (including fill characteristics), and other relevant facts and circumstances. For example, if a person's intent when placing a bid or offer was to cancel the entire bid or offer prior to execution and not attempt to consummate a legitimate trade, regardless of whether such bid or offer was subsequently partially filled, that conduct may violate CEA section 4c(a)(5)(C). . . .

---

a. "Banging the Close"

Before the Dodd-Frank Act's enhancement of the CFTC's enforcement authority, the CFTC's position was that "banging the close" was a violation of the Commodity Exchange Act's general anti-manipulation provisions. For example, a former portfolio manager for Moore Capital Management, LP, a registered commodity trading advisor, was found by the CFTC to have engaged in "banging the close" by having:

> Caused to be entered market-on-close . . . buy orders that were executed in the last ten seconds of the closing period for . . . [palladium and platinum futures] contracts in an attempt to exert upward pressure on the settlement prices of the futures contracts.

In the Matter of: Moore Capital Management, LP, CFTC Docket No. 10-09 (April 29, 2010), p. 2.

b. "Spoofing"

The CFTC has asserted its new anti-spoofing authority.

In the Matter of Panther Energy Trading LLC and Michael J. Coscia

CFTC Docket No. 13-26 (July 22, 2013)

ORDER INSTITUTING PROCEEDINGS PURSUANT TO SECTIONS 6(c) AND 6(d) OF THE COMMODITY EXCHANGE ACT, AS AMENDED, MAKING FINDINGS AND IMPOSING REMEDIAL SANCTIONS . . .

The Commodity Futures Trading Commission ("Commission") has reason to believe that from August 8, 2011 through October 18, 2011, Panther Energy Trading LLC and Michael J. Coscia violated Section 4c(a)(5)(C) of the Commodity Exchange Act (the "Act"). . . .

Beginning on August 8, 2011 through and including October 18, 2011 (the "Relevant Period"}, Panther Energy Trading LLC ("Panther") and Michael J. Coscia ("Coscia") (collectively, "Respondents") engaged in the disruptive practice of "spoofing" (bidding or offering with the intent to cancel the bid or offer before execution) through algorithmic trading utilizing a program that was designed to place bids and offers and to quickly cancel those bids and offers before execution.

Because the Respondents engaged in conduct that is, or is of the character of, or is known to the trade as, spoofing, the conduct violated Section 4c(a)(5)(C) of the Act, which, *inter alia*, makes it unlawful for any person to engage in any trading, practice or conduct on or subject to the rules of a registered entity that is, is of the character of, or is commonly known to the trade as, spoofing. . . .

Panther Energy Trading LLC is a trading company . . . [and] Michael J. Coscia is the manager and sole owner of Panther and has been registered with the Commission as a floor broker since 1988. . . .

During the Relevant Period, Respondents placed on Globex, CME Group's electronic trading platform, algorithmic bids or offers which they intended to, and did, cancel prior to execution, and therefore engaged in a disruptive trading practice known as spoofing, in 18 futures contracts traded on four exchanges owned by CME Group. The futures contracts in which the Respondents engaged in spoofing involved a wide spectrum of commodities . . .

Respondents made money by employing an algorithm that was designed to rapidly place bids and offers in the market and to cancel those bids and offers prior to execution. The following example of Respondents' trading in the Light Sweet Crude Oil futures contract is illustrative of how the algorithm worked. First, the algorithm placed a relatively small order on one side of the market at or near the best price being offered to buy or sell, in this instance a sell order for 17 contracts at a price of $85.29 per barrel, which was a lower price than the contracts then being offered by other market participants. Thus, the Respondents' offer was at the lowest, i.e., best, offered price. Second, within a fraction of a second, the Respondents entered orders to buy a relatively larger number of Light Sweet Crude Oil futures contracts at progressively higher prices: the first bid at $85.26, the second bid at $85.27, and the third bid at $85.28. The prices of Respondents' bids were higher than the contracts then being bid by other market participants. Thus, Respondents' placed their bids at the highest, i.e., best, prices. By placing the large buy orders, Respondents sought to give the market the impression that there was significant buying interest, which suggested that prices would soon rise, raising the likelihood that other market participants would buy the 17 lots the Respondents were then offering to sell. Although Respondents wanted to give the impression of buy-side interest, Respondents entered the large buy orders with the intent that these buy orders be canceled before the orders were actually executed.

In the above example, the program sought to capture an immediate profit from selling the 17 lots. Thus, if the program successfully filled the small 17-lot sell order, the large buy orders were immediately cancelled and the algorithm was designed to promptly operate in reverse.

That is, the algorithm would then enter a small buy order in conjunction with relatively large sell orders at progressively lower prices, which sell orders Respondents intended to cancel prior to execution. . . .

The episodes of bidding, offering, canceling, and, if the program successfully filled the small order, liquidation activity, occurred over a very short time frame. In some instances, the Respondents utilized the spoofing algorithm hundreds of times in an individual futures contract in a single day. During the Relevant Period, Respondents accumulated net profits of approximately $1.4 million using the spoofing algorithm. . . .

Section 4c(a)(5)(C) of the Act makes it "unlawful for any person to engage in any trading, practice, or conduct on or subject to the rules of a registered entity that . . . is, is of the character of, or is commonly known to the trade as, 'spoofing' (bidding or offering with the intent to cancel the bid or offer before execution)."

In this case, Respondents intended when placing bids or offers to cancel the bids or offers prior to execution. Respondents designed the algorithmic trading program to place orders on one side of the market to give the impression of market interest on that side of the market and to increase the likelihood that their smaller orders sitting on the opposite side of the market would be filled Respondents used an algorithm designed to cancel orders prior to execution. Consequently, Respondents, engaged in trading that was spoofing, in violation of Section 4c(a)(5)(C) of the Act.

Accordingly, IT IS HEREBY ORDERED THAT . . .

Respondents shall cease and desist from violating Section 4c(a)(5)(C) of the Act. . . .

Respondents shall pay a civil monetary penalty in the amount of one million, four hundred thousand dollars ($1,400,000), plus post-judgment interest. . . .

Respondents are prohibited from directly or indirectly engaging in trading on or subject to the rules of any registered entity (as that term is defined in Section 1a of the Act, as amended, and all registered entities shall refuse them trading privileges for a period of one year. . . .

Respondents shall . . . pay disgorgement in the amount of one million, four hundred thousand dollars ($1,400,000), plus post-judgment interest. . . .

---

4. *Position Limits and Cornering*

Commodity Exchange Act § 9(a)(2) in addition to criminalizing manipulation generally, as described in section C2 above, also prohibits "cornering" by making it a felony for anyone to "corner or attempt to corner any . . . commodity or knowingly to deliver or cause to be delivered . . . false or misleading or knowingly inaccurate reports concerning crop or market information or conditions that affect or tend to affect the price of any commodity. . . ." For physical commodities, in addition to the prohibition on cornering, a method of combating cornering is through position limits. Both the CFTC and designated contract markets have position limit rules.

a. CFTC Position Limits

CFTC rules impose position limits on commodity futures or options (algebraically converted into a "futures equivalent") on corn, soybeans, wheat, soybean oil, and soybean meal traded on the Chicago Board of Trade, hard red spring wheat traded on the Minneapolis Grain Exchange, cotton traded on ICE Futures and hard winter wheat traded on the Kansas City Board of Trade.[16] There is a general exemption for any *bona fide* hedging position.[17]

Note that, for the commodities for which the CFTC has not established position limits directly, the Commodity Exchange Act and the CFTC require designated contract markets to establish position limits or "accountability levels," both discussed below in section D4b.[18]

Note also that these particular position limits do not apply to swaps. For a discussion of position limits and swaps, *see* section D4c below.

For the purposes of calculating whether a person has exceeded position limits, positions in separate accounts are aggregated when they are commonly controlled or when "two or more persons [are] acting pursuant to an expressed or implied agreement or understanding. . . ."[19]

Commodity Futures Trading Commission v. Hunt

591 F.2d 1211 (7th Cir. 1979)

Swygert, Circuit Judge.

This case presents several issues arising out of a complaint brought by the Commodity Futures Trading Commission, pursuant to the Commodity Exchange Act, against seven members of the Hunt family and an affiliated company. The complaint was instituted by the Commission . . . to compel the defendants to comply with limits established by the Commission on the speculative position that any individual or group may have in soybean futures contracts.

The Commission's complaint alleges that from at least January 17, 1977 and continuing to the commencement of the court action, two brothers, Nelson Bunker Hunt and William Herbert Hunt, five of their children, and a corporation they control, had been exceeding collectively the limit of three million bushels that had been set for soybean futures contracts. . . .

[T]he district court . . . concluded that the Hunts . . . had acquired soybean futures in excess of the three million bushel limit prescribed by regulation . . .

The Hunts . . . [seek] to overturn the district court's declaratory judgment that the Hunts had violated the speculative limit . . .

[T]he Commodity Exchange Act . . . authorizes the Commodity Futures Trading Commission to set commodity trading limits. Congress concluded that excessive speculation in commodity contracts for future delivery can cause adverse fluctuations in the price of a commodity, and authorized the Commission to restrict the positions held or trading done by any individual person or by certain groups of people acting in concert. . . .

[The Commodity Exchange Act] provides for the aggregation of commodity positions for purposes of determining whether the speculative limit has been exceeded, when one person "directly or indirectly" controls the trading of another, or when two persons are acting "pursuant to an express or implied agreement or understanding. . . ." Thus, even though two persons acting in concert might each individually have a commodity position below the limit, if their combined position exceeds the limit they have violated the statute. Further, contrary to the arguments advanced by the Hunts, there is nothing in either the statutory language or legislative history which suggests that intent either to affect market prices or specific intent to exceed the speculative limits is a necessary element of a violation . . . A violation occurs simply when an individual or several individuals acting in concert exceed the commodity position limits set pursuant to the statute. . . .

Nelson Bunker Hunt and William Herbert Hunt were the principal family figures in these transactions. They are brothers, and the chief officers of the Hunt Energy Corporation. In mid-1976 N. B. and W. H. Hunt entered the soybean market. By August 1 each brother consistently held a long position at the three million bushel limit, usually for the closest delivery month. Through a series of purchases the date, timing, and size of which were virtually identical each brother, by January 1977, held a three million bushel position in March 1977 soybeans. Over the next six weeks each of the Hunt brothers entered into eight transactions on the same days, using the same broker, involving virtually identical quantities and prices. Throughout this time an employee of the Hunt Energy Corporation, Charles Mercer, prepared commodity position statements for the brothers reflecting their combined holdings and unrealized profits and losses.

On February 25, with both N. B. and W. H. Hunt at the personal position limit, N. B. Hunt ordered a purchase, through one of his brokers, of 750,000 bushels of May soybeans in the name of his son, Houston Hunt. On March 3 he ordered the purchase of 750,000 May bushels to be allocated equally among accounts he had opened on behalf of his three daughters. And, although the bank accounts of the various children lacked the funds to cover these purchases, the transactions were made possible by a short-term transfer of interest-free funds from their father's account. N. B. Hunt's children did not participate in these initial soybean transactions made in their names: they had nothing to do with opening the accounts, placing the first order, or arranging financing for their purchases. And once these family members had entered the soybean market, their transactions were added to the composite report sent to N. B. Hunt.

A similar relationship existed between W. H. Hunt and his son, Douglas. On March 1 W. H. Hunt and his wife transferred their interests in Hunt Holdings, Inc. to their three sons. Less than a week later Douglas Hunt personally and through Hunt Holdings, whose trading he controlled, began purchasing July soybeans. These purchases were financed in part by money advanced by his father. . . .

As of April 14, 1977 the Hunt family's collective position involved over twenty-three million bushels of old crop soybeans: over 10.8 million in May futures, 7.7 million in July futures, and 5.2 million in August futures. . . . [T]he evidence presented in the district court clearly indicates that the individual positions of the family members should be aggregated. Thus, the Hunt family soybean transactions constituted a violation of the Commodity Exchange Act. . . .

---

b. Position Limits Imposed by Designated Contract Markets

In addition to the position limits imposed directly by the CFTC, the Commodity Exchange Act and CFTC rules require designated contract markets to impose their own position limits or, alternatively, with CFTC approval, accountability reporting requirements that, instead of imposing a hard limit on the number of contracts that may be traded by any common enterprise, require notifications to the exchange once specified thresholds are exceeded and provide the exchange the opportunity to prohibit the acquisition of further positions.[20] As with the CFTC's position limits, there is a *bona fide* hedging exemption.[21]

In the following case, the question arose as to the extent of aiding and abetting liability for a futures commission merchant whose customer has exceeded position and accountability limits as well as engaged in "slamming the close" market manipulation. ("Slamming the close" is another phrase for "banging the close," discussed above in D3a.) We examined a related case, *Hunter v. FERC* in Chapter 3 in the context of evaluating a jurisdictional dispute that arose between the CFTC and the Federal Energy Regulatory Commission.

In re Amaranth Natural Gas Commodities Litigation

730 F.3d 170 (2d Cir. 2013)

Debra Ann Livingston, Circuit Judge:

In the fall of 2006, Amaranth Advisors LLC ("Amaranth"), a hedge fund that had heavily invested in natural gas futures, collapsed. A Senate investigation would later conclude that Amaranth, in the months leading up to its demise, had taken positions in natural gas futures and swaps so massive that its trading directly affected domestic natural gas prices and price volatility. Plaintiffs-Appellants, traders who had bought or sold natural gas futures during these same months, filed a complaint in the United States District Court for the Southern District of New York alleging that Amaranth had manipulated the price of natural gas futures in violation of the Commodities [sic] Exchange Act ("CEA"). Plaintiffs-Appellants also alleged that Defendants-Appellees J.P. Morgan Chase & Co., J.P. Morgan Chase Bank, Inc., and J.P. Morgan Futures, Inc. ("J.P. Futures") (collectively, "J.P. Morgan") had aided and abetted Amaranth's manipulation of natural gas futures through J.P. Futures's services as Amaranth's futures commission merchant and clearing broker. The district court . . . concluded that both Plaintiffs-Appellants' complaint and amended complaint failed to state claims against J.P. Morgan. . . .

We conclude that the district court did not err. . . .

The CEA prohibits manipulation of the price of any commodity or commodity future. . . .

NYMEX is a futures and options exchange based in New York City. . . .

One type of futures contract traded on NYMEX is for the delivery of natural gas. . . .

NYMEX is a designated contract market, or "DCM." As a DCM, NYMEX may offer options and futures trading for any type of commodity, but is subject to extensive oversight from the Commodity Futures Trading Commission ("CFTC"). . . . NYMEX [must] establish position limits and accountability levels for each type of contract that it offers for trading. A "position limit" is a cap on the number of contracts that a trader may hold or control for a particular option or future at a particular time, with exceptions provided for traders engaged in *bona fide* hedging. An "accountability level" provides that once a trader holds or controls a certain number of contracts for a particular option or future she must provide information about that position upon request by the exchange and, if the exchange so orders, stop increasing her position. At the time of the events alleged in the amended complaint, NYMEX had set a position limit of 1,000 contracts, net short or net long, for any natural gas future, applicable during the last three days of trading. NYMEX had also set corresponding accountability limits, which varied in size based on the trader's capitalization and applied at all times the future was traded. . . .

Amaranth . . . began to acquire large "spread" positions in NYMEX natural gas futures.[v] Specifically, Amaranth acquired "calendar" spreads between natural gas futures for different months. Since many homes and businesses use it for indoor heating, natural gas has a highly seasonal price that rises in the colder winter months and falls in the warmer summer months. By taking large spread positions, Amaranth was betting that the difference between these winter and summer prices would increase.

Amaranth started to build up short positions for the March 2006, April 2006, and November 2006 NYMEX natural gas futures, while at the same time acquiring a long position for the January 2007 future. The sizes of these positions were exceptional. Most traders consider control of only a few hundred contracts to be a substantial position; a position of 10,000 NYMEX natural gas futures contracts, meanwhile, will produce $1,000,000 in profit or loss for every cent of price change. Amaranth, however, soon acquired positions of over 40,000 March 2006 and 27,000 April 2006 contracts. These positions also represented a substantial share of the market. By February, Amaranth controlled over half of the open interest on NYMEX November 2006 natural gas futures contracts, and held a similar percentage of January 2007 contracts.

While Amaranth was building its spread positions during the first half of 2006, it also engaged in several unusual transactions, referred to by Plaintiffs-

[v] [N. 6] A spread position is created when a trader takes a long position in one future and a short position in another. The trader seeks to profit from changes in the difference between the two futures' prices, rather than from any absolute changes to the futures' prices themselves.

Appellants in their amended complaint as "slamming the close" trades. These trades all followed the same pattern: in the weeks leading up to a NYMEX future's expiration, Amaranth would simultaneously acquire a long position in the future and a short position in the corresponding swap on ICE. Then, during the last half hour of trading on the final trading day – the final settlement period – Amaranth would sell most or all of its long position, thus lowering the future's final settlement price. This would then lower the final settlement price of the corresponding ICE swap, allowing Amaranth to profit from its short position in that swap.

Amaranth engaged in these "slamming the close" trades for the March 2006, April 2006, and May 2006 NYMEX natural gas futures. . . . Subsequent investigations would reveal that Amaranth traders discussed "smashing" the settlement price of these NYMEX futures and directed floor brokers not to sell the contracts until the final minutes of trading.

In conducting these trades, Amaranth violated NYMEX position limits and accountability levels, which prompted investigations from both NYMEX and the CFTC. NYMEX also sought to limit Amaranth's trading for the June 2006 future, even contacting J.P. Futures, Amaranth's clearing broker, in May to remind it that Amaranth needed to remain below applicable position limits. Amaranth failed to heed these warnings, and on June 1 it appeared on a list of traders exceeding applicable accountability levels. Nevertheless, NYMEX's initial response to Amaranth's having again exceeded accountability levels was to recommend their temporary increase. Then in early August, NYMEX informed Amaranth that it should reduce its positions in the September 2006 natural gas future. Amaranth responded by shifting its positions in September and October natural gas futures to the corresponding swaps. . . .

By early September 2006, Amaranth had a total open position in natural gas futures and swaps of 594,455 contracts. The fund's ever-increasing positions kept the spreads between winter and summer natural gas prices artificially high. Indeed, energy traders would subsequently describe the spread between winter and summer prices as "clearly out-of-whack" and "ridiculous." The Senate Permanent Subcommittee on Investigations would later conclude that Amaranth "dominated" the domestic natural gas market in 2006, and "had a direct effect on U.S. natural gas prices and increased price volatility in the natural gas market." This investigation would reveal that Amaranth traders discussed using the fund's large positions to, among other things, "push" and "widen" spreads.

By September 2006, however, the market for natural gas moved in ways that disrupted Amaranth's positions. As the winter months approached, it became clearer that the price of natural gas would not rise considerably; the winter/summer price spreads in which Amaranth had invested consequently began to fall. Amaranth, faced with ballooning margin requirements, struggled to find the capital or credit necessary to continue buying large positions that could prop up prices. On the brink of collapse, the fund entered into negotiations with several investment banks to sell off its natural gas positions. These negotiations fell through, and on September 20, 2006, Amaranth sold most of its natural gas portfolio to J.P. Morgan. J.P. Morgan eventually earned $725 million from the takeover. Amaranth liquidated the remainder of its assets. . . .

As Amaranth's clearing broker, J.P. Futures "marked to market" Amaranth's positions on a daily basis in order to determine if Amaranth needed to deposit additional margin. This, along with J.P. Futures's other roles as a clearing broker, meant that it knew of Amaranth's positions and trading activity. As the clearing broker, J.P. Futures also knew when Amaranth violated NYMEX position limits or exceeded NYMEX accountability levels. Indeed, NYMEX contacted J.P. Futures directly in May 2006 to warn it about Amaranth's position in the June 2006 NYMEX natural gas future. Additionally, J.P. Futures knew of the positions Amaranth took in connection with its "slamming the close" trades. It similarly knew about the NYMEX and CFTC investigations into Amaranth's trading.

Throughout the class period, J.P. Futures continued to service all of Amaranth's trades, including those that put Amaranth's positions above applicable NYMEX position limits and accountability levels. On one occasion in late May 2006, J.P. Futures bypassed its own internal position limits for natural gas futures in order to clear a series of large trading transactions undertaken by Amaranth. During the summer months of 2006, J.P. Futures regularly granted Amaranth credit limit increases to support its positions on ICE. J.P. Futures facilitated Amaranth's transfer of positions from NYMEX natural gas futures to ICE natural gas swaps, which were beyond CFTC and NYMEX scrutiny. This transfer resulted in higher margin requirements for Amaranth, and thus increased fees and interest for J.P. Futures. . . .

[B]oth the CFTC and courts have determined that the standard for aiding and abetting liability under the CEA is the same as that for aiding and abetting under federal criminal law. . . .

As stated earlier, Plaintiffs-Appellants allege that Amaranth manipulated the price of NYMEX natural gas futures in two ways: (1) the accumulation of large open positions that artificially propped up natural gas calendar spreads; and (2) its "slamming the close" trades. Plaintiffs-Appellants allege that J.P. Futures had knowledge of these manipulative schemes because it had information on Amaranth's daily trading activity and open positions on NYMEX and ICE. This information also meant that J.P. Futures knew when Amaranth was in violation of NYMEX position limits or accountability levels. Plaintiffs-Appellants further allege that J.P. Futures performed multiple overt acts to assist Amaranth in its manipulations, including the clearing of trades, the extension of credit, and assistance in moving positions from NYMEX to ICE. According to the amended complaint, J.P. Futures assisted Amaranth because of the large commissions J.P. Futures earned from the fund's trading, as well as fees and interest it earned on the fund's margin deposits.

With respect to Plaintiffs-Appellants' first theory of manipulation – the building of large open positions – the amended complaint alleges, at most, a very weak inference that J.P. Futures actually knew of Amaranth's manipulative intent, much less that it intended to assist in carrying it out. This is for a simple reason: while J.P. Futures may have known about Amaranth's large positions in natural gas futures and swaps, such large positions do not necessarily imply manipulation. A trader may indeed acquire a large position in order to manipulate prices. But a trader may also acquire a large position in the belief that the price of the future will, for reasons other than the trader's own activity, move in a favorable direction. Put differently, large positions can be indicative either of manipulation or of excessive speculation. The amended complaint contains no allegation from which we can draw the conclusion that a clearing broker like J.P. Futures would know which is the goal of any particular large position held by a client.

This remains true even if a trader's positions violate applicable position limits and accountability levels. As the CEA explains, position limits and accountability levels are intended not only to prevent manipulation, but also "to diminish, eliminate, or prevent excessive speculation," "to ensure sufficient market liquidity for bona fide hedgers," and "to ensure that the price discovery function of the underlying market is not disrupted." 7 U.S.C. § 6a(a)(3)(B).[vi] This makes sense: excessive speculation, just as much as manipulation, can result in market illiquidity and artificial prices. If the violation of these restrictions does not necessarily entail manipulation, moreover, then neither should their evasion: that a trader shifts contracts from NYMEX to . . . [swaps] in order to maintain a large open position, standing alone, does not reveal why the trader seeks that large position. . . .

The allegations supporting Plaintiffs-Appellants' second theory of manipulation – the "slamming the close" trades – present a closer issue. In contrast to the acquisition of large open positions, J.P. Futures has provided no obvious legitimate economic reason why Amaranth would wait until the final minutes of trading to sell large quantities of a particular future. This type of trading activity, while not dispositive of manipulation, does strongly suggest it. Indeed, the district court found that "the timing of the sales are suspicious in themselves."

Still . . . we must consider J.P. Futures's alleged knowledge and intent regarding Amaranth's "slamming the close" trades in connection with J.P. Futures's alleged actions. The amended complaint does not allege that J.P.

[vi] [N. 16] Though . . . [7 U.S.C.] 6a(a)(3)(B) is specifically about position limits set by the CFTC, its description of their purpose applies to position limits and accountability levels generally. Indeed, 7 U.S.C. § 7(d)(5), which relates to position limits and accountability levels set by the exchanges, similarly states that position limits are "[t]o reduce the potential threat of market manipulation or congestion (especially during trading in the delivery month)." . . .

Futures did anything more to assist Amaranth in these trades than to provide routine clearing firm services. . . .

Plaintiffs-Appellants argue that the amended complaint also alleges that J.P. Futures performed "non-routine" tasks to assist Amaranth, including helping to transfer positions from NYMEX to ICE, extending credit limits, and bypassing internal position limits. But these acts, even if they are "non-routine," are alleged to have been performed only in connection with Amaranth's accumulation of large open positions. . . .

In sum, Plaintiffs–Appellants have cited no authority establishing that an FCM must at all times monitor its clients' trading in order to prevent manipulation. . . .

For the foregoing reasons, we AFFIRM the judgment of the district court.

---

c. Position Limits and Swaps

The CFTC had finalized a rule imposing position limits on swap transactions that referenced 28 specified physical commodities. This rule, however, was vacated.

International Swaps and Derivatives Association v. Commodity Futures Trading Commission

887 F. Supp. 2d 259 (D.D.C. 2012)

Robert L. Wilkins, District Judge.

Plaintiffs International Swaps and Derivatives Association ("ISDA") and Securities Industry and Financial Markets Association ("SIFMA") (collectively "Plaintiffs") challenge a . . . rulemaking by Defendant United States Commodity Futures Trading Commission ("CFTC" or "Commission") setting position limits on derivatives tied to 28 physical commodities.

The heart of Plaintiffs' challenge is that the CFTC misinterpreted its statutory authority under the Commodity Exchange Act of 1936 ("CEA"), as amended by [the] Dodd-Frank [Act]. The central question for the Court, then, is whether the CFTC promulgated the Position Limits Rule based on a correct and permissible interpretation of the statute at issue. . . .

A position limit "caps the maximum number of derivatives contracts to purchase (long) or sell (short) a commodity that an individual trader or group of traders may own during a given period." A position limit may impose a ceiling on either a "spot-month" position or a "non-spot-month" position. A "spot month" is a specific period of time (which varies by commodity under the rules) that immediately precedes the date of delivery of the commodity under the derivatives contract. . . .

The main issue in this case is whether the Dodd-Frank amendments to Section 4a of the CEA (codified at 7 U.S.C. § 6a)[vii] mandated that the CFTC impose a new position limits regime in the commodity derivatives market. It is undisputed that, prior to Dodd-Frank, the CEA vested the Commission with discretion to set position limits on futures and options contracts in commodity derivatives markets. . . .

Dodd-Frank went into effect on July 21, 2010. On January 26, 2011, the CFTC issued a Notice of Proposed Rulemaking ("NPRM"), stating that Title VII of Dodd–Frank "requires" the Commission "to establish position limits for certain physical commodity derivatives." At an open meeting on January 13, 2011 prior to the issuance of the NPRM, Commissioner Michael V. Dunn stated that, "to date CFTC staff has been unable to find any reliable economic analysis to support either the contention that excessive speculation is affecting the market we regulate or that position limits will prevent excessive speculation." Dunn also shared his "fear" that "at best position limits are a cure for a disease that does not exist, or at worst it's a placebo for one that does." Commissioners Jill Sommers and Scott D. O'Malia also expressed fundamental concerns with the position limits proposal before the agency. . . .

[O]n October 18, 2011, the CFTC adopted the Position Limits Rule by a vote of 3 to 2. Chairman Gary Gensler and Commissioner Bart Chilton voted in favor of the Rule, with Commissioner Dunn providing the third vote for the majority. Dunn stated that "no one has presented this agency any reliable economic analysis to support either the contention that excessive speculation is affecting the market we regulate or that position limits will prevent the excessive speculation." Dunn expressed his opinion that "position limits may harm the very markets we're intending to protect." Despite the fact that his opinion on position limits still "ha[d] not changed," Dunn voted in favor of the Rule because he believed Congress had required the Commission to impose position limits . . .

This case largely turns on whether the CFTC, in promulgating the Position Limits Rule, correctly interpreted Section 6a as amended by Dodd-Frank. Although both sides forcefully argue that the statute is clear and unambiguous, their respective interpretations lead to two very different results: one which mandates the Commission to set position limits without regard to whether they are necessary or appropriate, and one which requires the Commission to find such limits are necessary and appropriate before imposing them. . . .

The first question for the Court is whether Section 6a(a)(1) requires the Commission to find that position limits are necessary prior to imposing them. This is important, of course, because the so-called "mandate" of Dodd-Frank in Section 6a(a)(2) [to impose position limits on swaps] expressly incorporates the "standards" of paragraph (1). The relevant portion of Section 6a(a)(1) states:

[vii] [N. 2] This Court will refer to the statute by its United States Code number.

> For the purpose of diminishing, eliminating, or preventing such burden, *the Commission shall, from time to time*, after due notice and opportunity for hearing, by rule, regulation, or order, *proclaim and fix such limits on the amounts of trading which may be done or positions which may be held by any person . . .* under contracts of sale of such commodity for future delivery on or subject to the rules of any contract market or derivatives transaction execution facility, or swaps traded on or subject to the rules of a designated contract market or a swap execution facility, or swaps not traded on or subject to the rules of a designated contract market or a swap execution facility that performs a significant price discovery function with respect to a registered entity, *as the Commission finds are necessary to diminish, eliminate, or prevent such burden*.

§ 6a(a)(1) (emphasis added). . . .

[T]he Commission made necessity findings in its]past] rulemakings establishing position limits for 45 years after the passage of the CEA.

The CFTC argues that, although it made necessity findings in these prior rulemakings, the agency never stated that a finding of necessity was required. This argument is without merit. The plain text of the statute requires that position limits be set "as the Commission finds are necessary to diminish, eliminate, or prevent [excessive speculation]." § 6a(a)(1). The text does not state (nor has it ever) that the CFTC may do away with or ignore the necessity requirement in its discretion. There is no ambiguity as to whether the statute requires the CFTC to make such findings, and the CFTC has never apparently treated the statute as ambiguous on this point. Accordingly, the Court concludes that § 6a(a)(1) unambiguously requires that, prior to imposing position limits, the Commission find that position limits are necessary to "diminish, eliminate, or prevent" the burden described in Section 6a(a)(1). . . .

There is no question, as the CFTC argues, that Congress used traditionally mandatory language throughout the Dodd-Frank amendments to Section 6a. The CFTC relies on that language as support for its view that Congress stripped the CFTC of any discretion not to impose position limits even if the agency did not find it "necessary" or "appropriate" to do so. . . .

Upon a review of the entire Section 6a as amended by Dodd-Frank, the Court finds that there are at least two plausible readings of the statute. First is the CFTC's interpretation: that the CFTC was mandated to set position limits, that it was stripped of any discretion not to set limits, that it was not required to find (either implicitly or explicitly) that the imposition of position limits both generally and with respect to certain commodities was necessary, that it was not required to determine whether the actual imposition of limits was appropriate both generally and with respect to certain commodities, and that it was required to impose those limits expeditiously.[viii]

This interpretation, however, renders other parts of Section 6a mere surplusage. Significantly, it fails to give any meaningful effect to the very first clause of Section 6a(a)(2), which requires that the CFTC establish position limits "[i]n accordance with the standards set forth" in subsection (a)(1). . . .

The other plausible interpretation of Section 6a is the one that Plaintiffs offer. As Plaintiffs argue, "[t]he only reasonable reading of the Dodd–Frank amendments to Section 6a is that Congress intended the Commission to immediately gather evidence relating to whether excessive speculation was harming commodity markets and to impose position limits where necessary and appropriate to prevent an undue burden on the economy." In other words, Plaintiffs do not seem to contest that the CFTC may be required to impose position limits, but that that obligation does not arise until the Commission first makes a finding that such position limits are necessary to combat the burden described in 6a(a)(1). . . .

[T]he Dodd-Frank amendments to Section 6a are ambiguous and lend themselves to more than one plausible interpretation. . . .

The law of this Circuit, therefore, requires in this circumstance that the Court remand the rule to the agency so that it can fill in the gaps and resolve the ambiguities. . . .

Although the Court does not foreclose the possibility that the CFTC could, in the exercise of its discretion, determine that it should impose position limits without a finding of necessity and appropriateness, it is not plain and clear that the statute requires this result. . . .

Plaintiffs request that this Court vacate the Position Limits Rule and remand this matter back to the agency. The CFTC contends that, even were this Court to find in Plaintiffs' favor, the Court has discretion to – and should – remand the rule to the CFTC without vacatur. . . .

[A]s set forth above, the CFTC's error in this case was that it fundamentally misunderstood and failed to recognize the ambiguities in the statute. In circumstances such as this, our Circuit has found it appropriate to vacate the agency action on remand. . . .

[I]t would be far more disruptive if the Position Limits Rule were allowed to go into effect while on remand. . . .

For the foregoing reasons, the Position Limits Rule is vacated and remanded to the Commission . . .

[viii] [N. 6] So rigid is the Commission's view of the Dodd-Frank "mandate" that, at oral argument, agency counsel represented to the Court that the agency intended to eventually set position limits on derivatives tied to every non-exempt physical commodity.

In the wake of this ruling – and presumably guided by the findings of the court – the CFTC has proposed a new position limits rule applying to swaps.[22] The proposed rule, just like the rule vacated by the court in *International Swaps and Derivatives Association v. CFTC*, seeks to impose position limits with respect to swaps referencing 28 physical commodities.

d. Cornering

The position limits authority is just one means of preventing market manipulation due to the aggregation of positions. The CFTC also has enforcement authority with respect to attempts to "corner" the market.

In the Matter of Fenchurch Capital Management, Ltd.

CFTC No. 96-7 (July 10, 1996)

ORDER INSTITUTING PROCEEDINGS PURSUANT TO SECTIONS 6(c), 6(d) AND 8(a) OF THE COMMODITY EXCHANGE ACT AS AMENDED AND FINDINGS AND ORDER IMPOSING REMEDIAL SANCTIONS . . .

The Commodity Futures Trading Commission ("Commission") has reason to believe that Fenchurch Capital Management, Ltd. ("Fenchurch") has violated Sections 6(c) and 9(a)(2) of the Commodity Exchange Act, as amended ("Act"). . . .

The Commission finds [that] . . . Fenchurch is, and was at all times relevant to this matter, registered with the Commission as a commodity trading advisor and commodity pool operator . . . Fenchurch trades extensively in the U.S. government securities cash and futures markets, has held large positions in government securities futures contracts as part of arbitrage positions, and has taken large deliveries on several futures contracts. . . .

In June 1993, Fenchurch stood for delivery on a large futures position on the June 1993 Ten Year U.S. Treasury Note futures contract ("June contract") traded on the Chicago Board of Trade ("CBT"). During the last four business days of the delivery period and after the last trading day on the June contract, Fenchurch intentionally gained and maintained control over a dominant portion of the available supply of the cheapest-to-deliver Treasury notes on the June contract. Fenchurch increased its position in the issue through a series of repurchase ("repo") market transactions at a time when the notes were in tight supply . . . Fenchurch exacerbated the tightness in the supply of the cheapest-to-deliver notes by increasing its position and intentionally withholding the notes from the market. As a result, shorts on the futures contract were unable to obtain sufficient quantities of the notes and had to deliver a more valuable security without offsetting compensation. . . .

Through its conduct, Fenchurch increased and thus manipulated upward the value of its position on the June contract by cornering the available supply of the cheapest-to-deliver notes in violation of Sections 6(c) and 9(a)(2) of the Act. . . .

On June 21, 1993, the last day of trading on the June contract, Fenchurch stood for delivery on a long futures position of about 12,700 contracts. Fenchurch's position was 76% of the open interest on the June contract. At that time, the total open interest was the third largest to be satisfied by delivery in the history of the CBT 10 Year Note contract. The terms of the June contract allowed shorts to deliver any Treasury security in a basket of notes having certain maturity characteristics. Typically, one note in the basket becomes the cheapest-to-deliver based principally on coupon rates and times to maturity, and the price of the contract converges with the cash market value of the cheapest-to-deliver issue. Throughout the month of June 1993, the cheapest-to-deliver note on the June contract was the 8 1/2% February 15, 2000 United States Treasury Note ("8 1/2% note"). Thus, the settlement price of the June contract at expiration reflected the value of the 8 1/2% note in the cash market.

Shorts on the June contract could make delivery anytime during the delivery month, with the last delivery day being on June 30. Because long term interest rates were higher than short term rates in June 1993, it was most economical for the shorts to delay delivery until the last delivery day, if possible. When the notes are readily available in the market, acquisition and delivery of the notes occurs quickly and easily through use of the Federal wire. If there is no indication that the cheapest-to-deliver note is in tight supply, shorts generally prepare for delivery within a few days prior to the last delivery day. . . .

In June 1993, there were no signs that the cheapest-to-deliver note, the 8 1/2% note, was in short supply until Friday, June 25. . . .

As of June 25, Fenchurch was in a position to benefit from the developing scarcity of the 8 1/2% notes and the increased value of receiving the 8 7/8% notes on delivery. Fenchurch already held a sizable pre-existing position in the 8 1/2% note. In addition to its large futures position, Fenchurch also had entered into several repo transactions using the 8 1/2% note as collateral. . . .

With the developing scarcity of the 8 1/2% notes and the increasing value of receiving the 8 7/8% notes, Fenchurch proceeded to increase its position in the 8 1/2% notes to over $2 billion and withheld the notes from the markets. Fenchurch knew that if it acquired and maintained control over a dominant portion of the available supply of the 8 1/2% notes until delivery on June 30, shorts would have to deliver the more valuable 8 7/8% note on the June contract. Between June 25 and 29, Fenchurch borrowed the notes in the repo market at the increasingly low repo rates for the 8 1/2% notes and entered into overnight repo transactions with several counterparties using the 8 1/2% notes as collateral. . . . In negotiating each repo transaction, Fenchurch's repo trader ensured that the counterparty would not relend the notes to the repo market.

At the same time that Fenchurch was entering into new repo transactions in which it lent the 8 1/2% notes to counterparties who would not relend them to the market, Fenchurch was intentionally "failing" on various repo transactions, i.e., failing to return the notes to counterparties from whom it had borrowed them. By failing to return the notes, Fenchurch gave up the interest it would have received on the transactions. Several of the counterparties on the transactions in which Fenchurch failed to return the security were preparing to make delivery on the June contract. . . .

Fenchurch withheld from the markets a dominant portion of the available supply of the 8 1/2% notes [and] . . . increased substantially the value of its futures position, thus benefitting itself and the two pools it manages. . . .

In pursuing the course of action set forth above, Fenchurch attempted to manipulate and did manipulate upward the value of Fenchurch's long futures position in the June contract by attempting to corner and cornering the available supply of the cheapest-to-deliver notes on the June contract. . . .

Although the conduct here occurred after the expiration of the contract, Fenchurch nonetheless engaged in intentional conduct through which it controlled a dominant portion of the cheapest-to-deliver notes available for delivery on the June Contract and thus restricted the available supply of the cheapest-to-deliver issue. Fenchurch's conduct resulted in the value of the futures contract being artificially altered.

Fenchurch intentionally acquired and maintained its dominant position in the 8 1/2% notes at a time of tight supplies and as a result the shorts had to deliver the more valuable 8 7/8% notes. By receiving the 8 7/8% notes on approximately one third of its futures position, the value of Fenchurch's position became artificially high. The Commission believes that Fenchurch's activities . . . did not have an economic or business rationale but for an intent to restrict the supply of the notes in order to obtain delivery of a more valuable security. . . .

It is the Commission's responsibility to ensure that futures markets remain free of illegitimate forces throughout the trading and delivery periods. If longs are allowed to engage in conduct of the type found in this case, the price discovery function of the futures markets could be jeopardized. . . .

Based on the foregoing, the Commission finds that Fenchurch violated Sections 6(c) and 9(a)(2) of the Act. . . .

QUESTIONS AND COMMENTS

1. Why, at the time *United States v. Reliant Energy* was decided in 2006, had there never been a criminal prosecution based on the Commodity Exchange Act's anti-manipulation provisions? Why have the criminal provisions in the Commodity Exchange Act if the more common practice is to charge defendants with violations of the Federal mail and wire fraud statutes?
2. What are some of the reasons the Department of Justice might seek to criminally prosecute a defendant under the Federal mail or wire fraud

statutes? Familiarity with the statutes, abundant supporting case law, different standards of proof?

3. The "London Whale" lost JPMorgan more than $6 billion in total. In a context where the alleged manipulator absorbs such a significant loss does a CFTC enforcement action alleging market manipulation make sense?
4. As a practical matter, why might the plaintiffs in *In re Amaranth Natural Gas Commodities Litigation* have sought to make a claim against J.P. Morgan Futures, Inc., for aiding and abetting liability instead of focusing on claims against Amaranth itself?
5. Devise a market manipulation. Now evaluate the civil enforcement and criminal prosecution strategies you would employ if you were the CFTC enforcing the civil provisions of the Commodity Exchange Act and the Department of Justice enforcing the criminal provisions.

CHAPTER 14
PRIVATE ENFORCEMENT

A. PRIVATE RIGHT OF ACTION

1. Pre-1982

Before the Futures Trading Act of 1982, the Commodity Exchange Act contained no explicit private right of action. In the below case, the Supreme Court concluded that Congress had intended private parties to have the ability to make a claim for a violation of the Commodity Exchange Act.

Merrill Lynch, Pierce, Fenner & Smith, Inc. v. Curran

456 U.S. 353 (1982)

Justice Stevens delivered the opinion of the Court. . . .

The central question presented . . . is whether a private party may maintain an action for damages caused by a violation of the . . . [Commodity Exchange Act (the "CEA")]. . . .

[I]n a broad sense, futures trading has a direct financial impact on three classes of persons. Those who actually are interested in selling or buying the commodity are described as "hedgers"; their primary financial interest is in the profit to be earned from the production or processing of the commodity. Those who seek financial gain by taking positions in the futures market generally are called "speculators" or "investors"; without their participation, futures markets "simply would not exist."[i] Finally, there are the futures commission merchants,

---

[i] [N. 11] ". . . Speculators . . . embrace all representatives of the general public . . . who seek financial gain by taking positions in volatile markets. The principal role of the speculator in the markets is to take the risks that the hedger is unwilling to accept. The opportunity for profit makes the speculator willing to take those risks. The activity of speculators is essential to the operation of a futures market in that the composite bids and offers of large numbers of individuals tend to broaden a market, thus making possible the execution . . . of the larger trade hedging orders. By increasing the number

the floor brokers, and the persons who manage the market; they also are essential participants, and they have an interest in maximizing the activity on the exchange. The petitioners in these cases are members of this third class whereas their adversaries, the respondents, are speculators or investors. . . .

In the four cases before us, the allegations in the complaints filed by respondents are assumed to be true. The first involves a complaint by customers against their broker. The other three arise out of a malfunction of the contract market for futures contracts covering the delivery of Maine potatoes in May 1976, "'when the sellers of almost 1,000 contracts failed to deliver approximately 50,000,000 pounds of potatoes, resulting in the largest default in the history of commodities futures trading in this country.'" . . .

From the enactment of the original federal legislation [regulating commodity futures], Congress primarily has relied upon the exchanges to regulate the contract markets. . . . [T]he exchanges promulgated rules and regulations, but they did not always enforce them. In 1968, Congress attempted to correct this flaw in the self-regulation concept by enacting § 5a(8), which requires the exchanges to enforce their own rules.

The enactment of § 5a(8), coupled with the recognition by the federal courts of an implied private remedy for violations of the CEA, gave rise to a new problem. As representatives of the exchanges complained during the hearings preceding . . . 1974 amendments [to the Commodity Exchange Act], the exchanges were being sued for not enforcing their rules. The complaint was taken seriously because it implicated the self-regulation premise of the CEA. . . .

Congress could have removed this impediment to exchange rulemaking by eliminating the implied private remedy, but it did not follow that course. . . .

Congress in 1974 created new procedures through which traders might seek relief for violations of the CEA, but the legislative evidence indicates that these informal procedures were intended to supplement rather than supplant the implied judicial remedy. These procedures do not substitute for the private remedy either as a means of compensating injured traders or as a means of enforcing compliance with the statute. . . .

As the Solicitor General argues on behalf of the Commission as amicus curiae, the private cause of action enhances the enforcement mechanism fostered by Congress over the course of 60 years. . . .

---

of bids and offers available at any given price level, the speculator usually helps to minimize price fluctuations rather than to intensify them. Without the trading activity of the speculative fraternity, the liquidity, so badly needed in futures markets, simply would not exist. Trading volume would be restricted materially since, without a host of speculative orders in the trading ring, many larger trade orders at limit prices would simply go unfilled due to the floor broker's inability to find an equally large but opposing hedge order at the same price to complete the match." [H.R.Rep. No. 93–975, p. 1 (1974), U.S.Code Cong. & Admin.News 1974 ("House Report")] . . . , at 138.

In addition to their principal argument that no private remedy is available under the CEA, petitioners also contend that respondents, as speculators, may not maintain such an action . . .

The characterization of persons who invest in futures contracts as "speculators" does not exclude them from the class of persons protected by the CEA. The statutory scheme could not effectively protect the producers and processors who engage in hedging transactions without also protecting the other participants in the market whose transactions over exchanges necessarily must conform to the same trading rules. . . .

The legislative history quite clearly indicates that Congress intended to protect all futures traders from price manipulation and other fraudulent conduct violative of the statute. It is assumed, of course, that federal regulation of futures trading benefits the entire economy; a sound futures market tends to reduce retail prices of the underlying commodities. The immediate beneficiaries of a healthy futures market are the producers and processors of commodities who can minimize the risk of loss from volatile price changes on the cash market by hedging on the futures market.

The judgments of the Courts of Appeals [finding that a private right of action is available] are affirmed. . . .

---

2. *Futures Trading Act of 1982*

In response to the decision in *Merrill Lynch v. Curran*, Congress added an explicit private right of action to the Commodity Exchange Act via the Futures Trading Act of 1982.[1]

House of Representatives Report on the Futures Trading Act of 1982

H.R. Rept. 97-565 (May 17, 1982)

. . . At the time the Committee considered the bill, the Supreme Court had not yet resolved the issue of whether a private right of action could be implied under the [Commodity Exchange] Act. The Committee is of the view that the right of an aggrieved person to sue a violator of the Act is critical to protecting the public and fundamental to maintaining the credibility of the futures market.

To that end the Committee added a new section to the bill to provide specific authority for private rights of action for recovery of actual damages against violators of the Act. In order to recover the violation must have arisen from a transaction on the futures market, a regulated option or leverage contract, or participation in a commodity pool.

The Committee also specifically provided for liability for actual damages by a contract market, clearing organization of a contract market, licensed board of trade or registered futures association that failed to enforce a bylaw, rule or regulation made a condition of its designation or license. In addition, a cause of action could be brought against an officer, director, or employee who willfully aided or induced such a violation. The cause of action in these cases would be restricted to cases where the plaintiff had engaged in a regulated commodity transaction and could show that there was bad faith in failing to take the necessary action. Any action by a private litigant under the Act must be brought within two years after the date the cause of action accrued.

The Committee included these restrictions on the causes of action to avoid suits for speculative damages to assets that are affected by fluctuations in prices on the commodity market but which are not the subject of transactions on such market.

The availability of these remedies -- reparations, arbitration and private rights of action -- supplements, but does not substitute, for the regulatory and enforcement program of the CFTC and self-regulatory agencies. The Committee fully expects that these agencies will vigorously use the tools at its command to protect the investing public so that it does not become necessary to rely on private litigants as a policeman of the Commodity Exchange Act. . . .

The above-described provisions were enacted into the Commodity Exchange Act by the Futures Trading Act of 1982. They were amended by the Dodd-Frank Act to include swaps in their scope. There is a two year statute of limitations for private rights of action under the Commodity Exchange Act.

Commodity Exchange Act § 22

Private rights of action

(a) Actual damages; actionable transactions; exclusive remedy

(1) Any person (other than a registered entity or registered futures association) who violates this chapter or who willfully aids, abets, counsels, induces, or procures the commission of a violation of this chapter shall be liable for actual damages resulting from . . . the transactions referred to in subparagraphs (A) through (D) of this paragraph and caused by such violation to any other person –

(A) who received trading advice from such person for a fee;

(B) who made through such person any contract of sale of any commodity for future delivery (or option on such contract or any commodity) or any swap; or who deposited with or paid to such person money, securities, or property (or incurred debt in lieu thereof) in connection with any order to make such contract or any swap;

(C) who purchased from or sold to such person or placed through such person an order for the purchase or sale of –

(i) an option subject to [CFTC jurisdiction] . . . (other than an option purchased or sold on a registered entity or other board of trade); . . .

(iii) an interest or participation in a commodity pool; or

(iv) a swap; or

(D) who purchased or sold a contract referred to in subparagraph (B) hereof or swap if the violation constitutes –

(i) the use or employment of, or an attempt to use or employ . . . any manipulative device or contrivance in contravention of [CFTC] . . . rules and regulations . . .; or

(ii) a manipulation of the price of any such contract or swap or the price of the commodity underlying such contract or swap. . . .

(3) In any action arising from a violation in the execution of an order on the floor of a registered entity, the person referred to in paragraph (1) shall be liable for –

(A) actual damages proximately caused by such violation . . .; and

(B) where the violation is willful and intentional, punitive or exemplary damages equal to no more than two times the amount of such actual damages. . . .

(b) Liabilities of organizations and individuals; bad faith requirement; exclusive remedy

(1) (A) A registered entity that fails to enforce any bylaw, rule, regulation, or resolution . . ., (B) a licensed board of trade that fails to enforce any bylaw, rule, regulation, or resolution that it is required to enforce by the Commission, or (C) any registered entity that in enforcing any such bylaw, rule, regulation, or resolution violates this chapter or any Commission rule, regulation, or order, shall be liable for actual damages sustained by a person who engaged in any transaction on or subject to the rules of such registered entity to the extent of such person's actual losses that resulted from such transaction and were caused by such failure to enforce or enforcement of such bylaws, rules, regulations, or resolutions.

(2) A registered futures association that fails to enforce any bylaw or rule that is required . . . or in enforcing any such bylaw or rule violates . . . [the Commodity Exchange Act] or any Commission rule, regulation, or order shall be liable for actual damages sustained by a person that engaged in any transaction specified in subsection (a) of this section to the extent of such person's actual losses that resulted from such transaction and were caused by such failure to enforce or enforcement of such bylaw or rule. . . .

(c) Jurisdiction; statute of limitations . . .

The United States district courts shall have exclusive jurisdiction of actions brought under this section. Any such action shall be brought not later than two years after the date the cause of action arises. . . .

---

3. Limitations on the Commodity Exchange Act's Private Right of Action

a. Limitations on Parties Against Whom Claims Can Be Made

The limitation of the private right of action in Commodity Exchange Act § 22(a)(1) to claims against four categories of persons has been a cause of dispute as plaintiffs have propounded theories broadening the scope of possible parties against whom a private right of action under the Commodity Exchange Act is available.

One theory, backed by the CFTC and the Seventh Circuit, is that Commodity Exchange Act § 22(a)(1) permits a claim against a party not specifically enumerated therein if such party is an aider or abettor of a person in one of the four categories listed in § 22(a)(1).

Nicholas v. Saul Stone & Co. LLC

224 F.3d 179 (3d Cir. 2000)

Pollak, District Judge.

Appellants seek review of a judgment of the District Court of New Jersey granting defendants' motion to dismiss plaintiffs' amended complaint. . . .

According to the amended complaint, the plaintiffs . . . are persons who . . . were lured into improvident investments in the commodities market by Chuck ("Chuckles") Kohli, Nungambukkam Swamy Ramchandran, and certain corporate pawns of Kohli and Ramchandran known collectively as "Sigma." . . . The investors were told that the funds would be placed in a commodities trading pool and used to invest in commodities futures and options. . . . Plaintiffs further alleged that . . . the bulk of those investments failed. However, . . . investors seeking to withdraw their funds or profits were paid with the funds of later investors, thus creating the aura of success. The plaintiffs' pleadings characterized this structure as a Ponzi scheme. . . .

Kohli has since pled guilty to federal criminal charges stemming out of these events, and Ramchandran has since filed for bankruptcy. As a result, plaintiffs have undertaken to seek recoupment of their losses elsewhere.

Plaintiffs brought suit in the District Court for New Jersey against the FCMs used by Kohli, Ramchandran, and Sigma. . . .

Because of the various registration requirements (detailed below) laid down by the Commodities [*sic*] Exchange Act ("CEA") . . . Kohli, Ramchandran, and Sigma were, so plaintiffs alleged, under a duty to register with the Commodities [*sic*] Futures Trading Commission (the "CFTC") . . . ; they were also, plaintiffs alleged, obligated to become members of the NFA. Plaintiffs further alleged that Kohli, Ramchandran, and Sigma, in fact, did not register with the . . . [CFTC] or become members of the NFA, and hence that the various FCMs that accepted their business acted improperly. In particular, plaintiffs alleged that the defendant FCMs and their employees failed to inquire into the source of funds in the Sigma accounts or into the CFTC registration status and NFA membership of Kohli, Ramchandran, and Sigma. . . . Plaintiffs alleged that the FCMs and their employees, by failing to make the necessary investigation, directly violated the CEA, and aided and abetted violations of the CEA . . .

Appellants have raised numerous issues. Most do not, in our view, require discussion in this opinion because they have been fully and correctly canvassed in the District Court's comprehensive opinion. There are, however, a few issues arising under section 22 of the CEA which, we think, call for additional analysis. . . .

Subsection 22(a)(1) of the CEA creates a private right of action for "actual damages" caused by "[a]ny person . . . who violates this chapter [the CEA] or who willfully aids [or] abets . . . the commission of a violation of this chapter." . . .

A plaintiff may bring a private damage action against "[a]ny person who violates" the CEA when that person stands in one of four relationships with the plaintiff specified in subparagraphs (A) through (D) of subsection 22(a)(1). Each of the required relationships involves the "person" sued having given advice related to the sale of commodities, or having participated in a transaction related to such sales. Subparagraph (A) imposes liability on the "person" sued when a plaintiff "received trading advice from such person for a fee"; subparagraph (B) imposes liability on the "person" sued when the plaintiff "made through *such person*" a contract for futures or options thereon, or when the plaintiff deposited money or other property with "*such person*" in connection with a futures or options contract; subparagraph (C) imposes liability on the "person" sued when the plaintiff purchased from or sold to " such person," or placed through "*such person*" an order for, certain specified options or commodities contracts, or "an interest or participation in a commodity pool"; and subparagraph (D) imposes liability on the "person" sued when the plaintiff "purchased or sold a contract referred to in subparagraph (B) if the violation constitutes a manipulation of the price of any such contract or the price of the commodity underlying such contract." (Emphasis added). If the "person" sued has participated in one of the transactions specified in these four subparagraphs, then "such person" can be held liable "for actual damages resulting from one or more of the [specified] transactions . . . and caused by such violation" to the plaintiff. Thus, in order for a plaintiff to sue a defendant for directly violating subsection 22(a)(1), the defendant must (1) have violated the CEA, and (2) stand in an appropriate relationship to the plaintiff with respect to the violative conduct.

Appellants, in their amended complaint, alleged that the FCMs were liable under subsection 22(a)(1) to plaintiffs because of their participation in transactions described in subparagraphs (A), (B), and (C). In particular, appellants alleged that the defendant FCMs gave trading advice to Kohli, who was, so appellants alleged, in some sense, appellants' agent. Similarly, appellants alleged that the FCMs accepted orders of the kind described in subparagraph (B) from Kohli. And finally, appellants contended that the FCMs fell under subparagraph (C) insofar as they permitted Kohli, Ramchandran, and Sigma to sell to appellants interests in commodity pools in violation of the CEA.

Appellants do not contend that the defendant FCMs themselves stood in one of the listed relationships to one or more of the appellants. . . . According to appellants, the conclusion that "Defendant FCMs were dealing directly with Plaintiffs for purposes of violating 7 U.S.C. § 25(a)(1)(A)-(D)" follows from the fact that "Kohli, the acknowledged primary violator was the Plaintiff's [sic] agent." The District Court rejected appellants' theory, stating that "[p]laintiffs have provided no authority for allowing a [subsection 22(a)(1)] relationship to be established through an agency theory and there is no indication in the statute indicating the availability of such relief." Without deciding whether or to what extent an agency relationship can ever appropriately be used to establish a subsection 22(a)(1) relationship, we agree with the District Court that the agency theory invoked by appellants does not fit this case. For, as the District Court stated, "allowing such a theory in the instant case, where Kohli, although technically the agent of the plaintiff[s], was clearly not operating in plaintiffs' interests does not seem appropriate." Accordingly, the FCMs' transactions with Kohli (and/or Ramchandran and/or Sigma) do not suffice to make them liable to appellants under subsection 22(a)(1).

We turn, then, to appellants' alternate subsection 22(a)(1) theory – namely that the defendant FCMs can be found liable to appellants by virtue of having "aided and abetted" Kohli (and/or Ramchandran and/or Sigma) in violating the CEA.

The District Court held that the FCMs could not be liable under subsection 22(a)(1) as aiders and abetters based on its view that, in order to establish aider-and-abetter liability, a defendant must be in one of the four subparagraph-(A)-through-(D) relationships with a plaintiff. The District Court . . . reached this conclusion on the basis of language in subsection 22(a)(1) which appears to treat direct and aider-and-abetter liability in parallel terms. Thus, for example, subsection 22(a)(1) provides, "*Any person* who violates this chapter or who willfully aids [and] abets . . . the commission of a violation of this chapter shall be liable for actual damages resulting from one or more of the [specified] transactions . . . and caused by such violation to any other person – (A) who received trading advice from *such person* for a fee." 7 U.S.C. § 25(a)(1) (emphasis added). Each of the specified transactions in subparagraphs (A), (B), and (C) (the three subparagraphs invoked in the amended complaint) involves activity by "such person" – the antecedent of which appears to be a "person who violates this chapter or who willfully aids [and] abets . . . the commission of a violation."[ii] Accordingly, the syntactic structure of the statute seems to contemplate that "any person" who aids and abets can only be held liable if he is also "such person," i.e., a person who performs one of the acts enumerated in (A), (B), and (C). Under this reading of the statute, it would appear that – just as with direct violators of the CEA – a plaintiff can bring private causes of action against aiders and abetters only if they (1) aid and abet a violation of the CEA; and (2) themselves stand in one of the relationships specified in subparagraphs (A), (B), and (C). . . .

In holding that only "such persons" can be liable as aiders and abetters under subsection 22(a)(1) of the CEA, the District Court expressly rejected the position of the Commodities [*sic*] Futures Trading Commission ("CFTC"), as expressed in an amicus curiae brief, which had been filed by the CFTC in the then-pending appeal to the Seventh Circuit in *Damato v. Hermanson* [153 F.3d 464 (7th Cir. 1998)] . . . and which had been presented to the District Court in the present case by plaintiffs. The CFTC, in that brief, had argued that the reading adopted by the district court in *Damato* would unnecessarily limit aider and abetter liability:

> Indeed, requiring that the aider and abettor be "such person" within the meaning of subparagraphs (A) through (D) renders § 22(a) internally inconsistent and does violence to the clear intent of § 22. As indicated above, § 22(a)(1)(A)-(D) defines the persons who are appropriate plaintiffs under the CEA. It also sets forth the damages that may be recovered in a private right of action. It limits recovery to damages caused by the violation and "resulting from one or more of the transactions referred to in subparagraphs (A) through (D)." If "such person" under subparagraphs (A) through (D) referred to the aider and abettor (i.e., if the aider and abettor were required to have the direct relationship with plaintiff), then the only damages recoverable would be those resulting from the transaction between the aider and abettor and the plaintiff. This is nonsensical, because the plaintiff's damages result not from the act of the aider and abettor in providing trading advice or selling futures, options or pool interests to the plaintiff, but from the violation itself by the primary violator. . . . Thus, for the language of § 22

[ii] [N. 14] Although subparagraph (D) does not expressly refer to "such person," its operative focus is on transactions involving "a contract referred to in subparagraph (B)." We need not, however, address the ingredients of aider-and-abetter liability under subparagraph (D), since as the District Court noted, the amended complaint focused on transactions allegedly falling within subparagraphs (A), (B), and (C).

> to make sense, "such person" in subparagraphs (A) through (D) must refer to the primary violator and not the aider and abettor.

Thus, according to the CFTC, "§ 22(a) creates liability for an aider and abettor if (i) he or she assists in a violation of the Act, (ii) the plaintiffs' damages are caused by that underlying violation and (iii) the damages result from one of the transactions set forth in subparagraphs (A)-(D). There is no independent requirement that both the primary violator and the aider and abettor deal directly with the plaintiff."

After the District Court handed down its order dismissing the amended complaint . . . the Seventh Circuit . . . adopted the CFTC interpretation of subsection 22(a)(1).

In the instant case, appellants urge this court to follow the Seventh Circuit's adoption . . . of the CFTC approach to subsection 22(a)(1)'s aiding and abetting language. By contrast, appellees argue, *contra Damato*, that this court should look to the plain language of subsection 22(a)(1), and that – because the FCMs and their employees took no action described in subparagraphs 22(a)(1)(A) through (C) – the FCMs should not be liable as aiders and abetters. We find it unnecessary, however, to resolve this issue at this juncture. For even assuming that we were to follow *Damato*'s adoption of the CFTC approach, the defendant FCMs could, in any event, only be held liable if their conduct met the basic requirements of aiding and abetting. But plaintiffs, in their amended complaint, have not alleged such conduct. . . .

The closest that the amended complaint comes to alleging that the FCMs knew of the misconduct of Kohli, Ramchandran, and Sigma are the statements that the FCMs "were aware, or with required minimal due diligence would have discovered" that "Kohli, Chandran and the Sigma Entities were a fiction under the CEA," and that the FCMs "knew or recklessly disregarded facts showing that" Kohli, Ramchandran, and the Sigma Entities were engaged in various activities violative of the CEA. In essence, appellants have alleged, at most, that the FCMs acted recklessly, and that they knew or should have known of the violations by Kohli, Ramchandran, and Sigma of the CEA. But these allegations are a far cry from an allegation that the FCMs not only had knowledge of the intent of Kohli and the others to violate the CEA, but, as the Seventh Circuit put it in *Damato*, "the intent to further that violation." Accordingly, even if we were to assume arguendo the correctness of the CFTC construction of subsection 22(a)(1) . . . which was adopted by the Seventh Circuit in *Damato*, plaintiffs' amended complaint nonetheless falls short. Therefore, we conclude that the District Court acted properly in dismissing appellants' aiding and abetting claims. . . .

---

b. Limitations on Claimants

Commodity Exchange Act § 22 also limits the categories of parties who can bring a private right of action.

Klein & Co. Futures, Inc. v. Board of Trade of City of New York

464 F.3d 255 (2d Cir. 2006)

B.D. Parker, Jr., Circuit Judge:

Klein & Co. Futures Inc. is a futures commission merchant ("FCM") and a clearing member of New York Clearing Corporation ("NYCC"). Klein appeals the dismissal by the United States District Court for the Southern District of New York . . . for lack of standing to bring claims against Defendant-Appellees the Board of Trade of the City of New York ("NYBOT"), New York Clearing Corporation ("NYCC"), Norman Eisler, and others (collectively "NYBOT Defendants") under Sections 22(a) and (b) of the Commodity Exchange Act (CEA). . . . For the reasons set forth below, we affirm. . . .

As a FCM, Klein facilitated the trading and fulfilled certain obligations of its customers who traded through the NYBOT. Prior to May 2000, Defendant Norman Eisler, whose conduct is the focus of Klein's complaint, was the Chairman of the New York Futures Exchange ("NYFE"). The NYFE is a futures and options exchange designated by the Commodity Futures Trading Commission ("CFTC") as a contract market for the trading of commodities futures and options, including P-Tech Futures and Options ("P-Tech contracts"). Eisler was also a member of the NYFE's Settlement Committee for the Pacific Stock Exchange Technology Index Futures Contract & Options (the "Committee"). The Committee's primary responsibility was to calculate the price of P-Tech contracts for the purposes, among other things, of calculating margin requirements in customers' accounts.[iii] Eisler was also a customer of Klein and the principal of First West Trading Inc. ("First West"), another Klein customer. Eisler traded in P-Tech contracts for the account of First West. The trades were unsolicited and were made without input or advice from Klein.

Allegedly, Eisler, in his capacity as a member of the Committee, secretly manipulated the settlement prices of P-Tech contracts. This manipulation benefitted Eisler's P-Tech positions but, at the same time, caused Klein to miscalculate the margin requirements for the First West account. Around March 2000, the NYBOT began receiving complaints regarding the P-Tech settlement

---

[iii] [N. 1] P-Tech Futures and Options prices are based on a composite index of one hundred technology stocks compiled by the Pacific Stock Exchange. The prices of those stocks and the value of that index may change up to the close of trading. Therefore, the Committee was charged with setting the settlement price after the close of the market.

prices but failed to make proper inquiries or to place Klein or other members of the industry or public on notice of potential irregularities.

In early May 2000, Klein, based on the incorrect settlement prices, computed the required margin in First West's account at $700,000, but Eisler was unable to post that amount. Klein then contacted the NYBOT and expressed concerns regarding the illiquidity of the P-Tech contracts, Eisler's inability to meet First West's margin call, and his inability to liquidate First West's contracts. Klein reported that the First West margin deficit, if not covered, would impair Klein's net capital and cause Eisler significant losses. Klein requested that the NYFE Board halt trading in P-Tech contracts, but no such action occurred.

At that point, the scheme began to unravel. In mid-May, Eisler's NYBOT membership privileges were suspended and he was dropped from the Committee. Once this occurred, the remaining Committee members recalculated the settlement prices and First West's margin deficit ballooned to $4.5 million, an obligation it could not meet. As a result, Klein was required to take an immediate charge against its net capital, forcing it below the minimum required for clearing members of the NYCC and the New York Mercantile Exchange ("NYMEX"). Its membership privileges were suspended and Klein collapsed.

Klein then sued on various claims. Klein's first claim alleged that NYFE violated § 5b of the CEA by failing to enforce its rules, and sought a declaration that NYFE should be suspended as a contract market. Klein further alleged that the NYBOT Defendants violated the . . . CEA. . . .

The NYBOT Defendants moved to dismiss principally on the ground that Klein was not a purchaser or seller of futures contracts or options and, therefore, lacked standing under § 22 of the CEA. They also they moved to dismiss Klein's state law claims with prejudice on the ground that they were preempted by the CEA. The district court agreed and dismissed Klein's claims under the CEA for lack of standing. . . .

The court . . . reasoned that § 22 precluded an action by a plaintiff that "did not suffer its damages in the course of its trading activities on a contract market." . . . This appeal followed. . . .

CEA § 22 enumerates the only circumstances under which a private litigant may assert a private right of action for violations of the CEA. Section 22 includes two types of claims. Section 22(a) relates to claims against persons other than registered entities and registered futures associations. Section 22(b) deals with claims against those entities and their officers directors, governors, committee members and employees. The text of the two subdivisions requires that a putative plaintiff fall within one of the four required relationships set forth in § 22(a)(1)(A-D).

The common thread of these four subdivisions is that they limit claims to those of a plaintiff who actually traded in the commodities market. Specifically, the remedies afforded by CEA § 22(b) are available only to a private litigant "who engaged in . . . transaction[s] on or subject to the rules of" a contract market. The section contains another important limitation. Subsection 22(b)(5) provides that the private rights of action against the exchanges enumerated in § 22(b) "shall be the exclusive remedy . . . available to any person who sustains a loss as a result of" a violation of the CEA or an exchange rule by a contract market or one of its officers or employees.

Klein does not fall within any of the required subdivisions of § 22(a)(1)(A)-(D). To fit under one of the four, Klein must essentially either have (1) received trading advice from Eisler or First West for a fee; (2) traded through Eisler or First West or deposited money in connection with a trade; (3) purchased from or sold to Eisler or First West or placed an order for the purchase or sale through them; or (4) engaged in certain market manipulation activities in connection with the purchase or sale of a commodity contract.

Here, Klein was a FCM and a clearing member of the NYCC that cleared First West's trades through NYCC. Klein does not contend that it purchased or sold P-Tech contracts. Klein was not a trader of P-Tech contracts; nor did it own the P-Tech contracts at issue. To the contrary, Klein's complaint admits that it had no financial interest in the First West account and that all the trades in question were unsolicited by First West. Klein's losses were not the result of its purchases or sales in the commodities market. Klein functioned merely as a broker or agent that earned commissions for handling its customers [*sic*] trades. As a clearing member, Klein cleared their trades and was obligated to post margins for them as required. Under NYCC Rules governing clearing members, Klein was liable for its own failure to post the required margin on its customers' positions, whether or not Klein collected that margin from defaulting customers such as First West. In view of the provisions of sections 22(a) and (b) expressly limiting the categories of persons that can seek remedies under the statute we conclude, as did the court below, that a plaintiff such as Klein who falls outside those categories lacks standing. . . .

Klein contends that it has standing under CEA to challenge the NYBOT Defendants as a "forced" purchaser and seller of securities. Klein contends that the Supreme Court in *Blue Chip Stamps v. Manor Drug Stores*, 421 U.S. 723, 95 S. Ct. 1917, 44 L. Ed.2d 539 (1975), after confirming that the federal securities laws confer an implied private right of action, granted standing under § 10(b) of the Securities Act of 1934 to securities brokers as "forced" purchasers or sellers, in situations where they, as clearing members, suffered damages arising from obligations to guarantee their customers' trades. Klein argues that as a FCM and clearing member, it was subject to federal statutes as well as the rules and by-laws of NYBOT, NYFE, and NYCC that required Klein to maintain funds guaranteeing its customers' transactions on the contract market. In his brief on appeal, Klein asserts that it assumed "a very real investment risk that the commodity contracts its customers traded would maintain or increase in value, a risk that is identical to that taken by any purchaser or seller of a commodity contract who is granted standing under the CEA." In sum, Klein argues that it has standing because it faced essentially the same risks as a purchaser or seller of commodities contracts. We disagree. . . .

[R]egardless of whether the First West trading position rose or declined in value, Klein had no interest in any of the resulting profits or investments losses. . . . Thus, Klein's loss was a credit loss, not a trading loss. . . .

For the reasons discussed, the judgment of the district court is affirmed.

B. REPARATION PROCEEDINGS

The CFTC has broad powers to award reparations to parties harmed by a violation of the Commodity Exchange Act by an entity registered with the CFTC.[2] As with private rights of action, there is a two-year limit for bringing a claim.[3] Also, futures commission merchants can require customers who are eligible contract participants (i.e., non-retail) to contractually waive their right to seek reparation proceedings.[4]

Commodity Exchange Act § 14

Complaints against registered persons

(a) Petition for actual damages

(1) Any person complaining of any violation of any provision of [the Commodity Exchange Act] . . . or any [CFTC] rule, regulation, or order . . . by any person who is registered [with the CFTC] . . . may, at any time within two years after the cause of action accrues, apply to the Commission for an order awarding –

(A) actual damages proximately caused by such violation . . . ; and

(B) in the case of any action arising from a willful and intentional violation in the execution of an order on the floor of a registered entity, punitive or exemplary damages equal to no more than two times the amount of such actual damages. . . .

(e) Review

Any order of the Commission entered hereunder shall be reviewable on petition of any party aggrieved thereby, by the United States Court of Appeals for any circuit in which a hearing was held, or if no hearing was held, any circuit in which the appellee is located. . . . The appellee shall not be liable for costs in said court. If the appellee prevails, he shall be allowed a reasonable attorney's fee to be taxed and collected as a part of his costs. . . .

(g) Predispute resolution agreements for institutional customers

Nothing in this section prohibits a registered futures commission merchant from requiring a customer that is an eligible contract participant, as a condition to the commission merchant's conducting a transaction for the customer, to enter into an agreement waiving the right to file a claim under this section.

Although a Commodity Exchange Act violation needs to underlie any claim coming before the CFTC in a reparation proceeding, the CFTC has the authority to adjudicate related common law and state law claims, even if not grounded in the Commodity Exchange Act.

Commodity Futures Trading Commission v. Schor

478 U.S. 833 (1986)

Justice O'Connor delivered the opinion of the Court.

The question presented is whether the Commodity Exchange Act (CEA or Act) empowers the Commodity Futures Trading Commission (CFTC or Commission) to entertain state law counterclaims in reparation proceedings. . . .

The CEA broadly prohibits fraudulent and manipulative conduct in connection with commodity futures transactions. . . .

Among the duties assigned to the CFTC . . . [is] the administration of a reparations procedure through which disgruntled customers of professional commodity brokers . . . [can] seek redress for the brokers' violations of the Act or CFTC regulations. Thus, § 14 of the CEA provides that any person injured by such violations may apply to the Commission for an order directing the offender to pay reparations to the complainant and may enforce that order in federal district court. Congress intended this administrative procedure to be an "inexpensive and expeditious" alternative to existing fora available to aggrieved customers, namely, the courts and arbitration. . . .

The instant dispute arose in February 1980, when respondents Schor and Mortgage Services of America, Inc., invoked the CFTC's reparations jurisdiction by filing complaints against petitioner ContiCommodity Services, Inc. (Conti), a commodity futures broker, and Richard L. Sandor, a Conti employee. Schor had an account with Conti which contained a debit balance because Schor's net futures trading losses and expenses, such as commissions, exceeded the funds deposited in the account. Schor alleged that this debit balance was the result of Conti's numerous violations of the CEA.

Before receiving notice that Schor had commenced the reparations proceeding, Conti had filed a diversity action in Federal District Court to recover the debit balance. Schor counterclaimed in this action, reiterating his charges that the debit balance was due to Conti's violations of the CEA. Schor also moved on two separate occasions to dismiss or stay the District Court action, arguing that the continuation of the federal action would be a waste of judicial resources and an undue burden on the litigants in view of the fact that "[t]he reparations proceedings . . . will fully . . . resolve and adjudicate all the rights of the parties to this action with respect to the transactions which are the subject matter of this action."

Although the District Court declined to stay or dismiss the suit, Conti voluntarily dismissed the federal court action and presented its debit balance claim by way of a counterclaim in the CFTC reparations proceeding. Conti denied violating the CEA and instead insisted that the debit balance resulted from Schor's trading, and was therefore a simple debt owed by Schor.

After discovery, briefing, and a hearing, the Administrative Law Judge (ALJ) in Schor's reparations proceeding ruled in Conti's favor on both Schor's claims and Conti's counterclaims. After this ruling, Schor for the first time challenged the CFTC's statutory authority to adjudicate Conti's counterclaim. . . . Schor filed a petition for review with the Court of Appeals for the District of Columbia Circuit. Prior to oral argument, the Court of Appeals, *sua sponte*, raised the question whether CFTC could constitutionally adjudicate Conti's counterclaims . . .

[T]he Court of Appeals . . . ordered the dismissal of Conti's counterclaims on the ground that "the CFTC lacks authority (subject matter competence) to adjudicate" common law counterclaims. . . .

Our examination of the CEA and its legislative history and purpose reveals that Congress plainly intended the CFTC to decide counterclaims asserted by respondents in reparations proceedings, and just as plainly delegated to the CFTC the authority to fashion its counterclaim jurisdiction in the manner the CFTC determined necessary to further the purposes of the reparations program. . . .

Reference to the instant controversy illustrates the crippling effect that the Court of Appeals' restrictive reading of the CFTC's counterclaim jurisdiction would have on the efficacy of the reparations remedy. The dispute between Schor and Conti is typical of the disputes adjudicated in reparations proceedings: a customer and a professional commodities broker agree that there is a debit balance in the customer's account, but the customer attributes the deficit to the broker's alleged CEA violations and the broker attributes it to the customer's lack of success in the market. The customer brings a reparations claim; the broker counterclaims for the amount of the debit balance. In the usual case, then, the counterclaim "arises out of precisely the same course of events" as the principal claim and requires resolution of many of the same disputed factual issues.

Under the Court of Appeals' approach, the entire dispute may not be resolved in the administrative forum. Consequently, the entire dispute will typically end up in court, for when the broker files suit to recover the debit balance, the customer will normally be compelled either by compulsory counterclaim rules or by the expense and inconvenience of litigating the same issues in two fora to forgo his reparations remedy and to litigate his claim in court. In sum, as Schor himself aptly summarized, to require a bifurcated examination of the single dispute "would be to emasculate if not destroy the purposes of the Commodity Exchange Act to provide an efficient and relatively inexpensive forum for the resolution of disputes in futures trading." . . .

As our discussion makes manifest, the CFTC's long-held position that it has the power to take jurisdiction over counterclaims such as Conti's is eminently reasonable and well within the scope of its delegated authority. . . .

We therefore are squarely faced with the question whether the CFTC's assumption of jurisdiction over common law counterclaims violates Article III of the Constitution. . . .

Article III, § 1, directs that the "judicial Power of the United States shall be vested in one supreme Court and in such inferior Courts as the Congress may from time to time ordain and establish," and provides that these federal courts shall be staffed by judges who hold office during good behavior, and whose compensation shall not be diminished during tenure in office. Schor claims that these provisions prohibit Congress from authorizing the initial adjudication of common law counterclaims by the CFTC, an administrative agency whose adjudicatory officers do not enjoy the tenure and salary protections embodied in Article III. . . .

In the instant cases, Schor indisputably waived any right he may have possessed to the full trial of Conti's counterclaim before an Article III court. Schor expressly demanded that Conti proceed on its counterclaim in the reparations proceeding rather than before the District Court and was content to have the entire dispute settled in the forum he had selected until the ALJ ruled against him on all counts; it was only after the ALJ rendered a decision to which he objected that Schor raised any challenge to the CFTC's consideration of Conti's counterclaim.

Even were there no evidence of an express waiver here, Schor's election to forgo his right to proceed in state or federal court on his claim and his decision to seek relief instead in a CFTC reparations proceeding constituted an effective waiver. . . .

An examination of the relative allocation of powers between the CFTC and Article III courts in light of the considerations given prominence in our precedents demonstrates that the congressional scheme does not impermissibly intrude on the province of the judiciary. The CFTC's adjudicatory powers depart from the traditional agency model in just one respect: the CFTC's jurisdiction over common law counterclaims. . . .

It is clear that Congress has not attempted to "withdraw from judicial cognizance" the determination of Conti's right to the sum represented by the debit balance in Schor's account. Congress gave the CFTC the authority to adjudicate such matters, but the decision to invoke this forum is left entirely to the parties and the power of the federal judiciary to take jurisdiction of these matters is unaffected. In such circumstances, separation of powers concerns are diminished, for it seems self-evident that just as Congress may encourage parties to settle a dispute out of court or resort to arbitration without impermissible incursions on the separation of powers, Congress may make available a quasi-judicial mechanism through which willing parties may, at their option, elect to resolve their differences. This is not to say, of course, that if Congress created a phalanx of non-Article III tribunals equipped to handle the entire business of the Article III courts without any Article III supervision or control and without evidence of valid and specific legislative necessities, the fact that the parties had the election to proceed in their forum of choice would necessarily save the scheme from constitutional attack. But this case obviously bears no resemblance to such a scenario, given the degree of judicial control saved to the federal courts as well as the congressional purpose behind the jurisdictional delegation, the demonstrated need for the delegation, and the limited nature of the delegation.

When Congress authorized the CFTC to adjudicate counterclaims, its primary focus was on making effective a specific and limited federal regulatory scheme, not on allocating jurisdiction among federal tribunals. Congress intended to create an inexpensive and expeditious alternative forum through which customers could enforce the provisions of the CEA against professional brokers. . . .

It also bears emphasis that the CFTC's assertion of counterclaim jurisdiction is limited to [what is] . . . incidental to, and completely dependent upon, adjudication of reparations claims created by federal law, and in actual fact is limited to claims arising out of the same transaction or occurrence as the reparations claim. . . .

The judgment of the Court of Appeals for the District of Columbia Circuit is reversed, and the cases remanded for further proceedings consistent with this opinion. . . .

QUESTIONS AND COMMENTS

1. What are the merits of public v. private enforcement? Which do you believe is more effective?
2. Evaluate the economics of public v. private enforcement. How are each funded? How are awards distributed? Is one fairer than the other? What incentives are relevant with each method of enforcing the Commodity Exchange Act? What incentives do private litigants have? What incentives do public bodies such as the CFTC or Department of Justice or their personnel have?

3. Should Commodity Exchange Act § 22(a)(1) be read to exclude a private claim against a party aiding and abetting one of the four categories of specifically enumerated parties against whom claims can be made?
4. Are the barriers to a private claim by a market intermediary against a designated contract market effectively insuperable? Being mindful of the Second Circuit's decision in *Klein & Co. Futures, Inc. v. Board of Trade of the City of New York*, consider what factual circumstances might lead to a successful claim by a futures commission merchant against a designated contract market.
5. What are the pros and cons of a private right of action pursuant to Commodity Exchange Act § 22 compared to the pros and cons of a reparation proceeding pursuant to Commodity Exchange Act § 14?

CHAPTER 15
CROSS-BORDER ISSUES

A. BACKGROUND

In Chapter 4, we discussed foreign boards of trade, commonly known as FBOTs, in the context of commodity futures. The foreign board of trade registration category is only a solution for the question of in what circumstances can a non-U.S. board of trade access U.S. persons. Other questions arise with respect to commodity futures, centering around the extent of extraterritorial jurisdiction that can be asserted and whether Congress intended the Commodity Exchange Act to have extraterritorial effect.

With respect to swaps, historically a global unregulated market, numerous cross-border issues arise. Of particular regulatory concern is "regulatory arbitrage," i.e., where parties select the jurisdiction with the least burdensome regulations in an effort to avoid a jurisdiction with stricter regulation.

A challenge faced by regulators is how to maintain a global marketplace where parties can seamlessly transact across national boundaries without having the "race to the bottom" inherent in regulatory arbitrage. One remedy that has been attempted is to have international regulators agree to common standards, known as regulatory harmonization. Another is the promulgation of rules, known as anti-evasion rules, intended to prohibit the most egregious regulatory arbitrage. However, the question of whether a seamless global marketplace can cohabitate with heavy regulation has not yet been definitively answered.

B. FRAMEWORK FOR INTERNATIONAL DERIVATIVES COOPERATION

1. Group of Twenty

The framework that formed the basis for Title VII of the Dodd-Frank Act (i.e., the portion of the Dodd-Frank Act specifically focused on swaps) resulted from international commitments made after the Financial Crisis that had begun in 2007. These non-binding commitments were made by representatives of the governments that together comprise the "Group of Twenty," commonly known as the "G-20." The representatives attending the periodic G-20 meetings are generally among the most senior members of government responsible for macroeconomic policy and the members of the G-20 are intended to represent 85% of global gross domestic product.[1] The members of the G-20 are Argentina, Australia, Brazil, Canada, China, European Union, France, Germany, India, Indonesia, Italy, Japan, Mexico, Russia, Saudi Arabia, South Africa, South Korea, Turkey, United Kingdom, and the United States.

In the G-20's 2009 meeting held in Pittsburgh, nearly a year before passage of the Dodd-Frank Act, the broad contours of the forthcoming legislation were outlined.

Group of Twenty, Leaders' Statement

Group of Twenty Pittsburgh Summit (September 24 – 25, 2009)[2]

. . . We meet in the midst of a critical transition from crisis to recovery to turn the page on an era of irresponsibility and to adopt a set of policies, regulations and reforms to meet the needs of the 21st century global economy. . . .

When we last gathered in April, we confronted the greatest challenge to the world economy in our generation. . . .

We [have] assessed the progress we have made together in addressing the global crisis and . . . committed to additional steps to ensure strong, sustainable, and balanced growth, to build a stronger international financial system . . . and to modernize our architecture for international economic cooperation. . . .

The growth of the global economy and the success of our coordinated effort to respond to the recent crisis have increased the case for more sustained and systematic international cooperation. . . .

Since the onset of the global crisis, we have developed and begun implementing sweeping reforms to tackle the root causes of the crisis and transform the system for global financial regulation. Substantial progress has been made in strengthening prudential oversight, improving risk management, strengthening transparency, promoting market integrity, establishing supervisory colleges, and reinforcing international cooperation. We have enhanced and expanded the scope of regulation and oversight, with tougher regulation of over-the-counter (OTC) derivatives, securitization markets, credit rating agencies, and hedge funds. . . .

Yet our work is not done. Far more needs to be done. . . .

All standardized OTC derivative contracts should be traded on exchanges or electronic trading platforms, where appropriate, and cleared through central counterparties by end-2012 at the latest. OTC derivative contracts should be reported to trade repositories. Non-centrally cleared contracts should be subject to higher capital requirements. We ask the [Financial Standards Board] and its relevant members to assess regularly implementation and whether it is sufficient to improve transparency in the derivatives markets, mitigate systemic risk, and protect against market abuse. . . .

---

a. Financial Stability Board

During the Pittsburgh G-20 meeting, the G-20 declared itself "the premier forum for . . . economic cooperation" among its members.[3] It also saw the establishment of the Financial Stability Board as a body to coordinate and monitor the implementation of G-20 commitments.[4] In addition to the G-20 members, the Financial Stability Board includes the Netherlands, Singapore, Spain, Switzerland, and various international bodies.[5]

In the September 5, 2013, letter to all G-20 leaders, the FSB reported that:

> Not all G20 jurisdictions have implemented earlier commitments. Authorities should promptly introduce requirements for reporting of all derivatives trades to trade repositories, rapidly adopt rules for central clearing and trading on organised platforms. . . .

Letter from Mark Carney, Financial Stability Board Chair, to G20 Leaders, *Progress of Financial Reforms* (September 5, 2013), available at http://www financialstabilityboard.org/publications/r_130905.pdf (accessed June 27, 2014).

b. OTC Derivatives Working Group

The Financial Stability Board also has an OTC Derivatives Working Group, which has as one of its mandates the preparation of semi-annual "progress reports" on the implementation of the G-20 derivatives commitments. In its April 2014 progress report, it found that more than half of Financial Stability Board members had implemented derivatives trade reporting requirements, only three jurisdictions had implemented central clearing and on-facility trading requirements, and none had implemented margin requirements.[6]

c. OTC Derivatives Regulators Group

The OTC Derivatives Regulators Group is a forum for derivatives regulators established under the auspices of the G-20.

3. *International Organization of Securities Commissions*

The International Organization of Securities Commissions (commonly known as IOSCO) is another forum for national securities and futures regulators. In most nations, the securities and futures regulator is one body – the U.S. approach of separating the regulation of such products into two regulatory bodies, the SEC and CFTC, is not the norm and both are IOSCO attendees. IOSCO helps to coordinate the development of international standards on issues such as margin requirements and market manipulation.

Having examined the international framework that spurred and continues to drive implementation of common derivatives regulatory standards in the major economies, we now examine the CFTC's approach to cross-border issues with respect to: (1) the extraterritorial limit of the CFTC's jurisdiction; and (2) the CFTC's "substituted compliance" regime for recognizing regulation of derivatives as being comparable to U.S. regulation and, therefore, as satisfying U.S. requirements.

C. EXTRATERRITORIAL LIMIT OF CFTC'S JURISDICTION GENERALLY

The Commodity Exchange Act does not explicitly provide a test for determining the extraterritorial limit of the CFTC's jurisdiction, other than with respect to swaps. Therefore, for products other than swaps, caselaw is the primary resource. (For a discussion on the matters over which the CFTC has jurisdiction, *see* Chapter 3.)

In this area, Commodity Exchange Act precedents and securities law precedents have historically been treated nearly identically due to the statutes on which they are founded being largely silent on questions of extraterritoriality.

1. *The Historic "Conduct and Effects" Test*

Until the decision in *Morrison*, examined below, the applicable test was a "conduct" and "effects" test.

Psimenos v. E.F. Hutton & Company, Inc.

722 F.2d 1041 (2d Cir. 1983)

Lumbard, Circuit Judge:

Plaintiff John Psimenos, a citizen and resident of Greece, brought this action under the . . . Commodities [*sic*] Exchange Act ("CEA") . . . for damages resulting from Hutton's allegedly fraudulent procurement and management of his commodities trading account.

Hutton moved . . . to dismiss the federal claims for lack of subject matter jurisdiction. . . . Chief Judge Motley, holding that the alleged fraud was "predominantly foreign" and therefore outside the scope of the Commodities [*sic*] Exchange Act, dismissed the federal claim for lack of subject matter jurisdiction. We disagree with Judge Motley's reading of the jurisdictional limitations of the Act and, accordingly, reverse and remand for further proceedings.[i] . . .

In 1975, plaintiff became interested in investing in a commodities trading account with E.F. Hutton. Mathieu Mavridoglou, Hutton's agent and employee in Athens, told Psimenos "that his account would be managed in accordance with Hutton's standard procedures and with rules and regulations of the Commodities [*sic*] Futures Trading Commission." . . .

Relying on these statements, Psimenos opened an account with Hutton's Athens office, executing blank forms that granted Hutton discretionary authority to trade in his account. Although Psimenos directed Mavridoglou to seek conservative investments, Hutton's agents often used money in Psimenos' account to participate in unresearched and highly speculative and leveraged transactions.

By 1977, after having incurred heavy losses, Psimenos talked in Athens with Mavridoglou, and in Geneva with Mavridoglou and a Mr. Tome, another Hutton employee. Through these conversations, he was induced to have his account moved to Hutton's Paris office. At some point . . . Psimenos ordered trading halted in his account.

In 1981, Mavridoglou convinced Psimenos to move the account back to Athens and to allow trading in his account to resume. Mavridoglou told Psimenos that Hutton would recoup all his losses by assigning a new manager, Marios Michaelides, to the account. Michaelides was represented as a Hutton employee and qualified broker, though in fact he was not a Hutton employee,

---

[i] [N. 3] At our invitation, the Securities and Exchange Commission and the Commodities Futures Trading Commission each submitted a brief as *amicus curiae* urging us to find that the district court has subject matter jurisdiction to hear Psimenos' claim. The CFTC argues that trading on domestic commodities markets is sufficient to establish jurisdiction both because it involves substantial conduct in the United States and because it implicates the integrity of the United States markets.

and was not nor had he ever been registered with the Commodities [*sic*] Futures Trading Commission as a broker. . . .

Eventually, Psimenos lost in excess of $200,000. . . .

Although most of the fraudulent misrepresentations alleged in the complaint occurred outside the United States, the trading contracts that consummated the transactions were often executed in New York. The issue on appeal is whether that trading in United States commodities markets is sufficient to confer subject matter jurisdiction on a federal district court to hear a claim for damages brought by an alien under the Commodities [*sic*] Exchange Act.

We find that the district court has jurisdiction to hear Psimenos' claim. The trades Hutton executed on American markets constituted the final act in Hutton's alleged fraud on Psimenos, without which Hutton's employees could not have generated commissions for themselves. . . .

In construing the reaches of jurisdiction under the CEA, courts have analogized to similar problems under the securities laws which have been more extensively litigated. *See*, e.g., *Mormels v. Girofinance, S.A.*, 544 F. Supp. 815, 817 n. 8 (S.D.N.Y.1982) ("[s]ecurities cases and principles are used as persuasive aids to interpretation of the CEA").

Several of our decisions have explored the limits of subject matter jurisdiction under the federal securities statutes. Our major consideration concerning transnational transactions is "whether Congress would have wished the precious resources of United States courts and law enforcement agencies to be devoted to them rather than leave the problem to foreign countries."

Two tests have emerged, the "effects" test and the "conduct" test. Since we find that there is jurisdiction under the latter, we do not need to reach the question whether the effects test provides an independent basis for jurisdiction.

The conduct test does not center its inquiry on whether domestic investors or markets are affected, but on the nature of conduct within the United States as it relates to carrying out the alleged fraudulent scheme, on the theory that Congress did not want "to allow the United States to be used as a base for manufacturing fraudulent security devices for export, even when these are peddled only to foreigners." . . .

We find that under the conduct test, Hutton's activities in the United States in furtherance of the alleged fraud were substantial enough to establish subject matter jurisdiction. . . .

Viewing the conduct test in this light, it is clear that the trading conducted by Hutton on United States exchanges should be weighed in determining this court's jurisdiction. Just as Congress did not want the United States to be used as a base for manufacturing fraudulent securities devices, irrespective of the nationality of the victim, neither did it want United States commodities markets to be used as a base to consummate schemes concocted abroad, particularly when the perpetrators are agents of American corporations. . . .

Trading activities on United States commodities markets were significant acts without which Psimenos' losses could not have occurred, and are sufficient to establish jurisdiction. . . .

A contemporaneous Seventh Circuit case defined the conduct and effects test as:

> [T]he "conduct" and "effects" tests . . . were developed in cases brought under the antifraud provisions of the federal securities laws and have recently been applied in similar cases arising under the Commodity Exchange Act. The conduct test focuses on the foreigner's conduct within the United States as it relates to the alleged scheme to defraud. When the conduct occurring in the United States is material to the successful completion of the alleged scheme, jurisdiction is asserted based on the theory that Congress would not have intended the United States to be used as a base for effectuating the fraudulent conduct of foreign companies. Under the effects test, courts have looked to whether conduct occurring in foreign countries had caused foreseeable and substantial harm to interests in the United States.

Tamari v. Bache & Co. (Lebanon) S.A.L., 730 F.2d 1103, 1107-1108 (7th Cir. 1984).

2. *Presumption Against Extraterritoriality*

a. Presumption Generally

The conduct and effects test was utilized for decades until, in 2010, the Supreme Court determined that there is a presumption against the extraterritorial application of a statute and, where a statute is intended to have extraterritorial application, Congress would explicitly legislate such extraterritorial application. Although the case in question, *Morrison v. National Australia Bank, Ltd.*, was a securities law case, its findings apply to an analysis of the extraterritorial extent of the Commodity Exchange Act (other than with respect to swaps, since they have a distinct jurisdictional test discussed in section D below).

Morrison v. National Australia Bank, Ltd.
561 U.S. 247 (2010)

Justice Scalia delivered the opinion of the Court.

We decide whether § 10(b) of the Securities Exchange Act of 1934 provides a cause of action to foreign plaintiffs suing foreign and American defendants for misconduct in connection with securities traded on foreign exchanges.

Respondent National Australia Bank Limited (National) was . . . the largest bank in Australia. . . . Its [shares are not traded] . . . on any exchange in the United States. There are listed on the New York Stock Exchange, however, National's American Depositary Receipts (ADRs), which represent the right to receive a specified number of National's . . . [shares].

The complaint alleges the following facts. . . . In February 1998, National bought respondent HomeSide Lending, Inc., a mortgage servicing company headquartered in Florida. HomeSide's business was to receive fees for servicing mortgages (essentially the administrative tasks associated with collecting mortgage payments). The rights to receive those fees, so-called mortgage-servicing rights, can provide a valuable income stream. How valuable each of the rights is depends, in part, on the likelihood that the mortgage to which it applies will be fully repaid before it is due, terminating the need for servicing. HomeSide calculated the present value of its mortgage-servicing rights by using valuation models designed to take this likelihood into account. It recorded the value of its assets, and the numbers appeared in National's financial statements.

From 1998 until 2001, National's annual reports and other public documents touted the success of HomeSide's business. . . . But on July 5, 2001, National announced that it was writing down the value of HomeSide's assets . . . The prices of both . . . [the shares] and ADRs slumped. . . .

[P]etitioners Russell Leslie Owen and Brian and Geraldine Silverlock, all Australians, purchased National's [shares] in 2000 and 2001, before the write-downs.[ii] They sued National, HomeSide, Cicutto, and . . . three HomeSide executives. . . .

Respondents moved to dismiss for lack of subject-matter jurisdiction. . . . The District Court granted the motion . . . finding no jurisdiction. . . . The Court of Appeals for the Second Circuit affirmed on similar grounds. . . .

It is a "longstanding principle of American law 'that legislation of Congress, unless a contrary intent appears, is meant to apply only within the territorial jurisdiction of the United States.'" This principle represents a canon of construction, or a presumption about a statute's meaning, rather than a limit upon Congress's power to legislate. It rests on the perception that Congress ordinarily legislates with respect to domestic, not foreign matters. Thus, "unless

---

[ii] [N. 1] Robert Morrison, an American investor in National's ADRs, also brought suit, but his claims were dismissed . . . because he failed to allege damages. . . . Inexplicably, Morrison continued to be listed as a petitioner in the Court of Appeals and here.

there is the affirmative intention of the Congress clearly expressed" to give a statute extraterritorial effect, "we must presume it is primarily concerned with domestic conditions." . . . When a statute gives no clear indication of an extraterritorial application, it has none.

Despite this principle of interpretation . . . the Second Circuit believed that, because the Exchange Act is silent as to the extraterritorial application of § 10(b) [(the relevant securities law provision at issue)], it was left to the court to "discern" whether Congress would have wanted the statute to apply. This disregard of the presumption against extraterritoriality did not originate with the Court of Appeals panel in this case. It has been repeated over many decades by various courts of appeals. . . .

[T]he Second Circuit . . . excised the presumption against extraterritoriality . . . and replaced it with the inquiry whether it would be reasonable (and hence what Congress would have wanted) to apply the statute to a given situation. . . .

The Second Circuit had thus established that application of § 10(b) could be premised upon either some effect on American securities markets or investors or significant conduct in the United States. It later formalized these two applications into (1) an "effects test," "whether the wrongful conduct had a substantial effect in the United States or upon United States citizens," and (2) a "conduct test," "whether the wrongful conduct occurred in the United States." . . .

Other Circuits embraced the Second Circuit's approach. . . .

Commentators have criticized the unpredictable and inconsistent application of § 10(b) to transnational cases. Some have challenged the premise underlying the Courts of Appeals' approach, namely that Congress did not consider the extraterritorial application of § 10(b) (thereby leaving it open to the courts, supposedly, to determine what Congress would have wanted).

The criticisms seem to us justified. The results of judicial-speculation-made-law – divining what Congress would have wanted if it had thought of the situation before the court – demonstrate the wisdom of the presumption against extraterritoriality. Rather than guess anew in each case, we apply the presumption in all cases, preserving a stable background against which Congress can legislate with predictable effects.

Rule 10b–5, the regulation under which petitioners have brought suit, was promulgated under § 10(b), and "does not extend beyond conduct encompassed by § 10(b)'s prohibition." Therefore, if § 10(b) is not extraterritorial, neither is Rule 10b–5.

On its face, § 10(b) contains nothing to suggest it applies abroad:

> It shall be unlawful for any person, directly or indirectly, by the use of any means or instrumentality of interstate commerce or of the mails, or of any facility of any national securities exchange . . . [t]o use or employ, in connection with the purchase or sale of any security registered on a national securities exchange or any security not so registered, . . . any manipulative or deceptive device or

> contrivance in contravention of such rules and regulations as the [Securities and Exchange] Commission may prescribe. . . ." [Note that there is nearly identical language in the Commodity Exchange Act.]

[T]here is no affirmative indication in the Exchange Act that § 10(b) applies extraterritorially, and we therefore conclude that it does not. . . .

Petitioners argue that the conclusion that § 10(b) does not apply extraterritorially does not resolve this case. They contend that they seek no more than domestic application anyway, since Florida is where HomeSide and its senior executives engaged in the deceptive conduct of manipulating HomeSide's financial models; their complaint also alleged that Race and Hughes made misleading public statements there. . . . [I]t is a rare case of prohibited extraterritorial application that lacks all contact with the territory of the United States. But the presumption against extraterritorial application would be a craven watchdog indeed if it retreated to its kennel whenever some domestic activity is involved in the case. . . .

[W]e think that the focus of the Exchange Act is not upon the place where the deception originated, but upon purchases and sales of securities in the United States. Section 10(b) does not punish deceptive conduct, but only deceptive conduct "in connection with the purchase or sale of any security registered on a national securities exchange or any security not so registered."

Finally, . . . [the] probability of incompatibility with the applicable laws of other countries is so obvious that if Congress intended such foreign application "it would have addressed the subject of conflicts with foreign laws and procedures." Like the United States, foreign countries regulate their domestic securities exchanges and securities transactions occurring within their territorial jurisdiction. And the regulation of other countries often differs from ours as to what constitutes fraud, what disclosures must be made, what damages are recoverable, what discovery is available in litigation, what individual actions may be joined in a single suit, what attorney's fees are recoverable, and many other matters. The Commonwealth of Australia, the United Kingdom of Great Britain and Northern Ireland, and the Republic of France have filed *amicus* briefs in this case. So have (separately or jointly) such international and foreign organizations as the International Chamber of Commerce, the Swiss Bankers Association, the Federation of German Industries, the French Business Confederation, the Institute of International Bankers, the European Banking Federation, the Australian Bankers' Association, and the Association Francaise des Entreprises Privées. They all complain of the interference with foreign securities regulation that application of § 10(b) abroad would produce, and urge the adoption of a clear test that will avoid that consequence. . . .

The Solicitor General points out that the "significant and material conduct" test is in accord with prevailing notions of international comity. If so, that proves that if the United States asserted prescriptive jurisdiction pursuant to the "significant and material conduct" test it would not violate customary international law; but it in no way tends to prove that that is what Congress has done.

Section 10(b) reaches the use of a manipulative or deceptive device or contrivance only in connection with the purchase or sale of a security listed on an American stock exchange, and the purchase or sale of any other security in the United States. . . .

---

b. Presumption Applied to the Commodity Exchange Act

The precedent in *Morrison* regarding Securities Exchange Act of 1934 § 10b has been applied *mutatis mutandis* to the context of a claim under the Commodity Exchange Act.

Starshinova v. Batratchenko

931 F. Supp. 2d 478 (S.D.N.Y. 2013)

Kimba M. Wood, District Judge.

Russian citizens Tamara Starshinova ("Starshinova"), Marina Vasilyanskaya ("Vasilyanskaya"), and Rafail Tzentziper ("Tzentziper") (collectively, "Plaintiffs"), on behalf of themselves and as assignees for 551 individuals . . . bring this action seeking millions of dollars in damages for an alleged massive fraud involving various funds in which Plaintiffs invested. Plaintiffs' Amended Complaint alleges eleven causes of action, including violations of federal law under the Commodities [*sic*] Exchange Act [("CEA")] and the Securities Exchange Act of 1934 [("SEA")] and various state law claims.

Defendants Oleg Batratchenko ("Batratchenko"); Thor United Corp. (USA); Thor United Corp. (Nevis); Thor Asset Management, Inc.; Thor Opti–Max, LLC; Thor Real Estate Management, LLC; Thor Capital, LLC; Thor Futures, LLC; Thor Opti–Max Fund, Ltd.; Thor Guarant Real Estate Fund, Ltd. (BVI); Thor Real Estate Master Fund, Ltd. (BVI); Thor Realty Holdings, LLC; Optima Investment Holdings, Ltd.; and Thor Guarant, LLC (the "Thor Entities" and, collectively with Batratchenko, "Defendants") move to dismiss. . . .

Plaintiffs are all citizens of the Russian Federation. They bring this action on behalf of themselves and hundreds of other investors who seek to recover money that they contributed to investment programs managed and controlled by Defendants. Batratchenko, a U.S. citizen residing in Moscow, is the "co-founder, principal, officer, owner, employee, and/or agent" of the Thor Entities, a series of related domestic and foreign companies operating a number of "programs" that invest in U.S. and foreign stocks, commodities, and real estate.

This suit arises from Plaintiffs' investments in three of the Thor Entities' investment programs. . . .

Plaintiff Tzentziper invested $190,538.87 in Thor Optima and Thor Opti–Max between September 2003 and April 2010; Plaintiff Vasilyanskaya invested $37,017 of her own money and $80,000 of her son's money in Thor Optima between July 2004 and April 2010; and Plaintiff Starshinova invested $21,900 in Thor Optima between September 2004 and April 2010. Plaintiffs assert that these investments were made in reliance on various misrepresentations made by Defendants. . . .

Periodic account statements issued by the Thor Entities prior to 2008 reflected returns as high as 50%. . . . In 2008, Batratchenko sent investors a letter asserting that "the New York residential property market would need to experience a threefold decline" in order for the funds to lose money.

In 2009, . . . Batratchenko and the Thor Group claimed that the SEC had frozen . . . assets, and, "as a result of 'radical reform of the U.S. financial markets regulatory system,' the procedure for redemption or removal of funds . . . ha[d] changed and became more complicated." In late 2009, . . . the remaining investors sought to redeem their investments. . . . In August of 2010, Batratchenko sent a letter to all investors saying he could not return the funds because they were tied up in illiquid investments, such as real estate. . . .

Defendants argue that the *Morrison* decision [i.e. *Morrison v. National Australian Bank*] regarding the territorial reach of the SEA "applies with equal force" to Plaintiffs' claims under the CEA, and, because the transactions occurred abroad, these claims must be dismissed. Defendants also argue that Plaintiffs lack standing under Section 22(a) of the CEA. The Court agrees with both contentions. . . .

Although no case law directly addresses whether the *Morrison* reasoning applies to the CEA, the Court finds that such application is warranted. *Morrison* emphasized the "longstanding principle" that congressional legislation, "unless a contrary intent appears, is meant to apply only within the territorial jurisdiction of the United States." . . . Absent a "clearly expressed," "affirmative intention" to give a statute extraterritorial effect, courts are directed to "presume it is primarily concerned with domestic conditions." In short, "[w]hen a statute gives no clear indication of an extraterritorial application, it has none."

Pre-*Morrison* case law squarely determined that Section 4 of the CEA does not affirmatively indicate that it applies extraterritorially. . . .

Moreover, after reviewing the CEA in accordance with the principles of statutory interpretation laid out in *Morrison*, the Court finds no basis to conclude that the CEA applies abroad. First, the Court finds no language in § 4o [a general anti-fraud provision applying to commodity pool operators and commodity trading advisors] to support a finding that it applies extraterritorially. Like § 10(b), § 4o "[o]n its face . . . contains nothing to suggest it applies abroad." . . .

Petitioners, supported by the Solicitor General, argued in *Morrison* that Section 10(b)'s reference to "interstate commerce," which included commerce between "any foreign country and any State," justified extraterritorial application. The Supreme Court rejected this contention, and noted that "even statutes that contain broad language in their definitions of 'commerce' that expressly refer to foreign commerce do not apply abroad." Consequently, the reference to "interstate commerce" in Section 4o does not indicate Section 4o was intended to apply abroad.

Further, the provisions of the CEA that do mention extraterritorial application support the proposition that § 4o does not apply extraterritorially. Section 4(b) restricts the jurisdiction of the Commodity Futures Trading Commission ("CFTC") to persons "located in the United States," and notes that "[n]o rule or regulation may be adopted" under this subsection that requires the CFTC to approve any rules or contracts proposed by a foreign commodities board, or which "governs in any way" any rule or contract for a foreign board. These provisions that do refer to extraterritorial application emphasize that the CEA is not designed to apply abroad. In light of the text of § 4o, other provisions of the CEA, and pre-*Morrison* precedent, the Court holds that "there is no clear indication of extraterritoriality" in the CEA.

Thus, the scope of CEA § 4o is the same as SEA § 10(b): it applies to transactions involving entities listed on domestic exchanges, or to domestic purchases and sales where either party has "incurred irrevocable liability within the United States." . . .

Alternatively, even if the CEA were to apply extraterritorially, Plaintiffs' CEA claim must still be dismissed . . . Section 22 of the CEA "enumerates the only circumstances under which a private litigant may assert a private right of action for violations of the CEA." To have standing under Section 22, a private plaintiff must fall into one of four categories: a plaintiff must either have (A) received trading advice from Defendants for a fee; (B) traded through Defendants or deposited money with Defendants in connection with a commodities trade; (C) purchased from or sold to Defendants or placed an order for purchase or sale of a commodity through them; or (D) engaged in certain market manipulation activities in connection with the purchase or sale of a commodity contract. Plaintiffs' allegations do not support standing under any of these categories. . . .

Within days of the ruling in *Starshinova v. Batratchenko*, another judge sitting in the Southern District of New York, evaluating nearly identical facts stemming from the same fraud that was the subject of *Starshinova*, declined to unequivocally apply *Morrison* to the Commodity Exchange Act in the same way courts have applied it to questions of securities law by concluding that Commodity Exchange Act § 4o (generally prohibiting fraud by commodity pool operators and commodity trading advisors) and Securities Exchange Act § 10b – contrary to the decision in *Starshinova* – differ in ways that are substantive when applying *Morrison*.

The decision below demonstrates that the application of *Morrison* to questions of the extent of jurisdiction conferred by the Commodity Exchange Act may be an evolutionary process.

Loginovskaya v. Batratchenko

936 F. Supp. 2d 357 (S.D.N.Y. 2013)

J. Paul Oetken, District Judge.

Plaintiff Ludmila Loginovskaya ("Loginovskaya" or "Plaintiff") brings this action pursuant to the Commodity Exchange Act (the "CEA") against Defendants Oleg Batratchenko ("Batratchenko"), Tatiana Smirnova ("Smirnova"), John Does 1–20, and Thor United Corp., Thor United Corp. (Nevis), Thor Real Estate Master Fund, Ltd., Thor Asset Management, Inc. ("TAM"), Thor Real Estate Management LLC, Thor Capital LLC, Thor Futures LLC, and Thor Realty LLC (collectively "Thor Defendants" or "Thor Entities"). . . . Batratchenko and the Thor Defendants have moved to dismiss . . . For the reasons that follow, Defendants' motion is granted. . . .

Plaintiff entered into two investment contracts with Batratchenko and Thor United in 2006 and 2007 [and ultimately invested $590,000 and were allegedly defrauded] . . . .

The Supreme Court's decision in *Morrison v. Nat'l Australia Bank* held that the antifraud protections of § 10(b) of the . . . [Securities Exchange Act of 1934 (the "'34 Act")] apply only to "transactions in securities listed on domestic exchanges, and domestic transactions in other securities, to which § 10(b) of the Securities Exchange Act applies." . . .

Although the presumption against extraterritoriality is appropriately applied in all cases, not just those involving the '34 [Act], the presumption alone "is not self-evidently dispositive," but rather, "requires further analysis." Accordingly, in order for the CEA's protections to apply to a given set of investors – or prospective investors – asserting a private right of action for violations of § 4o, the fraud itself must be domestic in nature. Therefore, here, in order for the CEA to be applicable, the implicated fraud prohibited by the statute must be domestic. In a post-*Morrison* universe, however, determining whether actionable conduct falling within a given statute is domestic in nature presents complications for provisions whose language departs from that of § 10(b).

Prior to *Morrison*, the Second Circuit utilized the so-called "conduct" or "effects" test to determine the appropriateness of extraterritorial application of § 10(b). . . . *Morrison* replaced this "conduct" or "effects" test, interpreting the statutory presumption against extraterritoriality as rebutted only in instances where the securities involved are either (1) listed on domestic exchanges or (2) involved in a domestic transaction.

In Absolute Activist Value Master Fund Ltd. v. Ficeto, 677 F.3d 60 (2d Cir. 2012), the Second Circuit held that in the context of the purchase or sale of a security, the transaction occurs at the point "at which the parties obligated themselves to perform what they had agreed to perform even if the formal performance of their agreement is to be after a lapse of time." Thus, by extension, "the point of irrevocable liability can be used to determine the locus of a securities purchase or sale." According to the *Absolute Activist Court*, a plaintiff may sufficiently allege the existence of a domestic transaction by pleading facts that lead "to the plausible inference that the parties incurred irrevocable liability within the United States: that is, that the purchaser incurred irrevocable liability within the United States to take and pay for a security, or that the seller incurred irrevocable liability within the United States to deliver a security." In sum, the Court held that in the wake of *Morrison*, "a plaintiff must allege facts suggesting that irrevocable liability was incurred or title was transferred within the United States." The Court also underscored that "mere assertion[s] that transactions 'took place in the United States' [are] insufficient to adequately plead the existence of domestic transactions." . . . In *Absolute Activist*, the Court held that the "fact that two of the defendants resided in California," along with the allegation that the nonparty investors "subscribed to the Funds by wiring money to a bank located in New York," were insufficient to bring the relevant conduct – namely, the plaintiff-Funds' purchases and sales of U.S. Penny Stocks – within *Morrison's* transaction test.

Prior to *Morrison*, courts deciding commodities cases applied the same conduct or effects test as was used in the securities context. . . . Given this historic approach to CEA claims, together with the fact that the CEA case law addressing extraterritoriality has seemingly been abrogated by *Morrison*, it follows that *Morrison's* presumption against extraterritoriality, together with its requirement that the interests protected by the pertinent statute – here, the CEA – be domestic in nature, apply to the CEA claims in this case. The applicability of *Morrison's* transactional test to CEA claims under § 4o, however, is less clear, given both the language of § 4o and the Second Circuit's interpretation of the meaning of domestic "transaction" in the '34 Act context.

Section 4o operates differently from § 10(b). . . . Unlike § 10(b), which is transaction focused, § 4o is status-based, in that it prohibits commodity trading advisors, or associated persons or entities, from "employ[ing] any device, scheme, or artifice to defraud any client or participant or prospective client or participant," or from "engaging in any transaction, practice, or course of business which operates as a fraud or deceit upon any client or participant or prospective client or participant." In other words, there is no language limiting § 4o to actions performed "*in connection with the purchase or sale of*" a commodity [as is the case with § 10 b]. . . . In some sense, an application of *Morrison's* transaction test to § 4o nevertheless requires an analogous inquiry to that which is required under § 10(b): specifically, whether the interests bought or sold here – Plaintiff's interests and participation in Defendants' commodity pools – were purchased or sold domestically. . . .

From one vantage point, it seems logical to maintain the conduct or effects test in the context of CEA claims, given that *Morrison* explicitly abrogated that test with respect to securities, but not commodities claims. Be that as it may, the more powerful inference is, in fact, that the plain language of § 4o militates against finding that the transaction test is automatically appropriate in a § 4o, as well as a securities, context. In support of this position is the fact that the language of § 4o plainly contemplates fraud that extends beyond any initial transaction in which an interest in commodities was purchased. Moreover, § 4o's protection of prospective, as well as actual, investors creates a difficulty with respect to the application of *Absolute Activist*'s transactional definition: specifically, it is not clear how a "prospective" investor could ever incur "irrevocable liability," because such an individual, by definition, need not purchase an interest in commodities in order to fall within the plain language of § 4o. At the same time, the reality is that the conduct or effects test governed the extraterritoriality of the CEA prior to *Morrison*, and that *Morrison* abrogated that test. Thus, it is arguably illogical to maintain the abrogated test in the commodities context – particularly given that commodities and securities were treated analogously with respect to extraterritoriality prior to *Morrison*. Moreover, *Morrison* itself has since been applied to statutes other than the '34 Act, which would seem to broadly support its extension to CEA claims pursuant to § 4o. . . .

Although *Morrison* explicitly held that the presumption against extraterritoriality applies to all laws that are silent on extraterritorial application, the applicability of the transaction test outside of § 10(b) is not self evident. . . .

The terms of § 4o are broader than the "purchase or sale" language of § 10(b). Accordingly, Morrison's transaction test is not immediately applicable to § 4o. This particular antifraud provision, however, cannot be read in isolation from the rest of the CEA. Rather, § 4o must be read *in pari materia* with the other provisions of the statute, including, most importantly, that which confers a private right of action, § 22. . . .

Unlike the broad language of § 4o, which extends beyond the transactions contemplated in *Morrison* and *Absolute Activist*, . . . [§ 22(a) is] explicitly transactional in nature. . . .

Insofar as private litigants are concerned, § 4o necessarily reaches only conduct that is enumerated in § 22. To understand § 4o as separate from the transactional limitations of § 22 would be to read the requirements of the CEA's enumerated private right of action out of the statute. Given the presumption against extraterritoriality, it follows that in order for a private litigant to assert a viable claim pursuant to § 4o, one or more of the transactions enumerated in § 22 must be domestic in nature. . . .

This limitation reflects an explicit judgment by Congress to articulate the scope of the CEA's antifraud provisions within the realm of private rights of action.[iii] . . .

To summarize: The Court in *Morrison* held that a presumption against extraterritoriality applies in all cases as a canon of statutory construction. The presumption against extraterritoriality does not end the matter, however, as courts must determine whether the conduct covered by the statute at issue is "domestic" in relevant respects. . . . The CEA is silent as to its extraterritorial reach; accordingly, the *Morrison* presumption against extraterritoriality applies in full force. . . .

Plaintiff contends that . . . irrevocable liability was incurred in the United States, because (1) Plaintiff wired money to New York in exchange for the purchase of the commodities interest in Thor United; and (2) the investment memoranda that governed Plaintiff's purchase provided for a 15–day revocability provision, meaning "Plaintiff became bound only after the safe harbor period lapsed." This Court disagrees.

Though the terms of the Contract only became fully effective after the lapse of the safe harbor period, Plaintiff did not incur irrevocable liability in the United States within the reasoning of *Absolute Activist*. The contracts were negotiated in Russia, signed in Russia, and the meeting of the minds occurred in Russia. Though, by operation of the contract, Plaintiff could no longer remove her money from the pools in which she invested as of 15 days after the money had been wired to New York, under *Absolute Activist*, the "exchange of money" is a relevant, though not dispositive factor. . . .

It is the contract that gives rise to Plaintiff's irrevocable liability, and the contract at issue here was not domestic in nature, given the location of both the negotiations and the meeting of the minds. It is her signature that bound Plaintiff, not the wiring of money. While the exchange of consideration is relevant, as discussed, it cannot be the *sine qua non* of irrevocable liability. . . .

And finally, while Plaintiff did receive accounting statements created in the United States, and the alleged real estate fraud occurred domestically as well, these domestic activities occurred long after she had become bound by the terms of the investment memoranda.

In sum, Loginovskaya was irrevocably bound by the terms of the contract she signed. That relevant transaction – namely, the alleged purchase of an

---

[iii] [N. 12] It is worth noting that the CFTC has no such limitation on its own ability to bring suit, meaning that the applicable test to determine whether the prohibited conduct at issue was domestic in nature will necessarily vary depending on whether a private litigant sues pursuant to § 22, or whether the CFTC asserts its own cause of action (transactional when a private litigant asserts a claim and more broadly based when the CFTC brings a claim). Nevertheless, this result does not depart from Congressional intent, given the unequivocal delimitating effect of the private right of action that Congress chose to create.

interest in a commodities pool, along with the negotiations that led up to it – occurred in Russia. Although conduct that came later, and the potential fraudulent effects of that conduct, occurred domestically, through a series of domestic investments, those placements did not involve Plaintiff other than indirectly through the use of her funds, as she was already bound by the parties' agreements. And under *Morrison's* transaction test, the conduct or effects subsequent to the transaction at the core of a particular claim are irrelevant to the determination of extraterritorial application. Accordingly, Plaintiff fails to state a claim under the CEA. . . .

Loginovskaya raises difficult questions as to how to apply *Morrison* to the Commodity Exchange Act. It raises a possible distinction between the extraterritorial jurisdiction that the Commodity Exchange Act permits to be asserted by the CFTC and that which the Commodity Exchange Act permits a party making a claim through the private right of action available under Commodity Exchange Act § 22.

However, it is open to question whether the court in *Loginovskaya* is improperly morphing a statutory difference between Commodity Exchange Act §§ 4o and 22 on the *domestic* conduct to which the Commodity Exchange Act applies to a difference in analysis as to the Commodity Exchange Act's extraterritorial extent. Since the Commodity Exchange Act is silent as to the extraterritorial extent of both § 4o and § 22, *per Morrison*, neither § 4o nor § 22 should have extraterritorial effect and, where the facts are the same, a court arguably should come to the same conclusion as to whether a transaction is domestic or not, regardless of whether §§ 4o or 22 are invoked.

3. *Foreign Boards of Trade*

Foreign Boards of Trade, commonly known as "FBOTs," are facilities that offer access to U.S. persons to trade commodity futures and options with boards of trade not designated as contract markets in the United States. Whereas, in the past the CFTC has, on an *ad hoc* basis, permitted specific foreign boards of trade to provide U.S. persons access, these arrangements have now been formalized. *See* Chapter 4.

D. EXTRATERRITORIAL LIMIT OF THE CFTC'S JURISDICTION OVER SWAPS

As noted above, the Commodity Exchange Act does not, as a general matter, explicitly confer extraterritorial jurisdiction to the CFTC over the matters within its purview.

However, with respect to swaps specifically, the Commodity Exchange Act expressly addresses extraterritoriality.

1. *Statutory Limit*

When we evaluate the extent of the CFTC's extraterritorial reach with respect to swaps, the first resource is the Commodity Exchange Act, which expressly addresses its extraterritorial application to swaps transactions:

> *The provisions of this chapter relating to swaps that were enacted by the Wall Street Transparency and Accountability Act of 2010* [i.e. the Dodd-Frank Act] (including any rule prescribed or regulation promulgated under that Act), *shall not apply to activities outside the United States unless those activities –*
> (1) *have a direct and significant connection with activities in, or effect on, commerce of the United States*; or
> (2) contravene such rules or regulations as the Commission may prescribe or promulgate as are necessary or appropriate to prevent the evasion of any provision of this chapter that was enacted by the Wall Street Transparency and Accountability Act of 2010.

Commodity Exchange Act § 2(i) (emphasis added).

2. *CFTC's Position Generally*

In July 2013, CFTC staff issued "guidance"[7] as to how the CFTC can be expected to interpret Commodity Exchange Act § 2(i) in the context of: (1) what is a U.S. person, (2) what elements of the U.S. regulatory regime for swaps will non-U.S. CFTC-registered swap dealers and major swap participants be required to abide by in transactions with non-U.S. persons, and (3) standards for determining where non-U.S. regulatory regimes are "comparable" and deemed to be the equivalent of complying with U.S. regulations. This guidance will be referred to henceforth as the "Cross-Border Guidance."

3. *What Is a U.S. Person in the Context of Swaps?*

Among other things, the Cross-Border Guidance provides a definition of U.S. person. This definition is important because whether a counterparty to a swap is a U.S. person is in many cases a prerequisite for, as discussed below in section D4, determining the scope of the Dodd-Frank Act's application.

The Cross-Border Guidance defines a U.S. person "generally to include, but not be limited to" the categories listed in Figure 15-A.

Figure 15-A: Definition of U.S. Person

Category	Commentary
"(i) any natural person who is a resident of the United States."	The reference to a natural person means individuals, not partnerships, corporations or limited liability companies. Residency can be inferred via indicia such as primary residence or "permanent resident," i.e., "green card" status.
"(ii) any estate of a decedent who was a resident of the United States at the time of death."	An estate of a decedent is not likely to be a frequent entrant into the swaps market. If a person would have satisfied the U.S. person test in (i) while alive then their estate will be deemed a U.S. person.
"(iii) any corporation, partnership, limited liability company, business or other trust, association, joint-stock company, fund or any form of enterprise similar to any of the foregoing . . . (a "legal entity"), in each case that is organized or incorporated under the laws of a state or other jurisdiction in the United States or having its principal place of business in the United States."	The question of whether a legal entity is organized or incorporated in the United States is simple and objective. However, what constitutes having a "principal place of business in the United States"? This issue is discussed below in section D3a.
"(iv) any pension plan for the employees, officers or principals of a legal entity . . . unless the pension plan is primarily for foreign employees. . . ."	The central question is the class of beneficiaries of the pension plan, not the plan's jurisdiction of formation.
"(v) any trust governed by the laws of a state or other jurisdiction in the United States, if a court within the United States is able to exercise primary supervision over the	Whether a trust meets this standard or not may be difficult to assess. However, it should not arise often since such an entity is infrequently a party to a swap.

administration of the trust."	
"(vi) any commodity pool, pooled account, investment fund, or other collective investment vehicle that is not described in . . . (iii) and that is majority-owned by one or more persons described in . . . (i), (ii), (iii), (iv), or (v), except any commodity pool, pooled account, investment fund, or other collective investment vehicle that is publicly offered only to non-U.S. persons and not offered to U.S. persons."	This covers any private equity fund, hedge fund, commodity pool, or mutual fund (i.e., "investment company") that is not formed in the United States, yet is nonetheless owned mostly by U.S. persons. An exception is provided for such an entity that is publicly offered solely to non-U.S. persons even if it ends up majority-owned by U.S. persons.
"(vii) any legal entity . . . that is directly or indirectly majority-owned by one or more persons described in . . . (i), (ii), (iii), (iv), or (v) and in which such person(s) bears unlimited responsibility for the obligations and liabilities of the legal entity."	A legal entity formed outside of the U.S., the principal place of business of which is outside the U.S. and that is directly or indirectly owned by U.S. persons bearing unlimited liability for the entity, is considered to be a U.S. person. Though logical to have the U.S. person majority "pass through" the entity since, ultimately, U.S. persons that have unlimited liability bear the responsibility, this category should be uncommon.
(viii) any individual account or joint account . . . where the beneficial owner (or one of the beneficial owners in the case of a joint account) is a person described in . . . (i), (ii), (iii), (iv), (v), (vi), or (vii).	Any account held by a U.S. person, even if held overseas, will be treated as a U.S. person.

a. Principal Place of Business

The CFTC has sought to provide more detailed guidance on the concept of "principal place of business." A particular focus is on U.S. managers of non-U.S. investment vehicles. The CFTC's position has the potential to incentivize non-U.S. investment vehicles to use non-U.S. managers, if by doing so their regulatory burden can be lessened.

Interpretive Guidance and Policy Statement Regarding Compliance with Certain Swap Regulations

78 Fed. Reg. 45292 (July 26, 2013)

. . . [T]he Commission would generally interpret the term ''U.S. person'' to include also a legal entity that is not incorporated in the United States if it has its ''principal place of business'' in the United States. The Commission intends that this interpretation would generally include those entities that are organized outside the United States but have the center of direction, control, and coordination of their business activities in the United States.

The concept of an operating company having a principal place of business has been addressed by the Supreme Court. In a recent case, the Supreme Court described a corporation's principal place of business as the ''place where the corporation's high level officers direct, control, and coordinate the corporation's activities.''[iv] The Supreme Court explained that '''principal place of business' is best read as referring to the place where a corporation's officers direct, control, and coordinate the corporation's activities. It is the place that Courts of Appeals have called the corporation's 'nerve center.' And in practice it should normally be the place where the corporation maintains its headquarters – provided that the headquarters is the actual center of direction, control and coordination, i.e., the 'nerve center,' and not simply an office where the corporation holds its board meetings.''[v] . . .

The Commission is of the view that the application of the principal place of business concept to a collective investment vehicle may require consideration of additional factors beyond those applicable to operating companies. A collective investment vehicle is an entity or group of related entities created for the purpose of pooling assets of one or more investors and channeling these assets to trade or invest to achieve the investment objectives of the investor(s), rather than being a separate, active operating business. In this context, the determination of where the collective investment vehicle's "high level officers direct, control, and coordinate the [vehicle's] activities" – to apply the *Hertz* decision noted above – can involve several different factors.

The Commission is aware that the formation and structure of collective investment vehicles involve a great deal of variability, including with regard to the formation of the legal entities that will hold the relevant assets and enter into transactions (including swaps) in order to achieve the investors' objectives. Legal, regulatory, tax and accounting considerations may all play a role in determining how the collective investment vehicle is structured and the jurisdictions in which the legal entities will be incorporated. Many legal jurisdictions around the world have promulgated specialized regimes for the

---

[iv] [N. 193] *See Hertz Corp. v. Friend*, 559 U.S. 77, 80 (2010) (determining a corporation's principal place of business for purposes of diversity jurisdiction).

[v] [N. 194] *Id.* at 92–93.

formation of collective investment vehicles, which offer various legal, regulatory, tax and accounting efficiencies.

In view of these circumstances, the Commission believes that for a collective investment vehicle, the locations where the relevant legal entities have registered offices, hold board meetings or maintain books and records are generally not relevant in determining the principal place of business of the collective investment vehicle. Instead, as stated in the Hertz case cited above, the determination should generally depend on the location of the "actual center of direction, control and coordination," i.e., the "nerve center," of the collective investment vehicle.

Hertz focuses on the place where the "high level officers direct, control, and coordinate" the entity's activities. In this regard, the Commission believes that the focus should not necessarily be on the persons who are named as directors or officers of the legal entities that comprise the collective investment vehicle. As noted above, these legal entities are merely the legal structure through which the investment objectives of the collective investment vehicle are implemented. Rather, the analysis should focus on the persons who are the equivalent for the collective investment vehicle to the "high level officers" of an operating company because they direct, control and coordinate key functions of the vehicle, such as formation of the vehicle or its trading and investment.

The "high level officers [who] direct, control and coordinate" the collective investment vehicle may be those senior personnel who implement the investment and trading strategy of the collective investment vehicle and manage its risks, and the location where they conduct the activities necessary to implement the investment strategies of the vehicle may be its center of direction, control and coordination. In this regard, the Commission notes that the achievement of the investment objectives of a collective investment vehicle typically depends upon investment performance and risk management. Investors in a collective investment vehicle seek to maximize the return on their investment while remaining within their particular tolerance for risk. Thus, the key personnel relevant to this aspect of the analysis are those senior personnel responsible for implementing the vehicle's investment strategy and its risk management. Depending on the vehicle's investment strategy, these senior personnel could be those responsible for investment selections, risk management decisions, portfolio management, or trade execution.[vi]

[vi] [N. 201] The Commission understands that the collective investment vehicle may obtain the services of the relevant personnel through a variety of arrangements, including contracting with an asset manager that employs the personnel, contracting with other employers, or retaining the personnel as independent contractors. Thus, in this analysis, the Commission would generally expect to consider the location of the personnel who undertake the relevant activities, regardless of their particular employment arrangements.

The achievement of a collective investment vehicle's investment objectives may be closely linked to its formation. Decisions made in the structuring and formation of the collective investment vehicle may have a significant effect on the performance of the vehicle. Thus, for purposes of identifying the vehicle's principal place of business, the Commission may also consider the location of the senior personnel who direct, control and coordinate the formation of the vehicle (i.e., the promoters). The location of the promoters of the collective investment vehicle is relevant, particularly where the vehicle has a specialized structure or where the promoters of the vehicle continue to be integral to the ongoing success of the fund, including by retaining overall control of the vehicle. The location where the promoters of the collective investment vehicle act to form the vehicle and bring it to commercial life is relevant in determining the center of direction, control and coordination of the vehicle, and those promoters may be the "high level officers" of the vehicle referred to in *Hertz*.[vii]

Accordingly, the Commission will generally consider the principal place of business of a collective investment vehicle to be in the United States if the senior personnel responsible for either (1) the formation and promotion of the collective investment vehicle or (2) the implementation of the vehicle's investment strategy are located in the United States, depending on the facts and circumstances that are relevant to determining the center of direction, control and coordination of the vehicle.

Since the Commission recognizes that the structures of collective investment vehicles vary greatly, the Commission believes it is useful to provide examples to illustrate how the Commission's approach could apply to a consideration of whether the "principal place of business" of a collective investment vehicle is in the United States in particular hypothetical situations. However . . . these examples are for illustrative purposes only. . . .

Example 1. An asset management firm located in the United States establishes a collective investment vehicle outside the United States ("Fund A"). Typically, the formation of the collective investment vehicle by the personnel of the asset management firm involves the selection of firms to be the administrator, prime broker, custodian and placement agent for the collective investment vehicle. The legal entities comprising the collective investment vehicle enter into agreements retaining the asset management firm as

---

[vii] [N. 203] The Commission is aware that the boards of directors (or equivalent corporate bodies) of the legal entities that comprise a collective investment vehicle typically have the authority to appoint or remove the legal entity's investment manager, administrator, and auditor, and to approve major transactions involving the legal entity and the legal entity's audited financial statements. But since these functions are not key to the actual implementation of the investment objectives of the collective investment vehicle, and noting that *Hertz* focuses on the "high level officers" of the entity rather than its directors, the Commission would generally not view the boards of directors of the legal entities to be key personnel for the collective investment vehicle.

investment manager. Personnel of the asset management firm who are located in the United States will be responsible for implementing Fund A's investment and trading strategy and its risk management. Based on the above facts, the Commission would be inclined to view the principal place of business of Fund A as being in the United States,[viii] and therefore each of the legal entities that comprise Fund A would be within the interpretation of the term "U.S. person."

Example 2. An asset management firm located outside the United States establishes a collective investment vehicle located outside the United States ("Fund B"). Personnel of the asset management firm who are located outside the United States will be responsible for implementing Fund B's investment and trading strategy and its risk management. However, personnel in two offices of the asset management firm – one of which is located outside the United States and the other of which is located in the United States – will be involved in managing Fund B's investment portfolio. Although the personnel in the U.S. office may act autonomously on a day-to-day basis, they will be under the direction of senior personnel in the non-U.S. office regarding how they are implementing the investment objectives of Fund B. In terms of the asset management firm's internal organization, the personnel in the U.S. office report to the personnel in the non-U.S. office, who also generally hold higher positions within the firm. Because the personnel located inside the United States merely facilitate the implementation of the investment objectives of Fund B, for which senior personnel outside the United States are responsible, the Commission would be inclined to view the principal place of business of Fund B as not being in the United States.[ix] As a result, assuming that Fund B is not majority-owned

---

[viii] [N. 205] The collective investment vehicle's administrator generally handles day-to-day administrative activities. . . . The prime broker facilitates the execution of the vehicle's investment transactions, including swaps. The custodian is responsible for holding the vehicle's assets. The placement agent markets and sells shares to investors. The Commission generally considers all of these functions, although important to the collective investment vehicle, to be ministerial functions that are generally not relevant to the determination of the location of a collective investment vehicle's principal place of business. Thus, even if all of these firms and all the personnel performing these functions were outside the United States, the Commission would nonetheless be inclined to view the principal place of business of Fund A as within the United States. Additional elements that could be relevant to the determination include the location of the collective investment vehicle's primary assets, and the location of the collective investment vehicle's counterparties. However, the Commission believes that the location of these additional elements outside the United States should generally not preclude an interpretation that the collective investment vehicle's principal place of business is in the United States.

[ix] [N. 207] The Commission expects that in this example, this result would be the same if the asset management firm entered into a subadvisory agreement with an independent firm that employed the personnel in the U.S. office described in this example. That is . . . the relevant issue is whether the personnel who fulfill the key functions relating to its

by U.S. persons (as discussed further below), Fund B would not be within the interpretation of the term "U.S. person," and none of the legal entities that comprise Fund B would be U.S. persons (unless the legal entity was actually incorporated or organized in the United States).

Example 3. A financial firm located in the United States establishes a collective investment vehicle outside the United States ("Fund C"). The collective investment vehicle includes a single legal entity organized outside the United States, the assets of which are segregated into several separate classes. The U.S. financial firm arranges with several unaffiliated investment management firms to manage the assets in the various classes; an investment management firm affiliated with the U.S. financial firm may also manage the assets in one or more of the classes. Some of these investment management firms are located in, and others outside, the United States. Under the terms of the contracts between Fund C, the U.S. financial firm and these investment management firms, Fund C has delegated responsibility for the overall control of its investment strategies to the U.S. financial firm that established Fund C, and the U.S. financial firm will have rights to reallocate Fund C's assets among the investment management firms for various reasons, including the U.S. financial firm's discretion regarding Fund C's investment strategies. Based on the above facts, the Commission would be inclined to view the principal place of business of Fund C as being in the United States, even though some of the investment managers involved in implementing Fund C's investment and trading strategy are located outside the United States. Therefore, Fund C (including each of the legal entities that comprise Fund C) would be within the interpretation of the term "U.S. person."

The Commission recognizes that the structures of collective investment vehicles are complex and varied, and it does not intend to establish bright line tests for when the principal place of business of a collective investment vehicle would or would not be within the United States. Rather, the Commission's examples above are intended to illustrate the considerations that would be relevant to whether a collective investment vehicle's principal place of business is in the United States, within the framework of reviewing all the relevant facts and circumstances.

The Commission also understands that non-U.S. individuals, institutions, pension plans or operating companies may retain asset management firms in the United States to provide a range of asset management and other investment-related services. Where the individual, institution, pension plan or operating company is not within any prong of the interpretation of the term "U.S. person" . . . (including prongs (iii) and (vi) which relate to collective investment vehicles), then the Commission generally believes that the person would not come within the "U.S. person" interpretation solely because it retains

---

formation or the achievement of its investment objectives are located in, or outside of, the United States.

an asset management firm located in the United States to manage its assets or provide other financial services.

Based on the CFTC's above guidance, an investment vehicle must look at its sponsorship and its day-to-day management to apply a fact-specific analysis as to whether it is a U.S. person or not for these purposes.

b. Treatment of Bank Branches

Banks are unique in that, though one legal entity, the legal entity is comprised of a head office and branches. Branches are similar to offices of an ordinary corporation. They represent physical locations where the relevant legal entity is operating.

Unlike offices, branches – for specific purposes – are treated separately from the head office.[8] However, for the purposes of determining U.S.-person status, a branch of a bank, with some exceptions enumerated below in section D5, is considered to be the same legal entity as the bank.

This means that a U.S. branch of a non-U.S. bank is not a U.S. person since the legal entity, the non-U.S. bank, is not formed in the United States. However, the CTFC has stated that they have a "strong supervisory interest in regulating the [swap] dealing activities that occur with the United States, irrespective of the counterparty . . ." including if it is a non-U.S. bank operating through a U.S. branch.[9]

4. *Special Treatment of Non-U.S. Persons' Trades with U.S. Persons*

As discussed in Chapter 8, there is an $8 billion notional[10] *de minimis* threshold calculated on a rolling annual basis and aggregating the positions of all affiliated entities other than those already registered with the CFTC as a swap dealer, which allows a person engaging in swap dealing activities below that level to not register with the CFTC as a swap dealer. There is a *de minimis* level for potential major swap participants, also discussed in Chapter 8.

For the purposes of calculating swaps that have the potential to count toward this *de minimis* threshold, a non-U.S. entity need only calculate its swaps with U.S. persons. However, for this purpose only, and to address CFTC concerns as to U.S. persons directly or indirectly having significant swaps exposure to non-registrants, a swap with a non-U.S. entity guaranteed by a U.S. affiliate is deemed to be a swap with a U.S. person unless the U.S. affiliate is itself a swap dealer or affiliated with one or is a non-financial end-user. (*See* Chapter 10 for non-financial end-users.)

Also, even though a non-U.S. branch of a U.S. bank is, for other purposes, treated as a U.S. person since a branch is not a distinct legal entity, for the purpose of making this *de minimis* calculation it is treated as a non-U.S. person.

Otherwise, a non-U.S. entity might avoid trading with non-U.S. branches of U.S. banks for fear of adding to the swaps counting toward the non-U.S. entity's *de minimis* threshold.

5. Substituted Compliance

Some entities may be able to benefit from "substituted compliance," i.e., being able to demonstrate that another jurisdiction's regulations are "comparable." This can help avoid duplicative, overlapping regulations.

a. U.S. Persons

U.S. persons generally cannot take advantage of substituted compliance. They are required to comply with the law related to swaps and all of the rules related to swaps that are promulgated by the CFTC. Limited exceptions, outlined in Figure 15-B below, are available for U.S. swap dealers or major swap participants using a non-U.S. affiliate for all solicitations or negotiations or for non-U.S. branches of U.S. banks that are registered as swap dealers.[11]

b. Non-U.S. Persons

Most non-U.S. persons registered as swap dealers or major swap participants will, at least partially, be able to benefit from substituted compliance if they are able to demonstrate that they are subject to comparable regulation and, therefore, need not comply with duplicative CFTC regulations.

The extent of the benefit depends on which CFTC rules are in question and on the U.S. person status of the swap dealer or major swap participant seeking relief from CFTC requirements, as illustrated in Figure 15-B below. For more details on the requirements being referred to in the first column of the table, *see* Chapters 8, 9 and 10.

Figure 15-B: Application of Substituted Compliance[12]

	When Entity is Non-U.S. Entity Registered with CFTC as Swap Dealer or Major Swap Participant	When Entity is Foreign Branch of U.S. Bank Registered as a Swap Dealer or Major Swap Participant	When Entity is U.S. Swap Dealer or Major Swap Participant Soliciting and Negotiating Using non-U.S. Affiliate
First Category of Entity Level Requirements (i.e., capital adequacy, CCO	Substituted compliance available	Substituted compliance available	Substituted compliance not available

report, risk management, and swap recordkeeping, other than customer complaints and marketing materials)			
Second Category of Entity Level Requirements (i.e., SDR reporting, other than large swaps trader reporting, and records of customer complaints and marketing materials)	Substituted compliance available only if counterparty is non-U.S. person	Substituted compliance available only if counterparty is non-U.S. person	Substituted compliance not available
Category A of Transaction Level Requirements (i.e., clearing, margin, and segregation of uncleared swaps, swap trading relationship documentation, portfolio reconciliation and compression, real-time public reporting, trade confirmation requirements, and daily trading records)	Requirement not applicable if non-U.S. person is counterparty unless non-U.S. person is a foreign branch of a U.S. bank registered as a swap dealer or a non-U.S. person guaranteed by a U.S. affiliate, in which case substituted compliance is available	Substituted compliance if counterparty is non-U.S. person, a foreign branch of a U.S. bank registered as a swap dealer or a non-U.S. person guaranteed by a U.S. affiliate	Substituted compliance not available
Category B of Transaction Level Requirements (i.e., external	Requirement not applicable if counterparty is a non-U.S. person,	Requirement not applicable if counterparty is a non-U.S. person,	Requirement not applicable if counterparty is a non-U.S. person,

business conduct requirements)	a non-U.S. person guaranteed by a U.S. affiliate, or a foreign branch of a U.S. bank registered as a swap dealer	a non-U.S. person guaranteed by a U.S. affiliate, or a foreign branch of a U.S. bank registered as a swap dealer	a non-U.S. person guaranteed by a U.S. affiliate, or a foreign branch of a U.S. bank registered as a swap dealer

Additionally, some portions of the CFTC's swap regulatory regime apply to non-registrants, namely, for financial end-users, the clearing and on-facility trading requirements and, for all end-users, the reporting and recordkeeping requirements. When one of the counterparties is a U.S. person, all of these requirements apply, to the extent they would apply to the U.S. person. If two non-U.S. persons trade and one or both are guaranteed by a U.S. affiliate, substituted compliance is available. In all other cases, there is no obligation to comply with the above-referenced requirements.[13]

c. Comparability Determinations

To claim substituted compliance a party is required to be able to demonstrate that it is already complying with "comparable" requirements. Whether a regime has comparable requirements is a determination made by the CFTC.

Comparability determinations have been made – to different extents – with respect to the swap regulatory regime in place in Australia, Canada, the European Union, Hong Kong, Japan, and Switzerland.[14] Finding of comparability among Group of Twenty countries is to be expected due to the commitments on these core areas described in section B above.

6. Characterization of Cross-Border Guidance as Rulemaking

The CFTC's "guidance" has been challenged. Despite the complexity of the above Cross-Border Guidance, CFTC staff has characterized it as "guidance" and not as a rulemaking. Rulemakings require an affirmative vote of the commissioners and cannot be promulgated by staff decisions. Moreover, it requires compliance with the formalities of the Administrative Procedures Act.

In the following complaint, the Securities Industry and Financial Markets Association (commonly known as "SIFMA"), an industry association for the securities industry; the Institute of International Bankers, an industry association for non-U.S. banks operating in the United States; and the International Swaps and Derivatives Association sued the CFTC arguing that the CFTC staff, in promulgating the Cross-Border Guidance, had, in actuality, engaged in rulemaking without following the statutory conditions for promulgating a rule.

Securities Industry and Financial Markets Association v. Commodity Futures Trading Commission

Amended Complaint, Civil Action No. 13-CV-1916 (ESH)

This is a lawsuit under the Administrative Procedure Act ("APA") and the Commodity Exchange Act ("CEA") intended to halt an unprecedented and unlawful effort by the Commodity Futures Trading Commission ("CFTC" or "Commission") to regulate financial activity around the world without complying with fundamental requirements of agency rulemaking. The Commission has promulgated, in the guise of "guidance," an expansive new body of regulations under the Dodd-Frank Wall Street Reform and Consumer Protection Act ("Dodd-Frank") that seeks to extend the CFTC's authority and requirements across the globe. In doing so, the Commission failed to conduct the cost-benefit analysis required by law or to comply with other essential prerequisites of rulemaking under the APA and the CEA. This flawed attempt to act as the paramount regulator of international swaps trading, even where there is no significant connection with United States commerce, will harm investors, impair U.S. and foreign businesses, impose inconsistent, duplicative requirements on firms that are regulated by other nations, and exceeds the CFTC's lawful authority. . . . Plaintiffs are compelled to bring this action now to stop what is proving to be an unceasing effort by the Commission to regulate the global swaps markets through unpredictable "guidance" documents, advisories, and directives, and to force the CFTC instead to abide by the requirements for rulemaking laid down by Congress. Plaintiffs therefore seek a court order vacating the Commission's improperly promulgated cross-border rule and enjoining the CFTC from giving extraterritorial effect to its swaps regulations, until a valid rulemaking regarding extraterritorial application has been completed.

In adopting a series of rules under Title VII of Dodd-Frank, the Commission initially refused to address the crucial question of their application to parties or transactions abroad [by] . . . promising to address the issue at a later date. But the Commission never promulgated a rule on the extraterritorial reach of its Title VII regulations that complied with the strictures of the APA and the CEA. Instead, the Commission attempted to excuse itself from those requirements by issuing a sweeping, international compliance directive that it characterized as mere "guidance." This "guidance," referred to herein as the "Cross-Border Rule," spans 78 pages in the Federal Register and includes 650 footnotes and numerous charts and appendices; establishes a host of new regulatory definitions; and contains myriad directives for financial institutions and investors around the globe.

Despite calculated suggestions throughout the "guidance" that its terms are non-binding, the Commission has made clear at every turn that the Cross-Border Rule is intended to bind Commission staff and the public. Both the CFTC and Federal Register websites refer to the Cross-Border Rule as a "rule." As

Chairman Gensler declared when the Cross-Border Rule was issued, the Rule "provides that swap dealers, foreign or U.S., transacting with U.S. persons . . . must comply with Dodd-Frank's swap market reform." The Commission unambiguously confirmed that it was compelling compliance with the Cross-Border Rule – for some provisions after October 9, 2013, and for others after December 21, 2013 – by issuing an "exemptive order" providing limited temporary relief from compliance before those dates. . . .

The CFTC stands alone in attempting to implement Dodd-Frank by guidance rather than through the procedures required by law. The Securities and Exchange Commission ("SEC"), which . . . responsible for promulgating cross-border derivatives regulations . . . [with respect to security-based swaps], has proposed a cross-border rule that is subject to notice and comment and contains an economic and cost-benefit analysis. After considering the comments and conducting a complete cost-benefit analysis, the SEC intends to issue final rules relating to the cross-border application of its Title VII rules. . . .

The APA and the CEA establish vital rulemaking procedures that are intended to ensure care, thoroughness, and deliberation when promulgating regulations that could have a critical impact on the financial system, investors, and end-users of derivatives and commodities. The CFTC's willful evasion of those procedures sows unpredictability and confusion in the markets, produces irresponsible rules that are not cost effective, deprives the public of the opportunity to assist the government in developing smarter regulations, and undermines our Nation's settled framework for legislative rulemaking. . . .

In addition to these procedural errors, the Cross-Border Rule goes far beyond the CFTC's limited jurisdiction to regulate swaps outside of the United States, which encompasses – as relevant here – only "activities" that "have a direct and significant connection with activities in, or effect on, commerce of the United States." The Cross-Border Rule focuses largely on the status of market participants – such as whether one entity is a subsidiary of, or "guaranteed" by, another – not their actual "activities," as [CEA] Section 2(i) requires. The Commission justified this novel approach by assuming that it could regulate entities engaged in activities that, when "viewed as a class or in the aggregate," have a "direct and significant connection" with U.S. commerce. This deviates from the plain text of Section 2(i) by sweeping in a broad swath of "activities" that have only an indirect or insignificant connection to activities in, or effects on, U.S. commerce. . . .

Central to the Commission's regime for regulating cross-border swaps is the Cross-Border Rule's unprecedented definition of "U.S. person." That term is never used in Dodd-Frank and was never before defined in other CFTC rules. Instead, the Cross-Border Rule announced, for the first time, that in most circumstances, one's status as a "U.S. person" triggers application of all Entity- and Transaction-Level Requirements wherever in the world the "person" happens to be. By taking this approach, the CFTC sought to arrogate to itself unprecedented and unauthorized extraterritorial authority on the false premise that if a "U.S. person" enters into a swap transaction anywhere in the world, it automatically has "direct and significant connection with activities in, or effect on, commerce of the United States." . . .

QUESTIONS AND COMMENTS

1. In light of *Morrison* and its progeny, how would *Psimenos* be decided today?
2. Is there a reason grounded in statute to apply *Morrison* differently to the Commodity Exchange Act than it has been applied to the Securities Exchange Act?
3. Why does the CFTC put so much weight on where an investment fund is managed in determining whether a fund is a U.S. person? Could this have a chilling effect on the selection of U.S. fund managers?
4. Re-read Commodity Exchange Act § 2(i) in section D1 above. Is the CFTC's Cross-Border Guidance discussed in section D2 through D5 above reflective of the requirements of § 2(i)? What approach would you take to identify to what extent cross-border transactions would be subject to CFTC jurisdiction in light of Commodity Exchange Act § 2(i)?
5. If the plaintiffs in *SIFMA v. CFTC* prevail, what should be the remedy? Vacate the rule? If so, what could be the consequences of vacating the rule?
6. Are the plaintiffs' arguments in *SIFMA v. CFTC* meritorious?

ENDNOTES

Chapter 1 Endnotes

[1] McKinsey Global Institute, *Mapping Global Capital Markets 2011*, http://www.mckinsey.com/insights/mgi/research/financial_markets/mapping_global_capital_markets_2011 (accessed May 31, 2014).
[2] Bank for International Settlements, OTC Derivatives Statistics at End-December 2013, p. 14 (May 2014), *available at* http://www.bis.org/publ/otc_hy1405.pdf (accessed May 31, 2014). The so-called notional value, which will be discussed in Section B3 infra, was $710 trillion – more than three times the size of the world's financial stock. However, as will be seen, derivatives notional is not a good proxy to market value. Exchange-traded derivatives notional as of March 2014 equaled approximately $72 trillion. No gross market value figures were available. *See* Bank for International Settlements, Derivative Financial Instruments Traded on Organised Exchanges, *available at* http://www.bis.org/statistics/r_qa1406_hanx23a.pdf (accessed May 31, 2014).
[3] *Id.*
[4] *See* Henry Laurence, Symposium: The Rule of Law in the Era of Globalization, *Spawning the SEC*, 6 Ind. J. Global Leg. Stud. 647, 649 (1999).
[5] *See* Commodity Exchange Act § 1a(47) and Securities Exchange Act § 3(a)(68).
[6] A "bushel" is the main unit of measurement used to calculate grain. For wheat, it is equal to 60 pounds.
[7] If the option is "European" style, they would only have a right to exercise on a single date in a year's time. An "American" style option provides the right to exercise the option on any day. A "Bermudan" option is named thus due to Bermuda's position between the U.S. and Europe. It provides an exercise right on specific days.
[8] Physically settled off-exchange commodity swaps are rare. However, they are common enough to be on the regulatory radar screen, as illustrated by the Commodity Futures Trading Commission's effort to impose position limits on many commodity swaps, including off-exchange swaps with physical delivery of the commodity at certain locations. *See* Chapter 13.
[9] Or often slightly more, since the Law School Brewing Company's counterparty may embed a fee in the price to account for the credit risk it is exposed to, due to potential non-performance by the Law School Brewing Company, and a profit margin.
[10] Or often slightly less, since as noted in the preceding note, the Law School Brewing Company's counterparty may embed a fee in the price to account for the credit risk it is

exposed to, due to potential non-performance by the Law School Brewing Company, and a profit margin.

[11] This does not account for the time value of money, i.e., that money received later is worth less than money received earlier due to the fact that money received earlier could have been invested for a higher return. *See* Stephen A. Ross, Randolph W. Westerfield, and Jeffrey Jaffe, Corporate Finance, (5th Ed., McGraw-Hill Higher Education 1999), 64-75, for a description of this concept and associated formulae.

[12] Dodd-Frank Wall Street Reform and Consumer Protection Act, Pub. L. No. 111-203, 124 Stat. 1376 (2010).

[13] *See* Commodity Exchange Act § 1a(47)(a)(i).

[14] *See* Commodity Exchange Act § 1a(47)(iii) and (iv).

[15] *See* Commodity Exchange Act § 1a(35), 17 C.F.R. § 1.3(yyy), 17 C.F.R. § 1.3(aaaa), 12 U.S.C. § 78C(a)(55) and 17 C.F.R. §§ 240.3a68-1a and 240.3a68-1b.

[16] The Department of the Treasury granted an exemption for these foreign exchange swaps relying on authority conferred by the Commodity Exchange Act § 1a(47(E). *See* 77 Fed. Reg. 69694 (Nov. 20, 2012).

[17] *Supra* n. 2.

[18] The 1999 definitions have been supplanted by 2003 Definitions

[19] Berkshire Hathaway Inc., *2002 Annual Report*, 15 (2003) (available at http://www.berkshirehathaway.com/2002ar/2002ar.pdf) (accessed May 31, 2014).

Chapter 2
Endnotes

[1] *See* H.R. Rep. No. 93-975 (1974) and Richard Scott Carnell, Jonathan R. Macey and Geoffrey P. Miller, *The Law of Banking and Financial Institutions*, 739 (4th Ed., Wolters Kluwer 2009).

[2] *Board of Trade of City of Chicago v. Christie Grain & Stock Co.*, 198 U.S. 236, 246 (1905).

[3] *Gatewood v. North Carolina*, 203 U.S. 531, 536 (1906).

[4] *Oxford English Dictionary* vol. 2, p. 613 (Oxford U. Press 1989).

[5] Federal Trade Commission, *Report on the Grain Trade* vol. V, 330 (Government Printing Office 1920).

[6] David Hochfelder, *Where the Common People Could Speculate: The Ticker, Bucket Shops, and the Origins of Popular Participation in Financial Markets, 1880-1920*, 93 Journal of American History vol. 2, 335, 354 (2006).

[7] *Id.*

[8] Federal Trade Commission, *Report on the Grain Trade* vol. II, 128 (Government Printing Office 1920) and Hochfelder, 355.

[9] Pub. L. No. 67-66, 42 Stat. 187 (1921).

[10] *Hill v. Wallace*, 259 U.S. 44, 66-67 (1922). "It is impossible to escape the conviction, from a full reading of this law, that it was enacted for the purpose of regulating the conduct of business of Boards of Trade through supervision of the Secretary of Agriculture. . . . When this purpose is declared in the title to the bill, and is so clear from the effect of the provisions of the bill itself, it leaves no ground upon which the provisions we have been considering can be sustained as a valid exercise of the taxing

power. . . . There is not a word in the act from which it can be gathered that it is confined in its operation to interstate commerce. The words 'interstate commerce' are not to be found in any part of the act from the title to the closing section." *Id.*

[11] 262 U.S. 1 (1923).

[12] Grain Futures Act § 6(a).

[13] Commodity Exchange Act § 3(b) amending Grain Futures Act § 2(a).

[14] Grain Futures Act § 2(a).

[15] Mill feeds are "by-products from the manufacture of flour, namely, bran, middlings, shorts, reddog flour, etc." Purdue University Agricultural Experiment Station, *Commercial Feeding Stuffs Quarterly Report October 2, 1919-December 31, 1919*, Bulletin No. 242 (May 1920), 8.

[16] Commodity Exchange Act § 3(a) amending Grain Futures Act § 2(a).

[17] Commodity Exchange Act § 3(b).

[18] H.R. Rep. No. 93-975, 40-52. *See also* Roberta Romano, "the Political Dynamics of Derivatives Securities Regulation," 14 Yale J. on Reg. 279, 335, 337 (1997).

[19] *See* 76 Fed. Reg. 2083 (Jan. 31, 1976) and 76 Fed. Reg. 37681 (Dec. 22, 1976).

[20] 7 U.S.C. § 2(ii) (1993).

[21] *Board of Trade of the City of Chicago v. Securities and Exchange Commission*, 677 F.2d 1137 (7th Cir. 1982).

[22] For a further discussion of the Shad-Johnson Accord, *see* Chapter 2.

[23] *See Bank One Corp. v. C.I.R.*, 120 T.C. 174, 186 (2003) and Christian Johnson, *The Enigma of Clearing Buy-Side OTC Derivatives*, 29 Futures and Derivatives Law Report 11, n. 19 (2009), *citing World Bank: The IBM Deal That Opens a Cash Source,* Business Week, Sept. 7, 1981, 48. There are some arguments for an earlier date for the first modern over-the-counter swap going back as far as the 1960s. *See* Charles R. P. Pouncy, *Contemporary Financial Innovation: Orthodoxy and Alternatives*, 51 SMU L. Rev. 505, 529-531 (1998). Regardless, the IBM-World Bank swap appears to be the first to attract significant publicity.

[24] *See* Bloomberg, *J.P. Morgan's Debt Swapping Passes Lending as Top Money-Maker* (January 20, 2004) (available at http://www.bloomberg.com/apps/news?pid=21070001 &sid=anxEs_owYsv8) (accessed June 1, 2014).

[25] *See Bank One Corp. v. C.I.R.*, 186 and Pouncy, 530-532.

[26] International Swaps and Derivatives Association, *ISDA Market Survey, 1987-Present* (available at http://www.isda.org/statistics/pdf/isda-market-survey-historical-data.pdf) (accessed on June 1, 2014).

[27] *Id.*

[28] *See* Commodity Futures Trading Commission, *Regulation of Hybrid Instruments*, 54 Fed. Reg. 306984-01 (July 21, 1989) in which the CFTC exempts certain hybridized commodity options from regulation under the Commodity Exchange Act. *See also* Commodity Futures Trading Commission, *Policy Statement Concerning Swap Transactions*, 54 Fed. Reg. 30694-01 (July 21, 1989), n. 1 citing to exemptive authority in Commodity Exchange Act §§ 4c(b) and 4c(d).

[29] *See* Commodity Futures Trading Commission, *Statutory Interpretation Concerning Certain Hybrid Instruments*, 54 FR 1139-01 (January 11, 1989) that, unlike the exemptive relief related solely to commodity options in *Regulation of Hybrid Instruments* cited *supra* n. 27, is an interpretation presumably because the subject matter involved

futures, for which the CFTC did not at the time have statutory exemptive authority. As one commentator put it (*footnotes omitted*), "The difference between an exclusion and an exemption is that an exempt product may be a futures contract, while an excluded product may not." Rebecca Leon, *The Regulation of Derivatives and the Effect of the Futures Trading Practices Act of 1992*, 3 Journal of Law & Policy 321 (1994), 336-337.

[30] *Regulation of Hybrid Instruments*, 360684.

[31] Commodity Futures Trading Commission, *Statutory Interpretation Concerning Forward Transactions*, 55 Fed. Reg. 39188-03 (Sept. 25, 1990), 39189, n. 1.

[32] E.g., *see* Thomas A. Russo & Marlisa Vinciguerra, *Financial Innovation and Uncertain Regulation: Selected Issues Regarding New Product Development*, 69 Texas L. Rev. 1431 (May 1991), 1498 and C.A. "Cab" Baldwin, *Recent Changes in the Regulation of Commodity Sales and Derivatives*, 11 No. 3 ACCA Docket 76 (Summer 1993), 78 ("The parties settled the case at this point, but the multi-trillion dollar derivatives market was rocked by the implications of the court's reasoning.")

[33] Futures Trading Practices Act, PL 102-546, § 502.

[34] Commodity Futures Trading Commission, *Exemption for Certain Swap Agreement*, 58 Fed. Reg. 5587-01 (Jan. 22, 1993). One commentator described this at the time as a "parting gift" from Wendy Gramm, CTFTC chairman and wife of then-Senator Phil Gramm, to the growing swap industry. Frank Partnoy, *The Shifting Contours of Global Derivatives Regulation*, 22 U. Pa. J. Int'l Econ. L. 421, 436-437 *citing* Matt Rees, *Swaps Market: Farewell Gift from CFTC's Gramm for Swap Traders*, Bloomberg Business News (Jan. 14, 1993).

[35] Commodity Futures Trading Commission, *Exemption for Certain Contracts Involving Energy Products*, 58 Fed. Reg. 21286-02 (April 20, 1993).

[36] These tapes were initially subject to a protective order by the trial judge in *Proctor & Gamble* prohibiting their disclosure. After being leaked to Business Week, they were subsequently unsealed after motions by Business Week and Proctor & Gamble. *See* Business Week, "Business Week v. The Judge," October 15, 1995, available at http://www.businessweek.com/stories/1995-10-15/business-week-vs-dot-the-judge.

[37] Compiled from Business Week, *The Bankers Trust Tapes* (October 15, 1995) (available at http://www.businessweek.com/stories/1995-10-15/the-bankers-trust-tapes) (accessed June 5, 2014) and *In the Matter of BT Securities Corporation*, CFTC Docket No. 95-3 (Dec. 22, 1994).

[38] Note that with some types of swaps, such as physically settled foreign currency swaps, notional is exchanged by the parties.

[39] As noted below in section E2 this was superseded by the Commodity Futures Modernization Act and, as discussed in Chapters 7 through 10, the Dodd-Frank Act.

[40] *See* The Wall Street Journal, *Bankers Trust Names Newman Chief; Passed-Over President Shanks Resigns* (Oct. 20, 1995).

[41] New York Times, *Bankers Trust Settles Suit with P. & G.* (May 10, 1996) (available at http://www.nytimes.com/1996/05/10/business/bankers-trust-settles-suit-with-p-g.html?pagewanted=print&src=pm) (accessed June 5, 2014).

[42] *Id.*

[43] *The Bankers Trust Tapes*. For the claim of the Indonesian company, *see Bankers Trust International plc v. PT Dharmala Sakti Sejaherta and counterclaim*, [1996] C.L.C. 252 and

---

Bankers Trust International plc v. PT Dharmala Sakti Sejahtera & related action, [1996] C.L.C. 518.

[44] *See Proctor & Gamble*, 1276 *citing In re BT Securities Corp.*, SEC Release Nos. 33–7124, 34–35136 and CFTC Docket No. 95–3 (Dec. 22, 1994).

[45] For a survey of over-the-counter derivatives litigations in the era, *see The Shifting Contours of Global Derivatives Regulations*, 446-484.

[46] *See* Gary E. Kalbaugh & Richard A. Miller, *Master Agreements for OTC Derivatives*, in *Commercial Contracts: Strategies for Drafting and Negotiation*, § 25.04[C][24], n. 90 (Vladimir R. Rossman & Morton Moskin, eds., 3d ed., Aspen Publishers 2014).

[47] Commodity Futures Trading Commission, *Over-the-Counter Derivatives*, 63 FR 26114 (May 12, 1998) (hereinafter, the "1998 Concept Release").

[48] *Id.*

[49] *Ibid.* at 26115. The CFTC's 1998 Concept Release preceded by a few months the September bailout of hedge fund Long-Term Capital Management by a syndicate arranged by the Federal Reserve Bank of New York. *See* Government Accounting Office, *Report on Long-Term Capital Management*, GAO/GGD-00-3 (October 1999) and The President's Working Group on Financial Markets, *Leverage and the Lessons of Long-Term Capital Management* (April 1999).

[50] *Ibid.* at 26120-26127. Most of the concepts presaged the changes imposed by the Dodd-Frank Act in 2010, described further below.

[51] Ltr. from Robert E. Rubin, Secretary, Department of the Treasury, Alan Greenspan, Chairman, Board of Governors of the Federal Reserve System and Arthur Levitt, Chairman, Securities and Exchange Commission to The Honorable Newt Gingrich, Speaker U.S. House of Representatives (June 5, 1998) (available at http://www.treasury.gov/press-center/press-releases/Pages/cftcltr.aspx) (accessed June 5, 2014).

[52] *Ibid.* at 26114 & 26116.

[53] *Testimony of Brooksley Born, Chairperson Commodity Futures trading Commission Concerning the Over-the-Counter Derivatives market Before the U.S. House of Representatives Committee on Banking and Financial Services* (July 24, 1998) (available at http://www.cftc.gov/opa/speeches/opaborn-33.htm) (accessed June 5, 2014).

[54] Comments of the International Swaps and Derivatives Association to the 1998 Concept Release, CL 34, p.2 (October 13, 1998). All of the comments received are available on the CFTC's website at http://www.cftc.gov/foia/comment98/foi98--019_1.htm (accessed June 5, 2014).

[55] Comments of the Futures Industry Association to the 1998 Concept Release, CL 41, p.2 (October 13, 1998).

[56] Comments of the New York Clearinghouse to the 1998 Concept Release, CL 32, p.1 (October 13, 1998).

[57] Comments of the Chicago Mercantile Exchange to the 1998 Concept Release, CL 24 (October 12, 1998) and Comments of the Chicago Board of Trade to the 1998 Concept Release, CL 27 (October 13, 1998).

[58] PL 105-277 (October 21, 1998), § 760.

[59] Commodity Futures Trading Commission, *Concept release Concerning Over-the-Counter Derivatives*, 64 Fed. Reg. 65669 (November 22, 1999).

[60] *Ibid.*

[61] Comments of ABA Securities Association, American Bankers Association, The Bankers Roundtable, The Bond Market Association, Emerging Markets Traders Association, The Energy Group, Financial Markets Lawyers Group, The Foreign Exchange Committee, Futures Industry Association, International Swaps and Derivatives Association, Securities Industry Association and U.S. Chamber of Commerce to the 1998 Concept Release, CL 31, p. 1-2 (October 13, 1998).

[62] In addition to the clarity sought by the over-the-counter derivative marketplace, another motivation for passage of the Commodity Futures Modernization Act and, in fact an inducement for their support, was the futures exchanges' wish to offer futures based on single stocks or narrow-based securities indices, something banned by the Futures Trading Act of 1982. *See* William J. Brodsky [at the time Chairman and CEO of the Chicago Board Options Exchange], *New Legislation Permitting stock Futures: The Long and Winding Road*, 21 Nw. J. Int'l L. & Bus. 573, 576 (Spring, 2001) and section B4 *supra*.

[63] At this time, the President's Working Group was comprised of Lawrence H. Summers, Secretary of the Treasury, Alan Greenspan, Chairman of the Board of Governors of the Federal Reserve, Arthur Levitt, Chairman of the SEC, and William J. Rainer, Chairman of the CFTC. Brooksley Born had resigned as CFTC Chairman months beforehand.

[64] Available at www.treasury.gov/resource-center/fin-mkts/Documents/otcact.pdf (accessed June 5, 2014).

[65] This was ultimately narrowed by the CFMA to only agricultural commodities.

[66] *Over-the-Counter Derivatives Markets and the Commodity Exchange Act*, 33-34.

[67] Commodity Futures Modernization Act § 102, adding new § 2(c) to the Commodity Exchange Act.

[68] *See* Title II, Commodity Futures Modernization Act, "Coordinated Regulation of Security Futures Products."

[69] Commodity Futures Modernization Act §§ 302(a) and 303(a).

[70] *See Commodity Futures Trading Commission v. Zelener*, 373 F.3d 861 (7th Cir. 2004) and *Commodity Futures Trading Commission v. Erskine*, 512 F.3d 309 (6th Cir. 2008).

[71] PL 110–234 (Title XIII), 2008 HR 2419.

[72] Commodity Exchange Act, § 2(c)(2)(C)(i)(I)(aa).

[73] Commodity Exchange Act, § 2(c)(2)(C)(i)(I)(bb).

[74] Commodity Futures Trading Commission, *Regulation of Off-Exchange Retail Foreign Exchange Transactions and Intermediaries*, 75 FR 55410-01 (September 10, 2010).

[75] CFTC Reauthorization Act of 2008, §§ 13201 and 13202.

[76] Gary B. Gorton, *Misunderstanding Financial Crises: Why We Don't See Them Coming* (Oxford University Press 2012), 182. *See also* Financial Crisis Inquiry Commission, *The Financial Crisis Inquiry Report* (January 2011), xv (available at http://fcic-static.law.stanford.edu/cdn_media/fcic-reports/fcic_final_report_full.pdf) (accessed June 5, 2014).

[77] *Testimony of Alan Greenspan Before House Committee of Government Oversight and Reform* (October 23, 2008) (available at http://www.gpo.gov/fdsys/pkg/CHRG-110hhrg55764/html/CHRG-110hhrg55764.htm) (accessed June 5, 2014).

[78] *Misunderstanding Financial Crises*, 182 and Federal Reserve Bank of New York, *Financial Turmoil Timeline* (available at http://www.newyorkfed.org/research/global_economy/Crisis_Timeline.pdf) (accessed June 5, 2014).

---

[79] *The Financial Crisis Inquiry Report*, xxiii-xx-iv.
[80] *Testimony of Alan Greenspan Before House Committee of Government Oversight and Reform*
[81] This list is derived from *Financial Turmoil Timeline* and Federal Reserve Bank of St. Louis, *The Financial Crisis: A Timeline of Events and Policy Actions* (available at http://timeline.stlouisfed.org/pdf/CrisisTimeline.pdf) (accessed June 5, 2014).
[82] *The Financial Crisis Inquiry Report*, xiv, 50-51.
[83] *The Financial Crisis Inquiry Report*, 447.
[84] PL 11-203 (2010).

Chapter 3 Endnotes

[1] *Agricultural Swaps*, 75 Fed. Reg. 59666-01 (September 28, 2010), 59668 and 76 FR 6095-01, 6098.
[2] *Commodity Options*, 77 Fed. Reg. 25320 (April 27, 2012).
[3] Dodd-Frank Act § 712(d)(1).
[4] Dodd-Frank Act § 712(d)(3).
[5] This would be a derivative on a derivative.
[6] Securities Exchange Act of 1934 § 3(a)(68).
[7] The statutory definition appears to have minor errors. The definition provided is based on the summary in *Further Definition of "Swap," "Security-Based Swap," and "Security-Based Swap Agreement"; Mixed Swaps; Security-Based Swap Agreement Recordkeeping*, 47 FR 48208 (August 13, 2012), 48210, n. 10.
[8] *Ibid*. at 48291.
[9] Vacated as moot, 459 U.S. 1026 (1982).
[10] Legal Certainty for Bank Products Act of 2000 § 403 as amended by Dodd-Frank Act § 725(g). Before the Dodd-Frank, the Legal Certainty for Bank Products Act, in § 404, also provided an exclusion from the Commodity Exchange Act and CFTC jurisdiction for identified banking products developed after December 5, 2000. This section was removed by Dodd-Frank Act § 725(g).
[11] *Ibid*. at § 402(b).
[12] This presaged the conflict later resolved by the Shad-Johnson Accord. *See* Chapter 2.
[13] William T. Bagley, *Reign of Undue Process in Regulatory Agencies*, Forum (1977), p. 1.

Chapter 4 Endnotes

[14] In Chapter 9 we discuss trading facilities for swaps, instead of commodity futures. These trading facilities are known as "Swap Execution Facilities" or "SEFs."
[15] *See* http://sirt.cftc.gov/SIRT/SIRT.aspx?Topic=TradingOrganizations&implicit=true &type=DCM&CustomColumnDisplay=TTTTTTTT (accessed June 7, 2014).
[16] However, § 5(d)(19) of the Commodity Exchange Act prohibits a designated contract market from, unless otherwise required to do so by the Commodity Exchange Act, adopting "any rule or taking any action that results in any unreasonable restraint of

trade" or which imposes "any material anticompetitive burden on trading on the contract market."
[17] Swap execution facilities, commonly known as "SEFs," and derivatives clearing organizations, commonly known as "DCOs," also are required to comply with "core principles." *See* Chapter 9.
[18] E-mail from Richard A. Miller, Esq. (who formerly represented Spinale), January 2, 2014.
[19] *See*, e.g., *Strobl v. New York Mercantile Exchange*, 768 F.2d 22 (2d Cir. 1985).
[20] *Zimmerman v. Chicago Board of Trade*, 625.
[21] *See* Commodity Futures Trading Commission, *CFTC Emergency Authority Background*, http://www.cftc.gov/ucm/groups/public/@newsroom/documents/file/cftcemergencyauthoritybackgrou.pdf (accessed June 8, 2014).
[22] *See Klein & Co, Futures Inc, v. Board of Trade of the City of New York*, 464 F.3d 255 (2d Cir. 2006).
[23] *See* "A New Regulatory Framework for Clearing Organizations," 66 FR 45604-02 (August 29, 2001).
[24] Some also operated as exempt commercial markets, a now defunct category of CFTC registrant.

Chapter 5 Endnotes

[1] Only futures commission merchants are, at the current time, formally required to be National Futures Association members. However, the National Futures Association prohibits member futures commission merchants from transacting commodity futures with an introducing broker, commodity pool operator or commodity trading advisor which is not a member of the National Futures Association. Before the Dodd-Frank Act, this required, in effect, all introducing brokers, commodity pool operators and commodity trading advisors to be members of the National Futures Association. This arrangement, however, does not encompass the possibility of an introducing broker, commodity pool operator or commodity trading advisor engaged solely in swaps. *See* Chapter 8. The CFTC has, in lieu of the existing arrangement, proposed to directly require all such entities to be National Futures Association members. *See Membership in a Registered Futures Association*, 78 Fed. Reg. 67078 (November 8, 2013), 67079-67080.
[2] 17 C.F.R. § 1.3(aa).
[3] CME Clearing has provided clearing services for the Chicago Board of Trade since 2003. In 2007, the Chicago Board of Trade and the Chicago Mercantile Exchange, which operated CME Clearing, merged to form the CME Group Inc. *See* CME Group, *Timeline of CME Achievements*, http://www.cmegroup.com/company/history/timeline-of-achievements.html (accessed June 8, 2014).
[4] *Trading Places*, Motion Picture (Paramount Pictures 1983).
[5] 17 C.F.R. § 1.3(p).
[6] *See* 17 C.F.R. § 3.10(c)(1) and 1.7 C.F.R. § 1.3(y).

---

[7] This is not correct – an option to buy or sell a commodity in the future is a commodity option not a commodity future. This misstatement does not impact the rest of the opinion.
[8] Mark Dobrzycki, *F.B.I. Commodities 'Sting': Fast Money, Secret Lives*, N.Y. Times A1 (Jan. 30, 1989).
[9] *Id*.
[10] *U.S. v. Dempsey*, 724 F. Supp. 573 (N.D. Ill. 1989), 575.

Chapter 6 Endnotes

[1] Commodity Exchange Act § 1a(11).
[2] Commodity Exchange Act § 1a(10).
[3] In Chapter 8 we will see that these references to commodity futures have been expanded to also include swaps.
[4] *Commodity Futures Trading Commission v. Vision Capital Corp.*, 2007 WL 4246302 (D. Utah November 28, 2007), at *3.
[5] Commodity Exchange Act § 1a(10).
[6] The decision is *Commodity Futures Trading Commission v. Equity Financial Group*, 2006 WL 3359418 (D.N.J. November 16, 2006).
[7] *Commodity Futures Trading Commission v. Equity Financial Group, LLC*, 2007 WL 1038754 (D.N.J. March 30, 2007). After additional factual findings, the court ruled in favor of the CFTC on additional claims. *See Commodity Futures Trading Commission v. Equity Financial Group LLC*, 537 F. Supp. 2d 677 (D.N.J. 2008).
[8] *Commodity Futures Trading Commission v. Equity Financial Group LLC*, 572 F.3d 150 (3d Cir. 2009).
[9] Commodity Exchange Act § 1a(12)(A).
[10] Commodity Exchange Act § 1a(12)(C).
[11] U.S. Const. amend. I.
[12] Note that there is a similar exclusion in the Commodity Exchange Act's definition of commodity trading advisor. *See* Commodity Exchange Act § 1a(12)(b)(iv).
[13] The United States District Court for the District of Columbia found that *Lowe* was not distinguishable and that Commodity Exchange Act § 4m(1), as implemented by the CFTC, operated as an unconstitutional prior restraint. *See Taucher v. Born*, 53 F. Supp. 2d 464 (D.D.C. 1999). It was settled before appeals were heard by the Court of Appeals for the District of Columbia. *See Taucher v. Rainier*, 2000 WL 516081 (D.C. Cir. March 28, 2000).
[14] *Id*.
[15] *See Exemption From Registration as a Commodity Trading Advisor*, 65 Fed. Reg. 12938-01 (March 10, 2000), 12939.
[16] Commodity Exchange Act § 1a(11)(B).
[17] 17 C.F.R. § 4.5 (2002).
[18] *Additional Registration and Other Regulatory Relief for Commodity Pool Operators and Commodity Trading Advisors*, 68 Fed. Reg. 47221 (August 8, 2003).

[19] *Commodity Pool Operators and Commodity Trading Advisors: Compliance Obligations*, 77 Fed. Reg. 11252 (February 24, 2012). Note that due to "numerous errors," this was amended by a subsequent release, *Commodity Pool Operators and Commodity Trading Advisors: Compliance Obligations*, 77 Fed. Reg. 17328 (March 26, 2012).
[20] *See* 17 C.F.R. § 4.7(d) and 17 C.F.R. § 4.12(d).
[21] *See* 17 C.F.R. § 230.501(a).
[22] 17 C.F.R. § 4.7(a)(3).
[23] 17 C.F.R. § 4.7(a)(1)(vi).
[24] 17 C.F.R. § 4.12(b) and (c).
[25] *See Commodity Pool Operators and Commodity Trading Advisors: Compliance Obligations* (February 24, 2012) and the corrections in *Commodity Pool Operators and Commodity Trading Advisors: Compliance Obligations* (March 26, 2012).
[26] *See Commodity Pool Operators and Commodity Trading Advisors: Amendments to Compliance Obligations*, 76 Fed. Reg. 7976-01 (February 11, 2011), 7985-7987.
[27] *See Commodity Pool Operators and Commodity Trading Advisors: Compliance Obligations* (February 24, 2012), 11261.
[28] Commodity Exchange Act § 4m(1).
[29] Commodity Exchange Act § 4m(3).

Chapter 7 Endnotes

[1] Although the number of failures of insured banks in the aftermath of the Financial Crisis was unprecedented in modern times, a crisis among savings and loan banks in the late 1980s resulted, in 1989 alone, 531 failures, greatly exceeding the peak of 157 failures in 2010. *See* http://www.fdic.gov/bank/individual/failed/banklist.html *select* Failures and Assistance Transactions (accessed June 15, 2014).
[2] Congressional Oversight Panel, March Oversight Report. Available at http://www.gpo.gov/fdsys/pkg/CHRG-112shrg64832/pdf/CHRG-112shrg64832.pdf (accessed June 15, 2014), p. 114.
[3] Emergency Economic Stabilization Act of 2008, Pub. L. No 110-343, § 125(b).
[4] *Ibid.* at § 125(c).
[5] According to 12 U.S.C. § 5233, the Congressional Oversight Panel was required to terminate by December 31, 2009. However, an exclusion in 12 U.S.C. § 5211(a)(3) allowed for an extension.
[6] I.e., swap dealers, security-based swap dealers and, if not insured depository institutions, major swap participants and major security-based swap participants. *See* Dodd-Frank Act § 716(b)(2).
[7] The Dodd-Frank Act only references "insured depository institutions" in this context. However, the Federal Reserve via an Interim Rule has defined "insured depository institution" in this context to include uninsured U.S. branches and agencies of foreign banks. *See Prohibition Against Federal Assistance to Swaps Entities (Regulation KK)*, 78 Fed. Reg. 34545 (June 10, 2013) and 12 C.F.R. § 237.21.
[8] Dodd-Frank Act § 716(d).
[9] *See* Federal Reserve Act §§ 23A & 23B.

---

[10] Dodd-Frank Act § 716(c).
[11] Paul Volcker, *How to Reform Our Financial System*, N.Y. Times WK11 (January 31, 2010).
[12] Each of Morgan Stanley, Morgan Stanley Capital Management LLC, Morgan Stanley Domestic Holdings, Inc., Goldman Sachs Group, Inc., and Goldman Sachs Bank USA Holdings LLC were simultaneously approved as bank holding companies. *See Order Approving Formation of Bank Holding Companies* (Morgan Stanley, Morgan Stanley Capital Management LLC, and Morgan Stanley Domestic Holdings, Inc.), Federal Reserve Board, September 21, 2008, and *Order Approving Formation of Bank Holding Companies* (Goldman Sachs Group, Inc. and Goldman Sachs Bank USA Holdings LLC), Federal Reserve Board, September 21, 2008. Before this, each did not own subsidiaries engaged in commercial banking. Their focus was primarily "investment banking" activities, i.e., activities such as securities underwritings, and they owned no regulated banks other than industrial loan companies. Since industrial loan companies do not meet the definition of "bank" in Bank Holding Company Act § 2(c)(1) (they either have less than $100,000,000 in assets or take no demand deposits – *see* Bank Holding Company Act § 2(c)(2)(h)), their ownership did not result in Morgan Stanley or Goldman Sachs being subject to the strict regulatory regime applicable to bank holding companies. The industrial loan companies, however, were ineligible for Federal assistance from the Federal Reserve and these orders made possible the conversion of the industrial loan companies to banks that were eligible for Federal assistance.
[13] *Prohibitions and Restrictions on Proprietary Trading and Certain Interests in, and Relationships With, Hedge Funds and Private Equity Funds*, 79 Fed. Reg. 5535 (January 31, 2014) and 79 Fed. Reg. 5807 (January 31, 2014).
[14] *Id.*
[15] Note that this is the release issued by the Office of the Comptroller of the Currency, the Federal Reserve Board, the Federal Deposit Insurance Corporation, and the SEC. The CFTC issued a substantially identical release on the same day at 79 Fed. Reg. 5807 (January 31, 2014).
[16] Office of the Comptroller of the Currency, *Analysis of 12 CFR Part 44*, available at http://www.occ.gov/topics/laws-regulations/legislation-of-interest/volcker-analysis.pdf (accessed June 15, 2014), 1. *Ibid.* at 1, nn. 1 & 2.
[17] *See Exemption for Certain Swap* Agreements, 58 Fed. Reg. 5587-01 (January 22, 1993), 5589.
[18] Eligible swap participant were categories of transactions that the CFTC ruled were not commodity futures and, therefore, did not require to be traded on a designated contract market. *See* Chapter 2.
[19] *See Further Definition of "Swap Dealer," "Security-Based Swap Dealer," "Major Swap Participant," "Major Security-Based Swap Participant," and "Eligible Contract Participant"*, 77 Fed. Reg. 30596 (May 23, 2012).

Chapter 8
Endnotes

[1] *See* Dodd-Frank Act §§ 712(d)(1) & (3).

---

[2] *See* 17 C.F.R. § 1.3(ggg)(4).
[3] *Id*.
[4] Currently, there is no-action relief on this issue from the CFTC. *See* CFTC Staff Letter No. 14-34 (March 21, 2014). The proposed rule would effectively solemnize the no-action relief. *See generally Exclusion of Utility Operations-Related Swaps with Utility Special Entities from De Minimis Threshold for Swaps with Special Entities*, 79 Fed. Reg. 31238 (June 2, 2014).
[5] CFTC, *Provisionally Registered Swap Dealers*, available at http://www.cftc.gov/LawRegulation/DoddFrankAct/registerswapdealer (accessed June 16, 2014).
[6] These are Cournot Financial Products LLC and MBIA Insurance Corporation. *See* CFTC, *Provisionally Registered Major Swap Participants as of March 1, 2013*, available at http://www.cftc.gov/LawRegulation/DoddFrankAct/registermajorswappart (accessed June 16, 2014).
[7] Senate Committee on Agriculture, Nutrition and Forestry, *Reforming U.S. Financial Market Regulation*, S. Hrg. 11-799 (November 18, 2009), 13.
[8] *Ibid*. at 15, 22.
[9] *Ibid*. at 23.
[10] *Ibid*. at 45
[11] 17 C.F.R. § 1.3(mmm)(2).
[12] *See* Chapter 1.
[13] *See* 17 C.F.R. §§ 1.3(jjj) & (lll).
[14] The multipliers are in tabular format in 17 C.F.R. § 1.3(jjj)(3)(ii)(A)(i).
[15] Though the CFTC categorizes the general requirement to report swaps to a swap data repository, discussed in Chapter 9, and large swaps trader reporting requirements as entity level and only real-time public reporting requirements as transaction level, all reporting is treated herein as transaction level. *See Interpretative Guidance and Policy Statement Regarding Compliance with Certain Swap Regulations*, 78 Fed. Reg. 45292 (July 26, 2013), 45337-45339.
[16] Commodity Exchange Act § 1a(39).
[17] Commodity Exchange Act § 4s(e).
[18] *See Capital Requirements of Swap Dealers and Major Swap Participants*, 76 Fed. Reg. 27802 (May 12, 2011) and *Margin and Capital Requirements for Covered Swap Entities*, 76 Fed. Reg. 27564 (May 11, 2011), 27566, n. 4.
[19] *Capital Requirements of Swap Dealers and Major Swap Participants*, 27805-27806.
[20] *Capital Requirements of Swap Dealers and Major Swap Participants* and *Margin and Capital Requirements for Covered Swap Entities*.
[21] *Capital Requirements of Swap Dealers and Major Swap Participants*, 27805-27807.
[22] *Id*.
[23] *Margin and Capital Requirements for Covered Swap Entities*.
[24] For a general description of bank capital, *see* Richard Scott Carnell, Jonathan R. Macey, & Geoffrey P. Miller, *The Law of Financial Institutions*, 216-239 (5th ed., Wolters Kluwer Law & Business 2013)
[25] 17 C.F.R. § 3.1(e).
[26] U.S. Const. amend. V.
[27] 17 C.F.R. § 23.600(b).
[28] Commodity Exchange Act § 1a(39).

[29] *Further Definition of "Swap Dealer," "Security-Based Swap Dealer," "Major Swap Participant," "Major Security-Based Swap Participant," and "Eligible Contract Participant"*, 30607.

Chapter 9 Endnotes

[1] Commodity Exchange Act §§ 2(h)(2)(A) & (B).
[2] Commodity Exchange Act § 2(h)(2)(A).
[3] Commodity Exchange Act § 2(h)(2)(B).
[4] Commodity Exchange Act § 2(h)(2)(B)(iii).
[5] Commodity Exchange Act § 2(h)(8).
[6] Commodity Exchange Act § 2(h)(7).
[7] Commodity Exchange Act § 2(h)(1)(A).
[8] Commodity Exchange Act § 2(h)(7), 17 C.F.R. 50.50 and CFTC Letter No. 13-22 (June 4, 2013).
[9] Commodity Exchange Act § 2(h)(2)(A)(i).
[10] Commodity Exchange Act § 2(h)(2)(A)(ii).
[11] *See* 17 C.F.R. § 50.4.
[12] Commodity Exchange Act § 2(h)(2)(B).
[13] *Id.*
[14] Commodity Exchange Act § 2(h)(2)(C).
[15] Commodity Exchange Act § 2(h)(7)(A) and 17 C.F.R. § 50.50(a)(1)(iii).
[16] *See* CFTC No-Action Letter No. 13-22 (June 4, 2013).
[17] Commodity Exchange Act § 2(h)(7)(D).
[18] 17 C.F.R. § 50.51.
[19] 17 C.F.R. § 50.52.
[20] Commodity Exchange Act § 2(h)(7)(C)(i).
[21] *Id.*
[22] *Id.* and Commodity Exchange Act § 2(h)(7)(C)(ii).
[23] *See* 12 U.S.C. § 1243(k) and 12 C.F.R. § 225.86(d).
[24] Commodity Exchange Act § 2(h)(7)(E)(ii).
[25] *See* http://www.markit.com/product/isda-amend (accessed June 19, 2014).
[26] Commodity Exchange Act § 1a(50).
[27] For impartial access requirements of designated contract markets, *see* 17 C.F.R. § 38.151(b) and, for swap execution facilities, *see* Commodity Exchange Act § 5b-3(f)(2)(B)(i) and 17 C.F.R. § 37.202(a).
[28] 17 C.F.R. § 37.702(a).
[29] 17 C.F.R. § 37.10(a)(1) and 17 C.F.R. § 38.12(a)(1).
[30] 17 C.F.R. § 40.6(a) and (c).
[31] 17 C.F.R. § 40.5.
[32] 17 C.F.R. § 37.12(a)(2) and 17 C.F.R. § 38.11(a)(2).
[33] 17 C.F.R. § 23.432.
[34] 17 C.F.R. § 43.1(a).
[35] 17 C.F.R. §§ 43.3(b)(1) and (2).

---

[36] 17 C.F.R. § 43.4(d).
[37] 17 C.F.R. § 43.5 and 17 C.F.R. § 43.6.
[38] 17 C.F.R. § 45.3(a)(1).
[39] *Id.*
[40] 17 C.F.R. § 45.3(a)(2).
[41] 17 C.F.R. § 45.4(b).
[42] CFTC Letter No. 13-70 (November 15, 2013).

Chapter 10
Endnotes

[1] 17 C.F.R. § 23.430.
[2] 17 C.F.R. § 23.431(a).
[3] 17 C.F.R. § 23.431(a)(i).
[4] 17 C.F.R. § 23.431(d).
[5] 17 C.F.R. § 23.431(b).
[6] 17 C.F.R. § 23.433.
[7] See *Business Conduct Standards for Swap Dealers and Major Swap Participants with Counterparties*, 75 Fed. Reg. 80638-01 (December 22, 2010), 80646 and notes 65-69.
[8] 17 C.F.R. § 23.434(a).
[9] 17 C.F.R. § 23.401(c).
[10] For a list of the derivatives losses receiving the most significant media attention, *see* Edward S. Adams & David E. Runkle, *The Easy Case for Derivatives Use; Advocating a Corporate Fiduciary Duty to Use Derivatives*, 41 William & Mary L. Rev. 595 (2000). For a more recent example of a municipal derivatives loss, albeit one attracting less media attention, *see Hinds County, Miss. v. Wachovia Bank N.A.*, 708 F. Supp. 2d 348 (S.D.N.Y. 2010).
[11] 17 C.F.R. § 23.450(b).
[12] 17 C.F.R. § 23.450(c).
[13] 17 C.F.R. § 23.450(g).
[14] 17 C.F.R. § 23.451(b)(1).
[15] 17 C.F.R. § 23.451(b)(2). There is also relief in 17 C.F.R. § 23.451(e), which does not appear to differ from relief already provided by 17 C.F.R. § 23.451(b)(2)(i).
[16] 17 C.F.R. § 23.451(d).
[17] *Political Contributions by Certain Investment Advisers*, 75 Fed. Reg. 41018-01 (July 14, 2010), 41023, n. 68.
[18] Whereas Commodity Exchange Act § 4s(h)(5), the statutory basis for the regime on trading swaps as principal with special entities, incudes swap dealers and major swap participants, Commodity Exchange Act § 4s(h)(4), the statutory basis for the regime on acting as an advisor to a special entity with respect to swaps, applies only to swap dealers.
[19] 17 C.F.R. § 23.440(c).
[20] Commodity Exchange Act § 1a(39).
[21] Commodity Exchange Act § 4s(e).
[22] *See Swap Transaction Compliance and Implementation Schedule: Trading Documentation and Margining Requirements Under Section 4s of the CEA*, 76 Fed. Reg.

58176 (September 20, 2011), *Margin Requirements for Uncleared Swaps for Swap Dealers and Major Swap Participants*, 76 Fed. Reg. 23732 (April 28, 2011) and *Margin and Capital Requirements for Covered Swap Entities*.

[23] 17 C.F.R. § 23.700.

[24] *See* Commodity Exchange Act § 4s(l).

[25] *See* 17 C.F.R. § 43.4(a)(3).

[26] 17 C.F.R. §§ 23.502 and 503.

[27] *See* https://www2.isda.org/functional-areas/protocol-management/faq/8/ (accessed June 21, 2014) and https://www2.isda.org/functional-areas/protocol-management/faq/12/ (accessed June 21, 2014).

[28] *See* https://www.markit.com/Product/ISDA-Amend (accessed June 21, 2014).

[29] *Business Conduct Standards for Swap Dealers and Major Swap Participants with Counterparties*, 77 Fed. Reg. 9734 (February 17, 2012), 9769.

Chapter 11 Endnotes

[1] *See* Gary E. Kalbaugh, "Including Derivatives Providers in Intercreditor Arrangements," 44 No. 4 U.C.C. L.J. 409 (Nov. 2012), 420-422.

[2] 11 U.S.C. § 362(b)(6).

[3] *See* Dodd-Frank Act § 724(b).

[4] 11 U.S.C. § 362(b)(17).

[5] 11 U.S.C. § 547(b)(4).

[6] *Id.*

[7] 11 U.S.C. § 548(a)(1).

[8] *See* 11 U.S.C. §§ 546(e) and (g) and 11 U.S.C. § 548(d)(2).

[9] *See Lehman Brothers Special Financing Inc. v. Ballyrock ABS CDO 2007-1 Limited (In re Lehman Brothers Holdings Inc.)*, 2011 WL 9375423 (Bankr. S.D.N.Y. Nov. 3, 2011).

[10] *See* 12 U.S.C. § 1787(c)(8)(G) (credit unions), 12 U.S.C. 1821(e)(8)(G) (insured depository institutions), 12 U.S.C. 4617(d)(8)(G) (Federal National Mortgage Association, known as "Fannie Mae," the Federal Home Loan Mortgage Corporation, known as "Freddie Mac," and any Federal Home Loan Bank) and 12 U.S.C. § 5390(c)(8)(F) (covered financial company as defined in 12 U.S.C. § 5381(a)(8)).

[11] An advisory committee of the American Bankruptcy Institute Commission to Study the Reform of Chapter 11 has recommended that walk-away clauses be made statutorily unenforceable if triggered by a bankruptcy of the defaulting party. *See Financial Contracts, Derivatives and Safe Harbors Advisory Committee*, Full Committee Meeting Minutes/Summary (April 2, 2013), p. 2, available at http://commission.abi.org/sites/default/files/Minutes%20April%202,%202013%20Meeting%20of%20ABI%20Advisory%20Committee%20on%20Financial%20Contracts,%20Derivatives%20and%20Safe%20Harbors%20(00869734).pdf (accessed June 25, 2014).

[12] *Drexel Burnham Lambert Products Corp. v. Midland Bank PLC*, 1992 WL 12633422 (S.D.N.Y. November 10, 1992), 2.

[13] *Brookfield Asset Managementm Inc. v. AIG Financial Products Corp*, 2010 WL 3910590 (S.D.N.Y. Sept. 29, 2010).

---

[14] *In re Lehman Brothers Holdings Inc.*, 2009 WL 6057286 (Bankr. S.D.N.Y. September 17, 2009).
[15] *See Lomas and others v. JFB Firth Rixson Inc and others*, [2012] EWCA Civ 419, ¶¶ 31 and 35. For a similar decision in New South Wales, *see also Sims and Singleton as Liquidators of Enron Australia Pty Limited v TXU Electricity Limited & Anor*, [2005] NSWCA 12.
[16] *See In re Lehman Brothers Inc.*, 458 B.R. 134 (Bankr. S.D.N.Y. 2011), 138.
[17] *Ibid.* at 141, 144-145. *See also In re American Home Mortgage, Holdings, Inc.*, 501 B.R. 44 (Bankr. D. Del. 2013).
[18] *See* 11 U.S.C. § 1501 *et seq.*

Chapter 12 Endnotes

[1] *See* 7 U.S.C. § 2(ii) (1994). Or, relying on at least one District Court, an entity required to register as a board of trade. *See CFTC v. Noble Wealth Data*, 90 F. Supp. 2d 676 (D. Md. 2000), 687-692.
[2] For the Department of the Treasury's advocacy for an exclusion for foreign exchange transactions, *see Letter from Donald L. E. Richter, Acting General Counsel, Department of the Treasury*, S. Rep. 93-1311, 1974 U.S.C.C.A.N. 5843, 5587-5890.
[3] *See* 7 U.S.C. § 2(c)(2)(B) (2002) and 7 U.S.C. § 2(d)(1) (2002).
[4] 7 U.S.C. § 2(c)(2)(A) (2002).
[5] Pub. L. No. 110-246, Title XIII (2008).
[6] A new section, Commodity Exchange Act § 2(c)(2)(D), was also added by the CFTC Reauthorization Act of 2008 to enact similar provisions with respect to retail commodity transactions.
[7] *Regulation of Off-Exchange Retail Foreign Exchange Transactions and Intermediaries*, 75 Fed. Reg. 55410 (September 10, 2010).
[8] Commodity Exchange Act § 2(c)(2)(E)(ii)(1) requires the regulators of such entities to enact enabling rules, which has been the case for: (1) the SEC (*Retail Foreign Exchange Transactions*, 78 Fed. Reg. 42439-01 (July 16, 2013)), (2) the Federal Deposit Insurance Corporation (*Retail Foreign Exchange Transactions*, 76 Fed. Reg. 40779 (July 12, 2011)), (3) Office of the Comptroller of the Currency (*Retail Foreign Exchange Transactions*, 76 Fed. Reg. 41375 (July 14, 2011)) and (4) Federal Reserve Board (*Retail Foreign Exchange Transactions (Regulation NN)*, 78 Fed. Reg. 21019 (April 9, 2013)).
[9] *See* Commodity Exchange Act § 1a(47)(a)(i).
[10] *See* Commodity Exchange Act §§ 1a(47)(a)(iii)(VII) and (VIII).

Chapter 13 Endnotes

[1] *All Service Life Ins. Corp. v. Catling*, 171 F. Supp. 686 (S.D. Cal. 1959).
[2] A Ponzi scheme is where a fraudster solicits money from investors. The first to invest are given large returns based on money solicited from newer investors. These returns encourage more investment. Pay-offs continue until there are not enough new investors

to pay the false returns to existing investors. The scheme is named after Charles Ponzi, a perpetuator of such a fraud in the early twentieth century. *See Cunningham v. Brown*, 265 U.S. 1 (1924).

[3] *See U.S. Commodity Futures Trading Commission Continues its Aggressive Enforcement Program and Achieved Record Judgments during Fiscal Year 2007*, CFTC Release pr5396-07 (October 2, 2007) available at http://www.cftc.gov/PressRoom/PressReleases/pr5396-07 (accessed June 25, 2014), *CFTC's 2008 Fiscal Year Enforcement Roundup: Agency Files 40 Actions, Obtains Record Amount in Penalties and Fines, Discloses Crude Oil Investigation, Forms Forex Task Force*, CFTC Release pr5562-08 (October 2, 2008), available at http://www.cftc.gov/PressRoom/PressReleases/pr5562-08 (accessed June 25, 2014), *CFTC Enforcement Program Files 25% More Cases During Fiscal Year 2009 than in the Prior Fiscal Year*, CFTC Release pr5733A-09 (October 16, 2009), available at http://www.cftc.gov/PressRoom/PressReleases/pr5733A-09 (accessed June 25, 2014), *CFTC Enforcement Program Filings Increase 14 Percent in Fiscal Year 2010*, CFTC Release pr5918-10 (October 5, 2010), available at http://www.cftc.gov/PressRoom/PressReleases/pr5918-10 (accessed June 25, 2014), *CFTC Releases Annual Enforcement Results*, CFTC Release pr6121-11 (October 6, 2011), available at http://www.cftc.gov/PressRoom/PressReleases/pr6121-11 (accessed June 25, 2014), *CFTC Releases Enforcement Division's Annual Results*, CFTC Release pr6378-12 (October 5, 2012), available at http://www.cftc.gov/PressRoom/PressReleases/pr6378-12 (accessed June 25, 2014), *CFTC Releases Enforcement Division's Annual Results*, CFTC Release pr6749-13 (October 24, 2013) available at http://www.cftc.gov/PressRoom/PressReleases/pr6749-13 (accessed June 25, 2014).

[4] Commodity Exchange Act § 6(c)(4)(C)(ii)(I).

[5] Commodity Exchange Act § 6(c)(4)(C)(ii)(II).

[6] Commodity Exchange Act § 6(c)(10)(C).

[7] Commodity Exchange Act § 6(c)(10)(D).

[8] Commodity Exchange Act § 9(a)(5).

[9] *See* 18 U.S.C. §§ 1341 and 1343.

[10] 18 U.S.C. § 1001(a).

[11] Susan Abbott Gidel, *White Paper: Commodity Customer Protections and Regulations History and Potential Solutions for the Future 1938-2012* (February 14, 2012), available at http://av.r.ftdata.co.uk/files/2012/07/WHITE-PAPER-on-Customer-Protections-2012.pdf (accessed June 25, 2014). For the Commodity Customer Coalition generally, *see* http://commoditycustomercoalition.org/about/ (accessed June 25, 2014). For MF Global, *see* Chapter 11.

[12] Justin Scheck, *Deal for Reliant Energy Admits No Guilt in Fraud Case*, The Recorder (March 7, 2007) available at http://www.alm.law.com/jsp/article.jsp?id=900005553903&Deal_for_Reliant_Energy_Admits_No_Guilt_in_Fraud_Case#ixzz35lcbuRa9 (accessed June 26, 2014).

[13] *Cargill, Inc. v. Hardin*, 452 F.2d 1154, 1163 (8th Cir.1971).

[14] There is an exception for floor brokers and future commission merchants matching customer orders so long as they are executed at market price and in public on the floor of the exchange.

[15] It was the subject of one of the CFTC's uses of its emergency authority described in Chapter 4.

[16] 17 C.F.R. § 150.2.
[17] 17 C.F.R. § 150.3(a)(1).
[18] *See* Commodity Exchange Act § 5(d)(5) and 17 C.F.R. § 150.5.
[19] Commodity Exchange Act § 4a(a)(1).
[20] Commodity Exchange Act § 5(d)(5) and 17 C.F.R. § 150.5(e).
[21] 17 C.F.R. § 150.5(d).
[22] *See Position Limits for Derivatives*, 78 Fed. Reg. 75680 (December 12, 2013) and *Aggregation of Positions*, 78 Fed. Reg. 68946 (November 15, 2013).

Chapter 14 Endnotes

[1] Pub. L. No. 97-444 (January 11, 1983) at § 235.
[2] Commodity Exchange Act § 14(a).
[3] Commodity Exchange Act § 14(a)(1).
[4] Commodity Exchange Act § 14(g).

Chapter 15 Endnotes

[1] *See G20 Members*, available at https://www.g20.org/about_g20/g20_members (accessed June 27, 2014).
[2] Available at https://www.g20.org/sites/default/files/g20_resources/library/Pittsburgh_Declaration.pdf (accessed June 27, 2014).
[3] G-20, *Leaders' Statement: The Pittsburgh Summit* (September 24-25, 2009), p. 3, ¶ 19, available at https://www.g20.org/sites/default/files/g20_resources/library/Pittsburgh_Declaration.pdf (accessed June 27, 2014).
[4] *Id.*
[5] *See FSB member institutions*, available at http://www.financialstabilityboard.org/about/fsb_members.htm (accessed June 27, 2014).
[6] Financial Stability Board, *OTC Derivatives Market Reforms: Seventh Progress Report on Implementation* (April 8, 2014), p. 1-3, available at http://www.financialstabilityboard.org/publications/r_140408.pdf (accessed June 27, 2014).
[7] *Interpretative Guidance and Policy Statement Regarding Compliance with Certain Swap Regulations*, 78 Fed. Reg. 45292 (July 26, 2013). Note that this is currently the subject of a litigation dispute discussed below in section D6.
[8] *See* Geoffrey Sant, *The Rejection of the Separate Entity Rule Validates the Separate Entity Rule*, 65 SMU L. Rev. 813 (Fall 2012).
[9] *Ibid.*, 45351 at n. 513.
[10] It is slated to drop to $3 billion at an unspecified point, should the CFTC decide to lower it.
[11] Currently, according to a CFTC staff advisory, this requires all non-clerical employees, payments and tax responsibility to be outside of the U.S. *See Applicability of Transaction-Level Requirements to Activity in the United States*, CFTC Letter 13-69 (November 14, 2013). This position is subject to temporary no-action relief and is being

re-evaluated. *See* CFTC Letters 13-71 (November 14, 2013) and 14-01 (January 13, 2014). *See also Request for Comment on Application of Commission Regulations to Swaps Between Non-U.S. Swap Dealers and Non-U.S. Counterparties Involving Personnel or Agents of the Non-U.S. Swap Dealers Located in the United States*, 79 Fed. Reg. 1347 (January 18, 2014).

[12] *See Interpretative Guidance and Policy Statement Regarding Compliance with Certain Swap Regulations*, Appendices C and D.

[13] *Ibid.* at Appendix E.

[14] *See Australia: Certain Entity-Level Requirements*, 78 Fed. Reg. 78864 (December 27, 2013), *Canada: Certain Entity-Level Requirements*, 78 Fed. Reg. 78839 (December 27, 2013), *See European Union: Certain Entity-Level Requirements* 78 Fed. Reg. 78923 (December 27, 2013), *European Union: Certain Transaction-Level Requirements*, 78 Fed. Reg. 78878 (December 27, 2013), *Hong Kong: Certain Entity-Level Requirements*, 78 Fed. Reg. 78852 (December 27, 2013), *See Japan: Certain Entity-Level Requirements*, 78 Fed. Reg. 78910 (December 27, 2013), *Japan: Certain Transaction-Level Requirements*, 78 Fed. Reg. 78890 (December 27, 2013) and *Switzerland: Certain Entity-Level Requirements*, 78 Fed. Reg. 78899 (December 27, 2013).

GLOSSARY

Definitions are based on the usage common in the marketplace. Some of the terms also have special legal or regulatory definitions. Where this is the case, the marketplace definition is provided, followed by a citation to the legal or regulatory definition.

Affiliate: An entity that directly or indirectly controls, is controlled by, or is under common control with another entity.
American Option: An option that can be exercised by the holder of the option at any time during the term of the option.
Ask: *See* Offer.
Associated Person: A person who is associated with a futures commission merchant, an introducing broker, a commodity trading advisor, or a commodity pool operator who solicits or accepts orders or such person's supervisor. (Commodity Exchange Act § 1a(4))
Banging the Close: Disrupting the orderly execution of trades in the period before the market close. (Commodity Exchange Act § 4c(a)(5)(B))
Bid: Price at which a potential buyer is willing to make a purchase.
Bermudan Option: An option that can only be exercised by the holder at specified points during the term of the option.
Board of Trade: A trading facility for futures and commodity options. (Commodity Exchange Act § 1a(6))
Bucketing: Becoming a buyer or a seller of a position that was accepted as agent for execution on an organized market. (Commodity Exchange Act § 4b(a)(2)(D))
Call: An option agreement where the holder of the option has the right, but not the obligation, to buy an asset in the future from a seller for a pre-agreed amount.
Capper-Tincher Act: *See* Grain Futures Act of 1922.
Cash Settlement: A method whereby, in lieu of a physical exchange of assets referenced in a derivatives, parties exchange cash equivalents.
Cleared Swap: A swap for which a derivatives clearing organization has intermediated as counterparty for each of the original parties to the swap.
Clearing Determination: A determination by the CFTC that a category of swaps must be mandatorily cleared.

Close-Out Netting: Process by which multiple mutual present and future financial obligations, such as derivatives trades, documented under one instrument, such as an ISDA Master Agreement, are combined at termination of the instrument into one single amount due or payable by one party to the other.
Commodity: All goods, articles, services, rights, and interests other than onions and motion picture box office receipts. (Commodity Exchange Act § 1a(9))
Commodity Exchange Act of 1936: Statute amending the pre-existing Grain Futures Act of 1922 and, as amended, the statute that the Commodity Futures Trading Commission administers.
Commodity Futures Trading Commission or **CFTC**: Federal agency created by the Commodity Futures Trading Commission Act of 1974 to administer the Commodity Exchange Act.
Commodity Pool: A vehicle where funds are collectively pooled for the purposes of investing in commodity futures, commodity options or swaps. (Commodity Exchange Act § 1a(10))
Commodity Pool Operator: A person who solicits or accepts funds on behalf of a commodity pool. (Commodity Exchange Act § 1a(11))
Commodity Swap: Any swap that is not a credit, equity, or rate swap. *See* Credit Swap, Equity Swap, and Rate Swap.
Commodity Trading Advisor: A person who for compensation provides investment advice regarding commodity futures, commodity options, or swaps. (Commodity Exchange Act § 1a(12))
Confirmation: Means by which parties to a trade documented via an ISDA Master Agreement document the details of the trade.
Cornering: Purchasing available supply of a scarce resource for the purposes of obtaining a dominant market position. (Commodity Exchange Act § 9(a)(2))
Credit Default Swap: *See* Credit Swap.
Credit Swap: A swap where payments are calculated by reference to specified events related to third-party indebtedness.
Derivative: An instrument with a value derived from the value of an underlying asset. *See* Futures Contract, Option, and Swap.
Derivatives Clearing Organization: An entity providing clearing services in relation to commodity futures, commodity options, or swaps. (Commodity Exchange Act § 1a(15))
Designated Contract Market: A board of trade registered with the CFTC as a board of trade designated as a contract market. Designated contract markets are allowed to permit trading by retail participants.
Dodd-Frank Act of 2010: Statute providing the CFTC broad authority over swaps and the SEC broad authority of security-based swaps.
Eligible Contract Participant: A person who, based on its registration category or amount available for discretionary investment, is deemed to be non-retail and, therefore, among others, is permitted to be a swap counterparty. (Commodity Exchange Act § 1a(18))

End-User: A party to a swap who is not a swap dealer, security-based swap dealer, major swap participant, or major security-based swap participant. *See* Financial End-User and Non-Financial End-User.
End-User Exception: An exception from otherwise applicable clearing requirements available for some End-Users.
Equity Swap: A swap where payments are calculated by reference to one or more equity securities.
European Option: An option that can be exercised only by the holder at the maturity of the option.
Exchange: A central trading marketplace.
Financial Crisis of 2007: A global liquidity crisis that began in 2007 and resulted in the failure of numerous large financial institutions.
Financial End-User: An end-user that is a one of a number of entities engaged in financial activities described in Commodity Exchange Act § 2(h)(7)(C).
Financial Stability Board: An international body created by the Group of Twenty as a means of encouraging international economic cooperation.
Financial Stability Oversight Council: An inter-agency body responsible for assessing and responding to threats to U.S. financial stability and vested with, among others, the authority to require that a non-bank financial company submit to a strict supervision regime. (Dodd-Frank Act § 111)
Floor Broker: A person who directly places trades on a designated contract market on behalf of customers. (Commodity Exchange Act § 1a(22))
Floor Trader: A person with the right to place trades directly on a designated contract market on his or her own behalf. (Commodity Exchange Act § 1a(23))
Foreign Board of Trade: A board of trade outside of the U.S. Foreign boards of trade seeking to offer U.S. persons access are required to register with the CFTC. *See* Board of Trade. (17 C.F.R. § 1.3(SS))
Foreign Exchange Swap: *See* Rate Swap.
Forward Contract: An off-exchange agreement to buy or sell something for future physical delivery.
Future Trading Act of 1921: The first Federal statute enacted to regulate commodity futures. Was subsequently invalidated by *Hill v. Wallace*, 259 U.S. 44 (1922), and replaced by the Grain Futures Act of 1922.
Futures Commission Merchant: A person who solicits or accepts orders for commodity futures, commodity options, or swaps and, in association therewith, accepts money, securities, or property as margin for such transactions. (Commodity Exchange Act § 1a(28))
Futures Contract: A contract to buy or sell an asset at a pre-agreed price on a future date.
Futures Industry Association: Trade association for futures and exchanged-traded commodity options.
FX Swap: *See* Rate Swap.
Governmental Special Entity: A state, state agency, municipality, or government benefit plan. (17 C.F.R. § 23.451(a)(3))

Grain Futures Act of 1922: Statute following invalidation on constitutional grounds of the Future Trading Act of 1921 and the first successful Federal effort to regulate commodity futures.
Group of Twenty: Forum for international economic cooperation among the 20 most-developed economies.
Hedge Fund: A private investment vehicle structured to limit regulatory requirements and oversight.
Hedging: Entering into a transaction with the goal of mitigating an existing risk.
Interest Rate Swap: *See* Rate Swap.
International Organization of Securities Commissions: An international cooperative forum for national securities and futures regulators.
International Swaps and Derivatives Association: Trade association for derivatives other than futures and exchange-traded commodity options.
Introducing Broker: A person who solicits or accepts orders for commodity futures, commodity options, or swaps. (Commodity Exchange Act § 1a(31))
ISDA Master Agreement: Standardized agreement for the documentation of off-exchange derivatives developed by the International Swaps and Derivatives association. Most common variants are the 1992 and the 2002 ISDA Master Agreement.
ISDA Schedule: Part of the ISDA Master Agreement, the Schedule is the means by which parties modify, augment, or complete elections contemplated in the form ISDA Master Agreement.
Made Available to Trade Determination: A determination by the CFTC or a formal declaration by a designated contract market or swap execution facility that a category of swap already subject to mandatory clearing is now available to trade on a trading facility. Has the effect of requiring such swaps to be traded on-facility.
Major Swap Participant: A person, other than a swap dealer, maintaining a substantial speculative position in swaps or whose swaps exposure to counterparties could have serious adverse effects on U.S. financial stability. Additionally, any highly leveraged financial entity that maintains a substantial position in swaps, whether for hedging or speculation, is a major swap participant. (Commodity Exchange Act § 1a(33))
Major Security-Based Swap Participant: A person, other than a security-based swap dealer, maintaining a substantial speculative position in security-based swaps or whose security-based swaps exposure to counterparties could have serious adverse effects on U.S. financial stability. Additionally, any highly leveraged financial entity that maintains a substantial position in security-based swaps, whether for hedging or speculation, is a major security-based swap participant. (15 U.S.C. § 78c(a)(67))
Mark-to-Market: A method of valuing a financial position by assessing what price it would obtain if bought or sold in the marketplace.

Mixed Swap: A swap subject to CFTC and SEC jurisdiction because it combines elements of swaps subject to CFTC jurisdiction and security-based swaps subject to SEC jurisdiction. (Commodity Exchange Act § 1a(47)(D))
Narrow-Based Security Index: Generally, an index with nine or fewer securities or that otherwise is highly concentrated in a few securities. (Commodity Exchange Act § 1a(35))
National Futures Association: Self-regulatory organization for much of the futures industry.
Netting: *See* Close-Out Netting, Payment Netting, and Set-off.
Non-Financial End-User: An end-user that is not a financial end-user. *See* Financial End-User.
Notional Amount: An amount used in swap transactions as a multiplier to calculate swap payments.
Offer: Price at which a potential seller is willing to make a sale.
Off-Exchange Swap: Swap traded privately off-facility via bilateral agreement.
On-Facility Swap: A swap traded using a trading facility, such as a designated contract market or swap execution facility.
Option: An agreement whereby one party grants to the other a right, but not an obligation, to take a course of action. (Commodity Exchange Act § 1a(36))
Over-the-Counter Swap or **OTC Swap**: *See* Off-Exchange Swap.
Payment Netting: Process by which, if an amount is owed by X to Y and an amount is simultaneously owed by Y to X, these amounts are combined so that there is only one payment. For example, if X owed Y $100 and Y owed X $75, both obligations would be satisfied by X paying Y $25.
Physical Delivery: A settlement method where parties actually exchange an asset referenced in a derivative.
Position Limit: A limit on commodity futures and commodity options positions referencing certain physical commodities.
Prudential Regulator: The Federal Reserve Board, Office of the Comptroller of the Currency, Federal Deposit Insurance Corporation, Farm Credit Administration, or Federal Housing Finance Agency. (Commodity Exchange Act § 1a(39))
Put: An option agreement where the holder of the option has the right, but not the obligation, to sell an asset in the future to a buyer for a pre-agreed amount.
Rate Swap: A swap where payments are calculated by reference to a rate, such as an interest rate or foreign exchange rate.
Registered Entity: A derivatives clearing organization, designated contract market, swap data repository, or swap execution facility. (Commodity Exchange Act § 1a(40))
Retail Market: A market in which non-eligible contract participants may participate.
Securities and Exchange Commission or **SEC**: Federal agency created by the Securities Exchange Act of 1934 with the authority to regulate securities and security-based swaps.

Security-Based Swap: A swap that references a security or a narrow-based security index. The SEC has jurisdiction over security-based swaps. *See* Narrow-Based Security Index. (15 U.S.C. § 78c(a)(68))
Security-Based Swap Data Repository: An SEC registrant that provides a central recordkeeping facility for security-based swap transactions. (15 U.S.C. § 78c(a)(75))
Security-Based Swap Dealer: A market-maker or dealer in security-based swaps. The SEC has jurisdiction over security-based swap dealers. (15 U.S.C. § 78c(a)(71))
Security-Based Swap Execution Facility: A swap execution facility providing a platform for the trading of security-based swaps. Security-based swap execution facilities are regulated by the SEC. (15 U.S.C. § 78c(a)(77))
Self-Regulatory Organization: A private member organization that has the authority to make and enforce rules applicable to the members.
Set-off: Process by which off-setting obligations between two parties incurred under separate instruments are combined, resulting in one party owing a net amount to the other. For example, if X has borrowed $1,000 from Y and Y owes X $800 under a terminated ISDA Master Agreement, X might exercise a set-off right, if one is legally available, to pay $200 to Y and forgive Y the payment of the $800 under the terminated ISDA Master Agreement in full satisfaction of its obligation to repay the loan.
Shad-Johnson Accord: Agreement between then SEC chair, John Shad, and then CFTC chair, Phillip Johnson, by which the agencies agreed on the jurisdictional dividing line between their agencies. Ratified by Congress via the Futures Trading Act of 1982.
Slamming the Close: *See* Banging the Close.
Special entity: A Federal agency, a state, state agency, or municipality, a pension plan or endowment. (Commodity Exchange Act § 4s(h)(2)(C))
Speculation: Entering into a transaction that incurs an increased economic exposure in return for a potential economic reward.
Spoofing: A form of market manipulation whereby a party places a bid or offer without having an intent to trade. (Commodity Exchange Act § 4c(a)(5)(C))
Swap: An agreement to exchange payments periodically using predetermined pricing mechanisms. The CFTC has jurisdiction over swaps, except for security-based swaps. *See* security-based swap. (Commodity Exchange Act § 1a(47))
Swap Data Repository: A CFTC registrant that provides a central recordkeeping facility for swap transactions. (Commodity Exchange Act § 1a(48))
Swap Dealer: A market-maker or dealer in swaps. (Commodity Exchange Act § 1a(49))
Swap Execution Facility: A trading facility for swaps that is limited in participation to eligible contract participants. (Commodity Exchange Act § 1a(50))
Swap Push-out: A provision of the Dodd-Frank Act that effectively requires U.S. banks and U.S. branches or agencies of non-U.S. banks to, with certain broad

exceptions, conduct many swap activities through affiliates that do not benefit from the Federal Reserve discount window, Federal Deposit Insurance Corporation insurance, or similar assistance. (Dodd-Frank Act § 716)

Trading Facility: A facility that allows for access by multiple offerors and multiple offerees for the purposes of derivatives trading. (Commodity Exchange Act § 1a(51))

Treasury Amendment: An amendment to the predecessor bill of what became the Commodity Futures Trading Commission Act of 1974, which carved-out, among others, off-exchange foreign exchange transactions from the CFTC's jurisdiction.

Violating a Bid or Offer: Entering into a trade at a level lower than the highest bid price or higher than the lowest offer price. (Commodity Exchange Act § 4c(a)(5)(A))

Volcker Rule: A provision of the Dodd-Frank Act named after Paul Volcker, the former chair of the Federal Reserve Board. Requires that U.S. banks and non-U.S. banks with branches or agencies in the United States refrain from proprietary trading or investments in certain hedge funds or private equity funds. (Dodd-Frank Act § 619)

Wash Sale: Trades that off-set so that there is no economic impact to either party. (Commodity Exchange Act § 4c(a)(2))

COMMODITY EXCHANGE ACT-U.S.C. CONVERSION TABLE

Note that the following sections of the United States Code are contained in the same chapter as the Commodity Exchange without being, formally, a part of the Act: 7 U.S.C. § 13-1 (making it a misdemeanor to trade box office receipts or onions on a board of trade), 7 U.S.C. § 15b (Cotton Futures Act), 7 U.S.C. § 16a (grant of authority to CFTC to collect user fees and commissioning of National Futures Association report), 7 U.S.C. §§ 17a and 17b (severability clauses with respect to 1936 and 1968 amendments to the Commodity Exchange Act) and 7 U.S.C. §§ 27, 27a, 27d and 27f (Legal Certainty for Bank Products Act).

Commodity Exchange Act §	United States Code §
1	1
1a	1a
1b	1b
2	2
3	5
4	6
4a	6a
4b	6b
4b-1	6b-1
4c	6c
4d	6d
4e	6e
4f	6f
4g	6g
4h	6h
4i	6i
4j	6j
4k	6k

Commodity Exchange Act §	United States Code §
4l	6l
4m	6m
4n	6n
4o	6o
4p	6p
4q	6q
4r	6r
4s	6s
4t	6t
5	7
5b	7a-1
5c	7a-2
5e	7b
5f	7b-1
5g	7b-2
5h	7b-3
6(a)	8(a)
6(b)	8(b)
6(c)	9
6(d)	13b
6(e)	9a
6(f)	9b
6(g)	9c
6a	10a
6b	13a
6c	13a-1
6d	13a-2
7	11
8	12
8a	12a
8b	12b
8c	12c
8d	12d
9	13
10	17
12	16

Commodity Exchange Act §	**United States Code §**
13	13c
14	18
15	19
16	20
17	21
18	22
19	23
20	24
21	24a
22	25
23	26

TABLE OF CASES

Principle cases are italicized.

TABLE OF CASES

TABLE OF STATUTES

Principle sections of the statutes are in bold.

COMMODITY EXCHANGE ACT

DODD-FRANK ACT

11 U.S.C. (BANKRUPTCY CODE)

OTHER STATUTES

TABLE OF REGULATIONS

Principle regulations are in bold.

17 C.F.R.

INDEX

E

F

G

H

I

J

K

L

M

N

O